The Colonialist

Portrait of Cecil Rhodes, ca. 1885. Courtesy of the McGregor Museum, Kimberley, MMKP 8149.

THE COLONIALIST

The Vision of Cecil Rhodes

———◆———

WILLIAM KELLEHER STOREY

OXFORD
UNIVERSITY PRESS

Oxford University Press is a department of the University of Oxford.
It furthers the University's objective of excellence in research, scholarship,
and education by publishing worldwide. Oxford is a registered trade mark of
Oxford University Press in the UK and in certain other countries.

Published in the United States of America by Oxford University Press
198 Madison Avenue, New York, NY 10016, United States of America.

© Oxford University Press 2025

All rights reserved. No part of this publication may be reproduced, stored in a retrieval system, transmitted, used for text and data mining, or used for training artificial intelligence, in any form or by any means, without the prior permission in writing of Oxford University Press, or as expressly permitted by law, by license or under terms agreed with the appropriate reprographics rights organization. Inquiries concerning reproduction outside the scope of the above should be sent to the Rights Department, Oxford University Press, at the address above.

You must not circulate this work in any other form
and you must impose this same condition on any acquirer

Library of Congress Control Number: 2024950726

ISBN 9780199811359

DOI: 10.1093/oso/9780199811359.001.0001

Sheridan Books, Inc., United States of America

Contents

Introduction: Reconsidering Cecil Rhodes ... 1
1. Becoming an Englishman and a Migrant ... 9
2. Digging Diamonds ... 23
3. Growing Pains ... 39
4. Learning at Oxford ... 58
5. Entering Politics ... 74
6. Aiming North ... 96
7. Controlling De Beers ... 111
8. Amalgamating the Mines ... 138
9. Connecting a Country ... 162
10. Stealing Arcadia ... 182
11. Perpetrating a Fraud ... 199
12. Leading the Cape Colony ... 220
13. Multiplying Force ... 247
14. Consolidating Rhodesia ... 269
15. Fighting for Arcadia ... 287
16. Maintaining Mines ... 303
17. Raiding the Rand ... 322
18. Defending the Vision ... 349

19. Recovering the Vision	363
20. Falling Short	382
Conclusion: Perpetuating the Vision	401
Acknowledgments	415
Notes	421
Select Bibliography	467
Index	489

Map of Southern Africa, 1870–1890.

Introduction

RECONSIDERING CECIL RHODES

WHEN I FIRST visited the University of Cape Town in 1998, a greenish-bronze statue of Cecil Rhodes dominated the main campus vista. Raised high on a plinth, Rhodes sat enthroned at the center of knowledge and beauty. One of the most influential people in the history of the British Empire, he was dressed in everyday clothes, framed in the near background by UCT's tan and terracotta buildings and in the distance by the imposing Devil's Peak. His right foot was planted on a rock, his right elbow dug into his right knee, his right fist held up his chin, and his left hand clutched a scroll of laws. Rhodes gazed restlessly out into the distance. An inscription written by a friend was chiseled into the rock: "I dream my dream, / By rock and heath and pine, / Of Empire to the northward. / Ay, one land / From Lion Head to Line. / Rudyard Kipling." The poem portrayed the dream; the statue portrayed the vision.

This relic of the colonial past seemed out of tune with the values of the newly democratic "Rainbow Nation" of South Africa. I learned that the statue had been controversial for a long time. When it was unveiled in the 1930s, Afrikaner students complained that this tribute to a man who made a fortune in diamond and gold mining, served as the Cape Colony's prime minister, and led the colonization of Rhodesia still triggered memories of Rhodes's betrayal of their grandparents during the coup that he planned against the independent Boer republic in the Transvaal. Scholars noted some telling inaccuracies: one of my hosts showed me that instead of facing north toward Cairo, the endpoint of Rhodes's vision of an interconnected British Africa, the statue actually faced east, toward the Black townships of Langa, Guguletu, and Khayelitsha. For the historically conscious, the memorial was fitting. Defective in its details, the statue raised questions about its subject's larger vision.

In 2008, trouble flared up around the statue. Kipling's stirring lines, "I dream my dream," were spray-painted over with "F--k your dream of empire." These equally stirring words were scrubbed off, but the act of vandalism unleashed a deep rage about Rhodes, imperialism, and connections between the past and the present. A few years later, the statue incited Chumani Maxwele, a thirty-year-old UCT student and activist who was once arrested for saluting President Jacob Zuma's motorcade with a raised middle finger. On March 9, 2015, Maxwele appeared at the Rhodes statue bare-chested, wearing sports leggings and a pink helmet. On the plinth he placed two placards inscribed with words that defied the campus administration. Then he pushed past campus security officers, hoisted a portable toilet in the air, and doused Rhodes with brown slush. Maxwele knew how to attract attention. A friend of his filmed the incident on his cellphone camera and circulated the video. Maxwele himself made a statement to reporters:

> As Black students we are disgusted by the fact that this statue still stands here today as it is a symbol of White supremacy. How we can be living in a time of transformation when this statue still stands and our hall is named after Jameson, who was a brutal lieutenant under Rhodes? This poo that we are throwing on the statue represents the shame of Black people. By throwing it on the statue we are throwing our shame to Whites' affluence.[1]

Maxwele's protest kicked off weeks of demonstrations around the statue. The Rhodes statue was festooned with signs, including one that said: "Rhodes Must Fall." This became the moniker for a new student movement that linked the removal of imperialist statues with calls for campus reform and social justice. After much debate the university agreed to let the Cape heritage authorities remove the statue and put it into storage. Nearby, another statue of Rhodes remained in place at the spectacular Rhodes Memorial. In July 2020, an intruder vandalized it with an angle-grinder and graffitied the words "Racist, thief, [and] murderer." The statue has since been repaired. Questions linger.

Rhodes wanted South Africans of European descent to run a unified country for themselves, holding down Black African people while at the same time cultivating ties to the British Empire. He spent most of his forty-eight years (1853–1902) traveling between South Africa and Britain, so it was perhaps inevitable that the "Rhodes Must Fall" movement would spread from the University of Cape Town to the University of Oxford, specifically to Oriel College, where Rhodes had been a student and later became a generous benefactor. Oriel's administration was asked by "Fallists" to remove its own Rhodes statue from its Rhodes Building near the center of Oxford. The building, completed in 1911, was funded by a £100,000 bequest from Rhodes's will.

A Rhodes statue stands above High Street near the top of the building's façade. Most people walk by without noticing it, but for those who look up, Rhodes can be seen standing grandly but dressed plainly, as was his preference in life. On either side of him, Solomonic columns hold up an arch, whose interior is in the shape of a scallop shell, a Christian symbol of the pilgrim's courage and a Roman symbol of Venus's generative powers. Rhodes looks down over his left boot, which points halfway over the ledge. Beneath him are statues of King Edward VII and King George V, as well as four former heads of the college.[2]

If Rhodes had to fall, this statue on a precipice seemed ready, but Oriel College and the wider university community struggled to interpret their controversial benefactor. Prominent figures weighed in on the side of keeping the statue, making the point that Rhodes was indeed a racist, but so were most white Victorians. They argued that this morally ambiguous context constituted grounds for slowing down, lest the removal of Rhodes initiate the removal of many more statues. The members of "Rhodes Must Fall" responded forcefully by raising the stakes. They would not be satisfied with just the removal of the offending statue; they claimed that colonial ideologies pervaded the university, a situation that required drastic reform.[3]

These lines of argument were well delineated during an Oxford Union debate. Three students from Africa, Ntokozo Qwabe, Yasmin Kumi, and Athinangamso Esther Nkopo, argued in favor of removal and linked it to curricular reform. They were supported by King's College London's Barbadian history professor, Richard Drayton, who read a famous quote from Mark Twain: "I admire Rhodes. I fully confess it. And when his time comes, I shall buy a piece of the rope for a keepsake." Drayton's point was to show that opposition to Rhodes was nothing new. On the side of keeping the statue, things got complicated. Oxford's prominent English theology professor, Nigel Biggar, defended Rhodes's accomplishments and legacy, noting that on several occasions, Rhodes had spoken favorably about "civilized" African people. Oxford's prominent South African history professor, William Beinart, spoke critically about Rhodes and the statue, while articulating the hope that the university could focus its attention and resources on building future programs to support a better understanding of Africa. The BBC's English presenter, Sophia Cannon, expressed the view that the statue could be kept as a way of challenging academic minds.[4]

The debate over Rhodes was part of a larger, early twenty-first-century reconsideration of the history of the British Empire. Starting around 9/11, when Prime Minister Tony Blair joined US president George W. Bush in making interventions in Afghanistan, some commentators recalled the liberal imperialism of the nineteenth century with fondness. Such nostalgia was skewered by professional historians. One of the foremost historians on both sides of the Atlantic, Simon Schama, called these rosy memories of imperialism to be "offensive and insulting."[5] To move beyond nostalgia and gain knowledge of Rhodes, Oriel College tapped William Beinart to prepare a full analysis that was intended to inform any decisions about Rhodes and his statue. Beinart's negative conclusions about Rhodes were contested by Nigel Biggar and by others who saw the record as mixed. In 2020, the college's board of governors leaned toward removing the statue, an inclination confirmed by a blue-ribbon commission. The commission pointed out, however, that removing a statue from a building classified as "Grade II* Listed"—of national architectural importance—was going to be complicated from the perspective of heritage regulations. Even if all the required steps were taken and the Oxford City Council approved, the ruling Conservative Party's minister for culture, Oliver Dowden, made it clear that he would prevent any such changes. Rhodes still stands, his statue explained by an interpretive sign at street level.[6]

In Oxford and Cape Town, the lines of debate tended to be drawn along how to interpret antiquated symbols of racism amidst contemporary desires for inclusivity. But in Cape Town, Maxwele's protest was about more than racism. The activist spoke powerfully about the persistence of unequal access to infrastructure, a half century after the African National Congress (ANC) Freedom Charter promised to bring material benefits to all South Africans. In Maxwele's Khayelitsha neighborhood, indoor toilets and proper sewerage were still not universally available. The ANC government distributed portable toilets to township residents, who left them out on street corners to be disposed of by the municipality. The toilets stank, crawled with maggots, and swarmed with flies. Worse still, children played with them. The situation was intolerable, especially when compared to the modern amenities of Rondebosch, the historically white suburb where the university is located. Chumani Maxwele giving a "poo shower" to Cecil Rhodes's statue was his way of calling attention to the colonial origins of unequal infrastructure and the ongoing disparities of South African society.[7]

---◆---

In the mid-nineteenth century, Southern Africa had a sparse population mainly dedicated to small-scale farming and animal husbandry. The scale and scope of agriculture and trade were growing as white settler colonialism became more firmly established, and there were a handful of quarries and mines. The discovery of diamonds, just before Rhodes's arrival in 1870, and the subsequent discovery of the world's largest deposit of gold in the 1880s brought migrants to the mining cities of Kimberley and Johannesburg from all over Southern Africa and other parts of the world. As global investment and imported technologies poured into the mines, the region shifted from a reliance on human and animal energy to dependence on wood and coal. This energy transition fueled revolutions in farming, mining, and transportation, as well as major political and social transformations.

More than any other individual, Cecil Rhodes saw the need to consolidate the mining industry and to lay the groundwork for a supporting political, agricultural, and industrial infrastructure that would accelerate white settlement in the north and the dispossession and employment of Black people throughout the region. His business and political leadership propelled national unification, racial segregation, and spatial rearrangement. It changed the way in which people in South Africa thought about and experienced the world around them. It liberated and empowered the white minority while actively hindering the Black majority's striving for power and freedom. This new South Africa was dominated by mining and progressive farming, traversed by railroads and telegraphs, and traveled by Black migrant workers as they were pressured to leave their farms to labor on settler farms and industrial sites. By the time of Rhodes's death in 1902, the unified capitalist colonies controlled by self-governing white settlers loyal to the British Empire was starting to look very much like modern Southern Africa. More than a century later, it was Rhodes's colonialist achievements that presented so many obstacles to those who sought a country based on equality, including equal access to land, mines, and housing. The ANC's 1955 Freedom Charter did not mention him by name, but it amounted to nothing less than a call for the rooting out of the legacy of Cecil Rhodes. The section of the charter titled "The Land Shall Be Shared by Those Who Work It!" is clearly a rebuke to various initiatives by Rhodes:

> Restrictions of land ownership on a racial basis shall be ended, and all the land re-divided amongst those who work it to banish famine and land hunger; The state shall help the peasants with implements, seed, tractors and dams to save the soil and assist the tillers; Freedom of movement shall be guaranteed to all who work on the land; All shall have the right to occupy land wherever they choose; People shall not be robbed of their cattle, and forced labour and farm prisons shall be abolished.[8]

When it came to racial restrictions on land, labor, and mobility, Rhodes was the key mover in the colonializing process. Others participated, too, but it is hard to imagine the process developing so far without Rhodes. His grand vision for British imperialism and industrial capitalism grew out of technical challenges in diamond mining. His companies consolidated operations, buying up small claims and creating an advanced, industrial infrastructure of deep-level mines and large processing plants. To borrow a term used by US environmental historians William Cronon and Timothy LeCain, Rhodes's mining operations in Kimberley were "disassembly lines" in which ground was hauled up from tunnels, exposed, crushed, washed, and sorted. The precious stones were then shipped to faraway destinations, where they were further disassembled by being cut into jewels. The diamonds were then polished and sold. The buyers of the jewels had little reason to contemplate the original hole in the ground or the labor and engineering behind the diamond.[9]

The disassembly line is a useful concept for understanding diamond mining as well as gold mining, in which Rhodes invested and which, by 1890, was well on its way to becoming South Africa's greatest industry. This book takes the concept of the disassembly line one step further. Rhodes's mining companies depended on migrant labor. He encouraged migration through rural policies and recruitment measures in which African men were uprooted from their families and pushed to the mines from as far away as Mozambique. This social disassembly line provided labor to the mines, whose profits funded the work of Rhodes's British South Africa Company. The BSAC's private army murderously disassembled Ndebele and Shona societies to serve Rhodes's plan for the white settlers' Arcadia that came to be called Rhodesia.

Rhodes's social and material vision may be understood in the context of other important "system-builders" of the industrial age. Samuel Morse did more than invent the telegraph; he envisioned a trans-Atlantic network of communications. Thomas Edison did more than invent the light bulb; he envisioned the electric power grid. Henry Ford did not invent the car, nor did he invent the assembly line; he envisioned what it took to build a society that depended on mass-produced automobiles. These titanic system-builders all shaped societies and governments around the things that they produced.[10]

Americans were the source of many ideas and practices for Rhodes. Although he never visited the United States, he imagined the reunion of the upstart nation with the British Empire, a goal that helped to inspire the creation of the Rhodes Scholarships. He counted Americans among his most important associates, especially his chief engineers, Gardner Fred Williams and John Hays Hammond, who made major contributions to his diamond and gold mines, respectively. Rhodes relied on Williams to institute key practices, ranging from the construction and maintenance of deep shafts and tunnels under the old, open-pit mines to the development of segregated compounds for African migrant laborers. Hammond helped to identify the most productive sites of gold mining on the Witwatersrand and played a key role in the attempted overthrow of the South African Republic, the independent Boer state known then as the Transvaal. More broadly, many of Rhodes's ideas about the consolidation and expansion of his businesses resembled those of the US robber barons Vanderbilt, Rockefeller, and Carnegie, who were much in the news during his lifetime. Like those American monopolists, Rhodes used corporate power to bring order to an unruly society. He, too, hoped to retire to idyllic circumstances and bankroll philanthropies and universities. Of course, there were key differences between Rhodes and his fellow monopolists. They generally preferred to work in the political shadows, while Rhodes played a prominent role in leadership.[11]

Rhodes's active involvement in politics, particularly his rule as prime minister of the Cape Colony, is well known. It is less well known that in his early days on the diamond fields, the classically educated young Englishman gained a strong command of technical details, on full display in his speeches, letters, and reports. In addition to supervising technical experts like the mine engineers Williams and Hammond, Rhodes had a close relationship with railway engineer Charles Metcalfe and supervised two well-known architects. He hired Sydney Stent to design Kenilworth, a model village near Kimberley whose main purpose was housing De Beers's white workforce but whose secondary purpose was to surveil the workers in ways that were different from the prison-like compounds designed for Black miners. And six hundred miles to the southwest in Cape Town, renowned imperial architect Herbert Baker received his first commissions from Rhodes, including the renovation of Rhodes's home, Groote Schuur, and the building of a cottage for Rhodes at one of his vineyards, Boschendal, as well as construction of the nearby workers' village of Languedoc. Rhodes imagined that, on his own lands, he could be a beneficent lord, which led him to take a strong interest in the planning of buildings and communities.

Although previous biographies have addressed Rhodes's political career, none have examined the ways in which his career was oriented around ideas about managing environment, geography, and technology. The political, social, and economic vision of Cecil Rhodes depended on technical advances in diamond mining at Kimberley and gold mining in the Transvaal, as well as agriculture in the Western Cape and Rhodesia, now called Zimbabwe, and the extension of roads, railways, and telegraphs to connect all these spaces. Sometimes, Rhodes's reach exceeded his grasp. Beyond Zimbabwe, his British South Africa Company established nominal governance in what is today Zambia, which only became effective in the decades after his death. The limits of geography and technology also circumscribed his unsuccessful efforts to control Nyasaland, now called Malawi, and Katanga. These frustrations still did not stop him from concocting outlandish ideas for governing Uganda and for stretching the rail and telegraph lines from the Cape to Cairo.

Rhodes experienced limits and successes. All his efforts hinged on managing a transcontinental social network. He was adept at working with engineers, bankers, and partners to build his businesses and the British Empire. Throughout his career, Rhodes bridged the disparate interests of investors and politicians in Britain and Europe, connecting them all to the needs of businessmen and engineers in Southern Africa. Like many of his fellow Victorians, Rhodes overlooked Africans' creativity and adaptability with technologies and their own practices for managing natural resources. This book aims to explore the full scope of Rhodes's engagement with the social and material world, while acknowledging the thorny long-term problems that were implicit in his projects.[12]

Over the course of his three decades in South Africa, Cecil Rhodes lived a paradoxical life. He became a key figure in the country's transition from a patriarchal, slaveholding backwater to an industrialized nation that made an important contribution to the world economy. He acquired most of his wealth from advanced industrial mining corporations, yet he hoped to live as a throwback, a feudal lord on his estates in Rhodesia and the Western Cape. He was involved in developing the region's modern roads, railways, and telegraphs, but he did so to support an older, more authoritarian social order. One thing was clear: every step forward in infrastructure or industry empowered white people and disempowered Black people. A complex figure, admired and detested in his own time, Rhodes deserves to be understood on his own terms, both for what he achieved and for the lasting and often damaging impact he had on Southern Africa.

I

Becoming an Englishman and a Migrant

ON JULY 5, 1853, Cecil Rhodes was born in Bishop's Stortford, a market town about thirty-five miles north of central London. The town got its name from a ford on the River Stort, which passes to the east of the town and flows southward to the River Lea, eventually connecting to the Thames at London. The easy river trip to London had encouraged trade and settlement ever since ancient times. The town's location also put it at a crossroads of conquest. In Rhodes's day, schoolchildren learned about the shift from the Romano-Britons to the Anglo-Saxons, whose later kingdom bordered on the part of England ruled by the king of Denmark. England was only unified in the mid-eleventh century, when, in 1060, the Bishop of London bought the estate near the ford, giving the town its name of Bishop's Stortford just in time for the Norman Conquest of 1066.[1]

Young Cecil Rhodes walked and rode on the roads near his hometown, seeing the remnants of cross-cultural conquest and domination, from Stone Age forts to the Norman castle.[2] The town's connections to industry were as deep as its connections to conquest. Bishop's Stortford was home to brick-making and iron-working dating to the Roman period. By the early modern period, the town's economy was anchored by the malt industry, with malt houses located near the Rhodes family home. The finished malt was sent to brewers downriver to London. Bishop Stortford's malt industry began in the early seventeenth century, reaching its peak in the late eighteenth century.[3]

Young Rhodes, the future builder of mines and railroads, might have seen the connections between industry and infrastructure. In 1766, to better serve the malt trade, the British Parliament gave permission to the townspeople of Bishop's Stortford to canalize the Stort River. A canal company dredged the river and built towpaths and fifteen locks down to the Lea River, which had been progressively canalized since the Middle Ages. The benefits of better connections between the sites of production, processing, and marketing may have made an impression on young Rhodes when he first visited South Africa, which had only just begun to develop roadways and railways. At home, British travelers were benefiting from the network of roadways constructed during the eighteenth and early nineteenth centuries, even if that network was often in a state of disrepair.[4]

The roads and canals that connected Bishop's Stortford to London ensured that the town became more than just a site of malt production. It was also home to many other small businesses linked to trade, especially inns and taverns. The town even had a sort of temple to commerce, the Corn Market, designed in the Greek Revival style, giving it the façade of a Greek temple. Built in 1828, the Corn Market—and buildings like it all around Britain—were closely associated with nationalism, reason, authority, and commerce, all with a tinge of secularism. Every day, young Rhodes walked past the Corn Market. It was the symbolic connection of his small hometown to the wider world of trade.

A town that lived by trade could die by trade. By the time of Rhodes's childhood Bishop's Stortford's economy was in trouble. The arrival of the railway in 1842 at first signified exciting new connections to London and the rest of the country, but instead travelers bypassed the town, which sent the local stagecoaches and inns into decline. The development of rail networks meant that it was now easier and cheaper for other locations with newer facilities to ship malt and beer to London. Rhodes and his family lived practically next door to a malthouse and may have been aware of the decline of this business. At an early age, it almost certainly occurred to Rhodes that industrial technologies such as the railway had a transformative power and that it was better to be ahead of technology's curve than to be behind it.

The Rhodes family prospered during England's commercial and industrial development. Cecil often spoke fondly of his farming ancestors. His father, Francis William Rhodes, was descended from farmers and tradesmen who moved from Cheshire to London in the 1720s. Quite wisely, the Rhodes ancestors bought land around west-central London, in the vicinity of what later became the University of London. Francis William's great-grandfather, William, was the proprietor of a 300-acre dairy farm between what became Mecklenburgh Place, Brunswick Square, and the Foundling Hospital. In the 1730s William Rhodes bought more land nearby and opened several businesses. William's son, Samuel, recognized the potential of their lands for urban development. Not only did Samuel begin to construct housing and speculate in real estate, but he also opened brick and tile kilns, using the soil that was being stripped from construction sites to create valuable building materials. Much of this London property remained in the possession of members of the Rhodes family, some of whom were buried in the Old St. Pancras churchyard. In the 1890s, distant relatives of Rhodes sold him a two-and-a-half-acre estate in London's Dalston neighborhood that ultimately passed to the Rhodes Trust.[5]

As Britain industrialized, the Rhodes family branched out from farming to real-estate development and small-scale manufacturing. Cecil's grandfather, William Rhodes, the third son of Samuel, became quite wealthy in his own right by further involvement in land speculation. William's son, Francis William (Cecil's father), was born into prosperity in 1807. The eldest of eight children, Francis William was educated at the elite Harrow School and at Trinity College, Cambridge, where he studied to become an Anglican priest.

The Reverend Francis William Rhodes turned his own vision to church and community, helped by a family fund that supplied him with the substantial yearly sum of £2,600. In 1833, Francis William took up his first appointment as the curate of a small church in Brentwood, Essex, and soon after married nineteen-year-old Elizabeth Sophia Manet, from a Swiss family that lived in London. In 1835, Elizabeth Sophia died while giving birth to their first child, Elizabeth. Even after the loss of his young wife, Francis William appears to have succeeded in Brentwood. He waited until 1844 to marry again, this time to Louisa Peacock. Louisa and Francis William were an odd couple in certain respects. For Victorian newlyweds they were relatively old—Francis William was thirty-seven and Louisa was twenty-eight. He was tall, thin, and stern while Louisa was short, plump, and jolly. Even so, both were from successful, middle-class families. Louisa's family was from Lincolnshire, where her grandfather owned land and founded an important local canal company. Louisa's father, Anthony Taylor Peacock, served as a member of the British Parliament in the 1850s. The Peacocks, like the Rhodeses, used landowning as the springboard to prosperity and prominence.[6]

In 1849, successful politicking within the church resulted in Francis William Rhodes being promoted to be the vicar of St. Michael's in Bishop's Stortford. An impressive large Gothic church with a high steeple, it was the main church of its parish, with a substantial congregation plus oversight over several smaller churches nearby. It is not hard to imagine the impression that St. Michael's made on young Cecil Rhodes. Sitting adjacent to a classic English churchyard, the church is grand and inspiring. Looking down the main aisle, the side columns and gothic arches highlight the carved wood screen and choir stalls, all the workmanship of fifteenth-century craftsmen. The elevated, carved-wood pulpit, where Francis William preached his sermons, dated to the seventeenth century. While the church is a classic Gothic structure that reminds visitors of the medieval Catholic past, its interior is rather plain, indicating the influence of the Protestant Reformation. The exterior of the church also hints of power and struggle, with its rooftop ringed with crenellated battlements. The positioning of the church on top of a hill tends to emphasize a sense of domination.[7]

The Rhodes family was fruitful and multiplied. When the Rhodeses arrived in Bishop's Stortford, they already had fourteen-year-old Elizabeth, plus Herbert, four; Edith, two; and Louisa, one. The family lived for a short while in the vicarage, before moving in 1850 to a large Georgian house called Thorleybourn. Like many upper-middle-class English families, they employed servants, including a cook, a head governess, and a head housekeeper, as well as several younger nannies, maids, and "houseboys." Over the course of 1850 to 1861, Francis William and Louisa added to their family. First there was Basil, who was born in 1850 but who died in infancy. He was followed by Francis William, known as Frank, in 1851; Ernest, born in 1852; and Cecil, born on July 5, 1853. Frederick, born in 1854, died in infancy. Louisa continued to have more children: Elmhirst in 1858; Arthur in 1859; and Bernard in 1861. In that year, Cecil was eight years old, living in a household with nine siblings and half a dozen servants.[8]

There are only sparse records of what it was like to be a young member of the Rhodes family. Cecil and his siblings appreciated trips to Lincolnshire to visit his mother's family and especially her outgoing sister, Sophy Peacock. These family visits involved romping in the country and may have helped Cecil to develop a lifelong enjoyment of riding and camping. Young Cecil was remembered for being reserved, at times even withdrawn. His nanny recalled episodes in which Rhodes hid, moaning to himself, unwilling to communicate his feelings. A friend and early biographer, Lewis Michell, interviewed Cecil's acquaintances at school. "He is described as a slender, delicate-looking, but not delicate, boy, and as possessing a retiring nature, and a high, proud spirit. One of the assistant masters recalls him as a bright, fairly clever lad, with nothing dreamy about him." Michell learned that none of the boys called him Cecil—all of them called him Rhodes, an indication, perhaps, of distance or social awkwardness. Later in life, he was noted for having quiet, sensitive moments of abstraction, combined with a sense of adventure.[9]

The education of the Rhodes children reflected the aspirations and realities of life for an upper-class English family in the nineteenth century. Francis William and Louisa had enough resources for a growing household, but the costs of private education began to outstrip their means. The oldest son,

Herbert, was educated at Winchester, while the second son, Frank, was educated at Eton. By the time Cecil was old enough to attend a public school, it appears not to have been an option. He remained enrolled at the Bishop's Stortford Grammar School, where he was an average and unremarkable student, fond of cricket. His best subjects were French and religion, while his favorites were history and geography. In 1869, at the age of sixteen, Cecil Rhodes left school and studied languages and mathematics under his father's tutelage. He developed a fascination with classical history, philosophy, and religion. Even so, the fact that young Cecil did not sit for an Oxford entrance exam right away may indicate that his skills in Latin and Greek were lackluster.[10]

Rhodes had a particularly strong interest in the history of the Roman Empire. This was a topic with great contemporary resonance, as Britain extended its dominion across the globe. The specific works on his father's reading list are unknown, but we do know that by the time of Cecil's involvement in South Africa, he often discussed with friends his favorite works, *The History of the Decline and Fall of the Roman Empire* by Edward Gibbon and the *Meditations* of Marcus Aurelius. According to Gibbon, the era of Marcus Aurelius was a golden time, when absolute powers were wielded by virtuous and wise rulers who delighted in the image of liberty even as their subjects were mostly not yet worthy of it. Gibbon's analysis held great appeal to youths like Cecil Rhodes who were educated in the classics and aspired to imperial service. Marcus Aurelius advocated broad awareness and intense focus while doing the dirty work of empire building. Gibbon explained the emperor's attachment to the Stoic philosophers, which taught him to submit his body to his mind, his passions to his reason; to consider virtue as the only good, vice as the only evil, all things external as things indifferent. He advised others to be "just and beneficent to all mankind."[11] People must focus on the good, while practicing detachment from superficial distractions. Achieving distance and perspective on emotions was considered important, especially in challenging circumstances. Rhodes imitated Marcus Aurelius in certain other key respects. The emperor had tremendous resources at his disposal, but he preferred to live life without luxuries. Rhodes, too, had the resources to dress well and live lavishly, but most of the time he dressed casually and preferred simplicity.[12]

Rhodes grew up in a period marked by tension over approaches to empire-building, especially between intellectual liberalism and popular authoritarianism. Britain's government became more representative, thanks to the parliamentary reforms of 1832 that extended the franchise and made representation more geographically even, but intensifying nationalism tended to support the traditional institutions of the monarchy, the aristocracy, the army, and the navy.[13] In 1833, the freeing of the slaves became the single greatest accomplishment of liberal politicians, yet racist reaction and colonial authoritarianism built slowly and steadily for the rest of the nineteenth century. In the 1840s, the repeal of the Corn Laws was another triumph for liberals, but Britain's unsatisfactory interventions in the Irish famine cast a long shadow over the supposed benefits of free trade. Liberal efforts to reform India seemed to be repaid with backlash and rebellion. The Indian rebellion of 1857 appeared to result from liberal overreach and was repressed, with popular support, by a scorched-earth campaign that involved outright racism and horrific reprisals. The 1866 rebellion by free Black people in Jamaica divided British opinion, between those who were sympathetic to Jamaican desires for freedom and those who supported Governor Edward Eyre's bloody crackdown.[14]

As the tall, slender, blue-eyed, auburn-haired Rhodes entered his teenage years, he almost certainly heard these conflicts being discussed. Reports reached England ever more quickly, thanks to the advent of steamships and telegraphs and foreign newspaper correspondents whose coverage was enhanced by the new technology of photography. British news contained reports of the rebellions in India and Jamaica, as well as news about the Crimean War and the Second Opium War. Rhodes probably learned about the Civil War in the United States, too, which was followed closely in Britain and throughout Europe. When Rhodes was seven years old, Abraham Lincoln was elected on a pledge to stop the spread of slavery, not to emancipate the slaves. When enslaved people started to take advantage of wartime conditions and take freedom for themselves, Lincoln issued the Emancipation Proclamation. The newly freed African Americans attained more freedoms thanks to passage of the Thirteenth, Fourteenth, and Fifteenth Amendments, but readers in England knew that the cause of full freedom for African Americans proved to be unacceptable to most white people for decades to come. White pessimism about Black abilities in the United States were paralleled in France and Britain and their far-flung colonial empires, where there were still many obstacles in the way of colonial subjects becoming full citizens.[15]

Migration from Britain to Southern Africa was commonplace when Herbert Rhodes sailed on a small ship from London to Durban, the main port of Natal, arriving on April 23, 1868.[16] The colony of Natal was still very young. British colonization had only begun in 1831, with a small settlement of merchants landing on the coast and establishing contact with the Zulu kingdom. In 1838, groups of Boer trekkers who entered the region defeated the Zulu leader, Dingane, at the Battle of Ncome, also known as Blood River. An alliance between the Boers and Dingane's brother, Mpande, resulted in the 1840 division of the territory between the Zulu kingdom, to the north of the Thukela River, and a Boer republic called Natalia to the south. The British government, fearing a mass flight of Africans from Boer rule, annexed the colony in 1842. Around the time of the handover, British speculators bought most of the Boer land claims at low prices, then persuaded the colonial authorities to approve the claims. The landowners sponsored various schemes to attract more European settlers, yet those who did arrive often found themselves unprepared to farm in Natal's soil and climate. The arrival of European settlers was a mere trickle compared to the inflow of African migrants from around the region, on the order of 100,000 people. Many settlers turned to trading and began to rent land to African tenant farmers.[17]

African tenant farmers prospered under the policies of the colonial government's specialist in "native affairs," Theophilus Shepstone. Shepstone began to implement a system for governing African people that later came to be known as "indirect rule," which saved money by giving great latitude to chiefs who cooperated with British overlords. Loyal chiefs were assigned reserved "locations" and allowed to govern through "traditions" that were being written down and codified into law. Traditions related to property, polygamy, and bride price proved difficult for some Europeans to support. While old customs seemed "barbaric" to some settlers, to others they seemed likely to keep African workers on their own land—and not working for colonial farms and enterprises. A colonial "hut tax" was believed to put some pressure on Africans to earn wages, but Shepstone's native policies set aside land for groups of African people, not individuals. This made it difficult for land to be bought and sold, either to individual Africans or to European settlers. European settlers were restricted to their own large reservation. There, African workers were welcome, provided they lived on white farms or in townships where their mobility was restricted. In 1856, settler politicians were permitted by Britain to form a legislative council. Shepstone's system for separate and supposedly equal development still resonated throughout Southern Africa for the next hundred years.[18]

The Natal economy grew during the late 1850s and early 1860s. Much of the growth was based on speculation about future production of exports such as sugar and cotton. Chronic shortages of labor and capital persuaded big landowners to import indentured labor from India and to raise funds through a Natal Land and Colonisation Company, floated in London in 1861. Shepstone and the Natal government promoted cotton cultivation during the 1850s, but cultivation never fully took hold. The disruption to cotton and textile production during the US Civil War (1861–65), combined with a financial crisis at the Cape, persuaded Natal bankers to withhold credit and to demand repayment from farmers and merchants who owed money. In the middle and late 1860s, widespread bankruptcy was followed by government retrenchment. Settler protests accomplished little. Settler frustration over the lack of land, labor, and capital was directed increasingly toward Natal's African people. The key settler anxiety had to do with being a minority among an African majority. Africans came to be portrayed as settlers or "refugees" themselves, while colonial anxieties came to focus on fears of sexual encounters and the availability of African labor for white enterprises. In the late 1860s, settler ideology became increasingly racist and hostile.[19]

In some ways this was a favorable time for Herbert Rhodes to arrive in Natal. He received a grant of two hundred acres from one of the colony's immigrant schemes. His allotted land was located forty-five miles west of Durban in the valley of the Umkomaas (or Mkhomazi) River, about twelve miles from the nearest white settlement, Richmond. He intended to plant cotton, which had been scarce on world markets during and after the American Civil War. Herbert had success in meeting colonists and clearing the land. His early efforts at cotton cultivation revealed that he still had little knowledge of growing, processing, and marketing. In 1870, the seventeen-year-old Cecil Rhodes emigrated to Natal, to join Herbert's social network and to assist his efforts at cotton-farming. Cecil may have been encouraged by some of the guidebooks that he brought along, including one book by Louisiana native Joseph Lyman, who declared that the decline in cotton consumption after the US Civil War was an "unnatural state of things." He predicted a recovery for cotton, based on the growing demand for manufactured goods. For all planters who shared his sanguine expectations, Lyman provided a concise guide to cotton cultivation, as well as ginning and marketing.[20]

The prospect of all-male company and brotherly guidance may have appealed to Cecil.[21] His father supported the idea of farming in Natal and so, apparently, did Aunt Sophy, who lent young Cecil two thousand pounds (about $260,000 in today's dollars). Few British emigrants had such strong backing.

By the time of Cecil's arrival, Herbert had done the hard work of clearing forty-five acres of bush and planting it with cotton. And Herbert was gone. In November 1869, he took part in a small expedition of off-duty British soldiers from the 20th Regiment. They rode for several weeks, ascending the Drakensberg and riding for the Vaal River. In January 1870 they found diamonds near the bed of the river. Herbert came away with a few small stones. He and his companions were getting in at the very beginning of South Africa's mineral revolution.[22]

The European "discovery" of diamonds was built on a longer history of migration, settlement, and trade in the arid northern part of the Cape Colony. The area was populated by Tswana-speaking Tlhaping and Rolong people, as well as Dutch-speaking, mixed-race people called Griqua and Kora, and San people (formerly known as "Bushmen"). In the late 1830s, Dutch settlers called "voortrekkers" entered the area, migrating north after the British freed enslaved people. The Boer migrants formed a settlers' republic in the area called the Orange Free State. Similar voortrekker republics were formed in Natal and the Transvaal.[23] The British sought to stabilize the northern frontier, but it proved too expensive. They kept Natal but allowed the Transvaal and the Orange Free State to become independent, subject to British "suzerainty." Technically this meant that the British claimed oversight of the Free State's foreign relations.

Political expediency had been allowed to overshadow geographical vision. It took only a few years for the British government to recognize that allowing the two Boer republics to be formed was a mistake. The Boer migrants were soon provoking African neighbors by taking cattle and land. Along the republics' borders, conflict seemed constant, yet this was not the only problem. As the Cape Colony took steps toward achieving responsible government, it began to seem that a united South Africa might be the most economical way forward. Boer independence stood in the way. Then, in the 1860s, ancient gold mines were discovered to the north in Mashonaland, in what is today northeastern Zimbabwe, while in Matabeleland, in southwestern Zimbabwe, small-scale gold mining began at Tati. By the time diamonds were discovered in Griqua territory, near the Orange Free State and the Transvaal, unification under British oversight began to seem essential. In 1868 the British government accepted an invitation from the Sotho paramount chief, Moshoeshoe, to turn Sotho lands into British territory. The same thing was about to be done to the diamond fields.

The diamond rush developed in a seemingly remote area that had long-standing patterns of migration and trade. The "Road to the North," sometimes called the "Missionary Road" and the "Hunters' Road," stretched from the diamond fields north into the territory of the Ndebele state centered on Bulawayo, in Matabeleland. Starting in the 1820s, merchants and hunters traveled north from the Cape, exchanging firearms and brandy for tons of ivory and for other animal products, such as skins and feathers. Missionaries traveled the roads, too, spreading knowledge of Christianity as well as European-style farming and material culture. David Arnot, a mixed-race legal clerk from the Northern Cape, advocated for the northward expansion of British rule up the Missionary Road. (The idea of an imperial Road to the North was not original to Cecil Rhodes.)[24]

Supporters of Britain and the Boer republics vied for access to land, cattle, and mobility. It came as a surprise to everyone that the residents of the Northern Cape were sitting on top of vast mineral resources. In the late 1860s, after years of economic and environmental distress, a diamond rush began with seemingly random discoveries. Diggers lacked the expertise to assess the value of the finds until a scientist in Grahamstown, Dr. William G. Atherstone, confirmed one stone to be a 21.25-carat diamond worth £500. The British governor of the Cape Colony, Philip Wodehouse, purchased the diamond and had it sent to the colony's display at the Paris Exhibition. The gem came to be known as the Eureka diamond.[25]

The area began to yield more precious stones. Toward the end of 1867, the Cape Colony's magistrate at Hopetown, Lorenzo Boyes, visited van Niekerk's farm to see if more diamonds could be found. Boyes worked with local Boers and their African "servants," who together gathered and sifted pebbles for two weeks. This appears to have been the first systematic search for alluvial diamonds. During 1868 more small diamonds were found by local people and a handful of outside prospectors. Some outsiders remained skeptical about the existence of a diamond field. One English expert, J. R. Gregory, visited Hopetown and its vicinity and reported that there was no diamond field—the gems had been deposited by ostriches. It was not until March 1869, when Schalk van Niekerk bought a large rough diamond from a young Griqua shepherd who was also known locally as a "witch-finder," that the potential value of the find began to be understood. The shepherd was delighted to receive 500 sheep, ten oxen, and a horse and thought he had gotten the better of van Niekerk. The stone, later known as the Star of South Africa, was an 83.5-carat diamond that van Niekerk sold to local merchants, Lilienfeld Brothers of Hopetown, for £11,200. Soon after, the Lilienfelds sent the stone to England, where it changed hands several more times. Eventually William Ward, the Earl of Dudley, bought it for his wife, paying £25,000.[26]

By the time the Star of South Africa was identified, it was becoming apparent that alluvial diamonds could be found on both sides of the Vaal River. The rise and fall of the river appeared to have washed gems onto the surface in current and former channels. Amidst the gravel deposits of basalt, sandstone, and quartz there were colorful pebbles of agate, garnet, and jasper, along with occasional diamonds. The early stories of the diamond fields emphasize the activities of Europeans, but most of the diamonds were being discovered by Tswana or Griqua people. Local chiefs controlled the trade, possibly because finders brought diamonds to them as a kind of tribute. The town of Dikgatlong, on the Vaal River thirty miles northwest of present-day Kimberley, was the location of the Tlhaping chief, Jantjie Mothibi. His settlement appears to have played a central role in the early trade. During 1869, as Herbert Rhodes and other European adventurers were exploring the area, formal diggings were established along the Vaal River, and control of diamond hunting passed into the hands of Europeans.[27]

By the start of 1870, there were almost a thousand diggers near the Vaal River. By the end of the year, their numbers had risen to somewhere between 5,000 and 10,000. They made their way mostly from South Africa's port cities, riding for upwards of six weeks to the "river diggings," where they set up camps, sheltering in wagons and shanties. The largest mine camps were located at the village of Klipdrift, later called Barkly West, twenty miles northwest of present-day Kimberley, just across the Vaal River. From there, the river diggings stretched along the Vaal another twenty miles west and northwest toward Delportshoop. Miners dug with picks and shovels and used the small river's water to wash the soil in sifting screens to reveal any diamonds. Miners marked their claims. Miners who ventured a few miles from the river into the interior found that alluvial diamonds appeared to be common on two Boer farms, Bultfontein and Dorstfontein. The children of Dorstfontein's proprietor, Van Wyk, even found diamonds in the dried mud walls of their home. The source of the mud, the farm's pond, Dutoitspan, was scoured for diamonds. Soon it became a major digging site.[28]

Hundreds of prospectors began to "rush" or forcibly occupy the mostly arid area, called the "dry diggings." Meanwhile, a group of merchants from Port Elizabeth purchased the Bultfontein farm and began the process of evicting squatters and making more formal plans for a proper mine. That farm, together with Dorstfontein, was then bought by a group of diamond merchants from London. The new owners issued an ultimatum to the diggers to leave the property, but without the backing of a police force, the company had to give in to the diggers, who agreed to pay a license fee for the right to prospect for diamonds. Starting in April 1871, more diamonds were found at the neighboring farm, Vooruitzigt, which belonged to the De Beers family. With the price of diamonds starting to decline, merchants began to attempt to create monopolies over the dry diggings, pressuring some diggers to return to the riverside. Concessions and dispossessions fueled conflict between British, Dutch, Tlhaping, and Rolong authorities, all of whom had different legal understandings about land.[29] Miners took the law into their own hands and formed committees to govern the assignment of claims and to adjudicate disputes over boundaries.

When Herbert Rhodes arrived at the River Diggings, as they were called, miners were using technologies that were easy to construct and understand. They were introduced by diggers who had experience with "placer" or surface mining in Australia and the US West. The simplest technique was to shovel a load of pebbles and dirt onto a "cradle," a kind of sieve that could be rinsed with the river's water. A more advanced technique involved building four simple devices. First, the rocks were placed in a "Long Tom," a trough with running water and a comb to help identify stones with potential. Second, the rocks were washed in a larger cradle built into a heavy wooden frame, with several layers of perforated screens. The screens were rocked back and forth—hence the name. The third simple machine was called a "Babe" or "Baby," named after its inventor, an American named Jerome Babe who built the first one at the River Diggings. The baby was a screen that was hung in the air, attached by leather reins to four posts. The pebbles were bounced up and down, or "pulsated" on the baby. The fourth device was a cylinder made with either wire screen or perforated metal. This, too, appears to have been invented on the diamond fields. The cylinder was dunked in a deep trough and spun around until potential gems were separated from rock. These machines seem primitive by later standards, but they were highly portable and easily modified and repaired with minimal equipment. They were well suited to small-scale mining operations.[30]

During this early phase of surface diamond mining, the workforce began to divide along racial lines. The miners who arrived from Europe, Australia, and the US West were familiar with doing all manual labor themselves. On the diamond fields of the early 1870s, there were still some African and mixed-race men who asserted rights of ownership over claims, but soon their ownership became prohibited.[31]

Cecil Rhodes did not travel immediately to see Herbert on the diamond fields. Cecil arrived in Durban on September 1, 1870, and was hosted by Dr. Peter Sutherland, Natal's surveyor-general, the official in charge of mapping out landholdings. Sutherland told Cecil that Herbert had left for the diamond fields. Sutherland himself had an interest in geology, but it is not clear to what extent he influenced Cecil's thinking about diamonds. The main value of Cecil's stay with Sutherland was that he was introduced to many colonists. He met African people for the first time, too. During several rides around the colony, he and Sutherland got to stay with African families in their homes, happily sampling local beer. After a month of learning his way around, Cecil, a teenager without farming experience, began to manage the Rhodes farm for several months until his brother's return. Conditions were unlike anything in Bishop's Stortford. Access to the farm lay on a steep path. Cecil lived in a hut and cooked on a campfire. He was helped by one servant and occasional African laborers. When Herbert returned after a few months, the two Rhodes brothers both pitched in with manual labor, cultivating cotton and clearing more land. Herbert came and went, restless for opportunities.[32]

The Rhodes brothers made social and business connections by playing cricket, the sport that Herbert and his brothers learned in Bishop's Stortford. Within several months of Herbert's arrival, he was playing for the Richmond team against William E. Shepstone, the son of Theophilus Shepstone. Over the course of the next months, William Shepstone and two of his brothers started to play on the same side as Herbert.[33] Cricket provided entrée into the settler world and into the world of colonial policymaking. Cecil wrote to his mother that attending cricket matches had less to do with playing and more to do with socializing. "You are obliged out here," he wrote, "if you wish to be at all respected, to just go to a cricket-match, and a dance or so. It is twenty times better than going into town for a spree, as a great many do out here…it is astonishing what a lot of useful knowledge you pick up at one of these matches."[34]

The landscape of Natal made a strong impression on young Rhodes. In one letter to his mother about a journey to hunt birds, he reported that "I never saw such an extraordinarily beautiful place in my life. It is not possible to picture or fancy such a place. The water ran the whole way down the hill, over immense boulders of stone; a thick brush being on each side filled with tremendous great aloes and cactus.…And there hundreds of feet below us lay stretched out the whole valley with our huts looking like specks, and in the distance there were hills rising one above the other, with a splendid blue tint on them."[35]

Many of his early letters describe the sense of awe and wonder that he felt when gazing at the Natal landscape. In one he describes a riding trip through a forest in the Drakensberg Mountains: "It fills you with a sort of awe to get right into the heart, to look up and see those immense trees, whose tops you can hardly reach with your eye, to feel the deathlike silence, suddenly broken either by the shrill cries of parrots, or else by the chatter of the monkeys. And then, in a minute everything is still again, and you feel as if you were in an immense tomb, shut out from every living creature. We stopped only about one day there, and then rode back. You have a splendid view of the Drakensburg from there, looking so near, within half an hour's ride, and yet miles and miles away. I believe that to see the sun rise in Natal from the top of the Drakensberg, is one of the finest views in the world."[36]

Rhodes described African scenery and African people. In one of his early letters home he wrote to his mother using a term that was becoming an epithet: "The K-----rs rather shock your modesty. They many of them have nothing on, excepting a band round the middle. They are fine-looking men, and carry themselves very erect. They all take snuff, and carry their snuff-boxes in a hole, bored through their ears. They also pay great attention to their hair and carry porcupine quills in it, with which they dress it. You often see them sitting down in groups, dressing each other's hairs, and picking the fleas out. The most disagreeable thing about them is their smell. I don't think anything equals the smell of a party of K----r women on a hot day if you pass on the lee side of them." Early biographers of Rhodes claimed that African people found him sympathetic, but it seems that Rhodes's negative attitude toward African people resembled that of his fellow colonists. Rhodes told his mother about his hopes for using African people as laborers: "There is a great satisfaction in having land of your own, horses of your own, and shooting when you like, and a lot of black n-----s to do what you like with, apart from the fact of making money."[37]

The 250-acre Rhodes cotton farm fared better in its second season. The Rhodes brothers and thirty-odd African workers were cultivating the crops more appropriately. Cecil's letters home indicate that he arranged for planting and picking carefully. Cecil even began to invest small amounts of money with Dr. Sutherland, who, acting as an agent, bought shares in a Natal railway. Cecil was already showing signs of financial acumen.[38] He was also cultivating the right connections. On May 25, 1871, after the harvest came in, Cecil attended the annual meeting of the colony's agricultural society, where he exhibited a sample of his cotton. The *Natal Witness* reported that the evening dinner was attended by the colony's leaders and most prominent settlers. The local newspaper reports many long after-dinner political speeches, all initiated by toasting. When one settler proposed that a man should offer the traditional toast, "To the Ladies," Rhodes rose in response, possibly his first public speech according to his friend and biographer, Lewis Michell.[39] As a youth Rhodes was showing a bent for networking and speaking.

2

Digging Diamonds

FARMING AND INVESTING presented modest opportunities for Herbert and Cecil Rhodes. Diamond mining involved greater opportunities as well as greater risks. The local newspaper, the *Natal Witness*, regularly published stories about the exploits of the colony's young men at the diamond fields. In the semi-arid area twenty miles to the southeast of the Vaal River, at the present-day site of Kimberley, significant deposits of diamonds were starting to be found on four farms: Bultfontein (1869), Dutoitspan (1870), De Beers (May 1871), and Vooruitzigt (July 1871). The dry diggings began to yield large quantities of diamonds and started to attract thousands of miners. By the end of 1871, there were approximately 50,000 miners living in the area, including African and European people from around the region and the world. The diamond fields may have had a population larger than Cape Town's.[1]

The diggers in this new, rich territory needed order. Mine claims, by their very nature, required a legal framework. Order could be established through customary practices, local government, or colonial legislation. Diggers' committees, a common practice in California, spread to Kimberley via American and Australian miners. Government by digger's committee implied government by experts in the craft of mining, but the specific need for arbitration, together with the general need for social and economic order, in turn necessitated seemingly inevitable (and resented) interventions by the governments of the Cape Colony and the Orange Free State.

The key legal issue involved rights to claims. At the early alluvial diamond diggings near the Vaal River, claimholders paid rent to property owners. In 1870, when the dry diggings started to open, the landowner at Bultfontein charged miners a monthly fee. The owner at Dorstfontein (later called Dutoitspan) took a similar approach, until he sold the land to a company in April 1871. When the company attempted to close off the mine to tenants, the miners rushed the land and forced the company to rent to them. In subsequent months, diggers rushed the Vooruitzigt farm, which contained the sites that became Old De Beers or Old Rush (later called De Beers Mine) and

Colesberg Kopje (later called Kimberley Mine). The owners sold the property to merchants from Port Elizabeth, who in turn continued to extract rents from the miners.[2]

When Rhodes arrived, the Old Rush and the New Rush were not yet under the authority of the Cape's British governor and were still governed as diggers' republics. Among the diggers a consensus emerged to limit each miner to two claims, with each claim allowed to be subdivided. Portions of claims in the Kimberley Mine were set aside for paths, so that dirt could be hauled out more easily. To be valid, claims had to be worked on every day. Shortly after the start of mining at De Beers and Kimberley, the government of the Orange Free State sent out a surveyor who was empowered to organize the diggers' committees and collect license fees from miners. With so many miners discovering so many diamonds, it was only a matter of time before the government of the Cape Colony intervened. British annexation came in November 1871.

The arrival of Cecil Rhodes at the diamond fields coincided with the imposition of British rule over the region's varied population. Before the discovery of diamonds, this part of the Northern Cape was so remote and sparsely populated that there had never been much need to fix boundaries. The boundaries between groups were not entirely clear, nor were the boundaries between the states that ruled them. But the potential wealth of the diamond fields was causing conflicts. The region was contested by multiple groups, and the cultural geography of the area was difficult for outsiders to understand. A core misunderstanding had to do with politics. Nineteenth-century Europeans identified strongly with nations, linked by language, religion, customs, and a sense of borders, whereas African chiefdoms tended to take a more open approach to group membership. Chiefs were more willing to incorporate outsiders. Chiefdoms might involve people who spoke the same languages or had the same customs and sense of place, but cultural and geographical borders tended to be more fluid. As Southern African people met Europeans and went to work for them on the diamond fields, they were subjected to intense classification along European lines and split into "tribes."[3]

Local authorities were locked in conflict over the diamond fields. The Griqua chief, Andries Waterboer, hired Colesberg's mixed-race entrepreneur, David Arnot, as his agent. Arnot made the case that all the diamond fields, including the river diggings and the dry diggings, as well as the start of the road to the interior, belonged to Waterboer and his people, who numbered approximately one thousand. The nearby Tswana chiefdom, the Tlhaping, had ten thousand people and a claim to the region that was at least equally strong. The Tlhaping chief, Jantjie, had been pushing back against settler land purchases but had himself been taken advantage of by dodgy speculators from England. The unfair association with these speculators, together with his resistance, alienated Jantjie somewhat from British officials. Waterboer, through Arnot, maintained all along that he had sovereignty over the diamond fields. Arnot supported these claims by presenting old treaties with the British that extended back into the time of Waterboer's father.[4]

The politics of this open geographical space tended to favor the most powerful groups. The claims of the Tlhaping were strong but were overcome by the relationship that Arnot was maintaining between Griqua and British leaders. By 1871, Waterboer had little hope of managing the emerging boomtown himself, but Arnot knew that if Waterboer's claim to the region could be firmed up, then the Griqua leader could be pressured to assign the diamond fields to Britain. This would benefit Arnot personally, because Waterboer had assigned the exclusive rights to mine in the territory to Arnot and his partners. Unfortunately for them, the Cape Colony was not going to chase out the thousands of fortune-seekers who rushed the diamond fields, nor were they going to be made to pay fees to Arnot. Arnot and his partners learned a key lesson about mineral concessions granted by chiefs like Waterboer. The concession's value was relative to the chief's authority.[5]

Might made right. It seemed imperative to the most powerful regional player, the British, to keep the diamond fields out of the hands of the Orange Free State and the Transvaal. The Boer republics proclaimed sovereignty over the diamond fields and tried to exclude noncitizens from claim ownership. Diggers responded by starting to organize a republic of their own. In 1871, the British government responded to the disorder. The secretary of state for the colonies, John Wodehouse, the Earl of Kimberley, appointed a new governor of the Cape Colony and high commissioner for Southern Africa, Henry Barkly, with instructions to take control of the diamond fields.[6]

Barkly was an experienced colonial administrator. He had previously served as the governor of four colonies but had little knowledge of Southern Africa. He relied heavily on Richard Southey, an Eastern Cape settler who held the top Cape Colony post of colonial secretary, in effect the prime minister. Southey had extensive experience with the Northern Cape and the diamond fields. On arriving in South Africa, Barkly traveled immediately to Klipdrift, on the Vaal River, to assess the situation. While the Griqua chief, Waterboer, had submitted claims to the governor through Arnot, the Tlhaping chief, Jantjie, was not granted access and could not submit a legal case. Barkly, Southey, and their aides clearly preferred Waterboer, whose claims were represented eloquently by Arnot. To give the decision the appearance of competence and neutrality, Barkly appointed a commission to study the baffling details of the claims. Then Barkly returned to Cape Town. The commission that decided the fate of the diamond fields was headed by the lieutenant-governor of Natal, Robert Keate, a former governor of Trinidad and a famous cricketer. Keate's commission met in Bloemhof during April, May, and June of 1871 and predictably drew a boundary around the diamond fields, awarding them to Waterboer. Waterboer, through Arnot, then appealed for British "protection." Keate drew a line between the Transvaal, to the east, and the Tlhaping and Rolong territories to the west, preventing Boer access to the roadways north.[7]

Keate presented the British government with a legalistic fig leaf to conceal what Jantjie of the Tlhaping and the Boers of the Orange Free State and the Transvaal considered to be a naked theft of territory. Having some familiarity with land-theft themselves, the Orange Free State leadership protested that the leases assigned to them by Adam Kok's eastern Griquas permitted their own governance of the diamond fields. The English-speaking diamond diggers resented the Free State's intrusions, even though they preferred the Free State's racially discriminatory labor laws to the Cape Colony's ostensibly color-blind system. As a practical matter, the Orange Free State had few powers of enforcement, while the Cape Colony could call on Britain for armed help, albeit at great expense. The diggers knew that a stronger state like Britain was likely to administer the territory with a greater degree of regulation and scrutiny.[8]

Through clever rationalizations, the British commission assigned some of the world's most valuable real estate to Britain. The Keate Award outraged the Orange Free State government and the Tlhaping leadership. Five years later, a subsequent commission called it into question, but by that point, the diamond mines were going deeper and attracting heavy investments and the Tlhaping and Boer protests were essentially a moot point. Barkly encountered one final obstacle. Ideally Waterboer's territory would be incorporated into the Cape Colony, but the Cape Parliament refused to authorize funding, thanks to the influence of Boer members. The idea of Cape administration was also feared by diggers. In response, the Colonial Office created a new crown colony called Griqualand West as of October 1871 under a new lieutenant-governor, Richard Southey. Southey was empowered to act without any check on his actions by a representative government. Immediately his government started a conflict with miners by abolishing the diggers' committees and upholding the rights of landowners.[9]

News of Britain claiming the dry diggings set Herbert and Cecil Rhodes in motion. On September 1, 1871, one year after Cecil's arrival in Natal, the *Witness* reprinted a story from the *Diamond Fields* newspaper indicating that Herbert found a total of 110 carats of diamonds, with the best stones measuring 14, 16, and 28 carats.[10] The news about Herbert's discoveries raised questions about the wisdom of continuing to farm in Natal. In late October 1871, Cecil packed a shovel and a bucket and left Natal on a month-long journey in a two-wheeled "Scotch cart" pulled by oxen to join Herbert at Colesberg Kopje, the hill that was yielding diamonds at Vooruizigt. Cecil rode four hundred miles by himself, accompanied by several works of the classical authors and a Greek lexicon. Thousands of settlers were making their way in the same direction. From Pietermaritzburg, the road rises steadily toward the mountain range called the Drakensberg. On the other side of the Drakensberg, Rhodes continued westward, across the plains to Bloemfontein, the capital of the Orange Free State. From there he made his way to Kimberley.[11]

The mountains and the open expanses of the plains were said by his early biographer, Basil Williams, to have expanded Rhodes's view. Unlike what he had seen in Natal, the interior landscape is one of "the great unconfined spaces of the world," offering "vast plains, unending to the view." Williams knew many of Rhodes's associates and was sympathetic to colonialism. Williams made the point that the landscape helped to produce "a wide outlook on South African affairs." Williams believed that Rhodes "gained that clear direct gaze characteristic of those who have dwelt long in those sun-washed spaces, a gaze that seemed to be straining out to a far distant horizon and never finding the goal of his visions."[12]

Upon arriving at Herbert's claims on Colesberg Kopje, Rhodes described what he saw in a letter to his mother. The *kopje* was a

> small round hill at its very highest part only 30 feet above the level of the surrounding country, about 180 yards broad and 220 long; all round it a mass of White tents, and then beyond them a flat level country for miles and miles, with here and there a gentle rise. . . . I should like you to have a peep at the kopje from my tent door at the present moment. It is like an immense number of ant-heaps covered with black ants, as thick as can be, the latter represented by human beings; when you understand that there are about 600 claims on the kopje and each claim is generally split into 4, and on each bit there are about 6 blacks and whites working, it gives a total of about ten thousand working every day on a piece of ground 180 yards by 220. . . . Take your garden,

for instance, and peg the whole off into squares or claims 31 ft. by 31 ft., and then the question is how to take all the earth out and sieve it. All through the kopje roads have been left to carry the stuff off in carts like the following [rough diagram]; that is of every claim of 31 ft., 7 ft. 6 inches are not allowed to be worked, but is left for a road . . . the roads are the only ground that remain of the original level. . . . The carting on the kopje is done chiefly by mules, as they are so very hardy, and have so few diseases. There are constantly mules, carts and all going head over heels into the mines below as there are no rails or anything on either side of the roads, nothing but one great broad chasm below. Here and there where the roads have fallen in, bridges have been put, and they are now the safest part of the kopje. . . . On each side of every road there is now a continuous chasm from top to bottom of the kopje varying in depth from 30 to 60 ft.[13]

Rhodes saw the mines like an educated, middle-class, mid-nineteenth-century Englishman would, as a theater of the sublime and as a place to turn a profit. In an early letter to his family, Rhodes described the process of sifting the soil and his ambitions for the mine:

There are reefs all round these diamond mines, inside which the diamonds are found. The reef is the usual soil of the country round, red sand just at the top and then a black and white stony shale below. Inside the reef is the diamondiferous soil. It works just like Stilton cheese, and is as like the composition of Stilton cheese as anything I can compare it to. . . . They have been able to find no bottom yet, and keep on finding steadily at 70 ft. You will understand how enormously rich it is, when I say that a good claim would certainly average a diamond to every load of stuff that was sorted—a load being about 50 buckets. . . . Some day I expect to see the kopje one big basin where once there was a large hill.[14]

Rhodes's vision of the place was prescient. The hill called Colesberg Kopje did turn into a basin, one of the largest dug holes in history, when it came to be known as the Kimberley Mine, or "The Big Hole."

Young Cecil Rhodes enjoyed significant advantages over most ordinary diggers. Herbert had been digging for two years already and had accumulated enough capital to own two claims, plus a half share in one and a quarter share in another. Cecil began to earn money quickly—about £100 per week—and bought a quarter claim of his own. Capital was also used to buy rudimentary technology. Rhodes described the technical challenges. "To begin with," he wrote, "the ground is first picked, then the bumps smashed up, and you just put the stuff through a very coarse wire sieving, this lets the fine stuff pass through and keeps all the stones which are thrown on the side; it is then hoisted out of the claim, and either carried or carted to the sorting table, where it is first put through fine wire sieving which sieves all the lime-dust away. What remains is put on the sorting-table, and then one sorts away with a small scraper spreading the stuff out on the table with one scoop and then off with the next."[15]

Small-scale claim-owners still helped with some of the manual labor, but for the most part the work was done by African migrant workers. White claim-owners gave overall direction to the digging. They gave the day's instructions to white overseers, many of whom were migrants from the Cape Colony or from other mining regions in Britain, Australia, and the US West. The white overseers supervised a team of African workers who had migrated from different parts of Southern Africa. African laborers were often inexperienced and unable to speak English. They were subject to verbal and physical abuse, like those who had labored under slavery in the Cape Colony and continued to be subject to discrimination after emancipation. The three-tiered labor system had already been established in the copper mines of Namaqualand. These were located near O'okiep, five hundred miles west of the diamond fields. The copper mines and the diamond mines were separate from each other, but the labor system was quite similar. The system was extended to Kimberley and eventually spread to the gold mines of the South African Republic, or Transvaal, where racial discrimination was built into the constitution.[16]

Earning money from digging was not the only way to succeed in the sprawling mining camps emerging around Colesberg Kopje and De Beers Mine. Herbert possessed the social polish and the quick wit that was lacking in Cecil, but his younger brother was still able to step into his social circle, living and dining with a close group of upper-middle-class Englishmen and colonials who eventually called themselves the "Twelve Apostles." In this group Cecil made lifelong friends and business connections. Among them was John X. Merriman, also the son of a clergyman, who had been a member of the Cape Parliament's House of Assembly since 1869. When Parliament was out of session, Merriman was in Kimberley, representing a syndicate of diamond buyers. His conversations with Rhodes were not recorded, but through Merriman, Rhodes had access to inside information about economic development and infrastructure building.[17]

Rhodes made the acquaintance of several other people who became important to his network. One was John Blades Currey, soon to be the colonial secretary of the new colony of Griqualand West. Rhodes met his future business partner, an athlete from Harrow and Cambridge named Charles Dunell Rudd, as well as other present and future men of influence in South African business and politics. He became friends with Sidney Shippard, an Oxford graduate and a future colonial administrator in Southern Africa, who served as attorney-general of Griqualand West from 1873 to 1877. Rhodes shared meals with Jacob Barry, who would later become an attorney and judge. Rhodes also dined regularly with the witty novelist and poet William Charles Scully. Two artists were present, too: Henry Charles Seppings Wright, future caricaturist for *Vanity Fair* and the *Illustrated London News*, and the future impressionist painter Norman Garstin.[18]

An artist—most probably Garstin—wrote a letter to Rhodes's friend and biographer, Lewis Michell, describing what it was like to be with Rhodes in these early days in Kimberley. The town was dusty and the mines were dangerous. A claimholder like Garstin or Rhodes "sat amongst his K----s, in the blinding sun and dust, passing the sifted granules of tufa before his dazzled eyes." They could see nearby "great heaps and mounds" of tailings piling up, while "mound and mine were black with men moving and working with ant-like activity." As for Rhodes, the artist remembered "his tall, delicate figure crumpled up on an inverted bucket, as he sat scraping his gravel surrounded by his dusky Zulus."[19]

Looking back on these days, Rhodes's messmates located the origins of Rhodes's vision in his mining experiences. Scully later wrote that "Rhodes was somewhat intolerant in discussion."

> After dinner it was his wont to lean forward with both elbows on the table and his mouth slightly open. He had a habit, when thinking, of rubbing his chin gently with his forefinger. Very often he would sit in the attitude described for a very long time, without joining in whatever conversation happened to be going on. His manner and expression suggested that his thoughts were far away, but occasionally some interjection would indicate that, to a certain extent, he was keeping in touch with the current topic. Indeed, it often seemed to me that the larger part of his brain was dealing with something of which no one else had the cognizance.[20]

His fellow diggers recall the tall, thin Rhodes, dressed simply, sitting quietly at the edge of the mine, thinking about it, or standing or sitting, quietly by himself, on a street corner or outside a tent. Conventionally biographers have thought that it was during these moments that Rhodes imagined the consolidation of the mining claims, from the standpoint of finance and engineering; the potential profits; and the prospects for using these profits to unite South Africa and expand it north of the Limpopo into Central Africa. None of these speculations have been documented, but Rhodes indisputably gained an early understanding of the technical complexities of mining.

Rhodes found himself living in a difficult urban environment. The boomtown's population of 50,000 was divided into 20,000 Europeans and 30,000 Africans. Soon the town was named Kimberley after Britain's secretary of state for the colonies. The African migrants came from all around the subcontinent, while the Europeans came from around the world. The place was a wild mix of languages and traditions. In Rhodes's letters to his mother, he did not mention physical hardships, but these were worthy of note. Kimberley is dry, with an average annual rainfall of only sixteen inches. Temperatures swing between cool winters, with average temperatures of around fifty degrees Fahrenheit, to warm summers, averaging eighty-five degrees. Water had to be trucked to the town from the Vaal River at great cost. One bucket cost nine pence or more. Nearly all food and drink needed to be shipped from South Africa's port cities. Kimberley had virtually no local agriculture. The miners lived in tents and shanties, with the most rudimentary arrangements for sanitation. Flies were everywhere. Fire and disease were ever-present dangers. Dust swirled about, and the noise of digging and traffic was incessant. Order was preserved by rough justice. Those accused of stealing or smuggling diamonds had their tents burned down by vigilantes.[21]

The miners used the old, straightforward technologies to sift the gems from the yellow ground, which was worthless crumbly rock. Technically the yellow ground and the blue ground below it are classified as breccia, the geological term for naturally occurring concrete. The breccia could be spread out and allowed to disintegrate in the sun and rain, revealing pebbles that were potentially gems, but since space and patience were often lacking, the breccia was more likely to be pulverized with hammers and shovels. Next the beaten rocks were spread on rocking tables to shake off the lighter pebbles and dust before running them through the cylinder sieve. Miners still used the "Long Tom" washing trough; the "Cradle" sieve; the "Babe" pulsator; and the "Cylinder" centrifuge. The Rhodes brothers used other simple pieces of equipment, too, such as picks, shovels, wheelbarrows, carts, scrapers, and rakes. At Colesberg Kopje and the three other nearby mines, the miners at the dry diggings added a few steps to the processing of the diamonds from the surrounding rocks. The deeper mines necessitated a process for workers shoveling the ground up, in stages, and eventually using buckets to haul up the crumbly rocks to the top of the pit. There were early attempts to introduce power sifting. In 1871, one group of Americans used a steam engine to power a pulsating cylinder, but the contraption did not last for very long. In these early years, miners preferred to use the simpler, reliable methods that yielded plenty of large, high-quality diamonds.[22]

As diamond mining took off, the diamond fields became the scene of intense competition among diamond buyers. Initially the market was informal, with merchants on horseback, called "kopje-wallopers," buying diamonds on the spot from diggers. Mainly these buyers were Jewish in origin, as were the merchant firms like Mosenthal Brothers and Lilienfeld Brothers of Cape Town and Port Elizabeth, whose networks connected them to Britain and continental Europe. Dealers were required to pay a license fee that rose, in the early years, from £25 to £50. By 1875, colonial records list 185 licensed dealers and 81 brokers. Many diamond dealers also invested in mining and in businesses near the mines. Licensed dealers often funded informal, poor brokers who bought diamonds in the shadows. From small dealers to large trade houses, the diamond-dealing business depended on the analysis of diamonds, focusing on their size as well as their shape and their color. "Rough" or uncut diamonds were sold in London's Hatton Garden and Holborn Viaduct to buyers from Amsterdam and Antwerp, where most cutting and polishing firms were located. Buyers paid careful attention to the susceptibility of rough diamonds to cutting and polishing.[23]

In late 1871 and throughout 1872, Cecil worked for Herbert, supervising laborers at the two claims. For half the year they were joined by their brother Frank, who had just finished his studies at the Royal Military Academy, Sandhurst, and was awaiting his first assignment as an officer. In early 1872, Herbert went to Natal to attend to the farm and to welcome Frank to South Africa. Cecil was left in charge of the claims and appears to have suffered from the stress. The hard labor in a harsh climate, combined with the challenges of supervising a business, coincided with the death of a friend, John C. Thompson. These factors, likely combined with the effects of tobacco, alcohol, and dehydration, brought about a spell in which he suffered from chest pains and shortness of breath. The spell required him to stay with John Blades Currey and his wife, Mary, who "nursed him back to health."[24]

Still only eighteen years old, Cecil Rhodes confronted mortality by writing his first will. In it, he made an unusual gesture: he left his possessions not to his family members or friends but to Britain's secretary of state for the colonies, Lord Kimberley, to advance the cause of British colonial rule. As biographer Robert Rotberg points out, this is the first indication that Rhodes coupled thoughts of mortality with thoughts of empire building. Rhodes's sense of destiny eventually became bound up with "the idea," his ambition to extend European settlement far to the north. It is around this time, in May 1872, that he made his first journey north. Herbert returned to Kimberley with Frank. Frank took charge of the family claims at the diamond diggings so that Herbert and Cecil could trek northward. There are few details about this trip. It may have lasted between four and eight months. Sources indicate that the brothers rode 125 miles north to Vryburg, then continued another 100 miles north to Mahikeng, then known as Mafeking, 190 miles east to Marabastad, Pretoria's market area. They had heard that gold was being panned in the vicinity but did not find any themselves. On the way back to Kimberley, the brothers stopped at Roodeport, near Johannesburg, where Cecil bought a 3,000-acre farm. His motivations for buying it are not clear. In a letter to Natal's surveyor-general, Peter Sutherland, Rhodes described the farm as being "of no earthly good and only sunk money."[25]

Rhodes kept expanding his network of associates. During his first year at the diamond fields Rhodes befriended Charles Dunell Rudd, who became a long-term associate. Nine years older than Rhodes, Rudd was born in Norfolk, the son of a merchant and shipbuilder with business ties to South Africa. Rudd attended Harrow and Trinity College, Cambridge, where he spent three years but never earned a degree. An athlete, he later claimed that he "overtrained" for the mile run and left for South Africa to restore his health. He spent several years traveling to Mauritius, Sri Lanka, and throughout South Africa with some of the best-known adventurers of his day, including stints with John Dunn, the English merchant who became a Zulu chief, and the German explorer Eduard Mohr. With the help of his brother, Thomas, a merchant in Port Elizabeth with R. E. Wallace and Company, in 1871 he arrived at the diamond fields, where he struggled to establish himself as a merchant, insurance agent, and diamond dealer. It was around this time that he became acquainted with the Rhodes brothers.[26]

Rudd mentored Rhodes in business practices, showing him how to be versatile and adaptive. They worked shoulder to shoulder at Herbert's claims, supervising the digging and sorting of diamonds, while Rudd also worked in various businesses for his brother's company. Rhodes spent some of his time working as Rudd's clerk. Their first two years together, 1872 and 1873, are poorly documented. We know that as prices fell and Herbert sold his claims, Cecil and Rudd shifted away from the New Rush (Kimberley Mine) toward buying claims

The De Beers Mine, 1872. Courtesy of the McGregor Museum, Kimberley, MMKP 4447.

in the Old Rush (De Beers Mine), known to be more productive than the Kimberley Mine, which generally produced higher quality diamonds.

Rapid changes were under way at the mines. As a way of making money, white claim owners turned increasingly to regulating Black migrant workers, particularly their mobility. For decades, white settlers had limited success in pressing colonial governments for vagrancy laws. In July and August of 1872, new rules were put in place. Black migrant workers were required to register at a Servants' Registry Office, where they obtained daily passes until they found work. When they had a job, they received a longer-term pass, which the law required them to produce whenever white men asked to see it. When employment ended, another pass had to be secured. Black men without a pass could be fined five pounds, imprisoned for two months, and flogged with twenty-five lashes, at a time when most of the English-speaking world was repealing flogging. Further rules that were imposed on Black workers were related to the material characteristics of diamonds. Small and highly portable, diamonds were easily stolen and fenced. Rules were imposed to prevent Black workers from stealing diamonds. Employers, called "masters," could search their "servants" at any time. Any diamonds found on a servant were assumed to belong to the master. Diamond theft could be punished by a year of prison and fifty lashes, a sanction that was potentially lethal.[27]

Diamonds were also a luxury good that made diggers vulnerable to downturns in the world economy. In countries that bought luxury goods, the early years on the diamond fields were a time of prosperity. The conclusion of the US Civil War (1865), the opening of the Suez Canal (1867), and the unification of Germany (1871) had fueled an economic boom. Spectacular growth occurred in railways and shipping, the keys to modern mobility, while improvements were also made in agriculture, mining, and industrial production. Rhodes's early years in South Africa coincided with a period of great optimism in the world economy. Yet in May 1873, a panic on the Vienna Stock Market caused share values to decline worldwide. In all the industrial countries, prices began to fall, sparking labor unrest and causing bankruptcies, including some famous ones, like Jay Cooke's Northern Pacific Railroad. The newly opened Suez Canal suffered from a lack of investment in steamships, which were better adapted to canal travel than sailing ships. By 1875, the ruler or "Khedive" of Egypt was forced to sell his shares in the Suez Canal Company to the British government, which had the help of bankers from the Rothschild family. From 1873 to 1879, the world economy experienced a Great Depression. In Britain, the downturn lasted even longer, until the mid-1890s. At the outset of the depression, diamond prices fell along with other commodity prices.

While prices fell around the world, Kimberley's diggers were also struggling with technical problems. Miners were used to working in what they called the "yellow ground" near the surface, which was somewhat loose and easily worked with picks and shovels. By 1873, diggers were mainly excavating the next stratum, the harder "blue ground," which needed to be dug out, carted, spread out, and weathered on fields, called "floors," for upwards of a year before it was amenable to crushing and sifting, a costly process. The discovery of the blue stratum of rock, more difficult to work, also raised questions about whether the mines would still yield plentiful diamonds. With diamond prices starting to decline, many producers felt squeezed. The cost of African labor was rising, as were the prices of goods sent by wagon from the Cape Colony's ports. Capital was scarce. Diamond miners studied their decreasing margins and wondered if they had the wherewithal to continue production, let alone to buy more claims and better equipment.[28]

Rhodes, Rudd, and a significant portion of Kimberley's diggers continued to believe that the mines had the potential to produce more diamonds, although doubts were raised thanks to their limited and speculative knowledge. A memoir of diamond mining published by a digger under the pseudonym "Fossor" in 1872 explained that "the looking after and finding of diamonds is . . . a very ticklish puzzle, books will not assist the search, geological lore and learned theoretical maxims don't seem to do any good, they give way to practical lessons, and the most specious theories of the most profound stony philosophers, have been utterly confounded by the diggings in South Africa."[29] In the late 1860s and early 1870s, a half dozen learned guides and pamphlets were circulating that sought to explain the geology of the Griqualand West diamond fields.[30]

The Cape Colony had an active amateur scientific scene with a strong interest in geology and diamonds. Members of the Cape elite as well as educated immigrants played a large part in local scientific discussions, while there was a great deal of pride in Cape Town's scientific institutions, especially the South African Library, founded in 1818, and the Royal Observatory, founded in 1820. The *Cape Monthly Magazine*, which published essays about science, history, and literature, became a forum for educated Europeans living in South Africa to report and discuss local scientific discoveries.[31]

During Rhodes's early years at Kimberley, the *Monthly* ran a series by a geologist, Dr. John Shaw, who was conducting a study on the origins of diamonds. In articles published in 1870 and 1871, he noted that diamonds tended to be found on or near the small hills, or *kopjes,* that dot the flat landscape near the Vaal River. Shaw noted that these *kopjes* tended to be sedimentary. He also noted the existence of salt pans and theorized (correctly, as it turned out) that the area was at one time washed by a sea that eroded rock formations around the *kopjes.* He also theorized (incorrectly, as it turned out) that diamonds were likely to be found in bulk below the initial layers of sedimentation, particularly in riverbeds.[32] In 1871, another local geologist, E. J. Dunn, theorized that diamonds were spread around the surface by a massive sandstorm. That same year, a German geologist, E. Cohen, visited the Kimberley mines and was able to observe that the yellow diamond-bearing soil was going deeper within the confines of a border of shale. He developed the theory that is still current, that diamonds were formed deep under the earth, under high pressure, and were blasted to the surface in volcanic pipes. Subsequently, the action of water and sedimentation spread them around the surface, which explains why they were initially discovered by alluvial mining. Following the theory, when the pipes were found, the diamonds could be mined deeper and deeper. Dunn then tried to claim Cohen's theory as his own. The dispute played out in the pages of the *Cape Monthly Magazine*.[33]

As knowledge of geology improved, miners dealt increasingly with floods and rockslides. Making matters even more difficult, mining supplies were becoming more expensive, mainly owing to the lack of sufficient transportation. White colonists were used to turning to the Cape Colony's government for help with infrastructure. In the early nineteenth century, the Cape administration supported economic development by building roads and mountain passes, as well as docks, lighthouses, reservoirs, and jails. To complete expensive projects, the Cape's government became more effective.[34] Growing budgets and rising expenditures generated some of the momentum for the colony to achieve a more representative government. Nation building and infrastructure building were linked together in settler ideology. In 1848, one governor, Harry Smith, dedicated Michell's Pass, saying that it "was an undertaking which would do honour to a great nation instead of a mere dependency of the British crown."[35]

Smith received instructions from the Colonial Office to begin drafting a more representative constitution. In 1853, the year Cecil Rhodes was born, the Cape Colony achieved a parliament elected by voters of any race who possessed £25 worth of property. The lower house of the Cape Parliament was called the House of Assembly, with two representatives from each parliamentary district. The upper house, called the Legislative Council, had eight members from the Western Cape and seven members from the Eastern Cape. Members of the Legislative Council had a property qualification of £2,000. The governor, appointed by London, was still the official head of state in the Cape Colony. He also served as the queen's high commissioner for Southern Africa, which meant that he oversaw relations with neighboring states. The colonial secretary in Cape Town was appointed by London, too. In 1872, two years after Cecil Rhodes arrived in South Africa, the British government gave the Cape Parliament's lower house, the House of Assembly, the right to choose its own prime minister and thereby control its own domestic policy. The first prime minister, John C. Molteno, formed a cabinet from members of the House of Assembly, including a commissioner of crown lands who directed infrastructure policy and helped district road boards to manage local problems.[36]

White farmers, diggers, and merchants were clamoring for a better network of roads, railways, and harbors. Choices had to be made about the direction of development. Port Elizabeth, in the Eastern Cape, was much closer to Kimberley than Cape Town. Port Elizabeth lay 450 miles due south of Kimberley, while Cape Town lay 600 miles to the southwest. In both cases, wagons and stagecoaches crossed a mountain range then had to move through the dry landscape of the Karoo. Crammed with people and their food, drink, and luggage, the wagons moved at seven or eight miles per hour, stopping every three or four hours to change horses and drivers. Port Elizabeth was the obvious choice for starting a journey, but Cape Town was the traditional seat of government, and the Western Cape's Dutch-speaking farmers held great influence over policy. It was hoped that better roads and eventually a railroad would make the journey across the Karoo less challenging. At first, Cape Town's two private railway companies began to construct piecemeal extensions to their line. In 1871, investors in Port Elizabeth built a railway to Uitenhage, just outside of town. In 1873, public meetings took place in nearly every town in the Cape Colony to advocate for railway connections.[37]

As South Africa developed as a nation, European settlers developed colonial infrastructure and benefited from its capacity to move and enable people. Black African people had a different experience. In Rhodes's day, increasing race-based restrictions meant that infrastructure tended to channel them into limited options.[38] Within these confines, new opportunities did present themselves, but only in the context of great challenges. In the early 1870s, nobody could have predicted that Rhodes would be at the center of such major shifts. For a short time, he left South Africa, returning to England to further his own education.

3

Growing Pains

IN AUGUST 1873, for the first time in three years, Cecil Rhodes decided that it was time to return home to Bishop's Stortford. Going home to England was a matter of push and pull. The Kimberley economy was struggling in the midst of a global depression, and at home Rhodes's mother, Louisa Peacock Rhodes, was gravely ill with an unspecified illness. Rhodes wanted to visit her one last time. After traveling by coach and ship for several weeks, Rhodes arrived in time to say farewell before Louisa's death in November. At this difficult time, Rhodes took several steps that had significant meaning for his developing plans. He was earning about £10,000 per year (approximately 1.3 million pounds in today's money), a considerable sum for a youth. Much of his money was invested in diamond digging and associated businesses in Kimberley, along with some shares in the Durban Point Railway. He owned a farm on the Witwatersrand, as well as real estate in London. Yet while Rhodes was at home, he applied to study at the University of Oxford. Rhodes was not a keen scholar, but many of his acquaintances on the diamond fields had university educations. Education seemed like a key part of the formula for an entrepreneur's success.[1]

In Rhodes's day, applications to Oxford were handled somewhat informally, as candidates applied personally to the master of each college at the university. Most admitted students were graduates of one of Britain's rigorous public schools such as Eton, Harrow, or Rugby. A few others were accepted from less-well-regarded day schools. By these standards, Rhodes did not make a strong candidate for admission. He had only attended the day school in Bishop's Stortford and received private tuition from his own father. Rhodes was also older than most students and, from the point of view of faculty members, may have seemed tainted by his rough experiences in a colony. His desire to lead a double life as an English undergraduate and a South African mine owner made him less of a prospect for Oxford colleges, at least for an honors degree. Rhodes interviewed with the master of University College and failed to gain admission for a non-honors or "pass" degree.[2] Next, Rhodes tried

Oriel College, which he may have heard about from Sidney Shippard, his friend from Kimberley who had studied there, or from his father, an Anglican priest, since during his formative years Oriel's professors had challenged the authority of the Church of England.[3]

Rhodes was accepted to Oriel College and began his studies in the fall or Michaelmas term of 1873. Rhodes enrolled just in time for the term but not in time to have a room in the college, so he rented an apartment around the corner, where he prepared for the preliminary examination in Latin, Greek, and mathematics. Rhodes's mother's death interrupted his studies. While he was grieving, legend has it that Rhodes caught a chill while out rowing, setting him back physically. He did pass his exam, ensuring his place at Oriel, where he intended to pursue a pass degree. Shortly thereafter, for reasons that have not been fully explained, at the end of his first term, in December 1873, Rhodes returned to Kimberley. At the diamond mines there were immediate challenges and opportunities. Completing a degree could wait.[4]

Rhodes got back to Kimberley at a time when many miners were leaving. Some miners, like Herbert Rhodes, were restless spirits and left for adventures to the north. More practical miners simply noted that the global economic downturn, combined with the material challenges of working in the deeper mine pits, made diamonds lose their sparkle. The miners who remained debated the extent to which they should invest in efficiencies, especially mechanization. Cecil Rhodes may have sensed opportunity. In retrospect, these were key years of transition toward larger-scale, capital-intensive mining around the Kimberley Mine and the De Beers Mine, as well as the less productive mines at Dutoitspan and Bultfontein.

These were also key years for the development of the supporting economic, political, and social infrastructure. Ideas for a unified, industrialized South Africa can be traced to debates that were in the air around Kimberley in the mid-1870s, which were, in turn, shaped by the environmental circumstances of the mines as well as the political currents of the times. A new political situation in the Cape Colony was helping European settler politicians to link national development to infrastructure. The increasingly independent settler government had incentives to use infrastructure projects for patronage. Along these lines, in 1874 the Cape's newly "responsible" government, led by John C. Molteno, embarked on an ambitious program of legislation. Molteno led a government effort to build railways, telegraphs, and harbor facilities, as well as a new parliament building. The construction opened many opportunities for practical politicking. Molteno, who was married three times and was the father of nineteen children, must have been accustomed to making decisions about the fair distribution of resources. His rail plan answered the pleas of many communities of settlers for access to rail lines. Delivering a railway station to a community put members in Molteno's pocket, while opening avenues for patronage jobs. Patronage became the basis of responsible government, even as the "Molteno Plan" was intended to help European settlers in the region to achieve economic development and political independence. Settler clients were awarded contracts and facilities, while African people heard paternalistic rhetoric and received inferior treatment.[5]

The centerpiece of Molteno's plan was the development of the Cape Government Railways. Lines stretched in politically astute directions. The politicians of the Western Cape got a line that extended from Cape Town all the way to Beaufort West, Molteno's own constituency. Eventually the plan was for this line to run to Kimberley. The line from Port Elizabeth was funded as far into the interior as Cradock, thus serving the prosperous businesses and separatist politicians of the Eastern Cape. Most of the legislators were pleased by the plan, although some communities, like Grahamstown, felt excluded. Farther up the coast, East London got its line, too. The total cost of all the railways was the enormous sum of £4.75 million, to be paid for with loans raised for different segments of the lines. Borrowing the full sum relieved the colony's local authorities of paying traditional fees and raising new taxes.[6]

To save money the railway planners reached a key technical decision to diminish the gauge of the tracks, from the standard gauge of 4 feet, 8.5 inches used in most of Europe and North America, to 3 feet, 6 inches. The narrower gauge made the tracks less expensive to construct. The narrower tracks also allowed for tighter curves, meaning that the track could be built to follow geographical contours more closely. The savings of 10 percent on construction costs were soon lost in other ways, since wider-gauge trains travel faster and bear more weight. A less expensive railway was more easily sold to the white settler population by pragmatic politicians, who hoped to reap the quickest benefits. As the railway system developed during the 1870s, there was another way in which the construction favored European merchants, farmers, and diggers over African people. The system was being built to facilitate the sending of resources from the interior to the coast, where ships could send goods to world markets. In the words of Molteno's son and biographer, "The fundamental idea of the scheme was to avoid lines parallel to the coast, and to proceed from points on the coast as directly as possible towards the interior."[7] This became the predominant pattern in rail construction in Southern Africa and eventually all through the continent.

The Molteno Plan resulted in the hiring of many hundreds of unskilled workers from African and European communities, giving many people their first taste of temporary work in an industrial setting remote from their homes.[8] And as in the early years at Kimberley, railway workers were supervised by a collection of contractors and subcontractors who enforced discipline without much oversight by police or courts. Labor recruited from Britain also played a major role in railway construction, making up one-quarter to one-third of the workforce. These workers were not all skilled blasters and masons. There were also large numbers of less skilled "navvies" who were transported from Britain. Some were used as ordinary laborers, others supervised African men, too, as "gangers" and subcontractors. Race was not a complete barrier to being assigned to unskilled labor. Dutch-speaking farmers came to work unskilled jobs on the railways, too, especially during 1877–1878, when the region faced a bad drought. Many factors made railway work in the 1870s different from the mines, but in some ways the histories are similar. As early as 1875, industrial unrest and tough bargaining on the part of railway workers of both races persuaded the Cape government to begin recruiting labor farther in the interior, where they began to compete with the diamond mine owners for workers. Colonial officials reported that the competition was starting to drive rises in wages. When diamond mining slumped in 1876, African workers left the diamond fields and headed for the railways. The two sectors competed for labor out of the same pools.[9]

The Cape Government Railways became one of the most significant achievements of responsible government, as well as one of its greatest expenses. National infrastructure development was a key aspect of the Molteno Plan, but Molteno himself had little interest in imperial support. Until the end of his term in 1878 he consistently pushed back against British interference. Molteno's projects were not based on a national or international vision. He was strictly a pragmatist who sought development, revenue, and patronage. By building harbors, roads, and railways, as well as library facilities, he identified useful items for boosting the economy.

When Rhodes returned to Kimberley in 1874, he and Rudd began the gradual process of buying claims and enlarging their interests. Like other miners, they also worked to improve the mines' infrastructure. They discovered the physical constraints of the mines and the limits of the available technology. As the pits went deeper, pathways crumbled and bridges tumbled. To overcome the increasing technical challenges, the miners created systems of simple machines, consisting of leather buckets, ropes, and pulleys. As loads got heavier and mines went deeper, miners installed rope-and-pulley systems on grooved wheels, powered by hand-cranked windlasses installed around the edges of the pits. Cranking the buckets up to the top worked best for claims along the outer rim of oval-shaped pits; the inner claims were not able to have such systems pass above the outer claims. Soon this problem was solved by miners building three-tiered platforms, with the higher levels connected by ropes to the farther claims. Workers turned windlasses to haul up the buckets. When the buckets arrived, the rocks were dumped down a chute, then carted off to a sorting ground. American mine engineer Gardner Williams used vivid language to describe the system of removing rocks from the pits:

> So thickly together were these lines set, that the whole face of the vast pit seemed to be covered by a monstrous cobweb, shining in the moonlight as if every filament was a silver strand. Never has any eye seen such a marvelous show of mining as was given in this grand amphitheatre, when the huge pit was sunk far below the surface level; when the encircling wreath of the chasm rose sheer and black like the walls of a deep, gloomy canyon, or the swelling round of a demon's caldron; when a downward glance from the perch of a platform made weak heads reel; when thousands of half-naked men, dwarfed to pygmy size, were scratching the face of the pit with their puny picks like burrowing gnomes; when thousands more, all grimy and sweating and odorous, were swarming around the pit's mouth, dragging up loads of diamond-sprinkled ground and carrying off their precious sacks; when hide buckets were flying like shuttles in a loom up and down the vast warp of wires, twanging like dissonant harp-strings, with a deafening din of rattling wheels and falling ground; and where every beholder was wonder-struck at the thought that this weird creation in the heart of South Africa had been evolved by men for the sake of a few buckets of tiny white crystals to adorn the heads and hands of a few fanciful women.[10]

By the time Rhodes returned from Oxford, in March 1874, miners were replacing hand cranks with "whims," large wheels turned by horses. Horsepower increased the capacity of mine owners to haul out the rocks and dirt. Steam-powered hauling seemed inevitable at Kimberley, yet it remained very challenging—and very expensive—to transport steam engines and coal across the Karoo. In 1874, Rhodes gained local recognition at Kimberley by becoming one of the entrepreneurs to introduce steam engines to the mines. The engines were not initially used for hauling rocks but for pumping water.[11]

Steam-powered mine pumps had been in use in England for more than a century. Many of Kimberley's miners had migrated from Cornwall and other mining regions, where they saw such engines in operation. These engines consisted of a simple piston and a reciprocating beam. A plunger moved up and down in a cylinder, creating enough suction to pump water. The engines also burned scarce fuel at an alarming rate. Only high savings in efficiency, and the prospect of higher prices for diamonds, made the use of steam engines appealing.

Pumping lay at the nexus of thorny problems in environment, technology, and politics. During the cooler months, from May to November, it hardly rains at all, but from December to April, it can rain between two and three inches per month, with the greatest intensity in February and March. Heavy rainfall in the early months of 1874 drained into the open-pit mines, where it combined with the water of underground springs, leaving pools of water where the miners needed to dig. Virtually unable to work, miners now deserted the pits in even greater numbers. Kimberley's population dipped to 8,000 Europeans and 10,000 Africans. It was the problem of water, together with the problem of rocks, called "reef," falling from the walls into the mine, that persuaded claimholders to form mining boards. The board members had the authority to assess a tax on all owners to pay for keeping the mine clear of water and falling rocks. It was in this arena of technological and environmental management that Rhodes gained early experience in politics.

The entrepreneurs who mastered mine pumping built a great deal of influence. While too much water was present in the mines, there was a shortage of water outside, where water was needed to rinse diamond-bearing soil. There was a shortage of drinking water, too. A successful pumping contractor benefited many people in the community. Several of Rhodes's associates began to recognize this, including Charles Rudd, now a partner in R. E. Wallace and Company. Rudd and his associates speculated in mine shares as well as businesses related to mining, ranging from a local telegraph service in Kimberley to ice-making machines. Rhodes was employed by Rudd at R. E. Wallace in the months before his departure for England, and when he returned, he went back to work for Rudd, who was then preoccupied with the problems of pumping. His brother, Thomas Rudd, was then the largest claimholder in the De Beers Mine. Without pumping, his brother's shares were sure to lose value, but at the same time, effective pumping depended on ownership of the deeper claims in the pit. Pumping contractors also gained leverage over other claims.[12]

In Charles Rudd's employ, Rhodes made forays into pumping at De Beers Mine, Kimberley Mine, and Dutoitspan Mine. Pumping gave him experience with a key technology of mine modernization as well as a wide exposure to claimholders. He was also involved from the beginning in South Africa's transition to steam-powered industrialization. To run the pumping engines, it was prohibitively expensive to buy imported British coal in Port Elizabeth or Cape Town and then load it on ox-wagons and haul it to Kimberley. The railway did not reach Kimberley for another decade. The most common fuel burned on the diamond fields, for heating and for pumping, was firewood from local trees, especially the camelthorn tree. In 1873, a settler family might burn one wagon load of wood per month. By that point in time, the trees in the area around Kimberley had already been scalped. Every morning, contractors like Rhodes procured firewood from "wood-riders," mainly Tlhaping men from the north, who used their earnings to buy liquor and other goods to sell back home. As a result of the trade in firewood, their own home areas also started to be denuded of trees.[13]

Rhodes first attempted to bid for pumping at the Kimberley Mine. There, an influential claimholder, William Hall, already ran steam pumps. In fact, Hall had brought the first steam engine to Kimberley, installing it at the edge of the Kimberley Mine to haul buckets of dirt along a wire tram system, earning him the nickname "Tramway" Hall. His influence at the Kimberley Mine made it difficult for the mining board to offer anybody else a contract. Rhodes and Rudd discussed buying claims that could be used to better support pumping, but they decided that they lacked pull with the board and turned next to the Dutoitspan Mining Board. At Dutoitspan, their bid to install one pump was clearly inferior to Hall's proposal to install three, but Rudd's personal connections with the mining board chairman carried the day. The Kimberley newspapers, one of which was owned by Hall, decried the decision, but Rudd and Rhodes were now established as contractors at Dutoitspan. There was only one problem: Rhodes and Rudd did not have a steam engine. They knew from advertisements in the Cape newspapers that a steam pump was for sale in the village of Victoria West. To buy it, Rhodes rode eight days across the Karoo and paid £1,000, much more than market value. The Dutoitspan Mine contract brought in £500 per month, which easily covered the purchase and the operating expenses, generating a good profit by the third month. In time, Rudd agreed to let Rhodes become the sole pumping contractor at Dutoitspan. Rhodes was not an engineer and had a layperson's understanding of steam engines. Sometimes he had to learn from mistakes. Rudd's pump at the De Beers Mine worked well enough during the dry season, but when seasonal rains started in December 1874, the pump was overwhelmed and the mine flooded. Rhodes stepped in, and together with an engineer, James McKenzie, he made a successful bid to install better pumps and keep the mine dry.[14]

The intervention by Rhodes and McKenzie came at a time when the diamond fields were beset with political problems that were inextricably linked with the technical problems of production. By mid-1872, the problems of multiple claims in open-pit mines started to become acute. This was especially true at the Kimberley Mine, the richest of the four mines, where the pit was being dug deepest. As the mine went deeper, the pathways down and around the claims collapsed, one by one. Miners built wooden platforms around the edge of the pit, then extended a heavy hemp rope down to their claim. Rawhide buckets were suspended from grooved wheels and hauled back and forth from top to bottom. Almost every claim owner came to use this system, so that the open pits were covered with cobwebs of heavy ropes. As the platforms grew bigger, the ropes were replaced by wire cables, and buckets were replaced by larger iron carriers, big enough to carry heavy loads and even to transport miners between the edge and the pit. The wire haulage systems were powered by windlasses positioned behind the platform and turned initially by laborers and next by mules and horses. The "Long Tom" troughs were replaced by larger rotary washers, big circular pans in which the gravel was rinsed and cleaned by devices that resembled spinning combs. As the technology developed, the labor force remained racially stratified. African migrants assigned the most menial tasks were supervised by white overseers, who took their orders from the claim owners. Claim owners needed to invest ever-increasing amounts of capital in mine operations, even as the pit experienced problems with flooding and collapses of reef.[15]

Even the most casual observer could see that with hundreds of claims and thousands of workers sharing the same open pits, the hauling, pumping, and processing equipment was crowding the space and being used inefficiently. The same might be said for the labor. It is estimated that more than ten thousand workers were at the mines. Entrepreneurs like Rhodes, McKenzie, and Rudd believed that ever more capital was required to dig deeper holes, pump more water, and buy better equipment. The larger the capital outlay, the more it made sense to increase the size of holdings. Production by large companies seemed to hold the greatest promise of financial and technical dynamism. In 1874 at least one large company was in the process of floating shares on the London stock market. Small claimholders correctly perceived a threat to their interests. Merchants, too, preferred to have many small claimholders as customers and feared the prospect of large companies dominating the market for supplies. Small claims were also preferred by the government of Griqualand

West. Lieutenant-Governor Richard Southey spoke in theoretical terms about the need for a free economy to support smallholders. In fact, the government depended on smallholding for income from fees. In the early 1870s, disputes between miners and landowners were resolved by implementing a system in which the government collected rents and delivered them to the landowners, taking a portion as government revenue. Revenue also depended on the collection of licensing fees from claimholders. The interest of the government tended to align with smallholders, too.[16]

To satisfy the fashions of London, Paris, and New York, networks of people brought together technologies and natural resources to produce a commodity that dominated a colony's economy. To find valuable stones, diggers migrated from other parts of Southern Africa and from all around the world, inspired by stories of fabulous discoveries. Upon arrival, they discovered that the mine seemed to be in the middle of nowhere yet was ever more connected to the rest of the world every day. This was a revolutionary moment in South African economic history, but the structures of the old slave society still influenced who performed manual labor and who ran things. And in this freewheeling mining town, markets were restricted to preserve a moral economy of small-scale entrepreneurs. Investment poured in from financial centers and from personal savings. The equipment demonstrated noteworthy improvements, even as overlap continued between pre-industrial and industrial processes. First men turned the cranks that pulled the wheels that hauled the rocks, then it was done by horses, then it was done by steam engines. The men and the horses were not surpassed so much as they were shunted into doing other industrial tasks. Cecil Rhodes saw the entangled elements and imagined making them more unified and productive.[17]

Shortly before Rhodes returned to Kimberley, the intertwined system of production and administration began to unravel. Locally, there was a drought in full swing. Globally, there was economic turmoil. Southey anticipated a decline in revenue and decided to support the diamond industry through government intervention. One key act was to broker a deal that solved a key complaint of the diggers, the continued private ownership of the land of the Vooruitzigt Estate that comprised the De Beers and Kimberley mines. The provincial government, in consultation with the Cape governor, Henry Barkly, and John X. Merriman, the commissioner of crown lands and public works, bought the 17,000-acre estate with £100,000 in debenture stock. As soon as this was done, much of the land was auctioned off to investors who were keen to participate in the development of the city of Kimberley. The mineral rights at the De Beers Mine and the Kimberley Mine were reserved

The Racial Division of Labor: Operating Washing Gear at the Kimberley Diamond Mines. Courtesy of the McGregor Museum, Kimberley, MMKP 6376.

to the Crown, but anyone who officially registered a claim could own the minerals as property.[18]

Southey made another set of decisions about land use that had profound consequences for Rhodes's future plans. The government hoped to stabilize the colony by introducing settlers of European descent. Southey used a convenient legal fiction to declare much of the Tlhaping land to be vacant and therefore available to settlers. The Keate commission had ruled that the territory belonged to Waterboer, who assigned it to the colony. Southey had personal authority to grant titles to land. He said that he only recognized Tlhaping titles to lands that were occupied by farms—and nothing broader. Southey assigned land claims to colonists in an area north of the Vaal River, but colonists were not able to occupy the land, because the Tlhaping living there objected to their presence. Tlhaping were still expected to pay rent to the owners. In 1877, when rent payments were not made, Southey's successor, Major Owen Lanyon, declared the area to be "native locations," where the chiefs were to be left in place but were required to pay a hut tax to the colonial administration.[19] Southey's policies laid the groundwork for segregation, but he also refused to make special regulations for African workers, on the grounds that such policies were racially discriminatory and therefore contradicted British law. This decision alienated nearly every white mine-owner, large or small. The high-handed attitude of Southey's principal assistant, Rhodes's friend, John Blades Currey, made Southey's administration even less popular.[20]

Traditional understandings about political consultation and personal conduct remained important to the white settlers, even as the advantages of larger mining companies were starting to be realized. The open-pit mines were still governed by diggers' committees elected directly by each claimholder. To preserve "Diggers' Democracy," each claimholder was restricted to two claims. This practice had originated as a law when the mines were briefly thought to be under the jurisdiction of the Orange Free State. Although not recognized as a law in the British colony of Griqualand West, it continued as a moral practice. It had brought a degree of equality, but it also created technical problems. When open-pit mines have multiple claimholders, the diggers needed to work uniformly, otherwise higher claims tended to collapse into lower claims, resulting in disagreements and litigation. In Kimberley, miners who let their claims go unworked for more than three days were even liable to be dispossessed. "Claim-jumping," as the practice was called, undermined notions of private property, yet it was an effective way to put moral pressure on small-scale owners to continue digging uniformly. There were also ways to get around requirements for small-scale ownership. Budding monopolists hid their purchases of additional claims by paying straw men to buy claims.

In 1873, feeling the need for greater state regulation, Southey accepted the recommendation of a mining commission and established boards for each mine and oversight by a government inspector. The boards for the De Beers Mine and the Kimberley Mine began to meet in mid-1874 and soon proved they lacked the ability to satisfactorily regulate the problems of production. The key regulation was Ordinance No. 10 of 1874, which fixed the limit on individual claims to ten. In the eyes of the small diggers, this increase seemed significant and threatening, but in the eyes of aspiring capitalists a ten-claim limit was still a major restriction. The boards did not have enough authority to prevent claims being bought by miners who were acting as stand-ins for larger buyers.[21]

While Rhodes was away in Oxford, Southey convened a Diamond Fields Commission to study the business and politics of the mines. The conclusions favored ending Diggers' Democracy. The Mining Ordinance of 1874 abolished the diggers' committees and replaced them with mining boards, which were elected proportionally. Owners of quarter-claims or less were allotted one vote. Those holding more claims were given a maximum of three votes. Mining boards hired inspectors who could warn inactive owners, threatening them with the forfeit and auction of their property. Aspiring consolidators of claims pressed for even more concessions, such as representation based on the value of claims, not the number of claims.[22]

Over the course of 1874, when Rhodes was back in Kimberley, diggers started directing their grievances against changed mining practices toward the colonial government. The old diggers' committees formed "vigilance committees," the US West term for quasi-judicial armed gangs. The vigilantes patrolled the camps, arresting anybody thought to be violating the laws. They were particularly tough on African people, many of whom were arrested for operating illegal "canteens" or saloons. The vigilantes also entrapped diamond thieves and smugglers, in the process causing so much trouble themselves that the colonial government discontinued the practice of paying rewards for catching thieves. White miners blamed Black miners for IDB and hoped to exclude them from buying licenses to claims. The presence of American miners may have made calls for racial discrimination more strident, while the presence of Irish and Boer nationalists may have pushed the malcontents toward calls for a republic. A dozen small claimholders, led by an Irishman, Alfred Aylward, formed themselves into a Committee of Public Safety, ominously named after France's governing council during the revolution's Reign of Terror. Aylward rode to Bloemfontein to discuss republican prospects for Kimberley with the president of the Orange Free State, Jan Brand, an act of treason. In April 1875, the rebels deposed Southey, hoisted a black flag, and proclaimed a diggers' republic. Southey sent for British troops, and three months later, 250 redcoats appeared in town. The revolt ended and the ringleaders were brought to justice. Most were treated lightly, with many of them returning to respectable occupations in the community. Aylward shifted north to the Transvaal, where he pursued his anti-British, republican agenda for years to come.[23] To some extent, Cecil Rhodes sympathized with the diggers' grievances. All claimholders, large and small, complained about IDB and African laborers. Yet Rhodes sided with the government and answered Southey's call for volunteers to guard government buildings. Rhodes was consistently an empire loyalist, with reverence for queen and parliament, even though he wrote to his soldier brother, Frank, that serving as a guard was "frightful nonsense." Rhodes was bothered by the standoff between rebels and loyalists. "It was a most ridiculous sight to see" three hundred armed rebels "drilling and parading and the Government looking on quite helpless."[24]

After the rebellion, the diamond industry continued to struggle. Labor became scarce and was alleviated by "share-working," the mining equivalent of sharecropping. Share-working lessened owners' surveillance over claims, with the seemingly inevitable result that diamonds were hidden and smuggled out secretly.[25] Discussions of IDB often had a racial component. White settlers engaged in robust debate around the "native question," their term for policy toward African people. African people had the legal rights of British subjects, an approach that diverged from that of the nearby Boer republics, the Orange Free State and the Transvaal. The republics were nearby. Familiarity with the laws of the Boer republics increased pressure on Griqualand West and the Cape Colony to impose a stricter racial order.

Debates about race and power echoed as far away as London, where traditional liberals defended African rights against a growing tide of pessimism that was generated by the rebellions in India (1857) and Jamaica (1865). Prominent intellectuals like Thomas Carlyle argued that the old policies of "civilizing" African and Asian people were naïve, given their inferiority. The trend started before the 1859 publication of Charles Darwin's *Origin of Species*, but soon afterward, Social Darwinism began to inform historically pessimistic imperial policies.[26] In South Africa, debates about "the native question" were inflamed by the visit of an English historian, James Anthony Froude, a disciple of Carlyle and a friend of the secretary of state for the colonies, Lord Carnarvon. Carnarvon sponsored Froude's two lecture tours of 1874 and 1875, which became occasions for controversy. Froude spoke in favor of the unification of British and Boer colonies and republics, with Boer policies of racial discrimination put in place everywhere. Reconciliation between Britons and Boers would have to include atonement for the British occupation of the diamond fields, "one of the most scandalous acts recorded in our history." This was strong language to utter in a society that placed a high value on honor. He continued, "I could only regret that the English good name had been soiled by contact with so dirty a business, and we had broken our solemn word, too."[27] His accusations echoed those of the Boers; his exaggerations did not gain him much ground with British officialdom or Cape liberals like Molteno. Officials in London and Cape Town knew that the Boers of the Transvaal and the Orange Free State did not have a record of trustworthiness when it came to dealings with African people. Froude's views resonated with white miners and settlers.[28]

At the time of Froude's visit, the British government was seriously considering the political and economic problems at Kimberley and the Colony of Griqualand West. Carnarvon fired Southey and Currey and in November 1875 replaced them with an army officer, Major Owen Lanyon, a martinet who lacked Southey's ties to the settler community. Next, Carnarvon dispatched Lieutenant-Colonel William Crossman of the Royal Engineers to

Kimberley, with instructions to hold hearings and to decide if a Royal Commission should be appointed to investigate the colony. On the first day of the hearings, Wednesday, January 5, 1876, complainants unleashed inflammatory statements and accusations. Near the end of the day, Crossman started to hear about the De Beers Mine, where Rhodes's pump was not keeping the open pit dry. The De Beers Mining Board responded to Rhodes's failure by employing an engineer from the Mauritian sugar industry, E. Huteau, who succeeded in keeping the mines dry, even at the end of 1875, when the seasonal rains were starting again. On the day after Christmas, Huteau's pumps were sabotaged and stopped working. The mine flooded. The claimholders were seething.

Cecil Rhodes attended Crossman's hearing, perhaps sensing that his own involvement in pumping and mining-board politicking might be discussed. One witness, a Mr. Cowie, complained about the composition of the De Beers Mining Board. Board members were investing heavily in one portion of the mine to the exclusion of others. In his words, "There are a certain lot in the Mining Board interested in a certain gully. Everything done by the Board is done for the benefit of that gully." The board focused on that area, while taking tax revenues from all claimholders. The system of registering workers often resulted in unregistered workers being imprisoned, with prisoners being made available to the mining boards. Prisoners, too, were allocated to claimholders for work on the gully rather than other areas. To make matters worse, Cowie, backed by another witness, raised the possibility that someone had bribed Huteau with £300 to break his own pump.[29]

Seeking confirmation, Crossman ordered a policeman to find Huteau and bring him to the hearing. While the search unfolded, the hearing continued, with Rhodes still present. Cowie again raised the subject of representation on the mining boards, stating that "the members of the De Beer's board should be elected from sections of the mine. At present, one end of the mine has all the power at the board." Leaning toward agreement, Crossman commented that "the plan of dividing the mine into sections has already been advocated for the Kimberley Mine." From the audience, G. Hall agreed, too: "The high ground, he said, had no proper representation at the board. He had been in the mine during 1874, and had eight members to contend against the whole time." It is at this point that Rhodes spoke up, making a rare appearance in the written historical record of these turbulent years at Kimberley. "Mr. Rhodes," wrote the enquiry's reporter, "held quite an opposite opinion. He thought the high ground had an undue preponderance." This provocation, directed at Hall and Cowie, achieved Rhodes's likely aim of ending discussion. Crossman expressed frustration: "You have a Mining Board elected by yourselves. I hardly see how you can complain." An argument ensued between Cowie and Ward about the employment of a common resource, convict labor, which caused Crossman to end the debate. The record indicates that "some more discussion arising as to deep and high ground, Colonel Crossman said he could not go into such details."[30]

For the time being, Rhodes had succeeded in diverting the question of mining board corruption, making Cowie and Hall's complaints seem like a matter of opinion that could be resolved through democratic process. Having achieved this goal, Rhodes slipped out of the room before the policeman came back with Huteau. The Mauritian engineer was reluctant to testify, mainly because he promised the man offering the bribe not to speak his name in court. Crossman threatened Huteau with prosecution, but Huteau invoked the Victorian code of gentlemanly conduct: "I shall be sorry [to be prosecuted], but I swore not to tell the man's name, and I won't. I have given him my honour." Crossman retorted, "But this is a matter of compulsion; honour is out of the question. If you do not tell me on Friday [in two days] I shall fine you £20." The reporter noted that "Huteau inquired if he should render himself to an action for libel." The colony's attorney-general, Sidney Shippard, assured Huteau that he would be protected, "just as in any court of law." With these assurances, Huteau decided that while he had given his word not to tell the name of the briber, he could at least write the name on a piece of paper and hand it to Crossman, who then said, "Let Mr. Cecil Rhodes be called." The reporter noted "great commotion," then wrote, "Mr. Rhodes was sent for, but could not be found, and the Court adjourned until Friday amid much excitement." Two days later, Rhodes appeared before Crossman and publicly accused Huteau of perjury, a charge that resulted in Huteau's arraignment before Kimberley's High Court.[31]

Rhodes had every reason to expect favorable treatment from the court. He was friends with Shippard and also with Jacob Barry, who presided over the court as the "recorder" or chief magistrate. The two friends may have even advised Rhodes to bring the case to restore his honor. After a few months passed, Rhodes thought better of the perjury accusation. In March 1876, Rhodes's case against Huteau was dropped. In the meantime, the De Beers Mining Board decided that they had waited long enough for the replacement pumps, and they fired Rhodes. With his reputation damaged, the twenty-three-year-old Rhodes decided that the best course of action was to leave Kimberley and return to his studies at Oxford. Arriving there, he wrote: "My character was so battered at the Diamond Fields, that I like to preserve a few remnants."[32]

Crossman's intervention at Kimberley resulted in a short-term loss for Rhodes. In the long term, Crossman's investigation concluded with a blockbuster report that benefited Rhodes and other capitalists. The report recommended that restrictions on claim ownership be dropped and that companies be allowed to own as many claims as they wished. Mining boards should be given greater independence from government oversight, except for safety inspections, which should remain mandatory.

Crossman's report was heavily influenced by the testimony of a Cornish mining engineer, Francis Oats, who was at the beginning of a long career at Kimberley. Oats was born in 1848 and grew up in St. Just, Cornwall. He earned prizes and scholarships at school, but his family was so poor that as a teenager he had to go to work in the local tin mines. After tiring shifts, he was still able to work part-time as a teacher and study for his qualifying exams as a mine engineer. He rose to the rank of "captain," which meant that he supervised teams of miners underground. Oats had a promising career ahead of him, but Cornwall was no longer competitive with other parts of the world. Cornish miners had special skills with hard-rock mining, so they found themselves out of work in the UK, where soft-rock coal mining predominated, but in high demand in the US West and in other parts of the world, like Kimberley, where hard-rock mining was practiced. In 1874, Oats successfully applied for the job of government mining engineer in Griqualand West. By the time of Crossman's arrival, he had been studying the mines and getting to know members of the community, including Cecil Rhodes.[33]

Oats produced two reports that were submitted to Crossman and published with his endorsement. The mundanely titled "Enclosure No. 6" and "Enclosure No. 12" mapped out proposals for the future of the Kimberley mines, showing the ways in which politics and technology were intertwined. Claimholders or their companies were still only allowed to own four claims, a restriction that presented technical problems as the mine went deeper. Oats argued that digging deeper and wider was needed, but limits on claim holding prevented this from a technical and economic standpoint. He believed that "such vexatious restriction prevents home capitalists from investing." Oats asked for all restrictions on ownership to be dropped and for the mining boards of the four mines to be composed of claim owners represented "pro rata," with the owners of more of the mine getting more of the representation. He hoped this would eliminate corruption, particularly the disguising of the ownership of companies and the bribing of members of the mining board. The mining boards should then run the mines in the interests of the largest companies, "without any interference on the part of the Government, except where danger to life was concerned." Oats left it to Crossman and other colonial authorities to determine the degree to which safety and risk could be managed by finding a "happy mean" between "passively" or "actively" managing safety.[34]

For the sake of safety and profitability, Oats recommended that ever-more-powerful steam engines should be applied to the mines. Pumps were already using steam engines. The next engines to appear in Kimberley were winding engines. Winding engines pulled the wire ropes that hauled rocks out of the pit. Previously the rocks were hauled out by means of horse-pulled whims. Replacing horsepower was no small thing. To start a winding wheel from a resting position necessitated engines running at higher pressures and producing more torque than the usual pump engines. Winding engines needed to be more advanced than pumping engines.[35] Oats also examined the pumping operations in all the mines and acknowledged the technical assistance of Cecil Rhodes, who was known for his expertise in pumping. Oats also advocated better methods for removing reef and diamond-bearing rock. The most desirable approach involved digging shafts and tunnels deep under the ground, especially if prospecting shafts confirmed that diamonds could continue to be found at deeper levels. Even if prospecting gave good results, he regretted that deep-level mining was unrealistic, "on account of the large number of separate interests."[36]

Oats's views, according to Crossman, were the majority view of the remaining diggers at Kimberley. It was time to drop rules that restricted claim ownership. Consolidating claims would ensure efficient operations, which in turn would yield more government revenue. Crossman encouraged the formation of joint companies and, as an alternative, even suggested a cooperative society. A combination of owners would have a number of effects, including higher prices, higher margins, and more effective surveillance over workers. Larger diamond mines were more likely to attract capital investment. As for the government, Crossman concluded that Griqualand West should no longer be a separate colony. It was too small and almost completely focused around the municipality of Kimberley, making it an administrative oddity.

Crossman embraced another idea that was advocated by some of the mine owners: the closer regulation of the mobility of African migrant laborers. He hoped that these men, called "servants," would be "confined to their masters' camps, or compounds from sunset till sunrise, except provided with a special pass." He was concerned that race-based restrictions might not be legal in the Cape Colony, yet he wrote that "it is the law of the Free State, and appears to me to be as much for the benefit of the black man as for the comfort of the white. The natives do not wander about after dark except for the purposes of drinking or disposing of ill-gotten property."[37] At the same time, another Cornish mine engineer, Thomas C. Kitto, proposed that Kimberley's African mine workers should be placed in compounds much like the ones that he had seen used to quarter slaves near the mines of Brazil. In that country, wrote Kitto:

> The blacks are lodged in barracks, which are built in the form of a square, the outer wall being much higher than the inner wall; the roof slopes inside. The entrance to the place is by a large gate.... Men and women answer to their names while passing out at the gate in the morning and in the evening when entering.... an overseer locks up the premises each night.... the natives of South Africa, under European supervision, are capable of being made almost—if not quite—as good as the blacks of Brazil, provided they are dealt with in the same manner.[38]

Over the next decade, crime prevention and temperance would become the key reasons to institute a new system of closed diamond-mine compounds. The compounds became a system of restricting the mobility of African migrants that evolved simultaneously with the corporate consolidation of the mines. The vision of deregulation, consolidation, and compounding, which is sometimes attributed to Rhodes, in fact originated as a consensus view as early as 1875, a decade before compounds became common around Kimberley.

The Crossman Report made recommendations for the diamond industry and also for colonial politics. The process for winding up the colonial government of Griqualand West and incorporating it into the larger Cape Colony was complicated and prolonged, lasting from 1877 to 1880. The Cape Colony repealed restrictions on mining companies, saving administrative costs. The Cape continued the appointment of government mine inspectors yet saved money by allowing companies to employ their own security officers for the purpose of policing workers. Africans would be limited to unskilled jobs and were no longer be able to buy claims. The Cape government shut down shops that sold guns, liquor, and sex to Africans. All this was in keeping with the Cape Colony's gradual shift toward legal discrimination, seen first in the 1878 legislation that restricted gun ownership by Africans. In the late 1870s, there were many detailed debates over the loss of rights by Africans and the deregulation of Kimberley. That is the backdrop against which, over the course of the next decade, Rhodes developed three companies with far-reaching powers—De Beers, Gold Fields, and the British South Africa Company. It is also during this time that he became a member of the Cape Parliament's House of Assembly and worked against African rights and in favor of solidarity between Britons and Boers.

Cecil Rhodes and his fellow entrepreneurs were driving significant changes in South Africa's history that would have lasting effects. South Africa's majority African population was being excluded from ownership in the economy's most dynamic sector, mining. African people also found themselves excluded from access to land and finance. Meanwhile, they were being deprived of civic rights, a harbinger of future assaults on their rights to vote and to own property. Their mobility was restricted through pass laws, while proposals for putting them in closed compounds would further restrict the mobility of migrant workers. A "dual economy" was starting to be established, with different rules for white settlers and African people. White settlers received favorable treatment, while African people experienced many disincentives to participation. It is a classic point of political economy to say that inclusive economies produce long-term growth. By contrast, economies that generate wealth by extracting natural resources and discriminating against laborers may produce short-term profits but also tend to produce long-term poverty.[39] In the 1870s, aspiring monopolists at Kimberley were mainly responding to short-term opportunities and were blinkered by an intensifying racism.

4
Learning at Oxford

RHODES RETURNED TO Oxford for the Trinity Term in the spring of 1876. As a student he remained engaged in business on two continents. He managed investments and property in England and spent summer vacations in Kimberley. There, he invested his earnings in new partnerships with Kimberley's Jewish merchant capitalists, including Henry Barlow Webb of the London and South African Exploration Company and Samuel Woolf and Jules LeJeune of the LeJeune Company. He also visited the diamond dealers in London's Hatton Garden and kept up regular correspondence with Rudd. Nearing the end of his first term, Rhodes wrote to Rudd, telling his faraway partner that he was buying a better steam engine to be shipped to Kimberley. The description shows that Rhodes was learning the technicalities of steam power. "I must tell you," Rhodes wrote to Rudd, "that I have ordered an engine, one of Roley & Co.'s patents with gear under boiler. . . . It is 10 horses and I have impressed it on them that our pumping is continuous and our pulling out a secondary consideration, so the winding drum with the clutch gear are made expressly with a view to that." As to pumps, Rhodes indicated a preference for a pump in which the "cylinder and the pump is one and you can have your boiler quite separate. . . . They work with half the steam power and throw an enormous volume of water." Rhodes discussed winding engines with Rudd, too, but the 1876 letter is most striking for the way that it relates technical matters to larger ideas for their business. "You will be in the thick of bad times now," he advised Rudd, "but do not funk." Rhodes continued: "The application of machinery to diamonds will lick depreciation in prices."[1]

Given his continuing involvement in business, it is not surprising that he was only studying for an unambitious pass degree. Rhodes did manage to have an active social life. His wealth gave him access to activities and clubs that helped him advance his social network. He lived with friends outside of Oriel. He played polo and rowed. He was active in social clubs, including Vincent's Club, a club for sportsmen, and the Bullingdon Club, an exclusive club known for cricket as well as drinking and rowdy, destructive suppers.

Rhodes also belonged to the exclusive Oxford Drag Hunt. In a drag hunt, riders follow a pack of hounds around a course that has been "dragged" or smeared with bait. The dogs follow the scent, chased by horses and riders along a cross-country course with jumps. Rhodes was known among his friends as an ungainly rider, so only his personal popularity could account for his election as Master of the Hunt in 1876. His sociability does not appear to have been inhibited by his middle-class origins, his lack of elite schooling, or his years spent in the colonies. His budding fortune seemed to have been enough to gain entrée to exclusive clubs populated by the sons of the wealthy classes. Rhodes's contemporaries remembered him as a bit unusual. Eschewing fancy dress, he often wore the rough clothing of a colonial. For a young man who had already achieved a measure of maturity and independence, he seems to have enjoyed cavorting with undergraduates.[2]

Rhodes still set aside enough time to study for his degree. In the 1870s, most Oxford students followed a general course of study in the humanities, known as "Greats," which required them to read ancient Greek and Roman history, literature, theology, and philosophy in the original languages, plus modern works in ethics, politics, and economics. Students met weekly with tutors in their own colleges, while also attending newly instituted lectures by professors at other colleges.[3] This curriculum idealized national and imperial service and influenced the outlook of Cecil Rhodes and many of his contemporaries who would go on to serve as high-minded proconsuls of the British Empire while at the same time grappling with the base, material problems of how to extract resources from distant people in distant lands. That this very problem helped to precipitate the declines of the Athenian *polis* and the Roman republic was not lost on the faculty and students. The political and the economic improvement of the empire was a central concern of its most influential faculty members, such as Benjamin Jowett, a fellow of Oxford's Balliol College who later became his college's master and eventually the vice-chancellor of the University.[4]

Students and faculty at Oxford followed Jowett's associations between the study of the Greek and Roman classics and the building of the British Empire, even though many classical authors had mixed views of imperialism. One book familiar to Oxford students, *The Peloponnesian War* by Thucydides, presented the expansion of the Athenian empire as a form of tragedy. Another commonly read work, the *Histories* of Herodotus, questioned the accumulation of wealth and praised people who resisted imperialism. It is true that ancient authors described a world of imperial conquest, male dominance, and widespread enslavement. It is also true that an education in the classics did not ineluctably produce nineteenth-century ideologies of domination and oppression. Herodotus was fascinated by the diversity of human cultures and races.[5]

Among the classical Greek philosophers, Rhodes often turned for inspiration to Aristotle. The *Nicomachean Ethics* advised readers to achieve happiness by developing their characters through study and experience. Rhodes quoted from the *Nicomachean Ethics* on important occasions throughout his career. Given Rhodes's transformative leadership in business and public service, it is worth also remembering Aristotle's *Politics*. It opens with a discussion of relations between people in their households, the fundamental political unit. In Jowett's 1885 translation, Aristotle says that the slave "is intended by nature to belong to his master" and is an instrument of the master's action. "From the hour of their birth," writes Aristotle, "some are marked out for subjection, others for rule." The highest object is the fulfillment of nature, in which "the male is by nature superior, and the female inferior; and the one rules, and the other is ruled; this principle, of necessity, extends to all mankind." Relations of slaves and masters are made to seem natural: "the lower sort are by nature slaves, and it is better for them as for all inferiors that they should be under the rule of a master."[6] At least, according to Aristotle, slaves are capable of reason, which makes them better than animals.

Aristotle's naturalizing of hierarchy was supplemented, in Rhodes's reading list, by one of the most widely discussed books of the early 1870s, Winwood Reade's *The Martyrdom of Man*, first published in 1872 and widely circulated and read. Reade argued that the pressures associated with war, religion, and the environment had helped to advance Europeans above Asians and Africans. These lesser people, in turn, were stalled in their development by their racial proclivities, their religious beliefs, and their abundant resources. The key ingredient in advancement was a willingness to sacrifice and suffer—hence the title. One of Rhodes's late-in-life acquaintances, Princess Catherine Radziwill, reported that "he [Rhodes] always kept this momentous book beside him, and used to read it when he wanted to strengthen himself in some hard resolution or when he was expected to steel his mind to the performance of some task against which his finest instincts revolted even whilst his sense of necessity urged him onward." Rhodes confided in Radziwill that "you can imagine the impression which it produced on me when I read it amid all the excitement of life at Kimberley not long after leaving Oxford University. . . . That book has made me what I am."[7]

Reade believed that the political dominance of Europeans had to do with their more highly evolved intellects. This, to him, was a fact of nature. Near the start of *The Martyrdom of Man*, Reade writes: "*God made all men equal* is a fine-sounding phrase, and has also done good service in its day; but it is not a scientific fact. On the contrary, there is nothing so certain as the natural inequality of men. Those who outlive hardships and sufferings which fall on all alike owe their existence to some superiority, not only of body, but of mind."[8] Citing evolutionary theory, Reade wrote, "Let me ask those who admit the development of all civilized people from a savage state . . . how it is that Europeans have advanced (this involving a change in the structure of the brain), while others have remained in a savage state, others in the pastoral condition, others fixed at a certain point of culture, as the Hindoos and Chinese? The analogy [with natural selection] is perfect and the answer is, in either case, the same. Those forms remain stationary which are able to preserve their condition of life unchanged."[9] In Reade's view, the evolution of dominant races related closely to nature's conquest. He encouraged "the conquest of the planet on which we dwell; the destruction or domestication of the savage forces by which we are tormented and enslaved."[10]

Classical education helped educated Victorians understand the ties that bind people together, ranging from imperial domination to personal friendship. From his earlier reading of Marcus Aurelius, Rhodes knew that Stoic philosophers believed in an unemotional, reasoned form of friendship. One of Rhodes's strongest Stoic leanings found expression in socializing with a "band of brothers" dedicated to empire building. It was in keeping with this approach that we can understand how Rhodes managed a network of friends in business and later designed the Rhodes Scholarships, an international gathering of young male leaders at Oxford, chosen by reason, not by emotion.

There were other elements of friendship that were discussed by students in Greats. In 1871, Jowett published one of his best-known works, a four-volume, scholarly translation of Plato's *Dialogues*, which included the *Symposium*. There is no direct evidence to prove that Rhodes read or discussed this text, though it was read by most students enrolled in Greats. Plato's *Symposium* brought together notions of power and sexuality. In the central dialogue with Phaedrus, Socrates explains love, as it was explained to him by Diotima, a wise woman. First, according to Socrates, one lover will be physically attracted to another, in the context of being attracted to many other bodies. Next, the lover will find spiritual beauty in another body, even one that is not physically attractive. This spiritual attraction leads the lover to engage in higher forms of discourse, first in learning about the law and politics, and finally in the contemplation of science and beauty. It is love that inspires an escape from the cave of ignorance into the realms of higher knowledge. Jowett's translations of the *Symposium* and Plato's other dialogues became standard fare for Oxford undergraduates, many of whom, like Rhodes, were bound for positions of leadership.[11]

Oxford students knew that when Plato discussed love in the *Symposium*, he was not describing Victorian marriage; he was describing older men having sexual relationships with younger men. Jowett was apparently embarrassed by what was described, in hushed tones, as "the unspeakable vice of the Greeks," but Rhodes may have found these ideas persuasive, given his preference, later in life, for surrounding himself with younger men. To students who were pondering their sexuality, the message of authors like Plato was still clear: a special bond existed between men that could lead to order and knowledge.

Rhodes was not the only man to rebel against late Victorian ideas about settling down to marriage and home life. Rhodes even made pronouncements against marriage. In one undated letter written around 1876 or 1877, Rhodes wrote to a friend, "I hope you won't get married. I hate people getting married. They simply become machines and have no ideas beyond their respective spouses and offspring."[12] That being said, Rhodes left few traces of his love life, which made it easy for early biographers to avoid discussions of his sexuality. Rhodes kept company almost exclusively with men and on several occasions lived under the same roof with other men with whom he had a close friendship. This was not unusual. From the 1850s, through Rhodes's time at Oxford, to the 1880s, choosing to socialize mainly with men and asexual homoeroticism were quietly accepted. In the 1880s, the tide began to turn, particularly with an 1885 law that made sexual acts between men, either in public or in private, subject to a minimum jail term of two years.[13]

Rhodes made key contacts at Oxford with men who would later help him to press forward with imperialist projects and eventually transform his ideas into practice. One of his Oxford connections was James Rochfort Maguire, a young Irishman who was, like Rhodes, a son of a cleric and a fellow member of Bullingdon's. At Oxford, Maguire was a brilliant student of mathematics and law. On completing his studies in 1878, he was honored with a prestigious appointment as fellow of All Souls College. This was not enough for the ambitious Maguire. In 1883 he was called to the bar, and in 1886 he was elected to the House of Commons. Over the years, Maguire remained in touch with Rhodes and became part of some key enterprises.[14]

Another acquaintance was Charles Metcalfe. Metcalfe's family played significant roles in colonial administration, mainly in India. Metcalfe himself attended Harrow, then University College, Oxford. Known as an outstanding rugby player, he completed his degree in 1878. He then took an unusual step for a liberal-arts graduate of his day by joining an engineering firm,

Charles Fox & Sons, and working on railroad construction in England and Ireland.[15] Rhodes and Metcalfe shared a rare enthusiasm for Oxford students of that time: industry. Britain had the world's most advanced industrial economy during the nineteenth century, but few leaders in business or engineering were educated at Oxford and Cambridge.[16]

Rhodes's time at Oxford helped him to make important contacts. He may also have been exposed to some formative ideas that may only be inferred from context. George Parkin, a Canadian scholar and school headmaster, lectured at Oxford in 1873–1874 and summarized his ideas in a book published two decades later. He believed in the racial superiority of English-speaking people and believed that their nations could manage common interests through an Imperial Federation, linked by steamships and telegraphs.[17] Another historian, Arnold Toynbee, who coined the term "Industrial Revolution," was an undergraduate from 1873 to 1878, when he organized volunteers to help poor people in Oxford as a way to bridge the gap between scholars and the working classes.[18]

Key ideas about political culture were widely debated at Oxford during the 1870s. In those years, one of Rhodes's most important future collaborators, Alfred Milner, was a student and junior faculty member and remembered the powerful influence of one professor, Thomas Hill Green, on himself and on Arnold Toynbee. Green taught that moral good derived from critical self-reflection as well as through the purposeful engagement of the individual with society, with the ultimate goal of social improvement. Green's writing and teaching reformulated classical liberalism, which stressed the negative rights of individuals against the state as the basis of a good society.[19] Years later, Milner wrote, "Now the years which I spent at Oxford, and those immediately succeeding them, were marked by a very striking change in the social and political philosophy of the place, a change which has subsequently reproduced itself on the larger stage of the world. When I went up the *Laisser-faire* theory still held the field. All the recognised authorities were 'orthodox' economists of the old school. But within ten years the few men who still held the old doctrines in their extreme rigidity had come to be regarded as curiosities."[20]

There were other influential future leaders of the British Empire present at Oxford who were likely to have absorbed the same lessons about the empire as Milner and Rhodes. The future political leader H. H. Asquith was an outstanding student at Balliol College from 1870 to 1874. He studied with T. H. Green and later went on to a distinguished parliamentary career, serving as a Liberal M.P., Cabinet member, and prime minister from 1908 to 1916. Another imperial leader was educated at Oxford from 1879 to 1883: George Curzon, a prize-winning student at Balliol and member of Bullingdon's. He became the viceroy of India (1899–1905), leader of the House of Lords (1916–1925), foreign secretary of Great Britain (1919–1925), and chancellor of Oxford University (1907–1925).[21]

Oxford men like Curzon, Asquith, Milner, and Rhodes shaped the British Empire as it neared its apex in the late nineteenth and early twentieth century. When it came to inspiring future imperialists, possibly the most influential Oxford faculty member was the Slade Professor of Fine Art, John Ruskin. In 1870, Ruskin began his professorial appointment by giving a lecture that was not only well attended—it was printed and reprinted, achieving global circulation. In the lecture, Ruskin made the argument that the noblest art was produced by the noblest people. For his contemporaries to achieve the best art, he claimed, they needed to live frugally and to take up the responsibilities that the Empire demanded of them, especially since the British were "still undegenerate in race" and had "the firmness to govern, and the grace to obey." Ruskin recognized that much of Britain's power derived from superior science and technology, which had "made but one kingdom of the habitable globe." To support Britain's glory, subjects should not rally to the flag "that hangs heavy with terrestrial gold," but instead choose true glory without the promise of wealth. In building an empire, patriots should be prepared to "cast themselves against cannon-mouths for love of England . . . and who will gladden themselves in the brightness of her glory, more than in all the light of tropic skies."[22]

Much of Rhodes's vision was ultimately in accord with Ruskin's philosophy. Rhodes's associate James McDonald confided to Rhodes's architect, Herbert Baker, that once, in the 1890s, Rhodes spoke in conversation about the influence of Ruskin. Rhodes said, "Listening to Ruskin while at Oxford his lectures made a deep impression on one. One of them in which he set out the privileges and opportunities of the young men in the Empire made a forceful entry into my mind." The evidence is secondhand but still worth considering. Rhodes hoped that England would "found colonies as fast and as far as she is able . . . seizing every piece of fruitful waste land she can set her foot on and teaching her colonists that their aim is to advance the power of England by land and sea," and "to make England a centre of peace, mistress of learning and of the arts."[23]

If England were to have men who would "cast themselves against cannon-mouths," Ruskin believed that the leaders of society had to come to a stronger appreciation for the work of ordinary people and the things produced by craft. Craft involved the mindful contemplation of the arrangement of materials, contrary to industrial production, where people became cogs in a machine. Traditional craftsmanship was closer to nature, and nature was closer to goodness and truth. In 1874, Ruskin tried to teach this romanticized idea about the nobility of labor by recruiting students and faculty to help build a road across the marsh between the villages of North Hinksey and South Hinksey, just west of Oxford. Rhodes missed the experience—he had already left Oxford after his first term—but he must have heard of it. The project was discussed extensively. An account of the road building was given by one of the participants, Oscar Wilde, in an 1882 lecture entitled "Art and the Handicraftsman." Wilde wrote that Ruskin chided students for expending their useful energies on cricket and tennis, when they could be helping others. Ruskin told the students that "we should be working at something that would do good to other people, at something by which we might show that in all labour there was something noble." The students spent several months constructing the road, which they did not complete.[24]

Ruskin's thinking echoed that of his Oxford faculty contemporary, T. H. Green, in that they both hoped for students to build a better society through positive civic engagement. Ruskin was unusual in that he rebelled against orthodox notions of progress, hoping instead that a utopian society would revert to the production of simple, well-designed, beautiful but necessary products. One of Ruskin's students from the 1850s, William Morris, shared his teacher's love for older ways. Morris, who became famous as a designer and author, romanticized the connection between the craftsman and the materials in the preindustrial era. Morris's designs for housing, furniture, and decorations became some of the most important inspirations for the Arts and Crafts Movement. He, too, was well known at Oxford during Rhodes's student days. In the 1870s, Morris was living and working in the village of Kelmscott, twenty miles west of Oxford. His vision, like Ruskin's, of a future that incorporated idealized past technological practices, seems at first blush to be highly eccentric. Ironically, many Arts and Crafts products were expensive and could only be afforded by wealthy industrialists, whose own products ran contrary to Ruskin's ideals. Ruskin and Morris still influenced important utopians, such as Tolstoy and Gandhi, who put many of their ideas into action.[25]

Ruskin's emphasis on simplicity and craftsmanship can be seen turning up, like the influence of Marcus Aurelius, in Rhodes's preference for simple clothing and housing, as well as his interest, in the 1890s, in becoming a gentleman-farmer and a proponent of a South African variant of the Arts and

Crafts style. As a young man, Rhodes had worked with his hands at Kimberley, so Ruskin's emphasis on the nobility of manual labor may have resonated with him, although it must be said that Rhodes's later mining operations were highly industrialized and not especially sympathetic to workers.[26]

To prepare himself for a return to Kimberley, Rhodes took the initial steps to become a barrister, an attorney who is qualified to advocate for clients in court. Together with his friend Robert Yerburgh, he became a member of the Inner Temple, one of London's four Inns of Court responsible for the education of barristers. Student members like Rhodes were required to eat occasional suppers there. In addition to the sociable requirement of members' meals, the Inns of Court required a year or more of legal education in London before the student became eligible to take the examination for admission to the bar. Taking a membership and dining at the Inner Temple was the first step. Rhodes explained, in a letter to Rudd, that having a legal career as a backup would make him a bolder businessman. In 1876, Rhodes was in Oxford and wrote to Rudd, in Kimberley, that the lack of a profession caused him to lack "pluck" in three business deals, "through fearing that one might lose and I had nothing to fall back on," which cost them £3,000. Rhodes wrote, "You will find me a most perfect speculator if I have two years and obtain a profession. I am slightly too cautious now." A legal career may also have appealed to him as a backstop in case of failure on the Diamond Fields.[27]

Rhodes attended meals and paid fees at the Inner Temple but gradually lost interest in a legal career. He was more attracted to building a social network. On June 2, 1877, as Trinity (Spring) term was drawing to a close, Rhodes followed up on his agnostic leanings by officially joining the Freemasons. The university branch, known as the Apollo Lodge, was one of the leading social clubs available to undergraduates. Founded in 1818, the Apollo was open only to men who were students or faculty at the university. The Apollo was known to be especially formal and ritualistic—members wore full court dress—white tie, knee breeches, white stockings, and pumps. This may not have appealed to Rhodes, who preferred informality. Even so, he probably enjoyed the jolly, patriotic, all-male company. The Masonic lodge had one other member who would become just as famous as Rhodes. On the day of Rhodes's initiation, one of the officers of the lodge was a fellow member of Bullingdon's, Oscar Wilde, who reveled in the rituals and dress of the Masons, as they appealed to his aestheticism.[28]

Masonic symbolism was not as important to Rhodes as Masonic ideology. The Masons preached international brotherhood, calling themselves "citizens of the world." In the eighteenth century, the ranks of the Masons were highly diverse. By the time Rhodes joined the all-male organization it had become, in the words of historian Jessica Harland-Jacobs, "a primarily white, respectable, Protestant institution tied explicitly to the British monarchy." Membership was restricted yet global. Anywhere in the British Empire, men were able to forge social, political, and business links through the Masons. Membership was more than instrumental—it provided men with an identity that enhanced the Victorian age's increased mobility. It also provided men with a fraternal social organization, making it possible, through gatherings and rituals, to deepen friendships.[29]

On the very same day as his induction into the Masons, Rhodes began to write his second will, known as the "Confession of Faith," which plainly shows the influence of Freemasonry as well as Winwood Reade. Rhodes brought the first draft with him to Kimberley during his summer vacation of 1877. While attending to business, he worked on a second draft, which he had notarized on September 19, shortly before he returned to Oxford.[30] The "Confession" extended the simple imperialist patriotism of the first will, adding various ideas that influenced Rhodes while he was at Oxford: Freemasonry, imperialism, social Darwinism, and the key texts of a classical education, especially Aristotle's *Ethics*, plus, most likely, *The Martyrdom of Man*. The "Confession of Faith" gives a clear sense of Rhodes's early vision for the British Empire and South Africa.

The 1877 Confession opens with Rhodes wondering, in an Aristotelian vein, "what is the chief good in life." Rhodes passes over a "happy marriage" and "great wealth" to arrive at his conclusion, "to render myself useful to my country." Even early in his life, a nationalist vision was winning out over more mundane motivations. He laments that Britain's loss of the lands of the United States has limited the capacity of the English population to grow, a bad thing because "we are the finest race in the world and that the more of the world we inhabit the better it is for the human race." Surveying the parts of the world that are "inhabited by the most despicable specimens of human beings," he wonders, "what an alteration there would be if they were brought under Anglo-Saxon influence." Adding territory to the British Empire would bring about "the future birth to some more of the English race," while "the absorption of the greater portion of the world under our rule simply means the end of all wars."[31] Very early in his career, Rhodes supported the extension of a *pax Britannica*, with the object of populating the earth with more people like himself.

Rhodes then turns to solving the problem of how best to conquer the world and populate it with Englishmen. He writes, in a drafty style, that "I look into history and I read the story of the Jesuits I see what they were able to do in a bad cause and I might say under bad leaders." Next, he touches on his membership in the Masons. "I see the wealth and power they possess the influence they hold and I think over their ceremonies and I wonder that a large body of men can devote themselves to what at times appear the most ridiculous and absurd rites without an object and without an end." Yet according to Rhodes, secret societies still hold the potential for achieving greatness. "The idea gleaming and dancing before ones eyes like a will-of-the-wisp at last frames itself into a plan. Why should we not form a secret society with but one object the furtherance of the British Empire and the bringing of the whole uncivilized world under British rule for the recovery of the United States for the making the Anglo-Saxon race but one Empire. What a dream, but yet it is probable, it is possible." Blaming the loss of the thirteen colonies on "pig-headed statesmen" who make him feel "mad" and "murderous," he imagines a future filled with conquests. "Africa is still lying ready for us it is our duty to take it. It is our duty to seize every opportunity of acquiring more territory and we should keep this one idea steadily before our eyes that more territory simply means more of the Anglo-Saxon race more of the best the most human, most honourable race the world possesses."[32] And with the optimism of a young, idealistic man, he regards his grand vision as a practicable scheme.

The ideas that Rhodes articulated in his Confession of 1877 are more than a grab bag of Aristotle and Freemasonry. The document is best understood in the context of the broader intellectual milieu of Oxford in the 1870s. The Confession of 1877 also had a specific political context. In August, in between Rhodes's writing of the first draft and the second draft, the widely distributed journal *The Nineteenth Century* published an essay by the former prime minister, William E. Gladstone, entitled "Aggression on Egypt and Freedom in the East," in which the leader of the Liberal party made a strong case against further British expansion, in this case into Egypt. Gladstone spoke words of caution:

> But our first site in Egypt, be it by larceny or be it by emption, will be the almost certain egg off a North African Empire, that will grow and grow until another Victoria and another Albert, titles of the Lake-sources of the White Nile, come within our borders; and till we finally join hands across the Equator with Natal and Cape Town, to say nothing of the Transvaal and the Orange River on the south, or of Abyssinia or Zanzibar to be swallowed by way of *viaticum* on our journey. And then, with a great empire in each of the four quarters of the world, and

with the whole new or fifth quarter to ourselves, we may be territorially content, but less than ever at ease; for if agitators and alarmists can now find at almost every spot "British interests" to bewilder and disquiet us, their quest will then be all the wider, in proportion as the excepted points will be the fewer.[33]

Gladstone cast doubt on ideas for a trans-African empire. He was pushing back against broad imperialist objectives as well as a specific plan that was being discussed in the mid-1870s. An empire, a railroad, and a telegraph stretching from "Cape to Cairo" is a phrase most closely associated with Rhodes, but the catchphrase was first articulated by the former prime minister of South Australia, Henry Strangways, an advocate for imperialism who moved to London in 1871 and who was active in the Royal Colonial Institute. Strangways claimed that he "first mooted" the idea of a Cape-to-Cairo telegraph in 1875. The term itself may have been coined by Strangways but at around that time it came to be associated with a better-known imperialist, Edwin Arnold, who edited the influential newspaper the *Daily Telegraph*. Led by Arnold, the *Telegraph* had backed Henry Morton Stanley's expeditions in Central Africa from 1874 to 1877. While Stanley's expeditions were under way, in 1876 Arnold joined explorers Kerry Nicholls and James Augustus Grant in making a presentation to the Brussels Geographical Conference. The pamphlet was called "Remarks on a Proposed Line of Telegraph Overland from Egypt to the Cape of Good Hope." The recommendations were discussed in geographical circles and inspired future colonial subalterns.[34]

Rhodes did propose another idea that was original. In his 1877 "Confession of Faith" he built on his imperial interests and on his experience with Freemasonry to propose the creation of a secret society. The society's membership was to be recruited from men, who, like Rhodes, have "ample means" but who recognize, like Aristotle, that goodness does not come from "plunges into dissipation" or "travels" or going "into the far interior after the wild game," but from working for the greater good. Rhodes hopes that his secret society will reach out to such men who might otherwise be "compelled to pass [their] time in some occupation which furnishes him with mere existence." Upon being recruited to the Society, these men were expected to become advocates for imperial unity in colonial legislatures, where their duty was to "crush all disloyalty." Members of the Society were expected to own newspapers, too, because "the press rules the mind of the people." Rhodes's 1877 Confession left his fortune to Sidney Shippard and to the secretary of state for the colonies, so that they might "try to form such a Society with such an object."[35]

The scheme's core contained Aristotelian high-mindedness as well as contemporary biological notions of race, with an admixture of Social Darwinism and a whiff of Freemasonry. It is worth noting that in the early iteration of his thinking that is contained the 1877 Confession, Rhodes mentions Africa once, with no discussion of South Africa, diamonds, or engineering. His ultimate notion of the Greater Good involved the expansion of the British Empire by means of a secret society.

The best way to understand this vision for imperial unity is by putting Rhodes's ideas into context. During the second half of the nineteenth century, British intellectuals articulated fears that their country was declining relative to other countries—fears that could be overcome by uniting the Empire through federation. Closer imperial ties had been discussed before by British intellectuals, especially during the American Revolution. A consensus emerged at that time that the vast expanses of the oceans and the state of navigation and communication technologies militated against close ties. The idea of imperial federation can be thought of as a response to the political challenges of globalization, driven by the possibilities presented by the late-nineteenth-century revolution in communications and transportation.[36]

The new technologies shaped the consciousness of Rhodes and his generation, helping them to conceive of a world in which people could traverse vast spaces more quickly than ever before. The 1870s and 1880s were the key decades for the emergence of this shift in perception. *The Times* as well many leading authors spoke of the "shrinking" and "annihilation" of time, space, and nature. In 1871, the widely read *Contemporary Review* published an article by John Edward Jenkins that was typical of the discourse that linked imperial federation with the "conquest" of space. Jenkins wrote: "It may be said that every year we advance nearer to our dependencies both in time and facility of intercourse. At no very distant date steam communication with Australia will be so frequent, regular, and rapid, and the telegraph system so enlarged and cheap, that no practical difficulty would impede the working of a representative federal government." In 1875, W. E. Forster made a speech, "Our Colonial Empire," that was reported in *The Times*. Forster argued that "science has brought together the ends of the earth, and made it possible for a nation to have oceans roll between its provinces." In 1884, Forster was involved in the founding of the Imperial Federation League. He published a widely read essay in *The Nineteenth Century* in which he extolled the "political effect of steam and electricity," which he believed made possible political unity across the oceans. Even critics of imperial federation accepted that the perception of time and distance had changed radically.[37]

The Confession of 1877 does contain a noticeable silence about the mines, even though Rhodes knew they were the key underlying means of achieving his ends. The mines at Kimberley appear to have been only instruments for achieving the secret society and the unified Empire. In 1876, Rhodes sent a letter from Oxford to Rudd in Kimberley. The diamond business was slumping, yet Rhodes kept the faith in diamonds, partly because he had faith in technological improvements to mining. He encouraged Rudd to "knock along" with their ice-making machine, their steam pumps, and the ten-horsepower engine they used for hauling dirt out of the mines, knowing that these side businesses were likely to generate a steady stream of capital. Rhodes wrote that "the application of machinery to diamonds will lick depreciation in prices." As for prices, he wrote that "if bad times have got you in a mess, do not funk. They are temporary. Diamonds in themselves are more liked than ever, all the swells now wear them in preference to anything but the people hit in foreign loans have been as you can understand selling their houses and diamonds, dropping their carriages and horses in town."[38] The public's desire for diamonds was forecast to be strong, so it was a sensible business decision to buy machines that were capable of getting gems out of the ground more efficiently.

In 1877, Rhodes was back in Kimberley for his summer "long vacation" from Oxford. Over the course of the clear, sunny days and long, cool nights of the South African winter, Rhodes worked together with Rudd to advance their mutual business interests, while also dining and socializing with miners and visitors. On one occasion—the exact date is uncertain—Rhodes hosted a dinner party in his two-room, corrugated-iron shack. The guests were the government surveyor-general, John Padden, as well as H. J. Feltham, local branch manager of the Cape of Good Hope Bank. They were joined by David Arnot's friend Francis Henry Orpen and his brother, Joseph Millerd Orpen. Joseph Orpen was a convivial Irish polymath who had worked as a farmer, surveyor, and soldier and who was an experienced politician with knowledge of the region's various cultures and languages and with side interests in geology and paleontology. Few people knew the changing geography of colonial Southern Africa better.[39]

In a letter written in 1918, Joseph Orpen recalled his Kimberley dinner with Cecil Rhodes. The meal was memorable because after dinner, Rhodes laid out his scheme for British domination in Southern Africa. Orpen recalled that Rhodes made a striking statement:

> Gentlemen, I have asked you to dine... because I want to tell you what I want to do with the remainder of my life. I think if a man when he is young determined to devote his life to one worthy object and persists in that he can do a good deal during that life even it is to be a short one as I know that my life will be but he can do still more if he has a few like minded friends as I believe you to be who will just lend him a helping hand when they are able to do so. The object of which I intend to devote my life is the defence and extension of the British Empire. I think that object a worthy one because the British Empire stands for the protection of all the inhabitants of a country in life, liberty, property, fair play and happiness and it is the greatest platform the world has ever seen for these purposes and for human enjoyment. Everything is now going on happily around us. The Transvaal [after the 1877 annexation by Britain is] much better off than it was and is quietly settled under government. The Free State is perfectly friendly and can join us when and if it likes. It is mainly the extension of the empire northward that we have to watch and work for in South Africa.[40]

Joseph Orpen recalled that at the dinner, he and his brother, Frank, agreed with Rhodes that British government was the best. The five dinner companions pledged to work together to achieve the extension of the empire in Southern Africa. They promised to form a corresponding brotherhood, whose letters had a secret mark, the five dots of a dice. The letters have not survived but it is significant to note that Rhodes was building his network for achieving the goals that he set forth in the 1877 Confession. Rhodes may have been saying the same things to many other dinner companions during the late 1870s, as a way of extending his imperialist project through social networking.

While Rhodes was busy developing his political outlook, he lived a curious double life as an undergraduate socialite in Oxford and as a young entrepreneur in Kimberley. He returned to Oxford for the full academic year of 1877–1878. By the summer of 1878, he had only one term left to complete his degree. At that point he seemed to lose momentum. Some biographers suggest that he may have been affected by the death of his father in February 1878. That is likely, even though he does not seem to have been very close to his father, having visited him at his retirement home in Hastings only twice. Perhaps it was not family matters but rather the press of business in Kimberley that made it difficult for Rhodes to finish his degree until the fall of 1881.[41]

Rhodes's experiences at Oxford are not well documented, as he did not leave behind much in the way of correspondence or other written materials. Based on the available evidence as well as the context of his later life's trajectory, it does seem that Rhodes's time at Oxford shaped his vision. It was there that he most likely encountered lively discussions about evolution, religion, and imperialism. The classical education afforded by the university may have seemed out of touch with the technological developments that enabled imperialism. For young Cecil Rhodes, Greats provided a wider political context, orienting his thoughts strongly toward personal improvement and national service. Networking was important, too. At Oxford, he widened his social network to include the social and political elite of Britain. Rhodes returned to Kimberley in 1878 determined to pursue the amalgamation of the mines and to become a political leader. His experience and his connections at Oxford extended his influence, sometimes in ways that did not bear fruit for a decade or longer. The range of contacts that he made at Oriel, Bullingdon's, the Masons, and other clubs proved critically important for Rhodes's career. Over the course of the next twenty-five years, he articulated his ideas with more and more members of his network, particularly with politicians, bankers, engineers, and architects, many of whom worked with him. The development of his political and technical vision, by means of his network, forms the central element of his legacy for Southern Africa.

5
Entering Politics

SOON AFTER LEAVING Oxford, one term before earning a pass degree, Cecil Rhodes experienced another personal setback: the death of one more of the most influential men in his life. While the Reverend Francis William Rhodes had been a major influence over Cecil's development, there was not a strong emotional attachment and there is no documentation for Rhodes mourning his father. We do know that he was very much affected by another loss, the death of his older brother Herbert in 1879. Herbert was a larger-than-life, athletic figure who struck out for the interior of Southern Africa in 1872. For three years he lived in the Transvaal, near Pilgrim's Rest, where he prospected for gold. He ran a saloon called the Spotted Dog and was elected to the republic's legislature, the Volksraad. In 1877, Herbert grew restless again and joined friends seeking ivory and gold farther north. He journeyed two thousand miles, past the shores of Lake Nyasa, today called Lake Malawi, and up through modern-day Tanzania to Zanzibar. In 1879, he was back in Nyasaland, today called Malawi, to hunt elephants and prospect for gold. Shortly after Herbert's return to Central Africa, his friend, the famous hunter Frederick Courteney Selous, sent word to Rhodes that his brother had burned to death in an accident. The news shook Rhodes deeply.[1]

This personal tragedy occurred at a time of general stress in Southern Africa. In the late 1870s, there were major wars between the British and the Xhosa, Pedi, and Zulu, as well as lesser conflicts in the Northern Cape and Griqualand East. Colonial militia units became more active in defense of regional colonialism. In 1877, Griqualand West's militia, the Diamond Fields Horse, fought as far away as the Transkei and Pondoland—500 miles. In 1878, they fought closer to home. At the start of the year, a Griqua rebellion broke out to the west of Kimberley, in the Langeberg. The lieutenant-governor, Major Lanyon, together with the officer in charge of the Diamond Fields Horse, Captain Charles Warren, led the militia to the Langeberg to suppress the rebellion. Some of the British community's opinion leaders spoke out against the campaign. The "natives," noted Dr. Josiah Matthews, "were once, it must be kept in mind, the owners of the soil." They disputed the injustice of land transactions and tried their best to resolve things peacefully. Matthews blamed the rebellion on Warren, who was "hasty beyond description, autocratic to a degree, and bigoted in the extreme." Richard Southey went even further. Speaking now as a member of the House of Assembly, he said on the floor that "so gross was the injustice sustained by these people in the land court that had I been a Griqua, I too would have rebelled."[2]

Warren's force also attacked other African people. Around the same time as the Griqua rebellion, violence broke out between settlers and Tlhaping people. The Tlhaping residing in Griqualand West had seen much of their land expropriated under the administrations of Southey and Lanyon. Tensions boiled over in the early months of 1878, when Tlhaping fighters attacked settlers. In July 1878, Warren's 300 cavalrymen and a battery of field artillery fought against well-armed Tlhaping soldiers commanded by their chief, Jantjie, and his son, Luka, at the towns of Kuruman and Dithakong, 150 and 160 miles northwest of Kimberley. On both occasions, the settler militia carried the day—and carried off several thousand cattle, goats, and sheep. For the Tlhaping chiefdom the losses represented an economic disaster.[3]

Rhodes joined the Diamond Fields Horse after returning from Oxford in June 1878 and may have been present for the battles at Kuruman and Dithakong. He did participate in Warren's follow-up campaign, which consisted of riding a full circuit around the colony of Griqualand West, looking for Tlhaping and Griqua men who had resisted British authority. Many years later, Warren noted that Rhodes participated in one particular operation that took place in January 1879. The Cape governor and high commissioner, Bartle Frere, ordered the nonwhite population of the area to surrender their firearms, in response to fears of "risings of native tribes" during the Anglo-Zulu War. Warren asked Rhodes to be a witness to the disarming of an impoverished settlement of one hundred mixed-race Koranna cattle ranchers at Zoutpan, near Christiana, seventy miles north of Kimberley on the Vaal River. These Koranna were being encouraged by German missionaries to resist. Warren did not go himself but sent Rhodes with a small force under Major Rolleston. They rode out to the Zoutpan settlement, where they found the armed Koranna residents in a hostile state of mind. Arguments ensued, and when the weapons were being collected, a Koranna man shot a militia member dead and wounded another. The resisters were arrested and brought to the Kimberley jail. Rhodes was never in any danger but still felt it necessary to defend the heavy-handed approach to the Koranna in an article in the *Government Gazette*. His opinion about the Koranna indicates that he held classic attitudes about indigenous people. According to Rhodes, the Koranna were

> a race so utterly debased and fallen that many of them are frequently mistaken for Bushmen; they are not found like the Bechuanas, Basutos, Zulus, or other native races, inhabiting separate tracts of country with defined limits, but are scattered along the Orange and Vaal Rivers, and in the interior, mixed up with other tribes, generally without chiefs, and living under the most miserable circumstances. They never cultivate, but are dependent for existence on the milk of the few cattle they possess, and when this fails, on the scanty roots they can find in the soil. It is in behalf of a few remnants of such a race the Rev. Kallenberg (of the German Mission) claims the whole of the Bloemhof and Christiana districts, a territory containing two villages and an immense number of occupied farms. By his own showing he has encouraged them to lay claim to a territory in extent about 2,000 square miles. (A travelling gipsy tribe laying claim to the county of Yorkshire would be a fairly similar case.)[4]

South Africa's people and geography were being described in terms familiar to the English, with lands enclosed for the benefit of wealthy farmers and with "gipsy" tribes regarded with bemused hostility.

Looking outward from Kimberley, white relations with African neighbors were poor. Looking inward, Kimberley was developing from an unruly mining town into a more settled community. The administrations of Southey and his successor, Lanyon, placed restrictions on gambling, prostitution, and liquor. Roads were still rutted and bumpy, maintained ineffectively by the same convicts who dug the town's latrines. Fires were still a regular occurrence, but at least most residents were replacing their tents and shacks with sturdier housing made from corrugated iron. Businesses occupied more attractive structures, too, and there was even a handful of two-story buildings. The telegraph arrived in 1876, better connecting remote Kimberley with the rest of the world. And with the germ theory of disease gaining adherents, recognized sanitary standards started to be applied in the town. In 1877, the mining magnate Joseph B. Robinson led citizens in forming a municipality to address community sanitation. Town doctors complained that Kimberley "was perfectly honeycombed with cesspools," which they connected to outbreaks of disease. In 1879 they persuaded the town to establish a "pail-system" for the removal of "nightsoil" to the outskirts of town.[5]

Sanitation was not the only concern about public health. Sexually transmitted infections were prevalent, too; they were just not discussed openly. And in late 1882 and again in late 1883, Kimberley was ravaged by outbreaks of smallpox. Quarantines were hotly contested. During the first smallpox outbreak, Rhodes supported the approach of another young man, Dr. Johannes "Hans" Sauer, who had studied at Edinburgh. He was hired by the town council to inspect migrants at the Modder River crossing, near Kimberley, to quarantine the sick and to vaccinate the healthy. Sauer was called back when the second outbreak hit, but before he could arrive, some of the city's established practitioners, Dr. Josiah Matthews and Dr. Rutherfoord Harris, and the newly arrived Dr. Leander Starr Jameson, had issued a flyer stating that the outbreak was not smallpox. They were eventually joined by one of Cape Town's most prominent physicians, Dr. Edmond Sinclair Stevenson, as well as by Kimberley's well-known nurse, Sister Henrietta Stockdale. The doctors were under pressure from mine owners not to drive away African migrant laborers, so there were grounds for skepticism about their smallpox denialism. Stevenson wrote in his memoirs that "if it was smallpox a quarantine would be called, the result being that the comparatively large population, mostly n----rs and others, would be thrown out of work. . . . Needless to say we pronounced it chicken-pox, otherwise it might have led to serious trouble." Rhodes himself insisted that the disease was chickenpox and thereby downplayed the spread of infectious disease. Disease was one of the key risks of bringing so many migrant workers to the diamond fields.[6] Rhodes certainly stood to lose income if the outbreak disturbed work at the mine. The doctors were all in his social circle. Later he became close friends with Jameson and a patient of Stevenson's. Rhodes also befriended Sauer, whose sister was married to Harry Caldecott, the law partner of Frederic Philipson Stow, Kimberley's most prominent attorney and a member of the De Beers Mining Board. Sauer began to spend time with Rhodes socially and became a key supporter.

While the white community of Kimberley was showing signs of stability, Kimberley's African community was becoming diverse and vibrant. In the early 1880s, there were several thousand African migrants employed by the diamond mines and an additional 9,000 who lived on company allotments and in the locations just outside of Kimberley. The diamond miners typically worked all day at the rockface, with the noise and smoke of dynamite and dozens of steam engines. In the evenings they retired to small gatherings around the locations, to saloons, restaurants, and campfires. People from all around Southern Africa brought their songs and musical instruments and were able to watch each other dance. New modes of dress were tried, especially the cast-offs of Europeans, while at least five Christian denominations sought African converts.[7] Rhodes and most of his acquaintances had little curiosity about the culture of African migrants. They only had a general sense of what "tribe" people might have come from—and that method of classification was often faulty. White mine owners typically complained of the crime and the dangerous habits of the Black community, without spending much time or effort looking into it.

Rhodes preferred the company of Kimberley's leading men. In 1879, he made the acquaintance of Jameson, originally from Scotland, who had received his medical training in London. Jameson and Rhodes were the same age. They became fast friends and encouraged each other's ambitions. In the words of Robert Rotberg, who emphasized psychology in his biography of Rhodes, the two men were "unusually intimate." By 1880, they were living together in "bachelor quarters." Jameson may not have been the easiest roommate. He was described by some as a man who flirted and carried

Dr. Leander Starr Jameson. From *Cecil Rhodes: Man and Empire-Maker* by Princess Catherine Radziwill (London: Cassell and Company, 1918).

on affairs with both men and women, while Rhodes had little interest in women, either sexually or socially. The people who knew Jameson also described him as an impulsive gambler and card-player, subject to mood swings, leading at least one scholar to suggest that he may have suffered from bipolar disorder. It is also possible that Jameson self-medicated with morphine.[8]

The intimate textures of Jameson's relationship with Rhodes will never be known. They lived together in 1880 until Rhodes met another man, Neville Pickering, a new arrival who was four years younger and worked for a merchant firm. When Rhodes went to the Cape Parliament in 1881, he hired Pickering to be his private secretary. As Rhodes went back and forth from Cape Town, to Oxford, and to Kimberley, the two men appear to have grown fond of each other. From the correspondence of others in Rhodes's circle, we know that Rhodes enjoyed Pickering's boyish vivacity. They lived together in Kimberley from 1882 to 1886. There is no evidence regarding a sexual relationship, but one acquaintance, Graham Bower, the Cape governor's secretary and a former naval officer, commented that Rhodes and Pickering had an "absolutely lover-like friendship." One early biographer, Basil Williams, met Rhodes and knew many in his circle. Williams commented that "Rhodes had a romantic affection" for Pickering. "He never loved any one so well." Rhodes even rewrote his will, putting Pickering in charge of his legacy.[9]

As Rhodes was building his network, he was becoming acquainted with an important future business partner, Alfred Beit. Beit came from a prominent Jewish family in Hamburg and had learned the diamond trade in Amsterdam, the world's center for diamond cutting. Beit was the same age as Rhodes. In 1875, he moved to Kimberley, where he worked as the agent of Lippert and Company, his cousins from Hamburg who were prominent merchants and investors in South Africa. Beit ran Lippert's office in Kimberley, where he earned a reputation as one of the best judges of diamond quality and as a quiet, sophisticated person who could be trusted. His talent was to be able to predict the value that a stone might earn on the European market. Before Beit, Kimberley's diamond buyers were not trained to the standards of the metropolis. Beit's work brought him to prominence in Kimberley, so that when Rhodes returned in 1879, they were introduced by a friend. Soon after their first meeting, Rhodes walked by Beit's office late at night and saw the lights were on. Rhodes stepped in and said, "Hallo, do you never take a rest, Mr. Beit?" Beit replied, "Not often." "Well, what's your game?" "I am going to control the whole diamond output before I am much older." Bantering back,

Rhodes replied, "That's funny, I have made up my mind to do the same. We had better join hands." They did, eventually.[10]

In getting to know Alfred Beit, Rhodes was not only gaining access to an expert in diamonds and finance. He was engaging with a separate network of diamond buyers who were now becoming diamond-mine owners and investors. Beit soon partnered with a fellow German, Julius Wernher, son of a general and representative of Jules Porgès, an influential diamond merchant. In 1880, Porgès, Wernher, and Beit merged with the Kimberley Mining Company, owned by Isaac Lewis, Barnet Lewis, and Samuel Marks. Porgès led the company, which was registered in Paris and called the Compagnie Française des Mines de Diamants du Cap de Bonne-Espérance. It was known around Kimberley simply as the French Company. The French Company focused on buying up claims in the Kimberley Mine. Other merchants started their own companies, too, intending to consolidate claims. These included Woolf and Solomon Joel and the soon-to-be-famous boxer, entertainer, and merchant Barnet Isaacs, known by his performing name, Barney Barnato.

In the minds of many of Kimberley's prominent citizens, Barnato was associated with shady practices, especially IDB. Rhodes's partner, Fred Stow, wrote in his account of amalgamation that Barnato was "considered an adventurer of uncertain integrity, and unsavoury record, and many of his associates were under police surveillance." Stow still gave Barnato some grudging admiration: "Notwithstanding his antecedents this man by bold speculation and financial courage amassed a fortune."[11] In Kimberley, it was hard to be particular about one's partners, as illegal practices were widespread. The very nature of diamonds, with their small size and high value, made them very tempting to hide and steal. Diamonds were typically shipped to markets via the colonial mail service, whose post offices and stagecoaches were sometimes robbed. Small buyers minimized the risk of theft by selling to bigger companies, who could afford better insurance and security.[12]

Rhodes and Rudd began their own drive to buy up claims for their De Beers Mining Company. In 1874, Lieutenant-Governor Southey increased the maximum number of claims per owner from two to ten. Rhodes and Rudd began to purchase claims worth £4,000 in a rich part of the De Beers Mine known as Baxter's Gully. There they became partners with Robert Dundas Graham and E. Grey. In 1876, after the Crossman Report persuaded the authorities to allow unlimited claim-holding, the partners began to buy more, with Rudd often corresponding with Rhodes in Oxford. Over the course of two years, their total number of claims rose to forty, worth £9,000. In 1879, Grey sold out to his partners, but a slew of new partners was added:

miners named Runciman, Leigh Hoskyns, and W. Puzey, as well as H. W. Henderson Dunsmore and Graham Alderson. Several more companies remained in direct competition with Rhodes and his partners, but with the pit getting deeper and the technical challenges increasing, these companies merged with Rhodes, too. In 1879, the number of Rhodes and Rudd's claims rose to ninety, for a total value of £175,369. Rhodes and Rudd used these claims to form the De Beers Mining Company.[13]

A complete buy-up of the De Beers Mine seemed within reach. The next important merger was with the company owned by Fred Stow. In 1878, Stow and Robert English started buying up claims at the same time as Rhodes and Rudd. In 1879, Stow and English added another partner, George Compton, to establish a strong geographical position in the mine. According to Stow's account, he and his partners owned claims that ran from the north end to the south end, cutting off Rhodes and Rudd, who sought consolidation from weaker positions that ran from east to west. Rhodes approached Stow and "made overtures" to join forces. A "great intimacy" formed between the two men, who decided to set aside their rivalry and work together with their partners to establish the De Beers Mining Company. The company's operations were strictly limited to the De Beers Mine.[14]

The early De Beers Mining Company had plenty of competition. In the late 1870s, the diamond mines were in a state of transition. The use of better equipment was resulting in overproduction. Lower prices were resulting in lower wages. And lower wages caused workers to leave the diamond fields. Rhodes, Rudd, and Stow were not the only ones buying up claims; so, too, were many of the Jewish merchant companies with links to Britain and Europe. In the De Beers Mine, many claims were now owned by Alfred Beit and other competitors. The sums of money became so great that some historians note a shift from "merchant capitalism" to "industrial capitalism."[15]

Rhodes wanted to do more than just merge his and Rudd's interests with Compton, English, and Stow's. Stow reported that in 1881, he visited Rhodes in England, when his new partner was finishing his degree at Oxford. Rhodes presented Stow with a full-fledged plan to buy up all four mines on the diamond fields. Stow reported "folio after folio of intricate figures and calculations for arriving at a basis of valuation of the many conflicting interests. The labour bestowed upon the elaboration of this project must have been prodigious." Stow was still unimpressed and dismissed Rhodes's plan: "A cursory glance sufficed to convince that it was inherently faulty and impracticable." Stow was not convinced that the merger really helped their interests. Even worse, "the agents it was proposed to employ to conduct the financial arrangements did not inspire sufficient confidence. Neither their repute nor ability to carry the venture to a successful issue was re-assuring." Rhodes and Stow decided to pursue the amalgamation of the De Beers Mine first, since that "served the interests of our company best." Complete amalgamation of the four mines would have to wait.[16]

Throughout the early 1880s, the new De Beers Mining Company could only afford to buy up other mining companies one by one. Share prices rose, helped by a general availability of capital in these years. Those who sold out to De Beers were often undervaluing their holdings because they were perplexed by the technical problems of mining. The job of hauling up the blue ground was frequently interrupted by the reef collapsing into the mine, a significant danger that resulted in delays. A reef collapse could involve the fall of a few rocks, or it could be a thunderous avalanche. Every year, miners were killed and injured at the De Beers Mine. Still, it could be worse. At the nearby Kimberley Mine, the problem of collapsing reef was especially bad, as that mine was the deepest of the four—at four hundred feet—and had ground that was especially crumbly. Starting in 1878, the mining board and the mining companies began to spend large sums of money to remove reef. They even installed extra tramways for reef removal and dug three shafts along the outskirts of the crater, to help remove the useless, dangerous shale. Even so, the walls of the open pit continued to collapse into the mine. From 1878 to 1883, the mining board spent more than one million pounds on removal, but the reef kept sliding into the mine. By the time a massive slide happened in November 1883, the mining board was bankrupt. The geology and geography of the mine demanded a new approach.[17]

New technologies began to help to some extent. The men working in Kimberley's open pits had been using ancient tools for breaking rocks, such as picks, shovels, and drills. They also used black powder for blasting rocks until the late 1870s, when a more powerful explosive came on the market. Dynamite's main ingredient was nitroglycerin, which was discovered in the 1840s by an Italian chemist, Ascanio Sobrero. Liquid nitroglycerin had much greater explosive force than black powder, but it had a key disadvantage: it was unstable. In the 1860s, it was manufactured and sold by Sweden's Alfred Nobel, who called it "blasting oil." The substance was so terrifying and unreliable that it was banned in many places. Blasting oil arrived in South Africa in 1866, when a Mr. Andrews and a Mr. Saunders gave a demonstration to the Cape Town Harbour Commissioners. Andrews poured two tablespoons into a tin dish then lit the "patent safety fuse." The explosion blew the men backward with such force that they turned three somersaults. Amazed that they survived with minor shrapnel wounds, Andrews quipped, "Thank God it was only two tablespoons."[18]

Nobel's chemists worked to address these safety concerns. In the 1870s Nobel succeeded at mixing nitroglycerin with diatomaceous earth and packing the dry substance in sticks. Dynamite sticks became popular with miners in the US West and were soon introduced to Kimberley. Dynamite was safer than blasting oil, but it still presented challenges. The original dynamite worked well with hard rock, but its force had to be adjusted for softer rock. Over the course of the 1880s and 1890s, different strengths of dynamite became available. Dynamite blasting came to be understood precisely, and workers who learned how to use it properly became valued for their skills.[19]

Progress did not eliminate risks. On January 10, 1884, the dynamite storage magazines of the De Beers Mine's Victoria Company blew up. The sound of the initial explosion frightened townspeople, who ran out into the streets. Looking up into the sky, they saw a large, black cloud of smoke billowing over the mine. Over the course of the next few minutes, more explosions could be heard as cases of dynamite and other explosives, including boxes of bullet cartridges, were heard going off. Rocks and debris showered the town. The future manager of De Beers, Gardner Williams, was not present for the explosion, but his colleagues later told him that windows, lamps, and chandeliers were shattered. Bartenders watched their liquor bottles blow up, spreading spirits onto the floor in puddles of "dynamite cocktail." Two workers standing near the magazine were killed. The government mine inspector, William Erskine, was not able to identify the cause of the explosion but complained in his report that "the insecure condition of some of the magazines, their unguarded position, and the utter carelessness observed by owners or users have been already animadverted in my Report for 1882." The owners had been warned but had chosen to ignore the inspector. Now Erskine and his colleagues imposed simple rules on the construction and placement of "magazine huts." The incident underscores how diamond-mining companies were frequently overlooking worker safety. Every mine inspector's report provides details of accidents. Nearly every year, several workers were killed in each mine. Many were injured.[20]

The worst dangers came from rockslides and floods, which scared miners and investors. Erskine indicated that in late 1881, when he started his inspector's job, "some claim-holders did not seem at all confident about the permanence of the industry." Even after ten years of digging, there was still uncertainty about the mine's geology. "Many had the idea," he wrote, "that the diamondiferous ground had been deposited in some inexplicable manner in various holes or cups in the earth's surface." There was plenty of evidence to suggest that the mines had potential, but it was doubted by many claimholders. He wrote that "the probability of the diamondiferous magma being a true mine rock contained within the pipe of the producing volcano was then opposed and even ridiculed by some of the diggers of the period."[21] The investors who believed in the existence of the "diamondiferous pipes" held shares and bought more. The skeptics sold their shares and left the diamond fields.

Miscalculations by the skeptical claimholders helped Rhodes and his partners. In 1883 De Beers Mining Company and six other companies were left, along with three solo owners. By 1885, one of those individuals sold out to DBMC, and only three other companies held out. Rhodes kept the faith in the De Beers Mine, but if holding was an act of faith, it was also a self-fulfilling prophecy. A company that controlled the entire mine would be able to take full advantage of underground mining without negotiating with another company. And the bigger the company, the more advantages it could expect to have on the European diamond markets.[22]

Amalgamation also unfolded at the other diamond mines, driven by the same financial and geological considerations. At the Kimberley Mine, claims were bought up by several groups, each group aiming for total control. In 1881, new shafts were revealing that the blue ground stretched deeper. One of the most aggressive buyers was the founder of the Central Company, Francis Baring-Gould. His family belonged to the Devon gentry and were distant relatives of the Baring Brothers bankers. Baring-Gould's main rival was Joseph B. Robinson, founder of the Standard Company. Descended from the 1820 British settlers of the Eastern Cape, Robinson fought with the Boers of the Orange Free State against the Sotho and in 1867 established himself as one of the original diamond buyers. During the 1870s, he became a prominent citizen in Kimberley's business community, famed for his pith helmet and his foul temper. "Robinson was universally detested," according to historian John Flint. "He was an unprincipled, though highly successful, moneygrubber of unparalleled meanness and lack of charity."[23]

Diamond magnates and political leaders used the Crossman Report as a template for strategic decisions. The report recommended the deregulation at the mines, which entailed less of a need for a separate colony of Griqualand West. The colony, which had never amounted to much more than the administration of Kimberley and the old river diggings by the Vaal, was absorbed by the Cape Colony in 1880. Companies were given a freer hand to organize production. Colonial governance and corporate amalgamation were much discussed at Kimberley. So was the railroad, which was still closely linked to colonial politics.

Seen from the ground in the Cape Colony during the 1870s, railway construction was mainly about patronage for farmers and miners. Kimberley clamored for connections to Cape Town and Port Elizabeth. Even without a railroad, the diamond fields were at the center of South Africa's shift from preindustrial animal power to industrial steam power. Steam pumps could be fueled by Tswana wood, but that was an expensive proposition. It was also expensive to transport coal by ox-wagon. The mines needed timber supports, too, which were also expensive to ship overland. The cost of transport attenuated efforts to develop coal mining in the Eastern Cape and Natal, where low-quality coal had been discovered. In the late 1870s, Kimberley industrialists learned that coal fields were discovered south of Johannesburg near Vereeniging. This was still a significant distance for an ox-wagon to travel. Investors from the diamond fields made efforts to open coal mines in the Transvaal and the Free State, but these, too, foundered under high transportation costs.[24] Kimberley's residents and migrant workers complained that coal and timber were expensive, and food and most supplies were expensive, too. Passengers preferred train travel over wagon travel. But so long as Kimberley was a part of Griqualand West, it had no representation in the Cape Parliament. No patronage, no railroad.

Rhodes believed that the railway was central to the further development of Kimberley and its diamond mines—and that representation in Parliament was necessary to achieve that goal. In 1880, with negotiations about the absorption of Griqualand West in their final stages, Rhodes wrote to his old friend John X. Merriman, with whom he had often gone riding when they were both diamond diggers. Merriman was now a member of the Cape Parliament's House of Assembly and held the cabinet post of commissioner of crown lands, which involved him in every colonial development project. His portfolio included the expansion of Cape railways and telegraphs. Rhodes had visited him in Cape Town when passing through on his way to and from Oxford. In May of 1880, Rhodes wrote to Merriman to express his hope that Griqualand West be given plenty of representatives in the Cape Parliament. Rhodes was confident about future diamond production. "There is every chance of our prosperity lasting; the old fear of the mines working out is rapidly fading, for instance, the Kimberley mine, which is now 300 feet deep, has a shaft in its centre 180 feet below that level and no signs of a change, diamonds being found out of the stuff coming out of the bottom of it." Rhodes's real goal was to put pressure on the government to extend the railway from

Beaufort West to Kimberley. Rhodes recognized that Merriman hoped for the new government to move beyond patronage politics and become run in a way that was fair and professional. He genuflected in the direction of reform, saying that Merriman was "rightly opposed to that wretched system of making a railway to every village in the country for the sake of the political support of its members." But when it came to achieving a railroad connection to Kimberley, Rhodes asked Merriman to "show a consideration for this Province" and argued that it was "due" greater representation—and a railway line.[25]

When Rhodes formally entered politics in 1880, he made it a priority to promote railroads. At around the same time, he began to talk about securing access to the Road to the North, which started in Kuruman and went first to Molepolole, the capital of the Kwena Tswana, up to Shoshong, a well-known trading post, and all the way to the Ndebele border at Tati. From there, the road went across to the Ndebele capital at Bulawayo and up into Mashonaland. The road was the key to travel north of Kimberley and was also a site of contests between Tswana chiefs and Boer settlers. One of the earliest voices to call for British control belonged to David Livingstone, who argued in 1852 that keeping the road British was the best commercial and humanitarian policy. Rhodes and his colleagues imagined that the original wagon trails of the missionaries and hunters would be developed into railways, with telegraph lines beside them. This would further a larger vision, in which the territory of Southern Africa would be incorporated in a settler state that excluded African people from power.[26]

When Cecil Rhodes first arrived at Durban and Kimberley, it was common for people to refer to their home as "South Africa," even though the country was divided into two British colonies, two Boer republics, and several independent chiefdoms. The official borders of all these political units were contested and were crossed easily. In the more remote northern interior, borders between chiefdoms and states remained vague. Rhodes sought to expand the Cape Colony's borders and to give settlers the sense that this territory belonged to them as part of a national patrimony. Territoriality became linked to ideology. The identity of that new settler nation was inextricably linked with material and technological processes. Settler farms soon availed themselves of progressive techniques, even as they relied on old forms of racial domination. The mines went under the ground, using modern engineering. Railroads ensured the supply of labor, goods, and energy, while telegraphs enabled up-to-the minute management and quick appeals to the security provided by the state. A telegraph message from a remote area could result in the rapid dispatch of troops by rail to defend that very territory.

To advance his interests, Rhodes became a politician. In October 1880, Griqualand West formally became part of the Cape Colony. The territory received four seats in the Cape Colony's House of Assembly. Two seats were allotted to Kimberley and two were allotted to Barkly West, a small town 25 miles to the northwest. Barkly West lay beside the Vaal River and was the main town of the river diggers from the early days of the diamond rush, when it was known in Afrikaans as Klipdrift and in Koranna as Ka-aub, both of which mean "stony ford." The town was briefly the site of an independent diggers' republic, but by the mid-1870s, in the words of a famous visitor, Anthony Trollope, it was "half deserted."[27] The seats for Barkly West were ostensibly to represent rural people, most of whom spoke Afrikaans. Rhodes did not speak Afrikaans and still decided to campaign for one of those seats, rather than oppose the favorites in Kimberley—the popular Dr. Josiah Matthews and the wealthy Joseph B. Robinson. In November 1880, Barkly West chose Rhodes to represent them, along with his friend Frank Orpen.[28]

Rhodes was only twenty-seven years old when he took what would become the lifelong job of representing Barkly West in Cape Town. Rhodes had some learning to do. In the House of Assembly, which then met in the Good Hope Masonic Lodge, he spoke plainly and lacked the quick-wittedness that is prized in parliamentary debate. He had trouble following the rules: he dressed in tweed suits, not in the traditional black frock coat, and referred to fellow members by their names and not by their constituency, which was the traditional practice. Rhodes spoke in short bursts and even fidgeted and giggled while others made formal addresses. This could be taken as evidence that Rhodes was a political lightweight, although he was certainly succeeding at calling attention to himself. He may have been testing the waters for a populist style, which appealed to Britons and Boers disaffected from the polished attorneys and landowners seated in the Cape Parliament. Rhodes eventually earned admiration for his simple, direct style.[29]

It soon became apparent that Rhodes's business background helped him cultivate a talent for deal-making. Rhodes felt most at home with fellow English-speakers but recognized that English-speaking politicians were divided against each other. For decades many Eastern Cape settlers wanted to separate from the Cape Colony and to form their own province. There were differences between the Eastern Cape and the Western Cape over policies toward Africans and Boers. Rhodes observed that the Cape Dutch, led by journalist Jan Hendrik Hofmeyr, voted as a unified bloc. Rhodes calculated

Jan Hendrik Hofmeyr. Wikimedia Commons.

that if he could ally himself with Hofmeyr and the Cape Dutch landed interests and then swing just enough of the English-speakers to support the Dutchmen, he had a chance of orchestrating a permanent majority in the Cape Parliament's House of Assembly. This insight came as a surprise to most Cape politicians, who thought of British and Dutch identities as separate. It may have helped that Rhodes shared an interest in Freemasonry with Hofmeyr, who was then the grand master of the Grand Lodge of South Africa.

One particular issue divided the Dutch and the British: the British occupation of the Transvaal. In the 1870s, the republic had been undermined by financial problems, theological disputes, and by poor relations with the Pedi chief, Sekhukhune. In 1877, the Transvaal's president, Thomas Burgers, left the country. Britain's Conservative prime minister, Benjamin Disraeli, ordered British forces to occupy the Transvaal and appointed Theophilus Shepstone as administrator. The Boer leadership was unhappy with the situation, tolerating it until the Pedi and Zulu were defeated in 1879. In December 1880, a Boer rebellion broke out against British rule. At this time, the British government changed hands from the Conservatives to the Liberals, with

William Gladstone starting his second term as prime minister. Gladstone had always been unenthusiastic about imperial expansion, but while campaigning for his parliamentary seat in Midlothian, near Edinburgh, in 1879, he made an especially fiery speech against imperialism that was widely reported. Gladstone criticized imperial wars in South Africa and Afghanistan, even going so far as to seek empathy for Britain's enemies: "Remember the rights of the savage, as we call him. Remember that the happiness of his humble home, remember that the sanctity of life in the hill villages of Afghanistan among the winter snows, is as inviolable in the eye of Almighty God as can be your own."[30] In 1881, after the Boers defeated the British at Majuba, Gladstone declined to intervene any further. The Transvaal regained its independence, while agreeing to grant the British government nominal suzerainty over the territory.

The ending of the First Anglo-Boer War, as it was called, was a difficult moment in the relationship between the British and the Boers on their northern borders. In Britain, anger about the war and about Gladstone's decision started to turn public opinion back in favor of imperialism. It was on the heels of Gladstone's much-criticized decision that Rhodes entered the Cape Parliament's House of Assembly in April 1881 as the representative of the Afrikaner district of Barkly West. Rhodes, still a proud supporter of British imperialism, understood the outlook of the Cape Dutch, who considered the winelands of the Western Cape to be their homeland. The region, with its vineyards extending from gabled houses up toward the slopes of beautiful mountains, gives visitors an idyllic impression. Behind the sunny surface, Cape Dutch landowners relied on a work force made up of mixed-race or "Coloured" workers who were descended from slaves and Khoisan people. They were joined by increasing numbers of workers who were migrating from different parts of Southern Africa. Some lived on the farms themselves, others walked to work from town, and many were subject to coercion. Workers were paid limited amounts of cash, supplemented by access to housing and with rations of alcohol, known as the "tot." The day began with the ringing of the old slave bell and was punctuated every couple of hours by tots of cheap white wine and brandy. The system fostered alcoholism and dependency.

For their own part, the Dutch farmers were under economic pressure. After the abolition of preferential tariffs in 1861, farmers shifted production to low-quality alcohol for domestic consumption. The cheap local brandy was known as "Cape Smoke" for the way that it burned the throat. Stiff competition caused smaller farmers to sell their land and for the scale of production to increase, financed by cooperative local lenders. Opportunities to work in the mines put pressure on wages.[31]

The Dutch farmers who were left formed organizations to preserve the culture of wine and grapes as well as the broader Dutch South African culture that was coming to be known as Afrikaner, or in those early days, Afrikander. Changing times had generated an aggrieved political climate. One organization, the Afrikaner Bond, was founded by strident anglophobes. Another organization, the Boeren Beschirmings Vereeniging (Farmers' Protection Society), promoted the economic interests of Western Cape farmers. It was led by Jan Hendrik Hofmeyr, who was elected to the House of Assembly in 1879 to represent the college town of Stellenbosch. By the time Rhodes became a member in 1881, Hofmeyr was the leader of the entire Afrikaner bloc, and in 1883 the Farmers' Protection Society formally joined the Afrikaner Bond. Hofmeyr demonstrated great skill in holding together the diverse interests of the Afrikaner cultural movement. He had little interest in Cabinet appointments and preferred instead to orchestrate his influence from behind the scenes, earning him the nickname of "The Mole."[32]

Rhodes visited the Western Cape and got to know the wine growers personally. Rhodes, following Ruskin, was attracted to traditional rural society, but initially he allied himself with the Western Cape farmers out of pragmatism. The support of the Afrikaner farmers would smooth access to the Road to the North, which ran through Boer territories, and the farmers and the mine owners had a mutual interest in cheap, accessible labor. In the short term, in 1881 the alliance with Hofmeyr put Rhodes in opposition to the prime minister, John Gordon Sprigg, who represented a rural district of the Eastern Cape. Sprigg had angered the Bond in 1878, when one of his first acts as the new prime minister was to support a tax on wine.[33]

Rhodes's new allies in the Afrikaner Bond had close ties to newspapers published in Cape Town, Paarl, and Stellenbosch. These newspapers were the key means for transmitting political news and for shaping public debate, so Rhodes followed suit and bought a newspaper. In the 1870s, the *Cape Argus* was the Cape's newspaper of record. It printed parliamentary debates and records of other official business, while its press also printed government documents. The *Argus* was owned by Saul Solomon, the most famous liberal member of the Cape Parliament. Solomon, an articulate defender of African rights, a "friend of the native" in principle, sold the newspaper to its editor, who was secretly backed by Rhodes. At that moment Cape liberals lost—and Rhodes gained—control of an important news outlet.[34]

The main story in the news was the Cape Colony's war in Lesotho, then known as Basutoland. It was established policy to protect Basutoland from the land-hungry settlers of the Orange Free State. Like their Boer neighbors, the Sotho were accomplished horsemen who were heavily armed. Under the influence of French Protestant missionaries, many Sotho people had embraced capitalism. They managed the farms that fed Kimberley, and some Sotho men went to work at the diamond mines. The cash that they earned bought Western-style clothing, which seemed desirable from the perspective of the Cape, and firearms, which seemed problematic. As the Cape and Britain drifted toward a new, conservative policy of expansion and confederation, the Sotho stood in the way.

Under the leadership of the Cape's prime minister, Gordon Sprigg, the colonial parliament passed a Peace Preservation Act that allowed the governor, Bartle Frere, to proclaim districts in which African people had to surrender their guns. Racial discrimination was against the law in the Cape Colony, and this was a plainly discriminatory measure. It provoked resistance on the part of liberal members of the Cape Parliament as well as the missionaries in Lesotho. The Peace Preservation Act represented was the first racially discriminatory law passed by the Cape's "responsible" government. Several prominent Sotho chiefs rebelled, and Sprigg was forced into an expensive and unpopular campaign in the mountains of Basutoland. The governor, Bartle Frere, had actively supported Disraeli's imperialism, as well as the scheme to confederate the South African colonies. After the election of Gladstone in April 1880, Frere was asked to step down. The failed confederation effort and the failed campaign in Basutoland had Rhodes and other members of parliament sharpening their knives for Sprigg when the session opened in April 1881.[35]

The Cape's expensive campaign against the isolated mountain kingdom of Basutoland was getting in the way of developing the railway to Kimberley and the Road to the North. Sotho resistance on difficult terrain ensured that the Cape's campaign was costly, sapping funds for public works such as railway and road construction. Both Rhodes and Sprigg believed that settler interests should be favored over imperial interests, while they also believed that African people were lesser beings who should be subject to discrimination. Ideological consistency was not always discernible in Cape politics. Rhodes made a pragmatic choice in opposing Sprigg. The Cape prime minister was slowing down railway building and was disliked by Rhodes's new allies in the Afrikaner Bond.

On April 19, 1881, and again on April 25, Rhodes made parliamentary speeches in favor of the rights of Africans, in this case to own firearms. This may seem ironic given Rhodes's racial views. He began the second speech with a claim to racial knowledge, based on his experience at Kimberley: "We are well aware at the Fields that there will be war. Our boys tell us so. I have a hundred of my own, so I know. My boys say, 'We cannot help it, Baas [boss]; we mean fighting."' The speech drips with paternalism yet makes a point of pragmatism. "It does not matter to Griqualand West members which party is in power," Rhodes claimed. "Any railway extension at all," even moderate ones, "must come to Kimberley." The Sotho war was hindering railway development and the development of South Africa as a whole. Rhodes favored a milder, less sweeping approach to gun control and stated that he favored shifting responsibility for Basutoland from the Cape government to the British government. Rhodes helped to swing several votes against Sprigg, who was forced to step down as prime minister in May 1881. Sprigg was replaced by Thomas Scanlen, who teamed up with Rhodes's allies, Merriman and Hofmeyr, in forming a cabinet.[36]

Rhodes found himself drawn into the major political debates of the day, but he still maintained a focus on the railways and on the economic development of Kimberley. Kimberley's residents approved. When Rhodes spoke there on August 3, 1881, he addressed the injustice of disarming the Sotho, who had earned their guns through hard work. Rhodes was careful, though, to show his loyalty to Britain's "native" policy and expressed the desire to defer judgment to the colonial governor, who was also the "high commissioner" traditionally in charge of relations with the people beyond the Cape's borders. Mainly Rhodes emphasized the importance of the railway to Kimberley. He faulted Sprigg's approach, which involved borrowing heavily to continue the expensive war against the Sotho. The speech was reported in the *Cape Argus,* which noted that while Rhodes's previous speeches had been disparaged by the Cape Town newspapers for their direct and informal rhetoric, this speech had been "an exhibition of oratorical skill and dialectical power" that resulted in a "perfect tempest of cheering."[37] Rhodes's investment in newspaper ownership was paying off.

On the heels of this triumph, Rhodes traveled to England, where he spent his final term at Oxford. He earned his degree in December 1881 and quickly returned to South Africa. When the Cape Parliament came back into session, the new prime minister, Thomas Scanlen, was still trying to manage the conflict in Basutoland. Negotiations had to be concluded with multiple chiefs, some of whom had remained loyal and some of whom had rebelled. Scanlen tried new approaches, including employing a special emissary, General Charles Gordon, hero of the Taiping Rebellion and former administrator of the Egyptian Sudan. Gordon had a reputation for personal bravery as well as for campaigning against corruption and slavery. He spent the early months of 1882 with Cape forces, then in August rode up into the mountains of Basutoland. At the very same time, Scanlen named Rhodes to be a special commissioner, together with two other appointees, charged with determining war reparations.

Rhodes and Gordon spent several months working simultaneously in Basutoland. Gordon's negotiations with the rebellious chiefs went well. The chiefs especially appreciated how Gordon came to their meetings unarmed, with an openness to their views. The general came to an understanding with the chiefs, but proposals for new administrative arrangements fell on deaf ears in Cape Town. At the end of 1882, Gordon resigned and left. Rhodes's job was easier—accounting for the war's losses and proposing ways of making up for the damage. For one week, Rhodes and Gordon worked together in the same village—Hlotse—where the two imperialists went for long walks together. Rhodes advised Gordon to be more mindful of his employers in the Cape government. Gordon, who was twenty years older than Rhodes, revealed that he had an offer of employment in the Congo from King Leopold of Belgium. He asked Rhodes to accompany him, but Rhodes felt committed to South Africa. In any case, Gordon's plan fell through when he realized Leopold's bad motives. Two years later, Gordon again asked Rhodes to work as his assistant, this time in Khartoum, Sudan, where the Anglo-Egyptian government was trying to put down a rebellion led by the Islamic reformer Muhammad Ahmad bin Abdullah, known as the Mahdi. This was an invitation that would appeal only to a special sort of man. Gordon was reputed to be a repressed homosexual who was attracted to younger men, so there may have been some romantic interest. Rhodes was, at that time, living with Neville Pickering. Had Rhodes joined Gordon, the two empire builders might have died shoulder to shoulder in Khartoum at the hands of the Mahdi's soldiers. Instead, Gordon died alone.[38]

As for the chiefs in Basutoland, they proved resilient in their negotiations. They asked to be ruled by London directly, as a separate colony, with powers still reserved for themselves. The Cape government was exasperated by the negotiations and wanted to be rid of responsibility for the territory. In 1884, Gladstone agreed to make Basutoland into the separate Crown Colony of Basutoland. This was a setback for Rhodes and others who sought a confederation of all the states of Southern Africa. Even so, in Basutoland, Rhodes learned a great deal about one of many rural areas supplying labor and food to Kimberley.

As the Cape government moved toward "de-annexation" of Basutoland, on July 18, 1883, Rhodes made a speech in the House of Assembly that delineated his geographical and political vision. The thirty-year-old addressed the failures of disarmament in Basutoland and referred to the disturbed country as a "volcano" of discontent. Rhodes opposed the idea of his ally, Hofmeyr, to let Basutoland rule itself, lest British rule antagonize the Orange Free State, which had designs on Sotho territory. Rhodes used these details as a springboard to introduce a new version of confederation. "I have my own views as to the future of South Africa," he said, "and I believe in a United States of South Africa, but as a portion of the British Empire. I believe that confederated states in a colony under responsible government would each be practically an independent republic, but I think we should also have all the privileges of the tie with the Empire." Building a unified, settler-run confederation had one obstacle, the majority African population, but this could be overcome. "We are now at the junction of two paths," Rhodes said, "one path leads to peace and prosperity in this country, by the removal of native difficulties, leaving us free for the development of the country; the other path leads to ruin and disaster." Euphemisms like the "removal of native difficulties" indicated Rhodes's disposition toward social disassembly.[39]

In the eyes of Rhodes and the other diamond mine owners, one of the key "native difficulties" was IDB. In 1881, while Rhodes was away in Oxford, his fellow mine owner in the Cape Parliament, Joseph B. Robinson, organized a Diamond Mining Protection Society to pressure for a crackdown on IDB. It was nothing new for the mine owners to complain about IDB, but two of them now sat in a closely divided house, where they could exert leverage. Rhodes and Robinson disliked each other personally but were still willing to join forces to regulate IDB. A special parliamentary committee was formed, chaired by Merriman and including Rhodes and Robinson. After extensive hearings in 1882, the committee recommended a harsh, extra-constitutional approach to accused African diamond thieves. Most of the proposals passed the Cape Parliament as the Diamond Trade Act of 1882. Record-keeping at the mines was improved. Surveillance was ramped up by increasing the number of guards and building new "searching houses." Men who possessed uncut diamonds and who were suspected of theft were presumed guilty, not innocent. Entrapment, or "trapping," was legal. People and packages could be searched without a warrant. Intrusive body searches of African miners were allowed. Those caught were now tried by a special court, with one member with legal training and others with experience in the diamond business. Punishments for IDB were made severe—upwards of fifteen years in prison. Rhodes and Robinson advocated the reintroduction of flogging as punishment for IDB. Flogging proved unacceptable to a majority of the Cape Parliament, which still passed the rest of the constitutionally dubious recommendations into law.[40]

Rhodes's views on flogging were extreme, even by the standards of his times. The restrictions that he proposed showed the ways in which his racial ideology was linked to pragmatic policymaking at the diamond fields. His aspirations in business and politics were interrelated. In the Cape Parliament's next session, in 1883, a Precious Stones and Minerals Act re-established each mine's mining board but included a key provision in support of the aspiring monopolists: as soon as one company owned nine-tenths of any mine, that mine's board was abolished and the company simply ran its own mine. Rhodes clearly furthered his plans for monopoly by means of legislation.[41]

6

Aiming North

IN THE EARLY 1880s, Rhodes began to use his growing influence in the Cape Parliament to protect its northern territories. The Vaal River runs from the Drakensberg and flows southwest toward Kimberley. From near there it flows all the way to the Molopo River, forming the lower boundary of a vast, semi-arid region. European hunters, traders, and missionaries had visited the dry region north of the Molopo many times over the course of the nineteenth century, giving the resident Tswana people familiarity with the outsiders' strengths and weaknesses. At the same time, Tswana identity was continuing to be formed, shaped in part by interactions with European "others" as well as their own ideas about language, nationhood, and material culture.

Tswana people were governed by separate chiefdoms, all of which shared elements of language and culture. By this time, many Tswana people practiced Christianity and European agriculture. Rhodes and the settlers at Kimberley were mainly acquainted with the southern Tswana chiefdoms south of the Molopo River, the Tlhaping and the Rolong. North of the river the principal Tswana chiefdoms were the Ngwato, in the north, ruled by Khama; the Kwena, in the center, ruled by Sechele; and the Ngwaketse, in the south, ruled by Gaseitsiwe and his heir-apparent, Bathoen. The leaders and the people of these chiefdoms were all wrestling with the benefits of European farming and trade, while trying to keep Boer settlers and alcohol at arms' length.[1]

Rhodes and other prominent people knew that the northward expansion of British colonialism was only possible if the Boers of the Transvaal could be kept from acquiring the Road to the North, which ran along the eastern edge of Tswana territory. After the brief British occupation of the Transvaal ended in 1880, it was "well known," according to a speech that Rhodes made in the Cape Parliament's House of Assembly on May 5, 1882, "that parties of [Boer] freebooters were anxious to establish a new republic on the border, and this colony ought not to alter the boundaries of the country as handed over to us." Rhodes did not know yet that the president of the Transvaal, Paul Kruger, was behind these efforts to cut off the Road to the North. Kruger planned instead to expand his territory westward. He also aimed to complete the Transvaal's rail connection eastward to Maputo, located in the southernmost part of Portuguese Mozambique. The capital of Mozambique, which is 325 miles due east from Pretoria, was then called Lourenço Marques; its harbor was known as Delagoa Bay. Kruger's rival plan for expansion along an east-west axis was part of a larger geopolitical context in which Belgium was expanding its claims in the Congo and Germany was becoming more aggressive in what is today Namibia and Tanzania.[2]

The strategic Road to the North was indeed vulnerable to a Boer takeover. Transvaal Boers seized land from the Rolong and Koranna. Several lesser chiefs favored cooperation with the Boers and gave them land as a form of payment. Several more favored the British and had land taken from them. Missionaries expressed concerns, but to the Boers of the republics and the Cape, the expansion of Boer territory was intended to convert the interior spaces of Southern Africa into settler-dominated, racially exclusive farming communities.

Rhodes was not particularly concerned with the rights of African people. Mainly he feared losing the Road to the North, so he asked the Cape Parliament to take up the matter. This was a complicated request. He was building alliances with the Afrikaner Bond, whose members supported the Boer incursions, even though, in 1881, the Transvaal had imposed tariffs on Cape products and proved unwilling or unable to keep Boer trekkers out of the territory of the Tswana. In 1882, two Boer republics were founded on the Road to the North. One, centered on Vryburg, was called Stellaland; the other, just to the north, was called Goshen. Both received support from the Transvaal and from the Afrikaner Bond.

Rhodes was horrified that the two Transvaal-sponsored miniature republics of Stellaland and Goshen might block the Road to the North. He felt impelled to gain the territory for the Cape Colony, yet he had to operate under the constraints of his alliance with the Cape Afrikaners. It worked to Rhodes's advantage that the proclamation of the republics of Stellaland and Goshen irritated the Colonial Office in London. The "Imperial Factor" often stood in the way of ambitious colonial politicians like Rhodes, whose hunger for land and resources often conflicted with African rights that were guaranteed by Britain. In the case of Stellaland and Goshen, the Colonial Office and Rhodes shared an interest in the Road to the North and worked in tandem. Not only were London officials offended by Boer challenges to British territorial sovereignty, but they were also alarmed that the Boers appeared to be encouraged by the German government. The Germans were establishing their authority in Namibia, while they were also supporting the Transvaal and negotiating with the quasi-independent Mpondo chiefdom in the Eastern Cape over a possible protectorate.[3]

Mindful of German and Boer competition, Rhodes became involved in claiming the vast spaces of the African interior for the British Empire. In May 1883, Cape Prime Minister Scanlen appointed Rhodes to be a member of the parliamentary commission that was investigating boundary claims in Griqualand West. For the next several months, Rhodes held his own meetings in the contested area and reached the self-serving conclusion that the Boers living there preferred to be part of the Cape Colony. He came up with an ingenious and somewhat less than honest solution to the problem of Stellaland and Goshen. Rhodes claimed that the Boers ought to remain on their new land but should be ruled by the Cape Colony, whose laws would give them more secure title than the laws of the republics. Stronger title would, of course, confirm the extortion of land from southern Tswana residents, but that did not concern Rhodes. Rhodes claimed that he could not show evidence of Stellaland and Goshen's support for Cape annexation, but their preference would become clear after they were annexed. From May to June of 1883, Rhodes lobbied Scanlen hard, repeatedly sending him telegrams to persuade him of the importance of the tiny new Boer republics. "You must act at once," Rhodes argued. "The key of the position is to stop Lord Derby from giving the Transvaal the right to extend" its territory westward. "Don't part with one inch of territory to Transvaal. . . . The interior road runs at present moment on edge of Transvaal boundary. Part with that, and you are driven into the desert . . . if you part with the road you part with everything."[4]

Scanlen was not persuaded that Rhodes's Road to the North was important enough to merit intervention. By contrast, Rhodes so feared nonintervention that even though he preferred settler government to imperial government, he began to court the intervention of the Cape's British governor and the Colonial Office in London. Imperial intervention was still better than Boer control. To improve relations with Britain, Rhodes cultivated a friendship with Graham Bower, the private secretary to the governor and high commissioner, Hercules Robinson. Bower and Rhodes persuaded Robinson that the Road to the North was one of the keys to South Africa's future. Robinson, in turn, was beginning to persuade Lord Derby, the secretary of state for the colonies in London, although Rhodes did not realize it.[5]

The Cape government and the British government were now under steady pressure from another corner, the missionary and humanitarian lobby. One of the most persistent advocates of the rights of colonized peoples was the

Hercules Robinson. Mitchell Library, State Library of New South Wales.

Reverend John Mackenzie, a prominent member of the London Missionary Society who had spent most of his career proselytizing Tswana people at Kuruman and Shoshong. Mackenzie denounced Boer incursions from the pulpit in South Africa and continued to do so while he was on leave in Britain in 1882 and 1883. Mackenzie's memoir of these times shows his passionate feelings about the perils facing African and mixed-race people north of Kimberley. He was especially concerned about what might happen if the large and diverse spaces near the Road to the North came under Transvaal law:

> The Transvaal is a country as large as France. Its population consists of some 50,000 whites, and some 600,000 to 700,000 natives. It is a fundamental Transvaal law among the Boers that no coloured person is the equal of a white person, either in Church or State. No coloured person can own land in the Transvaal in his own right. No coloured inhabitant of the Transvaal can move about his own country without a pass. White men, strangers or citizens, need no pass. There is no official recognition or registration of coloured people, either at birth, marriage, or death.[6]

Looking back on the 1880 withdrawal of British forces, Mackenzie vented his frustration: "No warning from the High Commissioner was given to the chiefs; no reply to their offer of obedience and submission; no advice as to the future; the policemen just left—the military occupation of three years ended; and Bechuanaland [Botswana] became what every confidential adviser and commissioner of Her Majesty said it would become—the abode of anarchy, filibustering, and outrage."[7]

Thanks to humanitarian pressure, Mackenzie was appointed by Hercules Robinson, the high commissioner, to be a "deputy commissioner" in the territory. Even so, the British government was not willing to make specific commitments to the different Tswana chiefdoms or the settler republics of Stellaland and Goshen, which had merged into one republic called Stellaland in August 1883. Legally speaking, the territory was under British suzerainty, meaning that Britain oversaw the external relations of the people who lived there. There was no specified legal relationship with the people who lived there—suzerainty was only a proclamation of overall dominance. Mackenzie began to shore up the Tswana chiefdoms and to guide Stellaland away from the Transvaal and toward the British.

John Mackenzie. Wikimedia Commons.

With Mackenzie beginning his work around Stellaland and Goshen and a Transvaal delegation preparing to visit London to negotiate boundary claims, on August 16, 1883, Rhodes rose in the House of Assembly and gave a speech that was indicative of his smaller and larger motives regarding territorial expansion. He forced his fellow members to grapple with his geographical vision, pronouncing that "the question before us really is this, whether this Colony is to be confined to its present borders, or whether it is to become the dominant state in South Africa—whether, in fact, it is to spread its civilisation over the interior." Rhodes harped on this theme of civilization, building common ground with fellow members by saying, "I am no negrophilist, and I hold to the distinct view that we must extend our civilisation beyond our present borders." This was part of a process, according to Rhodes, in which "the natives are bound gradually to come under the control of the Europeans." Echoing the sentiments and rhetoric of Oxford professor John Ruskin, Rhodes argued "that it is the duty of this colony, when, as it were, her younger and more fiery sons go out and take land, to follow in their steps with their civilised government." In other words, racially justified land theft ought to have government backing. The land appeared to be a desert in the hands of African people, but in the hands of Europeans it was "capable of great development."[8]

It was an age-old practice for European colonists to declare indigenous land to be *terra nullius*—empty land—and to use that as a pretext for taking it. In fact, while the area was semi-arid, Tswana had practiced cattle ranching there for a long time. Rhodes must have known this, at least in part because he knew that Tswana ranchers supplied meat to Kimberley. Meanwhile, Kimberley also depended on the Tswana area for firewood, at least until the railroad could bring coal from Port Elizabeth or Cape Town. "What we now want is to annex land," said Rhodes, "not natives." Passing from racism and greed to guilt, Rhodes clinched his argument by invoking the Cape Colony's railway debt of £14,000,000. If the railway could only go so far as the border of the Transvaal, where tariffs were prohibitive, then the Cape government's investment was not likely to make money.[9]

During this speech, Rhodes did make one significant feint. He opposed imperial intervention because it might result in oversight. He even said, "We want to get rid of the Imperial factor in this question, and to deal with it ourselves, jointly with the Transvaal." In fact, Rhodes was willing to accept any help in protecting the Road to the North. Cape governor Hercules Robinson was persuaded by Rhodes and Scanlen to take up the problem with the home government. Robinson offered to help pay the costs of annexing Stellaland

and Goshen by sharing customs duties. When the Transvaal's president, Paul Kruger, traveled to London to meet with the secretary of state for the colonies, Lord Derby, in February 1884, the two men struck a deal. Derby agreed to drop the British claim of suzerainty over the Transvaal and to reduce the Transvaal's debt and the powers of the British representative in Pretoria, while Kruger agreed to reduce some tariffs and to drop claims to Stellaland and Goshen, leaving the Road to the North open.[10]

The agreement seemed to be a victory for peace and stability in the region. Almost immediately, pro-Boer and pro-Imperial activists overstepped the bounds. Transvaal commandos rode east into Zululand and west into Bechuanaland, the colonial-era name for Botswana, while Mackenzie persuaded two chiefs to agree to a British protectorate in their territories, thus moving beyond a mere proclamation of suzerainty toward a *de facto* protectorate. Mankurwane of the Tlhaping and Montshiwa of the Rolong found it advantageous to have the British guarantee their security. Mackenzie held talks with Gerrit van Niekerk, the leader of Stellaland, making an amicable arrangement for van Niekerk to become a deputy commissioner and for the farmers' properties to be guaranteed by Britain. Mackenzie then raised the British flag over Vryburg. This seemed to be a step toward reconciliation and order, but Rhodes was adamantly opposed to the likes of Mackenzie advocating the landholding rights of Africans and Boers who lay astride the Road to the North. Mackenzie's claim was better than control by the Transvaal, but it was still problematic from Rhodes's perspective.[11]

Under pressure from Rhodes, Robinson sent a letter of reprimand to Mackenzie. The governor and high commissioner wrote, "You are not authorized to hoist the British flag as that implies sovereignty and Bechuanaland is just a protectorate." Robinson suggested that Mackenzie's actions could start more conflicts. "Come down here at once," wrote Robinson. "I have asked Mr. Rhodes to proceed from Kimberley to Vryburg and he is authorized to act as Deputy Commissioner." While Rhodes and his allies were whispering in the ear of Robinson, Rhodes was working to neutralize and remove Mackenzie. He even tried to get him out of the way by buying him ownership of a newspaper in Grahamstown. Rhodes indicated that he wanted to help the unemployed Mackenzie, but the missionary declined to become Rhodes's client and continued to lobby against white settler interests. Rhodes traveled north with Frank "Matabele" Thompson, an acquaintance from the diamond fields who owned a farm in the area and spoke the Tswana language. He became one of Rhodes's key assistants as he developed an interest in expanding settler influence in the north.[12]

Rhodes's efforts to control and occupy the Road to the North were helped by external events. The liberal government of Gladstone and its members, like Derby, preferred colonial trade and mission work over territorial conquest. Even so, the situation in Stellaland and Goshen had them caught in a difficult position.[13] Concerns about the Transvaal and Namibia persuaded the British government to take an uncharacteristic approach to the political instability along the Road to the North. The British government sent the British army at great expense. A force of 4,000 regular soldiers, including a famous regiment of cavalry from Ulster, the Inniskilling Dragoons, and three observation balloons, was sent north under the command of the upright Charles Warren. A prominent Freemason, he had gotten to know Rhodes and other prominent miners and settlers during his earlier assignment, when he surveyed the boundaries of Griqualand West and commanded the Diamond Fields Horse. After a successful posting to Egypt, Warren was promoted to lieutenant-colonel and given the title of special commissioner. At the insistence of Governor Robinson, Rhodes joined Warren. At Warren's insistence, so, too, did his friend and Rhodes's nemesis, John Mackenzie. Warren hoped that the missionary, with whom he shared an interest in moral reform, would use his connections in negotiations with the Tswana. This stirred much resentment in Rhodes, who had made promises to the Boers at Vryburg and had also intrigued to have Mackenzie removed as commissioner to the region. Rhodes and Warren were once friends; now the spit-and-polished Warren distanced himself from Rhodes and his dirty flannels, slouch hat, and casual shoes. It did not help that Rhodes, together with his young aide, Harry Currey, and their two mixed-race servants had arrived in camp with an ample supply of Guinness stout and Scotch whisky, which they shared with Warren's officers. Warren, who was known for sobriety, did not appreciate Rhodes's approach and made it clear to him that in the field he was going to be outranked and taking orders.[14]

In December 1884, Warren's force rode the railroad line that was being built to the north. The line ended near Kimberley, where a bridge still needed to be completed over the Orange River. The troopers crossed the river with the help of friendly Boers, who signed on to assist with further transport needs. As Warren's column approached Vryburg, the rustic village that was the capital of Stellaland, the parties to all the area's conflicts either vanished or agreed to Warren's proclamation of a vast formal British protectorate called British Bechuanaland. Warren learned that Goshen was still reluctant to accept British rule. British troops marched into the capital, Mafeking, to find that Boer fighters had departed. Warren soon learned that not only had they left, but they were the very same Boer farmers he hired to help with his transport problems.[15]

The Warren Expedition appeared to be a success. A few thousand redcoats gained control of a large area without firing a shot. Warren was an engineer by training, with extensive experience in Palestine. In between his assignments in South Africa, he worked in England as the chief surveying instructor of the British Army. Along the Road to the North, he put his training to use in infrastructure development. As Warren's troopers rode north, they installed wooden telegraph poles and strung wires, all the way from Barkly West to Vryburg and north to Mafeking, a total distance of 225 miles. The telegraph followed the line of conquest along the Road to the North. When Warren's soldiers left in August 1885, they took the wires but left the poles. These became the property of the new British crown colony of British Bechuanaland, which replaced the wooden poles with metal ones and realigned the telegraph along the line of the railway that was built several years later.[16] Telegraph construction, like infrastructure development generally, was closely aligned with imperial expansion.

Warren and his troops appeared to achieve security along the Road to the North, but Boer influence remained strong. When Warren received his commission from Robinson, he agreed to honor Rhodes's agreements with the Boer landholders of Stellaland. And then, in January 1885, Warren, Rhodes, and Mackenzie rode to the border of the Transvaal to meet with the president, Paul Kruger, who had been invited to discuss the new British crown colony of Bechuanaland. Against the advice of Rhodes, Warren brought along Mackenzie, who had previously accused Kruger and his Boer colleagues of stealing land from the Tswana. During the meeting, Kruger refused to acknowledge the existence of the British crown colony of Bechuanaland.[17]

After this inauspicious and inconclusive meeting, Rhodes was given the assignment of negotiating with the Stellaland Boers, who were being given title to the land they had taken. Warren criticized Rhodes for making too many concessions. Rhodes resented Warren's insistence on the primacy of imperial interests and African rights over settler land acquisitions. When Warren repudiated the agreement with the Stellaland Boers, Rhodes resigned from his commissioner's position and expressed his discontent with Warren in the Cape Parliament, which was now meeting in the newly opened Houses of Parliament. Rhodes's Dutch supporters became hostile to the long-term goal of incorporating Bechuanaland into the Cape Colony. The dispute between Rhodes and Warren even spilled into the pages of *The Times* in London. Warren, together with Mackenzie, rode to meet the key Tswana chiefs, Khama, Gaseitsiwe, and Sechele. They told Warren and Mackenzie that they were willing to open large portions of Tswana lands for white settlers. The British soon learned that they were offered lands that were disputed by neighboring chiefdoms, a shrewd move on the part of Khama, who offered land on his northeastern border that was also claimed by his rival, Lobengula, king of the Ndebele.[18] Khama saw the new relationship with the British as a way of increasing his own power. Working with the British gave him security against rival Boers and Ndebele, while the acquisition of literacy and new technologies had the potential to strengthen his administration.

Warren and Mackenzie were smitten with Khama, the teetotalling Ngwato chief who was known as *kgosi*, or king. They were less taken with the Kwena and Ngwaketse chiefs, Sechele and Gaseitsiwe, who negotiated for better arrangements. In April 1885, when Warren was enjoying Sechele's hospitality at Molepolole, the chief told the general, "We do not want any protection. We are strong enough to protect ourselves." Sechele wanted Warren to put a better offer on the table than mere protection. Warren also visited Gaseitsiwe, considered to be mild mannered, but even he took a firm line with Warren, saying that he "no longer believe[d] in England's power to protect the black man."[19]

Warren and Mackenzie were still pleased to be able to extend British protection throughout Tswana territory, but Rhodes maneuvered behind the scenes against them. Warren outright accused Rhodes of foul play. In September 1885, under pressure from Rhodes and from the British government, the governor, Robinson, intervened in Rhodes's favor with the Colonial Office in London. Just as Warren was preparing to leave South Africa for his next assignment, he learned that Britain was going to define the territory of the new Crown Colony of British Bechuanaland to include only the area south of the Molopo River; that is, it would be restricted to the area populated by the southern Tswana. The area to the north remained only a British protectorate. Robinson actively discouraged white settlement in Khama's territory by sending the new Bechuanaland Border Police to arrest settlers who trekked into the area.[20]

The new colony of British Bechuanaland protected the southern Tswana chiefdoms from the Boers. This protection came at a price. Inside the territory, British administrators allowed Boer settlers to keep their land. Tswana people were allowed to remain on land near their settlements, but they lost rights to extensive lands used for grazing and timber harvesting. Agriculture became more widespread, bolstered by unusually good rainfall in the initial decade of British rule. Soon it became clear that even under optimal conditions, there was not enough land to support the population. The British

King Khama III. Wikimedia Commons.

authorities required African people to pay a hut tax in cash, pressuring them to earn wages on Boer farms. That approach appears to be straightforward, but farmers often reneged on wages. African men had the option of working in Kimberley, but the mergers of the mining companies had already resulted in fewer jobs for miners. The other options were not good. With every passing year, hunters had to travel farther into the interior. The trade in hides, feathers, and firearms shifted to the Kalahari and even to Angra Pequena, then called Lüderitz, 650 miles away on the coast of Namibia. Taken together,

British colonial policies toward southern Tswana people were reducing them to poverty and dependence.[21]

The Tswana experience of colonialism was not something that concerned Rhodes. He focused on the extension of the Road to the North, relying on his social network for support. He leaned heavily on Sidney Shippard, now serving as the resident commissioner of Bechuanaland. Rhodes also made the acquaintance of Edward Maund and Ralph Williams, young officers who were dispatched to Matabeleland by Warren to share the news of the Bechuanaland Protectorate with Lobengula, the Ndebele ruler. After Maund and his assistant, Ralph Williams, returned, they met Rhodes at a campsite. During the conversation, Williams reported that Rhodes then spoke of securing a much more extensive Road to the North, stretching all the way to Lake Nyasa and Lake Tanganyika. Rhodes's vision of conquest and settlement was taking on a new objective even farther north.[22]

Rhodes's grand visions still had to take into account the realities of human geography. Matabeleland lay to the northeast of Khama's lands in the new Bechuanaland protectorate. Matabeleland was home to the centralized kingdom of the Ndebele or "Matabele" people, with its capital at Bulawayo. With a language and culture akin to that of the Zulu people, the Ndebele people had migrated from Natal to their current location, in Matabeleland, in the southwestern part of modern-day Zimbabwe, in the early nineteenth century, incorporating many different sorts of cultures along the way. Like the Zulu people, they were portrayed by settlers as fierce, at least in part to justify taking sovereignty from them and partly because British authorities in Africa and Asia had a predilection for identifying certain linguistic or cultural groups as "martial races."[23]

Rhodes also heard stories about the land beyond the Ndebele chiefdom, called Mashonaland, after the Shona people who lived there. It was thought that Shona people lived in small chiefdoms that were paying tribute to the Ndebele kingdom. The reality was more complex: there was a wide variety of states, some tiny, some large, some paying tribute, some not. Europeans stereotyped the Shona people as docile, while their region was thought to be suitable for settlement. There was also another type of exaggerated story being spread by European hunters and explorers who passed through Mashonaland—stories that told of the presence of gold jewelry and ancient mines. Centuries earlier, there had, indeed, been extensive gold mining in the area. Samples of Mashonaland gold had been appearing in South Africa. Rhodes was intrigued.[24]

Rhodes may have learned about Mashonaland and Matabeleland from his brother Herbert, but his imagination appears to have been stoked by Williams and Maund. Rhodes established a good rapport with Maund, who was a fellow Freemason, educated at Cambridge, with whom he had lengthy conversations in his corrugated-iron shack in Vryburg. Rhodes got along well with Williams, too, writing to him in July 1885 a long letter in which he complained bitterly about Mackenzie, Warren, Khama, and activists and politicians in London and Cape Town who were concerned about the rights of African people. Rhodes suggested to Williams that the easiest way forward was through the "much despised Cape politicians." Rhodes perceived that he "recognize[d] fully that the best chance of tapping the lake system of central Africa is through the Cape Colony." With the right political support, he imagined a railway being built all the way to the great lakes of central Africa. "I feel assured that with our railway system extended along the healthy ridge of the centre of Africa we can beat any attempted colonization by Germany, from either East or West coast, & seize the Lake system of Central Africa, & as you are aware this is the object of all my endeavours."[25]

It is important to note that in 1885, Rhodes was not yet considering a colony of white settlement north of the Limpopo. In his letter to Williams, Rhodes reviewed the proposed idea of white settlement in Tswana territory stretching from Vryburg all the way north to Tati, bordering Matabeleland, and derided it as "ridiculous," seeing as the area consisted mainly of "waterless flats." Proposals to settle farther north were ridiculed, too. "Fancy putting down English settlers in that fever-stricken country between Khama & the Zambezi or even Khama & Sechele. Amongst those who are acquainted with the country, the thing is so absurd that it would not be discussed."[26] Rhodes may have been doubtful about prospects for settlement in Bechuanaland and Matabeleland, but he was determined to persist in his plans for imposing colonial rule and building railways through those territories and then north to the Great Lakes. In the letter to Ralph Williams, Rhodes complained about those who stood up to him: "Up to the present I have only reaped abuse, & had to suffer the lowest insinuations from my fellow countrymen."[27]

The debate over the Road to the North indicated that mobility was a point of contention between powerful Europeans and Africans. Rhodes and other promoters of expanded white settlement hoped for an extended swathe of territory linked up by railroads and telegraphs. In November 1885, the railroad finally reached Kimberley. It would be very expensive and take a very long time to construct a railway from there to Vryburg, let alone all the way to Cairo. Territorial visions of national domination were not the only motives for developing railways. White farmers in the Eastern Cape and the Western Cape preferred the creation of a more extensive national market.

And finally, the mineral disassembly lines of the diamond and gold mines were drawing labor from rural areas increasingly linked by railways to Kimberley and Johannesburg. Black workers were conveyed by rail to the mines while white politicians who could deliver a railway to a community would be favored with white money and white votes. The construction of the infrastructure was opposed by the owners of the wagon companies, who stood to be put out of business, but Rhodes was more troubled by challenges posed by Boer nationalists in the Orange Free State, the Transvaal, and the Afrikaner Bond. These Afrikaners feared that national unification would bring domination by English-speakers, whose laws at the Cape were more favorable toward African people than the laws of the Boer republics. Boer ambitions to remain independent were fueled by surging pride in Afrikaner culture and language.

In the 1880s, rivalries among the four different colonial states thwarted the efforts of Rhodes and his allies in the Cape Colony to build a common market in South Africa. The next-best thing was to be involved in separate railway-building initiatives. In 1883, in the Transvaal, there was an early effort to construct a railway connection to the Portuguese port city of Lourenço Marques, on Delagoa Bay. The American entrepreneur in charge of the railway, Edward McMurdo, raised money by creating a company and floating it on the London Stock Exchange, but these funds were not sufficient to contend with the engineering challenges that emerged during construction. Negotiations over connecting Kimberley to the Transvaal failed. The 1886 discovery of gold at the Witwatersrand provided the president of the Transvaal, Paul Kruger, with enough revenue to continue the work of building a railway line to Delagoa Bay. A survey was completed at the end of 1887. Kruger was confident enough of constructing an independent railway to Delagoa Bay that he declined to join the customs union of the Cape Colony and the Orange Free State. In any event, the Cape's main ports, Port Elizabeth and Cape Town, were much farther away than Lourenço Marques. The Colony of Natal's main port, Durban, was only twenty miles farther from Johannesburg than Lourenço Marques. Natal had lower tariffs than the Cape, but at the time, it still seemed wise from Kruger's perspective to pursue the Transvaal's interests separately through negotiations with the Portuguese. Lourenço Marques, on Delagoa Bay, was supporting the building of a stronger state in the Transvaal, a challenge to the plans for colonial confederation that had been the dream of British settlers at the Cape.[28]

Rhodes's plans for a settler state, united by railroads and telegraphs, resembled developments in Europe and North America during the nineteenth century. The spread of railways and telegraphs—with the administrative and financial support of governments—united people within national territories and gave them a sense of belonging. When railroads brought rapid communication and movement, they diminished the usefulness of local dialects and regional loyalties; they strengthened a sense of national space. Railways and telegraphs also increased international connectedness. The same technologies that brought national cohesion also enhanced the operation of global economic and political networks. Ideological and material ties linked together geographic spaces into a sense of territoriality.[29] In settler colonies, indigenous people did not form part of this cohesive vision. Their voices were given little consideration.

7

Controlling De Beers

RHODES'S PLAN FOR settler expansion along the Road to the North was closely related to his ability to make money in mining. The broader idea of filling in vast territories with white settlers connected by railroads and telegraphs was linked to another idea about geographical space—that riches lay under the ground for those who could imagine and carry out the organization of a subterranean world of tunnels, equipment, and miners and then connect that artificial world to the resources above. As the miners dug deeper, daily decisions were shaped by the promise of finance and technology and by the limits of geography and geology. The diamond fields and hopefully, soon, the gold fields, had the potential to pay for settlement up north. This is the vision that began to animate Rhodes even as its breathtaking scope gave pause to some of his partners and rivals. To most miners, the business decisions at De Beers seemed contingent. To Rhodes, the business decisions at De Beers opened new horizons up north for white settlers. The essence of Rhodes's idea was to turn the noisy, dusty town of Kimberley into the engine that powered the expansion of settler colonialism in South Africa.

At the start of the 1880s, the De Beers Mine was an awesome sight. Like the nearby Kimberley Mine, it had become a large open pit, 29 acres in area and 180 feet deep. On any given day in 1881, Cecil Rhodes, his partners, or any visitor could walk to the edge of the mine and catch a glimpse of an impressive industrial spectacle.[1] The edge of the open pit was lined with wooden derricks, which raised up the aerial tramways so their trucks could travel back and forth from the top to the bottom. Introduced one by one in the 1870s, the tramways now covered the open pit. If the tramway wires were stretched from end to end, they would run for six and a half miles. Down in the pit, there was only one shaft, dug by the Victoria Company. The rest of the activity involved excavating the blue ground and the reef from the open pit. The pit swarmed with as many as 260 white "overseers" and 1,800 African migrant workers, while around the edge there were also 230 horses and 35 mules. Three pump engines ran constantly, removing more than 17,000 gallons of water every hour. The tramways and the shaft were powered by a thundering chorus of forty-six steam engines that consumed £57,000 worth of firewood in that year. After hours, most of the engines shut down. Then it was time for blasting the open pit with dynamite.

The open pits were dynamic craters that presented significant dangers to the workers. The mines were ever-shifting spaces that held rocks, water, miners, and all their equipment.[2] Miners in Kimberley's open pits were especially vulnerable to slides of blue ground and reef. In 1881 alone, eleven accidents took place in Kimberley. Five African workers were killed and twelve were injured. The mine inspector, William Erskine, tended to blame the victims, not the engineers, for the toll of deaths and injuries. In Erskine's 1881 report, he wrote:

> In low workings, labourers are endangered by careless working of higher ground; and the stolid stupidity shown in handling the simple appliances at tip-stages and platforms has resulted more than once in fatal accident.
>
> When warned of coming danger, many natives appear to lack brain action. They pay the most idiotic inattention to repeated shouts from the overseers to clear out of danger. The majority of accidents to K----rs are owing to this strange absence of intelligence.[3]

Perhaps the African miners were not able to understand English. Perhaps the background noise made it difficult to understand instructions. It is easy to condemn the racism of Erskine's statement. It is also worth thinking about the ways in which prominent members of the white community were so blinded by ideology that they did not recognize the dangers of the mine to miners who could not understand English.

The open pits became even more dangerous as they went deeper. Rockslides killed people, but they also slowed production by necessitating the clearing of reef. The key to preventing rockslides was to dig shafts and tunnels under the ground. In 1881, that expensive process had already started in both the De Beers Mine, where the Victoria Company had one shaft and a tunnel, and at the Kimberley Mine, where the reef and blue ground were even more crumbly and underground mining was even more desirable. The Kimberley Mine already had three shafts that were operated by the Central Company, the French Company, and the Mining Board. It was plain to see that underground mining, also called deep-level mining, would work most efficiently if one company controlled each mine. Even greater efficiencies were likely if only one company controlled all the mines.

In the 1880s, Rhodes and his associates made sure that De Beers invested steadily in better equipment. As early as 1882, the company was benefiting from upgrades. A new hauling engine increased the number of loads of blue ground and worthless shale by 50 percent. In 1885–1886, a new set of hauling engines was installed. Skips were now pulled up to a tipping device that was invented by a De Beers engineer. As De Beers bought out neighboring companies, the older machines of those companies were taken offline. The overall number of machines declined with amalgamation, as did the total amount of horsepower employed. In some years mechanization appears to have lost ground, with hand labor increasing. Horses, mules, and oxen were still important, but the days of older modes of transportation were numbered. A new tramway, complete with an embankment, connected the mine to expanded "floors," the fields near the mine where the blue ground was spread out and weathered.

The floors were curious places, fields strewn with rock being crumbled by the sun and rain. So many loads of blue ground had been put down that in 1887 the company bought a nearby estate, Kenilworth, so that blue ground could be sent there, too. There was more to the floors than met the eye. All that unprocessed blue ground—100,000 loads of it by 1885—could be thought of as a cash reserve. In 1885, Rudd shared these thoughts about a reserve of rocks with the annual meeting: "We have no actual cash reserve fund, but we have always treated it as invested in ground on the floors.... [Blue ground] is always going through the process of weathering and really develops the resources of the Company; and as long as we can keep anything like 100,000 loads on the floors I think we are fairly safe without a large reserve. That may be a subject afterward for discussion."[4] When Rudd said "safe," he meant safe from floods and other disasters, as well as labor unrest. If the mine had to shut down, at least the blue ground on the floors could be processed.

There were clear benefits to making the transition from open-pit mining to underground mining. Excavating the large open pit required the expansion of the circumference of the mine and hauling off the worthless shale reef. As the pit went wider and deeper, the costs of removing reef went higher. It was a frustrating dynamic. Then, in November 1883, a rockslide from the mine's edge dumped 250,000 cubic yards of reef across the bottom of the pit. It all had to be removed—a great waste of time and money. By 1884, it was clear to Rhodes, Rudd, and their partners that as the pit went deeper, more worthless shale would have to be removed. At the annual meeting of 1885, Rudd indicated to the audience that for every load of blue, De Beers was removing a load of worthless shale. If open-pit mining were to continue deeper, it would soon require one-and-a-half loads of worthless rocks to be hauled for every load of blue. Around the edges of the blue ground, there were many marginal loads of "inferior blue" being hauled out, too, which would not be needed to be removed and processed if companies shifted to underground mining. In his report, Rudd articulated what every miner must have known: that underground mining reduced "deadwork," the effort and expense that is not directly related to removing valuable minerals.

> In open working we do more than a load of dead work for every load of blue hauled, and in the future it would be 1½ of dead work to every load of blue.... And in favour of underground working, I may add that we will do away with that tremendous quantity of inferior blue which we have been forced to put over our floors, because it was too good to throw away, and which has always reduced the average yield of the really good blue.... All the stuff coming from underground will be really good ground.[5]

Rudd reported that "your Directors, having this in view, are making speedy preparations for underground working." Nearby, at the Kimberley Mine, two other companies were willing to take greater risks in order to address that mine's peculiar geological challenges. When compared to the De Beers Mine, the Kimberley Mine yielded more diamonds but also required more ground to be removed. In 1883, the Central and the French companies began to dig vertical shafts down from the area outside the rim of the pit. The shafts went straight down until they reached a depth lower than the pit. At that point, several hundred feet under the ground, horizontal tunnels were dug under the pit.

A rockslide at the Dutoitspan Mine, just outside of Kimberley, showed just how dangerous an open-pit mine could be. Dutoitspan had a complex pattern of ownership and never produced the quality or quantity of diamonds as the De Beers and Kimberley mines. When the pit reached a depth of more than two hundred feet, the northern edge showed signs of impending collapse. One day, in March 1886, an enormous avalanche of reef fell into the pit, killing eighteen miners. The rockslide occurred during the lunch hour, when most miners were outside of the pit, or the death toll would have been higher.[6]

Rockslides and all the other challenges of open-pit mining were less of a problem in underground mines, but there was a steep learning curve when it came to digging shafts and tunnels through the crumbly blue ground. Rudd reported that in November 1884, on the north side of the De Beers Mine, the company began work on sinking a thousand-foot shaft. Lesser shafts were begun on the West End. Rhodes, Rudd, and their fellow directors still had to convince shareholders of the value of underground mining. In 1885, they dug a test hole to 380 feet, being careful to keep that blue ground separate from the open-pit blue ground spread on the floors. The blue ground from the shaft contained greater numbers of carats than the blue ground from the open pit. Soon after, another level was opened at 500 feet, producing good-quality blue ground.[7]

De Beers's entry into underground mining was supposed to be "speedy." Speed could be costly as well as dangerous. For these reasons, Rhodes and De Beers approached the engineering challenge conservatively by making "an expert makeshift." During the early 1880s, Rhodes and his partners hired Edward Jones, a professional engineer with experience in Cornwall and Wales, who was working in the Kimberley Mine. De Beers had never employed professional engineers, and it took some getting used to Jones and his team. In 1881, when the Jones team was first hired, Rhodes wrote to Rudd that "Jones good man that he is makes the money fly. He spends about £6,000 per month. I'd not complain of him but still it is the old story these swell men will not work cheaply and you cannot make them. Jones personally I am extremely fond of but he piles up the white men and expenses frightful." Rhodes paid him personally by selling £3,000 of his own shares "for this reason that expenses were awful and my power with him for checking was nil." Rhodes groused to Rudd that "there is an explanation for everything but the broad fact remains that he works at double the cost we used to. Defend me from swell engineers." In spite of Rhodes's frustration with costs, Jones's shaft was a success, as were several more that followed. Jones dug a shaft inside the pit, in its deepest part, by using a traditional technique that he had employed at the Kimberley Mine. He had workers build a square timber frame that resembled a coffer dam. Workers stood in the center of the frame and dug out the hole. As the vertical shaft went deeper, permanent timbers were added to the exposed walls. Such a shaft had some advantages. The excavated earth was all blue ground that could be processed. Still, there were problems. The shaft began in a deep area where it was exposed to the possibility of rockslides from the edge of the pit. Even so, Jones's coffer-dam vertical shaft seemed to be a good solution.[8]

The De Beers partners spent the next few years debating how best to go about underground mining. As late as 1886, with work started on shafts and tunnels, Rudd represented the view of the De Beers directors when he said to the annual meeting that "it was at one time thought that underground workings were a necessity." He continued: "Difficulties so great have been encountered in the underground workings, especially in separate holdings, that we are determined to devote a certain proportion of our profits every year to making the reef safe and trying as long as we can to continue the output from the open." This statement was greeted with shouts of "hear, hear." Amalgamation was still not complete, which made determining the placement of shafts and tunnels quite challenging. Meanwhile, the open pit continued to pose problems. On December 30, 1885, an enormous rockslide in the West End required four months of work and £35,000 worth of expenses, eating up that quarter's dividends. In that fiscal year, the company removed more worthless rock than ever before. In 1886, Rudd once again looked forward to better underground workings. He reported to that year's annual meeting that it would "require an organized, systematic plan of underground working, one that will be successful and safe.... The underground workings at the present time, with separate holdings, are especially objectionable from the fact that so many men must, as time goes on, incur the risk of losing their lives in these works."[9]

Rudd was promoting a safer and more systematic approach to underground mining. It was one thing for entrepreneurs with a basic understanding of engineering to supervise the excavation of an open pit; it was altogether a different matter to design and dig a system of mine shafts that were safe. Discussions about risk easily become discussions about organization. It was apparent to Rhodes, Rudd, and their associates that underground mining required an upgrade in management. The manager himself knew this. Robert English had been serving as company manager ever since De Beers merged with Compton, Stow, and English in 1881. In 1884 he asked to be replaced, thinking that it was "impossible for one man" to manage the mine. The annual report indicated that De Beers hoped to find outside experience. "Your directors," stated Rudd, "desire to profit by the experience of other companies." Rudd and Rhodes discussed finding a replacement but dragged their feet for three years. They appointed De Beers director John Morrogh as a stopgap measure. Morrogh arrived on the diamond fields in the late 1860s and had risen to be a member of the De Beers Mining Board. In the early 1880s, he managed Barnato's De Beers Central Diamond Mining Company, which was another company working the open pit. Morrogh joined forces with Rhodes and Rudd but lacked the technical knowledge to develop deep-level mining. He did not last long as their manager and returned home to Ireland in 1887.

The De Beers partners supervised their managers carefully and met with them often. Rhodes kept up with the details, often doing so from a distance by using the telegraph service. During the mid-1880s, as he traveled back and forth between Kimberley, Cape Town, and England, he left much of the everyday decision-making to his fellow directors, especially to Stow and Rudd, even though Rudd was also busy as the owner of several small businesses in Kimberley and was a fellow member of the Cape Parliament's House of Assembly. In turn, Stow and Rudd relied on the managing engineers, like Thomas Andrews, to run the operations of the De Beers Mine. Rhodes had such charisma that even when he was not chairing, his partners still gave him full credit for leadership. In 1884, Fred Stow was chairing the company and gave the annual address to the shareholders' meeting. He thanked Rhodes profusely, saying that his "services have been invaluable to the Company." According to Stow, "He has devoted the whole of his time to the interests of the company. He was here constantly day and night. Whilst he was in Kimberley one felt a sort of security in remaining away from the works, because of the knowledge that the directorship could not be in better hands than his."[10] The next year, when the company was chaired by Rudd, the same, exact paragraph was inserted into the report. It is not clear whether this plagiarism was a backhanded slap at Rhodes or simply a rubber-stamp of grateful recognition. Or maybe Rudd was too busy to care.

Entrepreneurs, engineers, and bankers who were involved in De Beers Mining Company were trying to manage a seemingly unruly natural and social environment by communicating between the rockface, company headquarters nearby, and faraway investors. Rhodes and his partners, managers, and contractors had to keep production going in the midst of cave-ins, floods, fires, and coordinating a large workforce. When seen from this complex, networked viewpoint, the vision of Cecil Rhodes, as enacted at the diamond fields in the 1880s, may seem more defensive than forward-thinking. Yet Rhodes remained mindful of larger objectives.

In 1886, he defended De Beers from a buyout orchestrated by his old friend, John X. Merriman, who was aiming to amalgamate the mining companies. Merriman and Rhodes were both still members of the House of Assembly, had many mutual acquaintances, and still went riding together, but in Kimberley, they found each other on opposite sides of amalgamation. The drive to purchase shares was started by two diamond merchants who held significant positions in Dutoitspan and Bultfontein: Charles Roulina and Charles Posno. They began to work on a plan of amalgamation of all the diamond mines, employing Merriman as the front man. Merriman gained the support of Joseph B. Robinson, archrival of Rhodes, who owned many shares in the Kimberley Mine. Posno was backed by two bankers from Paris, who provided access to £600,000, enough to make strong bids for shares in the Kimberley and De Beers Mines.[11]

When Merriman and Robinson began to work together on building the Unified Company, Kimberley mine owners began to worry. They tended to support strict controls over labor, and Merriman's liberal leanings gave them pause. Many of them also found Joseph B. Robinson obnoxious and undependable. When Merriman began approaching shareholders and prices began to rise, Merriman learned that Robinson was already overextended and could not support further purchases. Having a reserve of funds or shares was especially important, because one of the key owners at the Kimberley Mine, Francis Baring-Gould of the Central Company, was holding out for a higher price. Robinson's shortcomings hurt the deal but did not scuttle it. Instead, owners of small claims in the mines—and owners of small businesses more generally—began to speak out against the merger, fearing the inevitable layoffs and the decline of local merchants. Try as they might, they, too, could not stop the merger. It was torpedoed by Rhodes.

Rhodes was not one to let his friendship with Merriman stand in the way of making money. At first, Rhodes hesitated about Merriman's proposed buyout of De Beers. Merriman indicated in a letter to his wife, Agnes, that he had persuaded Rhodes to sell and even talked him into returning to England, where they could both live as wealthy gentlemen and serve together in the British Parliament. Rhodes brought along his De Beers partner, Fred Stow, and seemed poised to allow De Beers to be bought out. At that moment, Rhodes reversed course and began to approach fellow mine owners about a scheme of his own. The plan involved swapping shares to create a jointly controlled amalgamated company. Rhodes knew that his own company's directors opposed this idea, on the grounds that it undervalued their shares. Rhodes confessed to a mutual friend, Harry Currey, that his scheme was merely put together to block Merriman's Unified. As predicted, the De Beers shareholders resisted both schemes, and both failed. Merriman wrote to his wife that "Rhodes is the same in business and politics, tricky, unstable, and headstrong." Rhodes calculated that he would make more money by first strengthening the position of his company by finishing the job of amalgamation at the De Beers Mine. Rhodes's friend Dr. Hans Sauer recollected in his memoirs that around this time, he often saw Rhodes "seated on the edge of the De Beers' mine, gazing intently down into its depths, absorbed in his reflections." When Sauer asked Rhodes what he was thinking, he replied, "I was calculating the amount of blue ground in sight and the power that this blue ground would confer on the man who obtained control of it all."[12]

In describing Rhodes's drive to buy up the mines himself, one of the earliest biographers, Michell, paused his narrative to describe his friend's personality. Michell knew Rhodes well, having served as his longtime personal banker. Beyond an inner circle of close friends, Rhodes, in Michell's words, "possessed few intimate friends," and, in a reference to Merriman, "not even to all of them did he disclose his hand." Michell continued: "Mere acquaintances disliked his moody silences, varied with fits of rather boisterous fun. They considered him exclusive, morose, rough, and overbearing. And it must be admitted that he was a good hater, violent when thwarted, and at times blunt to the point of rudeness. It is difficult to be sufficiently unconventional to shock a mining camp, but he shocked it." Michell explained that Rhodes's "mask of indifference" was explained by his striving "strenuously for wealth." For Rhodes, "wealth was power" and helped him to achieve his "ripening policy of Northern expansion."[13]

Having thwarted Merriman's attempt at consolidation, Rhodes persuaded his partners at De Beers to buy up the remaining claims in the De Beers Mine, backed by Alfred Beit and members of his network. In 1885, De Beers Mining Company bought the claims of the Eagle Company and the Australian Gully Block Company. In 1886, Rhodes and his partners bought the Elma Company and the United Company, leaving the Victoria Company, managed by Francis Oats, to be the remaining large company standing in the way of complete control of the mine. In 1886, De Beers Mining Company started to buy shares of Victoria. Rhodes appears to have wanted to pressure Victoria but to remain on good terms with Oats, a longtime acquaintance. Rhodes put pressure on Victoria by working with Beit to take control of two smaller companies nearby, the Gem Company and the Oriental Company.[14]

Rhodes's dealmaking skills are usually emphasized over his knowledge of finance and engineering, but his correspondence during the final stages of amalgamation shows that he had a strong grasp of financial and technical matters. Technical awareness enabled him to guide his colleagues in small-scale tactics as well as overall strategy. The valuation of each holding was calculated based on estimates of carats per load of blue ground and its varying shades of color, which mostly look bluish gray to the untrained eye. With the claim purchases putting pressure on Oats's Victoria Company, Rhodes and Stow, who were both in Kimberley in June and July of 1886, wrote letters back and forth detailing their tactics. One letter gives the flavor of the correspondence. It involved the purchase of the Oriental and Gem companies. "We are inclined to take this Co. on a basis of £6000 a claim for whatever they have @ 500' level so as to confine the Victoria on that side." Rhodes then advised about the opposition's tactics. "Oats however is disposed to obstruct our policy, & is I fear making mischief for us, back with them & with Schwab's Co. We cannot however afford to quarrel with him yet, as we are driving through the Victoria claims to prove those of the Gem Co. & until that work is completed we must maintain friendly relations with him."[15]

The amalgamation of De Beers involved tricky spatial and social dynamics. Rhodes and his partners strove to buy up rivals who then became their shareholders. Then those shareholders were courted in such a way that they supported the next round of purchases, sometimes in a matter of weeks or months. With partners and investors located in Kimberley and Cape Town, as well as Johannesburg, London, and Paris, the diplomacy with shareholders could get complicated, especially as the mines themselves could change value suddenly, with floods, rockslides, and discoveries affecting the market in company shares. Rhodes's correspondence with Stow indicates the complexities:

> When the first cable was sent you stating that they were in bad flight, a heavy fall of NE reef was expected, which would have stopped them entirely besides which the extent of the floating reef was believed to be much greater than it had been proved to be when that [telegram] of the 31st was sent. Feltham [H. J., Cape of Good Hope Bank] says he explained to you on the 14th ulto. [June] why it was considered desirable to send the explanatory cable stating who "we" were who promised support. We thought that without explanation you might suppose both Rudd & I were in Cape Town, whereas if you knew I was here & was a party to the promise, with those who were known to be @ Kimberley, you would see your way to act, acting sure of a majority; - it was not thought desirable to speak with Rudd & Mosenthal, seeing that they had been consulted, thought there was no reason to fear opposition from either of them. If Feltham is such an impracticable fellow it might be desirable to buy him out. I offer you the suggestion for what it may be worth if we should again re-open negotiations.[16]

The final purchases were supported by Stow as well as by Beit, Porgès, and members of their diamond-buying networks in Britain and continental Europe. To facilitate the deal-making, the share purchasers based themselves in London. Network members were able to disguise their purchases so that Oats did not learn that they were associated with De Beers until it was too late. In April 1887, Rhodes informed Victoria that a majority of shares were owned by allies of De Beers. This forced Oats and the other leaders of Victoria to yield. The amalgamation of the De Beers Mine was complete. Oats remained on good terms with Rhodes, and at the end of the amalgamation of all the mines, he joined the board of Rhodes's new company, De Beers Consolidated Mining.[17]

To enhance the value of the mining companies, Rhodes and the other diamond barons had to continually maintain and improve operations. The rocks had to be removed from the ground and processed as efficiently as possible. The laborers had to be recruited and sent to the mines as cheaply as possible. The transportation of labor, timber, coal, and food to the mines was central to mining operations. There was constant pressure to make mobilization more efficient. Timber, coal, and food could obviously be shipped and stored, but labor needed to be kept alive and it could always walk off. For those reasons, labor was mobilized and then it was immobilized. In the 1870s and 1880s, the diamond barons discussed and then created the closed compounds, where workers were put under surveillance and had their mobility restricted.

Restrictions on African migrant workers had much to do with whites' racial fears of Black workers. Historians of the diamond industry have argued that the imposition of different restrictions on white and Black workers reflected the mine owners' desire to divide racial groups against each other and thereby have greater power over a potentially multiracial working class. But Rhodes's efforts in farming, railways, and the Road to the North reveal that imperialists and industrialists took steps to increase their own mobility, traveling and transporting cargo on the railroads and steamships while at the same time restricting the mobility of African people. This aligned with trends globally, just as it was a sign of things to come in South Africa under apartheid.[18]

Kimberley's Black workers experienced threats to their freedom. White claimholders and the local government developed informal and formal rules for punishing African workers who refused to obey orders and stole diamonds, at the same time as African claimholders were being intimidated by violence. In 1872, African workers were required to register and receive a pass from a magistrate. "Wanderers" and "loiterers" could be punished by being whipped, imprisoned, or by being made to work. Employers were permitted to conduct body searches of workers to control IDB. Leaving work before the end of a contract was punishable by flogging, as were other offenses. In the late 1870s, efforts to codify these rules by Major Lanyon were struck down when they came to the attention of the Colonial Office. Even so, the restrictions continued to be practiced, and infractions by African workers piled up in magistrate's courts.[19]

Surveillance and restricted mobility were achieved by designing closed compounds, structures that eventually became widespread in the South African mining industry. The idea of enclosing African migrant workers in compounds appears to have been circulating in Kimberley, since they were recommended by Francis Oats in Colonel Crossman's report. Oats's fellow Cornish engineer, Thomas C. Kitto, had mined for diamonds in Brazil and had seen compounds there, at a time when slavery was still legal.[20] His own four-part report in the 1879 *Government Gazette* explained how compounds worked. The idea of compounds continued to appeal to influential people in Kimberley. Government mine inspector William Erskine promoted compounds for African workers as a way to achieve an honest and healthy workforce:

> It is now generally accepted that the best safeguard against illicit traffic will be obtained in housing mining employés in compounds, so as not only to bring them under better control, but also to separate them from the bad influences incidental to frequenting any questionable canteens or stores. The effect upon K----rs of providing regular barrack accommodation on their employers' floors, where they would be well housed, regularly looked after and attended to in sickness by a medical officer, where they could provide themselves with food and clothes worth the money paid for them, and where in moderation and under restraint from excess they could procure wholesome liquors; would be undeniably beneficial.[21]

At that time some of the larger mining companies started to develop rudimentary compounds. By 1884, as the drive for amalgamation entered its final years, De Beers owned several African migrant workers' barracks listed in the annual reports as "4 K----r Houses" on Warren Street and "1 K----r Compound" at De Beers Terrace. These had been acquired from mining companies that merged with De Beers. At the time, the structures were thought to be uncontrolled and unhealthy, while also being demoralized by alcohol, disease, and smuggling.

From the company's perspective, it was a good idea to search miners. The first official report by Erskine estimated that in 1881, IDB claimed 25 percent of all mined diamonds. The De Beers Mining Company reported that it was making progress against IDB. Its 1883 annual report boasted that the introduction of a new searching system had resulted in greater yields. In February 1883, the company found 658.25 carats in the mine and 1,108.25 on the floors.

In March, when a new searching system was introduced, the mine yielded 1,123.5 carats and the floors 1,530.75. The total increase of 998.25 carats was attributed to better searching—workers who had stolen diamonds may have put them back before being searched.[22]

Miners of all races resented the searching. In April 1884, white miners went on strike at all four mines. They singled out Cecil Rhodes as one of the capitalists who was causing their ill treatment. Hundreds of miners demonstrated against the big companies. Most of the demonstrations were peaceful, but in one incident, guards at the Kimberley Central Company shot and killed six white miners. The city government deputized company guards who patrolled the streets, and while the Cape government mobilized troops, over the course of ten days the strikers' ranks thinned and the strike fizzled out. Leaders of the large companies took matters a step further, announcing blacklisting and banning unions.[23]

The De Beers Mining Company was unapologetic about searching white miners. The annual report for 1884, likely prepared by the chairman, Rudd, and the manager, Robert English, stated that while their actions "have been characterized by some as coercive," they planned to persist with searching and continue the amalgamation. As they moved forward, better management of labor and mining was needed. The report claimed that "the diamond mining industry can only be carried out successfully under proper and effective searching rules and regulations," which at the time meant stricter criminal laws and putting laborers in closed compounds. They also announced that soon they would have "an organized plan for underground working."[24]

The company used the 1884 strike as an excuse to reform its approach to labor and thereby strengthen the company's business. The company's claims in the De Beers Mine were worked by approximately two hundred white contractors and overseers, who hired African migrant workers and were paid by the piece, usually amounting to two shillings per load of blue ground. It was expected that a contractor could deliver at least 1,000 loads in a day. In the mid-1880s, production costs declined as digging became more efficient. De Beers reduced the number of contractors from 200 to 40 and insisted that they use only laborers who were supplied by the company. Eliminating outsiders from the workforce guaranteed a higher level of skill and reduced the amount of IDB.[25]

The next step in securing the mines was to close the compounds. African migrant workers had to agree to have their mobility completely restricted. The miners began to sign six-month contracts that required them to always remain in a closed compound, even when they were not working down in the mine. The mines were connected directly to the compounds, where migrant workers would have access to food and basic services and consumer items. The miners spent six months underground or in the compound, although some chose to extend contracts. At the end of their contract, they were searched before they left. In 1885, the French Company and the Central Company constructed closed compounds for laborers at the Kimberley Mine. In 1886, Rhodes and his partners at De Beers made a commitment to building a large, five-acre compound of their own at the west end of the mine. It had a large yard, with high walls all around. Barracks were put in place along the wall and constructed in such a way that the windows and doors faced into the yard. No windows faced out. The doors to the outside were locked. The yard was open to the air but completely covered with fine wire mesh, so that hidden diamonds could not be tossed over the wall to smugglers.

The closed compounds bore a resemblance to slave lodges or prisons. De Beers did, in fact, supplement their free laborers with 300 convicts obtained from the Cape Colony with the help of the local magistrate, Edward Judge, and John Merriman, who was then the commissioner of public works. De Beers built a special compound for the prisoners and paid for the guards. The convicts were not employed in the mine, only on the floors. Rudd explained the company's motive in employing prisoners: "convict labour is not very

De Beers Mine Compound. Courtesy of the McGregor Museum, Kimberley, MMKP 829.

much cheaper than free labour but we certainly have the advantage of a guaranteed supply, and also we think we have a little more check over the stealing of diamonds."[26] Prison laborers were prized for their low wages and easy coercion. In addition, they could usually serve for longer than the ordinary migrant worker's six-month contract. If prisoners learned a skill, the company might profit from it longer. Erskine applauded De Beers for employing convict laborers and compounding them, saying that "not only will this be a means of utilizing the labour of the large number of convicts lately employed in unremunerative brickmaking, but housing so large a number in the Mining Area will prove a relief to the strained capacity of the Gaol."[27] Two years later, with the amalgamation nearly complete, the company reported that it was content with convict labor and hoped to add more prisoners to the workforce. A new contract for more convicts was signed with the government.[28]

There was some opposition to the closed compounds. In the mid-1880s, humanitarians began to observe that the compound system tended to work to the benefit of the company and to the detriment of workers. In 1885, the House of Assembly debated a bill to limit the amount of time that migrant workers could be compounded. Rhodes spoke vehemently against such regulations, restating the importance of stopping IDB. Merriman, who usually defended humanitarian measures, stated that the compounds benefited African mineworkers. Dr. Matthews still represented Kimberley in the Cape Parliament's House of Assembly, and he, too, spoke in their favor, calling them "magnificent." The bill to regulate the compounds failed.[29] The merchants of Kimberley also complained about compounds, saying they caused shopkeepers to lose business. In 1886, Rudd announced that De Beers was replacing its scattered barracks with the single large compound at the mine's west end, disregarding the concerns of merchants and humanitarians.

The compounds required professional management. Rhodes's companion from the days of the Warren Expedition, Francis "Matabele" Thompson, was hired to manage them. Rhodes frequently visited Thompson's ranch on the outskirts of Kimberley, but there was more to the hire than friendship. Thompson's fluency in the Afrikaans and Tswana languages gave him an advantage as a labor recruiter and compound manager. He contacted Tswana, Sotho, and Pedi chiefs and arranged for them to send laborers. The chiefs typically took a cut from the earnings of the young men. Thompson housed the young men in the compound while it was being built, before the gates were closed. He predicted that when the gates closed, the miners would object to the restrictions, so he made sure to order extra laborers from the chiefs. On the day when he closed the compound, the men were outraged. Thompson announced that liquor would no longer be allowed, further aggravating the workers. When a strike broke out, some of the De Beers partners were worried enough to send the workers rations of brandy. Rhodes remained Thompson's key supporter. With more workers on the way from the chiefs, Thompson did not feel pressured enough to capitulate. A few days later, the miners returned to work, resigned to the imposition of the closed compound.[30]

Liquor and traditional African beer were prohibited inside the compound. Rhodes and De Beers's other owners were not teetotalers, but it was a common belief among the Victorians that non-Europeans were not sufficiently evolved to be served alcohol safely. By contrast, it was thought that alcohol helped Europeans to adjust to warm climates.[31] De Beers did make a small concession to the compounded miners: on special occasions they were served a ration of mildly alcoholic ginger beer. And the miners were permitted to indulge in dagga, the South African word for cannabis.[32]

The miners took their work assignments from the white mining contractors. De Beers expected the contractors and miners to work in twelve-hour shifts, a day shift and a night shift. The workers went from the compound directly to the rock face yet were not paid for the time it took to travel back and forth, so most had a thirteenth, unpaid hour at work. (In 1892, De Beers agreed to the workers' suggestion to change the mines to three eight-hour shifts.) When the shift concluded, workers could eat, or relax in the yard, or sleep in the barracks. An infirmary provided health care. A company store sold food and supplies to the men in what was called the "truck system."

The searching of miners was carried out systematically, a sign of the increasing professionalization of mining and the closing of the compound. During the mid-1880s the method of searching was documented by photographer Robert Harris, whose images may have been used for training purposes. They give us a good idea of standard procedures for searching. When the miner was at the end of his contract, he was brought to an open area just outside of a shed. He stripped naked in front of a white manager and several African assistants, held up his hands, and opened his mouth for the assistant to see. His body was checked to see if he had sewn any diamonds in his muscle tissue, even the bottoms of his feet. He extended his penis and pulled back the foreskin, to show that he was not hiding diamonds under there. Then he squatted down, leaned forward, touched his head to the ground, and reached around with his hands to spread the cheeks of his buttocks. The miner held this pose, balancing on his head and grimacing, for the purpose of displaying his anus. A Black assistant approached and held a candle to the miner's anus

De Beers Workers Being Searched. Courtesy of the McGregor Museum, Kimberley, MMKP 10,700.

to have a good look, then the white inspector inserted an enema into the miner's rectum and squeezed the bulb. The miner hastily squatted back down and emptied his rectum into a container for all to see.[33]

In later years, the enema yielded to another system. Miners who were about to be discharged were taken to a large room or courtyard. They stripped naked, exchanging their clothes for blankets. Each miner's hand was covered with a fingerless glove, locked on the wrist by a chain. The gloves prevented the miners from removing diamonds from their excrement. The miners spent four or five days together, naked except for their gloves. The gloves caused awkward fumbling with spoons, pipes, and other implements. The miners' feces were duly collected by inspectors, placed on sieves, and washed with jets of water until stolen diamonds were either found or not found. It was the latest technology for diamond washing. There were reports of diamond-swallowing thieves who were caught this way, although the main object of the system was deterrence.[34]

The closing of the compound worked well from the company's perspective. In 1887 the directors, in their annual report, congratulated the shareholders "on the complete success which has attended the system of compounding the free native labourers, and which has falsified the predictions of evil, in which the opponents of that system so freely indulged." The report boasted that witnesses from Europe and South Africa observed "the manifest content of the inmates." The word "inmate" might have been a

Freudian slip, but the report described the social engineering of the compound with pride. The inmates were

> in fact well housed and provided with fuel, they are supplied at current rates with good wholesome food, they are free from the temptation to indulge in strong drink, a large swimming bath has been provided, and the general sanitary condition is as nearly perfect as it can be; while for those who are sick or suffering from injuries, a hospital has been erected in which they are treated by the Physician, who attends daily.... Certain ministers of Religion attend and give rudimentary instruction, and lastly, the fact that a large number of men whose contracts have expired offer themselves for re-engagement, is conclusive evidence that the solid advantages which the Compound System ensures to them are fully appreciated.[35]

Although the compounds resembled prisons and were designed to regulate the freedom and mobility of African migrant workers, some historians have noted that workers managed to develop a culture of their own that resisted the restrictions and retained some autonomy. Compound culture was largely invisible to Rhodes and his partners and managers. The mining companies had to attract young men from faraway regions, and wages were competitive. The process of amalgamation occurred during a time of depression, so wages were initially depressed while the number of miners fell. In 1882, 17,000 African miners earned an average weekly wage of 30 shillings. A few years later, the number of miners declined. Wages fell as low as 20 shillings, but by 1890, a total of 5,840 African miners were earning an average weekly wage of 32 shillings. In the early 1890s, a slump in the gold and diamond industry resulted in weekly wages being reduced to the low twenties, but these were still among the highest wages paid in South Africa. Wages in the diamond industry's closed compounds were often better than mine wages on the Witwatersrand and better than mine wages in Britain.[36]

The mine owners recognized that as their operations went underground, they had to attract and retain workers who learned all the technical skills of underground work. The possession of skill generated pushback against management's rules. There were complaints about the limits placed on alcohol in the compounds. Some workers chafed under the careful tracking of loads mined by the managers and the tracking of daily work and absenteeism on written "tickets." Workers were able to associate and enjoy leisure time together. Wages were high compared to the outside. One worker named

"Charlie" was asked by a labor commission what he thought about mining in Kimberley and living in the closed compound, and he replied, "I would prefer [to work on] the outside if I could get the same wages there."[37]

Rhodes and his fellow monopolists were doing more than just responding to the need for experienced labor in a competitive market. Some felt that their technological and moral superiority gave them the right to govern the lives of African workers. When African migrants were not supervised and cared for, it was thought that they might become susceptible to bad influences and become a threat, but if they were treated as children and given tutelage, they might become responsible and productive. Progressive paternalism was an approach taken by many nineteenth-century industrialists in Britain. They set up special dormitories and villages for workers, while arranging educational and religious opportunities for them. Missionaries were allowed to visit. Many observers approved of the compounds and believed that the mineworkers' productivity tended to improve under the compound system, lending credence to paternalistic notions that it was possible to achieve the gradual "uplift" of Africans.[38]

The system of compounding labor and mining underground was thought to decrease the risks of accidents and IDB, but confinement to the tunnels and the barracks resulted in an increase in respiratory illnesses. Although it is difficult to translate nineteenth-century medical descriptions to modern diagnoses, inhaling dust appears to have caused problems that resemble silicosis. Miners were reported to have pneumonia as well as "phthisis," the old term for tuberculosis. The close quarters enabled the spread of respiratory diseases. The miners also experienced problems with ankylostomiasis, or hookworm, a debilitating disease acquired by walking barefoot over damp earth. Scurvy, a deficiency in Vitamin C that is caused by a lack of fruit and vegetables in the diet, was also present. Some people at the time blamed scurvy on the ban on brewing traditional African beer, which is rich in B vitamins and contains some Vitamin C, but the disease had more to do with the miners' preference for cheap, filling carbohydrates over expensive fruits and vegetables. By the mid-1880s, the piping of drinking water from safe sources was cutting down on intestinal diseases, as was the policing of compound sanitation by company doctors. A quarantine station helped to reduce the introduction of infectious diseases, while an infirmary opened at the compound to care for sick workers.[39]

Closed compounds and amalgamation gave Rhodes and the shareholders of De Beers a greater sense of security about diamond mining. At the same time, Rhodes and his partners began to explore opportunities to mine for gold in the Transvaal. The allure of riches was great, although in the mid-1880s there was not yet a sense that gold mining was going to be more profitable than diamond mining. Rhodes became interested in gold mining partly through his partners in Kimberley and partly through the international network of engineers and bankers he met during the De Beers amalgamation.

In the early 1880s the Rothschild banking family was considering deepening its investments in gold mining, which had begun to be mined in the northeast Transvaal in the area near Lydenburg and Pilgrim's Rest, where Herbert Rhodes once lived. Alluvial gold was found in other parts of the Transvaal, too, but none of the discoveries appeared to be valuable until 1884, when a significant reef was found in Barberton, near the border with Swaziland. A gold rush followed the discovery, and for a year, the mines at Barberton attracted many investors. The Barberton boom of 1884 became a bust by 1886, a cautionary tale for investors and engineers.

For savvy investors like the Rothschilds, who were increasingly interested in Southern Africa, Barberton gave them reasons to seek professional engineers as consultants. While British engineers were strongly preferred and Americans were thought to lack enough training and technical skills, an exception was made for the London engineering firm of Edmund de Crano and Hamilton Smith, expatriate Americans who became the key consultants to the Rothschilds. An American associate of de Crano and Smith was working in the eastern Transvaal. Gardner Fred Williams was a professional engineer from Michigan who was educated at the University of California at Berkeley. After postgraduate training in Germany, Williams worked in salt mining and gold mining in California, Utah, and Nevada. In 1884, a British company paid Williams to travel to the Transvaal and manage its gold operations at Pilgrim's Rest. Williams had experience in hydraulic gold mining, the practice of blasting mineral-rich earth with pressurized water. The process produces ore but it also produces so much silt that rivers flood and ecosystems are destroyed. Williams managed the mine at Pilgrim's Rest during late 1884 and early 1885 but quickly came to realize that hydraulic gold mining could not be profitably done in the area.

Williams disappointed his employers at Pilgrim's Rest but enhanced his personal knowledge of South Africa. He traveled through the Witwatersrand, where prospectors were beginning to discover gold. Williams also visited the capital of the Transvaal, Pretoria, where he met State President Paul Kruger. In 1885, Williams passed through Kimberley just as underground mining was getting under way there. It was during this visit that Williams had a fateful meeting with Rhodes.[40] Rhodes invited Williams to the Kimberley Club, where they had supper together and then talked into the wee hours of the morning. He pumped Williams for information about gold mining in the northeast Transvaal and also shared his ideas for the Kimberley diamond mines. The next day, Rhodes gave Williams a tour of the De Beers Mine and made an interesting discovery. Rhodes said, "I hear that you are going to England on the same steamer as I am. I look forward to further talks with you on the future of South Africa." Williams and Rhodes parted company for a short time but did take a steamer together. Many years later, Williams's son, Alpheus, wrote that on board the ship Rhodes's "mind was definitely centred on the two major points, amalgamation and the British expansion to the north" but that "strange as it may seem he had very little to say on the method of mining that would be necessary when the open mine became unworkable, although he constantly referred to the trouble they were having from falls of reef." Williams traveled from England all the way back to California, never intending to come back to South Africa. Rhodes predicted a return.[41]

Rhodes was right. Edmund de Crano and Hamilton Smith recruited Williams for more consulting work in the Transvaal, where Rothschild bankers continued to assess the prospects for gold. The northeast Transvaal was still a site of mining activity, but attention was shifting to the Witwatersrand, forty miles south of Pretoria. The Witwatersrand was essentially a long ridge. When mining prospectors surveyed the area's surface layers of sedimentary and igneous rocks, they observed outcroppings of conglomerate, gold-bearing quartz reefs. It seemed natural enough to assume that the ridge was the place to buy mining claims. Prospectors provided samples of gold to a Kimberley merchant, Fred Alexander, who invited the diamond industry's magnates to private showings. It is known that Rhodes and Rudd viewed the samples, together with Joseph B. Robinson and other diamond magnates. Rhodes was also learning about gold from his friend Dr. Hans Sauer, who had recently traveled to Lydenburg, Barberton, and the Witwatersrand. He brought samples to Rhodes to persuade him to underwrite a reconnaissance mission.

In January of 1886, Rhodes decided to look at the Witwatersrand for himself. Together with Rudd, Sauer, and Sauer's brother-in-law, Harry Caldecott, the De Beers attorney, Rhodes rode north to see Langlaagte and to take in the Witwatersrand. Rhodes wrote to Rudd that "the belief in the Randt," referring to the Witwatersrand, "is increasing daily."[42] They camped out and explored the area, looking for alluvial gold and hints of reefs, while other visitors to the area were exploring and buying mining claims. One of the other key visitors to the area was Robinson, who was under financial pressure at Kimberley. Judging that the Witwatersrand gold discoveries were significant,

Robinson obtained financial backing from Alfred Beit and began to purchase claims.

There were technical, geological reasons that led some prospectors to underappreciate the gold deposits on the Witwatersrand. The best-known deposits of the nineteenth century were found in California, Australia, and New Zealand, where gold was embedded in quartz reefs similar to Pilgrim's Rest and Barberton. The quartz reef was quarried and hauled out in buckets or tramways powered by steam hauling engines. The rocks were processed in stamp mills powered by steam engines. At the top of the mill, fist-sized rocks were fed into roller crushers. The pebbles could then be run through another crusher, with ball bearings inside, before being mixed with water and sent into the battery of stamps, steel-tipped cylinders that moved up and down and smashed the quartz and water into powdery slurry. The pulverized quartz was then fed into copper-lined tanks, where mercury was used to separate the gold dust from the quartz dust.

The gold of the Witwatersrand was found not in quartz reefs but in conglomerates of pebbles set in a finer grained matrix of other rocks. These were laid down as layers in sedimentary formations. The layered structure was nicknamed "banket," after a Dutch nut cake. The gold could be found either in the pebbles or in the matrix. Some of the banket had high yields when crushed and processed with mercury. Other claims with banket contained higher proportions of pyrites, which required uneconomical amounts of mercury for processing. It did not take an experienced mine engineer to realize that the processing of gold at the Witwatersrand needed to be done differently from other locations. As stamp mills and mining gear spread across the Witwatersrand, speculators wondered if the milling of this ore had the potential for profits. Capital would need to be massive, much greater than the investment at Kimberley. There was also a particular need for infrastructure. The Witwatersrand was in a remote area that lacked a rail link, so equipment, miners, and gold had to be hauled by ox-wagons and stagecoaches.[43]

Rhodes, Rudd, Caldecott, and Sauer lacked training in geology, but they knew enough to pan, dig, and scrape at whatever they could find on the surface. The four men reached different conclusions. Rudd was known to be cautious and had hesitations about investing heavily at the Witwatersrand. Rhodes hesitated, too, sensing that he was out of his element with gold. Caldecott did not make any useful contribution. In a letter to Rudd, Rhodes commented that "Caldecott is terrible. He does nothing and pays nothing." Sauer made a better impression. "Sauer with all his faults I like. He is very good on diggers committee and fairly looks after our interests. He also is capital for dealing with boers as to their properties. I do not grudge him his good scrip."[44] Sauer felt optimistic about the Witwatersrand and regretted that his companions were less enthusiastic. During their visit, they came across a farm owned by the Du Plessis family. The farm was then on the market. Sauer thought it was likely to contain significant gold deposits. Rudd suspected foul play on the part of the owners. Rhodes decided to pass on the purchase. Soon enough, Sauer was proven correct. Robinson bought the Du Plessis farm and the neighboring farm, too. Gold was discovered and by 1891, the farms were valued at £15,000,000.[45]

Rhodes preferred the diamond fields, where he had a solid understanding of the business. Many years later, Sauer reported Rhodes's early thoughts about gold on the Witwatersrand: "It is all very well; but I cannot see or calculate the power in your claims." He was puzzled by his inability to see the deep seams of gold. "When I am in Kimberley, and have nothing much to do, I often go and sit on the edge of the De Beers mine, and I look at the blue diamondiferous ground, reaching from the surface, a thousand feet down the open workings of the mine, and I reckon up the value of the diamonds in the 'blue' and the power conferred by them. In fact every foot of blue ground means so much power. This I cannot do with your gold reefs."[46]

Sauer persisted in advocating for purchasing land on the Witwatersrand. He hired three Afrikaner assistants to help him line up multiple farms he thought Rhodes should consider. Rhodes dispatched the De Beers mine engineer, Edward Jones, so that he, too, could advise about the decision-making. Many other prospectors were there, beginning to make purchases, but Rhodes still had cold feet. Sauer commented, "As a matter of fact, Rhodes, like most of the men in South Africa then, knew nothing of gold mining, and still less of gold-bearing ore bodies, and in the back of his mind was the fear that the whole thing might turn out to be a frost. If he had taken up all or the greater part of the properties which I had secured under option for the matter of a few thousand pounds, he would undoubtedly have become one of the richest men that has ever lived."[47]

While Rhodes was considering claim purchases on the Witwatersrand, he received troubling news from Kimberley. Neville Pickering was dying. Pickering and Rhodes had lived together since 1882. In 1884, while Pickering was working as the secretary at De Beers, he fell from a horse into a thorn bush. Thorns punctured his legs, leaving him with a persistent bone infection. Jameson treated him without success. Pickering recovered somewhat and was able to work part-time at De Beers, but after Rhodes left for the Witwatersrand, in October 1886, a message arrived from Kimberley with the news that

Pickering was on his deathbed. Unable to buy a ticket on that day's coach, Rhodes rode instead on the top with the baggage for three hundred miles.

The scene at Pickering's bedside was pathetic. William Pickering, Neville's brother, summoned Jameson, but treatment did not help. Rhodes was completely focused on his friend, whose last words were reported to be: "You have been father, mother, brother, and sister to me." Soon after, he died in Rhodes's arms. The funeral was attended by Kimberley's most prominent residents, several of whom wrote that Rhodes was beside himself with grief. Years later an associate of Rhodes, David Harris, told a story to Sauer's brother-in-law, the gold magnate Percy FitzPatrick, that he entered the De Beers boardroom one day to find Rhodes and Willie Pickering crying on either side of a table, pushing Neville's watch back and forth to each other, saying again and again, "No, you are his brother," and "No, you are his greatest friend."[48] Rhodes was taken in by Jameson. They lived together in Jameson's cottage, which was just down the road from the Kimberley Club, where they took their meals.

After Pickering's death, Gardner Williams returned to the Transvaal. De Crano and Smith, Rothschild's American engineers, tasked him with assessing the Transvaal's potential for investment, this time analyzing the Witwatersrand. At the end of 1886, Williams passed through Kimberley and met with Rhodes. Rhodes was starting to feel confident about the Witwatersrand and had just written to Rudd that "the general feeling tends to more faith in the Rand on account of the healthy state of the climate and facilities for work and the enormous quantities of auriferous deposit."[49] Rhodes updated Williams on the amalgamation and the technical challenges at the mines, acknowledging his need for a highly trained engineer. Rhodes offered Williams the position of general manager at De Beers. Williams told Rhodes that he was considering the offer, but first he needed to complete his work for de Crano and Smith. In January 1887, Williams traveled by wagon from Kimberley to the Witwatersrand and then Pretoria. Much to his surprise, he was visited by Rhodes, who was traveling back to the area with Alfred Beit, Hermann Eckstein, and Jules Porgès, who had been buying gold shares. The men sought the advice of Williams.

Many stories have been told about how Williams predicted that the Witwatersrand was unlikely to be a profitable source of gold. Sauer even claimed that Williams said to him, "Dr. Sauer, if I rode over these reefs in America I would not get off my horse to look at them. In my opinion they are not worth hell room." Williams was later teased about this mistake, but several engineers have contested this story, including Williams's son, Alpheus. It appears that Williams advised Rhodes that some of the properties might be

Gardner Fred Williams. Library of Congress Prints and Photographs Division, LC-DIG-npcc-13,010.

expensive to mine, and Rhodes, who was putting most of his financial effort into the amalgamation of De Beers, did not buy as many gold-mining claims as he could have.[50]

Soon afterwards, Williams accepted the offer to be the general manager at De Beers. Having this highly skilled engineer gave the company greater credibility with the Rothschilds and other influential investors, especially at a time when Rhodes was seeking financial backing for the amalgamation. The senior partner, Nathaniel, 1st Lord Rothschild, knew through de Crano, Smith, and Williams about the technical challenges faced by the Kimberley diamond mines.

"Natty" Rothschild was one of the wealthiest people in Britain and had an international network that allowed him to maneuver at the highest levels in finance and politics. From 1865 to 1885, he served as a Liberal member of the House of Commons. In 1885, he inherited his father's title and became the first member of the House of Lords to practice the Jewish faith openly. A friend of the Prince of Wales, Rothschild supported imperialism and was allied with Joseph Chamberlain's Liberal Unionists. Rothschild bridged politics and finance, and like many of the financial and industrial leaders of his day, he was well known as a philanthropist. He had strong interests in helping the Jewish community of London and was a strong advocate for Jews who lived under the Russian empire.[51]

The need to impress the Rothschilds helps to explain why Rhodes and Rudd hired Williams even at the same time as they were discounting his advice about the Witwatersrand. When Rhodes rushed to Pickering's bedside, he left Sauer on the Witwatersrand, telling him to consider more exploration and claim purchases. Sauer had many opportunities to buy claims, but Rhodes was overwhelmed by Pickering's death and ignored the messages. Many of the best claims were being bought by Robinson, backed by Beit. Not until the last weeks of 1886 did Rhodes resume his interest in the Witwatersrand. He persuaded Rudd to travel to London, where he hoped to raise the funds to purchase claims before they were acquired by Beit, Porgès, and Robinson.

In February 1887, Rudd and Rhodes partnered with Caldecott in the formation of a company based in London called Gold Fields of South Africa. It would have been easier to form the company in the Transvaal, but Rhodes and Rudd appear to have wanted the respectability that came with incorporation in London. Rudd had clear instructions from Rhodes: "1. Get as much money as you can. 2. Order a large quantity of machinery. 3. Draw a Trust with very wide powers. 4. Obtain us a good remuneration or else the Company is not worth working for." Rudd arranged for Gold Fields' articles of association to be flexible, with the company permitted to mine anywhere. Over the course of 1887, Rudd sold shares to the tune of £250,000.[52]

The capitalization was less than the value of their major competitors, but it was still a considerable sum. Rudd included his brother, Thomas, a London banker, on the board of directors, a connection that helped the new company to obtain further investments in the City. Rhodes's correspondence with Rudd shows that the two partners were ebullient. In December of 1886, Rhodes wrote to Rudd, "There is no doubt the discovery of good things has only just commenced. There is plenty of time and money will command almost anything." Rhodes stated his belief that "there are plenty of really good things awaiting hard work and development.... The general feeling tends to more faith in the Rand on account of the healthy state of the climate and facilities for work and the enormous quantity of auriferous deposit."[53]

Faith in the Rand was famously justified. In several years' time, Rhodes's shares in Gold Fields provided an annual income estimated at £300,000 to £400,000, while shares in De Beers generated £200,000.[54] As much as this may seem like a lot of money, Rhodes could have done better, had he been quicker to invest in properties on the Witwatersrand. His companies formed an interlocking network of investors and directors. Over time, the need to invest more money in gold mines motivated him to make profits at De Beers and to explore for more gold north of the Limpopo. For Rhodes the gold mines became more than just a money-spinner. They became a part of his broader thinking about making money through northward colonial expansion. Expansion was helped by the flexibility of the Gold Fields articles of association, which allowed the company to mine elsewhere. The soon-to-be-created De Beers Consolidated Mining Company would have the same degree of flexibility. Both companies became instruments in Rhodes's expansion of the British Empire in Southern Africa.

8

Amalgamating the Mines

RHODES RESUMED THE chairmanship of the De Beers Mining Company in 1887, a crucial time in its history. The directors were finishing the amalgamation of the De Beers Mine and moving toward acquiring Kimberley's three other diamond mines. Corporate amalgamation was closely connected to the commencement of underground mining and the compounding of labor, both of which were still just getting started. Amalgamation engaged Rhodes in intense planning and negotiating. Always, at the back of his mind, the amalgamation of the diamond mines was related to his broader plan for regional colonialism and its need for infrastructure.

Rhodes made a key decision for the future of the company in entrusting Gardner Williams with resolving the technical problems of deep-level mining. Williams completed his work on the Witwatersrand and returned to Kimberley in May of 1887 to begin his new appointment as the general manager of the De Beers Mining Company. Williams was at Rhodes's side when he gave important speeches to the shareholders at the De Beers annual meetings of 1887 and 1888. Rhodes's speeches indicate the range of his abilities, the depth of his interest, and the opportunism of his vision. Both speeches contained dry recitations of technical details. New machinery was purchased. New pumps were installed. The new closed compound began to operate. As Rhodes reported details of those developments, he also sounded notes of triumph. In 1887, he reported that "it was a struggle to keep the Mine open." Yields were lower than expected, but all was well because of "the success attendant on the working of the sloping shaft has surpassed the expectations of your Directors." Rhodes boasted that work had begun on digging the sloping shaft on the western side of the mine, "by which means the output from that side could be doubled without difficulty, owing to the enormous area at their disposal." Rhodes reported that the amalgamation of the mine was easily within reach.[1]

Rhodes's speech to the 1887 meeting indicated that material factors were pulling owners toward amalgamation. That year, De Beers was "struggling" with somewhat lower yields while making the transition from open-pit mining to underground mining. "All of you who are diggers," he said to the Kimberley audience, "are aware that there comes in the history of this and the other mines a struggle against the reef," by which he meant the seemingly ineluctable need to remove more and more reef from an open pit that was being dug deeper and deeper. Now the "dead work" of clearing reef was diminished, "because we have entirely adopted the underground system." Rhodes credited the former chief engineer, Edward Jones, with the insight that the company should pursue underground mining. Rhodes noted that some directors had been reluctant to make the change. "The Directors, influenced perhaps by an old digger feeling…continued the open working perhaps far beyond the time when they should have abandoned it." Rhodes saw the move to underground mining as a bold solution that ensured the future productivity of the company. "We are justified, we think, in stating to our Shareholders that as far as we can see the amount of Blue before us is practically without limit." Diamonds continued to be found as shafts were sunk deeper. The mine had already gone 700 feet below the surface. Rhodes noted that "it would be like a story from the Arabian Nights to try and estimate what the Mine contains and will yield to us by the simple process of deepening the shaft." With sight limitless—and with consolidation moving forward rapidly—Rhodes announced plans for more shafts: a vertical shaft through the former holdings of the Gem Company and a second sloping shaft for the West End. He forecast that "the value in the Mine is almost beyond your reckoning."[2]

Company growth was remarkable. In seven years, the De Beers Diamond Mining Company's capital increased six times, from £200,000 to £1,265,000. Dividends rose from 5 percent to 16 percent, which continued to rise steadily even after the December 1885 fall of reef in the West End cost the company an extra £41,000 to remove. Labor practices had been changing, too, and Rhodes was pleased with the existing system of underground workings and miner compounding. He agreed that the compounds reduced diamond stealing and kept the supply of laborers steady. There were 214 white miners working underground, together with 1,350 compounded African miners. The latter were recruited and housed by the company and supervised and paid by contractors. Williams hoped to have 2,300 African miners in the West End Compound, to maximize the labor available to the contractors.[3]

Initial efforts at deep-level mining faced numerous technical challenges. The diamond-bearing "blue ground" tended to crumble when tunneling exposed it to air. The ground at the Kimberley Mine crumbled more than the ground at the De Beers Mine. That being said, the De Beers Mine was becoming more dangerous. The government mine inspector, Erskine, reported that the yearly average number of fatalities, which hovered around five or six workers per thousand in the early 1880s, climbed to about twelve or thirteen per thousand in the late 1880s.[4]

In his first report, Williams summarized the wrenching technical changes at the De Beers Mine. There had not been a slow changeover from open-pit mining to underground mining. Instead, according to Williams, "sufficient time was not given to prepare the latter before the works in the open mine had to be abandoned on account of the *debris* falling from the sides of the mine." The instability of the surrounding reef dictated an immediate change. Nonetheless, Williams, like his new employer, had faith in the mine's future. "That the 'blue' will continue to be diamond bearing to an unlimited depth there can be no doubt," he said, pointing to the clear boundary between blue ground filled with diamonds and the surrounding reef. According to Williams, "The inference is that the diamonds were crystallized at a great depth and were thrown up with the blue ground and were not formed in situ."[5]

The maps from the De Beers Annual Report for 1888 give further indication of Williams's professionalism. As mining became industrialized and mines went deeper, professional mapmaking became essential to mine management. Specialist surveyors used theodolites and transits to determine the distances, widths, and angles involved in tunneling, feeding this data to mine engineers, who often supervised the drafting of maps. Many engineers took pride in their maps—as Williams must have done. He used his maps as illustrations in his 1905 history of diamond mining, which made the case that while the risks of deep-level mining were great, he was a responsible engineer.[6]

Another important trend in the mine was to mechanize processing. Mechanization predated the arrival of Williams by several years. In the mid- to late 1880s, the weathering, crushing, and washing still resulted in a mix of rocks and minerals that necessitated a great deal of hand-sorting to pick out the diamonds. The more that the company relied on workmen for sorting, the more that it was exposed to human error and theft. Near the floors the company installed new rotary washing gear. In 1886, the company reduced hand-sorting considerably by purchasing a pulsator to be used after rotary washing. In the pulsator, known to the miners as a "jig," the washed slurry of pebbles and diamonds was fed into a tank where it rested over screens. The machine pulsed water up and down so that the diamonds and other heavy minerals sank to the bottom. The valuable mix left the pulsator through a bottom drain, to be screened and sorted by hand, while the remaining slurry of tailings exited near the top. Hand-sorting was still required but was much less time-consuming.⁷

As the De Beers Mine neared the end of amalgamation, the company kept upgrading equipment. In 1887, under the supervision of Williams, De Beers installed new hauling gear, a new crushing machine, and two new washing machines. Output increased, not only because De Beers acquired more claims but also because mine operations became more sophisticated from a technological perspective. Old problems, like water in the mine, were addressed with new systems. As the mine went underground, more water needed to be pumped out. The rotary washers and the pulsator required a great deal of water. Circulating water from the mine to the rotary washer and the pulsator in the processing plant was one of the only ways in which the mine sustained itself; almost everything else that the mine required had to be imported. In 1886, the fall of debris in the West End disrupted the De Beers pumps, forcing the company to contract with the Victoria Company even as it was being bought out. In August 1886, the De Beers pumps were functioning again. Nearly 15,000 gallons were pumped out every hour, all of it sent to the floors to be used by the washers and the pulsator. In 1888, the company ordered new pumps from Cornwall and began construction of a reservoir in Kenilworth.⁸

Underground mining was clearly the way forward, which presented technical challenges. The first experimental shaft of Edward Jones at De Beers was not stout enough to be used permanently. At the West End, De Beers began work on its first sloping shaft. By May 1887, with the amalgamation of the mines entering its final stages, the sloping shaft made it possible to open tunnels that reached galleries at 600 and 685 feet. These were thought to be capable of producing between 1500 and 2400 loads per day. By May 1888, the combination of underground mining and the amalgamation of holdings meant that the number of loads of blue per day was approximately 2500—ten times the amount hauled in 1881—with hardly any "dead" ground being moved. De Beers continued to push for more shafts. One vertical shaft began to be sunk through the holdings of the old Gem Company. Following the examples at the Kimberley Mine, another vertical shaft, called the "Rock Shaft," was started in 1886. It was excavated 841 feet down through the rock just outside of the blue ground. By 1888, it was almost connected to the mine tunnels in the blue ground.⁹

Almost immediately after the final amalgamation of the De Beers Mine, Rhodes began the campaign to control the Kimberley Mine. Rhodes was challenged by Barney Barnato, who was even richer. Barnato was born Barnet Isaacs to a Jewish family in the East End of London. He was raised in

Whitechapel, a neighborhood known for overcrowding, poverty, and crime. In 1873, together with his brother and two nephews, he migrated to Kimberley, where he changed his name, worked odd jobs and performed as a boxer and entertainer. Rumors circulated that he also was involved in IDB. He was able to parlay his cash into ownership of shares of the Kimberley Mine. His company, Barnato Mining, was one of several large companies remaining in the open pit. Barnato may have been the wealthiest mine owner in Kimberley when a large fall of reef in 1884 forced him to merge with another company, the British Company. Still in charge, Barnato listened to his engineers and decided to begin digging a shaft under the ground, following the example of Joseph Robinson's Standard Company, which Barnato took over in mid-1885 by paying agents to circulate rumors that Standard's underground mining operations were dangerous and likely to fail. The rumors drove down share prices, which Barnato then bought. He merged the Barnato and British Companies into Standard and retained the Standard name.[10]

The geography of the Kimberley Mine shaped the next battle for ownership. Barnato's Standard Company owned a large block of claims on the east end of the mine. The Central Company, owned by Francis Baring-Gould, controlled the west end. In between them lay the Compagnie Française des Mines de Diamants du Cap de Bonne-Espérance known as the French Company. It was owned by Jules Porgès. There was also a collection of small claims of W. A. Hall and Company known as Hall's Claims. In mid-1887, Rhodes entered the bidding war for claims in the Kimberley Mine, lining up the backing needed to buy the Hall's Claims from one of the principal owners, the Cape of Good Hope Bank. Rhodes began to buy up any available shares of the Hall's Claims, but when he tried to buy shares from the bank, he was scooped by an outside investor, Donald Currie, the owner of the Castle Shipping Line, one of two companies that carried the mail and most of the cargo between Britain and South Africa. Currie was a wealthy businessman, influential in London and Cape Town. He was also a member of the British Parliament, representing West Perthshire in Scotland. On the voyage back to Britain in February 1888, he encountered two young agents sent by Rhodes to persuade him to sell. He almost did, but when he reached land, he learned that Rhodes and his agents were offering a lower price than the value of the shares. Currie was outraged by what he considered to be dishonorable conduct and spurned Rhodes and his offer. Rhodes responded by dumping his own shares at a lower price to depress the value of Currie's shares. Rhodes hoped this aggressive move would put pressure on Currie to sell. Currie decided to hold the shares at a lower price just to spite Rhodes.[11]

It was well known that Rhodes and De Beers were keen to amalgamate all four mines, but in mid-1887, Barnato was emerging as the dominant player. In July 1887, he entered an alliance with Francis Baring-Gould. Baring-Gould and Barnato merged their two companies, the Standard and the Central, to form the Kimberley Central Company. Barnato held the most shares. At this point, the only major holding left for purchase in the Kimberley Mine was the French Company, worth £1,500,000. Rhodes lined up half of the money by trading shares of De Beers Mining Company with members of Beit's French and German network. Beit, who had a reputation for honesty and humility, then helped Rhodes to approach London's most influential venture capitalist, Nathaniel, 1st Lord Rothschild.

Natty Rothschild spent the 1880s and 1890s increasing his investments in mines around the globe. He knew enough to consult carefully with his engineers. When it came to investing in De Beers, Rothschild deferred to Gardner Williams, who had previously advised him about the Witwatersrand. Williams wrote an assessment of the effects of amalgamation on the diamond industry, arguing that bringing together all the mines promised handsome returns. Williams passed his report to Rothschild's consulting engineer, Edmund de Crano. The House of Rothschild studied the report with interest, but they were not moving fast enough for Rhodes. A few weeks after Williams began work for De Beers, he and Rhodes boarded a ship for England, arriving in July 1887. Rhodes and Williams were joined by de Crano for a meeting with Natty Rothschild at his London headquarters, New Court, an imposing, Italian-style palace in the City. It appears that the engineers played an important role. There was no written record, but Williams's son, Alpheus, who succeeded to his father's position at De Beers, wrote in his memoir that many years later Rothschild told him, "Williams, your father never took credit for the very important part that he played in the amalgamation of De Beers, let me tell you it was he who made me decide on what I did at the time."[12] Rothschild, Rhodes, and their partners and investors recognized that it took an engineer of Williams's experience and stature to make deep-level underground mining safe and profitable.

In the first week of August 1887, the offer of a loan by Rothschild set the stage for the amalgamation of the diamond mines. Rothschild made £750,000 cash available to Rhodes, plus £200,000 in debentures, a type of unsecured loan. The price of the funding was high. Rothschild received 50,000 shares of the amalgamated company, worth £750,000, plus half the difference between the value of the shares in August and their value in October. With this funding, Rhodes and his partners began to buy shares of the Central Company.

Soon, they were caught off guard by Barnato. He had been buying shares of the French Company and knew that Rhodes was making an offer. Rhodes owned one-fifth of the Central Company and Barnato owned one-fifth of the French Company. This gave Barnato intelligence about Rhodes's interest in the French Company. Barnato struck first. In September, Barnato offered the French Company's shareholders £1,700,000, which amounted to £300,000 more than Rhodes had offered. Rhodes responded with a counteroffer. He bought the French Company but then let Barnato buy it from him with shares of the Central. Barnato believed that the Rothschilds would then become the real owners, not Rhodes, but this was not correct: the shares were held by the De Beers Consolidated Mining Company. Rhodes did have to borrow even more money from the Rothschilds—an additional loan of £300,000 was used to buy shares of the Central Company, entitling Rothschilds to almost 6,000 shares of the amalgamated De Beers. Rhodes was now able to buy a significant position in the Central.[13]

Barnato and Rhodes drove hard bargains yet had different motives. Rhodes was certainly out to make money, but his overarching concern was to bankroll his vision of populating the subcontinent with British settlers. Barnato had no such desire—nor did many of Rhodes's partners in De Beers. Even Rudd, who went along with Rhodes's schemes, was mainly interested in making money. If Barnato did not buy out De Beers immediately, he could wait. Besides, most knowledgeable miners thought that the Kimberley Mine would produce greater quantities of superior diamonds than the De Beers Mine. The addition of Williams to the management of De Beers meant that the De Beers Mine could anticipate an advantage in terms of efficiency in underground mining, but still the Central could be more productive in terms of quality. Barnato demonstrated this point by putting increasing numbers of diamonds up for sale. The Central Company was big enough that it could remain independent and negotiate maximum leverage over the market. By contrast, Rhodes was in a hurry to fulfill his plans for extending colonization in Southern Africa. He wanted control over De Beers more than he wanted to become richer. He felt pressure to finish the amalgamation because the time seemed right for developing the Road to the North and for gaining control of northern territories such as Matabaleland and Mashonaland. Rhodes was ready to pay handsomely for Kimberley Central, thus satisfying his own territorial ambitions as well as Barnato's desire to make money.[14] To achieve this goal as quickly as possible, Rhodes started to work cooperatively with Barnato. In October 1887, Rhodes sent an interesting letter to Stow. "The great comfort I feel now is that the goal is reached." Rhodes explained that Barnato "is working in everything with me and has given me his pledge to go the end with me, and B[aring] Gould though a weak man has made up his mind to go with the tide."[15] Baring-Gould held out longer than Barnato, but Rothschild funds persuaded him to fold, too.

In December 1887, Rhodes gathered the De Beers directors and convinced them to join him in a final, aggressive push to acquire control of the Kimberley Central Company. To increase De Beers's holdings in Kimberley Central from one-fifth to three-fourths it cost an estimated one million pounds. The key player was Alfred Beit, who had good connections with European financiers. He persuaded Rothschild and Porgès to lend more money, while he contributed a quarter of a million of his own funds. Beit placed such a big bet on the buyout at least in part because he disliked Barnato.

Barnato agreed to the final terms of the purchase and did quite well from the swap of shares. For every ten shares in Kimberley Central, he was paid fourteen shares of De Beers. It was Barnato's price for supporting other features that were not standard. The new company, De Beers Consolidated Mining, could invest in anything as it saw fit, not just mining and not just in South Africa. The company also had an unusual structure. It would be run by five "life governors." The first ones would be Rhodes, Beit, and Stow, together with Baring-Gould and Barnato. They were entitled to run the company as they wished, without consulting ordinary shareholders. The ordinary shareholders were eligible to earn dividends on the first 30 percent of profits. The remaining 70 percent was divided five ways among the life governors.

The deal was finalized thanks to the persuasive powers of Rhodes. He wooed Barnato over lunch at the Kimberley Club—the club that had excluded Barnato on account of his Jewish origins, his reputation for IDB, and his flamboyant personality. Rhodes soon proposed Barnato for membership and even sponsored him as a candidate for the Cape Parliament's House of Assembly. Stow did not completely trust Rhodes and Beit, and he disliked Barnato intensely. Stow sneered in his memoir that Barnato's "antecedents were freely discussed and our opinions differed but little as to them. I urged the expediency of keeping him where he was, without our circle." Rhodes had given his word to Barnato and could not give in to Stow's request. After a week of sulking, Stow relented, then Barnato got cold feet about the deed of trust, which gave the company permission to enter any sort of transaction. The final meeting between Rhodes and Barnato lasted all day and into the early hours of the morning, accompanied by copious drinking and smoking. When Barnato finally agreed to the deed of trust, he said, "Some people have a fancy for one thing, some for another. You want the means to go north, if possible, so I suppose we must give it to you."[16]

The process of consolidating the diamond mines was almost complete. On the London stock market there was a temporary flurry of controversy over the concept of the life governorships and the participation of Barnato, followed by a lawsuit by shareholders in the Central Company. Amalgamation still moved forward, with further support from Rothschild and his representative in Kimberley, Paul Dreyfus, who worked out many of the details of refinancing the debts of the old companies.[17]

De Beers Consolidated Mining was incorporated in March 1888. It was immediately challenged by a lawsuit filed in the Cape Colony's Supreme Court. Shareholders in the Kimberley Central Company, led by Baring-Gould, filed a lawsuit alleging that the De Beers merger was illegal. The unusual deed of trust for the new company meant that it was not a similar company, as the law said that it was supposed to have been. When the court's ruling favored the plaintiffs, Rhodes carried out a surprise legal maneuver. He and his partners in De Beers were still the main owners of the Kimberley Central. Rhodes and De Beers liquidated the Kimberley Central Company and put its assets up for sale. Conveniently enough, the De Beers Consolidated Mining Company was ready to purchase those assets immediately. The merger was finalized.[18]

Amalgamation may have been driven by technical and financial concerns, but it resulted in the creation of a powerful company. De Beers Consolidated Mining Company had the classic powers of a monopoly to undermine competition and pressure laborers, combined with broad powers to make investments outside of the diamond-mining industry. With the amalgamation of Kimberley's two principal diamond mines almost finished, Cecil Rhodes addressed the annual meeting on Saturday, May 10, 1888. He mixed mastery of technical details with rhetorical showmanship. He explained that yields were lower than hoped for and attributed this problem to the geology of the mine. "We have always been hampered by the fact that we had to work at the higher levels, and our ground has been mixed with the dead blue lying above the shale in the Victoria portion of the mine." Rhodes urged investors to have faith: "I am confident that when we work upon our deeper levels we shall have as satisfactory yields as in the past." The development of deep-level mining required much patience. Rhodes stated, "You must remember that there was in the past no great faith in underground working, and we attempted to continue open work as long as possible." Rhodes reported that Williams "states that he has now practically in sight seven million loads of blue. The other levels are nearly completed, and there is not the slightest doubt that we could go on with these underground works practically ad infinitum." The prospect of infinite amounts of diamonds inspired Rhodes. The logical objection to such a prediction of expanded production had to do with overproduction, but Rhodes was not worried. "I feel now perfectly confident we can put out practically an unlimited supply of blue, and I feel also confident that in the future the results of our industry will not be spoilt by an over production."[19]

As the company moved to corner Southern African diamond production, Rhodes felt obliged to reflect on the nature of the new company's governance, as most shareholders of the combined companies found it to be structured in an unusual way. Rhodes recognized that many objections were being made to the arrangement but that the new company's economic importance suggested that it should have a special structure of governance. In Rhodes's opinion, the life governorships protected investors: they were "the greatest safeguard you can possibly possess. And I'll show you why." Rhodes predicted the creation of more value. "It will not be long," Rhodes argued, "before this industry will be yielding from three to four millions per annum, and I would point out to you—it is a mere sum, if you will work it out—that the value of the property, with the increase we expect, will be practically almost equal to the whole value of the Colony of the Cape of Good Hope." The importance of the company justified the structure, according to Rhodes. "We have got an industry," he said, "which is almost like a government within a government." Shareholders got the leadership of four or five devoted men who held a very large stake in the company's success. Rhodes saw the life governorships as a step that mitigated risk for investors. Investors had three risks in the past: "that the depth of the mine was doubtful"; that the underground tunnels might have to use large supplies of timber; and that there might be overproduction. "Now I wish to point out that risk is over and done with."[20]

As the chief wirepuller for the De Beers merger, Rhodes managed an extensive, transnational network of people and materials. Yet much like the overall project of imperialism, such a grandiose and complex network had its vulnerabilities. Each component was susceptible to failures that could threaten the entire plan. On July 11, 1888, disaster struck at the vision's material heart. A fire broke out at the De Beers Mine that killed twenty-four white miners and 178 Black miners. One of South Africa's worst industrial disasters, it revealed weaknesses in Rhodes's corporate, material, and political network. The disaster also exposed what it was like to work inside one of South Africa's first deep-level mines.

The fire began on the night of Wednesday, July 11. As word of the fire spread, hundreds of relatives and rescuers rushed to the mine shaft entrances and jostled near Williams, yelling suggestions. A newspaper reporter observed that Williams "kept his head through all that deluge of ideas and plans from inefficient interfering busybodies is a marvel. I suppose he got a little 'snappy' but the wonder is that he did not use a revolver or a club." One member of the crowd yelled at Williams, "I call it murder." Blamed in public, Williams turned to two mineworkers, instructing them to ask for the heckler's permit. When this was not produced, the miners "quietly escorted him out, and so got rid of him."[21] The company's first response to blame was to silence an accuser.

By sunrise on the next morning, smoke could be seen billowing out of the De Beers Mine's two main shafts. It was becoming clear to everyone in Kimberley that a terrible accident had occurred, raising fears about husbands, sons, and friends who might be trapped. Newspapers reported people standing at the edge of the mine, waiting for any information. "Wives were there who rushed with streaming eyes to the front as each [rescued] man ascended, one poor woman pushing aside the people impatiently saying, 'My God! Let me pass and see if that's my husband.'"[22]

De Beers Mine Fire of 1888, Showing Miners Standing on the Edge of the Open Pit, Awaiting News, while in the Distance, by the Headgear, Smoke Billows from the Shaft. Courtesy of the McGregor Museum, Kimberley, MMKP 4806.

Forty-three white miners and several hundred Black miners were trapped in the Gem Shaft. The shaft had been kept open just barely enough to suck air down into the mine but not open wide enough so that men could easily pass through. The No. 1 and No. 2 shafts were "upcasts," meaning that they blew the air up, so the fire, which appeared to be coming from the 500-foot level, blocked the flow of air through the upcasts. Miners survived, trapped, in tunnels below 500 feet or in subsidiary shafts like the "downcast" Gem. There the miners waited, aware of the possibility that as the disaster unfolded, the Gem Shaft could shift and become an upcast, making the smoke and flames rise toward them. In the mine fire's best-known story of heroism, a white miner, Harry Paull, led a successful effort to climb up the Gem Shaft from the 500-foot level to the aperture—described as a crack—at the 340-foot level that led to the open pit. The miners had to climb through narrow passageways, removing bodies as they went. They managed to climb up to the airway's crack, where they hammered their way out to safety.[23]

Paull then went back down into the mine, leading a small party to search for more miners. According to the *Daily Independent,* that was when "one of the saddest scenes in connection with the De Beers disaster occurred." The newspaper reported that "two of the rescuers saw a crowd of natives at the mouth of the nearest tunnel below. The rope was quickly thrown down and the rescuers took it in turn to pull up the K----rs one by one. When 166 K----rs had been dragged up the white men were so utterly exhausted with the terrible labour, and with the stifling smoke that they had to go away and leave four K----rs to their fate. The poor fellows were last seen with their arms uplifted towards the hole piteously crying, 'Baas, baas!'" A second attempt was made to get them out, but that failed.[24]

There were also stories about the heroism of African miners. One "boy" called John Zulu carried his heavy "baas" all the way "up a ladder way choked with the dead bodies of natives." Another African miner, a "colonial native" known as Jim, "saved the lives of three of the Europeans working in the Mine." He found one European miner unconscious and carried him 600 feet through smoking tunnels and shafts to safety. When the newspaper reporter asked him why he made such a dangerous rescue, "he answered that if he had died it would not matter much, but if the 'baases' died it would matter a great deal."[25] Such stories reinforced colonial beliefs that workers from dominated groups are supposed to be loyal.

Shortly after Paull's final rescue attempt, William Erskine, the government inspector of mines, ordered the rescue work to stop, judging it to be too dangerous, especially given the low chances of finding more men. An exhaust fan was being used to remove smoke from the No. 2 shaft. On Friday, when there was no more hope of finding trapped survivors, the entrance to No. 2 was battened down and a blower installed to blow air down into the mine, to drive smoke and steam up and out of No. 1. When the smoke cleared, workers started to run the skips down the shaft and removed dead miners' bodies by the cartload.[26]

With Williams working around the clock to lead the rescue efforts, the De Beers management debated how to explain the situation to Rhodes, who was not there. Telegrams flew back and forth between the De Beers secretary, William Pickering, and the various De Beers directors in Kimberley, Cape Town, and London. At the time of the fire, Rhodes and Rudd were in Cape Town for the parliamentary session. Both men were members. Initial correspondence between Pickering and Cape Town shows that he hoped Rudd would come to Kimberley, not Rhodes.[27] As the bodies were being pulled from the mine, Pickering wrote to his counterpart in London, "The news will be a terrible blow to Mr Rhodes on his arrival." The copy of the sent telegram had those words underlined in blue pencil by another De Beers employee, possibly by Williams, who also added three underlined exclamation points, "!!!"[28] A few days later, a telegram from Pickering, this time to Rhodes's flatmate in Cape Town, the city's port captain, M. H. Penfold, reported that "the work of extracting bodies will be something too awful and will take days" and that it was a good idea to "try and keep Rhodes with you until mine is clear for the sight will upset him and we cannot afford to have him laid up although I must confess all of us would be pleased to see him."[29] As the rescue attempts ended and the grim work of recovery continued, the next day Pickering wrote that he was "pleased to hear Rhodes is not coming just yet."[30]

In Britain, the law required that a mine accident be followed by an official investigation. Two days after the disaster, with miners still staggering out of the old Gem Shaft, and with "many thousands" of people "besieging" the mine, the *Diamond Fields Advertiser* wrote: "There are loud demands in some quarters for a Government enquiry, but they are made in a tone which indicates that the clamourers have already prejudged the matter and that their cry is only another method of declaring that 'somebody must be hung.'" The editor counseled patience. The newspaper anticipated that in South Africa's first major mine disaster, a commission would be created.[31]

Establishing liability required investigators to use common-law concepts familiar to engineers and miners in Britain and North America. The doctrine of "assumed risk" implied that when employees started a job, they were familiar with the risks. The doctrine of "contributory negligence" meant that injured employees could not be awarded compensation if they were partially to blame for the accident. And the doctrine of the "fellow servant" meant that if a fellow employee caused the accident, the owner could not be blamed. Legally speaking, it was very difficult to blame an accident on the owner, either in a lawsuit or in an inquest.[32] The problem with these legal doctrines was that they envisioned an ideal worker, free to choose any workplace, always careful, never under pressure to produce at a higher pace. Yet miners who were paid by the load were often in a hurry and disliked performing extra duties related to safety. They even had a name for it—"deadwork"—an ironic usage that reflected the risks as well as their annoyance with maintenance work that did not pay. The miners found themselves in a difficult situation, having to choose between safety and wages. Mine owners like Rhodes kept expenditures on safety to the minimum. They often felt that by instituting a safety measure, they might be implying the mine was unsafe, increasing their liability.[33]

In Kimberley, risks were heightened by the numbers of miners, as well as by the newness of the deep-level mines. Many of Kimberley's white miners had migrated from the copper, tin, and lead mines of Cornwall. Of these, many had also worked in Australia and the US West. Migrant Cornish miners, nicknamed "Cousin Jack" for their clannishness, were known for their skill at "hard rock" mining, as contrasted with working in "soft rock" coal mining.[34] The Cornish miners were known to have a blind spot when it came to safety. In Cornwall, miners shared risk with mine owners and had a "cavalier attitude to safety."[35] Cornish names frequently appear in the newspaper accounts of the De Beers fire.

On the Monday after the accident, an editorial in the *Diamond Fields Advertiser* assigned general blame to the mining company. Did the rich mine owners "disregard the safety of the poor human factor, the mere labourer and mechanic, who is in their eyes often the least notable element in their great plans and schemes of wealth-making?" There was specific mention of a safety issue. Shortly before the fire, Shaft No. 2 was temporarily blocked, meaning that "there was no provision for escape existing in the contingency of a fire in No. 1 shaft." The newspaper suggested that the mining company as well as the government inspectors might be blameworthy and called for a "rigid and impartial enquiry" by commissioners who "must be appropriately selected to satisfy the Diamond Fields public."[36]

As the recovery effort continued, the colonial government announced the appointment of a commission of enquiry. The members were Edward Judge, the civil commissioner of Kimberley; J. M. Crosby, the resident magistrate of

Cape Town; and W. M. Grier, chief inspector of public works. These men held positions of responsibility within the civil service, but none of them had any experience in mining, and their lack of expertise became the subject of contention between different factions in Kimberley politics and in the Cape Parliament.[37] On Friday, July 20, the commission held its first meeting in Kimberley. Immediately the chair announced that the commission was under government instructions to keep the hearings behind closed doors. A public outcry about company efforts to silence the truth resulted in the opening of the hearings.[38]

The hearing, now open, continued with testimony from William Erskine and from the assistant inspector of mines, William Hambly, both of whom were engineers. Erskine put it gently: Williams knew the inspectors, and he knew the rules. If Erskine had known about the accident that closed the No. 2 shaft, he would have closed the mine. Hambly said the same thing. The No. 1 shaft did not provide enough of an escape route for all the miners. The remaining Gem Shaft was known to be unsafe.[39]

Given the trust that Rhodes placed in Williams during the amalgamation of De Beers, the fire put the Californian in the difficult position of having to give a credible explanation for the accident. In his testimony, Williams described how the rail trolley, known as a "skip," derailed and blocked the newly opened No. 2 incline shaft. Contradicting the inspectors' recommendation, he went so far as to claim that No. 2 shaft was not fully disabled and that in a last resort, the ventilation shaft could be used as an escape. Shortly after Williams's decision to keep the mine open, a fire did break out, most likely in a cavern off one of the exploratory shafts, named the "Friggens Shaft," at the 500-foot level. The No. 1 and No. 2 shafts were upcasts, so the smoke rose, asphyxiating all miners above 500 feet. The miners at the 700-foot level were trapped, but they were not killed. The timbers in the No. 1 shaft burned up, closing the shaft completely; the No. 2 shaft did not have such bad damage, but it did have one cave-in that blocked it completely. Trapped miners had to climb up to the open pit through narrow shafts that were once used for exploration and that were now just used for ventilation. On the surface, unaware of the extent of the damage, Williams and a group of engineers and miners made heroic efforts to rescue 685 trapped miners. At first, they tried to pull men up from the 600-foot level by hauling a skip up the No. 1 shaft, but when the skip reached the 300-foot mark, the hauling wire overheated and snapped, plunging four men to their deaths. Most of the miners trapped below the 500-foot level took another route, escaping over the course of a day by climbing out of the mine through an exploratory shaft that was a downcast.[40]

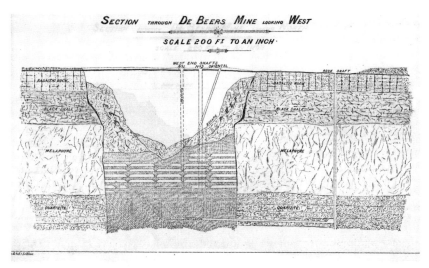

Map of the De Beers Mine at the Time of the Fire, Showing Shafts Sloping from the Edge, and Deep-Level Tunnels in the Blue Ground. De Beers Mining Company Annual Report of 1889.

During the commission hearings and a related coroner's inquest, Williams and Rhodes's other engineers were concerned to divert blame from the design of the mine and from their decisions about safety. Instead of taking some of the blame for themselves, the engineers scapegoated African miners. One of the assistant engineers under Williams, Joseph Gouldie, had helped to design the underground works in the De Beers Mine. In his testimony, he stated that he "considered De Beers underground works...the safest mine that I was in." He assessed the mine's risk favorably, while admitting that "smoking was allowed and natives might have matches." "Carefully watched," African miners were known to "carry about candles but not to light fires."[41] The "overman" who had worked three years below for De Beers, a Cornishman named William Tregonning, thought that the mine was "safe enough." He discounted the possibility that an old, disused forge was being used again near the Friggens Shaft, then mentioned that "in some places in the mine the timber is dry. In some parts of Friggens shaft it is dry. About the 500 it is dry." Another engineer, Grier, emphasized that the tragedy was caused by the timing of the fire and the skip accident. Additional shafts were already being dug—the "Rock Shaft" and the "Oriental Shaft" slated to open in several months—which gave miners even more avenues for escape. Crosby added that he did not anticipate both shafts becoming upcasts, a factor in the smoke killing the men in the mine's middle levels.[42] The foreman, Tregonning, described one problematic practice. "No fires are allowed in the mine," he told the commissioners, "but the K----rs sometimes make fires against orders."[43]

Concerned about the risks of an African workforce, the commission recalled the assistant mine inspector, William Hambly, who then said that ignoring rules underground could not be blamed on weak management. Instead, ignoring rules had to do with the stereotypical proclivities of African miners. Hambly was a Cornish engineer, with experience mining for tin, copper, and lead before coming to South Africa in 1885. Hambly testified that "I do not think that unskilled black labour should be used in underground works in these mines, because they don't know when there is danger, and they are naturally indifferent. They have made fires in the mine, and they require great watching to prevent their doing so. They are not allowed to make fires or to carry lights about. They are conducted from place to place by an overman. Every precaution is taken to prevent fire or any other accident.... The De Beers Mine is very dry and therefore the timbers become very dry and very inflammable. The wood chiefly used is pitch pine and deals [pine boards] in the shafts and tunnels. Ironwood is used for props and legs for sets of timbers in the drives."[44]

The management decision to use highly flammable wood as part of the mine's construction meant that miners had to be supervised carefully. African miners were led everywhere by white foremen, but blaming them was unlikely if Hambly proved his claim about the riskiness of African miners. Rhodes's plan for De Beers involved risky digging, deeper and deeper into the Kimberlite pipes. The underground mining was very costly; costs could be offset by importing unskilled and risky African labor. Rhodes's developing plan for railways and telegraphs stretching into the African interior planned to bring laborers to Kimberley in ways that were cheaper, quicker, and safer. This would squeeze the job prospects and salaries of arguably less risky white mineworkers, who had resisted Rhodes's monopolizing schemes for more than a decade. White miners like Tregonning and inspectors like Hambly had an interest in portraying African miners as unreliable.

Even with these contradictions, once the commission's arc turned toward blaming African miners, the narrative of the mine fire's origins began to fall into place. One miner, a white contractor named Harrison Lawson, speculated about risky African behavior around the Friggens Shaft. "The natives were allowed to go into the engine house and they used to go and lie down about there and smoke and have candles there. I suppose they must have left a candle there which caught the timbers."[45] More speculative testimony followed. The next day, Crosby recalled that on the night of the fire, "When I got to the top of Friggens's shaft I don't remember whether there were any natives there. There were no white men above. I knew that natives do lie about there." The tallyman, Thomas Lewis, described miners using "naked candles" in the vicinity of the intersection of the Friggens Shaft and the vertical shaft. Another tallyman, John Smith, testified that at five minutes before six o'clock, he passed near the entrance to the Friggens Shaft. "I saw some natives lying about up the top of that shaft as I passed. Some of them had open candles in their hands, and they had stuck candles in the ground. I did not see any candle in any dangerous position. They were natives who had come down for night work."[46]

As more white miners testified about the carelessness of African workers, it began to seem like the supervisors were culpable to some degree. One miner, Joseph Jones, testified: "I did not see any natives about there, nor did I notice any ran as we went. The natives are in the habit of going into the mine before their time and lying about there because it is a warm place. There is a steam pipe there. They have open candles there, and there is no one to look after them because their overseers have not yet come down. I think the natives must have left some small candles burning there when they went to their work." Supervisors pushed back. Crosby testified shortly afterwards. "Natives were allowed candles in De Beers Mine," he stated, "but not to light fires."[47] Foremen supervised African workers and told them when—and when not—to light lamps or tobacco pipes.

These precautions seemed sensible, but some white miners believed that it was not enough. One Cornish foreman, John Vingoe, described the mine's rules about where candles and lamps could be used and also mentioned the lack of a safety system. Water and hoses were available, but no instructions were given as to their use: "We have hoses underground, and we can turn water onto any part of the mine where there is wood in two minutes; we are not provided with extincteurs [extinguishers]. There is no system for putting out fires, nor any special instructions as to what is to be done in case of fire."[48]

Even with the evidence of poor design and poor management, Williams, the head engineer, and Erskine, the government inspector, were relieved of blame by the commissioners. One commissioner, Edward Judge, pronounced that "if I had only two shafts, and one became disabled and I expected to get it repaired within 24 hours I think I would risk keeping my men in the mines. An outbreak of fire is looked upon as a very unlikely contingency in a mine."[49] White inspectors, managers, and miners all avoided responsibility for the fire. While they were distancing themselves from the causes of the disaster, bodies, mostly African, continued to be carried up from the mine.[50]

It is difficult to locate African testimony, but several Black miners were brave enough to testify and to resist being made into scapegoats. A miner called "George" or "Juni" indicated that when the fire started, he was stationed near the entrance to the Friggens Shaft. He testified that "some one said there was fire, and then I and others ran up the three ladders with buckets to put it out. We came on the fire and found the bags round the pipes burning, but no wood was burning. I did not see what had set the bags alight. I saw no candle about. The pipes are covered all the way with sacking. The sacks are put on to prevent the pipes burning men going down the ladders." He described the scene of panic that followed, with "a rush for the ladders and the men trampled on one another." Then he returned to the causes of the fire. "None of the natives to whom I have spoken know how the fire originated. The natives are not in the habit of lying about the spot where the fire began, they hang about the blacksmith forge. The sacking that was burning would very easily catch fire. It was very dry from the heat of the pipe. A native going down with a candle could easily set it alight."[51]

Several more African miners testified with the help of the local court interpreter. One miner, a teenager with the racist nickname "Piccaninnie," described the scene of panic near the entrance to the Friggens Shaft. He claimed that "I did not go to the white man and light a candle before the fire." Instead, he told the commission that the miners already "had lights where we were." Another African miner, Philip Musa, said much the same thing. In his words, "The white men do not prevent us carrying candles about. The white men supply us with candles." Their supervisor, Thomas Lewis, and the engineer, Crosby, confirmed that they saw Piccaninnie ask for a light after, but not before, the fire. Crosby admitted that when he went down the Friggens Shaft, he saw the steam pipe covered with sacking, but he insisted that the design was not a problem. He assessed the risks of the situation and gave the miner a light. "I did not consider it at all dangerous to allow the boy to go up and down that shaft with a lighted candle. It is not to my knowledge that it is one of the principal duties of overmen and others to see that the natives do not carry candles and to prevent them carrying lighted candles. I can stand by it that I lit the boy's candle and quite innocently, too." As for the pipes that were wrapped in dry sacking, "A careless person might set fire to the sacking," according to Crosby, "but it would be carelessness."[52] Talk of miner carelessness was the classic way for management to shift blame from themselves to workmen.

The testimony continued in this vein, with skilled white employees blaming less skilled African miners, but with the white employees indirectly raising concerns about the mine's design. On Saturday, June 28, the company's mechanical engineer, Thomas Andrews, was testifying about the system of hoses that were put in place to prevent engine fires, either in the head gear or in the engine houses below ground. When it came to the mine itself, he said that "there was no provision for putting out fire in the mine as we never thought of fire as a source of danger." The African miners had testified that the fire started in the sacking that had been wrapped around the pipes near the Friggens Shaft. Andrews added a key speculation: "It is quite possible that natives, seeing that I had put sacking round pipes elsewhere in the mine, may have put sacking for their own protection round the pipe. Twill sacking would be highly inflammable." He added that in the absence of white workers, "the fire may have arisen from the natives lying about there smoking."[53]

One of the least skilled white workers, a Cornish lamp-trimmer named Bernard Curgenven, had the job of walking along with African miners as they moved from the searching room, at the head of the mine, down to the 500-foot level, where he stood at a gate, lighting candles and putting them into lanterns, until a group of workers needed to be escorted back up. All workers going up the shaft had to show him a pass. His station was 100 feet from the Friggens Shaft where he had a good standpoint for watching activity nearby. On cold July nights, Curgenven faced a problem. "The natives for night duty begin coming down in the mine about half past 12 and keep on coming down all the afternoon. They say they come down because it is cold in the compound. They scatter all about the mine and do congregate about the top of Friggens' shaft, although it is not allowed. The overman's assistant and I have driven them away from there frequently." At 4:30, just before the fire, he left his station to go up, and "fixed the candle on the lantern" beforehand. He observed several African miners and chased them up. As for lighting in the shaft, it was dark. "If I were going down," he claimed, "I should take a candle."[54] Several more of the less-skilled white workers backed up Curgenven. One of them, Martin Dever, mentioned that "the natives used to lie about at the top of Friggens' shaft, and I used to clear them away from there. They had short stumps of candles which they would stick about in the timber there. There was no deal. It was Colonial timber which would not easily burn." Candles were impossible to carry lit through the Friggens's shaft, because the downward draught blew too strongly.[55]

While Kimberley waited for the findings of the commission to be made public, on July 31, the ministers of Kimberley provided a mass burial service for the African mineworkers who died in the fire. The company identified the bodies and provided a list of 163 names that was published in the newspapers two days later. For the most part, the names of the workers were known—only three were labeled "unknown"—and their geographic origins were listed, with half coming from Basutoland and the rest coming from Mozambique or the Cape Colony. Most names seemed authentic, but others had nicknames. There were four "Piccaninnies" and several that were more inventive, such as Parafine, after the lamp oil, and Pasop, Afrikaans for "Watch it!"[56] On July 31, the body of the last African miner was buried. On the next day, August 1, the De Beers Consolidated Mines Company began to operate as one fully unified enterprise.

With a disaster interfering in the De Beers Mine's productivity, and with questions reported in the press about the mine's design, the shareholders of the new De Beers Consolidated Mines Company held a public meeting. The *Independent* reported "a large attendance," including most of the directors. Rhodes arrived in Kimberley and took the president's chair, aiming to conduct business as usual. He spoke at length about the final details of the merger, which involved De Beers paying the Central Diamond Mining Company £120,000 for 7,000 shares. Rhodes was present and admitted that this was more than he wanted to pay for the final acquisitions but indicated that "other interests came into play, and he gave way." The negotiations involved assigning value to the Central's machinery. It appears that Rhodes ceded money to the owners of the Central, to avoid delay. The De Beers shareholders showed their support with a motion that was made, seconded, "and carried unanimously and with acclamation." Rhodes moved on to deny claims of holding back from the market large parcels of diamonds, then passed over the disaster quickly, reassuring the audience that the miners' families were receiving "ample compensation" and that an insurance fund was going to be established soon.[57] The technical and managerial problems of the fire were not even mentioned.

It fell to others to continue the discussion of the mine fire's origins. A week later, Hambly spoke about the risks of employing unskilled African labor and blamed the company for not training them properly. "I am of opinion that native labour should not be employed in any chambers or stopes in those mines because dangers such as broken ground and ground seeming detached from the reefs that the boys from want of a practical knowledge of mining cannot detect or realize the dangers in which they are placed. The same remarks will apply to the same class of labour in sinking winzes, passes, or shafts or in putting up rises." He believed that "the native might be educated in mining" but that "no native should be appointed to any place such as I first mentioned unless the Manager of the Company was convinced in his judgment that he (the native) was capable of taking the work in hand, and that he (the Manager) was prepared to hold himself responsible for the natives' actions."[58]

The mine manager did not see it that way. Gardner Williams blamed the fire on the African workers who loitered near the shaft entrances during shift changes, times when supervision was lax. Williams and other white miners may have felt uncomfortable with loitering, a classic, passive, and often imagined form of rebellion against the race-based restrictions on underground activity. The official commission agreed with Williams but only to a limited extent. The commissioners wrote that it was likely that the African miners, who "used to lie about the top of Friggens' shaft," while "smoking or sleeping but always with lighted candles near them," somehow ignited the dry timber supports.[59] The commissioners noted that there were problems with the design of the mine. They noted the inadequacy of firefighting equipment and noted another design flaw—Rule 16 required "winding shafts"—shafts with cables pulling skips—to have enough room for ladderways. And they pointed out that if Williams had followed the rules correctly, he would have reported the accident to the inspector within twenty-four hours and he would have closed the mine, pending a discussion with the inspector.[60]

The commissioners struck a balance between miners' carelessness and the need for miners to carry lights "owing to insufficient fixed lights"—a design flaw. The commissioners also explained why workers liked to spend extra time down the shaft in the winter. They wrote, "We are told that the natives for the night shift were in the habit of going down into the mine early in the afternoon, because it was warmer there than in the compound."[61] The investigation of the mine fire revealed a key oversight by De Beers's engineers when they designed and built the compound: the lack of warmth during the winter months of July and August, when nighttime temperatures in Kimberley can fall below freezing. Cold miners may have been sneaking down into the shaft and camping out to keep warm. Cheap treatment of miners may have been an indirect cause of the fire.

How much did Crosby, Williams, and the other De Beers engineers really know about workplace practices? The compounds were associated with surveillance and regulation, but work in the mine's shafts, tunnels, and stopes afforded the miners relative freedom from supervision.[62] Apologists for imperialism often cited the benefits that came from the spread of Western notions of freedom, which were later taken up by anti-imperialist political movements that used Western ideas to advocate for their own liberty. In the case of the De Beers Mine fire, it is worth considering another type of freedom. Deep in the heart of Rhodes's most important moneymaking enterprise, there was a freedom that bordered on unruliness. It appears that hundreds of feet below the ground, a miner had a free moment, ignored the rules, and lit a match. A decision that was trivial, contingent, and free set on fire a costly and strategic piece of imperialist infrastructure.[63]

Rhodes's vision for a white-dominated Southern Africa rested on the regimented productivity of African mineworkers. His planning extended to places that most people's eyes did not see, the mine tunnels, where he probably never even ventured himself. Getting diamonds out of the ground was intended to pay for future investments in the gold fields to the north as well as expansion into South-Central Africa, both of which interested Rhodes greatly in the late 1880s. In July 1888, the only obstacle was a lawsuit by shareholders of the Central Company, who objected to the new company's operational latitude. They settled their suit after Rhodes offered them a larger payout. In 1889, with the lawsuit settled and the purchase of all four mines complete, De Beers Consolidated began operations under the overall management of Gardner Williams. Starting in those years, Rhodes's involvement in politics made it difficult for him to return to Kimberley for board meetings. During those absences, Rhodes appointed Williams to be his stand-in as life governor.

To keep investors investing and to keep the vision alive, the causes of the disaster were elided soon after the commission of enquiry made its report. Nearly a year after the disaster, on July 20, 1889, De Beers Consolidated Mines, Limited, had its first annual meeting. Rhodes and two other life directors, Beit and Stow, did not attend. Rhodes had business in England, allowing him to maintain his silence about the disaster. The chairing of the De Beers annual meeting was done by the only available life director, Rhodes's rival and new partner, the colorful showman Barney Barnato. He was pleased to announce that in the previous year, in spite of the fire and all the repairs, De Beers had still turned a profit of £448,000. He paid tribute to the miners who died and to their rescuers, including Williams, "a gentleman to whom I believe no person can attach the least blame." "That calamity," concluded Barnato, "was an act of God."[64] Attributing a disaster to God had been done many times before. It was a way of shifting blame away from human decisions, diminishing the responsibility of designers, owners, and regulators. The tensions inherent in Rhodes's technopolitical achievements were, in the end, covered up by theology.[65]

Instead of taking any responsibility for the fire, Williams speculated, many years later, that if the Friggens Shaft was burning, "It is probable that one of the native miners had sneaked off to the disused engine room on the 500-foot level, and placed a lighted candle so carelessly that the flame ignited the timbers, perhaps while the lazy savage was snoring on the floor." Williams admitted that "the precise cause of the fire was, however, never determined...."[66] His claim that "a lazy savage" started the fire is mildly surprising. He may have held the standard stereotypes about African mineworkers, but he also described African miners as industrious. In his book *The Diamond Mines of South Africa*, he wrote that "those who have travelled through the native centres, or have seen the negroes loitering about the towns, and have thought them lazy, indolent, beer-drinking beings, should visit the diamond mines... and they will get a new impression of the working capacity of these... uniformly active and industrious men... with nearly as much skill as most European miners."[67]

Given Williams's positive impressions of African miners, why did he blame the 1888 mine fire on a "lazy savage"? It might simply be dismissed as the racial remark of an engineer who was a man of his times, defending his reputation by blaming an unknown stranger whose precise identity and actions could not be determined. Several months before the fire, in the 1888 annual report, Williams had written that "there are fewer accidents under the present [underground] system than there were in the open workings. A very large majority of the accidents in the mine are due either to the carelessness or stupidity of the natives themselves."[68] Whatever "real" views Williams might have had of African workers, at key moments he had to persuade Rhodes and De Beers's investors that the mine was safe. He chose to do so in a way that tended to confirm their racial stereotypes.

When Williams considered a possible racial explanation of the fire, he faced a double paradox. The mines were going to bankroll the extension of settler colonialism. Rhodes's vision was based on treating African people as racially inferior, yet to agree with white miners that Africans were inferior, risky workers might suggest that importing them was a bad idea, even if it helped De Beers save money. The alternative explanation—that the mine was systematically unsafe—was an even less palatable explanation from the standpoint of Rhodes and his investors. Historians of South Africa have given the mine fire little more than a glance, yet it is an important part of the story of the development of infrastructure under Cecil Rhodes. Williams's narrative of miner carelessness was a way to make the disaster seem to have been the outcome of contingencies, rather than the outcome of significant problems in design and management.

9

Connecting a Country

RHODES HAS RECEIVED credit for playing an important role in the amalgamation of the diamond mines. He was bolstered by energetic partners and financiers, some of whom were former rivals. While finishing the negotiations surrounding amalgamation, Rhodes turned to some family business. His father, Francis William, had inherited properties totaling twelve acres in Dalston, a London suburb. When Francis William died in 1878, the holdings in Dalston were divided equally among Rhodes and his siblings. In October 1888, Cecil used his fortune to buy out all of them.[1] He also updated his will. The most recent will left his entire fortune to Neville Pickering. The new will left 2,000 shares to his siblings, to be divided equally. The shares, together with the payments for the property, were intended to provide the siblings with greater financial security. The rest of Rhodes's fortune was willed to Natty Rothschild, with directions for him to found a society of pro-Empire scholars along the lines of the Confession of 1877.

Rhodes managed his network of mine owners and financiers by sending flurries of telegrams and letters, all the while maintaining a high level of engagement with politicians at the Cape. The nature of his political engagement was changing. Before the mid-1880s his business affairs and his political efforts put him into closest contact with associates in England as well as English-speaking South Africans. When he became interested in the Witwatersrand's gold and in developing a colony of settlement to the North, he extended his relationships with Afrikaners. Closer relations would help to smooth the Road to the North and to ensure the profitability of mining in the Transvaal.

In February 1887, Rudd and Rhodes formed their Witwatersrand gold-mining claims into the company called Gold Fields of South Africa. Initially Gold Fields was not very successful. Historians and biographers have speculated that Rhodes was simply too busy with politics and with the amalgamation of the diamond mines to pay sufficient attention to the gold mines. It is also possible that Rhodes simply made ill-advised decisions in a business that he did not yet understand. Other Kimberley mine owners fared much better on the Witwatersrand. Robinson was a spectacular success. Porgès did well, too, by backing Beit, Hermann Eckstein, and James B. Taylor. Barney Barnato also made purchases that paid. Gold Fields had less success and even distanced itself from some claims by leasing them to other owners. Over the objections of some stockholders, Rhodes and Rudd then used Gold Fields funds to invest in De Beers and in a new exploration company, the British South Africa Company (BSAC), that Rhodes intended to use in developing territories and mining interests to the north.[2]

Making inroads in the north required Rhodes to engage more extensively with Afrikaner politicians in both Pretoria and Cape Town. Rhodes himself never learned to speak Afrikaans very well, nor did he immerse himself in Afrikaner culture, but the more time he spent in Cape Town and the nearby wine district of the Western Cape, the more he emulated the outlook of the owners. Rhodes secured support for his plan to control the Road to the North by working with the leader of the Afrikaner Bond, J. H. Hofmeyr, to protect Cape agriculture.

Through the alliance of Rhodes and Hofmeyr, the agricultural landscape of the Western Cape and the efforts of Afrikaners to protect their culture became closely linked to the industrial landscape of Kimberley and, ultimately, to the industrial landscape of the Witwatersrand and to rural areas throughout South Africa, as well as to the settler colony Rhodes had in view north of the Limpopo. On the surface these regions appear to be very different, but in the eyes of Rhodes, the traditional rural landscape and the new industrial landscape were all of a piece, as in Ruskin's formulation. The diamond mines paid for political influence, northern exploration, and white settlement. New laws set back the rights of African people, who were to be put to work in mines and on farms. Rhodes, an Englishman, worked with various Britons and Afrikaners to extend the racial discrimination of the pre-British Dutch Cape and the Boer republics to the rest of the country and beyond.

The reintroduction of racially discriminatory legislation did not originate with Rhodes. Legal discrimination was advocated by other prominent figures during the 1870s. Most famously, racist policies were suggested by the historian James Anthony Froude during his time as a Colonial Office adviser in South Africa. Froude openly admired the Boer republics' discriminatory practices, which he expressed in the context of increasing support for imperialism during Disraeli's Conservative prime ministership. The Cape government's gun-control law, the Peace Preservation Act of 1878, was the first openly discriminatory law. Its most prominent backers were the governor, Bartle Frere, and his prime minister, Gordon Sprigg. In his first years as a member of the House of Assembly, Rhodes saw for himself the problems of enforcing that law when it was applied to Basutoland. Nonetheless his partnership with the Afrikaner Bond in securing the Road to the North put pressure on him to support the rest of their discriminatory agenda. This did not involve much mental effort for Rhodes, who arrived in South Africa with many of the same racial attitudes as his English contemporaries. Now Rhodes joined forces with Afrikaners whose racial attitudes had emerged in the contexts of Cape slavery and frontier dispossession.

There were still key differences between Rhodes and Hofmeyr. The Afrikaner Bond hoped for greater cultural independence from Britain, preserving political ties out of necessity, while Rhodes hoped for a white-dominated colony of settlement that was strongly part of the British Empire. In between these positions there was plenty of room for Rhodes and Hofmeyr to maneuver. Rhodes avoided support for Afrikaner independence and steered clear of politically sensitive issues, such as a proposed new flag and the use of the Dutch and Afrikaans languages in official business. There was also a key point of tension over railways. The Cape Dutch favored the creation of a robust network of rails around the Cape's rural areas, which contrasted with Rhodes and his far-reaching plans. Despite some differences, Rhodes did support the Bond on some issues that contradicted his values. Rhodes was skeptical about religion, but he endorsed proposals by Afrikaner religious conservatives to enforce the sabbath, and he supported their desire for separate religious schools. Rhodes leaned toward free trade, yet he spoke in favor of tariffs that protected the Western Cape's vineyards and grain farms. To curry favor with the Bond, he supported irrigation schemes that benefited the Western Cape. And Rhodes the industrialist opposed state support for industries that might draw laborers away from the farms of the Cape Dutch gentry.

The key area of cooperation between Rhodes and Hofmeyr had to do with race. They were both keen on rolling back the Cape Colony's franchise, which was ostensibly race-blind, one of the pillars of the old colonial liberalism. In 1853 the franchise was set at the ownership of £25 of property; income of £50; or £25 in income plus paid room and board. Traditional liberals were united in the belief that Africans could be "civilized" by encouraging them to adopt European farming, build European-style houses, and wear European-style clothing. The power of African chiefs might as well be attenuated, according to Cape liberalism, and it was hoped that most African people would one day become full-fledged citizens and qualify for the £25 franchise. There were signs that this notion of progress was unfolding. From 1853 up until the end of the 1870s, more territory was added to the colony in the Eastern Cape, with its sizeable population. Many African farmers were prospering and qualifying to vote. Already African voters constituted a significant minority in many districts, and white candidates had to address their concerns. The Cape Dutch took this as a direct threat to their system of racial domination. Significant numbers of English-speaking politicians were uneasy with it, too. Racism formed the basis of collaboration between Rhodes and Hofmeyr on this key issue of the franchise. They hoped to take away the franchise from African and mixed-race people at the Cape.[3]

The Cape franchise was vulnerable to race-based modifications, even though any change in the law needed to give the appearance of being race-blind to win approval from the secretary of state for the colonies in London. A reconsideration of the franchise began in 1885, when the Cape Colony incorporated the Transkei and its large African population. The Afrikaner Bond held a congress in early 1886, when the party endorsed raising the property qualification; introducing a literacy test; requiring voters to establish that they were "men of substance"; and disenfranchising those holding land under communal tenure. One of the most racist of the English-speaking members of the Cape Parliament, Thomas Upington, proposed that the Transkei be given

The Houses of Parliament, Cape Town, Opened in 1884. Wellcome Collection.

two seats in the House of Assembly. One of the two members would be elected by white men according to the old £25 qualification and African men who owned £500 worth of property under individual tenure. The other member would be elected by a "Native Elective Council," which would be voted on by all men who paid the hut tax. Hofmeyr and the Bondsmen supported this bill, which was discussed on the floor of the House of Assembly in June 1886. Traditional liberals like Merriman excoriated the bill, arguing that disenfranchising so many African property owners might turn them against the colony. Rhodes took a stand against his friend Merriman and even against Upington. He did not want any Transkei Africans to be given the franchise, even under Upington's restrictive conditions. At that time, Rhodes also made the argument that the Cape franchise could be based solely on literacy tests, an idea that did not attract followers. It was too strong for the Cape Parliament, even by the standards of the day. Upington's bill also had to be withdrawn for lack of enough support.[4]

The 1886 debates over a racially exclusive franchise laid the groundwork for racially biased legislation to pass in 1887. The government was then being led again by Gordon Sprigg, who had the support of the Bond. Sprigg devised a revision of the franchise that did not contain discriminatory language yet was discriminatory in application. This was the same strategy that he had pursued ten years earlier, during his previous term as prime minister, when he steered the Peace Preservation Act through the Cape Parliament. In 1887 Sprigg's proposed restriction of the franchise was called the Parliamentary Voters' Registration Bill. It was a much simpler revision to the franchise than the one supported by Upington the previous year. Many African people in the Eastern Cape owned land in common with their relatives. Some owned some parcels of land communally and other parcels of land individually. White colonists only owned land individually. Sprigg proposed that communal landowners should not be given the vote. With such a rule, fewer African men would qualify to vote. It was claimed that this was a constitutional issue, but it was in fact a thinly disguised effort to disenfranchise more African men and to reduce their representation in the House of Assembly.[5]

The Voters' Registration Bill of 1887 became highly controversial. Resistance to the measure helped to coalesce members of the House of Assembly who held more liberal views, including Merriman and J. W. Sauer, a practicing attorney and Dr. Hans Sauer's brother. Sauer defended the old Cape constitution by resisting the discriminatory initiatives. Sauer and Merriman were joined by several talented young English-speakers who were also standing against the rising tide of racial discrimination. James Rose Innes was an attorney from the Eastern Cape who won election to the House of Assembly thanks to the support of Xhosa voters. One of Innes's key supporters was John Tengo Jabavu, an Mfengu man who was the editor of the Eastern Cape's bilingual Xhosa-English newspaper, *Imvo Zabantsundu*, which translates roughly as "Black Opinion." Jabavu and Innes were joined by the brother of novelist Olive Schreiner, Will Schreiner, who was then working as the attorney advising the Cape Parliament about drafting laws. The Cape liberal opposition spoke scathingly about the proposed changes to the franchise. Jabavu wrote editorials against the Parliamentary Voters' Registration Bill, calling it the "natives disrepresentation bill." Merriman called the bill a "miserable sham" that should be opposed on the grounds of liberty, justice, and expediency. Innes was alarmed at the prospect of magistrates being empowered to decide which Africans could vote and called Sprigg, Rhodes, Upington, and the Bond "extreme and retrogressive."[6]

Rhodes spoke in favor of passage. Most of the bill's supporters still wrestled with constitutional issues rather than racial issues, perhaps out of respect for the humanitarian lobby or the Colonial Office. Rhodes had no such qualms. He openly discussed how the disenfranchisement of Africans was an important part of his plan to populate the subcontinent with European settlers. On June 23, 1887, he made a speech that pandered to white South Africans who supported restrictions, including the Bondsmen, the Boers of the two republics, and the colonists in Natal. "I prefer to call a spade a spade," said Rhodes, taking a dig at Sprigg and Upington. The ends justified the means, even unconstitutional means. Racially discriminatory legislation, then known as "class legislation," should be approved as part of a quasi-feudal order in which the white minority were to be lords. Rhodes continued:

> Does this House think it is right that men in a state of pure barbarism should have the franchise and vote? Either you have to receive them on an equal footing as citizens, or to call them a subject race. Well, I have made up my mind that there must be class legislation, that there must be Pass Laws, and Peace Preservation Acts, and that we have got to treat natives, where they are in a state of barbarism, in a different way to ourselves. We are to be lords over them.... The native is to be treated as a child and denied the franchise.... Why should we not settle all these differences between Dutch and English? I offer to the opposite benches the pomegranate; I ask you to clear away all grievances between me and you, and the native question is the greatest.... Does the House think for one moment that the Republics of the Transvaal

and the Free State would join with the Colony on its present native franchise? We must adopt a system of despotism, such as works so well in India, in our relations with the barbarians of South Africa.[7]

Rhodes made himself clear: racial discrimination was not only necessary; it would help to bring about regional unity. When constitutional concerns were set aside and the bill was voted into law, the Cape Colony took an important step toward instituting racial discrimination by revising ideas about geography. It is interesting to note, though, a recent study by historians Farai Nyika and Johan Fourie, who examined the statistical impact of efforts to restrict the Cape franchise. They found that restrictive laws did not reduce the numbers of voters as much as the legislators may have intended, possibly because the debates reached the ears of eligible, disengaged voters, who then registered themselves as an act of resistance.[8]

While working out a more restrictive racial order, Cecil Rhodes almost always supported the interests and outlook of the Afrikaner Bond. The members of the Bond were content to keep the Western Cape winelands organized along quasi-feudal lines and to support the discriminatory policies of the Boer republics. The Bond's ideology was racist in a conservative way; Rhodes was racist in a way that was characteristic of nineteenth-century progressive imperialists, who advocated the transformation of extensive territorial space by the movement of white settlers and their material practices. Rhodes hoped that the "open spaces of South Africa" would be populated with more settlers who would spread British notions of civilization, especially individual land tenure, to African "barbarians." Implicit in this model is the progressive notion that barbarians will become civilized eventually. The timeline was not clear. Would this take years, decades, or centuries?

The alliance between Rhodes and the Bond involved compromises. Rhodes generally favored free trade, but to gain the support of Bondsmen, Rhodes consistently supported customs legislation that protected the Afrikaner wine and grain farmers of the Western Cape. Afrikaner farmers did have hesitations about progressive industrialization, but the prospect of gaining new markets on the Witwatersrand persuaded the Bond to support Rhodes's scheme to connect South Africa with railways. The railway reached Kimberley in 1885, to much celebration. Now Rhodes hoped that the government would support the extension of the railway beyond the Cape, into the Orange Free State, the Transvaal, and Natal. Rhodes hoped to use the railway as the basis of a Southern African customs union, which was a way to maximize free trade within a region while still protecting members of the Afrikaner Bond as much as possible from competition. Free trade and free movement among the subcontinent's four principal states were intended to deliver prosperity and to further the cause of white unity.

Rhodes proposed a clever way for the railways to deliver his plan. The Western Line of the railroad was reaching from Cape Town to Kimberley, while a Midlands Line connected Port Alfred and Port Elizabeth, the principal ports of the Eastern Cape, to Grahamstown and the interior. In 1884, the Midlands Line reached a junction with the Western Line at De Aar, making it possible for trade from Port Elizabeth and Cape Town to reach Kimberley, where the first train arrived in 1885. The next intended route led from Kimberley across the border of the Orange Free State to Bloemfontein. From there, the railway could be built to run northward, across the border of the Transvaal to reach the booming mining town developing at Johannesburg.

There were several problems with Rhodes's plan for unifying South Africa with a railway network. The Cape Colony, the Orange Free State, and the South African Republic collected customs duties at points of entry. Any loss of customs revenue had to be offset. But the major obstacle standing in the way of a united South African railway was that the Transvaal was already constructing a railroad from Pretoria due east to Lourenço Marques, on Delagoa Bay in Portuguese Mozambique. Not only was this the shortest distance from the Witwatersrand to a port, but the Transvaal's leader, Paul Kruger, also saw the line to Delagoa Bay as the best guarantee for his country's independence. "Every railway that approaches me," said Kruger, "I look upon as an enemy, on whatever side it comes. I must have my Delagoa Bay line first, and then the other lines may come."[9] As far as Kruger was concerned, it seemed better to depend on a line through the minimally administered Portuguese territory than a line connected to the British colonies at the Cape or Natal.

Rhodes, working at cross-purposes to Kruger, introduced a clever plan to the floor of the House of Assembly in 1886. Rhodes argued: "If the Delagoa Bay Railway were carried out, the Union of South Africa would be indefinitely deferred." Rhodes proposed the immediate construction of a government railway from Kimberley to Pretoria: "If that is not done this session it will be too late; the interests of the Transvaal will be turned towards Delagoa Bay, and their commerce will go with their interests," he urged. "From being connected in commerce union will come, and that is the only way in which it can come."[10] The Bond supported the idea, but in Pretoria, it did not seem fair that the ports of the Cape Colony would still be able to collect duties on imports that were shipped by rail to the landlocked Boer republics, which would then not be able to collect duties. Negotiations dragged on into

1889. In that year, the Cape reached a customs union agreement with the Orange Free State but not with the Transvaal and Natal, which began talks toward their own separate customs agreement. By that time, it was hard for the Cape Parliament to see the agreement with the Free State as a victory—in 1889 the two Boer republics signed a defensive military alliance.[11] Even so, the railroads were so beneficial for farming and mining that within a few years the Boer republics allowed the Cape to build railroads into their territory. It was an unusual case of a state-owned railroad building infrastructure in what was, technically speaking, two other countries. The Cape Colony bankrolled the effort. From 1886 to 1889, under Gordon Sprigg's leadership, the Cape government spent an average of 13.7 million pounds per year, necessitating heavy borrowing.[12]

Rhodes believed that the economic benefits of a line from Kimberley to Johannesburg were clear. In his speeches, Rhodes discussed the importance of the growing trade in gold, as one might expect, but he also discussed the importance of the rails carrying coal. Coal fields were developing in the Transvaal that could supply Kimberley. Farmers and merchants from around South Africa were likely to benefit from easier access to new markets. Bondsmen who invested in coal mining in the Eastern Cape's Stormberg Range might lose out economically if Kimberley stopped buying their coal, but Rhodes said they should think in a more public-spirited way about mobility. "I would put it to the Bond members that they ought, above all things, to regard South Africa as a whole," urged Rhodes. "I feel that the present is a golden opportunity that may not soon recur."[13]

The debt raised concerns, but the results of the construction were spectacular. In 1888 the decision was made to extend the Midland Line. It already ran from Port Elizabeth to Colesberg, twenty-five miles west of the Orange River ford at Norvalspont, so named because people forded it by riding a pont—a pontoon craft attached to a wire that was pulled back and forth by horses turning large wheels. A bridge was built over the river, and the line reached Bloemfontein by 1890. Construction began on a second line from the Eastern Cape town of Springfontein that crossed the Orange River at Bethulie, site of a spectacular bridge. Meanwhile, starting in 1891 the main line was built from Bloemfontein to the Vaal River crossing point at Viljoensdrif, the border of the Transvaal. Kruger was still keen to complete the railway from Johannesburg to Delagoa Bay, but the Transvaal was still short of money. In exchange for the Cape contributing to the cost of the Delagoa Bay railroad, Kruger allowed the Cape to build the line from Viljoensdrif to Johannesburg. It was completed in September 1892.[14]

The opening of the rail link to Johannesburg was a major step toward unifying the economies of South Africa. As Rhodes became involved in this ambitious political and technical project, he needed to engage builders who had more experience with the technologies in question. One of the most interesting people in Rhodes's network was James Sivewright, the Cape's expert in telegraphs who was also involved in railroads and utilities. Born in 1848, Sivewright was educated at the University of Aberdeen and worked in the British government's telegraph service during the early 1870s. In 1878 he moved to the Cape, where he served as the general manager of telegraphs from 1878 to 1885. He received an award for his services during the Anglo-Zulu War and was recognized for his ambitious plans for a network of telegraphs. One major plan involved a Cape-to-Cairo telegraph, which was superseded in 1879 with the opening of the undersea cable from Durban to Aden. Afterwards Sivewright focused on local matters. He unified the telegraph services of the Cape Colony and Natal under his own leadership, at a time when the project of confederation was being taken off the table. He pursued telegraph connections in the Boer republics, too.[15]

Sivewright was known as a technician and as a schemer. By the early 1880s, the revenues of the telegraph service were declining, and he started to pursue other opportunities. In 1883, he became a member of the Afrikaner Bond, an unusual move for an anglophone but a good move for building the credibility of his business ventures. In 1885 he was elected to the Cape's House of Assembly as a Bondsman. Sivewright became involved in financial speculation over telegraph companies and became an entrepreneur in Johannesburg at the exact moment when the gold boom began. He must have known Rhodes from Cape politics in the 1880s, but the first record of a meeting comes from Kimberley in 1887, when Sivewright dined with Rhodes and bought shares of De Beers. Sivewright was still the leading technical consultant for telegraphs in Southern Africa and may have hoped for a contract to run cables along railway tracks under Rhodes's influence. Sivewright may have also raised the fact that he was working for a railway company that hoped to build lines connecting the Cape's ports with Kimberley and the Witwatersrand.[16]

Like Rhodes, Sivewright managed and invested in many different types of businesses. Like Rhodes, he mixed business with politics. And like Rhodes, his involvement in the details of business and politics expressed a wider technical and political outlook. Both men believed that settler colonies had the potential to govern themselves while maintaining ties to Britain. Rhodes tended to emphasize imperial ties more than Sivewright, who leaned more toward local autonomy. That difference was significant, but they both believed that technologies were important for establishing white rule. In 1916, just before he died, Sivewright published an essay in a magazine, *The African World*, that summed up his thoughts on settler colonialism:

> The ideal of empire was a collection of free, self-governing States... honourably bound to respect the local internal independence of their neighbors, and to regard that as sacred as they would their own, but all of them bound together by ties of common interests, and by the need for a common defense—a collection of States where the sword and the rifle as instruments of government had to make way for steam and electricity, and where the railway and the telegraph were welding all the component parts into one mighty whole.[17]

Sivewright and Rhodes worked together to advance this kind of thinking in South Africa. Their collaboration reached its highest point during the negotiations over the Transvaal railroads in 1891 and 1892. When Sivewright achieved success, he telegraphed Rhodes triumphantly, "You rest satisfied there is nothing which your greatest enemy could possibly object to."[18]

Sivewright, like Hofmeyr and other Bondsmen, needed to be treated well if Rhodes was to enjoy success beyond the Limpopo. Geographically speaking, the railway could either go through the South African Republic or run to the west of it, along the Road to the North and through the Bechuanaland Protectorate. Even if the railway skirted to the west of the Transvaal, good relations with the Boer republics were still important. The Afrikaner Bond could help. Rhodes also had to manage officials of the imperial government who saw South African developments in the context of international politics. The discovery of gold in the Transvaal catapulted the frontier republic to international importance.

Three European powers were becoming more interested in Southern Africa. The Portuguese were beginning to imagine that they could govern all Central Africa, from Angola on the Atlantic Ocean to Mozambique on the Indian Ocean, even though they did not have the army and navy to back up such hopes. And now, into the mix, came a newly unified Germany, with territorial ambitions of its own. The British government acceded to German claims in South-West Africa, today called Namibia. The decision was controversial at the Cape, which also had claims to ownership. In 1891, Rhodes even employed an expert to survey the mining potential of South-West Africa and decided not to become involved in the country.[19] Farther north, the Belgian

King Leopold's so-called Congo Free State was grasping the interior of Central Africa. In Nyasaland, there was enough of a British presence to warrant a claim of "effective occupation," the term used at the Berlin Conference of 1884–1885 to denote that a European country had signed treaties with indigenous rulers and installed an administration with a police force. The Liberal government of Gladstone and the Conservative government of Salisbury were wary of extensive involvement in such a conflict-ridden territory as Nyasaland, even though it occupied a key position on the proposed Cape-to-Cairo connection by rail or telegraph.[20]

It was in the context of German expansionism, conflicts in Nyasaland, and Portuguese ideas about a territory running from one coast to the other that the British governor and high commissioner, Robinson, considered Edward Maund's report about his visit to Lobengula, the ruler of the Ndebele. True to the stereotypes formed by previous travelers, Maund reported that Ndebele territory stretched from the Limpopo to the Zambezi River. He mentioned the area's wealth but had little to say about the Shona people who lived there. Maund reported that he heard tales of ancient gold diggings and that he "knew of no country better adapted for European colonization." According to Maund, Lobengula could be persuaded to accept British protection against the Boers. Maund believed that Ndebele forces were weak and estimated that they could be defeated by 1,500 British cavalrymen.[21]

In October 1885, Maund and his report reached the Colonial Office in London. While in London, Maund even met with Rhodes again to discuss opportunities to the north of the Limpopo. Rhodes seized the moment to publicize his own emerging vision for Southern Africa. It was quite different from the traditional humanitarian imperialist vision that Charles Warren was publicizing on his simultaneous visit to London. On the same day that *The Times* reported on a speech by Warren and the responses of Barkly and Maund, the Empire's leading newspaper also published a long letter by Rhodes. The letter detailed Rhodes's complaints about Warren, who had been criticized by Robinson for disregarding instructions and for alienating Boer settlers. Rhodes asked, "Are we to set party against party and [the British] race against [the Dutch] race? Is tribal animosity to be our ruling feature, as it is that of our savage neighbours?" Complex relations between and within African and Boer states were thus reduced to "us and them" formulations and labeled "tribal animosity."[22]

In his letter to the *Times*, Rhodes delineated his emerging ideas for colonization in the north. This was his debut on the stage of public opinion in Britain. He urged cordial relations between Britons and Boers and stoked fears of German intervention, writing, "It must not be forgotten that we are no longer the only powerful European Power with territories in this part of Africa, and it was possible for the German Empire, by extension through Damaraland and Lake N'gami, to cut off our settlements." German imperialism and the profit motive justified the extension of the Bechuanaland Protectorate all the way through Ndebele and Shona territories to the Zambezi, to incorporate much of modern-day Zimbabwe. Beyond that boundary, more markets in Central Africa could be tapped.[23]

In his letter to the *Times*, Rhodes argued that prospects for Mashonaland were especially attractive. "Within the territorial limits of Lobengula, the Matabele King, and subject to his jurisdiction, lies Mashonaland." Thus were the complexities of Ndebele–Shona political relations made understandable for a British audience. "Of the capabilities of this country there can be no question." He then described his vision for the territory:

> It has been frequently traversed by reliable explorers and is known to have pastoral resources and mineral wealth such as do not exist in any other portion of Africa, south of the Zambezi. It is peculiarly favoured as to climate, for it is situated on a high plateau, and is free, over a large portion of its extent, from the malarious influences which render the coast districts on both sides of the continent so dangerous to European life. The reports of recent explorers state that the country contains numerous quartz reefs with exceedingly rich auriferous indications, and their information is supported by the old Portuguese records of the 16th century, which relate that at that date large quantities of gold were obtained from the mines worked in this district, amounting, in one year, to a sum, reckoned in our currency, of nearly three millions sterling.[24]

Rhodes had similarly grand plans for the lands north of the Zambezi River, in what is today Zambia and the Great Lakes region, "with its vast population, and its almost unlimited market for the consumption of our manufactures." Rhodes proposed building a railway to connect Nyasaland to the Cape. "Over 500 miles of this a railway has been already constructed," he continued, "leaving only a distance of 350 miles to the borders of Mashunaland, and of about 200 miles further to the Zambezi." The area was healthy for Europeans, he claimed, who might settle there. With the plan for the railroad in place, a political plan could be developed:

With such objects in view, I would urge the formation of a Crown colony in Bechuanaland, the retention of a protectorate in the territory which Khama strictly possesses, and the opening up of communication with the Matabele King for the extension of that protectorate through his dominions to the Zambezi.[25]

This was not exactly a practical proposal. Rhodes could take comfort in the return to power of the Conservative Party a few months earlier in June 1885. The new prime minister, Robert Cecil, the Marquess of Salisbury, had shown few qualms about imperial expansion. In 1878, while foreign secretary, Salisbury responded to critics of empire building in no uncertain terms: "if our ancestors had cared for the rights of other people, the British Empire would not have been made."[26] With an unabashed imperialist now leading the British government, Rhodes could assume that Ndebele territory was safe from German encroachment. The challenge was to persuade Salisbury to support Rhodes's idea of productive white settlements, connected by rail to the Cape.

Rhodes built leverage over the British government through his social networking. He was particularly skilled at turning personal encounters to political advantage. In June 1887, on a voyage from England to South Africa, while walking on the deck, Rhodes met the Irish politician John Gordon Swift MacNeill. MacNeill, a law professor in Dublin's King's Inns, had recently been elected to the British Parliament and was voyaging to Cape Town by himself for a vacation. Rhodes recognized an opportunity. All of Ireland was then part of the United Kingdom, thanks to the Act of Union of 1801. MacNeill was a Protestant and a nationalist. He was a member of the Irish Parliamentary Party, which was led by Charles Stewart Parnell, one of the most powerful men in the United Kingdom. So long as the Liberal Party and Conservative Party were equally popular among British voters, Parnell's Irish Parliamentary Party held the balance of power in the House of Commons. Governments could be made and broken by Parnell and his 85 disciplined colleagues, who used their leverage to press for Home Rule, the centerpiece of which was for Ireland to regain its separate parliament while remaining a part of the British Empire.[27]

Rhodes knew that friendship with MacNeill would create an opening for gaining leverage in British politics. The news of the day indicated that Parnell was still pushing for independence after the failure of a Home Rule Bill and the collapse of Gladstone's government in 1886. A separate parliament for

Ireland was unacceptable to Rhodes, who preferred an imperial parliament, where self-governing colonies such as Australia, Canada, New Zealand, and South Africa would all be represented, along with Ireland. Rhodes's ideas for imperial governance were linked to his hope to empower white settlers. With this broad agenda percolating in his mind, Rhodes invited MacNeill to Kimberley to give a presentation about Home Rule. While riding on the train through the Cape Colony, Rhodes offered the Irish Parliamentary Party £10,000 (the equivalent of one million dollars today) if Parnell's followers would support a future Home Rule Bill that retained some form of Irish representation in an imperial parliament. MacNeill asked Rhodes to put the offer in writing, which he did, after he and Jameson hosted MacNeill in Kimberley as their guest. On returning to London, MacNeill presented the letter to Parnell, who agreed to meet Rhodes.

In June 1888 Rhodes was in London, and MacNeill invited him to a dinner with Parnell at the House of Commons. Over the course of this meal and several more meetings, Rhodes discussed Irish representation with Parnell and persuaded him that even if Ireland achieved Home Rule and had its own parliament, Ireland's contributions to imperial defense meant that a number of Irish members should remain in the British Parliament. Rhodes then paid Parnell in two installments. Word of the £10,000 contribution reached the Cape, where politicians were puzzled. Rhodes was not known to have an interest in Ireland, a country he never visited, nor did he seem to have a reason to support a political party that opposed imperialism. After receiving the first check, Parnell told MacNeill that he thought the Cape Parliament was too small a stage for Rhodes, that he belonged in Westminster. "What a pity," he said, "that Rhodes is not in the Imperial Parliament. As it is, he will not live in history." When Rhodes made the contribution in June 1888, he still did not have a clear plan for expanding British colonialism into Mashonaland and Matabeleland. That plan developed soon after meeting Parnell, and when the charter for Rhodes's British South Africa Company was considered in 1889, the Irish nationalists were silent. In 1892, the next Home Rule Bill contained provisions for an Irish parliament as well as Irish representation in the British Parliament. In their quest for independence from Britain, the Irish nationalists allowed themselves to be bought by an imperialist. Rhodes described Parnell as "the most reasonable and sensible man I ever met."[28]

Thanks to successful networking, Rhodes gained leverage in Westminster. He now needed his social network to help him achieve leverage in the Ndebele capital, Bulawayo. Lobengula, the Ndebele ruler, attracted many visitors. In a normal year, Lobengula permitted parties of Boer hunters to pass through his territory. With the gold rush in full swing at the Witwatersrand, dozens of prospectors hoped to find even greater gold deposits in the lands to the north. Several of the British visitors, including Maund, claimed that they saw gold-bearing quartz reefs. Visitors came to Bulawayo from the Transvaal and the Cape, and even from Germany. They reported on Lobengula's regal bearing and good judgment. The king indicated that he was not interested in gold miners arriving in his country. His indunas, or councilors, advised him strongly against accepting payments from the visitors, who hoped to obtain permission to dig for gold. A former sergeant from the Warren Expedition, Frank Johnson, formed a small group of veterans and obtained permission to pan for gold in the Mazoe River, to the northeast of what is today Harare. His reports of success fanned even more interest in the region. The governor and high commissioner, Hercules Robinson, received a letter from Sidney Shippard, Rhodes's old friend and the administrator of Bechuanaland, who was responsible for relations with the Ndebele. In the letter, Shippard imagined that the entire area north of the Limpopo could become a prosperous British colony. "The Power that can acquire that territory and also secure Delagoa Bay," he wrote, "will hold the key of the wealth and commerce of South and Central Africa." Shippard hoped that the colony would be linked to Lourenço Marques, on Delagoa Bay, a "future San Francisco of the Indian Ocean."[29]

The same stories about the riches of Mashonaland circulated in Pretoria and on the Witwatersrand. The Transvaal's border commissioner, the politician and general Piet Joubert, found a merchant named Pieter J. Grobler who was familiar with Matabeleland and Mashonaland and sent him north to renegotiate an old treaty of friendship with Lobengula. Grobler persuaded Lobengula to sign the treaty, which stipulated the mutual recognition of each country's independence, as well as the appointment of a Transvaal consul in Bulawayo who would have authority over Boer hunters and merchants who were allowed to pass through. Grobler returned to Pretoria, then prepared to go back to Bulawayo as the Transvaal's consul. The terms of the treaty were kept secret, but Maund's and Rhodes's friend Ralph Williams, who was recently appointed British consul in Pretoria, learned of Grobler's mission and sounded an alarm.[30]

Shippard had just sent his own emissary to Lobengula, John Smith Moffat. Moffat was an older man, born in 1835, the son of Robert and Mary Moffat, famous missionaries to Tswana people. From 1859 to 1865, John Smith Moffat worked as a missionary among neighboring Ndebele people and maintained a friendship with Lobengula. In 1879, he went to work for the British colonial administration. Shippard appreciated Moffat's sterling reputation as well as his ability to speak the Tswana and Ndebele languages. He arranged for Robinson to appoint Moffat as assistant commissioner in Bechuanaland, making him responsible for British relations with Lobengula and the Ndebele leadership. Shippard thought Moffat was the perfect person to send to Lobengula to secure British rights along the Road to the North. Moffat, for his own part, did not realize the extent to which Shippard and Rhodes were taking advantage of him until several years later.[31]

If, in the distant future, the territory between the Limpopo and the Zambezi were to be filled with British settlers, there was a key next step. Shippard used Moffat to formalize a relationship between the British Empire and Lobengula. Warned that Grobler was on his way to Lobengula's court at Bulawayo, Shippard sent a letter to the king, asking him not to grant concessions to miners or farmers without first consulting Moffat. A concession was a document in which indigenous authorities exchanged some of their sovereignty for payments. The paying individuals and companies were then vested with economic or political powers. Ever since the seventeenth century, the method was used extensively by chartered companies to gain authority in the colonies. In the 1880s, European concession-seekers were active in "unclaimed" parts of Africa. Leopold, the Belgian king, sent his officers to the Congo for the purpose of reaching agreements and making treaties with hundreds of African chiefs. British businessmen took a similar approach in East Africa, while in the rest of Africa there were French, Portuguese, and German concession-seekers making hundreds more concession treaties. These treaties had to be written to be valid. Some were detailed documents that were negotiated extensively; some were sketchy. The treaties often assigned political authority to individuals and corporations—who were recognized by their own home countries as legitimate rulers who could raise armies, levy taxes, and administer justice.[32]

Moffat arrived in Bulawayo in November 1887 and was kept waiting. When Moffat finally did speak with Lobengula, the king stated clearly that he did not wish to be "protected" by the Transvaal. On the contrary, reported Moffat, "I think he wants to be left alone." Moffat was patient, and in February 1888 he persuaded Lobengula to agree that his territory was within Britain's sphere of influence. Lobengula also agreed not to cede any part of his territory to another country. The scene was set for a showdown on the return of the Transvaal's emissary, Grobler. He arrived, presented his credentials, and returned to the border to fetch his wife and belongings. He never made it back to Bulawayo. He and his companions had been involved in liquor-smuggling and horse-trading, earning a bad reputation among the Ngwato leadership. Under orders from Khama, a party of Ngwato men tracked Grobler near the border. After a series of skirmishes and escapes, Grobler was fatally wounded.[33]

With a British sphere of influence approved, mining companies began to scheme for concessions in lands under Lobengula's control. At this moment, Rhodes began to be outpaced by his rivals. Rhodes could do only so much. These months saw him leading the complex negotiations involved in the amalgamation of the diamond mines into De Beers Consolidated Mining. Important deals were being struck on the Witwatersrand. Meanwhile, in Cape Town, Parliament was in session, and Rhodes was actively involved in legislating, his multitasking fueled by cigarettes and alcohol. He benefited from regular horseback riding and time spent outdoors hunting and shooting, but still the physical and mental demands of his activities were great. From February to July 1888, it began to look like the press of business might cause Rhodes to miss out on opportunities for taking land, digging mines, and extending colonial settlement into South-Central Africa.

Keeping up with intelligence from Bulawayo presented challenges, since there was no telegraphic connection north of Kimberley. News of Moffat's agreement with Lobengula arrived by messenger, then spread by telegraph to Cape Town and to the Colonial Office and London society. There was considerable overlap between the traditional leadership classes and the financiers who provided the capital for expanding the empire. A network of potential investors had already formed without Rhodes's knowledge. It was initiated by Frank Johnson, the army sergeant who met Lobengula in the early months of 1887 and got permission to pan for gold in Mazowe in the northeast corner of Mashonaland. Johnson and his business partner, Maurice Heany, were refused a mining concession by Lobengula. They went south and obtained a mining concession from Khama. The concession entitled them to prospect for gold in 400 square miles of Ngwato territory. Johnson and Heany promptly sold the rights to a shady former major in the Spanish army, Francisco Ricarde-Seaver, who was backed by a French mining fund, the Caisse des Mines de Paris. Ricarde-Seaver quickly flipped the Ngwato mining concession, selling it to two well-known investors, George Cawston and Lord Edric Gifford.[34]

Like Rhodes, Gifford and Cawston had a strong network of supporters. Gifford was a well-known former officer in the British Army who had won the Victoria Cross during the Anglo-Ashanti War. Gifford followed his renowned commanding officer, Garnet Wolseley, to South Africa, where he played aide-de-camp to the "Modern Major General" during the Anglo-Zulu War. In 1880, Gifford wrote to Lobengula, offering him £100 for mining rights in Matabeleland. The offer was refused. The Colonial Office appointed Gifford to be colonial secretary in Western Australia (1880–83) and Gibraltar (1883–87). Cawston was a socialite investor who was active in the City of London. In April 1888, the two men used the Ngwato mining rights as a platform for creating the Bechuanaland Exploration Company, also known as the Exploring Company. The company attracted prominent investors, including members of the Mosenthal family, London merchant bankers with extensive experience in Port Elizabeth and Kimberley. With this backing, Gifford and Cawston incorporated their company, whose object was to find gold in the region and to ensure access to the interior by building railways. In late May 1888, Gifford wrote to the Colonial Office to ask them to discuss with him the construction of a rail link running from Kimberley through British Bechuanaland to Vryburg and Mafeking.

It is sometimes thought that the railway from Kimberley along the Road to the North was Cecil Rhodes's main vision. The construction of this specific part of the line from Kimberley through British Bechuanaland actually originated with Gifford and Cawston's Exploring Company. They hired one of Britain's best railway engineering firms, Charles Fox and Sons, which sent Charles Metcalfe to Southern Africa. Metcalfe, who had been at Oxford with Rhodes, was to spend three years surveying the future line. Metcalfe even exchanged letters with Shippard about extending the railway farther north, to the gold fields at Tati, in Ndebele territory, and from there to Mazoe, in Shona territory, up to Tete in Mozambique, on the Zambezi River. Many years later, Metcalfe wrote that he and Shippard had been influenced by the idea of the Cape-to-Cairo railway, which was being openly discussed by Rhodes and by some members of the British government.[35] Ominously for Rhodes, another old friend, Edward Maund, was also starting work for Gifford and Cawston. Maund arrived in Cape Town in June, with instructions to travel upcountry, meet Lobengula, and secure a mining concession granting the Bechuanaland Company access to Lobengula's sphere of control.[36]

Rhodes's network of friendships guarded him against these potential rivals. Rhodes was visiting London in June 1888 for discussions with Parnell and Rothschild, when supporters told him about the activities of Cawston, Gifford, and Maund. They were cultivating the secretary of state for the colonies, Henry Holland, Viscount Knutsford, as well as Robert Herbert, the permanent undersecretary at the Colonial Office. Herbert was the key contact. A graduate of Eton and Balliol College, Oxford, he became the first prime minister of Queensland, Australia, at the age of twenty-eight. In 1871, he returned home to serve in the number two post in the Colonial Office. He was aware of most of the important developments in the British colonies and had a keen interest in South Africa. It may have helped that Robert Herbert was a relative of Henry Herbert, the Earl of Carnarvon, who had served as secretary of state for the colonies under Disraeli and had advocated for South African confederation. Robert Herbert and Lord Knutsford appeared to be supporting Cawston, Gifford, and Maund, but the men at the top of the Colonial Office were also aware of Rhodes's interests.

An unknown insider, possibly Herbert himself, suggested to Rhodes a way to outmaneuver his rivals and obtain concessions in Matabeleland and Mashonaland. Rhodes wrote to Shippard that a contact at the Colonial Office told him that the British prime minister was reluctant to spend money on colonial expansion. The contact told him that Rhodes should work on a different approach, creating a chartered company instead. These were private companies that the British government allowed to govern territories. The most famous were the East India Company and the Hudson's Bay Company, which had ceased to govern territory in 1857 and 1869, respectively. The model of the chartered company was revived somewhat during the budgetary constraints of the 1880s, with the chartering of the British North Borneo Company in 1881 and the Royal Niger Company in 1886. Gifford and Cawston floated the idea of a chartered company to Herbert, but he believed that the Exploring Company did not have strong enough backing to make it work. Rhodes, with deep pockets and connections, might be able to do so. The one thing that Rhodes did not have was a concession from Lobengula. Without that, the British government was unlikely to approve a charter. This gave Rhodes a strong motive for sending representatives up to Bulawayo.[37]

Rhodes's network helped him in Cape Town, too. Rhodes had a particular point of leverage over Gifford, Cawston, and their agent, Maund. For them to build a railway through British Bechuanaland, they needed permission from the Colonial Office, but to start that line in Kimberley, they also needed permission from the Cape Colony to build a 50-mile segment of track from Kimberley to the Vaal River crossing at Fourteen Streams. When Maund arrived in Cape Town in June 1888, and when Metcalfe arrived in July, protocol dictated that they meet with the governor, Hercules Robinson, in his capacity as high commissioner to the rest of Southern Africa. Robinson knew about Rhodes's plan to use the resources of De Beers to "open up" the interior of South-Central Africa. When Robinson met with Maund and Metcalfe, he treated them with detachment, informing them that Rhodes's plans also had to be taken into consideration. It is likely that Robinson had Rhodes in mind when, in July 1888, he directed Moffat to return to Bulawayo. Moffat's instructions were to make sure that Lobengula did not make any concessions to any companies without Robinson's consent.[38]

10

Stealing Arcadia

RHODES'S OVERALL PLANS had two key components—closer ties between Britain and its colonies of settlement and the expansion of white settlement into the interior of Southern Africa. Spreading settler colonialism required him to transcend material limits, including the vast expanse of territory to the north; the available technologies of transportation, communication, mining, and agriculture; and the capital that was required for the project. Undaunted by the fire at the De Beers Mine, Rhodes set out to use the broad powers of the De Beers and Gold Fields bylaws to invest in a mission to Bulawayo, the location of Lobengula's court.

On August 1, 1888, the day on which the De Beers Consolidated Mining Company began to operate as a fully unified enterprise, Rhodes wrote to his old friend Shippard, the British administrator of Bechuanaland, to let him know that he was working on his "old idea" and on obtaining a concession from Lobengula before another group did. Gifford and Cawston's Exploring Company was likely just to obtain a mining concession and "will do nothing but simply tie the country up." By contrast, Rhodes planned to get a broad concession that could be used by De Beers to form a chartered company and rule the country. "I got my trust deed through with all its increased powers," Rhodes wrote, "and only hope I may be able to use them.... If country is given to others De Beers will have nothing to obtain in return for offer to pay expenses of government."[1] Rhodes hoped for something bigger and set in motion his personal network. He wrote a follow-up letter to Shippard, saying that "my plan is to give the chief whatever he desires and also offer H. M. [Her Majesty's] Government the whole expense of good government. If we get Matabeleland we shall get the balance of Africa. I do not stop in my ideas at Zambezi and I am willing to work with you for it."[2]

A few weeks after the mine fire, Rhodes was in Kimberley and learned that Charles Metcalfe was passing through town on his way north to survey the railroad line for Gifford and Cawston's Exploring Company. Personal networking paid off again. Over dinner, Rhodes persuaded Metcalfe and his partner, R. W. Murray, to join forces with him. The two engineers then advised Gifford and Cawston that they should partner with Rhodes. Rhodes followed up by engaging his key contact, Hercules Robinson, to apply political pressure on Gifford and Cawston. Robinson advised the Colonial Office that in his opinion, the Exploring Company was not competent to build a railway. Robinson's message effectively stalled the efforts of the Exploring Company and pushed Gifford and Cawston toward association with Rhodes.[3]

Rhodes was capable of influencing policy at the highest levels, but like all members of the Cape Colony's House of Assembly, he still had to campaign for office. On September 28, 1888, Rhodes addressed a public meeting in his constituency of Barkly West. The small town was an unlikely venue for a grand speech, except for a skilled politician like Rhodes, who had a knack for explaining how his larger territorial vision related to seemingly provincial concerns.

Rhodes addressed his Barkly West constituents by appealing to their sense of spiritual geography. "Consider it, gentlemen," he said, "to you, who are 'waiting by the river.'" Rhodes was making a play on words. The town of Barkly West was located on the north bank of the Vaal River, and "Waiting by the River" was a popular hymn, written in the early 1880s by the Americans James Henry Fillmore and Lucinda Bateman. The river in question was the Jordan, but in the context of Barkly West, the first verse delivered a bonanza of references for Christians and imperialists: "We are waiting by the river, / Strong and weak, and young and old, / Till the boatman comes to bear us / To the far-off streets of gold." For Rhodes, white territorial expansion across the Vaal River was to become an inspired hunt for mineral riches. Maybe Rhodes thought about his brother Herbert, who had "crossed the river" in the search for gold. Rhodes carried on with his speech, telling the audience:

> You are miners by birth, by education, and profession; and I believe you are as capable of developing the far interior as you have been of developing the alluvial wealth of the Vaal River. If you have any faith in me as your member, it is because you know I have not confined my political attention to advocating a Barkly pump. My ideas have always been directed towards the broad question of South African politics, and I believe that, if I succeed in the object of my political ambition, that is, the expansion of the Cape Colony the Zambesi, I shall provide for you in the future success in the prospecting for, and the production of, gold far beyond that which has occurred to you in the development of your property on the river.[4]

Rhodes's vision of material success and territorial expansion was now wrapped in spirituality and interwoven with his expanding ego. He went on with his speech, denying that he had ambitions to serve in the British Parliament, because he considered "that no grander future can belong to any statesman than that of dealing with the complicated questions of South Africa, and the enormous expansion that lies before us in the dark interior." Rhodes appealed to the audience to "share in that development," telling white settlers that they, rather than outsiders, should do the work. "I am tired of this mapping out of Africa at Berlin; without occupation, without development, without any claim to the position the various countries demand." African countries could be more than just open spaces, devoid of white settlers. Rhodes's preaching continued: "I have faith that, remote as our starting-point is, the development of Africa will occur through the Cape Colony... we shall be able to obtain the dominant position throughout the interior." He urged his audience to "always remember that the gist of the South African question lies in the extension of the Cape Colony to the Zambesi."[5]

According to Rhodes, frontier expansion drove South Africa's success as well as its spirit. This was an argument that resembled the American notion of "Manifest Destiny" that was then being turned into a thesis by a University of Wisconsin historian Frederick Jackson Turner, who argued that the challenges of life on a westward-moving frontier shaped his country's character and politics. Like Turner's thesis, the grandiose and problematic vision of Cecil Rhodes has a certain ineluctable and tragic element to it. Starting in 1888, the British government claimed that the lands beyond the Limpopo River were in a British sphere of influence. This announcement was made to preempt the Transvaal from making inroads; little planning was done for the territory. The stalling of Gifford and Cawston's Exploring Company bought Rhodes time to do much more than simply prepare a proposal for a rival railroad and mining concession. Rhodes received a tip, possibly from Robert Herbert of the Colonial Office, that a chartered company was likely to be looked upon favorably if Rhodes were able to obtain a concession from Lobengula. Rhodes now sought the right for a chartered company to govern South-Central Africa. Rhodes knew that Maund was traveling into the interior on behalf of Cawston and Gifford's company. Rhodes began to move quickly to organize his own effort to gain a concession. As a first step he sent a young man, Ivon Fry, to deliver a gift to Lobengula. Fry's mission was followed by a more substantive group of concession-seekers. Rhodes himself had to remain in Kimberley, to finalize the purchase of the Kimberley Mine and also to work with Gardner Williams on the De Beers Mine's recovery from the fire.

The mission to the north was led by Charles Rudd, Rhodes's cautious business partner. Rhodes knew that Rudd did not believe in any grand schemes and was acting mainly out of his interest in De Beers and Gold Fields. Rhodes wrote to his confidant, Shippard: "I am quite aware that you cannot act freely with him, but in case he lays the groundwork the objects are the same as though he does not know our big ideas, he will try and obtain what he desires for our Companies whose trust deeds I shall use for the objects I have in view."[6] Rhodes added two more men to Rudd's mission, James Rochfort Maguire and Francis "Matabele" Thompson. Thompson, who had been working for two years at De Beers as the head of the compounds, was needed for his language skills. Rochfort Maguire, an attorney and an old friend from Bullingdon's in Oxford, had recently worked in the colonial service as the assistant to Graham Bower. Maguire was needed for his social connections and his legal background. He was also an Irishman and a nationalist, and Rhodes, fresh off his meeting with Parnell, may have been considering giving support to Maguire as an Irish candidate for Parliament.[7]

Maguire, Rudd, and Thompson were not the only ones making their way on the Road to the North. Colonial administrators, Christian missionaries, and business competitors vied to try their luck with Lobengula. There were many possible outcomes, which raised concerns for Robinson and his advisers. In July 1888, Robinson ordered Moffat, Shippard's assistant commissioner in Bechuanaland, to go to Lobengula's court and insist that any future concessions have the approval of the British governor. British officials were supposed to be neutral, but Robinson had become a friend and admirer. When the governor and high commissioner's representative, Moffat, visited Lobengula's court, Rudd observed that "Moffat took the chance of putting in a good word for us."[8]

The stage was set for a key decision by Lobengula. Many concession-seekers were either already in Bulawayo or headed in that direction. The two main rival parties, representing the Exploring Company and the British South Africa Company, left Kimberley in August. Rhodes's rival, Maund, left Kimberley first, in early August, but during his travels on the Road to the North, he pursued opportunities to gain concessions with Khama and arrived at Bulawayo in mid-October. Rudd, Thompson, and Maguire left Kimberley in mid-August, avoided distractions, and arrived at Bulawayo in late September. Their early arrival allowed Rhodes's representatives to hold the field for a few crucial weeks. On getting there, Rudd, Maguire, and Thompson found Lobengula to be a skilled negotiator. In the first meeting, the leader welcomed them and accepted their gift of one hundred gold sovereigns. Then he advised them to go and get some sleep. Three days later, Lobengula asked

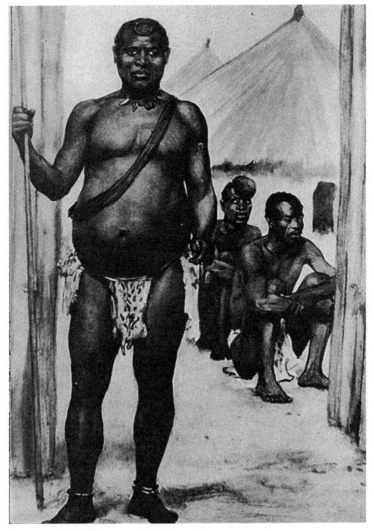

Lobengula. Drawn by Ralph Peacock, based on a sketch by E. A. Maund. Alamy.

them questions about many subjects, distracting from the main objective of Rhodes's three emissaries. They tried to steer the conversation back to the right to mine gold. Lobengula advised them to talk to his indunas, then he stalled for time. This was clearly a negotiating ploy, but Thompson opined that "the native mind moves slowly." In his memoir he remembered that "we were reduced to spending every day in our little camp, most of the time playing backgammon or reading."[9]

While the three emissaries waited for weeks at Bulawayo, Maund's party arrived and had to settle down and wait, too. Several other groups of concession-seekers were also encamped near Lobengula's residence. British officials were not supposed to take sides, but support was lining up in favor of Rhodes's scheme. In October, Shippard himself traveled to visit Bulawayo, with an escort of sixteen troopers of the Bechuanaland Police, commanded by a British Army major, Hamilton John Goold-Adams. When the group crossed into Ndebele territory, they were shadowed by an armed party, who taunted them but never attacked. Threats did not deter Shippard. As far as he was concerned, Lobengula was "an old savage" who could not prevent mining and settlement. Reflecting on the visit, Shippard wrote that "the accounts one hears of the wealth of Mashonaland if known and believed in England would bring such a rush to the country that its destiny would soon be settled whether the Matabele liked it or not."[10] Shippard arrived at Bulawayo in mid-October, ready to conduct important business. Shippard did not advocate openly for Rhodes and Rudd, but he did suggest that Rudd represented Rhodes and the queen. Shippard also raised questions about Rhodes's rivals, advising Lobengula that he would be better off reaching an agreement with one large company, rather than a collection of small ones. He reminded the chief that Robinson had final approval over any concessions.[11]

Shippard was biased in Rhodes's favor; he was also strongly biased against Ndebele people. Shortly after the meeting with Lobengula, Shippard wrote a letter to a colleague that revealed the depths of his hostility. According to Shippard, Central Africa did not need a railway, so much as it needed

> a liberal supply of Gatling guns, magazine and Martini-Henry rifles with bayonets and a good field battery with the proper men to handle the same effectively. I do not think that I am naturally of a cruel or bloodthirsty disposition, but I must confess that it would offer me sincere and lasting satisfaction if I could see the Matebele Matjaha cut down by our rifles and machine guns like a cornfield by a reaping machine and I would not spare a single one if I could have my way.[12]

With this grim harvest on his mind, Shippard left Bulawayo. The next and most important move was made by Rudd. His journey had been difficult, and the stay at Bulawayo had been hot and unpleasant. Rhodes was sending letters, pestering Rudd with advice. If Maund presented a problem, Rhodes wrote that it would be time buy out "those guinea pigs" Cawston and Gifford. Rhodes insisted that the "Interior Company must be De Beers and Gold Fields."[13] If Lobengula had doubts, he could be told that the concession meant that the company was "working for him." Rhodes suggested gifts for Lobengula, even a steamboat for the Zambezi. Rudd sent multiple requests to Lobengula for a meeting, which were turned down, repeatedly, until one day in late October, the king met with Rudd, who shared the proposed concession agreement. Further delays ensued, while Rudd consulted Lobengula's indunas. Several indunas were skeptical of Rudd and advised Lobengula to limit the size of the concession if he agreed to one at all. It was known that the Swazi king, Mbandzeni had been taken advantage of by European concessionaires.[14]

At noon on October 30, 1888, Lobengula sent for his induna, Lotshe, as well as Thompson and the English missionary Charles Helm, who acted as an interpreter. Helm's religious affiliation may have given reassurances to Englishmen and Ndebele alike that the proceedings were legitimate. The men at the meeting had a final discussion of the terms of the concession. When they were done, Thompson found Rudd and told him to bring the text of the concession. Lobengula was ready to sign. The written text of the concession says that Rudd, Thompson, and Maguire were expected to deliver to Lobengula an armed steamer for the Zambezi; one thousand Martini-Henry rifles; 100,000 rifle cartridges; and a payment of £100 every month. In exchange, Lobengula gave them "complete and exclusive charge over all metals and minerals situated and contained in my Kingdoms Principalities dominions together with full power to do all things that they may deem necessary to win and procure the same and to hold collect and enjoy the profits and revenue." The term "my Kingdoms Principalities dominions" was defined as "Matabeleland, Mashonaland, and all other adjacent territories." In that area, all other concession-seekers were excluded. Lobengula signed by marking the paper agreement with an X.[15]

It seemed that Lobengula had just given Rudd and his companions "full power to do all things that they may deem necessary" to dig for minerals and to make a profit in his territory. That afternoon, before anything could be changed, Rudd packed up and rushed back to Kimberley. Rhodes was delighted with the agreement. "Our concession is so gigantic," he wrote to Rudd, "it is like giving a man the whole of Australia." Others saw problems. Rhodes and Rudd soon learned that they were not the first ones to be promised mining rights by Lobengula. In 1884, Lobengula granted rights to the region's minerals to four British traders and promised two of them rights to the same space that had just been promised to Rudd. Rhodes met with several of them in Johannesburg in January 1889 and bought them out. Maund's group was promoting their claim at Bulawayo and posed a greater threat. They claimed to have been granted a concession for the Mazoe River valley, which would have contradicted the territorial claims related to the Rudd

Concession. For several months Rhodes had been advising Rudd about how to deal with Maund. "If you find him a dangerous antagonist," Rhodes advised, "take him over personally, or if he represents the Bechuanaland Prospecting Association join hands and give their Company a share." Rhodes was concerned that Maund and his colleagues had ambitions as great as his own. "Their aims are very large, including a Charter and the whole interior so we must best them, or join hands as you deem fit."[16]

Some started to wonder if Lobengula really could deliver what he promised. Rhodes's plan for territorial expansion was based on Lobengula's portrayal of tributary relationships with Shona people. In reality, it was not clear that Lobengula's writ extended so effectively to "Mashonaland and all other adjacent regions." The situation was complicated and unfamiliar to Europeans accustomed to their own notions about sovereignty. Shona groups near Matabeleland tended to be in a tributary relationship with Lobengula, while farther Shona groups sometimes decided not to pay tribute and to take their chances with being raided by Ndebele fighters. The extent of Lobengula's power was often misunderstood by British visitors. Lobengula was powerful, but his authority depended on the cooperation of chiefs who ruled various subgroups.[17]

Misconceptions about Ndebele politics extended from Bulawayo to London. When word of the agreement reached Whitehall, the senior staff member at the Colonial Office, Edward Fairfield, wrote to his superior, Robert Herbert, that Lobengula did not really govern the Shona; he was mostly interested in intimidating them and stealing from them. Fairfield did suspect Rhodes of shady dealings, writing to Herbert, "At best, I fear that our doings as to Mashonaland are a transaction into which we have been hustled by interested parties." Herbert responded by defending Rhodes and Rudd and even Lobengula. "Whatever may be the actual truth about Lo Bengula—and I certainly doubt his being anything like as bad as Mr. Fairfield makes out—it will never do for us to admit any doubt of his right over Mashonaland, or to open the door one inch to Portuguese claims."[18]

The territoriality of the Rudd Concession was problematic, and there was also confusion about whether the document represented the negotiation accurately. Not long after the meeting between Lobengula, Thompson, and Lotshe, the missionary translator, Helm, indicated to his superiors that Thompson had given verbal reassurances that went beyond the scope of the written document. The document gave broad powers to the concessionaires, but according to Helm, Thompson made verbal promises that only ten Europeans were to come to the country at any time. They were only supposed to dig for gold in one place at a time. The mines were intended to be far away from settlements. Helm soon had his claims backed up by Lobengula himself. In February 1889, Lobengula argued that he had not given Rudd rights in all his territories. Instead, he had promised Rudd a concession in a specific location, between Tati and the Ramokgwebana River. Furthermore, he had told Rudd that he was only allowed to dig "one hole." Lobengula then repudiated the text of the Rudd Concession.[19]

Lobengula's fury was not Rhodes's only problem. There were also legal problems from the perspective of the Cape government. Rudd, Thompson, and Maguire promised Lobengula one thousand rifles and a hundred thousand cartridges. It was widely known that Cape law prohibited the sale of firearms across the colony's borders. Shippard made the case to Robinson that, as far as the Ndebele were concerned, laws against the proliferation of firearms should be considered a moot point and overlooked. Shippard argued that Ndebele fighters were incapable of learning to use modern rifles. Giving them rifles that they could not use might even lead them to become less skilled with their assegais, their short stabbing spears. As implausible as this might seem, such arguments about African skill had been used before during Cape debates about gun proliferation. They were enough to give Robinson cover when he defended the Rudd Concession in letters to the Colonial Office. Privately, Shippard wrote to Robinson that he intended to issue a special permit for the weapons and ammunition to be delivered across borders. Robinson knew that he should not approve the permits. His chief staffer, Graham Bower, recalled that he discussed Shippard's letter with Robinson. Robinson said, "We will take time to answer that letter," and put it in a drawer. When the word of the gun shipments reached the public, there was an outcry. Cape prime minister Gordon Sprigg asked for Robinson and Bower's papers to be laid on the table. Bower wrote years later that they refused, in the knowledge that the Cape Parliament was about to adjourn a few days later. The Anglican bishop of Bloemfontein, George Knight-Bruce, had recently concluded a tour through Matabaleland and Mashonaland, with Lobengula's permission. The bishop openly criticized the idea of giving the Ndebele weapons when they would turn them against their Shona neighbors. Rhodes intervened with the bishop and later boasted to Rudd that Knight-Bruce had become a "cordial supporter."[20]

According to the terms of the Rudd Concession, 500 rifles were due right away. Rhodes purchased the rifles in Cape Town. The merchant arranged permits for them to be sent to De Beers in Kimberley in two shipments of 250 each. After that point, Rhodes did not apply for permits to send the rifles to

Lobengula, because the permits might have been denied. The rifles were packed up on wagons and driven north, transported by traders who were joined, at the border, by two close associates of Rhodes, his housemate, Jameson, and another Kimberley doctor, Frederick Rutherfoord Harris. Jameson may have been given the job because he had earlier treated Lobengula for an illness and been made an honorary induna. Jameson and Harris were met at the border by Maguire, who was on his way back. He informed them that he was exhausted by his stay at Bulawayo and needed to return to Cape Town, even though he and Thompson had promised Lobengula they would remain. Maguire fervently wished that Rhodes would ride to Bulawayo to meet Lobengula. Maguire wrote to Rudd, "I hope you will understand how very damaging this is." By "this," he meant the absence of Rhodes, who was in a strong position to fend off rival concession-seekers and answer questions about the terms of the agreement, particularly the parts about rifles and gunboats. "We have throughout been advised to keep things smooth until Rhodes arrived and now apparently he is not coming. For four months we have been playing John the Baptist and now there is no Christ!"[21]

Rhodes, no messiah, preferred for others to do the dirty work of empire building. If things went wrong with Lobengula and the gun shipment, Rhodes's absence gave him plausible deniability of involvement. The absence bothered Maguire, who wrote again to Rudd to urge a visit from Rhodes:

> If Rhodes, with the many great claims on his time and attention which undoubtedly exist, is not prepared himself to take an active personal part in this enterprise, well and good, there is nothing more to be said except that in my opinion it greatly diminishes the value of our concession or rather position. If on the other hand, as I have always hoped, he takes a strong personal interest in the affair a grievous error has been made, by his not coming up. There is no use extending or even excusing your ramifications unless you know that things are right at the fountain head. What is primarily wanted is things to be made clear here and set upon right lines.[22]

Rhodes remained in Cape Town and London so that he could better defend the concession. Cape politicians were concerned about the arms deal. Merriman stood up in the House of Assembly and asked a question about the weapons shipment. And the Cape government, with Gordon Sprigg serving again as prime minister, asked the governor and high commissioner for a certificate absolving it from any responsibility for the arms deal. It was plainly illegal. Even Rhodes admitted to Rudd, "I am slightly nervous as to getting guns through, but will do my best."[23]

Meanwhile in Bulawayo, Maguire and Thompson were under strain because Lobengula was convinced that he had been duped. He said that he had only granted permission for Rudd to mine in "one hole," a point that he increasingly needed to stress on account of Ndebele politics. After the signing of the Rudd Concession, some indunas were on the brink of rebellion. In November 1888, Shippard suspected one induna, Gambo, of plotting a coup with the assistance of Boers from the Transvaal. Thompson and Maguire remained in Bulawayo, mollifying the king, but another concession-seeker, William Tainton, persuaded him to go public with his concerns. In early February 1889, with help from Tainton, Lobengula published a letter in the *Bechuanaland News*, in which he alleged that there was a "great misunderstanding" about the Rudd Concession and that he planned to investigate. In March 1889, an indaba, or political meeting, was called. Lobengula did not participate but was informed of the proceedings. The indunas interrogated Thompson, Maguire, and Helm for two full days, making them sit outdoors in the sun. Many of the indunas' questions were prompted by the rival European concession-seekers. The interrogation did not reveal anything new, but Rhodes's representatives sensed hostility.[24]

Lobengula put additional pressure on Rhodes by making a shrewd maneuver. The king found a way to contact the British government without going through Thompson, Maguire, Moffat, Shippard, Robinson, or anyone else in Rhodes's corner. Lobengula asked Maund to escort two indunas, Babayane and Mshete, on a visit to London. Maund's party acquired one more member, Johan Colenbrander, a frontiersman from Natal, to be the translator. Colenbrander had been working for a separate group of concession-seekers, funded by Beit's alienated relative, Edouard Lippert. Lippert's group was making common cause with Cawston and Gifford's group in resisting Rhodes and the Rudd Concession.

Lobengula gave his emissaries clear instructions. They were told to deliver a letter to the queen complaining about Portuguese incursions. They were also told to make verbal remarks denouncing the Rudd Concession. They were welcome to share the letter before the meeting with the queen, but the complaints about the Rudd Concession were to be kept confidential until the meeting. Lobengula promised that if Maund accomplished the mission successfully, he might be granted a concession of his own. The group was instructed to stay away from Rhodes's associates. Maund, Colenbrander, Babayane, and Mshete set off for the Cape Colony, avoiding British

Bechuanaland and riding instead through the Transvaal. Maund and his party did travel through Kimberley, though, where Maund was cornered by Rhodes and Jameson. They invited Maund to their home, where they pressured him to join forces. Maund did not give in, honoring his commitment to Cawston and Gifford and his understanding with Lobengula. The men parted angrily, with Rhodes threatening to prevent Maund and his fellow travelers from visiting London. When Maund's group arrived in Cape Town, Robinson attempted to stop their travel by discrediting Maund and the indunas. Soon Rhodes arrived, bearing news. In London, the secretary of state for the colonies, Lord Knutsford, advised Cawston and Gifford that if they worked together with Rhodes, they would have a better chance of receiving a charter for a company. Cawston and Gifford had powerful backers in London, but in Cape Town, Robinson was known to be partial to Rhodes and to have powerful London connections of his own. Everyone knew that Rhodes held a great deal of influence in Cape Town and Kimberley as well as a strongly developing relationship in the City of London with Natty Rothschild. Apprising the situation, Cawston and Gifford accepted Knutsford's advice and capitulated to Rhodes by telegrams.[25]

Rhodes was pleased by the merger of interests with Cawston and Gifford. They had the ability to access financiers in elite circles in London. And Rhodes was now Maund's employer, too. Robinson had the power to give or withhold official accreditation to the indunas. Robinson and his secretary, Graham Bower, interviewed the indunas on three occasions, but the indunas discerned from the union of Cawston, Gifford, and Maund with Rhodes that they should not mention that the main point of their mission was to convey Lobengula's objections to the Rudd Concession. Ostensibly, their mission was still to deliver a letter from Lobengula to Queen Victoria that complained about Portuguese incursions into his territory. The visit of the indunas to England showed that, for a moment, Ndebele leaders could take advantage of new kinds of mobility and communication. On February 6, 1889, Maund, Colenbrander, Babayane, and Mshete set off for England. The next day, Robinson received a telegram from Knutsford, in London, informing him that the queen was unlikely to have time to meet with the envoys since she was preparing for a trip to Europe. The mission of the indunas seemed to be in jeopardy.[26]

Personal connections helped the mission to overcome the obstacles presented by the busy royal schedule. Maund had his own contacts in London, who could be relied on to communicate with the Colonial Office. The indunas were helped even more by a random encounter. On board the ship,

Babayane and Mshete made the acquaintance of Lucy Cavendish, who was active in British politics. Her husband, Frederick Cavendish, was a prominent Liberal who had been appointed to the sensitive position of chief secretary for Ireland, but on his first day in office, he and his chief staffer were knifed to death by Irish nationalists. After a period of mourning, Lucy Cavendish made a name for herself as an advocate for women's education. When she heard about Rhodes from Babayane and Mshete, she is likely to have known that Rhodes was a supporter of Parnell. Her negative experiences with Irish nationalists may have predisposed her to believe the indunas' concerns about the Rudd Concession. Lucy Cavendish listened to the case presented by the indunas and was determined to help them.[27]

By another coincidence, a prominent Scottish politician, Schomberg Henry Kerr, the Marquess of Lothian, boarded the ship at Madeira. A Conservative, Lothian was then serving in the British government as the Scottish secretary. Cavendish introduced Lothian to Mshete and Babayane, who were promised assistance. When the ship landed, arrangements were made for an interview with Knutsford. Knutsford wisely did not trust Colenbrander's interpreting, so he requested that yet another prominent passenger on board the *Moor*, the celebrity big-game hunter and former companion of Herbert Rhodes, Frederick Courteney Selous, to join the meetings. Knutsford's choice of Selous as an interpreter was not exactly going to bring more objectivity. Selous, whose father chaired the London Stock Exchange, was thought to have the ability to influence African people. Having Selous in the meeting with Knutsford may have balanced the inclinations of Lucy Cavendish.[28]

Queen Victoria's audience with Babayane and Mshete on March 2, 1889, attracted much attention in the press. Given that Rhodes and his new partners had laid the groundwork so extensively, the meeting did not go well for the imperialists. The indunas presented their letter, which complained about Portuguese encroachments. The letter was received without controversy, but to the surprise of their English companions, the indunas also delivered Lobengula's verbal message, in which the king expressed his annoyance with concession-seekers and asked the queen's advice. Knutsford and his staff took twenty-four days to prepare an official response in the queen's name. During that time, Maund edited a version of the induna's verbal statement to include a request that a trustworthy representative be sent to Bulawayo. He was angling for the job.

While the government letter was being composed, Babayane and Mshete built their own network by visiting humanitarians. Their cause was taken up by John Mackenzie, who had pushed back against Rhodes among the Tswana five years earlier during the Warren Expedition. Mackenzie recruited well-known public figures to his South Africa Committee. The group was chaired by Joseph Chamberlain, the Birmingham manufacturer turned influential reform M.P. He believed in the integrity of the British Empire and during the Home Rule debate led his Liberal Unionists into an alliance with the Conservatives. Chamberlain was then one of Britain's most influential politicians. Chamberlain and Mackenzie were joined on the committee by Thomas Fowell Buxton, the leader of the Aborigines Protection Society; Wardlaw Thompson, head of the London Missionary Society; and William T. Stead, editor of the *Pall Mall Gazette* and one of Britain's first investigative journalists. Stead's book about child prostitution, *The Maiden Tribute of Modern Babylon*, landed him in jail. Rhodes attempted to visit Stead and supported him publicly, cementing their friendship. The South Africa Committee's ranks were filled out by more public figures who, like Chamberlain, supported an improving, reforming, "progressive" imperialism. To govern territories consistently, they preferred direct imperial rule over African people, not the quasi-independent settler rule that was supported by Rhodes.[29]

Joseph Chamberlain asked about the Rudd Concession during parliamentary question time. Rising before the House of Commons, he addressed the undersecretary of state for the colonies, Henry de Worms, a prominent member of the Conservative party who was a relative of Rothschild. Chamberlain asked a leading question:

> I beg to ask the Under Secretary of State for the Colonies whether, in view of the character of the concession said to have been recently granted by the Chief Lo Bengula to Messrs. Rudd and Rhodes.... Her Majesty's Government will take any steps to call the attention of the Chief to the disadvantages and dangers to the peace of the country incident to such a monopoly; and, whether, in the event of Her Majesty's Government extending at any future time a protectorate over the Colony now under the sphere of British influence, they will refuse to recognize the concession in question.[30]

Chamberlain and the South Africa Committee hoped for British rule, but Henry de Worms could not satisfy them. He and the government that he represented were willing to offer advice to Lobengula and even to send an adviser to Bulawayo. Even so, the government hesitated to interfere in any concessions, except to raise one objection to the arms shipment. In a follow-up question on March 26, 1889, the prominent Liberal member Henry Labouchère asked Henry de Worms to verify terms of the Rudd Concession, including whether Lobengula was going to be given a gunboat. The answers, in both cases, were affirmative, but De Worms distanced himself from the decisions, saying that they were Lobengula's to make. Lobengula was still the sovereign.[31]

The queen's letter to Lobengula was most likely drafted by Herbert, Fairfield, and other staff members of the Colonial Office and then reviewed and signed by Lord Knutsford on March 26, 1889. The final draft was written in the faux-African voice made popular by the adventure novels of Rider Haggard:

> The Queen advises Lo Bengula not to grant hastily concessions of land, or leave to dig, but to consider all applications very carefully.
>
> It is not wise to put too much power into the hands of the men who come first, and to exclude other deserving men. A King gives a stranger an ox, not his whole herd of cattle, otherwise what would other strangers arriving have to eat?
>
> Umsheti and Babaan say that Lo Bengula asks that the Queen will send him someone from herself. To this request the Queen is advised that Her Majesty may be pleased to accede....
>
> Upon this and other matters Lo Bengula should write, and should send his letters to the High Commissioner at the Cape, who will send them direct to the Queen. The High Commissioner is the Queen's officer, and she places full trust in him, and Lo Bengula should also trust him. Those who advise Lo Bengula otherwise deceive him.[32]

Knutsford was advising Lobengula to be more trusting of British officials, when Shippard and Robinson were plainly helping Rhodes. It would seem to be a contradiction that Knutsford was suggesting that Lobengula should be wary of concessionaires who seek to exclude other concessionaires. Was the Colonial Office starting to side with Lobengula and the humanitarians over the Rudd Concession? Knutsford was merely acknowledging humanitarian concerns. He had already suggested the merger of Cawston and Gifford's company with Rhodes and Rudd's company, which implied that he favored a chartered company. Months later, when the letter arrived at Bulawayo and Babayane and Mshete read it, they were surprised by some of the contents. In their presentation to Queen Victoria, they never asked for a representative to be sent to Lobengula. Lobengula confirmed that he had never asked for a

British emissary. The idea appears to have originated with Maund, who wanted the job for himself.[33]

While debates over representation took place, the arms were about to be delivered to Lobengula. Rhodes knew that he could rely on his old friend Sidney Shippard to overcome the legal obstacles. The controversial shipments were taking place at a time of political transition. The old Cape governor and high commissioner, Hercules Robinson, had been replaced by an acting governor and high commissioner, General Henry Smyth, a Crimean War veteran who was then in command of British forces in Southern Africa. Smyth was asked by Sprigg to make enquiries to Shippard about the arms shipments. Shippard delayed his response by using a technicality. He denied Sprigg's request, writing, "I should be glad to know with what object the Cape Ministers are instituting enquiries into matters which do not appear to affect the interests of the Cape Colony. I am not at present prepared to furnish the information desired by them. If Your Excellency wishes to confer with me personally on the question raised by Ministers' memorandum I will proceed to Cape Town." This reply annoyed Smyth, who called Shippard's bluff and ordered him to Cape Town, where Shippard pretended to know nothing about the ultimate destination of the shipments. Sprigg advised Smyth that Shippard's written response "is of course merely an evasion of the question at issue." Smyth sent the full exchange of letters to the Colonial Office, where a staff member, Frederick Graham, wrote in the margins, "Sir Gordon Sprigg evidently thinks that the rifles were meant for Lobengula…and I daresay he isn't far wrong." Graham or another official penciled in the margin "!" but nothing was done. Shippard, loyal to Rhodes, got away with lawbreaking and insubordination.[34]

Shippard was an experienced and convincing liar. His nickname among Ngwato people was *Marana-make*, "the father of lies." King Khama knew that even a liar could be used to advantage. The rifles had to pass through Ngwato territory to get to Lobengula. Shippard communicated with Khama to make sure that the arms merchants' caravans were not disturbed. In January, two shipments of 250 rifles each went across the border, followed by the remaining 500 in March. Khama stated his price. He insisted that the British provide him with modern rifles, too. With Shippard's connivance, he was sent 800 Martini-Henrys, the same weapon promised to Lobengula. The Ndebele and Tswana recipients did not realize that the Martini-Henry, a single-shot, lever-action breechloader, had just been superseded by the British Army's new Lee-Metford, a bolt-action breechloader that used magazines holding eight to ten cartridges. Lobengula and Khama received Martini-Henrys that were modern enough for a fight with African neighbors but that would not give an advantage in a fight with Europeans in the years to come. In fact, since the Martini-Henry used factory-made brass cartridges, in certain respects the weapons increased Ndebele and Tswana dependency on Europeans.[35]

The British government and the Cape government had used arms deals to cement relationships with African chiefs who lived along the colony's borders ever since the early nineteenth century. The arms deals with Lobengula and Khama were the last in a long line of transactions involving loyalty and weapons. In 1889 and 1890, Britain and the other colonial powers in Africa negotiated a treaty that restricted trading in liquor, slaves, and firearms. Old-fashioned muzzle-loaders could be sold anywhere that banned the sale of slaves, but "precision arms" like the Martini-Henry rifles could only be sold to licensed individuals who agreed to have their weapon stamped. The British negotiated an exception for Africa below 22 degrees south latitude, which included Bechuanaland but excluded territories to the north. Lobengula was not going to get any more rifles unless more British officials became willing to look the other way.[36] Meanwhile in Bulawayo, Lobengula was accepting the monthly cash payments but was refusing to allow Jameson and Harris to deliver the rifles that were supposed to clinch the deal. Maguire met Jameson and Harris and told them that he could no longer stay in Bulawayo. In Bulawayo and in London, the Rudd Concession was in trouble.[37]

II

Perpetrating a Fraud

RHODES AND HIS associates took over Zimbabwe gradually, involving members of his network in small, questionable acts, in such a way that ever-widening circles of people became comfortable with the theft of territory. Rhodes enrolled his critics and rivals in his project by offering them money and a share in his vision. At no point did Rhodes simply pay people for their support in a simple transaction or "quid pro quo." Instead, he used his money and his powers of persuasion to help them to imagine that their own projects could be a part of his own.

Rhodes, a thirty-six-year-old entrepreneur still relatively unknown in England, promoted his plan by activating a transcontinental network of people and technologies. The Rudd Concession and its promises of a steamboat and weapons was only the first step. Material things promised to Lobengula, such as rifles and a steamboat, were just the start of what Rhodes intended to do. The Ndebele king was unaware that verbal reassurances given during negotiations counted less than written concessions that he could not read for himself. By the time Lobengula determined that he was a victim of fraud and grand larceny, it was too late. Rhodes had already moved on to the next stage of his campaign for land and money. To get more of both, Rhodes had to do more than trick an unlettered African monarch. Rhodes had to take the Rudd Concession and use it to gain the support of the ruling classes of the United Kingdom.

Rhodes arrived in England in late March 1889, a few weeks after Babayane and Mshete's audience with Queen Victoria. To achieve his goal of gold mining and white settlement in Mashonaland Rhodes's principal gambit was to take his one shaky asset from north of the Limpopo—the contested Rudd Concession—and transform that piece of paper with Lobengula's "X" into a sturdier document, a charter for a company. Initially the Rudd Concession was owned by Gold Fields, which had used its flexible corporate bylaws to put up the money for Rudd, Thompson, and Maguire to travel to Bulawayo. The key rival was the Exploring Company, owned by Cawston and Gifford. In the spring of 1889, Cawston and Gifford were pressured by the Colonial Office to join forces with Rhodes. The three men then merged their two companies into one company, Central Search Association. Central Search then bought all claims to African mineral rights from Gold Fields and from the Exploring Company. It also bought the claims of the Austral Africa Company, owned by Rider Haggard's brother, Alfred Haggard, and his partner, John Wallop, who was the second son of the Earl of Portsmouth and the nephew of the Earl of Carnarvon. Wallop was three years younger than Rhodes, attractive, and a lifelong bachelor, precisely the sort of man that Rhodes liked to work with. However, Wallop's involvement in a rival claim meant that he could use his aristocratic connection to hinder Rhodes's activities. Rhodes decided to buy out Wallop and Haggard and include them in the new company as a way of avoiding another potential challenge to the Rudd Concession.[1]

During these purchases, no money changed hands, only claims to mineral rights. Central Search still had to be given a nominal value that was based on its claims. This nominal capital was divided into shares that were assigned to the new partners based on the negotiated value of their claims. The negotiations took place in London, where Rhodes, joined by Beit, spent seven weeks bargaining with Cawston, Gifford, Edward Maund and his brother, John. The meetings were recalled years later by Maund, who wrote in favorable terms about his former nemesis. "I soon saw that Rhodes and Beit dominated the position. The former by his personality, the latter by his shrewd grasp of details." Maund continued:

> I now saw Cecil Rhodes in a totally different light to the brusque Rhodes I had met in Bechuanaland.... Now, here in London, I saw him the Man of Affairs, moderate, affable, and encouragingly jolly, ready to consider and yield to the opinions of others that, while taking broad views himself, he generally deferred to Beit regarding details.[2]

Maund recalled that Rhodes was highly persuasive:

> And when he spoke of his ideas of working, he electrified us with his fervour. The really Great Man towered above the pettifoggers who visioned Shares, Debentures, & Profits. He spoke of the enterprise from the standpoint of "England must do it" for the benefit of her future, and as a duty to civilization, to open the way through savagedom to a new Colony which would make homes for our overteeming population. How I drank in his vigorous words & metaphorically

threw my cap in the air, when I remembered he had joined our Board and I was to have the extreme gratification of working for this Mountain of Energy. He was splendid on this Imperial Subject.[3]

Rhodes's persuasive powers and his enthusiasm for broad, dynamic plans helped him to turn critics into supporters, by giving them the sense that they were participating in something bigger than themselves. This was the context that Rhodes established as he and five other gentlemen sat at a table in London and transformed the ill-gotten Rudd Concession into a thing of value and an instrument of power. Soon after the London negotiations concluded, Maund was given the assignment to go back to Bulawayo and insinuate himself into Lobengula's court as a trusted adviser. The expectation was that Maund would persuade Lobengula that the Rudd Concession was nothing to be concerned about. Maund was also given the task of buying up any additional concessions that might become available.[4]

Meanwhile in London, Rhodes turned the distribution of paper shares to his advantage. He used the shares to recruit accomplices, by means of a practice that was not technically illegal, but which was certainly questionable. Rhodes offered prominent supporters the option of buying shares at prices that were lower than their anticipated value. For example, in 1889, as Robinson was stepping down as governor, he bought 250 shares of Central Search worth £1 each. Soon afterwards, Robinson learned that Central Search was going to be bought by a successor company, United Concessions, by paying ten to one. He now owned 2,500 shares of United Concessions. By 1893, he had amassed 6,250 shares, which he sold for a profit. Graham Bower thought that the practice was fishy and refused such an offer. Rhodes made these kinds of offers to friend and foe alike. One former friend in the Cape Parliament, James Rose Innes, criticized the way in which Rhodes used gifts of shares to corrupt politics and complained of the extent of the practice, which spread from London to Cape Town.

> He [Rhodes] offered to members of [the Cape] parliament, and other prominent persons, the opportunity of subscribing at par for parcels of chartered shares then standing at a considerable premium. It was delicately put; the idea was to interest the selected recipients in northern development. Of course the recipient paid for his shares, but equally of course they were worth far more than he paid. In effect it was a valuable gift, which could not, one would think, be accepted without impairment of independence. Yet there were acceptances in unexpected

quarters. A list of the ground-floorers who came in when the shares were above par would be interesting.[5]

With the Central Search Association holding the Rudd Concession, Rhodes could organize the chartered company in such a way that it controlled the territory previously claimed by Lobengula. Rhodes did the work of organizing during June and July of 1889, when he met with prominent Britons. He promised shares of the proposed British South Africa Company to potential opponents, key among them leading journalists. William T. Stead, of the *Pall Mall Gazette*, had been a part of the South Africa Committee and was also an enthusiast for an imperial federation that included the United States. Rhodes paid off a £2,000 libel judgment that had gone against Stead. Rhodes also persuaded Flora Shaw, a well-known foreign and colonial correspondent for the *Times*, to join his camp. The deputy editor of the *Fortnightly Review*, John Verschoyle, met with Rhodes and took an instant liking to him. He, too, would become a key supporter.

Rhodes used his social connections to raise his profile and build his credibility. He met with Angela Burdett-Coutts, a banking heiress thought to be the richest woman in Britain. A serious art collector, she had made a career for herself as a philanthropist, giving money to a wide range of causes. She supported several charities in Africa and had even endowed the bishopric of Cape Town. In 1889 Burdett-Coutts was impressed enough by Rhodes to arrange for an introduction to her friend, the Prince of Wales, Albert Edward, the son of Queen Victoria and the future King Edward VII. "Bertie" once praised Burdett-Coutts for being "after my mother the most remarkable woman in the kingdom."[6]

Rhodes was well on his way to forming the British South Africa Company's board from prominent individuals. Rhodes approached Donald Currie and another shipping magnate, William Mackinnon, founder and president of the Imperial British East Africa Company. Both men declined, as did Lord Balfour of Burleigh, who held a position at court and who worried that his position as the junior whip in the House of Lords might create a conflict. Rhodes then persuaded another well-placed aristocrat, James Hamilton, the Duke of Abercorn, to be the BSAC's first chairman. A prominent landowner in Northern Ireland, he was the nephew of Lord John Russell, who served twice as prime minister, and was also the nephew of one of the richest men in England, the Duke of Bedford, who owned 250 acres in Central London and an estate in Bedfordshire. Abercorn served as a Conservative member of the House of Commons before acceding to his father's title in 1885, when he became an active member of the House of Lords. He was a staunch opponent of Irish Home Rule, which, in Conservative circles, balanced Rhodes's connections to Parnell, and he was also a good friend of Salisbury's. He was an ideal candidate to preside over the BSAC, from Rhodes's perspective, as he was not the sort of person to show great interest in the operations of the company.[7]

Rhodes scored another social coup by recruiting Alexander Duff, the Duke of Fife, to be the BSAC's first vice-chairman. In addition to being a prominent landowner in Aberdeenshire, Scotland, he, too was a member of the House of Lords, where he was a respected Liberal. He brought a special social connection for Rhodes: Fife was married to Princess Louise, daughter of the Prince of Wales. In addition to connections and status, Fife brought in another board member, Horace Farquhar, a private banker who invested the money earned from selling some of Fife's landholdings. Farquhar was one of the principal investors in Cawston and Gifford's Exploration Company. Appointing him to the board of the BSAC was a conflict of interest, as that company leased the Rudd Concession from the Central Search Association and its successor, the United Concessions Company, but technically it was not against any rules.[8]

It is significant that many investors were land-owning aristocrats. Rhodes pitched a new country for white settlers in Mashonaland that might inspire landowners who had nostalgia for Britain's traditional rural society—a society that for decades had been under pressure from international economic competition. In 1846 the British Parliament repealed the tariffs on imported grains, known as the Corn Laws, which protected rural elites. Without protection, the overall economic depression of 1873–1896 hit the big aristocratic estates hard. The downturn was exacerbated by the expansion of agriculture in the United States as well as Argentina, Canada, and Russia. Grain imports from Russia and the Americas made it difficult for English landowners to compete, a dire situation for the estates of the aristocracy. The Westminster Parliament remained committed to free trade, almost as an article of faith.[9] The English agricultural depression was widely discussed in the 1880s, when Rhodes was laying the groundwork for a new British settler society in Mashonaland. Rhodes's vision of re-establishing Arcadia in Mashonaland, controlled by a private company and relatively unregulated by the British government, may have made the chartered company appealing to nostalgic aristocrats. The promise of company shares also held out the prospect of easing financial strains.

Aristocrats like Fife and Abercorn gave the board of the BSAC an upper-class sheen. They gave Rhodes the credibility he needed to gain access to the capital held by Britain's landed classes and London's investors.[10] To round out the board, Rhodes sought a distinguished philanthropist who could help deflect any future criticism by humanitarians. Rhodes reeled in Albert Grey, heir to the Earl Grey of Northumberland and a former member of the House of Commons, where he was known as an ardent reformer and a progressive imperialist. Like Stead, he was a member of the critical South Africa Committee. Grey was known to be a man of integrity, which made him a useful tool for Rhodes. He became deeply involved in the administration of the BSAC.[11]

With another member of the South Africa Committee in the bag, Rhodes reached to involve Lord Salisbury himself. Rhodes gave Salisbury's son, Robert Cecil, the position of counsel to the board of the BSAC. Cecil was talented but still in his early twenties, with little experience.[12] In addition to hiring his young son, Rhodes helped Salisbury to solve a thorny political problem related to Central Africa. Nyasaland (present-day Malawi) was well to the northeast of any territory promised by the Rudd Concession, separated from Mashonaland by a large western salient of Portuguese Mozambique. In 1878, the African Lakes Company, backed by Scottish missionaries, began efforts to convert the people of Nyasaland's Shire Valley to Christianity and to teach them European-style farming. The effort was failing, and as a result the African Lakes Company could not be made into a chartered company. The 1884–1885 Berlin Conference of the European powers agreed that territorial claims had to be backed up by "effective occupation" by treaties, administration, and policing. The Portuguese authorities in Mozambique spent the late 1880s sending expeditions into parts of Mozambique and into the Shire Valley. The area became the scene of fighting among Europeans, Swahili slave traders, and local African chiefdoms supported by the company and even by British soldiers. In 1888, in Johannesburg, Rhodes met with one of the principal investors in the African Lakes Company, Alexander Livingstone Bruce, the son-in-law of David Livingstone and a relative, by marriage, of John S. Moffat. Bruce was also friends with Albert Grey and was related to the Scottish politician Lord Balfour of Burleigh. Alexander Livingstone Bruce had access to the corridors of power through his relatives and through his missionary contacts. Based on his conversations with Rhodes, he favored incorporating the African Lakes Company within Rhodes's BSAC.[13]

Rhodes wanted territory for the BSAC, and Salisbury needed an easy way to create a British presence in South-Central Africa. In 1888, Salisbury was in conversation with Harry Johnston, a thirty-year-old British diplomat who had served in West Africa. Johnston was an ardent imperialist who was fully aware of the problems presented by Portugal in Mozambique and Nyasaland.

He even had thought about creating a Cape-to-Cairo British zone in Africa, years before Rhodes advocated for a similar transcontinental vision. Salisbury encouraged Johnston to publish his views in the *Times*. On August 22, 1888, with the De Beers Mine still damaged and with Rudd and Maguire on their way to Bulawayo, an anonymous essay appeared in *The Times* that was written by Johnston, titled "Great Britain's Policy in Africa, by an African Explorer," which was indicative of European feelings of entitlement and capacity when it came to African territory.

> From this western shore of Lake Nyasa [Lake Malawi], along the course of the Loangwa River, through a country rich in gold, tin and iron, we may eventually extend our rule over the relatively short distance which at present separates our recently acquired protectorate over the middle Zambezi from the British settlements on Lake Nyasa. Thus, if our Government only grants some measure of support to the British agencies, commercial and evangelical, which have obtained such a footing in the Lake region, our possessions in South Africa may be linked some day to our sphere of influence in Eastern Africa and the Egyptian Sudan by a continuous band of British domination. The day will come, let us hope, when the African Lakes Company will shake hands with the British East Africa Company on the northern shores of Tanganyika; and Emin Pasha will rule in England's name and for the interests of civilization on the Albert Nyanza and the White Nile.[14]

Before sending Johnston to Nyasaland, Salisbury dispatched him to Lisbon, where he persuaded the Portuguese authorities to relinquish claims that connected Mozambique all the way across to Angola, while granting Portugal the Shire Highlands. This development was met with resistance in Scotland as well as in humanitarian circles. Salisbury preferred the direct British administration of Nyasaland, but the British treasury could not afford it. At the very least he wanted to send Johnston to secure treaties with chiefs that guaranteed a British presence in the area. Rhodes and Johnston had an all-night conversation about the future of Central Africa. After hours of scheming together, over breakfast Rhodes wrote a check to Johnston for £2,000, for the purpose of covering Johnston's immediate expenses in Nyasaland. Rhodes promised that the BSAC would pay £10,000 more. That money was enough to pay further expenses in Nyasaland as well as the cost of establishing a British presence in the territory to the west, in what is today Zambia. Salisbury appreciated the favor from Rhodes and accepted the deal.[15]

It was in this way, in the faraway city of London, that the fates of millions of people and roughly 470,000 square miles of territory in today's Zimbabwe, Zambia, and Malawi were presumed to be decided. Over the course of the next two years, while Johnston was busy with treaty-making, Rhodes used the BSAC to buy up almost all the shares of the African Lakes Company. He tripled the size of the BSAC's area of operations and ingratiated himself with Salisbury, who decided to support the BSAC's application for a charter. Salisbury did not want Britain to have the responsibilities of governing large portions of South-Central Africa, so he entrusted them to Rhodes, based on Rhodes's experience in politics and business, his powers of persuasion, and his network.[16] Salisbury also knew that the obscure, colonial Rhodes had Parnell in his pocket and that Parnell held the balance of power in the House of Commons. An alliance with an Irish nationalist and a colonial businessman might require aristocrats to set aside longstanding prejudices, but such an alliance might keep Lord Salisbury and the Conservative Party in power.

Rhodes created the BSAC's board of directors with the help of Gifford and Cawston as well as Rothschild. Rhodes needed their help. Although he was gaining prominence as a business leader and as a member of the Cape Parliament, his social background was not impressive to the likes of the Cecils, Duffs, Hamiltons, and Russells, not to mention the royal family. Social networking was important for the credibility of projects that needed to be financed. Among financial leaders, credibility had to do with one's status as a gentleman. The motto of the London Stock Exchange, where many of South Africa's diamond and gold shares were traded, was *Dictum Meum Pactum*, "My word is my bond," a reminder that landed aristocrats and their code of gentlemanly conduct were still consequential. Credibility also had to do with how gentlemen presented themselves. It was not enough for South African mine owners to send telegrams back and forth to London; they applied for financial support in person, by taking ships to England or by meeting with the agents of the financial houses sent to South Africa. The applicant for credit had to have the correct bearing and confidence. Any transaction depended on the bankers' sense of the person borrowing the money.[17]

The idea of a chartered company helped both Rhodes and his prominent allies. A charter could be granted so that Rhodes could use the sanction of the British government to establish his own personal rule over Lobengula's territories and the lands to the north. A charter gave the British aristocrats some leverage over Rhodes, who was only just beginning to be known as a credible person in high society. If he behaved badly, the charter could be revoked. Rhodes achieved some leverage, too. A revocation of the charter would make Britain responsible for governing the BSAC's territory. A revocation also had the potential to diminish the value of aristocratic shares in the BSAC.

The entire scheme of Rhodes and his transcontinental network was based on the Rudd Concession, which was now repudiated by Lobengula. The scheme was funded, in large part, by De Beers and Gold Fields. To avoid scrutiny, Rhodes enrolled more and more prominent people in his scheme. During these meetings, Rhodes and his partners in the Central Search Association did not disclose that the proposed chartered company, the BSAC, was not the owner of the Rudd Concession; it was merely a licensee. If the BSAC went bankrupt, it did not have this asset to sell. The ownership of the concession by another company would mean that investors and the British government would be responsible for all debts. Meanwhile, if the BSAC went under, Rhodes and the Central Search partners would still have the full value of the Rudd Concession.

Lobengula was only tricked once, but BSAC investors were tricked twice. They thought that the Rudd Concession was legitimate when it was contested, and they thought that it was owned by the BSAC, when it was owned by Central Search. The Colonial Office learned about the true ownership of the Rudd Concession in 1891 and told Rhodes that had they known about the true ownership in 1889, they would not have recommended the charter's approval. These moralizing claims themselves appear to be questionable, as Robinson, one of the shareholders of Central Search, must have known about the ownership of the Rudd Concession.[18]

Colonial officials and BSAC investors could have pried into the details, but in 1889 they took Rhodes at his word. The more that prominent people backed Rhodes's scheme, the more likely it was that they would be joined by even more prominent people. If Rothschild said that Rhodes could be respected and lent money, then people like Abercorn, Fife, and Grey could back him, too. Friendships and family ties produced emotions that clouded good judgment. And to make his supporters feel good, Rhodes was promoting a grand scheme that promised to do good things and make money at the same time, a recognized ploy of con artists. It took only a few years to demonstrate that the BSAC could not make money in Mashonaland, at which point Rhodes's backers were so deeply committed to the scheme that they were willing to keep it going against their better judgment.[19]

Rhodes campaigned in person and through his proxies. One of his key supporters for achieving dominance on the Road to the North was the railway engineer Charles Metcalfe, an acquaintance from Oxford, who had been surveying for the Bechuanaland Railway. Metcalfe lent public support to Rhodes's ideas for dominating the lands along the Road to the North in a well-placed magazine article. In March 1889, while Rhodes was involved in the BSAC negotiations with the Exploring Company and the Colonial Office, Metcalfe published "The British Sphere of Influence in South Africa," in the *Fortnightly Review*. The article was co-authored with Francisco Ricarde-Seaver, who had sold the Ngwato mining concession to Cawston and Gifford and who was now involved in gold ventures. The article argued for the colonization of Bechuanaland by "some powerful company or corporation, which might include the countries shown within the sphere of British influence." "This has been our practice in the past," the article continues, citing the former East India Company, as well as the more recent North Borneo Company.

The article publicized one of Rhodes's key ideas at a key moment. Near the start of the article, Metcalfe and Ricarde-Seaver applauded Rhodes's hopes for a transcontinental railway. In a passage that starts by manipulating nationalist sentiment, they wrote that "it is indeed vital to British interests in Africa that there should be an open road into the interior." They then stoked nationalism by mentioning local and global rivalries, citing that the British government was confronted with "the plans of the Transvaal Boer and the Germans to join hands and cut us off from the interior." Next the authors introduced the rhetoric of sports competition, stating that "we must recognise the fact that there is positively a race for the interior." Citing secret knowledge to back an unverifiable claim, they wrote, "It is not generally known that there has been actually a proposal to cede to Germany a strip of territory extending from east to west right across the continent north of the Zambesi." Such a move threatened Britain's ultimate ambition: it "would have effectually barred the passage of the iron track that must ultimately join the Cape with Cairo, and carry civilization through the heart of the dark continent." Thus did Metcalfe and Ricarde-Seaver do Rhodes's bidding, by playing on their educated audience's patriotic emotions and by conditioning them to think about geography and mobility as linked to Britain's national objectives. Near the conclusion, Metcalfe and Ricarde-Seaver wrote, "A word as to the way in which the countries within the British sphere of influence in South Africa should be civilised and developed. The chief means plainly is the iron way: this is the great civiliser, the great developing force of the nineteenth century." The article claimed that ideologies of civilization and imperialism were advanced by railway construction and found their best expression in the form of government by Rhodes's chartered company.[20]

By early June of 1889, the charter for the British South Africa Company had achieved the approval of enough influential people in London to move forward. Inside the British government, there were only two voices that steadfastly opposed chartering the BSAC, the senior staffers at the Colonial Office, John Bramston and Edward Fairfield. They were overruled by the secretary of state for the colonies, Lord Knutsford, and the permanent undersecretary, Robert Herbert. The decision was final, even though the Colonial Office received a letter in mid-June, written by Lobengula on April 28, in which the Ndebele king once again repudiated the Rudd Concession.[21]

When informed of Lobengula's letter, Rhodes assigned Maguire, then in London, to write a response. Maguire argued that Lobengula was illiterate, and his letter had not been witnessed by a missionary, therefore the letter could not be believed. Trustworthiness depended, once more, on social vouching. Furthermore, as the rifles were then in Bulawayo, it could be said that Lobengula had accepted the concession. That, it turned out, was an overstatement. While it was true that the rifles reached Bulawayo, they were also still being held by an agent of Rhodes and had not been taken by Lobengula. Maguire was just giving Britain's leading lights reasons to keep believing Rhodes. The financiers and the aristocracy played along. It was easier to turn a blind eye than to question the wrongdoings of prominent people with many supporters. A visit to the Colonial Office by Robinson, who had just stepped down as governor and high commissioner, provided final reassurances about Rhodes and Lobengula. Robinson, the recipient of shares in Central Search, was a trusted "old hand" at Southern Africa.[22]

Robinson smoothed over the continuing drama at Bulawayo. Lobengula's second letter to Queen Victoria repudiated the Rudd Concession. The Colonial Office responded with an acknowledgment. Lobengula's second letter crossed with Knutsford's letter of March 26, 1889, in which Queen Victoria recommended that Lobengula be wary of concession-seekers. Before crafting a response, Lobengula waited—and expected Moffat to wait—until Babayane, Mshete, Colenbrander, and Maund returned to Bulawayo. They only arrived on August 5. The next day, Lobengula called a meeting of all the envoys, British and Ndebele. Moffat translated Knutsford's letter into Tswana, a language that was understood by Lobengula and probably by most of the African men who were present. It was at this point that Mshete and Babayane objected to the queen's reference to Lobengula's request for a British adviser, which they had never asked for, but other than that Lobengula seemed pleased with the letter. The British backed his claim to Mashonaland over the Portuguese. On August 10, the king had a response written. It was witnessed by Moffat and addressed to Shippard, in the expectation that he would forward it to the governor and high commissioner in Cape Town and that from there it would be sent to the Colonial Office and the queen. In the letter Lobengula reaffirmed his claim to Mashonaland over the Portuguese. He declined the offer of a British adviser. Then he took a jab at the Rudd Concession. "The white people are troubling me much about gold. If the Queen hears that I have given away the whole country, it is not so. I have no one in my country who knows how to write. I do not understand where the dispute is, because I have no knowledge of writing." He concluded: "I thank the Queen for the word which my messengers give me by mouth, that the Queen says I am not to let anyone dig for gold in my country, except to dig for me as my servants."[23]

In London the creation of the chartered company was still moving forward. The list of preliminary investors was circulating. Rhodes had no way of knowing about the conversations in Bulawayo, let alone that Lobengula's dangerous letter was on its way to London. He returned to Cape Town in early August 1889, letting his London attorney, Bourchier Hawksley, work out the details of the BSAC charter application to the Privy Council. The application could be sunk by the arrival of Lobengula's letter. Unbeknownst to Rhodes, Sidney Shippard was giving timely help. Lobengula's letter was sent by rider from Bulawayo down the Road to the North. The road passed through the Bechuanaland Protectorate to Shippard in Vryburg, the capital of British Bechuanaland. The journey from Bulawayo to Vryburg could take several weeks. The letter was sent in mid-August. It is not known exactly when Shippard received the letter, but it was forwarded to Cape Town on October 14. Even by the most generous estimate, it appears that Shippard kept the letter in a desk drawer for at least a month. The letter was then sent by ship to London, where it arrived at the Colonial Office on November 18. The charter had already been granted on October 29.[24]

While letters were being sent (or not sent) to London, there was further drama in Bulawayo. Francis "Matabele" Thompson was still Rhodes's resident representative. He was often harassed by Ndebele men, with Lobengula's knowledge. When tensions over the concession grew, Lobengula threatened Thompson personally and demanded to see the original Rudd Concession again, so that he might have it compared with the copies. On September 10, Lobengula was so enraged that he executed the pro-concession induna, Lotshe, and three hundred of his relatives, by having them clubbed to death. Thompson was present for Lotshe's killing and sensed that he might be next. He fled toward Bechuanaland, riding bareback so fast that the horse dropped dead from exhaustion, forcing Thompson to walk the rest of the way.[25]

Lobengula was frustrated by his conversations with Maund and wanted to speak with Rhodes—"Ulodzi"—himself. Rhodes claimed to be too busy with politics in Cape Town and business in Kimberley but prevailed upon Dr. Jameson to represent him. Jameson's mission was to "square" the king, in other words, to bring him around to full support for the concession and the BSAC and the inevitable movement of white settlers into his territory. This was a tall order, but Jameson did make inroads. He traveled north to Bulawayo, collecting Thompson, who was ordered by Rhodes to return. In Bulawayo, Jameson was welcomed back into the king's inner circle for his medical knowledge and his diplomatic charm. Lobengula suffered from gout. To relieve the king's pain, Jameson began to give him injections of morphine, but even a consciousness-altering painkiller could not get Lobengula to permit white miners to begin digging for gold in Mashonaland.[26] In a meeting on October 18, 1889, Jameson backpedaled and asked if Lobengula would at least be willing to grant what he said he had granted, "digging one hole" near Ramokgwebana. Jameson's ploy gave Lobengula the impression that the BSAC was backing down from the Rudd Concession, which gave access to all of Mashonaland. Nothing could have been farther from Jameson's intent. He simply wanted to get his foot back in the door without arousing the suspicions of BSAC shareholders. Jameson wrote in his correspondence that his actual plan was "to bounce him [Lobengula] by saying we will accept a hole at Ramaquaban to be with…letting the whole country question slide by."[27]

While Jameson was installed at Lobengula's kraal, Rhodes was 1,400 miles away in Cape Town, negotiating a partnership between the Cape Colony and the BSAC. The BSAC appeared to have raised a great deal of money in London; in fact, it was undercapitalized, given the expenses of railway construction and colonial settlement. Rhodes asked Sprigg for help in constructing the railway line to the north. The BSAC had only half a million pounds to dedicate to the project, fully half of the company's capital. Sprigg agreed to let the Cape help Rhodes with the construction. In exchange, the Cape Government Railways were allowed to buy the line from the BSAC as soon as it was finished. Gifford protested. Up until this point, the Exploring Company had joined the BSAC's charter but had not yet sold its railway interests. Metcalfe had already been paid by the Exploring Company to survey the route. Rhodes was using his connections with the Cape government and the British government to put pressure on Gifford and Cawston to sell out at a lower price. The Cape government ultimately wound up contributing three-quarters of a million pounds to the construction.[28]

Lobengula and Jameson did not realize it until the news arrived later, but in England, the debate over the Rudd Concession became a moot point on October 29, 1889, about one year after the king put his "X" mark on the paper. When the queen approved the charter, the fraudulent Rudd Concession was turned into a warrant for the transformation of South-Central Africa. In the charter, the company was given a clear southern border, just across the Limpopo River from the Transvaal. The eastern border was clear, too: the "Portuguese Dominions" of Mozambique. But the northern and western borders were not yet set. Rhodes and Salisbury knew that the territory could include territory that, in the diplomatic term of the day, was under "effective occupation." The borders also depended on negotiations with Belgium over Katanga and with Germany over South-West Africa.

The charter document did not grant the BSAC sovereignty over this territory. Instead, it empowered the BSAC to negotiate with African rulers and to obtain rights to govern lands. The British government reserved the right to terminate any agreements that appeared to be against British interests and reserved the further right to terminate the charter itself. The BSAC was given the right to have its own police force and was allowed to enforce the law "in such ways and manners as it shall consider necessary." The company was to remain British but was to respect African customs, a nod to the humanitarians. African customs had not been experienced firsthand by the staff at the Colonial Office, whose knowledge derived from information provided by administrators like Robinson and Shippard.[29]

With the charter in hand, it was time to value the company and distribute shares of the stock. Rhodes insisted, over the hesitations of Cawston, that the company should be valued at one million pounds (equivalent to one hundred million dollars today). This was divided into one-pound shares. Most of the shares were fully paid up by the investors. Some of the shares were partly paid, at three shillings to the pound, with a call date (or deadline for full payment) established in advance, giving those investors time to secure funds. Shareholders were not allowed to sell their shares before two years, since values were likely to rise after that time. That way the market value would be higher than the par value, or the value assigned when the stock was first issued. Keeping shares off the market for two years gave Rhodes a window of time in which he could pursue risky policies in Mashonaland without negative financial repercussions. When the million pounds of BSAC stock was first issued, £750,000 was either fully or partly paid. A sum of £50,000 was used for buying out rival concession holders. Then £200,000 was held in reserve.[30]

Principal Shareholders in the BSAC (Source: Keppel-Jones, Rhodes and Rhodesia, 129–130.)

Investor	One-pound shares	Network information
De Beers Consolidated Mining	211,000	Rhodes a director
Gold Fields of South Africa	97,505	Rhodes a director
Exploring Company	75,000	Cawston and Gifford's company
Cecil Rhodes	45,212	Personal funds
Matabeleland Company	45,000	Ochs Brothers (diamond dealers), owners of a doubtful concession from Lobengula
Alfred Beit	34,100	De Beers director
Barney Barnato	30,000	De Beers director
Rochfort Maguire	18,695	Rudd's assistant in Bulawayo
Charles Rudd	17,897	Rhodes's long-term partner
Francis "Matabele" Thompson	12,291	Negotiated Rudd Concession; De Beers compound manager
Rhodes and Alfred Beit	11,100	Personal funds
Lord Edric Gifford	10,300	Exploring Company
Nathaniel, 1st Lord Rothschild	10,000	Backer of De Beers merger
Duke of Abercorn	9,000	Chair of BSAC Board
Albert Grey	9,000	BSAC Director
Horace T. Farquhar	8,000	Director of BSAC
Earl of Fife	8,000	Vice-Chair of BSAC Board
Edouard Lippert	7,100	Estranged cousin of Beit, financed Boyle and Renny-Tailyour
Alfred Beit and George Cawston	6,475	Personal funds
Hermann L. Eckstein	6,000	Associate of Porgès, investor in Gold Fields
Alfred Haggard	5,375	Concession-seeker, Austral Africa Exploration Co., brother of Rider Haggard

(Continued)

Investor	One-pound shares	Network information
J. Stevenson	5,268	Unknown
Donald Currie	5,000	Steamship magnate, rival during De Beers merger, director of De Beers
J. Seear	5,000	Unknown
G. Zwilgmeyer and H. A. Smart	5,000	Unknown
Alexander L. Bruce	4,570	African Lakes Co. director, connected to Scottish missionaries
Archibald R. Colquhoun	4,500	Explorer, author, first BSAC administrator of Mashonaland
Leander Starr Jameson	4,500	Rhodes's long-term associate
Frank Johnson	3,825	Manager of Cawston's Bechuanaland Exploration Co., prospecting partner of M. Heany
Edward R. Renny-Tailyour	3,700	Gold prospector, partner of F. Boyle and ally of E. Maund
H. F. Tiarks	3,340	London banker
Rutherfoord Harris	3,250	Associate of Jameson and Rhodes
George Cawston	3,236	Exploring Company
Harry J. Borrow	3,000	Concession seeker, partner of A. E. Burnett
Frank Boyle	3,000	Rival gold prospector, partner of Renny-Tailyour, ally of E. Maund
Maurice Heany	3,000	Gold prospector, partner of Frank Johnson
Tielman J. Hofmeyr	3,000	Member of the Afrikaner Bond, brother of J. H. Hofmeyr
John O. Maund	3,000	London banker, mountaineer, director of Exploring Co., married to Mary E. Baring of the banking family, brother of E. Maund
Hercules Robinson	3,000	Ex-governor and high commissioner
David Christiaan de Waal	2,500	Member of the Cape Parliament, Afrikaner Bond, brother-in-law of Hofmeyr
Thomas Leask	2,250	Owner of doubtful concessions

Investor	One-pound shares	Network information
Col. Charles Euan-Smith	2,000	British consul in Zanzibar, adviser to Salisbury
Charles Metcalfe	1,820	Engineer building Bechuanaland railway, future builder of railways for BSAC
Edward Burnett	1,575	Concession-seeker, partner of H. Borrow
Dennis Doyle	1,500	Scout, translator, and transport rider from Natal
Bourchier Hawksley	1,500	Rhodes's London attorney
Edward A. Maund	1,500	Exploring Company concession-seeker
Charles Dilke	1,200	Liberal reformer and imperialist, forced to resign from House of Commons after an 1885 sex scandal
Lt. Col. J. C. Willoughby	1,000	British Army, future officer of BSAC Police
Maj. Hamilton Goold-Adams	900	British Army, Bechuanaland Border Police
African Lakes Company	850	Nyasaland developers about to be merged into BSAC
J. H. de Villiers	750	Chief justice of the Cape Colony, decided the final lawsuit in the De Beers merger
Rider Haggard	720	Author, brother of concession-seeker Alfred Haggard
T. Fowell Buxton	500	Humanitarian, head of Aborigines Protection Society
Johan Colenbrander	500	Scout and translator from Natal, associated with E. Maund and E. Renny-Tailyour
Charles Mills	350	London representative of Cape Colony's government, introduced Rhodes to many influential people in London
Maj. H. L. Sapte	100	British Army, adviser to Gov. Loch
H. U. Moffat	50	Son of John S. Moffat; officer of Bechuanaland Police

By far the biggest shareholders in BSAC were De Beers and Gold Fields, with many shares held by individuals who had been part of these companies, such as Barnato, Beit, and Rhodes. Rhodes also doled out shares of the chartered company to those who might contest its access to the Rudd Concession, including the principals of the Exploring Company, Cawston and Gifford, as well as a long list of prospectors who had their own dealings with Lobengula. Rhodes distributed shares to buy the good will of powerful men, ranging from Fowell Buxton, the head of the famous Aborigines Protection Society, to Hercules Robinson, the former governor, to J. H. de Villiers, chief justice of the Cape Colony. Soon some of the men on the list were employed by Rhodes in colonizing Mashonaland.

The new British South Africa Company then licensed the Rudd Concession from the Central Search Association. The BSAC was now in business. The finalizing of the BSAC made it possible to inflate the shares of the Central Search Association and to reincorporate it into the new United Concessions Company, with a total capital of £4,000,000 ($600,000,000 in today's currency). Once again, the company's nominal value was divided into share portions derived from the commitment of individuals to the venture. The largest single portions went to Charles Rudd's brother, Thomas, and his business partner, H. D. Boyle. Rhodes's companion, Jameson, and their assistant, Francis "Matabele" Thompson, were also included, as was Hercules Robinson, whose services had been very important to Rhodes. An American named Harry Moore was included, too, because he maintained that he had his own concession from Lobengula.[31] Except for Harry Moore and John Wallop, all these shareholders also owned shares in the BSAC. The BSAC was designed never to have any competition for the right to license the Rudd Concession from United Concessions. The United Concessions' ownership of the Rudd Concession was not disclosed to the British government until several years later, after trouble in Mashonaland and Matabeleland coincided with the public selling of BSAC shares.

During the negotiations, the railroad played an important role. As the deal was going through, all shareholders expected that funds were likely to be earmarked for railroad construction. Railways were necessary for the profitability of the BSAC, but there were significant challenges to construction. The government of the Transvaal still hoped that its own railway could be constructed through very difficult terrain to Delagoa Bay in southern Mozambique, a deep-water port that was not controlled by the British. The Transvaal government used its ties to the Afrikaner Bond in the Cape Parliament to steer Cape railways along the Road to the North. The extension of the railway line was then discussed by representatives of the Cape, British Bechuanaland, and the Bechuanaland Protectorate, led by the Exploring Company and pushed by Gifford. The discussions became bogged down in details having to do with rights to land, water, and minerals. Even so, Gifford, Rhodes, and directors of the BSAC promised £500,000 for the extension of the railway from Kimberley up to Vryburg. The charter was granted without a firm agreement.[32]

The money for railroad construction from Kimberley to Vryburg was eventually gotten from the Cape Colony, which assumed most of the responsibility for that part of the line. Initially, Hofmeyr and the Bond were reluctant to grant Rhodes this support because they hoped to foster railway links to the Transvaal, not tracks that bypassed their compatriots in the Boer republic. The failure of free-trade negotiations between the Cape Colony and the Transvaal resulted in Hofmeyr becoming more open to funding railway development along the Road to the North, with Sivewright advising both Hofmeyr and Rhodes.[33] The BSAC received substantial land grants of thousands of square miles to go along with the tracks. In January 1890, Herbert, at the Colonial Office, wrote that "Mr. Rhodes has, I think, made a clever political-financial arrangement." In eleven months, the line from Kimberley to Vryburg was open, and the Cape bought the line soon after.[34]

When Britain's Cape Colony negotiated with the independent Boer republics over railways and free trade, a key background tension had to do with policy toward African people. The Cape gave the rights of citizenship to African people, while the Transvaal did not. The Transvaal legislature's hesitations over free trade had everything to do with their suspicions about the Cape's perceived liberal tendencies, even as Rhodes, Hofmeyr, and Sivewright were attempting to shift Cape policies more in the direction of the republics. Tensions over racial policies had a direct impact on the development of railroad lines.

While the complicated negotiations over railroads, finances, and concessions dragged on, talks in Bulawayo remained tense. Jameson continued sweet-talking Lobengula, injecting him with morphine and calling him "n----r" behind his back. Moffat was there, too, and on November 12, 1889, he broke the news of the charter to Lobengula. Moffat must have had advance notice of the charter—it was a three-week ride from Bulawayo to Vryburg. The news only caused Lobengula to be more skeptical of the British. In the words of historian Arthur Keppel-Jones, "The queen, in her last letter had advised him not to give the whole herd to the first comer, had now done herself what she had told him not to do."[35]

Jameson reported his exhaustion with the conversations. "Tiresome was no name for it," he wrote about a November 28 meeting. According to Jameson, Lobengula and the Ndebele indunas were "like a lot of silly children—repeating and repeating." Talking with them was a "grand exercise of patience," unwitting testimony to the skill of his negotiating partners in not being rushed. Finally, on December 9, Jameson got something he could use against Lobengula. He described the conversation that he and Moffat had with the Ndebele leader. "Well king you have given away Tati—let us begin from above Tati, and look from there 'upwards' where we will not interfere with your people or their kraals." Lobengula gestured his agreement and waved a hand toward the south. Then Jameson wondered what would happen if the BSAC could not find gold there. According to Jameson, Lobengula replied: "Come to me and I will let you dig there." Then Lobengula waved his hand in the direction of Mashonaland. This vague speaking and gesturing was interpreted by Jameson as permission for the BSAC to mine in Mashonaland, essentially confirming the original Rudd Concession, even though Lobengula had denounced it repeatedly. Jameson wrote to Harris that he and Moffat interpreted Lobengula's wave to be "a ratification of the original concession," or "as near a ratification it is possible to get from a k----r."[36]

Jameson did not know that Rhodes, too, was getting tired of Lobengula. Two days before Lobengula made his waving gesture, on December 7, 1889, Rhodes approached Frank Johnson and Maurice Heany to take out a contract on Lobengula's life. The plan was for Johnson and Heany to raise 500 troopers to attack Bulawayo. They would pretend to detect an Ndebele attack on the Ngwato, then use the fabricated attack as the excuse for killing or capturing Lobengula and as many of his indunas as possible. Rhodes agreed to pay Johnson and Heany £150,000 each and to settle on each of them 100,000 acres of land. While in the Ngwato capital with some of his recruits, Heany got drunk and was overheard bragging about the planned coup. A missionary took the story to Mackenzie, who, even though he was Rhodes's opponent, expressed concerns about what would happen to the force at the hands of the Ndebele army. Shippard got wind of the plot, too, and since the rumors were circulating widely, now had to inform the new governor and high commissioner, Henry Loch. The hot-tempered Loch called Rhodes to his office, where Rhodes denied the plot and blamed Johnson, who then had to come to Cape Town for his own dressing down. There were no consequences for Rhodes, except that he had to abandon the plot against Lobengula.[37]

More peaceful tactics seemed advisable. The colonial authorities and the members of the BSAC composed another letter to Lobengula through an elaborate drafting process. The first draft originated at the new BSAC office in London and was signed by Abercorn. It went to the Colonial Office, where it was accepted by Knutsford and signed as a letter from the queen. The influence of the BSAC network was not made plain. The draft went to the governor's office in Cape Town and was then sent to Shippard in Vryburg and to Moffat in Bulawayo, who sent it back to Cape Town asking for permission to make more modifications. The final draft was sent to Lobengula from Vryburg, delivered by six troopers of the Royal Horse Guards. They arrived at Bulawayo on January 29, 1890, turned out in their dress uniforms. The letter informed Lobengula that "the wisest and safest course" was to reach an agreement with Rhodes and his representative, Jameson, to "arrange where white people are to dig," and to let Rhodes and Jameson be "responsible to the Chief for any annoyance or trouble caused to himself or his people." Lobengula saw through the letter. When the six guardsmen were leaving, he told them that "the Queen's letter had been dictated by Rhodes and that she, the Queen, must not write any more letters like that one to him again."[38] Even though this response had a defiant tone, for several months Lobengula's resolve had been diminishing. Rhodes and Jameson might have achieved their plan through further negotiation. Instead, they devised their next plan to use armed force.

12

Leading the Cape Colony

RHODES BUILT AMALGAMATED industrial companies that derived wealth from mining. Like his fellow monopolists in the United States, he embraced the values of the era's capitalism, ranging from paternalism and philanthropy to activism against organized labor. Unlike his fellow monopolists, Rhodes was elected to a legislature and even led a country. It was in his political capacity that he was able to integrate industry and society. For Rhodes's system to work, he urgently needed state support for infrastructure development. Rhodes's direct involvement in politics makes him stand out from the other tycoons of the late nineteenth century.

Rhodes came to be prime minister of the Cape Colony thanks in part to his interest in developing a regional rail network. Planning for railway lines to the north had to be articulated with the politics of Boer independence and gold mining in the Transvaal. In June of 1888, the Cape government of Gordon Sprigg introduced a railway bill in Parliament. There was a line proposed to be built from Kimberley to Fourteen Streams, and then presumably to Vryburg, Gaborone, and Bulawayo, but its main purpose was no longer just to be a Road to the North. It was a means to put pressure on the Orange Free State and the South African Republic, or Transvaal, by drawing their commerce in a westerly direction. The bill also proposed a line to be constructed starting in Colesberg, then to cross the Orange River toward Bloemfontein and Johannesburg. The Cape government was attempting to profit from the gold rush.

Rhodes's allies in the Afrikaner Bond came out against the bill, seeing how it was likely to undermine the Boer republics' independence. Rhodes needed the Bond as allies, and with his interest in gold mining, he decided it was best not to antagonize the republics. He argued against Sprigg's bill, thinking that the line from Kimberley to Fourteen Streams could be delayed. A delay gave Kruger a concession in negotiations to open the Cape lines to Johannesburg. Sprigg's bill passed, but his lack of tact soon caused problems. His announcement that British Bechuanaland was going to be taken over by the Cape caused humanitarians in London to immediately and successfully lobby against the annexation. Without the Cape's annexation of British Bechuanaland, Gifford and Cawston's Exploring Company would have to stop construction of their railway north. Rhodes had a short window of time to use his own company, the BSAC, to gain mining concessions in Mashonaland and Matabeleland; to secure the right to govern territory north of the Limpopo from the British government and from local chiefs; and to build the railway from Kimberley to Bulawayo.[1]

Rhodes was absent from the Cape Parliament during 1889, so that he could spend time in England working on creating the BSAC. He returned to the Cape in 1890 as a well-known entity in Britain and South Africa. He missed the first two months of the 1890 parliamentary session and arrived just in time to welcome the new governor and high commissioner, Henry Brougham Loch. A well-built Scot with a long, bushy beard, Loch started in the military before entering politics. As a young cavalry officer, he fought in the Anglo-Sikh War (1845–1846) and the Crimean War (1853–1856). He served as a British diplomat in the Second Opium War (1856–1860). During the Anglo-French advance on Beijing, he was taken prisoner and tortured. Loch survived the horrors and became known as a respectable administrator, first as the lieutenant-governor of the Isle of Man, and next as the governor of Victoria, Australia, before arriving in the Cape Colony in 1890. Loch inherited Robinson's senior adviser in Cape Town, the Royal Navy's Captain Graham Bower, whose official title was "imperial secretary." Compared to Robinson, Bower found Loch to be "hot-headed and impetuous, dashing forward one day & retreating the next." He was also an extravagant spender, a practice that did not go over well with a Colonial Office that was dominated by penny-pinching Liberals. When Loch toured Bechuanaland in 1890, he sought to make a good impression, but in the eyes of the Colonial Office, the hard-riding governor did not really need an escort of fifty British cavalry troopers. Loch exceeded his budget and received a reprimand.[2]

On his initial tour of Southern Africa, Loch was invited to a welcome banquet in Bloemfontein. Sprigg, the prime minister, was not able to attend. Rhodes was only a hundred miles away at Kimberley and filled in for the premier. This was an opportunity for Rhodes to make an impression and lay out the key issues in South Africa, as he saw them, for the information of the new governor and high commissioner. Rhodes's speech was characteristic, in that he urged the need for infrastructure, unity, and cooperation between Britons and Boers. He reminded the new British governor that the colonists could rule themselves without interference from Britain. For Rhodes, it was all of a piece. In recounting the history of "responsible government" for an audience in an

Henry Loch. Wikimedia Commons.

independent republic, Rhodes reminded Loch that "it was a credit to the people of the colony that they had the boldness to take into their hands the government of the country." He boasted that "if I may put it to you to-night, when we look back upon the period during which we have had that government, I think we need not be ashamed of ourselves." He bragged about railroads, education, and governing African people. "We have taken upon ourselves the construction of two thousand miles of railway; we have educated ourselves, and have had to rule the races in our charge, and I think you will say that credit is due to us." Political unity was tied to customs union and infrastructure. "It has fallen to our lot to be put in possession of ports on the sea-coast, and thus we were brought into connection with the neighbouring Republics." Referring to the Cape's customs agreement with the Orange Free State, Rhodes praised their parliament, the Volksraad, for reaching an agreement with the Cape Colony "to contribute a share of customs, and to spend its money on railways in their State: and when there is any profit on those railways they share it on a half-and-half basis." Rhodes concluded by urging the extension of the rail lines from Kimberley to the coal mines of the Free State, so that the diamond industry no longer had to rely on coal from Britain.[3]

Rhodes was walking a political tightrope. He had to balance advocating for railroads, harbors, and unity, with the Colonial Office's expectation that the Cape Colony would not overburden its finances. To pull this off, Rhodes also had to manage complex businesses and alliances. Railway construction presented opportunities for state-building and patronage. For both these reasons, the government of Cape prime minister John Gordon Sprigg had been pursuing its major railroad-building initiative in 1889 and at the start of 1890. In addition to building lines that would position the Cape Colony strategically against the Transvaal and the Orange Free State, Sprigg intended to intensify development within the Cape, where small towns and rural areas wanted links to the major rail lines. Nine new rail lines were proposed, to be started simultaneously. The main beneficiaries were farmers and traders, but the costs were high, more than seven million pounds. Critics argued that such a cost was prohibitive and that the service on the debt was too much for the Cape Colony's economy to bear.

Sprigg's pork-barrel railway bill frightened enough English-speaking and Afrikaans-speaking lawmakers that it failed, and Sprigg lost the house's confidence. Negotiations began over the formation of a new government. The Afrikaner Bond still had the most seats in the House of Assembly, but their leader, Jan Hendrik Hofmeyr, was reluctant to form a government and serve as prime minister. Besides, when Sprigg's government fell, Hofmeyr was away in the Transvaal, discussing railway links and a customs union with President Paul Kruger. The anglophone members were divided between liberals and conservatives and between easterners and westerners. Years of balancing between the anglophone and the Bond paid off for Rhodes, who emerged as the only candidate able to put together a governing coalition. It helped that Rhodes had befriended Hofmeyr and that Hofmeyr's brother, Tielman, and his brother-in-law, David Christiaan de Waal, had been given 3,000 and 2,500 shares of the BSAC, respectively, while smaller amounts were spread around to the Bond's lesser lights. Rhodes was confirmed as prime minister by Loch, the governor, on July 17, 1890.[4]

Rhodes put together one of the most unusual governments in the history of the Cape Colony by uniting two factions that usually opposed each other. On the one side, Rhodes had the backing of the Afrikaner Bond. Hofmeyr preferred not to be a cabinet minister, but two Bondsmen received key appointments. Pieter Faure, a prominent attorney, became minister for native affairs and James Sivewright became the commissioner for crown lands and public works. The Cape's infrastructure was now in the charge of the expert on electricity and telegraphy with conservative views on race. Sivewright's experience seemed to qualify him for his position; his penchant for patronage and kickbacks raised eyebrows. He had recently bribed his way into becoming the manager of the municipal gas and water companies in Johannesburg, and soon enough, customers were complaining about the service.[5]

In putting together what was then called the "Cabinet of All the Talents," Rhodes was also supported by a trio who represented different strains of Cape liberalism. Rhodes patched things up with Merriman to the extent that his old friend was willing to serve as treasurer and as deputy prime minister. For the next several years, Merriman also carried out many of the duties of the prime minister, so Rhodes could pursue his business interests further afield. Like Merriman, J. W. Sauer found Sivewright in bad taste but was willing to join Rhodes as colonial secretary, the position akin to the interior secretary or home secretary. James Rose Innes rounded out the team as attorney general, even though he, too, had questions about Sivewright and Rhodes.[6]

Rhodes's premiership of the Cape Colony, a public office, overlapped considerably with his leadership of powerful private companies, such as De Beers, Gold Fields, and the BSAC. The BSAC depended on the government at the Cape for connections to rails and telegraphs. Now the infrastructure development and political leadership of the Cape and the BSAC were embodied in the same man. In public, Rhodes promised that he would step back from conflicts of interest and let the governor review his actions. In private, Rhodes distributed shares of the BSAC to members of the Bond and eventually invited several of them on trips north to company territory. In public, he met his critics head-to-head: Sprigg, who challenged his right to be prime minister; John Laing, who pointed out the conflict between the Cape and the BSAC; as well as Thomas Upington and Thomas Scanlen. They were all brought over to Rhodes's side. Sprigg and Laing entered the government in 1893. Upington was given a judgeship.

Rhodes gave special help to Thomas Scanlen, the former Cape prime minister and leader of the opposition who had been an early supporter of Rhodes's northern plans. Outside of the Cape Parliament, Scanlen was an attorney. and he and his law partner, Edward Ridge Syfret, had Rhodes as a client in their Cape Town office. There, Rhodes would have seen the elderly David Arnot, the mixed-race man who once thought he owned a concession to the entire diamond fields, working as Syfret and Scanlen's clerk.[7] Scanlen was a quiet and uncontroversial figure. Nonetheless, his marital problems and financial difficulties were the talk of Cape Town. In 1888, his wife, Sarah Ann, left him and moved to England, a decision that was unusual by the standards of the Victorians. Rhodes did Scanlen a favor and helped him to leave the Cape. The former prime minister was appointed to be the chief legal adviser to the BSAC in Salisbury, where the firm of Scanlen and Syfret opened an office. There, Scanlen went beyond corporate law practice to take turns as the chief prosecutor and the company administrator. The overlap between personal, state, and corporate interests was part of a pattern.[8]

A few months after the start of his premiership, Rhodes returned to Kimberley, where he gave a speech that revealed his thoughts about leading the Cape Colony. He claimed that he did not want to be prime minister, out of concern for his other endeavors, but took the opportunity hoping that cooperation between Britons and Boers was going to cause "many of the cobwebs to be swept away and a much better understanding would exist between the different parties." Rhodes hoped for unity through local self-determination, stating that "the Government's policy will be a South African policy," aiming "to draw closer the ties between us and the neighbouring States." The first item of business was a meeting with representatives of the Orange Free State, "to extend the railway from Bloemfontein to the Vaal River," a journey of 200 miles that made possible train travel to the border of the Transvaal. When it came to the Transvaal, Rhodes said that he was "sure that if the Transvaal joins with us and the other States in a Customs Union, the sister colony of Natal will also join, and that would be one great step towards a union of South Africa. The projected extension of the railway will likewise prove that we are getting nearer to a United South Africa."[9]

To make the colonial economy work, the railways needed to connect to better harbors. Rhodes was mindful of the importance of harbors, and in 1890 he began an effort to purchase Delagoa Bay from the Portuguese. The harbor had interested the Transvaal for some time; the proposed railway from Johannesburg was supposed to go there but the project bogged down. Rhodes's idea to purchase Delagoa Bay pressured President Paul Kruger to work with the Cape Colony and the British. Ownership of the harbor was also intended to help the BSAC and Gold Fields. The British government refused to help with money. Rhodes put together a Cape Colony offer of £700,000, but this was refused. The Portuguese government was reluctant to part with any territory in Mozambique, on grounds of national pride. The German government made a failed bid for McMurdo's railroad but still managed to pressure the Portuguese government to not to help the British or the Cape. Rhodes spent several years pushing for the acquisition of Delagoa Bay, involving John X. Merriman, James Sivewright, and Rochfort Maguire, as well as Natty Rothschild, whose representatives worked behind the scenes in London and Lisbon. In 1893, Rhodes made one last push by sending a letter to his friend, Archibald Primrose, Lord Rosebery, who was then the foreign secretary in Gladstone's government. Rhodes lobbied hard for the acquisition of Delagoa Bay, by reviewing the port's potential for the gold trade and the Royal Navy. In the letter, Rhodes indicated the strength of his personal interest in developing a transcontinental telegraph: "I hope you will not forget about getting me the right of way." Rhodes benefited from his personal relationship with Rosebery and feared his friend might be tired enough of politics to retire early. Rhodes concluded the letter by giving characteristic, high-minded advice to the prime minister: "I do hope even if you have trouble next session you will not retire from politics.... No man who has the chance of dealing with the world and doing some good for his country has any right to please his own fancies."[10]

The failure to acquire Delagoa Bay was a small setback to Rhodes's plan for a new state, united by railroads and customs agreements. In his speech at Kimberley, Rhodes reminded the audience that plans for infrastructure were closely related to plans for racial discrimination. He anticipated a united South Africa but told a parable about a newspaper editor in the Free State who, when asked about "native policy," said that he would not "at any time forfeit my flag." Everyone in the audience knew that he was talking about more than feelings of independence. In the Boer republics, Africans had no rights. Rhodes followed by claiming to "feel some respect for the neighbouring States, where men have been born under Republican institutions and with Republican feelings."[11]

Rhodes's efforts to deepen the material basis of discrimination tended to provoke political turmoil. Rhodes was supported by members of the Bond, but their support of discriminatory measures was often resisted by the anglophone Progressives. This difference between Bondsmen and Progressives was overcome by occasional alliances between the Bond and Sprigg's anglophone, Eastern Cape conservatives. Opportunism and racism could bring together rivals from different backgrounds. The Eastern Cape conservatives were not part of Rhodes's governing coalition, but they still could be rallied to support discriminatory legislation.

The first racially discriminatory measure that Rhodes introduced was intended to bind the Afrikaner Bond more closely to the Eastern Cape anglophones. The measure had already been introduced and defeated several years before—Rhodes probably knew he could use it to stir controversy. The Masters and Servants Amendment Bill of 1890, unofficially called the Strop Bill, made it legal for a white employer to beat an African servant or farm worker. The bill allowed Rhodes to signal to the Afrikaner Bond that he shared their values. Even though it failed, Rhodes gained the loyalty of the Bond for his various northern projects. The bill was opposed vehemently by Progressives.

Progressive enmity was short-lived, except for a handful of people who never forgave him. Olive Schreiner, the country's leading novelist and an advocate for African rights and women's rights, was one such person. Rhodes had read *Story of an African Farm* and had met with Schreiner on several occasions. There may even have been the spark of a romantic relationship between them. In 1890, she sent a letter to invite Rhodes to visit and talk about ideas, "a favour to me & help me in my work," but Schreiner was mindful of "the conventionalities of Cape Town life" which made "it difficult for a man to visit a woman as he would another man."[12] When Rhodes was pushing the Strop Bill, Olive Schreiner ended their friendship. Encountering Rhodes at a dinner party, she excoriated him in front of the guests, concluding the critique by deliberately banging her head on a table so hard that she almost knocked herself unconscious. Once she thought that Rhodes was "the only great man and man of genius South Africa possesses." But now "the perception of what his character was in its inmost depths was one of the most terrible revelations of my life." She sensed that "below the fascinating surface, the worms of falsehood and corruption creeping."[13]

Olive Schreiner. Wikimedia Commons.

Triggering a campaigner against racism and sexism was proof to the Bond that Rhodes was willing to sacrifice friendships for the sake of the old rural society. Rhodes now set his sights on voting rights. Cape liberals had a historic attachment to race-blind legislation, even if few of them practiced racial equality in their personal lives. Rhodes and the Bond preferred a stricter franchise with a much higher property qualification that eliminated the voting rights of many African men. In 1891, one of Rhodes's associates had even removed one hundred African voters from the rolls at Kimberley, leaving only twenty.[14] In 1892 the franchise issue dominated the entire session of the Cape Parliament. Various proposals were made and hotly debated, including one by Hofmeyr, who suggested that African votes be offset by giving the wealthiest people in the colony two votes. Rhodes had difficulty managing these debates, at least in part because at one point during this time he fell from a horse, broke his collarbone, and suffered a concussion. After spending several weeks healing, he managed to pull together a compromise, the 1892 Franchise and Ballot Bill, which was passed into law. The franchise was kept race-blind, but the property qualification was changed. The requirement to own land worth at least £25 was increased to £75. The law disenfranchised no one who had already voted, but an easily abused literacy test was introduced. Progressive support was secured partly through the introduction of the secret ballot, which Rhodes opposed but which he was willing to tolerate so that the Cape would limit African voting. The members of the Bond preferred taking all voting rights away from Africans, as was the practice in the Boer republics. The Cape's new franchise laws were a step in the republics' direction and toward Rhodes's goal of uniting South Africa's white governments. That being said, recent historical research suggests that the restrictions had less impact than Rhodes intended.[15]

When it came to racial politics, Rhodes was increasingly at odds with the Cape Progressives and increasingly at home with the Afrikaner Bond, particularly with their landed, cultured representatives. On the more industrial side of things, the telegraph expert and entrepreneur James Sivewright helped Rhodes make progress on his plan for rail development. As the minister in charge of the Cape's railways and telegraphs, Sivewright brokered a deal with the Transvaal's government. The Transvaal had struggled to raise the funds for its own railways, yet the independent-minded Kruger hesitated to join forces with the Cape Government Railway. Sivewright saw an opportunity to negotiate a complex agreement that unified the rail systems of the Cape and the two republics, helping them eventually to raise funds for construction. This opened the way for rail service connecting Cape Town, Bloemfontein, and

Pretoria. While negotiating technical and political unity, Sivewright was also using his position to line the pockets of his friends and associates. Rhodes signaled his pro-Bond values in 1891, when he arranged for Sivewright to receive a knighthood for brokering this deal. Progressives were predictably outraged.[16]

In time, though, even Rhodes was forced to confront Sivewright's corruption. Toward the end of 1892, Sivewright and Rhodes were traveling together on a trip to England, Europe, and Egypt, when an unflattering story broke in the *Cape Times*. The newspaper described how Sivewright had awarded a contract for railway food and beverages to a friend, James Logan, without opening the bidding to the public. A scandal broke, and it became clear that many of the Progressives no longer supported Rhodes's premiership. Ironically, since Rhodes was away, the Progressive deputy prime minister, Merriman, was running the government. On returning to Cape Town, Rhodes cancelled Logan's contract. Even so, it became clear that the Progressives intended to leave the Rhodes government, which would have caused it to collapse. Rhodes did not disavow Sivewright and leaned on Hofmeyr to help cast about for new cabinet members. At one point, the chief justice, Henry de Villiers, was even being considered as a caretaker prime minister. Merriman, J. W. Sauer, and Rose Innes all quit their positions and withdrew their support.

The Logan Scandal forced Rhodes to choose between Merriman and the Progressives, on the one hand, and Hofmeyr, Sivewright, and the Bond on the other. The Bond was the clear choice, since Rhodes was sympathetic to their racial views as well as their traditional practice of patronage and paternalism. The loss of the alliance with the Progressives caused Rhodes to court his old rival, Gordon Sprigg, leader of the Eastern Cape anglophones, who joined him in forming a second government. Sprigg replaced Merriman as the treasurer and became the deputy prime minister, too, managing most parliamentary business. Laing became the commissioner of crown lands and public works, while Will Schreiner served as the attorney general. Rhodes himself served as the secretary for native affairs. Sivewright was forced out of the Cabinet but remained in the House of Assembly and rejoined the Cabinet in 1896.[17] In the coalition politics of the Cape's House of Assembly, the new alliance was a minor revolution. The Easterners and the Bondsmen had a decades-long history of antagonism, even though their views of race and rural society were still largely consistent.

In 1894, Rhodes's new coalition handily won the Cape Colony's parliamentary election, garnering a majority of 58 out of 76 in the House of Assembly. Out of the 58 members who supported Rhodes, 40 of them were

Bondsmen. Some Bond members challenged the alliance with Rhodes on the grounds of corruption, and one even challenged him for the seat in Barkly West. Rhodes still won because the two seats in Barkly West and the two seats in Kimberley were in the pockets of De Beers. The election results meant that Rhodes's dependency on Hofmeyr was complete. Rhodes could pursue his vision for South Africa with the backing of white, rural conservatives and without Merriman and the Cape Progressives. Rhodes took a special interest in administering "natives." His attitude toward African people had been negative and critical ever since he set foot on African soil. The stage was set for innovation.[18]

With the new Rhodes government joining the Afrikaner Bond to the Eastern Cape anglophones, rural racial policies came to the fore. Nearly a century of wars between the Cape Colony and Xhosa people culminated in the Cape's sovereignty over the lands that ran between the Great Kei River as far east as the border with Natal. The Transkei, as this territory was called, was taken in 1877, and over the next decade, neighboring Thembuland and Griqualand East were taken, too. The area became the scene of violence and social disruption. At the start of 1894, with the new ministry in place, it seemed clear that the quasi-independent protectorate of Pondoland, between the Cape and Natal, would also be swallowed up soon. "Border incidents" involving accusations of raiding involved both colonial governments. Rhodes acted in February 1894, sending magistrates to oversee the protectorate's chiefdoms. The situation settled quickly, thanks to the arrival of a squadron of Cape Mounted Rifles. In April 1894, when Rhodes was touring the Transkei in a fancy carriage pulled by eight white horses, he crossed into Pondoland to deliver a message to the chiefs: they were going to manage their chiefdoms while answering to magistrates who were backed up by soldiers. This kind of indirect administration resembled the approach taken in Basutoland and the Bechuanaland Protectorate, as well as Zululand in Natal and Sekhukhuneland in the Transvaal. Such approaches did not sit well with Cape law. Rhodes now took up a legislative program to make Cape laws more compatible with his plan for the region.[19]

Rhodes knew full well about the connections between rural areas and the mining industry. The profitability of the diamond mines and the gold mines was tied to the labor of African migrant workers. They needed to be enticed and pressured to leave rural areas and travel to work on the diamond fields and the Rand. Migration to the mines had social repercussions. When young men left the countryside, they left families behind. Wives, children, and other relatives had to pick up the slack, not only in the form of farm labor but also in childrearing and craft production. In a society that was already suffering from the effects of colonial violence, families often became dependent on wages from the mines. Upon returning to the household, migrant workers brought home cash as well as elements of urban culture, ranging from material goods to religious values. Politics changed, too. Chiefs and lesser authorities yielded the young men of the community to mine recruiters and compound managers, while colonial authorities extended the reach of their government into the countryside.[20]

Rural areas were experiencing social and economic pressure. On top of this, the addition of the Transkei and other territories increased the Cape Colony's African population. The colony's population of 1.5 million was only 20 percent white. White colonists expressed concern that African populations continued to grow. Most of the Cape Colony's African families lived on land owned by whites. In the Western Cape, beloved of Rhodes and the heartland of the Bond, African and mixed-race people called "Coloureds" worked for landowners in exchange for wages and a "tot" or ration of wine. In other parts of the Cape Colony, peasants could pay rent or could engage in sharecropping. Most African peasants lived on land owned by whites, but in the Transkei, it was customary for African communities to hold collective title. Landholding was coming under significant strain. Rural areas seemed overpopulated, while the introduction of European agricultural techniques was often not suitable to local ecologies. Long-standing rural ways of life were under threat. Rural African people responded by taking up opportunities to join Christian churches and to attend European-style schools. Many able-bodied men migrated to the white-owned farms of the Eastern and Western Cape and to the diamond and gold mines.[21]

White settlers referred to these interconnected environmental, political, and social problems as the "Native Problem." Colonists debated the best ways to live cheek by jowl with African people and considered various forms of indirect rule and segregation. White farmers and mine owners insisted that any new system should provide access to reliable and inexpensive labor. Some white politicians and activists advocated for education and temperance. Others hoped that African people in the Transkei could be weaned from collective landholding and pushed to practice individual tenure, which would make it easier for whites to buy the land. Rhodes's approach to rural policy was influenced by his overarching commitment to unite the white communities of South Africa and to form a quasi-independent state loyal to Britain, stretching from the Cape to Central Africa.

Rhodes supported a new approach to segregation that white settlers were developing in a stressed rural district of the Eastern Cape called Glen Grey.

Thembu people in that part of the Cape mostly held the land communally. Starting in the late 1860s, Cape Colony magistrates began to distribute individual land holdings to prominent men who were cooperating with the colonial government. The key magistrate in the late 1860s and early 1870s was Edward Judge, who was later the Kimberley magistrate who chaired the investigation into the 1888 mine fire. Under Judge and his successors, the Cape was already encouraging individual landholding in Glen Grey while also helping a shift to capital-intensive agriculture. A hut tax was imposed, while administrators quietly hoped to introduce white settlement.[22]

Glen Grey entered the broader political consciousness of South Africa in 1893, when a report by three commissioners found that prominent Thembu men supported individual tenure. Individual tenure had many advantages in a modernizing economy. Land under individual tenure could be used as collateral for loans to purchase more land as well as seeds and implements. The evidence suggests that the farmers who had individual tenure were adopting European-style education and material culture. As some farmers prospered, others seemed to be becoming impoverished, especially, it was said, people who remained under communal tenure. Glen Grey and the neighboring districts of the Transkei were becoming a test case for addressing major questions about the relationship between customary land tenure and European ways to manage land and other natural resources.[23]

From the perspective of the Cape's governing white settler men, extending individual title to land was a two-edged sword. It might increase rural prosperity, and it might even result in sales to white settlers, but land ownership could also result in African men getting the right to vote, which Rhodes and the Bond opposed. The Bond was alarmed when a commission investigated disputes over land in Glen Grey and recommended that 8,000 male "heads of families" each receive individual tenure to lots of 55 morgen (115.5 acres, 47 hectares) and that sales to whites be restricted. Bondsmen found it undesirable for so many Thembu men to be enfranchised, presuming they could pass the literacy test. Rhodes devised a bill to solve these problems for Glen Grey and to provide a model for solving similar problems in much of the rest of white-ruled South Africa. In drafting what he called the "Native Bill for Africa," Rhodes worked closely with Hofmeyr and with two young advisers, Victor Sampson and William Milton.[24]

Rhodes was so determined to pass the Glen Grey Bill that he circumvented normal parliamentary procedures. Usually, a draft was introduced and discussed in committee, followed by debate on the floor of the House of Assembly. Revisions could be made before a vote. In the case of Glen Grey, the bill was drafted and discussed outside of the House of Assembly and presented in full, final form to the entire house for consideration. One of the most significant pieces of legislation ever debated in the Cape Parliament, the Glen Grey Bill was introduced near the end of the 1894 session, with Rhodes promising to continue the debate in 1895, if necessary. But when opposition to the bill grew, he decided to push it through before the 1894 session ended.[25] Like an experienced manipulator, Rhodes created time pressure and rushed judgment.[26]

The Glen Grey Bill granted African men individual tenure of plots of four morgen, not fifty-five, as was originally proposed. Primogeniture was imposed, to make sure that the plots remained an economical size and to pressure younger sons to migrate to white-owned farms and mines. The owners of the four-morgen plots were no longer qualified for the Cape franchise. Instead, residents were allowed to vote for representation in local councils that could introduce taxes and spend revenue on local projects. All men who did not migrate to another district for work were subject to a tax of ten shillings, one half of a pound. Europeans were not allowed to buy property in the area. Land that was not cultivated could be taken from its owner. Land could also be confiscated for unpaid debts. The bill was intended to uproot more African men and convey them to the mines and farms of white settlers.[27]

The first step of Rhodes's campaign for the bill's passage was to embark on a tour of the Transkei. Rhodes's critics were quick to recognize the fact-finding tour for what it was: political theater. John Tengo Jabavu, the Mfengu editor of the bilingual Xhosa-English newspaper, *Imvo Zabantsundu*, wrote, "It seems to us that Mr. Rhodes, who is responsible for the administration of Native Affairs, is taking his present run through the Transkei as a mere jaunt; and not as a journey for a serious study of Native problems." Jabavu pointed out that Rhodes had little time to speak with African people. Instead, he was "scampering through the Territories beyond the Kei" and he was "shooting, comet-like, through the territories, not caring to meet the people." Jabavu offered a critique of Rhodes's mode of travel: "From Capetown he came to Kei-road by train, and at the latter place he took a smart team of horses to Butterworth and Umtata in no time. The honourable gentleman has evidently overlooked the hundred thousand Natives in the vicinity of King Williamstown who look to him as 'their father.'" Instead of making a careful study of the area, "Mr. Rhodes seems to be running helter-skelter along the main road, hardly recognised by anybody save perhaps by an odd official at a halting place here and there."[28]

Rhodes now found himself in a public feud with Jabavu. The newspaper editor harped on the ways in which Rhodes and his cabinet lacked the

John Tengo Jabavu, with his son and biographer Davidson Don Tengo Jabavu. Wikimedia Commons.

knowledge to implement good policies in the Glen Grey District. Jabavu thundered that "there is no gentleman among those who compose the present Cape Cabinet who has shown any special acquaintance with Native character or understands Native wants; nor is there one in it in whom Natives can be said to place confidence." Rhodes and his colleagues were accused of acting out of ignorance and crass interest. "Mr. Rhodes, coming before Parliament," continued Jabavu, "representing in his most winning manner that he was by the Bill conceding this and that great advantage to the Glen Grey people; and then in an innocent way closing by exacting some privilege which people had heretofore enjoyed as a sort of *quid pro quo*."[29]

Rhodes and his own newspaper, the *Cape Argus*, were also supporting a bill to create racially segregated areas in the city of East London. Jabavu called this an effort at "harassing the Natives" and in response quoted a recent speech about "the elementary principles of British citizenship" by the Liberal Party's young star, Herbert Asquith, who had recently spoken about the importance of equality before the law in South Africa, calling it the "great ideal." Rhodes responded to Jabavu's criticism by avoiding an argument about first principles, preferring to make attacks that were *ad hominem*. "We should be careful about giving the Natives the franchise," said Rhodes. "They were like children, and could be led by one man."[30]

Rhodes introduced the Glen Grey Bill in a first reading, as was the custom. Then, when the bill was to have fuller consideration at the stage of the second reading, on July 30, he submitted the bill for consideration and gave a meandering oration. The transcript, published in the newspaper, gives insight into his approach to both African people and to his white male colleagues in the Cape Parliament. It was a hectoring, manipulative speech, filled with psychological pressure as well as erroneous information. He began with a false comparison to the United States, whose "labour troubles" were worse than South Africa's "native troubles." "When I see the labour troubles that are occurring in the United States," he declaimed, "and when I see the troubles that are going to occur with the English people in their own country on the social question and the labour question, I feel rather glad that the labour question here is connected to the native question." Colonial policy toward African people, which most listeners knew had been complex for centuries, was thus simplified. Knowledgeable house members had no opportunity to correct him.[31]

Rhodes's false claims about industrial unrest in the United States laid the rhetorical groundwork for him to defend the racial status quo in rural South Africa. According to Rhodes, South Africans had comparatively little to fear from "the natives." "In fact, I think the natives should be a source of great assistance to us." Here he injected a fear-inducing proviso: "At any rate, if the whites maintain their position as the supreme race, the day may come when we shall all be thankful that we have the natives with us in their proper position." And what if the "natives" were not kept in their proper position? South Africa might experience "those difficulties which are going on amongst all the old nations of the world."[32]

Rhodes stoked white fears by talking about a growing African population. "I find that they are increasing enormously.... They are multiplying to an enormous extent, and these locations are becoming too small." Putting it in Malthusian terms, "The old diminutions by war and pestilence do not occur" thanks to "our good government." He averred that "the natives devote their minds to a remarkable extent to the multiplication of children." The old stereotype of oversexed Africans was then followed by preposterous claims about the absence of politics. The reserves were overcrowded with people, meanwhile "the natives have had in the past an interesting employment for their minds in going to war and in consulting in their councils as to war. But by our wise government we have taken away all that employment from them. We have given them no share in the government—and I think rightly, too—and no interest in the local development of their country." The speech aimed to instill fear of overpopulation, yet never mentioned that during these "wars" in the Ciskei and Transkei, British and Dutch settlers had driven Xhosa people off their lands and forced them onto reserves. The history of how spaces became populated and depopulated was never referenced.[33]

The speech drips with a dismissive contempt for African people. "These are my premises," said Rhodes. "The natives know nothing about the politics of the country. They have told me time after time that they do not understand these politics. 'Leave us alone, but let us try and deal with some of our little local questions.' That is the common statement that they have made to me."[34] Again, one questionable claim was piled on top of another, then piled on top of another, before opposition members could make a rejoinder. Had Rhodes ever spoken with African people? Specific instances were not mentioned. African leaders and people had demonstrated time and time again that they understood colonial politics. Exactly which African people said they did not understand "these politics"? Rhodes did not say.

Continuing to deploy racial stereotypes, Rhodes claimed, "Further, it is our duty as a Government to remove these poor children from this life of sloth and laziness, and to give them some gentle stimulus to come forth and find out the dignity of labour." The millionaire advocate for the Strop Bill now spoke of gentle stimulation and the dignity of labor. Meanwhile, it was common in South Africa for Europeans to call Africans "children." The word implied that they deserved to be deprived of civic rights, but they could aspire to more as they grew to maturity at some unspecified date. As Rhodes said later in the speech, "Now, I say the natives are children. They are just emerging from barbarism." The "barbarian" epithet was thrown at editor John Tengo Jabavu: "I will say one thing in this House—that there was never a greater mistake made than by people who think that the native editor of *Imvo,* the native paper, has the confidence of the native people. And so the criticism and abuse which have been poured upon this Bill by this barbarian, who has just partly emerged from barbarism, are not to be taken any notice of."[35] Jabavu, for his part, decried the prime minister's infantilizing of African people, writing that "the most baleful mistakes in Native policy have resulted from actions conceived in this belief."[36]

Rhodes was following an argument made in 1853 by Thomas Carlyle, the conservative intellectual who claimed that African people could not be relied on to work for wages beyond subsistence and that the laws of supply and demand did not apply to them. African men needed other incentives besides wages to leave their homes. Rhodes proposed a labor tax of ten shillings on men who did not migrate to work on European farms or mines. He said:

> What I have found is this, that we must give some gentle stimulus to these people to make them go on working. There are a large number of young men in these locations who are like younger sons at home, or if you will have it so, like young men about town. These young natives live in the native areas and locations with their fathers and mothers and never do one stroke of work. But if a labour tax of 10s. were imposed, they would have to work.... These native young men are not in a position to marry and settle down, because they have not got cows. They are a nuisance to every district in the Transkei, to every magistrate in the Transkei, and to every location. We want to get hold of these young men and make them go out to work, and the only way to do this is to compel them to pay a certain labor tax. But we must prepare these people for the change. Every black man cannot have three acres and a cow, or four morgen and a commonage right. We have to face the question, and it must be brought home to them that in the future nine-tenths of them will have to spend their lives in daily labour, in physical work, in manual labour.[37]

Rhodes envisioned a rural area with nine-tenths of the male population engaged in labor for white settlers. Tax revenues would be spent on education, particularly "for industrial schools and training." Rhodes justified establishing industrial schools by manufacturing fear. Once again claiming to have traveled extensively through the Transkei, which he had not actually done, Rhodes said that he had "found some excellent establishments where the natives are taught Latin and Greek. They are turning out K----r parsons, most excellent individuals, but the thing is overdone. I find that these people cannot find congregations for them. There are K-----r parsons everywhere—these institutions are turning them out by the dozen. They are turning out to be a dangerous class." Rhodes proposed that the government should require attendance at industrial schools, rather than traditional schools, "otherwise these K-----r parsons would develop into agitators against the Government."[38]

Rhodes rambled on, hectoring fellow members of the House of Assembly by asking rhetorical questions: "Do you admit that the native question is most dangerous? Do you admit that you have done nothing for these people? Do you admit that in many parts of the colony these people have been ruining themselves?" He closed by suggesting that the entirety of the Transkei and Natal could become subject to the Glen Grey Bill and possibly even more territories. He added, "I may say the whole of the north will some time or another come under this Bill if passed by this House.... Indeed, you may say this is a native Bill for Africa."[39]

The "Native Bill for Africa" was an important step in the development of Rhodes's vision. The disassembly lines of the mines would be connected to the disassembling of rural African life. In his second term as prime minister, he used this opportunity to work out and legislate his ideas by managing shifting alliances. He continued to ally himself with the largely rural and conservative Bond and with Sprigg and the Eastern Cape conservatives. He dropped Merriman and the progressives. The political realignment gave Rhodes a chance to "gently stimulate" African men into farm work and mine work, at precisely the time when the Chamber of Mines was driving down costs by recruiting rural African workers. While the men might be away at the Rand or a white-owned farm, Rhodes hoped to keep their impoverished families on separate lands, struggling to make up for the lost labor of adult men, and unable to vote for members of the House of Assembly.

Rhodes's grand bill received criticism from several angles. Jabavu called it "drastic" and pointed out irregularities in parliamentary procedure, including a lack of full disclosure about the bill's effects, which he suspected were intended to be applied to the entire Cape Colony.[40] Merriman echoed Jabavu's earlier critique and said that the bill was based on superficial experiences and defective analysis. Rhodes had made only a brief visit, a "scamper through the Transkei" in which "he had gained a few ideas, put them into a Bill, and thought he was going to settle Africa." And Merriman wanted to know, if Africans were so lazy, how was it that Rhodes employed so many of them on the diamond fields? And turned their work into profit? All the progressives spoke out against measures that pressured African men to work. James Rose

Innes argued that the bill needed work and that it should not be pushed through the Cape Parliament before the end of the session, which was only one month away. Rhodes was at first amenable to Rose Innes's suggestion, but he tired of the criticism and knew that the Bond would deliver enough votes.[41]

After heated debate, Rhodes received enough support to push for final consideration on the last day of the session. When some members challenged Rhodes, he yelled "obstruction." More questions were raised, but Rhodes was prepared to outlast his critics. As the afternoon turned into evening, he refused to adjourn the House. He mocked his opponents by calling them followers of Jabavu. Rhodes pressed on with the bill all through the night, yielding only on the issue of temperance. The Bondsmen produced much of the cheap liquor sold in the Eastern Cape, so within his coalition, that part of the bill lacked full support. With temperance deleted, the bill passed largely intact. It was arguably the hardest fight surrounding any bill that Rhodes steered through the House of Assembly. Rhodes was proud of his achievement, keeping pro–Glen Grey (and anti-Jabavu) fan mail in his files. These are now contained in the Rhodes Papers at Oxford's Bodleian Library.[42]

The Glen Grey district resembled many of the districts in the Transkeian Territories. In October 1894, Rhodes succeeded in extending similar legislation to another Transkei district, Fingoland, populated mainly by Mfengu people, who had been among the region's key loyalists during the mid-nineteenth century. By the 1880s, forced disarmament and then changes to election laws were fostering a climate of resentment toward the colonial government. Bitter protests erupted against the extension of the Glen Grey Act, causing Rhodes enough concern that he visited the area in March 1895. The local magistrate arranged for Rhodes to speak at two public meetings, one at Idutywa, the other at Nqamakwe. Both meetings were attended by crowds of angry Mfengu men. Rhodes met their hostility with stubborn defenses of new landholding, government, and taxation. In Nqamakwe, he finished his speech with an explanation of the labor tax. When he turned to walk away, an Mfengu man yelled, "Hamba! Hamba! Asizi ku rola!" [Go! Go! We won't pay it!] More alarming to the colonial magistrates, resistance organizations were forming and were publicizing their protests outside of the district. Community leaders and ordinary people alike refused to cooperate. Rhodes held firm throughout the remainder of his term as prime minister, which ended in January 1896. Protests subsided, only to flare up again, especially after similar laws were extended to even more parts of the Transkei in the 1900s, where boycotts and nonviolent resistance were used against the government.[43]

The act and its likely consequences were characterized accurately by Jabavu. In October 1894, he described it as a premature experiment. "And experimenting with a million of Natives against their wish may be magnificent sport, and exciting to a degree, but so is larking in and around a powder magazine with a cigar in one's mouth. The end thereof may be peace, but it is more likely to be pieces." With petitions being sent to the British government and with the Aborigines Protection Society campaigning to repeal the Glen Grey Act, Jabavu made an accurate diagnosis: "There is at present a luminous halo around Mr. Rhodes. By a combination of good luck, good financing, clever share operations and conquest, he has become a much talked about man. But he may be that and be as far from being a statesman." Jabavu's goal was to bring African people around to the British way of life. This goal was hindered by Rhodes. "If our object is to cause suspicion and annoyance in the Native mind so that we may have the opportunity of employing against him the repeating rifle and the Maxim gun, we can safely give Mr. Rhodes carte blanche. But if we want to win them to our views, to loyalty, to a spontaneous development into a higher social life, we had better clearly recognize the fact that Mr. Rhodes should be one of the last men in the Colony to whom we should entrust the task."[44]

Over the next years, as the provisions of the Glen Grey Act were extended to even more districts of the Eastern Cape, district councils were appointed and began to meet to spend local tax revenues. The land tenure provisions were put in place. The labor tax was imposed, too, but it turned out to be difficult to collect and was eventually withdrawn. Much of the law was superseded in 1913, when the new Union of South Africa's parliament passed the Natives Land Act. The new law modified the Glen Grey Act and similar laws in other districts, but underlying attitudes about "opportunities" for "separate development" would prove long-lasting. Unfortunately, as Jabavu wrote, the provisions that allowed African people to govern themselves were "the mere sugar coating of the bitter pill—the pill which is to drive Natives off the lands secured them in perpetuity and for which they have the Queen's plighted word."[45]

The Cape Parliament was getting accustomed to passing "class" legislation, which meant, in the parlance of the day, legislation that was racially discriminatory. This was first done in 1878, with the Peace Preservation Act, and was done again in 1887, with the Voters' Registration Act. The passage of Glen Grey confirmed the discriminatory trend and became Rhodes's most significant legislative achievement. It pulled apart rural white settlers and Black Africans into separate landholding arrangements and separate governments.

Ever since the 1860s, a significant number of African farmers had been finding a niche for themselves in the colonial economy. Some were even beginning to prosper. The Glen Grey Act made it more difficult for African farmers to attain prosperity. African poverty was made to benefit white farmers and mine owners, who gained greater access to African labor. The act served the interest of racial discrimination while generating short-term profits for white settlers.[46]

The passage of the Glen Grey Act, with its apportionment of geographical space and political access, advanced Rhodes's vision of a white-dominated South Africa. It was aimed, in part, to hold together a conservative white coalition that was highly strained over another issue, the prevention of "sheep scab" disease. Sheep scab would seem like a relatively minor issue amidst larger colonial challenges, but this slow, quietly unfolding biological problem caused significant rifts among the very same white colonists whom Rhodes was trying to hold together.

Sheep scab, known in Afrikaans as "brandziecht" [fire sickness], was becoming widespread in South Africa. Sheep afflicted with the disease scratch on posts and pick at themselves until large patches of wool rub off, then the sheep keep scratching until burn marks and scabs appear on their bare skin. What little wool is left is often damaged and unsaleable. In the early nineteenth century, the disease was shown to be caused by mites, *Psoroptes ovis,* whose bites caused an allergic reaction and dermatitis on the sheep, thus making them scratch themselves. The mites spread from sheep to sheep as well as from fence posts and rocks, so the best preventative tactic involves isolating flocks from each other. By the end of the nineteenth century, the most effective solution was to dip all sheep in a tank filled with a solution of pesticide.

Sheep farming played an important role in the economy of the Cape Colony, and the best-educated and most prosperous sheep farmers pressed for mandatory dipping. They were led by Gordon Sprigg, who employed scientific methods on his own Eastern Cape farms. But many of the Eastern Cape's sheep farmers were impoverished and uneducated Boer shepherds who herded flocks in marginal areas and were disinclined to scientific solutions. They resented government intrusion and disliked how their educated betters dismissed their practical experience and local knowledge. These farmers made up a significant constituency within the Afrikaner Bond. So, too, did the growers of grapes and wheat in the Western Cape, who tended to be wealthier and better educated. They had seen the benefits of scientific agriculture when the Cape government, with strong support from Rhodes, helped them to maintain their farms by addressing the problem of the phylloxera, the louse that damages grapevines.

When it came time to discuss the outbreak of sheep scab, the Afrikaner Bond's meetings became acrimonious, with the antiscience, antiregulation farmers sensing the condescension of the proscience, proregulation farmers. The disdain of the rich farmers fueled the poor farmers' fulminations about tyranny, making them seem even more deplorable to the Western Cape gentry. The shepherds who opposed the Scab Bill threatened to trek with their sheep to German South-West Africa. The Western Cape's grape growers and wheat farmers worried that the underproduction of wool would hurt the South African economy. Prosperous anglophone sheep farmers like Gordon Sprigg pressed for government regulation through mandatory dipping and fencing, a move that threatened to blow up Rhodes's coalition. Rhodes's finely tuned network of people and materials was challenged by the need to get bugs off the sheep of rustic shepherds.[47]

Rhodes maneuvered successfully to hold his coalition together. Maintaining the different rural societies of the Cape and extending their discriminatory and exploitative practices northward was a key feature of Rhodes's plan, yet the day-to-day politicking required to advance his goals could be challenging. Hofmeyr found politics so tiresome that he resigned from his parliamentary seat in April 1895. Rhodes had greater incentives to stay the course. If his government were ever to lose the confidence of the House of Assembly, his role as head of the BSAC could be undermined. Rhodes recognized that the scientific approach to sheep scab was necessary, but he waffled and compromised enough to keep the antiregulation farmers from bolting out of the coalition. Rhodes's statements on the floor about Africans' immaturity and indolence were aimed, in part, at building common ground among rival groups of rich and poor white sheep farmers.

Amidst the rancor, Rhodes showed his commitment to the science of animal husbandry in interesting ways. Nineteenth-century animal and plant science depended on the exchange of specimens from one region to another in order to improve breeding stock. Rhodes spent November and December of 1894 conducting business in England. At the start of 1895, on the return to South Africa, he took a detour to Constantinople to visit the Ottoman Sultan, Abdul Hamid II. Hamid, like Rhodes, was interested in modernizing and unifying his country by the extension of railroads and telegraphs. And like Rhodes, he took a ruthless approach to restive populations in the borderlands, where he earned a telling nickname, the Bloody Sultan. Rhodes went to the sultan's court to discuss goats. Angora goats were being raised in the Cape

Colony for the production of mohair, but the South African goats were inferior to the purebred goats of Anatolia. The British ambassador arranged for Rhodes to have an audience with Hamid to discuss the acquisition of purebred Angora goats that would be used to improve the Cape breeding stock. The audience almost failed. Rhodes turned up at the palace dressed too casually and had to borrow a coat from the ambassador. Rhodes was annoyed that he was forced to wait until the end of the sultan's audience with an Indian prince, but in time he proceeded to have an amiable chat with Hamid and secured a gift of goats. Starting with that breeding stock, the Cape gradually increased its production of mohair.[48]

The debate over sheep scab disease continued in Cape politics. In March 1895, the annual meeting of the Bond managed to craft a compromise bill that was less restrictive. In May, two hundred sheep farmers arrived in Cape Town to petition Rhodes. He tried to win them over by inviting them to lunch at his home but still denied their request for a watered-down bill. Pressure from the grass roots continued. After further negotiations in the House of Assembly, Rhodes wound up compromising, allowing for experimental applications of sheep dip and promising to revisit the issue and address any problems in a follow-up bill in the 1896 session of the Cape Parliament.[49]

Rhodes owed his premiership to allies in the Afrikaner Bond, who held just under half of the seats in the Cape Parliament. The Bond had one requirement: the preservation of the colonial rural order. As prime minister, Rhodes tended to cater to the Bond's desires, reinforcing the rural order in the Western Cape and strengthening white colonist power in the Eastern Cape, too. This was more than a marriage of convenience, in which Rhodes exchanged support for the rural order for their support for his projects. He, too, believed in the old order. He fully bought into the old way of life. Whatever technical innovations he supported, such as approaches to the phylloxera outbreak in the vineyards or to the scab disease that afflicted sheep, he had a fascination with the way of life of the Western Cape's Dutch gentry.

While Rhodes supported the material interests of the Afrikaner farmers at the Cape, his renovation of a home near Cape Town indicated his sympathy with the Cape Dutch. Rhodes had been wealthy since his student days at Oxford, but he lived simply, especially when compared to fellow nineteenth-century monopolists. In Kimberley, he lived in Jameson's bungalow and took his meals at the Kimberley Club. Since his election to the House of Assembly, he resided in Cape Town, sharing a home on Adderley Street with Captain M. H. Penfold, the harbormaster. Rhodes ate at the Civil Service Club and at Poole's restaurant. Penfold took him under his wing, introducing him around to Cape Town society. Penfold even taught Rhodes to sail. After Rhodes was criticized for dressing too casually for the Cape Parliament, the captain helped to make sure that Rhodes at least had clean clothes to wear. As Rhodes became wealthier and his travels took him regularly to London, his private secretaries took on the task of his clothing, which had to become more formal. The Rhodes family still owned property in Dalston, but since there was no home there, Rhodes stayed at the Westminster Palace Hotel on Victoria Street. Starting in 1890, he was lodged in an expensive suite at the Burlington Hotel on Cork Street in Mayfair.[50]

Rhodes spent most of 1889 in London. When he returned to Cape Town and took up the premiership, he decided that he needed more formal living arrangements. He approached friends and colleagues about renting a home in the vicinity of Cape Town and settled on a large old farmhouse, a six-mile journey around Devil's Peak near the suburb of Rondebosch. The home was called Groote Schuur, Dutch for "big barn." The home dated to the eighteenth century, when it had been used by the Dutch East India Company for storing grain and wine. Rhodes became aware of Groote Schuur when it was being rented by Henry Barkly and Hercules Robinson. Rhodes rented the estate in 1890, then, two years later, he bought it. He also bought up the adjoining estates, totaling 1,500 acres.

Groote Schuur, Rhodes's Home in Rondebosch. Wikimedia Commons.

Rhodes's motives in purchasing Groote Schuur were not entirely clear. He was almost forty years old and perhaps sensing that he should settle down. He may have also wanted to blend in more with the landowners of the Western Cape, which Groote Schuur allowed him to do in style. Whatever his motives, Rhodes formed a strong attachment to Groote Schuur, as his contemporaries noted. His first step as owner was to decorate it with up-to-date furnishings from London, but in 1893, on making the acquaintance of a thirty-one-year-old architect named Herbert Baker, Rhodes embarked on a dramatic renovation. The roof was restored to the original thatch, while cheap wood fittings were replaced with traditional teak. Baker threw away the furniture and replaced it with Cape antiques.[51]

Baker and Rhodes aimed to make Groote Schuur into an important home for entertaining guests, who would be given a sense of imperial grandeur in the dining room, parlors, and verandahs. The private spaces were grand, too, including a famous master bathroom with an enormous granite tub. There was also a spectacular view of Devil's Peak from the upstairs bedroom window. It took Rhodes a little while to get used to such a large house. When the renovations were in progress, he took to sleeping out behind the house in the old slave quarters. He only moved into the house when Baker had the slave quarters demolished. The final renovation retained the simple, elegant lines of a Dutch farmhouse. Baker undid earlier renovations, exposing the beams on the interior to give a more rustic look. He used local materials and craftsmen, following along the lines of the Arts and Crafts Movement. The architectural highlight of the house, arguably, is the back *stoep,* the Dutch word for porch. Seated there, Rhodes and his guests saw the elegant landscaping rise toward Table Mountain, a sublime view.

At Groote Schuur, politicians, friends, and visitors were regularly hosted for luncheons, suppers, and evening entertainment. The grounds were planned and maintained with care and formed a spectacular backdrop for horseback riding with John Merriman, Jan Hofmeyr, and other influential men who sought Rhodes's advice as they sorted out the problems and objectives of the day. Inside the great house, Rhodes's tastes in decoration ran toward elegant simplicity. Rooms were graced with dark wooden furniture and Persian carpets. Wooden doors and chests were furnished with beautiful brass fittings. Rhodes lavished attention on the library, which was furnished with rare books and maps about Africa as well as an extensive collection of the Greek and Roman classics, consisting of several hundred bound volumes that had been specially translated for him by a team of British scholars. There were other telling artifacts placed around Groote Schuur. In his bedroom, Rhodes displayed a small gilded statue of the young Napoleon; an engraving of Napoleon crowning himself emperor; and a clock that was said to belong to Napoleon at St. Helena. He hung a childhood portrait of Herbert over his bed. Rhodes had a collection of archaeological artifacts from Zimbabwe and several items that had once belonged to Lobengula, including his seal, which produced his name and an image of an elephant, as well as a silver model of an elephant, containing a drinking cup, that had been found in the smoldering ruins of the chief's kraal. One of Rhodes's prized possessions was a soapstone bird from Great Zimbabwe. Several replicas in stone and wood could be found around the house, including beautifully carved birds atop the posts of the teak staircase. Sauer commented that Rhodes also kept a collection of stone phalluses from Zimbabwe, perhaps to remind himself of Bent's thesis of Phoenician colonization. The classically educated Rhodes may also have known that the Romans believed phallic pendants and statues brought fertility and luck. The masculine inclinations of Groote Schuur's owner were further demonstrated by the hiring of an all-male staff. Visitors who brought women servants were instructed to keep them out of Rhodes's sight.[52]

From architectural restoration to agricultural science, everything that Rhodes did to improve the Cape Colony was done with reverence for the old order. Groote Schuur signaled to the Afrikaner gentry of the Western Cape that he shared in their culture, even if he could not speak their language very well. Rhodes took care of the Bond through policy and through favors. In theory Rhodes had grown up as a free-trader, like many middle-class people in mid-nineteenth-century England, but as a politician tied to the Bond, he had to shift to protectionism. Cape vineyards and fruit farms, in which Rhodes soon had a personal interest, were protected by tariffs, even as South Africans expected to import cheap, unprotected goods from Britain. Mainly, Rhodes hoped to receive the benefits of the British connection without the costs. He supported the new idea of a system of tariffs between Britain and its colonies—known as Imperial Preference—and in 1894 even sent Hofmeyr to the conference in Ottawa that debated the subject. It was at home, though, that Rhodes took care of his supporters most generously. Supporters were sustained and opponents were "squared" by generous gifts of BSAC shares and by jobs and estates in BSAC territory.[53] Rhodes's aim was to maintain the old order at the Cape while uniting the four South African colonies into one self-governing state, connected to Britain, all the while spreading white settlement even farther north.

13

Multiplying Force

RHODES PUSHED FOR rapid colonization in the new territory of the British South Africa Company. He worked at high speed because the shareholders of the BSAC expected that in two years they would profit from their investments. Profitability in such a short time required decisive actions. Concessions needed to be granted. Mines needed to be opened. Farmlands needed to be taken. Spaces needed to be populated. Reports needed to be made. There was no time for a white settler society to evolve organically. It had to be forced, and Rhodes chafed against constraints that were at once material, political, and social. Half a million indigenous people would be pushed aside.

Mining prospects were thought to be best in Mashonaland, the northeastern region of today's Zimbabwe. Near the end of 1889, Frederick Courteney Selous returned to Southern Africa from his stay in London. He visited Rhodes in Kimberley and impressed upon him the urgent need to move on territory in Mashonaland, given the state of European rivalries and Transvaal expansionism.[1] Selous, Rhodes, and their colleagues believed that Shona capacities to resist were low. Some Shona chiefdoms had several hundred people; some had several thousand. Some Shona chiefdoms were well organized and armed; some were not. Groups of Shona people along the southwest border of Mashonaland were firmly incorporated within the Ndebele kingdom, which meant that the Rudd Concession was more likely to apply to them than the Shona groups that were farther away. Shona people were subject to being raided and having cattle and family members captured and taken by Ndebele raiders, but most of the Europeans who were familiar with South-Central Africa considered the Shona groups to be independent. The Portuguese could also make a plausible claim to dominance in the area. These complications were disregarded by Rhodes, who pushed ahead anyway.[2]

To access Mashonaland, Rhodes and the BSAC navigated several geographical and political obstacles. Selous advised Rhodes that there were several ways to get from the Cape to Mashonaland; none of them were easy. It was possible to travel through the Transvaal, but its government was committed to resisting

Frederick Courteney Selous. Library of Congress, LC-DIG-ggbain-00983.

British expansion generally as well as Rhodes personally. It was possible to go around the Transvaal by taking the Road to the North, which passed through Tswana and Ndebele territory, but Khama, Lobengula, and Rhodes were all suspicious of each other. Finally, it was possible to access Mashonaland from the east, by sailing to the port of Beira, in Mozambique and taking a combination of rivers and pathways westward through difficult terrain. The Portuguese colonial government of Mozambique, like the Transvaal, Tswana, and Ndebele, had little reason to assist Rhodes and the BSAC in accessing Mashonaland.

Rhodes began to sketch out a plan for armed gunboats to carry BSAC soldiers up the Zambezi River to the north rim of Shona territory. Company troops would disembark and march south into Mashonaland. Selous advised Rhodes that this plan was impracticable; the river had to be entered at its mouth in central Mozambique where Portuguese authorities would certainly resist. The river was also unlikely to be navigable by gunboats, even the shallow-draft vessels that Rhodes hoped to have built. And Rhodes was reminded that the area was infested with malaria-bearing mosquitoes and with tsetse flies. Rhodes and his colleagues at the BSAC knew that the flies caused sleeping sickness, which debilitated and killed horses and cattle. Rhodes and his colleagues even considered proposals to import camels, unaware that camels, too, were susceptible to sleeping sickness.[3]

Rhodes, on the advice of Selous, decided that the best way for the BSAC to access Shona territory was to go up the Road to the North as far as the borderlands of Ndebele territory and then pass around to the northeast to avoid conflict with Lobengula. In January of 1890, Rhodes and Selous met with Loch in Cape Town, joined by Sidney Shippard and Frederick Carrington, the commander of the Bechuanaland Border Police. Rhodes had first made Carrington's acquaintance in 1877, when the British officer led cavalry units in Griqualand West. Later, in 1885, Carrington served with the Warren Expedition. Carrington, Loch, and Shippard listened as Rhodes and Selous described their plan, which involved recruiting, training, and arming a force of 500 troopers. Their task was to escort a Pioneer Column of 300 miners on 100 wagons, accompanied by Tswana laborers, in a ride around Ndebele territory and up into Mashonaland. They were expected to avoid conflict. The broadly worded charters of De Beers and Gold Fields would allow sources of funding for the Pioneer Column. The amalgamation of the mines and the resulting layoffs of miners provided a ready source of recruits.[4]

Loch gave tentative approval to Rhodes's scheme, contingent on London's approval and the advice of Moffat and Khama. Khama was pleased at the prospect of Lobengula being menaced. Moffat was still stationed in Bulawayo and was understandably concerned about the prospect of war. When Loch wrote to the secretary of state for the colonies, Lord Knutsford, he and his senior staff were dismayed. They knew that Lobengula had not agreed to let in an armed band of several hundred troopers. Edward Fairfield commented that "the people in South Africa are getting out of hand." It seemed that the expedition was likely to provoke a war. The Colonial Office consulted the War Office, whose senior staff were equally concerned. It was hard to imagine that several hundred colonial soldiers could prevail over thousands of Ndebele fighters. Knutsford cabled Loch and instructed him that any incursion had to be approved by Lobengula.[5]

Loch conveyed the disappointing news to Rhodes. Both men found themselves in a difficult diplomatic position, having to balance the interests of the Cape and London in their efforts to reorganize the spaces of the African interior. Two parties of Transvaal Boers were organizing "treks" into the interior, with the object of seizing land. Their leaders announced having concessions from Shona chiefs, who claimed that they were not under Lobengula's "protection." When this claim got out, the Portuguese government laid its cards on the table and claimed these parts of Mashonaland. Rhodes wrote directly to Salisbury, who became concerned about the claims of the Portuguese and the Transvaal and swung his support behind Rhodes. With the diplomatic situation growing more intense by the day, James Sivewright, who had business in the Transvaal, persuaded Kruger to meet with Loch and Rhodes. Further complicating the picture, the Transvaal was involved in a different aspect of "northern" diplomacy over the future of Swaziland, where both the Transvaal and the British shared influence over the king. Loch insisted that to discuss Swaziland, Kruger would have to prevent the first trek that intended to go to Mashonaland. In March of 1890 the three men convened a meeting at a remote location on the Cape-Transvaal border, Blignaut's Pont, and signed an agreement to continue joint oversight over Swaziland. Kruger only agreed to prevent the first parties of Boers from entering Mashonaland. The BSAC would have to occupy the territory in order to prevent any future Transvaal trekkers from arriving.[6]

Under time pressure, Rhodes ordered multiple moves. Selous rode to Khama's court, obtained permission to organize a road-building party, then rode to Lobengula's court in Bulawayo, to ask permission to do the same, with the help of local labor. The country's first modern infrastructure project was going to be a road to facilitate BSAC domination. The road aroused the suspicions of Lobengula, who worried about giving easier access to the BSAC or any invading force, including Boers from the Transvaal. Selous was disappointed; he did not realize that Jameson lacked explicit permission from Lobengula for a BSAC presence in Mashonaland. Lobengula told Selous that he wanted to negotiate directly with Rhodes. "Go back and take Rhodes by the hand and bring him here," ordered the king. Selous rode for eleven days to Kimberley, where Rhodes declined to take up the invitation, fearing he might be kidnapped.[7]

Rhodes did know about the lack of exact permission and sent Jameson to meet with Lobengula again. Rhodes was in a rush but Lobengula, who also understood the value of time in negotiation, seemed to be stalling. Rhodes counted on the success of his friend Jameson. In late April of 1890, the doctor rode to Bulawayo. Working together with Moffat, Jameson held a succession of meetings with Lobengula. As before, Lobengula welcomed Jameson, who resumed the chief's injections of morphine. Jameson informed Lobengula of the anticipated size and power of the Pioneer Column and the plan to occupy a large area in Mashonaland. Jameson pushed Lobengula to let the Pioneer Column swing past Ndebele territory on their way to Mashonaland, to the northeast. At their final meeting in early May 1890, when pressed about the

Pioneer Column, Lobengula said, "I do not refuse, but let Rhodes come." Jameson wrote that "I have not got a refusal, but devilish little else... I have made him say in his own words that 'he does not refuse.' Surely that in a k----r is as good a ratification of his former permission, and we are justified in going on with the expedition into Mashonaland." Lobengula's half-permission looked weak in Cape Town and it looked weak in London, but external pressure from Mozambique and the Transvaal pushed the authorities to give Rhodes his wish. If a Pioneer Column entered Mashonaland, at least it could be used against any Boer trekkers or Portuguese soldiers who might venture into the vicinity. Meanwhile, it did not appear that Lobengula welcomed the Pioneer Column. The ruler of the Ndebele was preparing for war. He mobilized two new regiments and sent fighters to the northeast. Many Ndebele people concluded that conflict was inevitable and sent their cattle to the hills and harvested their grain early. The missionaries left, too. Lobengula sent his emissary, Mshete, to visit Loch in Cape Town, accompanied by Lippert's man in Matabeleland, Edward Renny-Tailyour. Loch dismissed them on account of their bias against Rhodes.[8]

Rhodes recognized that before he made a move on Mashonaland, he needed to consolidate his personal authority in the BSAC. The company board in London was dominated by Maguire, who acted as a proxy for Rhodes. Rhodes was also backed by Albert Grey, who had the strongest network and who managed government relations. Cawston and Beit had the most influence over financial decisions. In Southern Africa, the company could have set up a local board of directors, but instead Rhodes asked for—and was given—a free hand. In May 1890, the London board gave Rhodes a power of attorney to make decisions on behalf of the company in Southern Africa. Technically this meant that he was the managing director "on the spot." In 1891, Merriman remarked that "it is increasingly evident that the whole enterprise rests almost entirely on the personality of Rhodes. Without his interest it would go down like a pack of cards." Along the same lines, Grey wrote to Beit that "I must say I grudge Rhodes the honour of doing everything—supplying the foresight, the creative ability, and the funds required to make the Charter a success."[9]

What was it that made Rhodes, Jameson, and government officials so confident of the success of several hundred troopers and miners, when they were likely to be attacked by thousands of Ndebele warriors, as the Colonial Office and War Office had pointed out? One reason for confidence had to do with Rhodes's recruiting strategy. The civilians in the Pioneer Column were recruited and led by Frank Johnson. The group included about 200 recruits, less than the anticipated 300. Some were from prominent families in the Cape and Britain. The civilians of this "Pioneer Corps" were each promised fifteen claims and, as soon as it could be gotten from Lobengula, 1,500 morgen (3175 acres) of land. Johnson preferred recruits with military experience, for practical reasons, but Rhodes informed him to cast his net widely, pulling in people with social connections. In a memoir written many years later, Johnson recalled the written instructions that he received from Rhodes:

> Do you know what will happen to you? You will probably be massacred by the Matabele, or at least we shall one day hear that you have been surrounded and cut off! And who will rescue you, do you think? I will tell you—the Imperial Factor [a.k.a. the British government]. And who do you think will bring pressure to bear on the Imperial Factor and stir them to save you? The influential fathers of your young men![10]

In other words, in forming the Pioneer Column—whose object was to steal land for a sketchy company—Rhodes hedged his bets in the form of young men from prominent families who would be rescued, if necessary, by British taxpayers.

Loch got wind that Johnson, a former sergeant, was calling himself a major and recruiting troopers. Loch was willing to grant the BSAC the right to protect itself but could not countenance the formation of an amateur army. He insisted on the formation of a separate British South Africa Company Police, commanded by an experienced army officer and paid for by Rhodes and the BSAC. Rhodes gave Johnson the authority to draw £88,340 on the BSAC account to pay for all aspects of the expedition. To lead the armed BSAC Police, Loch chose Edward Pennefather, a lieutenant-colonel of the Inniskilling Dragoons who had served in the Anglo-Zulu War and the Warren Expedition. Pennefather was to recruit and train the BSAC Police in Bechuanaland with the assistance of the Bechuanaland Border Police. Over the course of several months Pennefather recruited several veteran officers, including his staff officer, John Willoughby, a graduate of Eton and Cambridge with previous service in the Royal Horse Guards.[11] All told Pennefather found 500 officers and troopers to protect Johnson's 200 pioneers, a high ratio of police to pioneers.

The BSAC Police, assembling near the border, and the civilian pioneers, assembling in Kimberley, all practiced how to ride and fight. Some were veterans and frontiersmen, but some were miners and members of prominent urban families and had little experience with soldiering. Although the uneven experience of the recruits raised questions, the Pioneer Column was protected by a modern arsenal. The troopers and many of the civilians were armed with revolvers and with Martini-Henry rifles, the single-shot, black-powder breechloaders that were the same as those used by the British army up until the end of the 1880s.[12] In trained hands the Martini-Henry rifles could fire ten to twelve .577 caliber bullets per minute and hit targets at a range of 400 yards.

Military analysts assess battlefield advantages of weapons, training, and tactics by using the concept of "force multiplication." A good arsenal can "multiply" the force of a small unit, making it as formidable as a poorly armed opponent's larger unit. The 500 BSAC Police troopers and the 200 members of the Pioneer Column were small compared to Lobengula's forces—some have estimated that Lobengula could call up between 8,000 and 15,000 fighters. But the Ndebele fighters had inferior weapons. They were generally armed with spears, while it is estimated that 20,000 were armed with older models of firearms. These varied considerably, from single-shot muzzle-loaders that could fire two shots per minute and were accurate to 50 yards, to the Snider-Enfield, the British Army's original breechloader of 1860, which was more challenging to use than the Martini-Henry but which had a similar range and rate of fire. Lobengula had also acquired 1,000 Martini-Henry rifles thanks to the Rudd Concession. It is difficult to determine how well the weapons were used by Ndebele fighters. Most British descriptions say that Ndebele fighters were poor marksmen, but commentary on African skill with firearms was unreliable and politicized. In the 1870s, when white politicians wanted to make Africans out to be dangerous, they described them as skilled marksmen. When white politicians wanted to demonstrate African racial inferiority, African gun owners were portrayed as unskilled. It is hard to know if there is much truth in the BSAC Police's descriptions of Ndebele skills with weapons.[13]

The force multiplication equation was straightforward. Ndebele forces needed numerical superiority and incredible bravery to get close enough to kill trained colonial soldiers who were wielding modern rifles. The BSAC Police further multiplied its force on the battlefield by bringing along two muzzle-loading seven-pounder rifled mountain guns. These were small, lightweight, mobile three-inch (75 mm) caliber cannons, that had been used in frontier fighting in India and South Africa since the early 1870s. The intimidating little cannons were portable in rough terrain and were well suited to defending positions. They multiplied a force's firepower significantly. Far more terrifying, though, were the BSAC Police's Maxim machine guns. One Maxim gun was assigned to each of the five units or "troops." The Maxim gun represented the latest in modern weaponry and was new to Southern Africa.

It weighed 60 pounds, too heavy to be a good offensive weapon but outstanding when used defensively. The small BSAC Police Force supplemented their five Maxim guns with an outmoded Gatling gun, the original hand-cranked machine gun first used in the American Civil War. They also carried with them a Maxim-Nordenfelt "Pom-Pom" gun, an oversized machine gun that fired a 1.457 caliber (37 mm) round weighing almost one pound. Like the regular Maxim guns, which were probably .577 caliber, the Pom-Pom gun could fire 400 rounds per minute. And finally, the BSAC deployed two 24-pounder Hale's rocket tubes with a supply of twenty rockets loaded with explosive warheads.[14]

The weaponry of the BSAC Police made them into a formidable force. One Maxim gun could fire 900 bullets in the ninety seconds that it might take Ndebele fighters to run across 400 yards of open ground. But the BSAC Police did not have one Maxim gun, they had five, for a total of 4,500 bullets in ninety seconds. The Gatling gun added 400 bullets per minute. When fighting in a defensive formation, a Maxim gun could be positioned at each point of the compass. The five machine guns, two cannons, and 500 rifles could lay down a withering fire, accurate to 400 yards, in the ninety-second space of time estimated for Ndebele soldiers to charge that distance. On the other side, Ndebele riflemen could only get off an accurate shot within that 400-yard range. Ndebele spearmen faced greater trouble. Most of their weapons were three-foot long assegais designed for stabbing, not throwing. And a thrown spear does not travel far enough. The BSAC troopers could concentrate their fire and inflict terrifying casualties on attackers while sustaining negligible casualties themselves. The BSAC Police might only be challenged if the ammunition ran out, or if the enemy decided to fight a different kind of battle.

The BSAC Police and the civilian Pioneer Corps were trained to defend their positions by circling wagons in the traditional South African "laager" formation. This formation helped to compensate for two problems. One problem involved disparities in numbers between the two fighting forces. The BSAC column may have had better weapons, but the larger number of Ndebele fighters made it difficult for the BSAC to go on the offensive during a pitched battle. A few hundred BSAC Police troopers with two cannons and five heavy machine guns were not likely to be able to give chase to thousands of Ndebele fighters. It is axiomatic in military theory that all things being equal, a fighting unit is stronger on defense than on offense.[15] The second problem involved communications. The inventors and manufacturers of the Industrial Revolution produced more powerful weapons, but they still had not produced effective means of remote mobile communications, a problem that only began to be solved by soldiers in the last two years of the First World War. In 1890, soldiers who were kept close together could be supervised effectively by experienced officers and sergeants and thereby maximize the power of their weapons. Keeping soldiers near each other in the laager formation prevented communications from being cut off or being misunderstood.

For the BSAC, success on the battlefield depended on luring the enemy into attacking heavily defended positions. The rifles, cannons, and machine guns, deployed in strategic offense and tactical defense by Pennefather and his officers, turned several hundred BSAC Police troopers into a new, deadly extension of the disassembly line. Like the dynamite, centrifuges, and pulsators at Kimberley, like the steam tractors that crushed the rocks strewn across acres of "floors," force-multiplying modern weapons were deployed by trained company employees to tear apart the bodies of Ndebele and Shona fighters and to blow asunder their military units. Lobengula and the Ndebele soldiers appeared to recognize that if they wanted to attack the Pioneer Column, the odds were not in their favor. They chose to watch and wait, but while they did so, the BSAC began to ride for Mashonaland.

The civilian Pioneer Corps was launched from faraway Griqualand West. The settlers mustered in Kenilworth, on the outskirts of Kimberley, supported by one hundred wagons, each pulled by sixteen oxen and accompanied by three African workers. Loch visited the column for a farewell banquet on April 17, joined by Rhodes, Shippard, Moffat, and a smattering of dignitaries. Soon after, the Pioneer Column rode to Mafeking, then moved up through Bechuanaland on the Road to the North, stopping just short of the border with the Ndebele kingdom. There they joined forces with the BSAC Police.[16]

The leadership structure of the Pioneer Column was divided. Johnson and Selous led the miners and settlers of the Pioneer Corps, and Pennefather led the BSAC Police. Selous supervised a team of 200 Ngwato laborers who were given the difficult job of clearing brush and creating a wagon track well ahead of the pioneers and troopers. To make the leadership structure even more complicated, the column was joined by Archibald Colquhoun, appointed by the BSAC to be the administrator of the territories about to be acquired in Mashonaland. Colquhoun was born in Cape Town in 1848. He worked as an administrator for the Indian Civil Service before embarking on a career as an explorer and author. He was best known for his books about his travels in Southeast Asia and China and for his heavy drinking. He was given 4,500 shares of the BSAC as part of his compensation. Colquhoun and Johnson were joined by Jameson, who had done the key negotiating with Lobengula.

He did not have an official role in the Pioneer Column but was there as Rhodes's emissary. The others did not realize that just in case of any trouble, Rhodes had given Jameson power of attorney, making him the ultimate authority over the Pioneer Column. Rhodes wanted to join the Pioneer Column himself, but exactly at this time he was becoming prime minister in Cape Town.

On June 27, 1890, Pennefather paraded his men before a special guest, the deputy commanding officer of British forces in Southern Africa, Major General Paul Methuen. Methuen reviewed the police at their camp and watched the Pioneer Corps practice defending their circled wagons. Methuen pronounced the BSAC Police ready at the end of June 1890, when Pennefather and Johnson ordered the Pioneer Column to cross the Thuli. From there they started their journey to Mashonaland.[17]

As the Pioneer Column and its 100 wagons skirted to the south and east of Ndebele territory, the BSAC Police prepared to maximize their force by using defensive tactics. As soon as the column crossed into Ndebele territory, near the Thuli River, the troopers began work on a fort. From there, in early July they moved in two columns to make it easier to circle the wagons in an emergency. Guided by Selous, the Ngwato laborers did the heavy work of road-clearing. Not only did this help the Pioneer Column to proceed; a cleared road made it easier for the group to be resupplied by wagons as soon as it reached its destination in Mashonaland. Ndebele fighters constantly watched the Pioneer Column and reported movements back to Lobengula. Lobengula sent messages challenging the arrival of the column, but he did not order an attack, possibly reflecting on the reports that he had heard about the lopsided wars between Africans and Europeans that were fought during the 1870s and 1880s. Lobengula was portrayed as a warlike tyrant but his initial encounters with the BSAC demonstrated that his initial preference was for diplomacy.[18]

By the first week of August, after much difficult work on the road, the Pioneer Column entered Mashonaland and continued to move in a northeasterly direction for about 220 miles. The column paused for a rest at Masvingo. A small group even made a side-trip to the ruins of Great Zimbabwe, where they hoped to find gold. When the Pioneer Column resumed its march northward, a detachment of troopers was left behind to build a frontier outpost, Fort Victoria. A message from Lobengula was received, ordering the column to turn back, but the column kept rolling. After two more weeks and 170 miles, the column rested again and began work on a third fort, named Fort Charter, located in a relatively remote area. Groups of settlers and miners began to drop out of the Pioneer Column to go and claim land. The remaining Pioneer Column proceeded northward. On September 12, after fifty more miles, the Pioneer Column halted and camped at a site that seemed suitable for another fort. They decided that they had arrived at their final destination. The next morning, at a ceremony on the present-day site of Harare, the Pioneer Column raised the Union Jack, fired a salute with the seven-pounder cannons, read a prayer, and named the place Fort Salisbury. They had ridden 340 miles from Fort Tuli, cutting a way for a wagon trail and starting construction on four forts. The pioneers dispersed to search for sites for their mines and farms, not paying much attention to the fact that the Rudd Concession only granted rights to minerals under the ground. The mining companies that formed were required to give 50 percent of their profits to the BSAC.[19]

Rhodes was excited about building the new colony in Mashonaland, with its anticipated white settlers and a gold-mining industry. To set the colony's borders, Rhodes needed the diplomatic support of the British government, but that was not entirely forthcoming. The boundaries between German South-West Africa (Namibia) and the BSAC had already been determined, but not the boundary between the BSAC and German East Africa, between what is today Zambia and Tanzania. By 1890, British territory was extending to Zambia as well as to Kenya and Uganda. Rhodes wanted to stretch it even further. To complete an all-British, strategic railway link from the Cape to Cairo required control of a strip of land running along the eastern side of Lake Tanganyika and then up past Rwanda and Burundi into Uganda or Kenya. The land on the east side of Lake Tanganyika was claimed by Germany. Rhodes was disappointed that during negotiations with Germany, the prime minister, Lord Salisbury, declined to support expansion in that area. Speaking in Parliament, Salisbury stated that he could "imagine no more uncomfortable possession."[20]

Salisbury's primary concern was to maintain peace between the European powers. European diplomacy framed Salisbury's thinking about Rhodes's problems with Portuguese Mozambique. Portugal and Britain had an alliance dating to the fourteenth century and now found themselves in a frustrating conflict over the interior of South-Central Africa. Portuguese explorers were visiting Mashonaland and attempting to float companies of their own. In 1889, Portuguese officers were in Manicaland, just to the east of Mashonaland, claiming territory that Rhodes wanted for the BSAC. To the north, in Nyasaland, today called Malawi, Harry Johnston had been aggressively signing treaties with chiefs since 1889, but so had Portuguese officers from Mozambique. Salisbury gave his full support to Johnston's efforts in Nyasaland by threatening a diplomatic break with Portugal. The Portuguese could not afford a conflict with Britain and decided to back down. In January 1890, the borders between Mozambique and Nyasaland were then drawn in Britain's favor, much to the consternation of nationalists and republicans in Portugal.[21]

The BSAC still needed access to the sea to survive. Rhodes turned to the project of building a railway from Fort Salisbury to the Indian Ocean. The best path for a railway was to run it from Fort Salisbury to the southeast, to Umtali (present-day Mutare), the capital city of Manicaland province. From Umtali, Rhodes's hope was to run the railway to Beira, on the coast, cutting through the territory of the Gaza kingdom, led by Gungunyana. The Gaza kingdom was formed in the 1820s, when the Zulu general, Soshangane, counquered the southern part of Mozambique between Manicaland and Delagoa Bay. Indigenous Tsonga people were subjugated and their culture blended with Zulu culture to form the Gaza kingdom's core ethnic identity, Shangaan, named for Soshangane. The Gaza kingdom held the upper hand over the Portuguese settlements on the coast and its authority extended westward into Shona territory. Rhodes's plan called for the railway to be built across Gaza territory, toward the Pungwe River, where it would follow the river down to its mouth in the harbor at Beira. The Portuguese had claimed the coast of Mozambique for centuries, but their claims to Manicaland and Gazaland were shaky. Gungunyana was technically paying tribute to the Portuguese government, but the Gaza kingdom had at its disposal thousands of trained fighters who could have easily crushed local Portuguese units. The Shona ruler of Manicaland, Mutasa, was only a Portuguese subject because he was also a subject of Gungunyana and feared his neighbor's military prowess.

Rhodes was not the first buccaneering foreign businessman to seek advantage in Mozambique's turbulent interior. Just to the north of Gungunyana's territory, in the mountains around Gorongosa, an ivory trader from Goa named Manuel António de Souza, known as Gouveia, set himself up as a feudal warlord in the 1850s and 1860s. With his company rule and his private army, he was a rival worthy of Rhodes and the BSAC. In addition, there were other companies forming in the Manica region. In the late 1880s, with the gold rush in full swing on the Witwatersrand, teams of American, British, and South African prospectors were combing Manicaland, working in cooperation with Gouveia and with the representative of the Portuguese colonial government, the Baron de Rezende. Foreign prospectors found quartz reefs and established multiple companies for the purpose of seeking concessions.

In the years before the BSAC Pioneer Column entered Mashonaland, the Portuguese government approved the creation of chartered companies to rule

Mozambique. The northern third of Mozambique was placed under the Nyassa Company, which was backed by London investors. The central part of Mozambique, between the Nyassa Company and the Zambezi River, was controlled by the Zambesi Company, which was owned by a mix of Portuguese and overseas investors. To the south, the area between the Zambezi and Sabi Rivers was given to the Mozambique Company. There were two provinces: Manica, to the west, along the border with Mashonaland, and Sofala, to the east, along the coast. Company rule was being put in place by a "man on the spot," Joaquim Carlos Paiva de Andrada, who worked with the local representative of the Portuguese government, the Baron de Rezende, and who befriended the ivory-merchant warlord Gouveia. The Mozambique Company was intended to be formally put in place in February 1891, but in November 1890 the plans were already well under way.[22]

In Mozambique and Mashonaland, there were two clashing visions. On the one hand, Rhodes sought to secure the BSAC colony by constructing a railway through Manicaland and Gaza territory to Beira, where harbor facilities could be constructed. On the other hand, the Portuguese envisioned a revived colonial empire and hoped that their own chartered companies would develop that same area. Rhodes decided to grab the territory for the BSAC but did not realize the complications that would ensue from tangling with a sovereign European nation, not to mention a robust African kingdom and a stolid British prime minister. Initially Salisbury had believed that Portugal's claims to the interior of Mozambique were "archaeological" and irrelevant to modern claims to African spaces. Salisbury's initial predispositions began to shift, thanks to his negotiations with Portugal as well as his concerns about Rhodes's aggressiveness. Rhodes seemed unwilling to play along with the larger goals of British foreign policy, a situation that was starting to irk Salisbury.

Rhodes's scheme to extend BSAC domains to Manicaland and Gaza territory was almost stopped at the outset by British border negotiations with Portugal. Rhodes wrote to the Colonial Office that it was "totally unnecessary" to let "such a Power as Portugal" claim territories in the interior of Mozambique. "Their frontier is the coast fringe and nothing more." In London, British officials were starting to find Rhodes tiresome. In internal communications, they mocked him as "The Prime Minister and Foreign Secretary of Great Britain as well as the Premier of S. Africa." Salisbury wrote to Abercorn that he "had enough" of Rhodes. Government officials much preferred to communicate with Cawston, who represented the BSAC in London, rather than with Rhodes. Yet independent-minded subordinates who crossed Rhodes received the full blast of his fury, none more so than Harry Johnston. Johnston had great latitude as the BSAC-funded administrator in Nyasaland, but Rhodes suspected him of supporting British negotiations with Portugal. Rhodes accused Johnston of "desertion."[23]

Rhodes was furious about the border negotiations. Soon he benefited from a mistake made by the Portuguese government. The Portuguese Parliament failed to ratify the January 1890 boundary treaty before the end of its session in mid-October. Formal implementation of the treaty had to wait until ratification in the next year. This opened a window of opportunity for Rhodes. While the treaty was still being discussed, in June and July of 1890, the Pioneer Column was headed toward Mashonaland. Portuguese claims to Manicaland and Gaza territory were about to be recognized in exchange for other concessions, but as ratification had not yet happened, the territory was technically still available. When the Pioneer Column reached Fort Charter, just short of its destination at Fort Salisbury, key members of the BSAC party rode east to Manicaland and Gaza territory. The group included Selous, Jameson, and Colquhoun, escorted by a small number of troopers. Rhodes had instructed them to meet with Mutasa, the chief who ruled Manicaland, to persuade him to give away mineral rights as well as land rights. The land rights could be used for a railroad right of way from Mashonaland to Beira on the east coast. Mutasa signed the concession agreement on September 14, 1890, while also informing the Portuguese that he remained loyal to them. Colquhuon, Selous, and the BSAC troopers returned to Fort Salisbury.

Next, Rhodes sent another BSAC representative, Dr. Aurel Schulz, to meet with the Gaza chief Gungunyana, who agreed to the same sort of concession that had been offered to Lobengula. In exchange for land and mineral rights, Gungunyana took delivery of a shipment of rifles and ammunition, which the BSAC snuck past Portuguese officials at the mouth of the Limpopo. When the goods were delivered, local Portuguese soldiers tried to collect £2000 in customs duties and were given a bond for the money. Gungunyana wisely declined to put anything in writing with the BSAC.[24]

As Rhodes became more interested in Mozambique, so did the Portuguese government. Portuguese politicians had the same nationalist and imperialist sentiments that were influencing leaders in Britain and other European countries. The Portuguese pursued the same territorial strategy as Rhodes and the BSAC, by laying claim to large spaces, just in case capitalist mining and agriculture became feasible. They were therefore concerned about the BSAC and the concession-seeking at Bulawayo, as well as Harry Johnston's efforts further north in Nyasaland. The "claim what you can" approach to territoriality blended opportunism, militarism, and imperialism.

Rhodes found himself challenged by the Portuguese and by their own chartered company, the Mozambique Company, for predominance in Manicaland. The BSAC sought railroad access to the sea in addition to minerals, while the Mozambique Company sought to consolidate rule throughout southern Mozambique. To make things more complicated, the Mozambique Company's main investors were British aristocrats, some of whom had a history of conflict with the investors in the BSAC. The Mozambique Company's most prominent investor was George Spencer-Churchill, the eighth Duke of Marlborough, who was the older brother of the British politician Randolph Spencer-Churchill, the father of the future prime minister, Winston Churchill. It was well known that the duke was burning through his inheritance and that his behavior was causing him to be ostracized by fellow members of the aristocracy. In one well-known incident in the late 1870s, George, then called the Marquess of Blandford, and his younger brother, known as Lord Randolph, implicated the Prince of Wales in a marital scandal, resulting in lasting enmity with the royal family. When George became the Duke of Marlborough in 1883, his wife, Albertha, divorced him for infidelity and abuse. She was the sister of the Duke of Abercorn, a key supporter of Rhodes. Marlborough's second marriage to a wealthy American widow was not recognized in high society.[25]

Occasionally the people in Rhodes's network were working at cross-purposes, at home and in the remotest areas. In November 1890, the BSAC clashed with the Mozambique Company over Colquhuon and Selous's visit to Mutasa and the chief's concessions to the BSAC. Andrada, Rezende, and Gouveia sent several hundred African soldiers to intimidate Mutasa and to reestablish Portuguese rule over his territories in western Manicaland. Mutasa sent for help to Fort Salisbury. The BSAC sent several dozen troopers in two groups, one commanded by Captain Patrick Forbes and the other by Lieutenant Eustace Fiennes. When Forbes, Fiennes, and their troopers arrived in Mutasa's territory, the Portuguese told them to leave. On November 15, 1890, the Portuguese arranged for a ceremony at Mutasa's court. With two hundred Portuguese soldiers standing by, Andrada, Gouveia, and Rezende ordered the Union Jack lowered and the Portuguese flag raised. Mutasa was forced to read a statement in which he denied that he had given concessions to the BSAC. At that moment, the troopers of the BSAC launched a surprise attack, scattered the confused Portuguese soldiers, and took Andrada and Gouveia prisoner. The two were marched off to Fort Salisbury and from there were sent to Cape Town.

In Portugal, there was public outrage directed at Rhodes and the BSAC. Rezende traveled to Lisbon and began to recruit youths and university students to fight against the BSAC for Portugal's honor. In England, the Mozambique Company's investors, including the Duke of Marlborough, predictably criticized the BSAC. The BSAC vice-chairman, the Duke of Fife, responded by pressuring Salisbury to recognize the weakness of the Portuguese and the fact of the BSAC's occupation of Manicaland. Salisbury, weary of Rhodes and the BSAC, remarked on Fife's "insolence" but quietly began to renegotiate the treaty with the Portuguese. Loch was called to London for consultations and sailed to England accompanied by Rhodes. Over the course of several weeks in January and February of 1891, they met with Natty Rothschild, who tried and failed to engineer a BSAC buyout of the Mozambique Company. Rhodes and Loch also met with government officials, culminating in a meeting with Salisbury and a meal with Queen Victoria at Windsor Castle.[26]

Rhodes and his agents were pushing the boundaries of British and Portuguese diplomacy. In January 1891, Dr. Aurel Schulz returned to Natal with his verbal concessions from Gungunyana in Gazaland. A follow-up mission resulted in Gungunyana signing a concession to the BSAC, but the chief hedged his bets by indicating that he did so as a Portuguese subject. Jameson and several BSAC colleagues made the trek from Umtali to Gungunyana to investigate. After a contentious meeting, the Britons made their way to the coast, intending to meet the BSAC steamer, *Countess of Carnarvon*, on its return trip to Durban. They found that a Portuguese gunboat had captured the *Countess*. Jameson and his BSAC associates were arrested and, Jameson snarled, kept "in the hold, with all the Portuguese and n----rs." He was imprisoned at Delagoa Bay for several months, until Rhodes bailed him out.[27]

The next major incursion into Portuguese Mozambique was entrusted to one of the BSAC's best officers, John Willoughby. He hired several steamboats and arrived at the mouth of the Pungwe River, at the port of Beira, with 250 troopers on board. Rhodes gave Willoughby two options. If he did not meet Portuguese resistance, he would land the troopers and march through Portuguese territory into the interior. If Willoughby's force met with resistance, he would provoke an incident. When several Portuguese gunboats met him in the harbor, he ignored the orders of the Portuguese captain, who then fired on him. It was only a blank shot, and Willoughby, having done his duty, decided to leave. Rhodes now had the material to arouse public indignation in Britain. Salisbury responded by sending a British gunboat from Zanzibar. He did so to strengthen his hand in negotiations with the Portuguese, though he disliked being manipulated by Rhodes.[28]

Rhodes continued to push. Just east of Mutasa's kraal in Manicaland, in the town of Massi Kessi, Andrada was assembling a small force of 100 student volunteers from Portugal and 120 African soldiers in Portuguese colonial service. The force advanced on Mutasa's kraal, where the BSAC had stationed 35 troopers. Andrada was keen to avenge Portuguese humiliation and was not thinking carefully. His inexperienced soldiers attacked the BSAC forces, who fought back professionally and drove off the Portuguese. Not only did Andrada lose the battle; he also lost the public relations war. The attack persuaded Salisbury to advocate for the BSAC to possess Mutasa's western side of Manicaland. Then Rhodes overreached and lost support, too. He ordered BSAC forces to attack Massi Kessi and to proceed to the coast and capture Beira. Loch was reaching the boiling point over Rhodes's amateur military campaign. He dispatched the Anglican bishop, Knight-Bruce, and a British army officer, Major Sapte, to deliver an order to the BSAC to stop. Loch wrote to Lord Knutsford, telling him that the BSAC should be subject to stricter government control. Salisbury decided to complete the negotiation of the Anglo-Portuguese treaty, giving the BSAC Mutasa's western edge of Manicaland but certifying Portuguese control over eastern Manicaland, Gazaland, and Beira. Rhodes was angry and resigned himself to negotiations.[29]

Rhodes's actions infuriated Portuguese public opinion, making negotiations more difficult for the BSAC. Rhodes turned to stealth tactics to get the BSAC access to the sea. His first move was to send Selous on an exploring mission to report on a possible route from Beira to Umtali, along the Lower Pungwe River. Selous wrote to Rhodes and described the difficulties encountered with swamps, forests, and high grasses, as well as tsetse flies. Selous's judgment was that "the 'Tse-tse' fly, which extends throughout the whole of the low country from the Pungwe to the Buzi rivers... will always render it impossible to make use of oxen, or any other domestic animals, as a means of transport between the east coast and Mashunaland. A railway, or something that runs on rails, must be built through the 'fly' country, and the question now is to decide upon the best route."[30]

With the report by Selous in his pocket, Rhodes used a "Trojan Horse" stratagem to get his way. Rhodes worked through Otto Beit, Alfred Beit's brother and business partner in Wernher Beit, to get control of the Mozambique Company's concession for the railway between Beira, on the coast, and the BSAC border. In late 1891, Otto Beit funded a business associate, Henry van Laun, in the purchase of the railway concession from the Mozambique Company. The British government was fully aware of the proceedings. A meeting then took place at the Foreign Office in London between board members of the Mozambique Company and the BSAC. The results were communicated in a letter from Salisbury's assistant directly to Rhodes. Rhodes's concession was called the Beira Railway Company, and Otto Beit was installed as the director.[31]

Rhodes intended for the railroad to run from the port of Beira westward to the border at Umtali, then to turn north and run to Fort Salisbury, the same route taken during his 1891 trip. To build the Beira line, Rhodes hired George Pauling, a railway contractor who had completed several short lines in the Cape Colony, including the final stretch of track from Kimberley to the Orange River. Pauling's subcontractors worked on the survey, a difficult task in a region replete with malaria and sleeping sickness. Pauling, who was famously tough, reported that in 1892 and 1893 his company "lost by death sixty per cent of these [white] men, including all the teetotallers. According to my experience, teetotallers do not stand a fever country even as well as excessive drinking." The dangerous terrain was made even less accessible by flooding. Building the railway was so difficult that as a temporary measure, two-foot gauge tracks were installed, so that slow-moving, "toy" trains could work their way around the topography until such a time as the land could be prepared for South Africa's standard gauge of three feet, six inches. Building the line was so challenging that it only reached Umtali in 1898 and Salisbury in 1899.[32]

While all the maneuvering for access to Mozambique was taking place, the territories to the north of the Zambezi River, in present-day Zambia, were not well known to Rhodes and occupied a secondary place in his thinking. Rhodes recognized that he needed to establish a border and to negotiate concessions, but there was only so much time and so much capital that he could invest in yet more territories. The best prospects for minerals were reported to be in Katanga, just north of Zambia in what is today the Democratic Republic of Congo and what was then King Leopold of Belgium's personal colony, the Congo Free State. Nyasaland was contested among Scottish missionaries, slave traders, and the Portuguese and British governments. What is today Zambia was largely unknown to Europeans. Rhodes had few ambitions in the area yet still felt it was important to make concession agreements with chiefs and take the first steps toward "effective occupation."

An opportunity to extend BSAC rule in Zambia practically fell into Rhodes's lap. The BSAC was approached by Lewanika, the Lozi king of Barotseland, the western third of today's Zambia. The Lozi kingdom was heavily involved in the ivory trade, a business that was declining. The trade put the Lozi in contact with European hunters who passed through Tswana and Ndebele territory on their way north to hunt in Barotseland. The most prominent hunter, George Westbeech, protected his trade by trying to maintain peace between Ndebele and Lozi leaders. Other visitors included Portuguese and British explorers. Lewanika was particularly impressed by Portuguese explorer Serpa Pinto and by the Scottish missionary, Frederick Stanley Arnot, who had been detained in Barotseland from 1882 to 1884 and taught the royal family to read.

Political struggles were endemic in Barotseland. Lewanika was deposed by rebels in 1884 and restored himself to the throne one year later after much bloodshed. As Lewanika was taking vengeance on his enemies, Lobengula launched a raid on Lozi territory. The raid was repulsed, but Khama suggested to Lewanika that his position could be strengthened by accepting the protection of a European power. The idea may have struck some advisers as strange: Lewanika is typically described as a proud and selfish king who believed in a divine right to rule over his people. He supported the reimposition of customary practices and was dismayed by missionary efforts to end polygamy. The idea of inviting British protection received lukewarm support from Lewanika's Lozi supporters, who were suspicious that their ruler was only making such a move to protect himself and the administrative and landholding reforms that he was putting in place.[33]

Lewanika's motives were also questioned by the French Protestant missionary, François Coillard. He was well known in Southern Africa for his previous work at Leribe among Sotho people and was now proselytizing in Barotseland and acting as a conduit to the British. In January 1889, Lewanika dictated a letter to Coillard that was sent to Shippard in Bechuanaland. In the letter, Lewanika asked Shippard to establish a British protectorate over Barotseland. Shippard received this extraordinary letter and forwarded it to London for the Colonial Office's advice. The Colonial Office was less than enthusiastic. It could be expensive to "protect" Barotseland and it did not seem necessary, either, but Shippard kept the idea in mind. When the BSAC received its charter in October 1889, Shippard told Rhodes about the possibility of enrolling Lewanika.

Rhodes seized this opportunity to push the BSAC into Barotseland. He immediately sent an emissary, a trooper from the Bechuanaland Border Police, Frank Lochner, to negotiate with Lewanika and Coillard about a concession. The Lochner Concession, as it was called, was more complicated than the Rudd Concession, thanks to the wariness of Lewanika and the interventions of Coillard. Lewanika agreed to grant the BSAC land and mining concessions in exchange for £2,000 per year, but rights to land and traditional forms of government were guaranteed to the Lozi people, and a mining concession had already been promised to Henry Ware, a hunter from Kimberley. The concession was questionable in one significant way. Lochner misrepresented himself as an emissary of the Queen, which led Lewanika to believe that he was making an agreement with the British government. When Lewanika complained to Loch, the governor and high commissioner assured him that the BSAC was chartered by the Queen, so Lochner was not engaging in anything deceptive. In fact, the agreement was dubious and caused bad feelings among the Lozi, the British, the Portuguese, and the BSAC for the next several years. At least Rhodes was able to purchase the mining concession from Ware.[34]

Rhodes's strategy in Barotseland was to hold the sizeable territory in case the BSAC might have a use for it later. The company took the same approach in Nyasaland, and in the lands of what is today eastern Zambia. Scottish missionaries had been active in Nyasaland since the explorations of David Livingstone, which took place between 1851 and 1873. The African Lakes Company supplied the Scottish missionaries and tried to establish what was then called "legitimate" trade in goods, not people. The area's slave traders resisted the African Lakes Company, which became involved in high-minded conflicts that did not help the bottom line. When Rhodes first met Harry Johnston, he was working as the British consul responsible for Nyasaland. They reached an agreement: that the BSAC would subsidize the African Lakes Company's administration in Nyasaland and Johnston would negotiate concessions with the African rulers who controlled northeastern Zambia.[35]

The BSAC secured claims in part to put itself in a good position to acquire Katanga, just to the north, a territory that appeared to be rich in minerals, especially copper. Katanga was also beginning to interest King Leopold of Belgium. In May of 1890, Rhodes organized a meeting at the Kimberley Club. Rhodes was still two months away from being named Cape prime minister, and the Pioneer Column was just getting ready to begin its journey. At that meeting, Rhodes was joined by some of his most important BSAC collaborators, including Harry Johnston, Rochfort Maguire, and Archibald Colquhuon. Also present was John Moir, who, with his brother, Fred, managed the African Lakes Company in Nyasaland. Those four and Rhodes were joined by two young explorers, Joseph Thomson and James Augustus Grant, Junior. Thomson had made a reputation for himself on two well-publicized expeditions around the Great Lakes region. James Augustus Grant, Junior, was the son of James Augustus Grant, Senior, who had explored the sources of the Nile. The son was a recent Oxford graduate who was then working for the

Bechuanaland railroad and hoping for something more than railway middle management.[36]

With Rhodes and Johnston taking the lead, supported by Cawston, the BSAC group hatched an extraordinary plot to take Katanga. The hubris of Rhodes and his fellow plotters was so great that they knowingly risked undermining Lord Salisbury, whose Foreign Office was negotiating with King Leopold's Congo Free State over boundary questions. Rhodes and Cawston recruited Thomson and Johnston recruited Alfred Sharpe, the administrator of Nyasaland. It was agreed that Thomson and Grant would travel from Nyasaland to Katanga along one route, while Sharpe would take another. The plan was for the two groups to meet up in Katanga and seek out the most powerful merchant king in Katanga, a Nyamwezi warlord named Msiri. Since the late 1850s, Msiri had controlled the region's trade in slaves, guns, copper, and ivory. Msiri used marriage alliances and ruthlessness to occupy and hold a central position. He traded along the traditional route, which extended from Lake Mweru up to Ujiji on Lake Tanganyika and from there to Zanzibar. He also had an established network that ran westward through Ovimbundu country to Benguela in Angola. Msiri's kingdom in southeastern Katanga, known as the Yeke or Garanganze kingdom, was centered on the city of Bunkeya. Msiri was conventionally portrayed as an arbitrary and cruel leader who decorated his compound fenceposts with his enemies' skulls.

Rhodes and his confederates hoped to get Msiri to sign concessions, but this did not happen, because both BSAC expeditions to Katanga failed. Sharpe did reach Msiri's court, but when missionaries translated the BSAC's proposals, he was expelled. Thomson and Grant's party never reached their objective at Bunkeya; Thomson got a bladder infection and his porters came down with smallpox. The illnesses were all so bad that Thomson, a trained geologist, overlooked evidence of northeastern Zambia's large copper belt. Thomson and Grant got within two hundred miles of Msiri's Garanganze court but had to turn back.[37]

Sharpe, Thomson, and Grant did not seize control of Katanga but they did lay the groundwork for BSAC control of northeastern Zambia. Thomson and Grant carried with them print copies of concession treaties that could be used to gain concessions from local chiefs. They managed to sign up thirteen chiefs, even though the BSAC explorers did not speak local languages, nor did any of the chiefs speak English. Through treaties, with their vague language and their "X" marks by chiefs who did not understand what they were signing, the British Foreign Office could now accept the transfer of this vast, culturally diverse region to the overlordship of the BSAC.

By the time Thomson was ready to mount a follow-up expedition to Katanga, he was informed that, during the boundary negotiations, the British government had given the region to King Leopold's company, the Congo Free State. Leopold decided to send armed parties to intimidate Msiri. Two expeditions with several hundred soldiers failed to make an impression. Leopold then hired a British army engineer from Nova Scotia, William Grant Stairs, to lead a force to take Katanga. Stairs, who had previously served with Henry Morton Stanley, recruited a force of four hundred men, half of them armed them with modern rifles. After a journey of several months they arrived at Msiri's capital of Bunkeya in December of 1891. When Msiri once again resisted European efforts to secure a concession in Katanga, they provoked him into a confrontation. Stairs's mercenaries shot Msiri and had him decapitated. A battle ensued, most of Msiri's followers fled, and his immediate successors signed the concessions. This ruthless approach delivered on the sorts of threats that small, heavily armed private armies could make in those days in South Central Africa. Rhodes missed his opportunity in Katanga, and in the next few years a formal boundary was negotiated. The BSAC's Barotseland became a separate territory from King Leopold's Katanga.[38]

In the 1880s and 1890s, Europeans imagined and enacted changes to African geographical spaces that are astonishing from hindsight. Bold visions of empire caused treaties to be signed, boundaries to be drawn, and maps to be shaded in new colors. Armed force lay behind every change. It was also becoming clear that within this expansive context, Rhodes was experiencing limits. The British government could still cut him and the BSAC out of important negotiations, while other European countries could stand up to him. And the geographical spaces were so vast that it was difficult to establish even mail service, let alone telegraphs and railroads. It was taking time— much time—to achieve true, effective occupation in South-Central Africa.

14

Consolidating Rhodesia

BY 1891, THE BSAC had worked out its boundaries in South-Central Africa. A final adjustment was made in 1894, when Malawi, known as Nyasaland, was separated from the BSAC. The company was still left with the vast territories known today as Zambia and Zimbabwe. Authority to administer these lands derived from concessions granted by chiefs, many of whom were swindled, to one degree or another, by Rhodes's representatives. It was one thing to claim territory and gain concessions; it was another thing to impose rule by a chartered company. In what became Zambia, BSAC administration only began in earnest in 1895, and it was still thin on the ground. Rhodes was running up against the challenges of time, money, and space. The share values available of the BSAC and, to some extent, the share values of some of its leading investors, De Beers and Gold Fields, depended on the impression that company activity made on the market. This pressure kept Rhodes busy. He made the most important decisions for the BSAC while also leading De Beers and Gold Fields and while serving as Cape prime minister, a job he started in July of 1890, at the same time as the Pioneer Column was pushing its way to Mashonaland. Rhodes decided that the BSAC would have to focus its attention on Mashonaland, the territory that was central to his plan for white settlement. Settlers had even started to call the land Rhodesia, attaching his personal name to every success and failure.

Over the course of 1890 and 1891, Rhodes and the BSAC overlooked important details. Technically speaking, Rhodes did not properly constitute the BSAC's legal and administrative authority. Rhodes knew that the Rudd Concession was owned by a separate company that assigned mining rights to the BSAC. The BSAC administrator in Fort Salisbury, Colquhoun, began to issue mining regulations and to organize the police and telegraph services, even though he did not have legal authority to do so. The Colonial Office went along with his actions. A specific set of challenges to BSAC authority revolved around mining rights. The plan had been for the BSAC to have other mining companies buy concessions and share the profits, with half going to the BSAC and half going to the mining companies. Furthermore, the Rudd Concession gave the BSAC mining rights and general authority, but not specifically the ownership of land, even though land was being given to members of the Pioneer Column. To complicate matters further, Lobengula was still angry with Rhodes and unlikely to further negotiate the expropriation of what he considered to be his own country. Lobengula also recognized the direction in which the situation was headed. "Did you ever see a chameleon catch a fly?" he asked the missionary, Helm. "The chameleon gets behind the fly and remains motionless for some time, then he advances very slowly and gently, first putting forward one leg and then another. At last, when well within reach, he darts out his tongue and the fly disappears. England is the chameleon and I am that fly."[1]

Lobengula's regrets and the impending pressure on the value of BSAC shares created an opportunity for a new swindle. This time, the mark was Rhodes. The con originated with Alfred Beit's estranged cousin, Edouard Lippert, a high-profile investor on the Witwatersrand and the initial developer of Johannesburg's well-heeled suburb, Parktown. Lippert, who held the dynamite concession from the government of the Transvaal, backed the perennial concession-seeker, Edward Renny-Tailyour, in an effort to buy a land concession from Lobengula, who relished an opportunity to get back at Rhodes. The grant of a land concession to a rival company could imperil the BSAC. In April 1891, Renny-Tailyour announced that he had obtained just such a land concession from Lobengula.

Lippert and Renny-Tailyour had Rhodes in a bind. Rhodes argued that the Rudd Concession gave the BSAC general oversight and therefore the right of approval over a land concession, but that position might not have stood the test of a court battle in England. Loch recognized the possibility for turbulence and asserted his right, as high commissioner, to grant permission for any such concession. He intervened in favor of Rhodes and ordered the Bechuanaland authorities to arrest Renny-Tailyour. Behind the scenes, the businessmen found a solution. Beit advised Rhodes to do a deal with Lippert. Rhodes agreed. Renny-Tailyour went back to Lobengula, and in November 1891 they confirmed an agreement. In exchange for £1,000 and an annual payment of £500, Lobengula granted Lippert the right to grant or lease farms in his territory. Renny-Tailyour and Lippert did not reveal to Lobengula their next move. They sold the land concession to Rhodes—an act of duplicity—for the price of £1,000,000. The sum was derived from BSAC shares, whose value might plummet in the absence of a land concession. Rhodes was played; so was Lobengula. The consequences were significant. The BSAC could now claim ownership of Lobengula's lands and assign titles to white settlers.[2]

Another tangle of legal and administrative issues surrounded the BSAC's authority to govern African people. The BSAC only had as much authority as it could derive from Lobengula, while the British government was reluctant to take land from what was still a foreign sovereign. The British government got over its scruples when Boer trekkers started to arrive from the Transvaal. In May 1891, an "order in council" proclaimed British jurisdiction and declared Mashonaland and Matabeleland to be a protectorate, subject to the oversight of the high commissioner, Loch. Nobody asked Lobengula for his consent. Meanwhile, while Loch, Rhodes, and Colquhoun operated on the understanding that they should refrain from governing African people, it was impossible to give the BSAC authority to govern just white people, as it was reasonable to predict disputes between miners and police, on the one hand, and Ndebele and Shona people on the other. The BSAC began to act as a government, appointing officers and assigning them to geographic areas, all on the flimsiest of legal pretexts. John S. Moffat, who still represented the British government at Bulawayo, described the details of these arrangements as a "palpable immorality." He stood on the sidelines and watched.[3]

Rhodes's stolen country had another significant problem. The leader of De Beers, Gold Fields, and the BSAC had floated a mining and land company without knowing much about local resources. By 1891 it was becoming clear that while there was some alluvial gold in Mashonaland, it was not a "Second Rand." The colony was going to have to rely on agriculture, but this was not a very good option. Mashonaland was far from markets and had no rail connections. If gold was not available in sufficient quantities, and if European-style agriculture was limited by lack of access to markets, the BSAC was at risk of collapse.

The situation began to take a toll on Rhodes's health. Rhodes was only thirty-eight years old and seemed to be aging rapidly. He had many stresses from his responsibilities in business and politics. He put his body under additional stress by smoking cigarettes and consuming large quantities of alcohol. At lunch he favored a cocktail called a Black Velvet, half champagne, half Guinness stout. In the afternoon and evening, he downed more of the same, plus brandy, whiskey, and wine. Biographers Robert Rotberg and Miles Shore estimate that Rhodes consumed more than half a dozen drinks each day, not unusual by Victorian standards, but still a lot. Rhodes was a hearty eater, too, enjoying fine dining on special occasions but generally preferring the traditional boiled, roasted, fatty, high-carbohydrate fare of the British middle classes. As a young man he had been tall and slender, but by 1891 he had gained considerable weight. The weight gain is explained, in part, by excessive eating and drinking. As a young man, Rhodes complained on several occasions about having "heart attacks," which may have been panic attacks or atrial fibrillation. On his 1891 trip to Mashonaland, fellow travelers noticed that Rhodes preferred to sleep in a chair, saying that lying on a cot or in a hammock made it difficult to breathe. This may have been a way of remedying the early stages of heart failure.[4]

Mindful of his own mortality, Rhodes developed plans for furthering his larger objectives. He had a long-standing plan to travel to Mashonaland, to finally see the land that he hoped would become a settler colony. While making preparations in Cape Town, in August and September of 1891, he wrote an important letter to W. T. Stead, his journalist friend, letting him know that he and Natty Rothschild were going to be named as the executors of his latest will. They were entrusted with Rhodes's scheme to create a secretive society of men to work together for the benefit of the British Empire. To that end, Rhodes sent Stead the original copies of his earlier wills. In the long cover letter, Rhodes reviewed the contents of the will as well as the politics of the British Empire, the Cape Colony, and the Road to the North.

In the will, Rhodes worried that his declining health might cause him to die before accomplishing his goal of putting his white settler colony on a sound footing. He was pleased that it was already being called "Rhodesia," and yet he compared himself to an inventor who fears that he might not get a patent approved before he dies. He criticized the British people and their government for their lack of ambition. The British were the "greatest people the world has ever seen" but do not "know their strength, their greatness, and their destiny." Instead, they are "wasting their time on their minor local matters." Rhodes wrote that the British, "being asleep, do not know that through the invention of steam and electricity and in view of their enormous increase they must now be trained to view the world as a whole and not only consider the social questions of the British Isles." He expressed his hope for the reunification of Britain and the United States under a "universal monarch" with a "federal Parliament." When it came to making imperialist priorities, Rhodes shifted seamlessly from one continent to the next. Rhodes brought the letter back to his desire for a colony in Mashonaland. "If I am worn out," which might easily have happened on his upcoming trip, "please remember never abandon Mashonaland. It is the key to Central Africa. It is very healthy, full of gold and dominates the situation. You have got it and believe me keep it. It is worth more than all your other African possessions. It is simply full of gold reefs."[5]

Rhodes now set out to see Mashonaland for himself. Rhodes and his servant, Antonio "Tony" de la Cruz, traveled with Frank Johnson of the BSAC and David Christiaan de Waal, Hofmeyr's brother-in-law and a member of the Afrikaner Bond. They sailed to Beira, on the coast of Mozambique, then traveled up the Pungwe River, disembarking for the long hike to Umtali and from there to Fort Salisbury. This was a difficult journey, to say the least, and Johnson remarked that Rhodes was often cross. In Mozambique, Rhodes screamed at the Portuguese ship's captain. On the road from Umtali, he became angry at De Waal's Shangaan servant and beat him. Finally, on reaching Salisbury, Rhodes was disappointed by the town, which was barely developed at all. When he arrived, he was greeted by a committee of townspeople, who handed him a list of complaints, mainly having to do with the high prices of imports and the lack of labor. The complaints were ultimately resolved by spending yet more money out of company funds. By this point, half of the company's capital of one million pounds was already spent, with no sign of likely profits. And adding to this aggravation, he found that Randolph Churchill was encamped nearby. Rhodes decided to camp next to him.

Churchill was a friend of Natty Rothschild and a Conservative member of the House of Commons. He supported the expansion of the empire and the modernizing and democratizing of the party. He was also known for his barbed tongue and his *ad hominem* attacks: after Gordon died at Khartoum, Churchill called Gladstone the "Moloch of Midlothian." Churchill had his own imperialist credentials. In 1885, he briefly served as secretary of state for India, during which time he advocated for aggression in Burma and let slip racial slurs. In 1886, he was at the start of an appointment as chancellor of the exchequer, when he committed a major gaffe. An intra-party dispute led him to threaten resignation in the expectation of gaining leverage; instead of giving Churchill what he wanted, Salisbury accepted his resignation.[6]

Churchill's older brother, the Duke of Marlborough, was an investor in the Mozambique Company, and Randolph Churchill had invested in the BSAC. He had little knowledge of Africa, so when two mining speculators invited him to Mashonaland, he took them up on it. To help pay for the extravagant trip, Churchill entered into a contract to provide articles to the *Daily Graphic*. He arrived in Cape Town in April 1891 and journeyed along the Road to the North in a heavy ox-wagon, passing through Thuli and Fort Victoria and arriving months later at Fort Salisbury. In the articles he sent back to his publisher, Churchill described the fascinating characters he met along the way, as well as his adventures as a hunter and his life of camping on a fancy safari. By day he shot animals; by night he sipped champagne.

Lord Randolph Churchill. Wikimedia Commons.

At Salisbury, Churchill wandered over to Rhodes's campsite and introduced himself. The two men and their companions shared a meal and spent a few days taking trips through the countryside. Churchill began to wax positive about the new settlement and praised Rhodes's continued optimism for the colony. The encounter was documented by De Waal in his own letters to a Cape Dutch newspaper, which were eventually translated and published as a book, *With Rhodes in Mashonaland*. De Waal wrote that Churchill got along so well with Rhodes that the two men discussed exploring together, although both men were not in the best of health.

The trip highlighted one of the BSAC's accomplishments, the installation of telegraphs. Churchill arrived in Salisbury at the very same time as the telegraph. Usually, the telegraph followed the railroad, but by 1890 the railroad from Kimberley only reached as far as Vryburg. Further railway construction faced financial and technical challenges. Telegraphs were deployed more easily. Stretching the lines from Vryburg through the territories of half a dozen Tswana chiefs still required complex negotiations on the part of Shippard.

The construction of the line through Palapye to Fort Tuli, on the border with Rhodesia, was done by Tswana men recruited with the permission of Khama. They reached Fort Tuli in late May 1891. The same Tswana men then built the telegraph line that followed the Pioneer Column's road, running from Fort Tuli to Fort Victoria to Salisbury. Challenges to the line's completion ranged from brush fires to lion attacks and labor shortages. Wooden poles were susceptible to being torn up by elephants, burned by brush fires, and eaten by termites. Because of the environment, iron poles were used for the southern half of the line, but for reasons of expense, wooden poles had to be used on the northern half. By early 1892, the telegraph connected Salisbury to the Cape Colony, allowing Rhodes to send and receive messages as Cape prime minister. Rhodes planned to construct a network of telegraphs within Rhodesia, connecting Salisbury to Bulawayo, while also planning for the line to reach north. Once again, the infrastructure of Southern Africa was built to serve the interests of imperialists.[7]

Rhodes left Churchill and together with De Waal, Johnson and Cruz rode from Salisbury in the northeast, sweeping southward and then turning west as they followed the trail laid down by the Pioneer Column. Like the Pioneer Column, the party planned to skirt around Matebeleland, lest they cross paths with the armed forces of Lobengula's subordinates. The party's aim was to follow the path all the way to Thuli, then cross into Tswana territory headed toward Palapye and then continue to the rail head at Vryburg. Along the way, Rhodes and his companions were joined by Jameson, Selous, and several others. Together, they made a detour to Great Zimbabwe, where they had one of their most interesting adventures. Rhodes was a romantic at heart, with a love for inspiring views and ancient ruins. The party had seen small ancient sites all throughout their trip, but the massive structures of Great Zimbabwe inspired awe. Rhodes believed that in ancient times, Great Zimbabwe was run by Phoenicians who mined alluvial gold. Rhodes wrote to Stead that "Zimbabwe is an old Phoenician residence and everything points to Sofala being the place from which Hiram fetched his gold."[8] European travelers had visited the site in previous years, with Karl Mauch publishing an account of his visit in 1871. In 1889, a South African hunting party arrived at Great Zimbabwe and looted the site. The thieves held a group of Shona people at gunpoint and hacked away the site's signature works of art, six large and two small soapstone statues of birds. Soon afterwards, one of the birds came into Rhodes's possession. At more than four feet tall, the large ones were too large to be spirited away easily, so they were buried near the site. Rhodes described them as depictions of "green parrots, the common bird of that district."[9]

Rhodes arranged for the BSAC to pay for a dig by archaeologists Theodore and Mabel Bent, who also received support from the Royal Geographical Society. The Bents traveled with two ox-wagons from Vryburg up the Road to the North, passing through Tswana territory. Khama arranged for them to hire twenty-five laborers. Together, the party rode on the route of the Pioneer Column, reaching Fort Victoria and then turning off in the direction of Great Zimbabwe. The Bents' heavy wagons necessitated the widening of an original pathway. Finally reaching the spectacular site, the Bents hired fifty more local laborers and spent June and July of 1891 digging up relics, including four of the hidden bird sculptures, which they removed from the country at the end of their stay. One item fascinated the Bents and early European visitors. In the Great Enclosure, there were the remains of two conical towers, one large and one small. The Bents believed that these resembled the enclosed stone towers in the Temple of the Obelisks in Byblos, Lebanon, and in other locations in the Mediterranean. The Phoenicians were thought to have built these structures in the shape of phalluses, a component of their worship of Baal. The Bents found several sculptures in the shape of phalluses, too. They believed that many other finds, including the Zimbabwe birds, resembled ancient Mediterranean and Arabic artifacts. In their wishful thinking, they discounted material evidence of medieval African origins, as well as African cultural connections to the site. Theodore Bent's report was published in a book in 1892. His account is filled with paternalistic remarks about African people, so it comes as no surprise that the archaeologists believed African people to be incapable of producing the monumental structures at Great Zimbabwe. The theory of ancient outsider construction and Shona incompetence lent support to the rule of the latter-day BSAC. During the 1890s, Rhodes continued to support research on Great Zimbabwe. At one point, he even sent an assistant to the Vatican Library for the sake of identifying records of Phoenician forts that might be compared to Great Zimbabwe. Tracings of illustrations were sent to Rhodes for his own consideration.[10]

While Rhodes and his friends were enjoying the ruins, Randolph Churchill was sending his letters from South Africa to London, where they were published serially in London's *Daily Graphic*. Churchill told entertaining stories about hunting, and, unfortunately for Rhodes, he gave a candid description of the prospects for mining and settlement in Mashonaland. Churchill wrote that he was unimpressed by "the vast tract of country between Fort Victoria and Fort Charter," which he found "unsuitable and grievous either for man or for domestic beast. Any profitable cultivation of this sandy soil is impossible. In a few spots here and there the natives raise poor crops of mealies. The climate is capricious and variable...." He continued with a dig at Rhodes: "Where, then, I commenced to ask myself, is the much-talked-of fine country of the Mashona? Where is the 'promised land' so desperately coveted by the Boers? On the low veldt, where the soil is of extraordinary fertility, fever and horse sickness afflict human beings and exterminate stock; on the high veldt, where neither of these evils extensively prevails, the soil is barren and worthless."[11]

Churchill's account also gave a mixed review to the area around Fort Salisbury. The settlement had a "thriving, rising, healthy appearance," with a small river serving 500 to 800 residents. "The settlers, hard at work, occupied with one business or another from dawn to dusk, wore an expression of contentment and of confidence." The settlement, located at 5,000 feet of elevation, had air that was "fresh and bracing." There were pretty views of Mount Hampden, and even "a hotel where was laid out a table d'hôte with clean napkins ensconced in glasses on the table." "But the necessaries of life," he added, "whether of food or raiment, were luxuries at Fort Salisbury, and costly in the extreme. Bread, meat, butter, jam had risen to impossible prices."[12]

Randolph Churchill wrote that the expenses of mining in Rhodesia could be afforded by successful entrepreneurs but that getting rich was not a sure bet. "At the time of writing these pages nothing definite or precise is known, or can be known, about the gold deposits of Mashonaland. There had been no one in the country possessing expert knowledge, on which reliance could be placed, and, even if there had been such persons, no sufficient development work had been effected to enable an opinion of any value to be formed. Many months, probably a year or two, must elapse before any certainty can be arrived at as to whether Mashonaland is a gold-producing country or not. Even if it turns out to be a country possessing gold deposits, the payable character of these depends entirely upon whether cheap and easy access to them can be gained." Churchill questioned whether it was worth building the various proposed routes to the east coast, 500 miles away. He concluded: "In my opinion, at the present time all that can be said of Mashonaland from a mining point of view is that the odds are overwhelmingly against the making of any rapid or large fortune by any individual."[13]

Randolph Churchill, a well-connected aristocrat and politician, had exposed one of the central weaknesses of Rhodes's British South Africa Company, confirming the suspicions of some of the City's financiers that the BSAC would not live up to its promises. Settlers complained about the high cost of imported goods. The company's expenses were also high, especially the cost of the 700 troopers of the expanded BSAC Police. In February 1891, shares were selling at £2.1.2. By June 1, shares had already dropped to £1.1.2. By February 1892, when all Churchill's reports had been published, the price was £0.12.6. It cannot be proven that there is a direct correlation between Churchill and the decline in BSAC stock, since the decline in value took place in the context of an overall slowdown in the London market that began in 1890, but Churchill's reports did not help BSAC shares.[14]

Some BSAC board members were concerned enough about the declining share values that they considered paying stock riggers to form a pool to raise the price. The directors in question proposed to pay the riggers £5,000 and agree not to sell their shares. The disreputable proposal was rejected by Cawston, Grey, Fife, and Abercorn, who had scruples about financial transactions. Grey summarized the board leadership's view, writing that he believed that a chartered company acted in the public trust. Even so, he was willing to let others act as their consciences saw fit. It is possible that the remaining board members attempted shady manipulations of the share price, as was alleged in reports published by the *Financial News* in April 1893.[15]

Rhodes worked to keep the BSAC afloat by using his transcontinental network to build the infrastructure that settlers needed in order to prosper. Rhodes hoped to connect Fort Salisbury to Beira by rail. The 1891 negotiations between Britain and Portugal left Manica Province in Portuguese hands, administered by the Mozambique Company, but the Beira Railway Company concession was bought by Henry van Laun and Otto Beit and turned over to the BSAC. The BSAC still lacked sufficient funds for these projects. Correspondence flew back and forth between Rhodes, Rothschild, and Horace Farquhar, who served as the London BSAC secretary, discussing borrowing money and even purchasing southern Mozambique from the Portuguese. John X. Merriman joined the discussions, too, visiting London as the Cape Colony's treasurer.[16]

Challenging financial circumstances persuaded Rhodes to make further changes at the BSAC. He decided to shake up the company's leadership. In

August 1891, Colquhoun was replaced as administrator by Dr. Jameson, a trusted friend who had never run an organization. The BSAC Police force was reduced in number and a colonial militia instituted as an inexpensive form of self-defense. Subsidies for food and merchant goods were reduced. And since capital was scarce, mining syndicates were granted increasingly large amounts of land in the hope that scale was likely to foster rapid development. Unsuccessful companies were treated leniently. Rhodes was aware that the large grants of land to companies conflicted with his vision of settlement by many individual white farmers, but he only slowed land distribution in mid-1893, by which time the colony's best land was in the hands of mining speculators, who were producing little gold.

Rhodes promoted the company heavily during his visits to England, distracting shareholders from fundamental problems by referencing grand schemes for infrastructure. At one such meeting, on November 29, 1892, he gave a rousing speech at London's Cannon Street Hotel, in which he described, in glowing terms, how his plans for the BSAC included stretching the telegraph line all the way through Central Africa, through the Sudan and up into Egypt. The next day's *Times* reported on the speech with a measure of skepticism, which was picked up by the editorial cartoonists of *Punch*. Soon, the humor magazine published a cartoon by Linley Sambourne featuring Cecil Rhodes, dressed as a British soldier, with one foot on Cape Town and the other on Cairo, holding up a telegraph wire. The title, "The Rhodes Colossus," was a pun on the giant statue of the Colossus formerly displayed on the Greek island of Rhodes. Classically educated Victorians would have known that it was once thought to be one of the "seven wonders of the world." The cartoon would also have called to mind the famous line that Cassius spoke to Brutus in Shakespeare's *Julius Caesar*: "why, man, he doth bestride the narrow world / Like a Colossus." Sambourne's depiction of Rhodes became one of the most recognizable political cartoons of all time.[17]

It is hard to know if Rhodes's efforts paid off. In April 1893, shares of the company climbed back up to £2.1.0. Soon afterwards, a worldwide crisis known as the Panic of 1893 caused share values to swing wildly. The price fluctuations continued for the next decade and ranged from a low of £1.0.0, the par value, reaching as high as £8.10.2 for a time in 1895. Share valuation seemingly had little to do with the actual production of gold from the mines of Mashonaland. Meanwhile, mining speculators, including Rhodes and Beit, acquired some of the most valuable landholdings.

The challenges did not diminish Rhodes's enthusiasm for Mashonaland. He knew that a handful of white settlers were unhappy, and that gold had not

Linley Sambourne, "The Rhodes Colossus," *Punch*, December 10, 1892. Wikipedia.

been discovered in sufficient quantities. Some of Rhodes's "yes men" encouraged their boss. Frank Johnson sent a letter in which he dismissed the advice of experts. "It is a pity the 'expert' does not encourage people a little more," wrote Johnson, "but I think we have reached the stage, when no one thinks twice as to what he says about a property, it is always a foregone conclusion that it will be condemned." Then Johnson gave examples of condemned mines that were producing modest results.[18] In hindsight it is difficult to determine the extent to which Johnson may have overestimated these mining properties, but Rhodes sent reassurances to the board in London and even sent Maund to deliver a personal message of confidence. Rhodes was trying to keep the bubble from bursting.

The BSAC depended on the backing of Natty Rothschild, who continued to support Rhodes through difficulties in Mashonaland and Matabeleland. Rothschild, who also played banker to the Churchill family, wrote to Rhodes that "it was no doubt injudicious on the part of Lord Randolph to cry down Mashonaland; but you may be certain of one thing, namely, that you have no warmer admirer than him, and perhaps it was as well that he should not have painted Mashonaland in too glowing colors, because it might have produced a rush into the country and in consequence, increased your transport and food difficulties." Mobility was, indeed, a key problem of the colony. So was money. Rothschild suggested in a letter to Rhodes that he saw considerable overlap between the northward territorial expansion policies of the Cape government and the BSAC.[19]

Rothschild disliked the idea of the BSAC using De Beers money to support expansionist policy. If "you require money for the purpose," Rothschild advised, "you will have to obtain it from other sources than the cash reserve of the De Beers Company. We have always held that the De Beers Company is simply and purely a diamond mining company." Anticipating Rhodes's objection, Rothschild believed that "it is quite possible that the Articles of Association may give you a loophole, but nowadays, people are disposed to construe all articles of association more severely than they used to do, and if it became known that the De Beers Company lent money to the Chartered Company, some De Beers shareholders," he hinted darkly, "might move for an injunction, and get up a an agitation to turn out the Board and put in their own nominees, which would be most undesirable." Rothschild worried that if the diamond industry's money was going to be used for public purposes, it could either be taxed more heavily or it could be nationalized. "Let that idea pass through your fertile brain and tell me what you think of it."[20]

Natty Rothschild was one of the most talented financiers and politicians of his generation, but even he fell for Rhodes's schemes. When questions were raised about Rhodes in Rothschild's social circles, he chose to defend Rhodes. In 1893, Lewis Harcourt, the son of the chancellor of the exchequer, recorded an argument between Rothschild and Churchill, at a reception at Rothschild's Tring Park manor. Churchill "attacked Rhodes and S Africa & Mashonaland most bitterly, said the country was bankrupt & Rhodes a sham and that Natty knew it and Rhodes could not raise £51,000 in the City to open a mine etc.

All this was to Natty's face and made him furious—so much so that he went out of the room for a few minutes to cool himself."[21]

Churchill was correct about Rhodes, yet many successful people continued to back the Colossus. Soon after the argument between Rothschild and Churchill, Rhodes misled the board about difficulties that were emerging with Shona and Ndebele people. When the BSAC bought the Lippert Concession, it was understood by Jameson and the BSAC that Lobengula was not going to collect any more tribute from Shona people. That was not understood by Lobengula. Parties of Ndebele soldiers still crossed into Mashonaland demanding tribute from Shona communities that had elected not to do so. Ndebele soldiers only menaced Shona people, studiously avoiding conflict with Europeans. Even so, Ndebele violence was still witnessed by colonial settlers, who understandably found the presence of Ndebele soldiers to be unnerving. Jameson took the attacks to be a provocation. He did not understand the tributary arrangements between Ndebele and Shona people. Shona people, according to Jameson, were under the jurisdiction of the BSAC.

Jameson complained about Ndebele incursions, but the BSAC's administration of justice was akin to vigilantism. In one instance in 1892, Jameson ordered the BSAC Police to "give a lesson" to a Shona chief named Moghabi who did not recognize BSAC authority. A patrol led by Captains Graham and Lendy killed the chief and torched his kraal. In another incident, white traders claimed that a prominent Shona village leader, Ngomo, had stolen some goods. Jameson requested that Lendy "take summary measures." Lendy led a BSAC Police patrol to Ngomo's kraal. The troopers surrounded the kraal and opened fire with a Maxim gun and a seven-pounder cannon. Twenty-one Shona people were killed, and all their cattle were captured. Lendy and Jameson's reign of terror met with disapproval in Cape Town and London. Graham Bower, still the governor's secretary, called the punishment "utterly disproportionate." Lord Knutsford threatened to cancel the BSAC charter. The BSAC board was worried but only issued mild reprimands to Rhodes and Jameson.[22]

A direct line of telegraphic communication between the forts, Cape Town, and London should have strengthened central control over the periphery, but throughout the run-up to war, Jameson, from his remote location, managed to manipulate the authorities in Cape Town and London. In August 1892, Gladstone became prime minister for the third time. The 82-year-old stalwart of the Liberal Party had been skeptical of empire-building for most of his long political career. Soon after Gladstone's government took charge at

Whitehall, Loch and Rhodes were summoned to London for a conference at the Colonial Office. The meeting had the potential to become difficult, but Rhodes turned it to his advantage. The new secretary of state for the colonies was the experienced Liberal politician George Robinson, the Marquess of Ripon, who had served as the viceroy of India in the early 1880s. In India, he had pursued a reforming agenda, but when it came to South African policy, his interventions were mild.

In October 1892, Rhodes and Loch arrived in Whitehall. The most immediate and pressing topic of conversation was the Bechuanaland Railway. Short of funds, the BSAC was not honoring its agreement to keep building the railway from Vryburg toward Palapye, 150 miles southwest of the border with Matabeleland. Loch suggested that Rhodes and the BSAC form a separate company to finish the railway. Rhodes agreed. At a follow-up meeting at the Colonial Office, Rhodes proposed that a new company, the Bechuanaland Railway Company, be created. Its debentures would be owned by the BSAC, which in turn would raise money by obtaining subscriptions from the Exploring Company, United Concessions, Gold Fields, and De Beers. Work on the line proceeded under this unusual structure, with Metcalfe as the engineer and Pauling as the contractor. Pauling recalled that while the corporate arrangements were unusual, Rhodes gave the project his personal touch. Pauling's contract was signed after midnight at the conclusion of a long dinner that he and Metcalfe had with Rhodes. This approach was nothing more than "crony capitalism" or the "band of brothers," with an admixture of complicated paperwork. The British government and the BSAC contributed to the railway company, in exchange for postal services and other support. Pauling hired his brother and his cousin to help manage the construction. The line to Mafeking was complete in October 1894 and would eventually reach Bulawayo in November 1897.[23]

The BSAC lacked funds for the Bechuanaland Railway, at least in part because Rhodes was spending money on building the shorter rail connection from the Mozambique coast, to run through the Manica region. Railroads and harbors involved enormous capital investments. Telegraph lines were less costly. In December 1892, Rhodes and partners from England and South Africa formed the Africa Trans-Continental Telegraph Company (ATT). Construction started simultaneously in Nyasaland and Rhodesia, with part of the line crossing through Mozambique. From Salisbury, the ATT line passed through difficult terrain to Mozambique's Mazoe mining district. From there it extended 40 miles northeast to the Zambezi River at Tete, still in Mozambique. Rhodes relied on advice from Harry Johnston, who knew the area well. In January of 1893, Johnston wrote a long letter to Rhodes, suggesting paths for the telegraph to take and describing the different rulers and groups of people along the route. Johnston invited Rhodes to visit the region and see the challenges for himself. Johnston advised that Rhodes could avoid "political troubles from the natives" by laying underwater cable the full length of Lake Nyasa, the old colonial name for Lake Malawi, and the full length of Lake Tanganyika, a very expensive proposition. Johnston informed Rhodes that "I find myself rather staggered at the idea of carrying an overland line from the north end of Tanganyika to Victoria Nyanza [Lake Victoria], because the people between the two Lakes are very hostile to the whites, and would certainly regard the telegraph line as an embodiment of witchcraft." However, it was Johnston's opinion that "a little expenditure of money would conquer their prejudices."[24] The 30-mile line that was stretched from Blantyre southwest to Chikwawa, in southern Nyasaland, opened in late 1894, but even nearby areas, such as Mount Darwin in Mashonaland, proved "more or less heavy bush," in the words of the construction supervisor, Patrick Forbes. The bush was so lush that it kept growing back. Forbes reported to Rhodes that "the line was surveyed & cleared right down to here 15 months ago but has grown up a good deal."[25] The line from Salisbury to Mazoe and Tete was nearly complete when the war between the British and the Ndebele and Shona broke out. Shona fighters attacked and destroyed the line. In 1897, a less vulnerable line was constructed that bypassed the parts of Shona territory that the BSAC considered to be unstable. The line was built from Salisbury in a southeast direction to Umtali (Mutare) on the border with Mozambique. From there the line was run north to Tete.[26]

Rhodes planned for the line to keep running all the way north, along the shores of Lake Nyasa, Lake Tanganyika, and Lake Victoria and from there up to Fashoda (Kodok) in the southern part of Sudan. Rhodes also hoped for a railway to eventually follow the path of the telegraph. In order to fulfill this mission, he had to obtain permission from all the colonial governments concerned, including the British authorities in East Africa and Egypt. The key person to persuade was Evelyn Baring, Lord Cromer, the controller-general of Egypt. Egypt was still technically an Ottoman dependency, but the ruler of Egypt, Ismail Pasha, had been bankrupted by the costs of the Suez Canal and the collapse of cotton prices. To ensure the repayment of debts, Ismail was forced to accept British and French oversight over his finances. As controller-general from 1877 to 1879, and as consul-general from 1883 to 1907, Cromer essentially governed Egypt, making him one of the most powerful proconsuls in the British Empire. Rhodes sought him out as an ally. In June of 1893,

Rhodes met with Cromer in Cairo. A telegram that Cromer sent to Rhodes indicates that they discussed the transcontinental telegraph, as well as the desirability of acquiring Delagoa Bay.[27]

With Cromer's help, British support for the telegraph was forthcoming, but Rhodes had to negotiate with the German government and also with King Leopold II of Belgium. Soon Rhodes encountered difficulties. In 1892, at a dinner meeting, he enlisted the help of the well-known imperialist explorer Henry Morton Stanley, who had advocated for a transcontinental telegraph in 1878, at the conclusion of his expedition through the Belgian Congo. In March of 1893, Stanley wrote to Rhodes to inform him that for months after their "frank & cordial conversation" the telegraph from Cape to Cairo "has engrossed all my spare time," apparently without any concrete achievement. Rhodes replied in a characteristic, brusque note:

Dear Mr. Stanley,

You can help me. Kindly go to the King of the Belgians and get me the right to come up his side of the Lake Tanganyika as far as Uganda with my telegraph. Be good enough to do this at once as it will influence me as to which side I shall take. I prefer the Belgians territory [to the Germans' territory].

Y/t [Yours truly]
C. J. Rhodes[28]

Rhodes's note to Stanley reeks of power and entitlement, with large swathes of territory and major infrastructure projects considered to be personal property. Such a domineering attitude worked well enough in the small pond of South African politics, but it may not have gotten Rhodes very far with first-rank schemers like Leopold. At home in England, Rhodes may have felt entitled to push his own government. In March 1893, the British government's secretary of state for foreign affairs, Lord Rosebery, approached the German government at Rhodes's request, making clear that support for Rhodes's rail-building schemes was not official policy. Rosebery learned that German investors were about to form a company to build a telegraph line in German East Africa that connected to Rhodes's lines.[29] Rhodes was not satisfied. In April 1893, Rhodes sent Rosebery a note:

You do not appear to get any further with the Germans. I felt sure they would do nothing. I hear from a private source they propose to grant a charter to a German Company for the territory along the shores of Lake Tanganyika.... It is just what I expected. If they do this I shall certainly retaliate....

You may say this will embarrass you as your only ally in Europe is Germany. Well you might let me know but I think you will agree that they are behaving most meanly towards my attempt to develop the dark continent by means of a trans-continental telegraph....

Consul [Harry] Johnston...telegraphs that he is coming to Capetown in May. Though we pay for everything I think he is like all Imperial officers, somewhat small minded and does not like to be considered or connected with a Chartered Co. It is human nature so I reminded him... that whether he liked it or not he must remember that the oil that kept the wheels going, came from us.[30]

Some weeks later, Rhodes pushed Rosebery again: "Still I think that if the ambassador at Berlin is worth anything," Rhodes wrote, "he could be able to explain to the young Emperor [Wilhelm II] the advantages of the telegraph to his enterprise and the alternatives through King of the Belgian's territory or else by a cable up the Lake Tanganyika." King Leopold was tending to side with the French in their efforts to build connections across the continent. Rhodes took a dim view of the French. "Whatever we do for the French," he told Rosebery, "we may rest assured that they will steadily maintain one sentiment towards us and that is they will dislike us in proportion to our prosperity," an ironic reference to the Christian practice of proportional tithing.[31]

With his penchant for drama and vision, Rhodes managed an expensive network of far-flung businesses that stretched from Cape Town and London to remote parts of Southern Africa. The final push to connect Rhodesia by rail began in 1893. By that time there were further changes to the British government. In 1893, Gladstone's efforts to hold together his minority government received a major setback. The government managed to pass the Second Irish Home Rule Bill in the Commons, only to have it massively defeated in the House of Lords, further undermining the leadership's credibility. The bill had the strong support of a handful of aristocrats in Gladstone's government, including Ripon. While Ripon supported less imperialism in Ireland, he supported more imperialism in Southern Africa. Ripon urged Loch to maintain the peace but also authorized him to move the Bechuanaland Border Police and an allied force of Tswana fighters into position near the Ndebele border. Loch, for his own part, contemplated British, not BSAC, rule over the Ndebele kingdom, but he was outflanked by Rhodes.

15

Fighting for Arcadia

IN 1893 RHODES was at the height of his powers. The premier of the Cape Colony led De Beers and played a prominent role in Gold Fields. His British South Africa Company was putting down roots in South Central Africa. In July 1893, Rhodes even proposed to the Colonial Office that the BSAC be paid £25,000 to govern Uganda. In private correspondence with Gladstone's foreign secretary, Lord Rosebery, Rhodes once again expressed the hope that telegraph lines could connect Uganda to BSAC territories to the south, by passing through German or Belgian territory. He even contemplated paying the Mahdi, Muhammad Ahmad bin Abdullah, so that telegraph lines could run from Uganda through the Sudan, all the way to Cairo. The Mahdi's forces had killed Rhodes's friend Charles Gordon only eight years earlier. The intended telegraph project had a total budget of three million pounds, a staggering sum of money. Rhodes believed that the BSAC shareholders could be persuaded of the telegraph's value. His appetite for geographical and technological power seemed boundless, but there were still obstacles and details to be dealt with in the territory governed by the BSAC.

The situation in Mashonaland and Matabeleland was unstable. Each month, the Ndebele ruler, Lobengula, collected the £100 in gold sovereigns promised by the Rudd Concession and tried to avoid conflict with the BSAC. Lobengula still objected to the agreement, as did many of the indunas. As settlement expanded, colonists objected to Ndebele tribute-gathering and intimidation of Shona people. White settlers witnessed theft, kidnapping, and murder but did not comprehend the underlying politics. Lobengula and the Ndebele leadership may have continued tribute-taking as a way of asserting themselves, even as they avoided a head-on collision with the heavily armed forces of the BSAC. As relations became tense between settlers and parties of Ndebele soldiers, Lobengula was not the only one who sought to avoid direct conflict. The Colonial Office's official position was to avoid conflict, too. The British government was unlikely to sanction an invasion of

Matabeleland, mainly for fear of the expense. London did allow British forces to defend themselves if they were attacked.

The telegraph lines that crossed Rhodesia started to become flashpoints for conflict. In December 1892, the telegraph wires in Kalanga territory, near the Lundi River, now called the Runde River, were cut. Kalanga people living nearby blamed Ndebele soldiers seeking tribute. It was not clear if the wire-cutters were resisting imperialism or stealing copper wire to make jewelry (or both). Jameson took the incident so seriously that he sent Lendy and a party of troopers to Lobengula's court. Shortly thereafter, when Kalanga people admitted the crime, Lendy still gave Lobengula a dire warning about interfering with the telegraph. In May 1893, a wire-cutting by Shona people near Fort Victoria was punished by assessing a fine in cattle. The local people paid the fine with cattle "on loan" from Lobengula, much to his anger and frustration. The wire-cutting incidents contributed to tensions between the BSAC and the Ndebele leadership.[1]

In hindsight the conflict that developed between the BSAC and Lobengula seems inevitable. In one incident, Lobengula was keeping cattle at the kraal of a Shona chief, but the cattle were taken by the BSAC. Lobengula protested vehemently to the BSAC and to Loch, resulting in Jameson sending the cattle back. Lobengula feared that he would give the BSAC a pretext for invading his country. Many Ndebele soldiers were running out of patience. In July 1893, Jameson staged a conference with several Ndebele indunas outside of Fort Salisbury. After the representatives departed, Jameson ordered Lendy and the BSAC Police to pursue and capture an Ndebele military formation. "If they resist, shoot them," he commanded. When stopped, the Ndebele soldiers did not resist; Lendy's patrol attacked them anyway, killing thirty men and mutilating some of the corpses. Victorious troopers bragged that the attack on the Ndebele had been "as good as partridge shooting" and that "fox hunting couldn't hold a candle to it."[2]

Jameson took the one-sided attack by Lendy as a major opportunity. He wrote to Loch, claiming that Ndebele fighters had attacked Lendy's patrol, putting the high commissioner on notice that conflict was possible. Rhodes recommended caution, sending Jameson a telegram that advised him to "Read Luke XIV.31." In the King James Version, this verse reads: "Or what king, going to make war against another king, sitteth not down first, and consulteth whether he be able with ten thousand to meet him that cometh against him with twenty thousand." Jameson misunderstood the Biblical quotation. Rather than meeting with Lobengula, Jameson began to recruit a larger and more threatening force of BSAC Police. Recruits were promised 3,000 morgen of land, plus twenty mine claims and a share of Lobengula's cattle. This approach was consistent with the practices of the past: for a century or more, promises of African cattle and land had been used to recruit militia members. Word leaked to the London press, where the BSAC was accused of starting a potentially bloody war that would be fought by mercenaries in the interest of preserving share values.[3] Influential members of the British establishment had just read Randolph Churchill's articles, now published in book form, in which he panned BSAC fortifications at Fort Charter and Fort Victoria:

> [They] appeared to be miserably weak constructions, which a few thousand Matabele [Ndebele] would probably rush with ease, attacking, as is their habit, in the dark just before daybreak. There is nothing to stop the rush of the savage foe, save a ditch from 3 to 4 feet deep, a mound from 10 to 12 feet high from the bottom of the ditch, and two or three strands of barbed wire stretched on weak posts. I thought that something in the nature of *chevaux de frise*—something in the way of wire entanglements, would be advantageous and easy of construction, but I was assured that such ideas were quite wrong and foolish. The officers of the police evidently disdain the Matabele, and have perfect confidence in their Martini-Henry rifles and their Maxim gun. I hope that they are right, but the African savage has often proved himself to be no contemptible foe, even against arms of precision.[4]

Loch, as Britain's high commissioner, invited Lobengula to send indunas to Cape Town for a discussion about improving relations. Lobengula chose to send his half-brother, Ingubogubo, as well as two indunas, Ingubo and Mantusi. Moffat was no longer working in Bulawayo, so escorting the indunas fell to James Dawson. Dawson, Ingubogubo, Ingubo, and Mantusi crossed the border into Bechuanaland, then stopped at Tati, which was occupied by the Bechuanaland Border Police. Dawson rode into town with the indunas, without explaining to anyone the purpose of the visit, then left them while he went to find water. While Dawson was having a drink, the commander of the Bechuanaland Border Police (BPP), Major Kenneth Goold-Adams, ordered his troopers to arrest the three Ndebele men. They fought back, but Mantusi was shot to death and Ingubo was killed by being clubbed with the stock of a rifle. Dawson and Ingubogubo were horrified but still proceeded on their mission. The meeting with Loch did not go well. Loch was not interested in helping Lobengula so much as he was interested in controlling him. The high commissioner refused to give the two emissaries permission to travel from Cape Town to London.[5]

Loch tried to control Ndebele resistance while also reining in the BSAC. When the Cape Parliament was in session, Loch and Rhodes met regularly in their roles as governor and prime minister. Rhodes became worried that Loch was interested in establishing direct British government control over Ndebele territory, when BSAC leaders were hopeful to find gold in Matabeleland. Meanwhile, Loch knew that up north, the BSAC was now being led by the impulsive Dr. Jameson. If a conflict broke out between the BSAC and Lobengula, the BSAC Police could reach Bulawayo and claim Ndebele territory before Loch's force, the BBP, could get there. Perceiving a threat from Loch, Rhodes gave him the slip. As soon as the Cape Parliament's session ended in mid-September, Rhodes snuck out of Cape Town and made his way north to Mashonaland, where he hoped to manage the looming conflict personally.

For Rhodes, the stakes were high. His vision of a white settler colony was at stake; so was his pocketbook. Rhodes was supporting the BSAC with investments from Gold Fields. In 1892, it seemed that Gold Fields did not have sufficient capital for extending its operations further in the deep-level mines of the Witwatersrand. Gold Fields merged with three other companies to form Consolidated Gold Fields. The new company now had the funds for digging deeper but was still held back by its investments in BSAC shares, which were declining in the months before Rhodes traveled north. If Rhodes defeated Lobengula and opened Ndebele territory for gold exploration, share prices might rise in the BSAC and in Consolidated Gold Fields, with the likely prospect of a future payout on the Rand.[6]

Rhodes sailed to Beira with the railway engineer, Charles Metcalfe; his private secretary, Gordon Le Sueur; and his servant, Tony de la Cruz. From Beira they planned to take the developing coastal route to the Mashonaland interior. The railway contractor, George Pauling, had constructed a narrow-gauge railway 75 miles into the interior, where the rail was met by an improved road. At Massi Kessi, they were joined by another key part of Rhodes's northern network, Hans Sauer. As Rhodes and his party traveled through Mozambique and into Manicaland, the Colossus played "hard to get." If Loch could reach him, the governor could send orders to stand down. The plan for the BSAC police to capture Bulawayo could be preempted by Loch's imperial force, the BBP.[7]

While Rhodes was en route, Jameson used the telegraph to manipulate Loch into permitting a war. During the first week of October 1893, Jameson informed Loch that an incident had taken place. An Ndebele force had crossed the border at the Shashi River and had taken cattle back to their side.

The Ndebele soldiers were pursued by BSAC Police, who retreated after being fired upon. Jameson also reported that Lobengula had gathered a force of 7,000 soldiers and sent them toward Victoria. The report was open to interpretation. Loch took the bait and authorized Jameson to defend Mashonaland and then, a few days later, to attack Bulawayo. The BSAC Police were not told to stand down, as Rhodes had feared. There was a race to see whether the BSAC Police under Jameson would get to Bulawayo before Loch's BBP, still commanded by Major Kenneth Goold-Adams. Goold-Adams's column consisted of 225 cavalry troopers armed with Martini-Henry rifles, two seven-pounder cannons, and five Maxim guns. They were supplemented by 1,000 Ngwato soldiers, half of whom were armed with Martini-Henrys. The Ngwato fighters were led by Khama himself. Loch hoped that the BBP troopers and their Tswana allies could reach Bulawayo before Jameson and the company troopers.[8]

Jameson's promises of land and cattle succeeded in attracting 650 white volunteers. Some of them were members of prominent families, like C. E. Judge, the son of the commissioner who investigated the De Beers mine fire. In a letter to his family, C. E. Judge expressed concerns that many of the recruits had come from the Transvaal and were unreliable. "I saw in the last Argus that arrived in camp," he wrote, referencing Cape Town's newspaper, "that Rhodes stated we were all mounted; he must have known at the time it was not true. The last batch that came up from Johannesburg to join were a horrible crew; they have looted us right & left."[9] The BSAC also recruited 900 Shona auxiliaries and more than a hundred drivers, cooks, and orderlies. The Shona auxiliaries were a mix of men from different groups with different motives. Some did not get along. Others had personal motivations for cooperating with the BSAC Police, including hopes to recover family members who had been kidnapped by Ndebele tribute-seekers.

The BSAC Police force was now commanded by a professional cavalry officer, Major Patrick Forbes. His troopers were hastily recruited but heavily armed. They carried Martini-Henry rifles and an assortment of revolvers and shotguns. They were supplemented by the machine guns, cannons, and rockets that entered the country with the Pioneer Column, as well as a Hotchkiss Gun, a lightweight, breechloading cannon developed for fighting in the US West that was taken from the Portuguese at Massi Kessi. The BSAC also brought two further acquisitions from the Portuguese: a pair of Nordenfelt guns. The Nordenfelt was a rapid-fire weapon designed in 1873, before the Maxim gun. It had five barrels, laid out in a row. A pull on a lever fired five rifle bullets simultaneously, while a push loaded the next five cartridges. The gun could be fired repeatedly by pulling and pushing the lever.[10]

Armed with this deadly combination of light artillery, machine guns, and breechloading rifles, the BSAC Police and the Bechuanaland Border Police rode quickly toward Bulawayo to avoid the rainy season, which starts in November. The BSAC Police set out in two columns, one from Victoria, the other from Salisbury. The columns were shadowed by Ndebele fighters who hoped to draw them into the woodlands. The Victoria and Salisbury columns met up and joined forces on October 16, 1893. On October 24, they crossed the Shangani River and set up their campsite at a place called Bonko close to a wooded area. The Salisbury group and the Victoria group each arranged its wagons in separate laagers, with pens for horses and oxen in between. In 1888, Sidney Shippard had expressed the hope that the Ndebele army would be "cut down by our rifles and machine guns like a cornfield by a reaping machine."[11] It had taken five years of BSAC maneuvering for an opportunity to present itself.

Before dawn on October 25, Ndebele general Mtshane Khumalo led several thousand Ndebele soldiers from different regiments in an attack on the BSAC position. The Ndebele men were armed with assegais as well as with rifles, although accounts suggest that they had not learned how to properly sight the Martini-Henrys that Lobengula acquired from the Rudd Concession. For four hours Ndebele fighters tried to charge their way to the circled wagons. Some managed to approach within a hundred yards, but they were no match for the concentrated fire of rifles, cannons, and machine guns. One white BSAC trooper was killed and six were wounded. Several dozen Shona allies were wounded or killed by friendly fire when they ran accidentally into the path of the machine guns. Ndebele forces suffered at least 500 casualties and retreated. Wounded Ndebele fighters were given special treatment by Dr. Jameson. "Jameson is a man who has very little respect for the truth," C. E. Judge wrote to his family, "& he has done a thing that disgusted all of us, taken wounded Matebele prisoners, got all the information out of them & then shot them. If ever this gets into the papers he will deny it of course but it is a fact all the same."[12]

The column packed up and over the next days, the troopers drew closer to Bulawayo. Ndebele fighters skirmished with BSAC scouts on patrol but could not cut them off or draw them out into ambushes. Lobengula was not present, but he had heard reports about the battle of the Shangani, and he ordered his generals to avoid attacking the BSAC laager with a frontal assault. Fighters from the two best Ndebele military units, the Imbizo and the Inqobo, boasted that they were braver than their defeated comrades. On November 1, they attacked at a place called Egodade near the Bembesi River. While BSAC orderlies were taking horses and oxen to drink at the river, members of the

Imbizo and the Inqobo lined up and charged. BSAC sentries were overrun while the animals' keepers struggled to get the beasts back into the pen. Bullets whizzed around the main force of the BSAC Police, hitting several troopers. The BSAC force returned fire with their rifles, cannons, and machine guns, inflicting heavy casualties. Ndebele fighters regrouped and charged two more times. Each time, the result was the same. John Willoughby was present and after the battle commented, "I doubt if any European troops could have withstood for such a long time as they had the terrific and well directed fire brought to bear on them."[13] The Anglican Bishop of Mashonaland, George Knight-Bruce, was also present at the battle and reported the terrifying effects of the machine guns. He wrote in his notebook that "it was a nasty ten minutes." When he went to find men who were wounded, he found none. He reflected that "it all made one realize what those terrible machine-guns mean. It must have required extra-ordinary courage to have come up the hill against the fire."[14]

The repeated assaults of Ndebele fighters on BSAC troopers armed with rapid-fire, high-velocity weapons may seem illogical or brave, but these battles were among the first in world history in which Maxim guns were used, and no soldier anywhere knew how to attack a position defended by these weapons. Early in the First World War, casualties were so high at least in part because many European officers still thought that machine guns could be overcome with bravery, a line of thinking that resembled the approach taken by Ndebele unit leaders in their early battles with the BSAC. In 1893, the Ndebele tactics against these unfamiliar weapons may not have been wise, but by the standards of the day they were typical. Lobengula had hesitated to make headlong attacks on soldiers armed with the modern weapons. He had preferred to wait, but the slow, patient approach had disadvantages. It had allowed the BSAC to impose itself on the unwilling country, which proved intolerable to many Ndebele leaders. Either way, it would be difficult for Ndebele leaders to win against the BSAC.

While the BSAC Police approached Bulawayo from the northeast, the BBP and the Tswana units were riding more slowly from the southwest. They were hindered by an outbreak of smallpox. Khama was concerned enough about the disease, and about the BPP's slow progress, that he withdrew his Tswana soldiers and ordered them home to tend their crops. Soon afterwards, on November 1, the BBP wagon train was attacked by Ndebele soldiers. The Ndebele commanders must have understood that attacking a moving column was a better tactic than attacking a fortified position, but still they met with little success. When Lobengula heard the news of the BBP and BSAC columns advancing toward him, he decided to evacuate Bulawayo and torch the town as he left. On November 4, as Lobengula and his followers fled, the BSAC Police column entered Bulawayo. Rhodes entered with them and gave a speech that defied Loch, Ripon, and Gladstone to impose constraints. He concluded by aiming vague threats in their direction: "if the Imperial Government interfered the consequences would be very unpleasant indeed." The exact consequences were not articulated. One thing was clear: Rhodes was getting more deeply invested in the outcome. Not only was he physically present; he had also contributed to the financing of the campaign by selling 40,000 of his BSAC shares.[15]

Key members of Rhodes's transcontinental network were happy with the results of the campaign, particularly investors. Natty Rothschild's cousin, Arthur de Rothschild, was pleased that the fighting resulted in "a little spurt in the shares of the Chartered Co."[16] Higher share values for the BSAC supported higher share values for Consolidated Gold Fields, which needed ever more funds to plow into deep-level mining, a very good investment. Yet many contemporaries were troubled by Rhodes's war. Even as he entered the smoldering wreck of Bulawayo in triumph, the news of the bloody campaign was beginning to undermine public support for the BSAC. In Cape Town, Loch was getting fed up with the problems caused by the BSAC. He called for ending BSAC rule and for imposing British colonial administration. In London, questions were raised about the BSAC in Parliament.

On November 9, 1893, Rhodes was denounced on the floor of the House of Commons by Henry Labouchère, a prominent Liberal who represented Northampton. Labouchère was a wealthy journalist and a critic of imperialism who led the Liberal Party's "Radicals." Skilled at stirring up controversy, he supported his magazine, *Truth,* by goading public figures into failed libel suits.[17] His new target was Rhodes. Labouchère used a parliamentary tactic—calling for a vote of adjournment—which allowed members to open a debate on any political topic. Labouchère addressed the news coming from what was coming to be called the "Matabele War." He gave a lengthy speech in the House of Commons in which he detailed the background history of the BSAC and laced into Rhodes's vision for a settler colony. On this day, Labouchère's speech was protected by parliamentary privilege, which means that members cannot be sued for statements made in Parliament. He was calling attention to himself and setting the stage for further provocations.

Labouchère's first criticism was directed at the concession. "Concessions were obtained very easily from African Monarchs, and generally they were fraudulent; the Monarch was asked to promise something in words, then it was reduced to writing, and the Monarch who could not read was asked to put his hand to the concession, with the result that he signed away a great deal more than he had ever promised." Labouchère reviewed the entire history of the Rudd Concession, of the visit by the indunas to the queen, and then the history of the Lippert Concession. "The Company disputed at first the validity of this concession," he said, "but giving up that contention they bought it, and they then considered it perfectly valid." The Charter was illegitimate, too, since Rhodes had not mentioned to the British government that the concession was owned by the United Concessions Company, not the Chartered Company. Rhodes and his colleagues, "having tricked Lobengula out of the concession, tricked the Colonial Office out of the Charter...at that time it was fully understood by the Colonial Office that this Company which was being created were possessors of the concessions. The Colonial Office then had never heard that the Search Company was only a dummy."

Labouchère went on at length, attacking the BSAC and impugning the motives and morals of Rhodes and his associates. Labouchère accused the BSAC of planting articles in the press that presented Mashonaland as "the land of Ophir," a reference to Bent's theories about Great Zimbabwe's origins in the ancient Middle East. The object was "to induce the British public, to believe that the best thing one could do was to buy a share in the Chartered Company." The fact that it was called a "Royal Charter" did not guarantee anything, but "investors, who were a very silly body of people, were led to suppose that in some way there was an assurance or guarantee that the Company was respectable, that the amount of capital was legitimate, and that the whole of the proceedings would be honestly conducted." The "pillars of the Empire" who owned the most shares were the real beneficiaries of inflated share prices after the first and second stock offerings. Labouchère "submitted that all this money had been, and would be, obtained under false pretences." It seemed that there was not much gold in Mashonaland, yet greed for gold and greed to maintain the value of BSAC shares inspired the attack on the Ndebele kingdom. And when the war was fought, the BSAC and its Shona allies committed atrocities, such as the killing of wounded Ndebele prisoners.[18]

Rhodes stood accused of being a crook and a greedy warmonger in the most public place in the United Kingdom. Sitting near Labouchère on the Liberal benches was none other than Rochfort Maguire, who had been present with Rudd in Bulawayo and who was now representing a constituency in Ireland. Maguire rose immediately to defend the BSAC. He did not attempt to deny any of the charges but instead provided context. Maguire made the shaky claim that at the time the charter was granted, the British government decided that a chartered company was the most cost-effective way to keep the territory out of Boer hands. Having made that choice about the economy of territoriality, "It appeared... that the financial relations of the Company to its shareholders was not a proper nor even a possible subject for exhaustive or satisfactory discussion" in the House of Commons. The ownership of the Rudd Concession by the separate Concessions Company was not concealed from the Colonial Office. "Lord Knutsford did not ask for information," Maguire said weakly, "but the fact that the matter was made public showed that there was no concealment." The matter had been made public several years after the fact. When it came to the war against the Ndebele kingdom, "the object of the Company was to peacefully and gradually develop the territories" and to "gradually civilise the Matabele—and to induce them to stop their raiding and to become well-ordered members of society like the natives of other parts of South Africa." It was known in Parliament that South African order was becoming even more racially discriminatory. The conflict was the fault of Lobengula and "his young men" who attacked colonial settlements and "assegaied the natives in the streets, including Black servants of the Whites, in front of their doors." In maintaining the security of the region, the BSAC was doing good work "without costing the English taxpayer one single farthing." Maguire summed up BSAC's intent, which "was to extend the railway and telegraphic systems, to encourage migration and colonisation, to promote trade and commerce, and to develop and work the mineral and other concessions under the management of one great and powerful organisation."[19]

In his long rebuttal Maguire did not respond to the key allegations about greed and about the trickery involved in the concessions. His shade was extended by supporters. The first to speak was the Liberal undersecretary of state for the colonies, Sidney Buxton, whose family was famous for philanthropy and whose uncle, by the same name, had become a prominent shareholder in the BSAC. Buxton defended the motives of Rhodes and the BSAC, noting that Labouchère's charge that the war was motivated by greed was not substantiated by proof, only by circumstantial evidence, and that this war was a necessary evil against the "hateful military system" of the Ndebele. If BSAC forces acted inappropriately, the proper course was to launch traditional parliamentary inquiries. As for questions about the concessions, that was for the shareholders to decide, as Maguire had stated.

A rising star of the Conservatives, Arthur Balfour, also defended Rhodes and the chartered company. Balfour referenced the BSAC's work on infrastructure and claimed that Rhodes was "extending the blessings of civilisation...railways, and telegraphs, and roads," a statement that elicited laughter from the benches of the Radicals. The discussion reached its climax with an intervention by Gladstone, who claimed that events in Matabeleland followed familiar colonial patterns that he had seen over the course of his long lifetime. He believed Rhodes to be a "very able man" who "enjoys the almost unbounded confidence of the free community in which he lives." Gladstone argued that Rhodes did not deserve to be "reduced to so low a point of moral character as to deserve that a censure of that kind should be pronounced upon him on the floor of the House of Commons."[20]

Gladstone had confidence in Rhodes, but this did not persuade Labouchère to change his plan. His next step was to goad Rhodes into filing a libel suit by publishing accusations in the press. Attacks on Rhodes and the BSAC were printed in the pages of several issues of Labouchère's magazine, *Truth*. Some readers wrote letters defending Rhodes's conduct during the war, giving Labouchère an opportunity to amplify his criticism: "The only names I know for such proceedings are robbery, piracy, and brigandage. These terms apply, of course, to the conduct of Mr. Rhodes, the Dukes of Fife and Abercorn, and the Chartered Company at large, as much as to the men who have enlisted under their flag on condition that they get a share of the spoils." Since robbery, piracy, and brigandage were statutory crimes and these words were printed and circulated to the wider reading public, Labouchère was daring Rhodes, Fife, and Abercorn to sue him for libel. On the next page of *Truth*, Labouchère continued his provocations by lacing into an article in the *Times* that praised Rhodes.

> The *Times* is so enraptured at Mr. Rhodes having, what it is pleased to call, "enlarged the Empire," that in gloating over the slaughter of the Matabele, it breaks out into rapturous laudation of that worthy.... And all this, as well as much more, in laudation of the head of a gang of shady financiers who forced on a war with the man through whose kindness they have pocketed millions; conducted it on the principle that "godless heathen" ought to be mowed down with Maxim guns if they happen to inhabit a country where there may be gold, and their envoys murdered, in order that a rotten Company might be saved from immediate bankruptcy, and the financing gang might be in a position to transfer more money from the pockets of British investors into their own.... My own belief is that Matabeleland will no more pay its expenses than Mashonaland. But what care Rhodes and his gang? They kill and steal in order to fool the British investor out of his money.[21]

Labouchère also had something to say about members of the press who wrote favorable articles about Rhodes. The newspapers "apparently hold the view that, where blacks are concerned who inhabit countries where there may be gold, the only proper way of dealing with the matter is to kill off the blacks, and, having seized the hills containing the gold, to bring out bogus Companies at home, and stock idiots with their shares, on nothing more tangible than the assurances of the robbers that they have gold in paying quantities to sell."[22]

These were ample provocations, but Rhodes and the BSAC directors wisely chose not to rise to the bait and file suit. Labouchère's claims could, indeed, be proven in court, which would then make them vulnerable to criminal charges for their conduct. Instead of foolishly initiating a lawsuit, Rhodes and the BSAC continued their business without defending their honor, practically admitting that Labouchère was right. This frustrated some in Rhodes's circle. John X. Merriman, an old friend who was now an opponent, wrote to John Blades Currey and asked him, "What do you think of Labouchère on the genesis of the Chartered Co.?" He answered the question for himself. "He is a horrid fellow but there is a damnable substratum of truth in much that he says. Rudd gravely suggested to me that Rhodes should on reaching England invite Labby onto a public platform to refute his statements. This would indeed be very high class sport but I doubt whether C. J. R. would come off top dog, and I advised Rudd to dismiss the project."[23]

Public criticism did not stop Rhodes from finishing off Lobengula. The king moved north with thousands of people and with most of his army intact. Rhodes sent Forbes and 158 BSAC troopers in pursuit. During the first week of December 1893, the column approached Lobengula's encampment near the Shangani River. A patrol of thirty-two troopers led by Major Allan Wilson was sent to capture the king. On finding the royal camp, Wilson's "Shangani Patrol" was surrounded by Ndebele soldiers, who killed the troopers in a pitched battle. BSAC reinforcements followed, with Rhodes, Jameson, and Willoughby riding together with Loch's military secretary, Major Sawyer. While the Ndebele fighting units held back the BSAC, Lobengula proceeded northward with a small group of followers. When the king learned that his forces were surrendering to the BSAC, he killed himself by taking poison.[24]

The Colonial Office got the message. At a time of growing concern about Afrikaner nationalism, Rhodes offered a form of British rule in Mashonaland and Matabeleland that cost the British taxpayers very little. Leaving Rhodes and the BSAC to plunder the two territories shored up the British position against the Transvaal. The historic parsimony of Gladstone's Liberal party now worked in Rhodes's favor. The secretary of state for the colonies, Lord

Ripon, spoke favorably about Rhodes. The Colonial Office and the British government decided to back Rhodes and authorized the BSAC to govern Ndebele lands as a colony. The Order in Council of July 18, 1894, allowed the BSAC directors to appoint the colony's administration, subject to the oversight of the governor and high commissioner in Cape Town. There would be only general oversight. Rhodes asked for—and received—the right for the directors to pass racially discriminatory legislation.[25]

The BSAC administration was expanded. Rhodes's brother Frank was named acting administrator under Jameson. Railway contractor George Pauling was made commissioner of public works and a well-regarded Cape attorney, Joseph Vintcent, became the chief judge. Vintcent's job was to give legal cover to conquest and dispossession. When Bulawayo fell, Rhodes instructed Jameson to treat Ndebele lands as conquered territories. In the context of colonial warfare, this signified official sanction for the plundering of land and cattle, which put inevitable pressure on African people to choose between starvation and becoming tenants of the conquerors on their own customary lands. About 5,000 Ndebele people had died from fighting, disease, or starvation, out of a pre-war population of 120,000. The looting began during the fighting. About 2,000 Ndebele fighters were killed in the 1893 war. Many remaining fighters and their families migrated to the north, competing with local African people for meager resources. Rhodes and the BSAC made plans for a company town to be built over Lobengula's Bulawayo, with the best land in the surrounding area, a country the size of Wales, set aside for a thousand white-owned farms. The lands claimed were ideal for cattle ranching, the traditional practice of the Ndebele people who lived there. White ranchers were able to buy, at auction, cattle looted from Ndebele herders by the BSAC. Other cattle were sold off to the Cape and to markets in neighboring countries. Ndebele losses are estimated to be as high as 200,000 head of cattle.[26]

In July 1894, Judge Vintcent chaired a land commission that took evidence and made decisions about allocating land and cattle. The process of determining the possession of land and cattle was complicated. The fighting had caused many Ndebele to flee to locations that were undesirable from the standpoint of farming, while many head of cattle were technically owned by Lobengula and were only being lent to Ndebele herdsmen. The commission began its work in October 1894. Commission reports indicate that Vintcent and his colleagues had some awareness of the complexity of the situation, but at the end of the process, in June 1895, the commission made things simple. Vintcent decided to "settle" Ndebele people on dry, rocky, unwanted "reserves" at Shangani and Gwaai. This meant that these Ndebele people lost control of their most valuable lands elsewhere. All of their cattle were put under the control of the company. A similar decision about cattle was applied to Shona people, on the grounds that during the war, they had taken advantage of Ndebele losses and engaged in rustling.[27]

The BSAC won the war and now paid back its supporters with land and cattle. This approach worked in the short term, but in the long term the seeds of future conflicts were sown. As far as most Ndebele and Shona people were concerned, the BSAC served no purpose except to steal their land and to terrorize them. The new laws created grievances, while in the event of a future conflict, the BSAC may have had technological advantages, but the Shona and Ndebele people still had vast numerical superiority.[28] BSAC resources were still very thin, and the company's access to railroads and harbors was still a work in progress. In sum, BSAC authority in Mashonaland and Matabeleland was thin. Maxim guns may have been deadly defensive weapons, but they did not guarantee strategic outcomes. If anything, as the weapons and tactics became familiar to people in South Central Africa, it became easier to imagine how to resist the BSAC more effectively.

Ndebele and Shona people mourned the loss of land and autonomy and resented the pressure to work for a small minority of white farmers and mineowners. As a final indignity, Rhodes and the BSAC took prisoner Lobengula's four sons, Njube (b. 1879); Mpezeni (b. 1880); Nguboyenja (b. 1881); and Sidojiwa (b. 1888), who might have eventually become heirs to the throne. Rhodes decided that he did not want to take a chance that the boys would grow up and one day lead resistance to the BSAC. The company had them sent to Cape Town, where they lived for a time at Groote Schuur and began to learn how to read and write. In short order, they were separated and educated in different places. The Rhodes papers contain an intriguing clue as to Nguboyenja's feelings about his education with Rhodes. A scrap of paper is included in one of the bound volumes, along with an archivist's note indicating that it was written by Ngubenja [Nguboyenja] and corrected by Rhodes. Under Rhodes's tutelage, young Nguboyenja wrote the following words:

>My dear mother
>I want to come home
>I am a noty
>Naughty
>Boy
>My name is
>Ngubenja[29]

Rhodes had returned to Cape Town for the year's session of the Cape Parliament. When the session ended, he returned to Rhodesia, on important business. He was accompanied by John Hays Hammond, the high-priced American mine engineer whom he had recently hired to manage Gold Fields's operations on the Witwatersrand. Rhodes had been promoting Mashonaland's wealth for years, but Churchill's criticism had so far turned out to be correct: there did not appear to be lucrative prospects for gold mining in Rhodesia. Rhodes wanted Hammond to establish, once and for all, that Rhodesia had the potential for mineral wealth.

Rhodes, together with Jameson, Willoughby, and other BSAC leaders, traveled with Hammond and three junior engineers as they surveyed Rhodesia. They spent the better part of two months together, during which time Hammond was especially keen to explore sites of ancient mines, particularly those in the vicinity of Great Zimbabwe, as well as the mines that were currently being developed. Fascinated by evidence of ancient mining, Hammond deduced that the old miners of Zimbabwe had used heat and water to extract quartz ore from the face of the veins and then crush it on hard

John Hays Hammond. Library of Congress, LC-DIG-ggbain-00807.

rock surfaces, which reminded him of the Mexican technique for stone-grinding corn. Most white visitors dismissed the achievements of the builders of Zimbabwe, but Hammond was impressed.

Hammond was less impressed about Rhodesia's resources. The country had mineral deposits, but they were not as great as the gold deposits of the Witwatersrand. Hammond concluded his report with devastating understatement:

> I consider it my professional duty to urge on the investing public the exercise of due discrimination in the selection of the properties on which money is to be expended in development; and, furthermore, to impress upon mining companies the necessity of establishing the commercial value of the properties before undertaking the erection of plants for the reduction of ores.[30]

The report produced a mixed reaction among the leadership of the BSAC. When Hammond returned to Johannesburg, he presented the report to the secretary of the BSAC, Dr. Rutherfoord Harris. Harris commented, "Well, if we have to depend on Hammond's geological report to raise money for this country, I don't think the outlook is encouraging." According to Hammond, Rhodes insisted that "Hammond is absolutely right. He's said everything he's justified in saying and the public will see that it's the report of a conscientious engineer, and give full credit to every word he says. If you don't like his report, you'd better go ahead and sell your Chartered shares." Hammond's record of Rhodes's words may not be exact, but he did at least convey Rhodes's subsequent approach. The report forced Rhodes to set aside the idea of a white settler colony that had fabulous mineral wealth. There could be a small mining industry in Rhodesia, but the BSAC colony would have to secure its prosperity by developing agriculture and its supporting infrastructure.[31]

Rhodes's plan for territorial expansion could easily have stopped there. From the perspective of colonialism, there was plenty enough for the BSAC to do in Rhodesia. There were also plenty of things to occupy Rhodes elsewhere. Rhodes was still prime minister of the Cape Colony and the lead partner of De Beers and Gold Fields. At the end of 1894 and the beginning of 1895, Rhodes's influence rested on the continued productivity of the diamond and gold mines and on the unusual deeds of trust of De Beers and Gold Fields, which allowed company funds to be used for political purposes. The diamond and gold companies maintained and even built their strength, but Rhodes was not able to overcome resistance to his projects that came from many quarters in the Cape, Rhodesia, Bechuanaland, and the Transvaal.

16

Maintaining Mines

AS BSAC FORCES were tearing through Mashonaland and Matabeleland, Rhodes was mindful that his bills were paid by his enterprises in Johannesburg and Kimberley. Five years had passed since the creation of the De Beers Consolidated Mining Company and the terrible fire. To support his overall vision of colonialism in the north, he hoped that his mining interests could be made more stable and predictable. As Rhodes himself wrote in 1893, he began to "look on De Beers as an investment and not a speculation." He expressed a "wish to make the property as safe as possible, and able to face all contingencies."[1] Rhodes, together with Gardner Williams, hoped that De Beers would introduce enough improvements so that it could run smoothly and predictably. They hoped for a time when they would only need to do the work of maintenance, the unexciting but important work done to keep businesses and infrastructures running.[2]

Gardner Williams designed the deep-level shafts, tunnels, and stopes that characterized future production in the De Beers Mine. When the merger was complete, he was put in charge of the engineering of the Kimberley Mine, too, a mine that needed to be rethought from a technical perspective. Just before the merger was concluded, the underground workings were shut down for safety reasons. The largest company in the mine, the Central Company, had dug shafts underground and had constructed galleries with unusually high chambers of fifteen feet. Winzes were used to remove broken-up pieces of blue ground to the surface. Williams later compared the underground workings to a honeycomb with fifteen-foot walls supporting the weight of the earth above. The walls began to crumble, an indication that the mine could collapse on top of the miners. The other companies in the mine were creating shafts, tunnels, and stopes that were equally unsatisfactory. Williams blamed the mine's defects on bad engineering and on bad relations between the owners of the different parts of the mine. At the end of 1888, the owners made the decision to deliberately collapse all the underground workings and to start tunneling all over again, using a better system designed by Williams.[3]

The new, amalgamated mining company faced the technical challenges related to the expansion of deep-level mining. The shafts went ever deeper. In 1893, both the De Beers Mine and the Kimberley Mine had tunnels deeper than 1,000 feet underground. By 1894, both mines reached 1,200 feet underground. In that year, with production running at maximum efficiency, more than 11,000 feet of tunnels were dug in the Kimberley Mine and more than 26,000 in the De Beers Mine. Below 800 feet, the underground water in the surrounding reef, combined with shifts in the reef, was causing "mud rushes"—the sudden, terrifying flooding of a tunnel with slurry. Several miners were drowned. In one case, two miners were trapped in a mud rush that left some airspace at the top. They were stuck in the flooded tunnel for twenty-eight hours before they were rescued. Two other miners ran from a mud rush toward the end of a tunnel and were stuck there for 95 hours. In 1894, Williams engineered a partial solution by digging drainage tunnels in the reef nearest the blue ground, but the challenge of mud rushes never completely went away.[4]

Technical challenges were compounded by challenges to the monopoly. The final stages of amalgamation took place in late 1888 and early 1889, when De Beers consolidated its ownership of Kimberley's two lesser mines, the open-pit mines at Bultfontein and Dutoitspan, which were still owned by multiple companies. Some owners in those mines saw the handwriting on the wall and sold out to De Beers. Others observed that so long as the De Beers monopoly was keeping diamond prices high, there was not sufficient incentive to sell. Both mines did face technical problems with falling reef, while the mining companies involved were unlikely to be able to afford digging shafts and tunnels. Rhodes, Beit, and Porgès debated how aggressively they should pursue Bultfontein and Dutoitspan. Given their leverage, they could start a price war or put pressure on company shares. Instead, it appeared that both mines were about to experience major problems with falling reef. Soon enough, the reef fell; it was as if the rocks were cooperating with the monopolists. Complex negotiations followed, some involving the governor, Hercules Robinson, others involving Donald Currie, the steamship magnate. The final push for a buy-up was financed by a network of banks headed by the House of Rothschild. In July 1889, Rhodes went to see Natty Rothschild in London and borrowed £1.75 million, on top of the £2.25 million that he borrowed in 1888 to finance the purchase of the Kimberley Mine.[5]

At the end of the amalgamation process, the De Beers Consolidated Mining Company, was producing 90 percent of the world's diamonds. With this monopoly in place, it could control prices by holding back reserve supplies of diamonds. In April 1890, De Beers closed Bultfontein and Dutoitspan and reduced production at other mines, laying off miners of both races. The timing was fortuitous. A few months later, the company was positioned well for an economic crisis. In November, the Baring Brothers bank failed, thanks to bad investments in Argentina. The ripple effects were felt as far away as South Africa, where several banks and gold mines failed. Public demonstrations against De Beers featured some of the same figures who had participated in the 1874 Black Flag Rebellion. They could not stop De Beers from maintaining its monopoly.[6]

Some competition did exist in South Africa. During the early 1870s, there had been rushes at three mines outside Kimberley. One happened at Wesselton, a few miles away, on the border with the Orange Free State. The two others happened inside the Free State, at Koffiefontein, sixty miles away, and Jagersfontein, a hundred miles away. Just as the amalgamation deals were being finalized, in 1889 the "Pam" diamond, weighing 241.5 carats, was discovered at Jagersfontein. It began to appear that the Jagersfontein, Koffiefontein, and Wesselton mines could be put into production and compete with the four mines that belonged to De Beers. Two of Rhodes's partners in De Beers went behind his back and invested in two of those mines. One of the wayward partners, Woolf Joel, had grown wealthy thanks in part to his association with his uncle, Barney Barnato. In 1889, Joel began to invest heavily in Koffiefontein. Another De Beers partner, Harry Mosenthal, part of the prominent merchant family, began to invest in Jagersfontein. Joel and Mosenthal bet that the riches forecast from the new diamond mines had to offset any possible losses from price declines due to an oversupply of diamonds. Rhodes's plan for funding his new British South Africa Company with diamond earnings would be collateral damage.

Rhodes learned about the unwanted competition from his own partners. He struck back aggressively by using De Beers money to bankroll "dummy" investors who bought enough shares to get on the company boards and to stop any increased output. In 1891, the Wesselton property owner allowed a rush of dozens of small-scale diggers, many of whom were unemployed miners from De Beers. At the end of 1891, De Beers purchased the property for £460,000 and allowed the landowner to continue production for five years until closure. As he had done in the past, Rhodes showed that he was a masterful strategist and diplomat who was also aware of the technical details of the purchase. In the run-up to the purchase, he wrote to Stow that "Wesselton is producing about 3000 carats a week but the stuff only realizes about 22/6 [22 shillings, 6 pence] per carat and runs about 15 carats to 100 loads. Of course there are parts that y[iel]d 20 carats to 100 loads.... On present production they make about £1500 per week clear even in the blue that part which gives 20 carats would be worked with a small profit but still damaging the diamond market so we must try to get a working arrangement with limitation of production so as to prevent flooding the market. We certainly have had bad luck to have a new diamond mine after 20 years freedom."[7]

Diamond prices could be controlled partly by buying up all possible sites of production and partly by manipulating the diamond market. Some of the De Beers board members, such as Barney Barnato and Alfred Beit, had connections to the ten firms that had, by 1890, come to dominate the London diamond-buying syndicate. Based in Hatton Garden, London's jewelry district, the ten firms also had offices near the Kimberley Mine. The three most influential companies in the London syndicate were Wernher & Beit; Dünkelsbühler; and L. & A. Abrahams, affiliated with Barnato. De Beers sold exclusively to these ten companies. When the De Beers office in Kimberley accumulated 50,000 carats, the gems were cleaned and sorted, then placed in tin boxes and carried to Wernher & Beit, where each of the ten companies was allotted a percentage. Each office sorted their own diamonds, dividing them into envelopes and placing them in their own sealed tin boxes. The boxes were taken to the Kimberley Post Office and sent to London. The packages of high- and low-quality diamonds arrived in Hatton Garden and were divided into more packages. Buyers from the cutting and polishing industry were invited for viewings or "sights" of the rough diamonds and were only allowed to buy packages of mixed quality. Those who complained would not be invited back.[8]

The arrangement with the London syndicate brought significant advantages to De Beers when diamond prices fell in the early 1890s, as part of a worldwide decline in commodity prices. Diamond prices fell 30 percent in 1891 alone. Shares in De Beers lost half of their value. The diamond sellers on the board put pressure on De Beers to limit production. Cooperation between De Beers and the syndicate would help to keep their companies afloat, while working-class miners and diamond-polishers were laid off. Rhodes had the further goal of using De Beers as a ready source of funds for the BSAC.

Rhodes and Williams took their response to the market downturn one step further, by falsifying data about production. In 1890, the board set a production target of 100,000, but Williams produced twice that amount. Rhodes had the extra diamonds shipped to Europe and sold in small batches to dealers who were outside the syndicate. He netted the enormous sum of £500,000 and invested it in consols, the safe bonds issued by the British treasury.

Rhodes's fellow director, Fred Stow, was working in the London office and was in on the scheme. He cooperated with Rhodes but expressed reservations in a letter written on September 17, 1890. Stow told Rhodes that "I have a great distaste for these secret arrangements. It is not a healthy tone in the conduct of the affairs of a concern and sooner or later there is sure to be some unpleasantness arising therewith." The syndicate members suspected something fishy. Beit suggested to Stow that he knew what Rhodes was doing, but when partners complained about the deception, Rhodes brought them in on the scheme. In early 1891, Rhodes informed Rothschild of the deception. Beit and Barnato found out, too, and began to negotiate their own deals with Rhodes and Stow. Stow found all the back-dealing exasperating. On May 22, 1891, he wrote to Rhodes that "I cannot approve of what you have done in taking all these people into your confidence and feel that your action has so complicated the scheme as to make it unworkable and that the future realization of the stuff will be attended with unnecessary sacrifice."[9]

Rhodes had extra leverage over the De Beers board because he was now so influential in politics. During the 1890s, he added key political figures to the board of De Beers, such as Hercules Robinson, Richard Solomon, and John Morrogh. As Cape prime minister he had the power to hurt partners who crossed him, while his popularity in South Africa and Great Britain gave him an advantage in the public sphere. Even with this level of influence, the amalgamation deal left him with several directors who were former rivals. Some, such as Francis Oats, became dependable allies, while others, such as Donald Currie and Francis Baring-Gould, remained wary. In funneling loans to the BSAC, Rhodes was breaking norms. Technically speaking, the unusual De Beers company deed of trust allowed it to invest in opportunities that had nothing to do with diamond mining. Unprofitable adventures were not excluded. The board tolerated investments in the BSAC for the sake of patriotism.

The De Beers Consolidated Mining Company typically held its annual meetings in the months of October or November. Participants tended to confirm the support of De Beers for the BSAC. At the annual meeting on November 9, 1892, Francis Oats substituted for Rhodes in the chair and made the case for making loans not only to the BSAC but to the Cape Colony, too. Oats began with a summary of De Beers policy successes for the year, then turned to loans, saying that "when the Chartered Company required money, we came to their aid, and I am quite sure, in my own judgment, that this £100,000 will be repaid to us.... The Chartered Company and the Cape Colonial Government are interests in which we have some identity of feeling and sentiment. We in this part of the world either stand or fall together.... We ought to be ready at all such times to come forward with whatever assistance we can give."[10]

In October of 1894, when Rhodes was prime minister of the Cape Colony, he spoke at the annual meeting and reiterated the points made by Oats two years earlier. He was keen to point out that the company was still making a profit and paying dividends during a recession. Even in a year when diamond prices were lower, Rhodes reported that De Beers was still able to contribute to its reserve fund comprising British consols, while also advancing £300,000 to the BSAC. He pronounced the investment in the BSAC to be worthwhile, not only for the "development of the North," but also for De Beers, because the BSAC reciprocated by giving De Beers the rights to all diamonds north of the Zambezi. Rhodes echoed Oats's statement about public spiritedness, saying that the investment in the BSAC "was undertaken not merely on a commercial basis, but with the idea of giving assistance in the development of the Interior," that is, the development of the interior for the benefit of colonial settlers. Rhodes reminded the shareholders that they might still make money from such public-spirited investments. The £75,000 spent on supporting the Cape Railways' construction of a line to Indwe was intended to benefit the company by reducing the price of coal deliveries to Kimberley.[11]

The decline in prices put pressure on De Beers to make production more efficient. The company achieved this through the deployment of better technologies at the Kimberley mines. Williams was able to do this, partly through his prior training and partly through continuous study. In 1892, he even toured mines in Germany and Montana to learn about cutting-edge methods. Williams pointed out in his history of diamond mining that it was not just the deep-level mining that kept the company productive and efficient. Success depended on the development of a factory complex for transforming the blue rock into diamonds.

Williams used the following illustration to put diamond processing in grand, inspiring terms that an audience of De Beers shareholders would have understood. By the late 1890s, every year De Beers miners were digging out of the earth four million tons of "blue ground," to produce "a few bucketfuls of diamonds." If all the blue ground were piled up, "It would form a cube of more than 430 feet...overtopping the spire of St. Paul's, while a box with sides measuring two feet nine inches would hold the gems." The example of St. Paul's is telling. As Williams knew from his days as a consulting engineer in the City of London, Christopher Wren's cathedral could be seen by walking a short distance from Broad Street, where the De Beers London headquarters was located, and from Rothschild's office at New Court, St. Swithin's Lane, the same street where the BSAC was headquartered. Williams understood the power of a graphic illustration to connect the network of people, papers, and telegraphs of the City of London to the rocks, workers, and machinery of remote, arid Kimberley.[12]

The transcontinental network depended on the processing of millions of tons of blue ground into buckets brimming with diamonds. The year-to-year development of processing machinery is chronicled in the annual reports from the 1890s and are summarized accurately in Williams's history. The blue ground exited the mines on board specially designed trucks that held loads of 1,600 pounds. The trucks rolled on rails on a slight decline, pulled along by a system of wires and pulleys connected to a steam-powered winding engine. The haulage system took the rocks to the floors, which now comprised several miles of flat, cleared fields that stretched out from the De Beers Mine and the Kimberley Mine. Out on the floors, workers detached the trucks from the wire tramway and hooked them up to teams of mules, which pulled them on sidings to their exact destination, an assigned rectangular section measuring 200 by 600 feet that could hold 50,000 loads. At the section, the contents of the trucks were then shoveled out and spread along the ground. The blue ground could be weathered for only three or four months, but Williams found that depending on the rainfall and heat, the Kimberley Mine's rocks needed six months, while the blue ground from the De Beers Mine was harder, taking upwards of a year. To hasten the natural weathering process, the original mining companies crunched the weathering breccia by using teams of mules to pull harrows across the floor sections. Amalgamation allowed Williams to justify larger, better-equipped floors, with much larger, heavier harrows pulled by steam tractors.[13]

When a section of blue ground was sufficiently weathered and harrowed, workers shoveled it back into the trucks, reconnected the trucks to the wire tramway, and let the tram pull the loads to the processing plant for washing. The washing facility was designed and built by a team of mechanical engineers employed by Williams. At this large structure, completed in 1894, washing was done first in two giant cylinders. The larger rocks fell to the bottom, where the lumps were inspected for large diamonds. Then a wire conveyor took the big rocks to a crushing mill, a six-story plant built on top of a heap of tailings, powered by an 1100-horsepower steam engine. The rocks were put through crushers, then screened, washed, and picked over by workers, who separated them into grades. For the larger rocks, the process could be repeated as many as three times. The small rocks did not need crushing in the cylinders. They passed through small holes to a circular washing pan with revolving arms that bristled with triangular teeth. The arms swept diamonds, gems, and other heavy minerals to the outside of the pan, allowing smaller worthless particles of dirt to pass through a screen.

In the next phase, sorting was done by machines and by people. All the potentially valuable pebbles that remained were loaded onto special, locked trucks and pushed to a combination of jigs, still called the "Pulsator" after the original jig installed in 1886. The pebbles were next washed through another machine invented by the De Beers mechanical engineers, a percussion table coated with axle grease. Valuable gems stuck to the grease, while tailings simply washed away. The remaining gems were washed with acid to remove any extra material, and then placed on a table, where trained workers sorted the different types of diamonds as well as rubies, emeralds, sapphires, garnets, and other valuable stones. All the valuable stones amounted to one-twelfth of one percent of the blue ground run through the plant.[14]

The mining and processing of blue ground required an extensive and diverse group of workers. White laborers made up one-sixth of the workforce, with jobs ranging from mechanical engineers to foremen and sorters. Most of the workers in the mine itself were African migrants. In the diamond-processing plant and on the floors, many of the African laborers were still convicts. If free labor at the mines were to go on strike, the convict labor at the floors and mills could still be compelled to produce diamonds from the blue ground that was on hand. By 1894 there were 800 convicts working in the diamond processing area. The size of the convict workforce persuaded De Beers to build a special barracks near the Pulsator. The total labor force "above ground" comprised 397 white men and 1,861 Black men, including the convicts. "Under the ground" there were 228 white men and 1,981 Black men. The workshops employed 417 white men and 273 African men. When De Beers was reaching new levels of productivity, the number of convicts kept rising. In 1898, there were 201 white men and 2,186 Black men "under the ground"; 507 white men and 1,714 Black men "above ground"; and 411 white men and 178 Black men in the workshops. Out of a total workforce of 5,197 men, there were 1,017 convicts, all employed "above the ground," increasing the fraction of incarcerated workers from one-sixth to one-fifth.[15]

The mines had a significant environmental impact. In 1894, the De Beers Mine was pumping 5,000 to 6,000 gallons per hour, while the Kimberley Mine was pumping 9,000 to 12,000 gallons per hour. The water was sent to the Kenilworth Reservoir, where Williams increased the height of the embankment. The reservoir could now hold 105,000,000 gallons, which was

De Beers Washing Gear. Courtesy of the McGregor Museum, Kimberley, MMKP 832.

made available to the new washing operation. While the crushed ground was being washed for diamonds, it was carried by water from one stage of the process to the next. The new plant required massive amounts of water: 400,000 gallons per hour.[16]

To pump the water and drive the machinery, large amounts of coal were used to fire all the engines. By 1893, Rhodes and Williams decided to stop buying coal from Britain and the Transvaal. De Beers was now able to obtain a supply mainly from the Stormberg town of Molteno, in the Eastern Cape. In Molteno, lower-quality coal had been mined and shipped to Kimberley since the early 1880s, when a railway line reached the area. Rhodes had even been an early investor in Molteno's coal-company shares. In the early 1890s, Molteno's coal production boomed, thanks to the opening of a more direct railway link to Kimberley. Ounce for ounce, the Molteno coal provided only 55 percent of the energy value of Welsh coal, but the supply of Molteno coal was easier to control. De Beers also continued the practice of purchasing firewood from Bechuanaland, contributing to that country's deforestation. Using wood and inferior coal was not a desirable long-term proposition. In 1894, Rhodes, in his role as the Cape Colony's prime minister, supported the opening of a rail link to Indwe, near Glen Grey, where De Beers started to obtain better quality coal, approximately 70 percent of the energy value of Welsh coal.[17]

In the 1890s, De Beers also made the sorting of diamonds more regular and stable. Each mine tended to produce certain kinds of diamonds. The color of diamonds tended to vary from mine to mine. The De Beers Mine was known for producing large quantities of yellow diamonds, with some production of dark-yellow and brownish diamonds as well as "silver Capes." The Kimberley Mine produced lighter yellows as well as many white diamonds. Light-colored diamonds were often produced at Dutoitspan, too, which also

The Open Pit of the Kimberley Mine in the 1890s. Courtesy of the McGregor Museum, Kimberley, MMKP 5334.

became known for blue-white stones. The diamonds from Bultfontein tended to be white but of lesser quality and size. After the diamonds went through the pulsator, they were cleaned and sent to the De Beers main office, where they were cleaned again and sent to a team of sorters—eight white men and two white women—who reviewed each stone with the naked eye and ranked the diamonds according to quality and color. The best diamonds were destined for jewelry; the worst were destined for industry. Either way, they were bought and sold by the London diamond syndicate.[18]

De Beers maintained its profitability through steady investments in technologies. The amalgamation resulted in layoffs, but for the white miners who remained employed, De Beers created a sense of stability by investing in a workers' village. The idea was first described by William Erskine in his 1882 and 1885 mine inspector's reports.[19] In 1889, Rhodes started working on the details. He directed De Beers to create a suburb for white workers called Kenilworth, located four miles to the north of the De Beers Mine. Rhodes referred to Kenilworth as his hobby. He hired an architect, Sydney Stent, for the basic design, which included simple cottages for workers built in the Arts and Crafts style. Kenilworth had long avenues lined with eucalyptus trees, which Rhodes had imported from Australia. There was a church named for one of England's saintly kings, Edward the Confessor. A steam-powered tramway called "Puffing Billy" took workers back and forth to the mines. Rhodes arranged for the suburb to have an orchard and a vineyard, with fruit to be distributed free to all residents.[20]

In creating an ideal workers' village, Rhodes was following in the footsteps of English industrialists like Titus Salt, the textile manufacturer of Bradford who created the workers' village of Saltaire, and John Cadbury, whose Birmingham chocolate-factory workers lived in the model village of Bournville. These model industrial towns provided demonstrably better conditions for workers, while providing the companies with a more reliable workforce. In Kenilworth, Rhodes had a club built for all white employees, where they had a "well fitted lavatory, and, at the back of the club, a bath room with apartments for six shower baths." These were intended "to attract the miners from spending their evenings in idle street lounging with time hanging on their hands. Mr Rhodes has expressed his desire that every employee of the Company shall be regarded a free member of the club."[21]

Kimberley residents took pride in the new worker's village, which was a major improvement over the jumble of corrugated iron shacks that once dotted the landscape. Commercial buildings were built, too. By 1894, Kenilworth was occupied by 171 adult men, 126 adult women, and 216 children, divided

Kenilworth. Courtesy of the McGregor Museum, Kimberley, MMKP 5491.

between cottages for families and the "bachelor quarters." The village's orchards were planted with 5,800 fruit trees. and the vineyard had 2,600 vines. Gardner Williams anticipated more growth.[22] From the company's perspective, fresh fruit and vegetables were not the only advantages of establishing Kenilworth. De Beers still had a problem with IDB. White workers had resisted the kind of body searches that were now commonplace in the African mine workers' compounds. By concentrating the white workforce in one location, De Beers simplified the work of surveillance.

Kenilworth's homes, club, school, and church provided white workers with a sense of domesticity that was an important part of the smooth running of the mines. Williams's account of the compounds for African workers stressed domesticity, too. By 1900 there were seventeen compounds on the diamond fields. Twelve were owned by De Beers, including the largest one, the four-acre compound at the west end of the De Beers Mine, with its dormitories, kitchens, and lavatories. A decade later, Williams showed his pride in worker domesticity by illustrating his book, *The Diamond Fields of South Africa*, with photographs captioned "Natives Making Coffee," "The Midday Meal," "Natives Playing Mancala," and even "Natives Smoking Indian Hemp."[23]

The compounds and Kenilworth were so intriguing that they attracted tourists. Picture postcards were even sold. When visitors arrived on Christmas

Day, they could watch as the African miners dove into the water for coins thrown in by the managers and directors. Dignitaries visiting Kimberley were given tours of Kenilworth and the west end compound. In 1895, the compound was toured by Oriel College's legal scholar, James Bryce. He described the origins of the workers in diverse parts of Southern Africa, then commented, in his detached, empirical style, but with a sense of wonder, that "they live peaceably together." He portrayed compound domesticity as a key element of peacekeeping. The miners "amuse themselves in their several ways during their leisure hours." He continued:

> Besides games of chance, we saw a game resembling "fox and geese," played with pebbles on a board; and music was being discoursed on two rude native instruments, the so-called "K----r piano," made of pieces of iron of unequal length fastened side by side in a frame, and a still ruder contrivance of hard bits of wood, also of unequal size, which when struck by a stick emit different notes, the first beginnings of a tune. A very few were reading or writing letters, the rest busy with their cooking or talking to one another. Some tribes are incessant talkers, and in this strange mixing-pot of black men one may hear a dozen languages spoken as one passes from group to group.[24]

The miners in "this strange mixing pot of black men" seem to have been making the best of the situation by living "peaceably together." The evidence could be interpreted to mean that the miners were resilient and sociable enough to find enjoyment and comradeship in this confined living space. Bryce connected the domesticity of life in the Kimberley compound to the broader benefits of white rule for African workers. He wrote that "to toss the gift of political power into the lap of a multitude of persons who are not only ignorant, but in mind children rather than men, is not to confer a boon, but to inflict an injury." This was evident from the experience of the United States after the Civil War, when "evils...followed the grant of the suffrage to persons unfit for it."[25]

Bryce approved of Rhodes's approach to the "native problem," but even Rhodes's critic, John Tengo Jabavu, wrote glowingly of a tour of the facilities of De Beers. Jabavu visited during the 1892 Kimberley Exhibition and called "the works down below" the "grandest and most magnificent undertaking we could ever expect to witness, even if we lived during the next one hundred years." The mines may have been magnificent, but the compounds, wrote Jabavu, "decided us to its favour as about the best thing that, in the multiplicity of interests involved, could be done."[26]

Behind the orderly scene of paternalism, other African voices told a story that was grimmer. The Cape government's "Protector of Natives" at Kimberley, G. W. Barnes, reported that Xhosa workers in the compounds were complaining about how managers coerced them by threatening them with vagrancy laws, took their money away, and even had them beaten with sjamboks, the Afrikaans term for a thick bullwhip made from the hide of a rhinoceros or a hippopotamus.[27]

Stabilizing production in Kimberley was important to Rhodes's overall vision, as earnings from diamond mining were plowed into the BSAC and other projects. Rhodes was fairly engaged in the work of De Beers and took pride in the success of his company. Gold mining was a different story. Rhodes made plenty of money in gold mining, but he tended to remain aloof from production, seeing himself as an investor and not a manager.

Rhodes and Rudd started the 1890s at a disadvantage. The claims that belonged to Gold Fields did have visible outcroppings of the conglomerate reefs that contained gold, but the mines turned out to be significantly less productive than mines owned by other companies. In 1889, Rudd explained to the shareholders in London that Gold Fields "had not quite fulfilled" expectations. He apologized, saying that "Rhodes and I had not done as well as men of our experience and knowledge ought to have done."[28] To make money, Gold Fields began to float and sell subsidiary companies and to lease its claims. Rhodes and Rudd even used Gold Fields money to invest in De Beers, where they anticipated better returns, and in the British South Africa Company, at best a questionable enterprise.

At the start of the gold-mining boom, superficial discoveries were straightforward to mine. The visible portions of the gold-bearing reef, known as outcroppings, were mined first. The reefs dipped into the earth, so when the miners finished with the visible parts, they dug trenches across the reef to follow it down into the earth. As soon as the reef got too deep for trenching, the miners had to sink vertical shafts, so that tunnels or "drives" could be dug into the reef at a depth of thirty or forty feet. From 1887 until mid-1889, the new Johannesburg stock exchange grew thanks to mining company shares. Savvy investors started to wonder if the shares were overvalued. Randolph Churchill understood the links between finance and technical knowledge. During his 1891 visit, he made the following observations:

> In the early days of the Randt, gold-field folly and fraud reigned supreme. The directors and managers were, as a rule, conspicuous for their ignorance on all matters of practical mining. The share market

was their one and only consideration, the development and proper working of the mines being in many cases absolutely neglected.... Millions of money have been literally thrown away. Bad machinery badly put up has been badly situated, badly worked. Many of the mines are at a standstill for want of capital, and most of them, so eminent experts assure me, are sadly behindhand with their development in view of the vast plant which has been erected.[29]

Up until mid-1889, it did not take much special technical knowledge to produce gold. The outcroppings of the gold reefs were somewhat weathered and responded well to the basic techniques of mining such as blasting and drilling. The gold ore was relatively easy to see in the conglomerate, and the somewhat weathered rocks were easy to process. Simple techniques of crushing, washing, and sorting produced what was called "slime." The gold was separated from the slime by letting it run over copper plates coated with mercury. The mercury stuck to the gold but then could be removed by baking it. But when the mines brought lower-grade ore to the surface, containing pyrites and other minerals, the old processing methods no longer worked. Some of the mining companies tried to hide this information, to preserve their share values, but in mid-1889 panic struck. Share values on the Johannesburg stock exchange declined by as much as 75 percent. Many firms were wiped out, and Johannesburg's population declined from 25,000 to 17,000.[30]

The gold industry found a path forward, thanks to better knowledge and better technology. Rothschild was the dominant buyer of raw gold, which was shipped to England for further processing. Rothschild's financial backing was sought by mine owners, who were aware that his investments had transformed De Beers into a powerful monopoly producer of diamonds. Rothschild was a canny investor and had some concerns about the prospects for gold mining. In 1887, the Rothschilds hired a well-known American engineer, Joseph Storey Curtis (no relation to the present author). The Harvard-educated Bostonian trained as a mine engineer at Freiberg and had extensive experience in gold and silver mining in the US West. When the Rothschilds sent Curtis to the Johannesburg area, his yearlong survey revealed important findings. Like the mine owners, he recognized the problems posed by the way in which the deeper mines were finding harder rock, making the ore more difficult to process. Curtis studied the ways in which the reef dipped down below the surface outcroppings. His studies with boreholes led him to suspect that the outcroppings were just the tip of long, extensive conglomerate gold reefs that kept sloping deep under the ground and toward the south.

Soon it was shown that the Witwatersrand was the northern rim of a basin that is 200 miles long and 100 miles wide. The layers of gold-bearing conglomerates begin along the northern and western ridges and extend downward toward the basin's center. Curtis shared his preliminary findings with Rothschild and with the founders of the emerging mine owning conglomerate, the Corner House, led by Hermann Eckstein, the former manager of a Dutoitspan diamond mining company. He was working together on the Rand with some other familiar faces from Kimberley, Jules Porgès and Alfred Beit. Beit shared the findings with his old friend Rhodes, even though Gold Fields and the Corner House were then rivals. Rhodes and Rudd sold off their shares in gold mines just in time and parked their money temporarily in shares of De Beers.[31]

Technical improvements in the processing of gold ore soon made it possible to overcome the obstacles of geology. The application of mercury to the lower-grade ores was uneconomical. The new MacArthur-Forrest process made it worthwhile to mine the lower-grade, pyritic ore. Crushed and sorted ore was poured over copper plates, further separated, then poured into large vats where it was treated with a solution of potassium cyanide, which separated out the gold from the rest of the conglomerate. The liquid gold solution was then sent through zinc shavings, a process that produced gold powder. Mine owners were able to draw on an expanding knowledge of geology and engineering to make gold mining more sophisticated and profitable.[32]

The profits of deep-level mining on the Witwatersrand could only be achieved through the investment of large amounts of capital in equipment and tunneling. Incline shafts in the outcrop mines reached 1,000 feet, while vertical shafts went even further in the deep-level mines. Horizontal tunnels called drives reached sideways far into the claims. With more ore to process, mine owners added more stamp mills. Rhodes and Rudd calculated that the best way to raise more capital was to turn Gold Fields into a different sort of company, a mining finance house. They partnered with Percy Tarbutt and with their business manager, Herbert Davies, who also owned several mining companies. Together the four men combined their interests and formed a new company. Instead of being a mining company, it was essentially an investment house that raised capital in London and owned majority shares of companies on the Rand that mined for gold, prospected for gold, or provided engineering or managerial services. The structure of Consolidated Gold Fields allowed professional services to be offered at lower cost to component mining companies, while spreading the financial risks of mining investments around a wide range of companies. Consolidated

Gold Fields also invested in De Beers, in the BSAC, and in the mining companies that operated in BSAC territory.

Consolidated Gold Fields began to operate in August 1892. Tarbutt and Davies merged their properties into the company and emerged as the dominant partners over Rhodes and Rudd, whose old Gold Fields company was comparatively less valuable. As much as they may have been accustomed to dominance in the diamond business, they still profited handsomely from gold because deep-level mining grew and the price of gold remained fixed. In the early 1890s, the Transvaal was the world's third-largest producer of gold, after Australia and the United States. In five years' time, the Transvaal was producing more than the other two countries. In 1892, Consolidated Gold Fields began its existence with its capital valued at £1,250,000. In 1893, its profits were £207,000. In 1894, its profits were £309,000. In 1895, Consolidated Gold Fields sold off some of its older properties and posted a profit of £2,540,918, the greatest profit that had ever been posted by any company registered in London. Rhodes's own personal share of the profits was £112,000, a staggering sum considering that he had not been involved in the active management of the company.

In February 1893, Beit and his partners in the Corner House formed Rand Mines Limited and invited Rhodes to be involved. The leading investors included Beit as well as Rothschild, Eckstein, and Lionel Phillips. Like Beit, Phillips had also started humbly in Kimberley and had become one of the most successful and ostentatious figures on the Rand. Rhodes was needed primarily for his strong network of connections with prominent investors. Rand Mines Limited soon became one of the dominant players in the gold mining industry. Rhodes still saw the gold industry as a form of investment. He had relatively little involvement in the industry's technical issues and did not attend company annual meetings. His stand-off attitude to gold mining contrasted with his deep involvement in De Beers and the BSAC.[33]

Profits could not be improved by raising prices because the price of gold was fixed on world markets. As the mines went deeper, the mining companies had to produce more and to cut costs. Some of the costs of production seemed unreasonably high, thanks to the government of the Transvaal. The government held a monopoly over dynamite sales, which, in 1887, it had turned over to Edouard Lippert, an old rival of Rhodes. Lippert bought dynamite in blocks from Nobel's French subsidiary and had it shipped to Leeuwfontein, near Pretoria, where factory workers made the dynamite sticks. The monopoly was known for overcharging its customers, resulting in a formal complaint by the British government in 1892. Lippert lost the concession in 1893, when the Transvaal allowed competition between Nobel's subsidiaries in France, Britain, and Germany. The competition lasted only for a few months. Soon the Transvaal took back the monopoly and gave the concession to Lippert's manager, Lambertus Vorstman, who bought mainly from the German syndicate, with Edouard Lippert acting as a seller's agent, much to the chagrin of the gold industry. When mines were shifting to processing the hard, low-grade pyritic ore, there was even stronger demand for dynamite, further squeezing gold producers. The government also levied unfavorable taxes on the gold industry. The taxes and the dynamite monopoly contributed to friction between the Transvaal's government and figures such as Rhodes, Beit, and Phillips.[34]

The industrial leaders on the Witwatersrand, nicknamed the Randlords, recognized that one of the best ways to ensure the continued profitability of the gold mines was to drive down the wages of the labor force. Labor was segregated by race in much the same way as it had been at Kimberley. White men held positions involving upper management, labor supervision, and machine operating. African migrant workers were assigned to jobs that were unskilled and semi-skilled. In rare cases, skilled African workers were paid a higher wage. Skilled white labor could be replaced by more efficient engineering, equipment, and management. The costs of less skilled Black labor could be brought down by better control of the labor market. Miners were funneled to the Rand from all around the region and were housed near the mines. Starting in 1889, the Corner House took the lead in forming a mine-owners' association, the Chamber of Mines, which worked with labor recruiters, represented by the Witwatersrand Native Labour Association and the Native Recruiting Corporation, to persuade young African men from rural areas to work in the gold mines. The larger the labor market and the more centralized the control of supply, the more the owners could drive down wages. The railways, in turn, enabled the process of introducing ever-greater numbers of African mine workers into the area. When the African men arrived on the Rand, the Chamber of Mines assigned them to their jobs.[35] The Chamber of Mines and the Randlords were successful in their effort to keep costs down by keeping wages low.[36]

Mining industrialists also worked to access cheaper fuel. Imported coal was expensive, due to the weight of the coal and the remoteness of the mines, while firewood was scarce, too. In the late 1880s, costs were lowered when a railway began to operate and coal was discovered on the East Rand, near Boksburg and Brakpan. The coal industry grew, thanks to the involvement of investors from the Rand and miners from Wales. By 1895, eight mines were producing 800,000 tons of coal every year and transporting it directly to the gold mines on a dedicated railway system.[37]

Cheaper coal saved money for the gold industry but increased the environmental costs. Coal-powered steam engines billowed soot into the air. There were other pollutants as well. In the early days, gold was processed with mercury, whose toxic properties had been known since ancient times. Mercury was dropped with the introduction of the MacArthur-Forrest process, which uses cyanide, a poison that kills animals and plants. Cyanide has an immediate, destructive effect on ecosystems, but unlike mercury it is soluble in water. The mine engineers knew that they were causing environmental problems. In addition to these toxic processing chemicals, the mine tailings were problematic. Fine tailings could often be washed down a stream, causing silting and flooding. Tailings could also cause salinization and thereby harm plants and wildlife. Rhodes's engineer, John Hays Hammond, had worked for the giant Bunker Hill mining company in Coeur d'Alene, Idaho, during the 1880s, where there had been controversies over tailings. It is reasonable to assume that Hammond's American colleagues knew about the hazards of tailings, since some of them had worked with him in Idaho.[38] Gardner Williams toured the hard rock mines of Montana and Idaho while on a study leave from De Beers. He, too, must have known about the environmental challenges related to tailings.

In the nineteenth century, mining companies developed techniques for managing tailings. Companies began to wash the fine tailings down into tailings dams, depositing areas that grew over time. The South African gold industry used this technique extensively. Tailings dams give the appearance of controlling mine waste but contribute to the acidification of groundwater, which in turn can cause unwanted elements to leach out of the surrounding soil.[39] The crushed conglomerate rocks of the Witwatersrand were dumped in big, ugly piles that contained arsenic, cadmium, lead, and uranium. On dry days, toxic elements blew around in clouds of dust, covering workers and neighbors in a ghastly powder. On wet days, the rain washed the toxins into the water table. Rain also washed sulphuric acid, a product of the oxidation of the pulverized pyrites in the tailings.[40] Everyone working near the mines could see the immediate effects of the pollution. The long-term environmental problems of tailings were not understood in the 1890s. Tailings were even sold to be used in the building of roads and railroads.[41] The impact of the mining industry's pollution, and its relationship to South Africa's struggles over race and class, have only begun to be understood more than a century later.

17

Raiding the Rand

WHILE ENACTING HIS vision of mobility and conquest, Rhodes derived financial support from De Beers in Kimberley and Gold Fields in Johannesburg. The expansion of colonialism also involved maintaining an alliance with the Afrikaner Bond, led by Hofmeyr, and the English-speaking settlers of the Eastern Cape, led by Sprigg. Rhodes also drew on a strong network of contacts in British finance and politics. In the early 1890s, politicians in London and Cape Town were becoming concerned about a surge in Boer nationalism in the Transvaal, which was taking place in the face of heavy British investments and significant numbers of British immigrants. But while Rhodes was imagining the ways in which the BSAC could be used against Kruger and the Transvaal, prominent people in Britain and South Africa were starting to question the wisdom of giving him further support.

Rhodes stoked the fears of the imperial government by working with his contacts in the Afrikaner Bond, such as David Christiaan de Waal, who had traveled with Rhodes through Rhodesia and who began to organize anti-imperial, prosettler rallies. De Waal planned a protest rally against British government interference in Rhodesia that became one of the biggest demonstrations in Cape history. On November 28, 1893, three weeks after the BSAC entered the ruins of Bulawayo, Hofmeyr wrote in the Bond's newspaper, *De Zuid Afrikaan*: "In Rhodesia, in which a brilliant victory was obtained, the whole North will open up with all these healthy highlands, gold veins, and thousands of industrious farmers" who "will soon settle there." He believed that Bond support for Rhodes was a proven success. Hofmeyr believed that Rhodes's success north of the Limpopo was likely to limit British power throughout Southern Africa.[1]

In January 1894, Rhodes traveled back to Cape Town, where he spoke in public and in private about the need for the imperial government to give him more of a free hand. In one speech, Rhodes rose to "thunders of applause," and then he summarized his career as a leader. "I had led an active life in the amalgamation of the diamond mines. I became the representative of a section of the community connected with the diamond mines." As a leader in business and politics, "in season and out of season I thought it would be a good and wise idea to obtain the unknown interior as a reversion to the colony of which I was one of the citizens. I had that idea. I advocated it in Parliament, and gradually I had the satisfaction of seeing your Hinterland grow from the Orange River to the vast interior." Rhodes reminded the gathering that in the mid-1880s, he worked with Robinson, the governor, to acquire the Bechuanaland Protectorate. In a private conversation, Robinson had told him, "Well, I think that is enough." Rhodes responded, "Do come with me and look at the blockhouse on Table Mountain."[2] Rhodes was referring to the King's Blockhouse on Devil's Peak. It dated to the late 1790s and today it can be accessed by hiking up a trail that starts near the Rhodes Memorial, a short distance from the University of Cape Town and Rhodes's home, Groote Schuur. According to Rhodes, he took Robinson to the blockhouse and invited him to look around at the view, which stretches from Table Bay to False Bay. Rhodes then claimed to have spoken the following words to the governor:

"Those good old people, 200 years ago, thought that blockhouse on Table Mountain was the limit of their ideas, but now, let us face it today. Where are we? We are considerably beyond the Vaal River, and, supposing that those good people were to come to life again to-day, what would they think of it and their blockhouses?" Then I said, "Sir, will you consider during the temporary period you have been the representative of her Majesty in this country what you have done? We are now in latitude 20." It was amusing when he said to me, "And what a trouble it has been." He next asked, "But where will you stop?" and I replied, "I will stop where the country has not been claimed."[3]

Rhodes may have made up this story, but it is still indicative of how the Colossus thought about territoriality. His words were summarized by the news reporter who was listening to Rhodes: "His plan was to paint on the map of Africa as British all those portions which were not occupied by other powers." Rhodes explained that he was reluctant for the BSAC to have a war against the Ndebele. "Having spent private means on the Beira and Mafeking railways and on the African telegraph, he was not likely to want to incur fresh obligations for a war. He tried to postpone action in every way, but he could not leave the people of Mashonaland exposed to the risk of having their servants slaughtered." Even so, according to the report, he was pleased to inform the audience that during the inevitable conflict, the BSAC did not "take a single sixpence from the heavily taxed people of England with their social difficulties." Rhodes noted that he had been unfairly criticized by Labouchère and the Aborigines Protection Society. When the speech concluded, Graham Bower raised his glass to Rhodes and offered a toast to "The Expansion of Africa."[4]

Cecil Rhodes's plan was to spread white settlement and British values throughout the subcontinent and to develop the region's natural and human resources. The most advanced technologies in mining and farming were deployed to make the land productive. These operations generated the funds that paid for the armed expeditions that secured even more territories. These, in turn, were being linked together by the extension of railroads and telegraphs. Laborers were drawn from African communities that were under new forms of colonial rule and were under pressure to pay taxes. This vision depended on a careful political balancing act that linked the actions of officials and investors in London with British and Afrikaner settlers in South Africa and with pressured African communities. Rhodes had to engineer a vast network of people, places, and things.

Rhodes's network was cultivated through personal relationships. The list of allies was long: John X. Merriman and Charles Rudd helped him to get his start at Kimberley and later made key interventions in finance and politics. J. H. Hofmeyr and Gordon Sprigg were often helpful in the Cape House of Assembly. De Beers never could have been merged into the world's most powerful diamond-mining companies without the engineering of Gardner Williams and the financial backing of Natty Rothschild. Additional financial backing from Alfred Beit was crucial to this and many other initiatives. On the Road to the North, key interventions were made by Sidney Shippard and Hercules Robinson. Further north, in what is today Malawi and Zambia, Rhodes depended on Harry Johnston. The railways that Rhodes imagined headed for the north were engineered by Charles Metcalfe and built by George Pauling. The rural architecture and landscape that was unfolding at Groote Schuur was very much the product of Herbert Baker, while Kenilworth was the product of a collaboration with Sydney Stent. The chartered company was supported by a long list of prominent investors, especially by Albert Grey and the Dukes of Fife and Abercorn. And it is unlikely that anybody other than Jameson could have persisted in negotiating with Lobengula.

By 1894, all these people formed a strong supporting network for Rhodes. Gold Fields was moving into a good position, too, thanks to the mine acquisitions and engineering decisions of John Hays Hammond, mostly centered on deep-level mining and ore-processing. Rhodes trusted Hammond with the leadership of Gold Fields and paid him more than any employee in the history of any of his enterprises. Hammond quickly turned the company in a profitable direction and became Rhodes's confidant. The American engineer's advice on Rhodesia's poor mining prospects was key, in that the BSAC could turn its focus more strongly to agriculture, while Gold Fields was freer to focus on deep-level mines on the Witwatersrand. Unfortunately for Rhodes, his hands-off management of Hammond—and his assignment of the mercurial Jameson to an inappropriate role at the head of the BSAC—resulted in a failure that set back many elements of the network.

When Hammond first arrived in South Africa, he was able to find employment thanks to his résumé, which combined the right professional training and accomplishments. Hammond was raised in San Francisco by relatives who had experienced the wars against Native Americans and Mexicans as well as the US Civil War. Educated at Yale and Freiberg, he had extensive experience with hard-rock mining in the Western Hemisphere. On the surface, Hammond seemed like a good fit for Gold Fields, but as historian Charles van Onselen points out, Rhodes and his circle failed to recognize that Hammond's background and personality combined elements that were problematic. Hammond's two-volume autobiography is filled with stories about defending one's honor through fistfights and gunfights. Hammond also had a record of starting trouble and then leaving. In Sonora during 1882 and 1883, Hammond and his wife, Natalie, together with another Californian engineer, Victor Clement, responded to repeated challenges from miners and insurgents by regimentation of the workforce and by arming themselves and fighting back. They left Minas Nuevas before the mines could be placed on an even keel. And just before they arrived in South Africa, Jack, Natalie, and Clement had brought regimentation and then conflict to the Bunker Hill and Sullivan mines in Coeur d'Alene, Idaho, where they left before difficulties had been resolved. Hammond was a fine engineer who was fond of trying to solve problems by means of force.[5]

Rhodes, usually a good judge of character, did not recognize that Hammond might be a source of trouble. If anything, Hammond's initial work as an engineer put Gold Fields on a track to greater prosperity. The brash American came to the Witwatersrand in 1893 and planned to work for Barney Barnato. Hammond and Clement brought with them a half-dozen other Americans with experience in mine management, engineering, and geology. Hammond's team evaluated a recent analysis by other American engineers and geologists.

These engineers had argued that the quartz reefs sloped downward into the basin at such a steep angle that they were likely to become unworkable. Hammond's team believed that was not the case. They predicted that the slope toward the basin was relatively shallow and that mines farther away in the basin were not only workable—they might also have higher quality ore. Barnato was reluctant to invest heavily in unproven claims and declined to follow Hammond's advice. Hammond decided to resign rather than work for someone who did not trust his opinions. When Rhodes invited Hammond to Cape Town, for a conversation at Groote Schuur, he jumped at the opportunity. "Rhodes was the big man of Africa," wrote Hammond, "and it was with him that I preferred to become identified, and I lost no time in accepting his invitation."[6]

Rhodes recommended that Consolidated Gold Fields hire Hammond and his team. Hammond was paid the extraordinary annual salary of £15,000, roughly equivalent to two million dollars in today's money. It was more than Rhodes ever paid any other employee. The management of the company was in the hands of Rhodes's brother Ernest, an officer in the British army who was unfamiliar with mining and who rubber-stamped Hammond's everyday requests. When it came to larger decisions, such as buying and selling mines, Hammond asked for Cecil Rhodes's personal approval first. The other company directors had no say in the matter, nor did the British engineers who were already present.

Hammond and his team earned their pay at Gold Fields. They advised Rhodes to sell holdings in mines that were based on visible outcropping and to buy three deep-level mines: the Robinson Deep Mine, just south of Johannesburg; the Simmer and Jack Mine, eight miles to the east; and the Sub Nigel Mine, thirty-five miles to the southeast. At the very same time, another well-known American engineer, Hamilton Smith—formerly Rothschild's consulting engineer—was presenting a similar analysis to Alfred Beit. Beit and Rhodes were both persuaded that the Americans' analysis was correct. Over time these deep-level mines became some of the richest gold mines in the world. The shift to deep-level mining helped the gold industry to recover from its slump and enter a phase of profitability. Rhodes was content to stand back and let Hammond run things. Rhodes knew that the money made on the Rand and at Kimberley was bankrolling his visionary colony of Rhodesia. Yet Rhodes's decision to work at a remove from Johannesburg and Hammond resulted in significant problems.

The understaffed Transvaal administration was thin on the ground and was still led by the conservative frontiersman Paul Kruger. Kruger brought a distinctive style to governance. At his home in Pretoria, he spent afternoons on his porch, rocking with a pipe in his mouth, letting citizens approach him with their questions and comments. Behind closed doors, he met with a small group of political advisers, all Afrikaners or Dutchmen from the Netherlands. He was in the regular habit of riding through rural districts of the Transvaal so that he could be available to his supporters. He belonged to a religious group known as the Doppers, who believed in literal interpretations of the Bible. All his life he maintained that the Earth was flat. His stolid, Bible-quoting wisdom attracted many of the Transvaal's Boers but was off-putting to the foreigners, known as *uitlanders*, who began to settle in the country in the late 1880s. They chafed under leadership that was so provincial. By contrast, they found Rhodes to be an appealing character, thanks to his steady efforts to connect the Transvaal and the Cape by rail and telegraph and his persistent advocacy for a customs union.

Kruger and the Transvaal establishment hoped to preserve their unique identity in the face of rapid change. When the gold rush began in the 1880s, the *uitlanders* could be dismissed as transitory people who were likely to leave as soon as the gold ran out, but people had now started to think that it would never run out. The development of the Rand brought higher tax revenues, but foreign professionals began to pose a problem for Kruger and the Transvaal establishment. The *uitlanders* brought economic opportunities, but also a secular, cosmopolitan outlook. Foreign miners became known for engaging in the typical activities of mining towns: drinking, gambling, and prostitution. In 1890, the socially conservative government of the South African Republic imposed a law requiring fourteen years in residence for citizenship. Only with citizenship could they vote or hold office in the Volksraad, the main legislative body. Instead, they were given a legislature of their own that could only make nonbinding recommendations to the main Volksraad on matters related to mining and the city of Johannesburg. Even though the *uitlanders* were being treated as second-class citizens, they were still expected to pay taxes and to participate in military service.[7]

The *uitlanders* were troubled by their status in the Transvaal. They were also troubled by the Transvaal government's contracting of public services to outsiders like Lippert, who was involved in the dynamite concession. Johannesburg's water supply was run by Barnato and Sivewright, whose performance resulted in many complaints. Further grievances revolved around labor issues. The deep-level mines required ever more African migrant workers, but mine owners complained that their efforts to discipline their African workers were hampered by the ineffectiveness of local law enforcement.

And the deep-level mines tended to be taxed more heavily, too, leading to more negative comments by the *uitlanders* about public services.[8]

Railway development became a flashpoint for conflict. The mining industry was keen to have better connections, in order to transport workers and equipment. In 1887, a Dutch company was given the concession to build and operate the Transvaal rail network. Construction was slow, and the Dutch company struggled to balance its books. The company built the lines that connected Pretoria and Johannesburg to the mining towns along the Witwatersrand, while working on Kruger's main strategic project, building a 350-mile line from Pretoria to Delagoa Bay, thus assuring a rail connection to Portuguese territory and less dependency on the British colonies, the Cape and Natal. The Pretoria-Delagoa line proved difficult to build. It passed through mountainous terrain, with significant areas infested by malaria-bearing mosquitoes, and only opened in October 1894. Another line to the coast, funded by the Colony of Natal, connected Durban to Charlestown, on the border with the Transvaal, in 1891, but Kruger delayed completion of the section from Charlestown to the Witwatersrand until December 1895, thinking it was better to finish the Delagoa line first.

Delays in construction were particularly frustrating to merchants and to the mining industry, which wanted to use the rails to transport heavy equipment. The *uitlanders* were in the early stages of organizing themselves. In 1892, a group of politically engaged professionals founded the Transvaal National Union, a nascent political party that pressed for change. The party was led by George Farrar, chairman of a mining company on the East Rand; Lionel Phillips, an associate of Beit who directed the Chamber of Mines; and Percy FitzPatrick, another associate of Beit and the future author of *Jock of the Bushveld*, South Africa's classic adventure story. During the 1892 election, representatives of the Transvaal National Union paid a visit to Paul Kruger, who told them off: "Go back and tell your people I shall never give them anything, now let the storm burst!"[9] Mine owners like Joseph B. Robinson and Barney Barnato were unwilling to chance a disruption to their profits and stayed out of politics. Rhodes and Beit also avoided involvement, until 1895, when they started to contribute to the National Union. The National Union, in turn, was influenced by the ideas of John Hays Hammond. Hammond, Rhodes, Beit, and Phillips were all affiliated with a range of mining companies, many of which were starting to become highly profitable. Kruger and his policies on taxes, labor, and dynamite stood in the way.[10]

It is worth noting that the *uitlander* political movement comprised mainly professional people and had little visible support among working-class whites.

The *uitlander* professionals may even have been resented by working-class white miners and small-business owners. Many of the miners bore some class antagonism against the professionals. Among the miners, there were many independent-minded Americans and Cornishmen who preferred the stability that good wages brought to their families over the high-minded rhetoric of the men with the smooth hands and clean fingernails.

Imperial officials started paying more careful attention to the *uitlander* professionals in June 1894, when Loch traveled to Pretoria for a meeting with Kruger. At the train station, the two men were settling into their carriage when it was surrounded by a mob of angry *uitlanders* who unhitched the horses and pulled the two men around town. Kruger wound up wrapped in a Union Jack, apparently unable to call on any police to help him. Loch was impressed by the spirit of the *uitlanders* and underwhelmed by the Transvaal's security forces. Soon thereafter, Loch met with Lionel Phillips and suggested that several thousand cavalry troopers could take Johannesburg, helped by the *uitlanders*. Still hot from his experience in the Transvaal, Loch ordered the Bechuanaland Border Police to prepare for action. He communicated his plan to the Colonial Office, where it was immediately vetoed by Lord Ripon, Gladstone's secretary of state for the colonies. Loch's plan was shelved, but Rhodes was made aware of it and began to sense some rivalry with the governor and high commissioner. Soon afterward, Rhodes began to hatch a coup plot of his own that involved an armed invasion from Bechuanaland and an uprising by the *uitlanders*.[11]

For a long time, Rhodes's plan for South Africa had involved the gradual absorption of the Transvaal and the Orange Free State into one nation. As Cape prime minister he supported the extension of the Cape's railways to the Transvaal and the development of a customs union. As Cape prime minister, he had also worked steadily with the Afrikaners of the Western Cape, which was appreciated in the republics. The progress toward a united South Africa seemed to be steady but slow. In the Cape Colony, Rhodes had promoted significant changes, such as the Glen Grey Act, but there he was willing to play a long-term game of steady rural transformation. In the north, however, he had once contemplated the assassination of Lobengula, and he encouraged BSAC agents to precipitate actions against the Portuguese and the Ndebele. This is the approach that began to be contemplated in the Transvaal.

In late 1894, Rhodes, Hammond, and Jameson started to plan to overthrow the government of Paul Kruger. They did not exactly hide their antipathy to Transvaal independence. On January 28, 1895, Jameson gave an address titled "South Africa" to an audience of 2,000 at London's Imperial Institute. He was introduced by the Prince of Wales, and the audience included Rhodes and most of the leadership of his companies: Beit, Cawston, and Maguire, as well as members of the British cabinet. Jameson presented them with a short history of South Africa that culminated with the BSAC conquest of Mashonaland and Matabeleland, "a settlement that has satisfied the Matabele nation." Now Rhodesia, as it was now called, was "a livable country, a payable country, a country which has succeeded in overcoming all its internal troubles." Jameson proposed a union of the Cape, Rhodesia, and the Orange Free State, together with a reluctant Natal and a defiant Transvaal. Unity of all five colonies and republics was "a proposition of practical politics which must inevitably come about."[12]

A plan took shape for overthrowing the South African Republic. Rhodes and Hammond formed a Reform Committee, a cadre of plotters drawn mainly from the principals at Consolidated Gold Fields and their acquaintances. Lionel Phillips led the committee, which included Victor Clement and Charles Leonard. The other prominent investors in the deep-level mines, Alfred Beit and his colleagues at the Corner House, were also instrumental. One committee member had military experience: Rhodes's brother Frank, who had twenty years of service in the British Army, followed by a brief administrative appointment to the BSAC in Mashonaland. The Reform Committee would be supplied with weapons sent from De Beers and stored at Gold Fields. On an appointed day, the Reform Committee would distribute the arms so that its members could take control of Johannesburg. Further arms would be stolen from the South African Republic's arsenal. Meanwhile, a force of BSAC Police, having gathered already in Pitsani, now called Pitsane, in Bechuanaland, would ride across the border into the Transvaal, aiming to join the rebellion in Johannesburg. The planned coup pitted the BSAC against the Transvaal's small professional army, who were backed by skilled reservists known as "commandos." The coup plotters did not hope for an outright victory; they merely anticipated that while the *uitlanders* and the BSAC Police fought in Johannesburg, the British government would intervene on their behalf. The governor and high commissioner would hopefully negotiate a peaceful settlement that would include the deposition of Kruger's government and the return of the Transvaal to British oversight.

While Rhodes and his colleagues made plans to remove Kruger from office, they were also working behind the scenes to have Loch replaced as governor and high commissioner. Loch was the first one to outline the plan for the two-pronged attack on the Transvaal, but Rhodes knew that he and Loch had different approaches to Southern Africa. Loch was, first and foremost, a British imperialist who was interested in preserving and extending the

British Empire. As such he was responsive to humanitarian criticism and willing to uphold laws that were ostensibly race-blind. Rhodes felt strong ties of loyalty to Britain but preferred that local settler governments be given latitude to deal with "the native question." Unlike Rhodes, whose political tactics were often unorthodox, Loch was an institutionalist. Rhodes knew that when the Colonial Office under Lord Ripon rejected Loch's idea of a coup in the Transvaal, Loch would do his duty and obey the order.

In July 1894, Rhodes and Loch corresponded about expanding the BSAC's territory and railway access in the Bechuanaland Protectorate. Loch reiterated his approval of the idea in a July 1894 letter to Rhodes, but in that letter, Loch warned Rhodes that the British government "would never consent to any pressure being put on Khama to oblige him to do so." Rhodes complained that when the BSAC received its charter, there had been an "understanding" that when the company was on its feet in Rhodesia, it would also be given Bechuanaland. "It was on account of this understanding," wrote Rhodes, "that we undertook the extension of the railway from Kimberley to Vryburg and subsequently to Mafeking." Rhodes was now using notions of guilt and honor to manipulate the Colonial Office. He concluded by saying that taking Bechuanaland was "natural" to his sense of territory: "A glance at the map will show that the Territory North of Mafeking, including Mashonaland and Matabeleland, will naturally form one state, and my desire is that nothing should mar this conception."[13]

In November 1894, Rhodes made a trip to England with the object of getting Loch removed from office. Rhodes brought with him two key advisers, Jameson and Rutherfoord Harris, the secretary of the BSAC in South Africa. During the visit, Rhodes was celebrated by London society; his participation in a shareholders' meeting of the BSAC was a triumph. Rhodes then used his power and connections to gain access to political leaders. Gladstone had retired as prime minister in March 1894, but the Liberal party was still in power. It was divided between the classic, thrifty Liberals who were skeptical of imperial expansion and other members, including Rosebery, who was now prime minister, who welcomed imperial expansion and a bigger navy. Rhodes and Rosebery agreed about many things. A decade earlier, Rosebery had advocated colonial representation at Westminster. From 1887 to 1892 he led an organization, the Imperial Federation League, that advocated closer ties between the mother country and the settler colonies.[14] Rhodes found Rosebery sympathetic and chose to deal directly with him.

Rosebery was a wealthy aristocrat and intellectual, educated at Eton and "sent down," or dismissed, from Oxford on account of his devotion to horse racing. Rosebery was a successful speaker and author who traveled in the highest social circles. He also suffered from prolonged depression after the death of his wife, Hannah de Rothschild, Natty Rothschild's cousin, in 1890. In October 1894, shortly before Rhodes's visit, he had also become embroiled in a scandal that touched on another acquaintance of Rhodes. Rosebery's private secretary and lover, Francis Douglas, Viscount Drumlanrig, was the brother of Alfred Douglas, the lover of Oscar Wilde. The Douglases were the sons of John Douglas, the Marquess of Queensberry, the notorious Scottish bully who had rewritten the rules of boxing. Queensberry was so incensed by his son's conduct with Rosebery that he followed them to the spa at Bad Homburg, Germany, where he burst in on them, brandished a dog whip, and threatened to flog them. Rosebery was saved only by the intervention of the sizeable Prince of Wales. Drumlanrig died in a suspicious shooting accident that was rumored to be either a murder or a suicide. Queensberry suspected foul play and threatened to expose Rosebery's homosexuality if he did not help him in his efforts against Oscar Wilde, Rhodes's acquaintance from Oxford, whom Queensbury blamed for corrupting his other son, Alfred. Soon afterwards, Queensberry would succeed in baiting Wilde into a libel suit that backfired and resulted in the brilliant author being prosecuted and imprisoned.[15]

Rosebery's personal dramas made it difficult for him to manage the day's political dramas, which included rivalry between his party's factions. Rosebery delivered a boost to Rhodes by arranging for him to be made a member of the Privy Council, the monarch's formal advisory body, comprising the leading politicians of Britain and the empire, as well as archbishops, senior judges, and members of the royal court. A *Times* editorial on New Year's Day, 1895, fawned over Rhodes. "It is clearly right," the editors wrote, "that a man playing so large a part in the field of Imperial and colonial expansion should now be formally associated with the governing forces of the Empire and admitted to his share in the councils of the Sovereign." The *Times* brushed off criticism of Rhodes, saying that it was not possible to "play so great a part in great affairs without doing many things displeasing on good grounds or bad to many people."[16]

Rosebery also made it possible for Rhodes to meet again with Queen Victoria at Windsor Castle. Victoria asked him to fill her in on his activities since their last meeting. Rhodes boasted, "I have added two provinces to Your Majesty's dominions." To this, Victoria replied, "I wish some of my ministers, who take away my provinces, would do as much."[17] Her ministers must have wondered about the remark, since none had lost any provinces. It is possible that she was referring to Liberal support for Home Rule in Ireland, which she opposed. Perhaps she had forgotten about Rhodes's support for Parnell.

When the ceremonial meetings were done, Rhodes met behind closed doors with Rosebery and senior members of the Liberal Party to sound them out about a coup in the Transvaal. The plan was not rejected. Rosebery's only real suggestion was to advise about timing. He suggested that Jameson and the BSAC forces should wait to invade the Transvaal until after the uprising in Johannesburg. Rhodes may have taken this as lukewarm approval of the raid. Rhodes next talked Rosebery into replacing Loch with Hercules Robinson, the retired governor and high commissioner. Not only had he helped Rhodes extensively during the late 1880s, but Rhodes had rewarded him by giving him substantial shares in the BSAC. Rosebery and Ripon went ahead with appointing Robinson, despite the protests of members of both political parties and even a question from Queen Victoria. William Harcourt, the chancellor of the exchequer and the leader of the government in the House of Commons, objected by saying that Robinson could not be "an impartial administrator"; he was plainly "the nominee of Rhodes," appointed to "carry out his political ideas and financial interests." Rosebery appointed Robinson anyway.[18]

Rhodes's trip to England had yet another purpose: to clear the way for his own personal control of Bechuanaland. Tswana territories had been divided since the days of the Warren Expedition. The Rolong and Tlhaping chiefdoms as well as the former republics of Stellaland and Goshen were located in the separate British colony of British Bechuanaland, between the Cape Colony and the Molopo River. From the Molopo River to the north, all the way to the Shashe River, was called the Bechuanaland Protectorate and is today the nation of Botswana. From south to north, it was the home of the Ngwaketse under Gaseitsiwe and the heir apparent, Bathoen; the Kwena under Sebele; and the Ngwato under Khama, all of whom were wary of Rhodes. In 1892, the BSAC began to fund the Bechuanaland Border Police, giving Rhodes some leverage over it. The BBP and Khama had helped in the campaign against Lobengula and the Ndebele. The Ngwato and Ndebele rulers were old rivals.

Rhodes coveted the Bechuanaland Protectorate for the BSAC and British Bechuanaland for the Cape Colony. He made efforts in the early 1890s and tried again to claim the territories in the wake of the war against Lobengula and the Ndebele people. While there was fighting, Khama allowed the BBP and the BSAC Police to use Palapye as a forward base. When the war was over, Rhodes visited Khama at the Ngwato court, the *kgotla*. It was the central legal and political institution, where chiefs were expected to be available to meet with any community member, high or low. Disputes that were brought to the *kgotla* were resolved in public, sometimes over the course of lengthy discussions, during which consensus was sought. In its consensus-building and its accessibility, the *kgotla* was a democratic institution that was also a theater for the wisdom of the chief. During his visit to the *kgotla*, Rhodes showed his characteristic scorn for African people. He lectured Khama in front of his counselors about how the chief was a deserter. After this public show of disrespect, Khama would become Rhodes's enemy. Khama was supported by a missionary who was present among the Ngwato, William C. Willoughby, who began to send critical information to Henry Labouchère for publication in *Truth*.[19]

Rhodes hoped to get the rights for the BSAC to mine and settle in the Tswana lands located in the Protectorate. Rhodes also remained interested in railway construction. Cape Town was connected to Kimberley by rail in 1885, and by the terms of its charter, the BSAC was supposed to complete the £500,000 segment from Kimberley to Vryburg. Rhodes used his influence and arranged for the BSAC to receive financial help from the Cape Colony, and when the line was done in December 1890, it was turned over to the Cape Government Railways. The BSAC charter obliged it to complete the line from Vryburg to Mafeking, but Rhodes was still short of funds. There was still an expectation that the line would reach Bulawayo. Rhodes's plan was for the railway to run north through the eastern part of the Bechuanaland Protectorate up into Rhodesia and beyond. The British government set aside a narrow strip of land along the eastern border of the Bechuanaland Protectorate, where the railway would be constructed. The plan was to sell the land on either side of the tracks to white settlers, following the example of the railroads in the US West. By this time, Rhodes was also thinking that the strip of land would be a convenient place for amassing BSAC troopers for an attack on the Transvaal.[20]

The Colonial Office supported Rhodes's plans to make the Bechuanaland Protectorate a part of the BSAC. As early as December 1892, Lord Ripon wrote to the senior staffer, Robert Meade, asking him to instruct "the Government officials in Bechuanaland and the Protectorate to use their endeavours to induce the Chiefs and people in the Bechuanaland Protectorate to grant to the British South Africa Company concessions of minerals, agricultural lands and town-sites, over areas not already made the subject of valid and recognised concessions to others . . ." One paragraph later, the following was underlined: "He [Ripon] will not recognise as valid any Concessions subsequent in date to the Charter granted to the British South Africa Company."[21] The BSAC was given permission to take the Bechuanaland Protectorate in much the same way as they had taken Mashonaland and Matabeleland.

Rhodes assumed that the BSAC absorption of the Bechuanaland Protectorate would go smoothly. In November 1894, he presented an official letter to Lord Ripon at the Colonial Office, asking "for an assurance from Her Majesty's Government that their policy is unchanged, and that when, in their opinion, the time has arrived, they will transfer the administration of the Protectorate to the Chartered Company, thus carrying out the terms of the Charter and the former assurances of their predecessors." Rhodes believed that informal assurances given earlier by the Colonial Office would smooth the way for BSAC rule over the Protectorate. Ripon indicated that he was still generally inclined to transfer the administration and warned Rhodes that "large and admiring classes in this country" supported preserving the independence of Khama.[22]

Loch disagreed with Ripon and preferred that the Bechuanaland Protectorate be made into a Crown Colony, not into BSAC territory. During a meeting with Ripon and the senior staff of the Colonial Office, the retiring governor and high commissioner made the case that BSAC rule was far from impressive. He compared BSAC rule in Rhodesia to "lynch law" and argued that putting the company in charge of the Bechuanaland Protectorate would be a "cruel wrong" against Tswana people. Loch recommended that the protectorate be annexed to the British Empire as a separate Crown Colony. That way, Tswana people would have the best protection against the BSAC and Rhodes.[23]

The British government rejected Loch's argument and gave Rhodes its continued support. The decision showed the strength of Rhodes's network in London. On November 30, 1894, a letter from Ripon to Rhodes confirmed the understanding that "the policy of our predecessors towards your Company" was "plain." The Colonial Office "contemplated the ultimate acquisition by the Company of administrative authority in the Protectorate." Rhodes only had to respect the alliance between Khama and Britain's temperance movement by making sure that the BSAC prohibited alcohol in the territory. In a follow-up letter written a few weeks later, Ripon's senior staffer, Edward Wingfield, expressed the hope that an upcoming visit by Rhodes to London would make it possible for a personal meeting "to deal with all outstanding questions relating to the concessions in the Bechuanaland Protectorate."[24] These included getting ready to pay the chiefs for any concessions that they had granted after the creation of the BSAC, on the assumption that the BSAC would take over all those rights. Rhodes did meet with Ripon, who wisely did not let Rhodes rush him into a decision. For a time, the status quo remained in place.

While Rhodes was still away in London, Loch was back in Cape Town for the last days of his governorship, courting Khama, the missionaries, and public opinion for a final move against the BSAC. Khama had reasons to be wary of Loch, who had generally been supportive of Rhodes, but he went ahead and boarded the train in Mafeking—his first train ride—and arrived in Cape Town in early January 1895. Loch arranged for Khama to have a VIP tour of the city, to see a parade of British soldiers, and to be welcomed on board a ship of the Royal Navy. Loch also sat down with Khama for a conversation. Loch warned Khama about the likelihood that a BSAC railroad would go through his territory and that he would have to pay taxes to support the administration of the Bechuanaland Protectorate. Khama seemed ready to bargain, insisting on the continued prohibition of alcohol. Khama visited Cape Town churches and temperance organizations and spent time with John Smith Moffat, who had recently been fired from the Bechuanaland Protectorate's civil service by the chief administrator, Sidney Shippard, for speaking critically about Rhodes.[25]

While British and Cape authorities considered Rhodes's and Khama's wishes, the BSAC promoted a scheme designed to get the company's foot in the door of the Bechuanaland Protectorate. It had its origins in 1893, when Rhodes had instructed a BSAC agent, Isaac John Bosman, to travel to Ngamiland, near Lake Ngami in the far northwestern corner of the Bechuanaland Protectorate. Rhodes used the area's proximity to the "Caprivi Strip" of German South-West Africa as a justification for promoting settlement from the Cape Colony. Bosman misrepresented himself to Sekgoma, who governed the area, by telling him that he was seeking concessions for the British government. Bosman presented the chief with five rifles, in violation of international agreements. Next Bosman persuaded Sekgoma to sign two treaties. The first treaty declared the mutual friendship of Sekgoma and the Queen. The second treaty, full of mistranslations, gave Sekgoma's land to the BSAC. In September 1894, with preparations ongoing for the BSAC to annex the Bechuanaland Protectorate, a young British army lieutenant, A. B. Walsh, discovered the fraud but allowed a small column of settlers and ox-wagons to move forward into Ngamiland. The Ngami Trek, as it was known, was paid for by Rhodes. The trek consisted of fifty-five Boer settlers who were under BSAC instructions to conduct reconnaissance and to peg claims. Sekgoma became alarmed and sought the intervention of Khama, who objected strenuously to the incursion. Khama, together with J. S. Moffat, worked to stop the trek. Loch hoped that the treaty could be renegotiated properly. A party of twenty-eight trekkers and troopers of the Bechuanaland Border Police followed a back road up into Ngamiland. A confrontation between Sekgoma and the BBP's captain, J. W. Fuller, occurred in May 1895 and effectively stalled the settlement scheme.[26]

With the BSAC annexation of the Bechuanaland Protectorate delayed, Rhodes pursued the Cape Colony's annexation of the Crown Colony of British Bechuanaland, located along the Road to the North, just south of the Bechuanaland Protectorate and west of the Transvaal. Rhodes smoothed the way by sending his confidant, Albert Grey, to meet with Ripon at the Colonial Office. Ripon told Grey that he approved of the idea; for the plan to move forward, the annexation only needed to be discussed by the full Cabinet.[27] The transfer was helped by the British government reinstalling Robinson as governor. Ripon allowed Robinson to announce, in his governor's speech to the Cape Parliament, that the annexation of British Bechuanaland would take place. In June 1895, the Cape Parliament voted to annex the territory. There were protests from Tswana people and petitions sent by the Rolong chief, Montshiwa, and the Tlhaping chief, Mankurwane, but these achieved little traction. Rhodes's friend, the colony's administrator, Sidney Shippard, reported in 1895 that Tswana people "thoroughly appreciate the blessings of British rule, under which they enjoy in peace the fruits of their labor."[28]

With British Bechuanaland under Cape rule, Rhodes decided to keep pressing for the Bechuanaland Protectorate to be given to the BSAC so that all the Tswana lands on the Road to the North would be subject to his authority. Rhodes's friend, the journalist W. T. Stead, wrote that at that moment, Rhodes "was at the zenith of his power." "In London and South Africa," Stead gushed, "every obstacle seemed to bend before his determined will."[29]

The next obstacle to be overcome was a surprise development in British politics. Rhodes had gone to great lengths to become acquainted with Ripon and Rosebery. The visit during the 1894–1895 winter had gone well, especially with the reappointment of Robinson as governor and high commissioner. But in June 1895, Rosebery resigned as prime minister. He had only served for a year, but disagreements between him and his Liberal Party colleagues, together with his personal problems, persuaded him to quit. Once again, the political winds were blowing in the direction of the Conservative Party. Queen Victoria named Salisbury as the caretaker prime minister. A few weeks later, an election confirmed the Conservatives in power.

When Salisbury appointed a new cabinet, he named Joseph Chamberlain to be the secretary of state for the colonies. Chamberlain was an opportunist who posed a threat to Rhodes's wishes. The new head of the Colonial Office began his career as a successful manufacturer of metal screws, then became the radical Liberal mayor of Birmingham. He was elected to Parliament in 1876. He was critical of Conservative Party leaders, especially Lord Salisbury, but when the Liberal prime minister, Gladstone, came out in favor of Irish Home Rule, Chamberlain changed sides. He led a faction of Liberals opposed to Home Rule, called the Liberal Unionists, into an alliance with the Conservatives. "Pushful Joe" Chamberlain joined Salisbury's government as the Secretary of State for the Colonies.[30]

Having Chamberlain in that position involved some risks for Rhodes. He knew that Chamberlain had spoken critically about the BSAC. Even so, Rhodes may have sensed that if Chamberlain could change his mind about Salisbury, he could also change his mind about other things. Rhodes sent Albert Grey to the Colonial Office for a fateful meeting with Chamberlain and two high-ranking staffers, Robert Meade and Edward Fairfield. They were joined by William Palmer, the Earl of Selborne, the undersecretary of state for the colonies. A Liberal Unionist, he was also the son-in-law of Salisbury. Grey's object for the meeting was to iron out any differences with Chamberlain. Grey brought two key principals in the BSAC: Rutherfoord Harris, the BSAC's secretary for South Africa, and Herbert Canning, the BSAC's secretary for London, who kept a record of the meeting. Grey pressed Chamberlain for a decision about giving the Bechuanaland Protectorate to the BSAC. Grey learned from Chamberlain that his support for transferring the Crown Colony of Bechuanaland to the Cape Colony was "practical proof of sympathy with Mr. C. J. Rhodes policy." Chamberlain agreed to the transfer "in order to ensure immediate further Railway Construction." The proposal to transfer the Bechuanaland Protectorate to the BSAC did not meet with his approval. "Although he is friendly," noted Canning, Chamberlain "considers cession Protectorate at any near date utterly impossible. His attitude on this point without compromise and decisive." Chamberlain refused an invitation to meet with Rhodes to discuss it any further, "that C. J. Rhodes must leave him alone for the present."[31]

Rhodes would not take "no" for an answer. The BSAC did not just want the Protectorate for a railway. The planned raid on Johannesburg would require a staging area somewhere on the border between the Bechuanaland Protectorate and the Transvaal. The BSAC secretary, Canning, noted, "We decided therefore to inform Secretary of State for Colonies guardedly reason we wish to have base at Gaberones [Gaborone], and advisable our presence in

Protectorate." Canning would have been a fool to write down the exact meaning of this, for legal reasons. Nevertheless, it does appear that Grey tipped Chamberlain about the BSAC plan to raid the Transvaal.[32]

When Chamberlain was told about the plan for the coup, he could have told Grey, Harris, and Canning that what they were proposing was illegal. That would have ended the meeting, but that sort of accusation could not be made lightly in a gentleman's culture. Furthermore, Rhodes and Grey would have "plausible deniability"—there were not any written records of a coup plot. A criminal investigation would have yielded little evidence. By not raising objections, Chamberlain became quietly enrolled in the plot. He was obliged by his government appointment to raise objections, and he did not. Backing out might end his political career. Rhodes now owned Chamberlain. At the end of the meeting, Chamberlain said that he was "heartily in sympathy with C. J. Rhodes policy." He could not, at that moment, approve a BSAC takeover of the Protectorate, thanks to the influence of the British temperance movement, but he was willing to approve giving the BSAC a narrow strip of land along the border, for the ostensible purpose of building the railway line to the north. The Road to the North was to have a new role in the infrastructure of imperialism. It was to become a staging ground for a coup against the Transvaal.[33]

Almost immediately, Rhodes made it known that railway construction would begin on the line from Mafeking to Gaborone. Maguire had a follow-up meeting with Chamberlain, at which the secretary of state for the colonies said that he did not favor the BSAC annexation of the protectorate—at least not for a year. That meeting was soon followed by another one between Grey and Chamberlain, in which they began to negotiate the size of the strip of territory along the eastern edge of the protectorate.[34] Rhodes succeeded in creating a sense of urgency, a familiar negotiating ploy used to cloud the judgment of a mark. Rhodes may also have felt pressure to coordinate timing with the coup plotters in Johannesburg.

Rhodes did not anticipate the next move of his opponents. Khama became aware of BSAC efforts to take his land. He knew full well what happened to his former enemy, Lobengula, when he reluctantly took up arms against the BSAC. Khama also knew of the success of Lobengula's indunas when they visited England. Khama decided to defend his chiefdom by mounting his own public relations campaign in Britain. Khama worked together with William Willoughby to organize a tour of Britain. Khama persuaded Sebele, chief of the Kwena, and Bathoen, chief of the Ngwaketse, to join his effort. The three chiefs arrived in London in September 1895 and spent two months traveling the length and breadth of Britain, from Southampton to Edinburgh.

Hosted by temperance activists and missionaries, they stopped at thirty towns and cities. They met with Chamberlain and the staff of the Colonial Office. They attended suppers, exchanged gifts, and toured the country's leading sites. They visited many churches. Everywhere they went, they acted in a quiet, dignified manner and won over the public with their message: that they valued the imperial government's protection and that they feared that if Cecil Rhodes and the BSAC were put in charge of their country, the Tswana people would be harmed by the company's greed and liquor.[35]

The travels of the three chiefs were covered by all the newspapers, which put pressure on the British government. Chamberlain called for a settlement of the difficulties between the three chiefs and the BSAC. Led by Albert Grey and Rutherfoord Harris, the BSAC delegates insisted on control over the entire protectorate. The chartered company was especially keen to complete the railway from Mafeking to Bulawayo, with plans to let it run along the eastern edge of the Bechuanaland Protectorate, on the border with the Transvaal. The three chiefs and their lead negotiator, Willoughby, all insisted on maintaining the current boundaries and the current political structure, too. On October 7, the BSAC offered the three chiefs reserved territories, based on a map drawn by Warren in 1885. The rest of the territory would be run by the BSAC, including a ten-mile strip along the border. The chiefs deliberated for several weeks, then rejected the offer. In a letter sent to the Colonial Office on November 4, they put their finger on how Rhodes viewed the territory of people on the Road to the North.

> You can see now that what they [the Company] really want is not to govern us nicely, but to take our land and sell it that they may see gain. And we ask you to protect us. . . . The Company have conquered the Matabele, and taken the land of the people they conquered. We know that custom: but we have not yet heard that it is the custom of any people to take the best lands of their friends. In Bathoen's country they seek a large piece of land, and in that land Bathoen's people have gardens and cattle posts. In Khama's country they seek nearly all the best parts. . . . Where will our cattle stay if the waters are thus taken from us? They will die. The Company wants to impoverish us so that hunger may drive us to become the White man's servants who dig in his mines and gather his wealth.[36]

The Tswana chiefs had a clear understanding of Rhodes's intent to put their country through the disassembly line. Sensing an impasse, Chamberlain called for a meeting at his office. The chiefs, the missionaries, and the BSAC agreed to Colonial Office arbitration. Chamberlain and his senior staffers, Meade and Fairfield, drew up a plan to divide the Bechuanaland Protectorate. The fateful meeting took place on November 6. The reservations offered to the chiefs were enlarged, but the company was still given control of most of what is today western and central Botswana, as well as the eastern strip. It is possible that by this point, Willoughby had been told of the impending coup, either by Colonial Office staffers or BSAC negotiators. His complicity may have put pressure on him to convince the three chiefs to take the deal. The chiefs gave in, securing promises to keep liquor out of their reservations and to keep the railway strip fenced off from the rest of the country. Grey and the representatives of the BSAC were satisfied with the agreement, but Rhodes, in Cape Town, was furious about the reservations. The Road to the North was open, but not as wide as he hoped. He complained that he had been defeated by "three canting natives. . . . The whole thing makes me ashamed of my own people." He told Rutherfoord Harris that "it is humiliating to be utterly beaten by these n----rs."[37]

Khama, Sebele, and Bathoen charmed the British nation and won the support of Christians. The trip culminated in an official luncheon for the chiefs at Windsor Castle with Queen Victoria, Chamberlain, and members of the court and Parliament. The three brought the missionaries William Willoughby and Edwin Lloyd to translate their remarks from Tswana to English. Lloyd interpreted as the queen's message was read by her daughter, Princess Beatrice, with the queen's assistant, Abdul Karim, at her side: "I approve of the provision excluding strong drink from their country." The queen was known to be fond of Scotch whisky, but she was persuaded to keep the chiefs' lands dry. "I feel strongly in this matter, and am glad to see that the chiefs have determined to keep so great a curse from the people." The queen's message thanked the chiefs for their obedience and gave them her best wishes for prosperity. The queen made no commitments, other than the prohibition of alcohol, but the event confirmed the high esteem that the nation felt for the three Tswana chiefs.[38]

Thanks to their successful public relations campaign, Khama, Bathoen, and Sebele got a better deal than the one that was given to the three lesser chiefs who ruled territory along the eastern edge of the Bechuanaland Protectorate. Lentswe, Ikaneng, and Montshiwa negotiated on site, with Frank Rhodes acting for the BSAC and Sidney Shippard representing the governor and high commissioner. The two Englishmen led the chiefs to believe that they were just ceding small landholdings that could be used for

BSAC Police campsites. Those three chiefs did not realize until later that the BSAC was also putting them under its legal control.[39]

Rhodes still whined and exaggerated about his inability to control all of the Bechuanaland Protectorate. In December 1895, he dictated a letter to Fife, the BSAC chairman, because he felt the need to "relieve my feelings" about the "Bechuanaland Settlement." He complained that "we have not been fairly dealt with." The "natives have been left with the whole country." He did "not look at it so much from a pecuniary point of view but from the broad point of South African politics." Territorial expansion was very much on his mind: "A large country as big as the British Isles will now be definitely beaconed and dedicated to these people." "Who are these people? They are not sixty thousand in number and the worst specimen of humanity—certainly in Africa—and perhaps in the whole world." He blamed the missionaries and the temperance advocates for creating a situation in which "huge reserves will have been beaconed by Her Majesty's officer and the natives will say that these were the solemn gifts granted by the Queen at Windsor and will appeal on every occasion to Her Majesty." The decision stood in the way of his ambitions for a united, white-dominated South Africa. "Even if federal union comes in Africa it makes it no better. These natives, through their missionaries, appeal again and again to the English people against the sentiment of Africa." Rhodes called the chiefs "drunkards and cowards" and said their visit to Britain was a "circus show." He was "deeply grieved" and summarized his views thus:

> For remember, as I have said before, a country as large as the British Isles, has been given to sixty thousand of the laziest rascals in the world, who never cultivate to any extent and whose chiefs now come out puffed with the importance of having seen the Queen and having been entertained by the leaders of English thought.[40]

Rhodes pouted that he could not have total control of the Bechuanaland Protectorate. He did get authority over the railway line that ran from Kimberley along the Road to the North, in Tswana territory that lay just west of the Transvaal's jurisdiction. In 1895, there was also trouble with the rail line that connected the Transvaal to the Cape. When Rhodes became prime minister in July 1890, a line had just been built from Port Elizabeth to Colesberg, and from there to Bloemfontein, with work under way to run the line north to the Vaal River border with the Transvaal. On the Transvaal side of the project, the line from Johannesburg to the Vaal River border was stalled thanks to financial challenges. Rhodes and Sivewright made an offer to Kruger for the Cape Government Railways to build the line inside the Transvaal and to operate it for two years. Kruger agreed to the arrangement, and the line was built and opened in early 1893. In December 1894, with the railway about to pass into the hands of the Transvaal government, Rhodes and Kruger engaged in a rate war. A meeting between the two men even resulted in them shaking fists at each other. Kruger decided to close the railway border crossing to freight traffic. Rhodes responded by encouraging Cape merchants and the *uitlanders* to form wagon companies that would ford the river and deliver the goods. Kruger responded by closing the fords, known in Dutch as "drifts." As the Drifts Crisis got worse, the British government protested strongly and even embarked troops on board ships bound for South Africa. The Cape and British governments even discussed an invasion of the Transvaal, agreeing to split the costs of an attack. In November 1895, after receiving an ultimatum from Chamberlain, Kruger backed down.[41]

While the Drifts Crisis was unfolding, and while the Tswana chiefs were ending their tour of Britain, Rhodes and his associates in Johannesburg and Rhodesia were laying the groundwork for the Transvaal coup. Toward the end of October 1895, Rhodes hosted a meeting at Groote Schuur. The main conspirators arrived from Johannesburg: Jack Hammond, Lionel Phillips, and Frank Rhodes. Charles Leonard of the National Union was also invited, in an effort to persuade him to join. Leonard hoped that the coup would succeed but wanted Rhodes to promise that the Transvaal would not necessarily be absorbed into the British Empire. Rhodes wanted the Transvaal to become part of a united South Africa that would in fact be part of the British Empire. Rhodes promised Leonard that he was mainly interested in protecting his investments in gold mining and that he hoped that any intervention by British forces would be only to "prevent bloodshed" and not to conquer territory. Everyone knew that Rhodes had influence over Robinson, which led Leonard to accept the assurances.[42]

As the plot unfolded, Rhodes began to suspect that the key player in Johannesburg, Jack Hammond, had republican sympathies of his own. Hammond admired Britain but still lacked the native British patriotism that Rhodes expressed over the course of his life. While Rhodes was busy as Cape prime minister, Hammond and his American colleagues worked on logistics. Arms were supposed to be shipped by Gardner Williams from Kimberley to Johannesburg, but secrecy necessitated small shipments, and Williams had fallen behind. To make up for the shortfall in weapons, Hammond began to emphasize the importance of the planned attack on the South African Republic's arsenal, located in the capital, Pretoria, forty miles to the north.

As Hammond worked on this new plot within a plot, his planning advanced to the point where he had objectives that diverged from Rhodes's. Unbeknownst to Rhodes, Hammond planned to rent a farmhouse near Pretoria and to keep a force of several dozen ex-miners there, ready to capture the arsenal and kidnap Paul Kruger. Hammond would keep the South African Republic intact while declaring that Johannesburg was to be a separate district, in an arrangement similar to the one in the US that defined the city of Washington, DC. Hammond's idea for preserving the South African Republic was not consistent with Rhodes's plan for a unified white settler state in Southern Africa under the British Empire.[43]

Hammond and the other plotters, including Frank Rhodes, Lionel Phillips, and Charles Leonard, left Groote Schuur and traveled back to Johannesburg, where they worked on the coup's final details with the Reform Committee. Rhodes used the unusual bylaws of his companies to arrange for Gold Fields to contribute £120,000 and for the BSAC to contribute £61,500—approximately 28 million dollars in today's money—to purchase weapons and ammunition. Jameson would bring 1,500 troopers, each carrying an extra rifle. The state arsenal at Pretoria held 10,000 more rifles, plus twelve million cartridges and a dozen cannons. The plotters were trying to create the same kind of advantage that they had against Ndebele soldiers, but the Boers would turn out to be a different sort of foe.[44]

In a remote southern corner of the Bechuanaland Protectorate, near the Transvaal border, a Rolong chief, Silas Molema, allowed Jameson to rent a large farm that was close to the border. Local Tswana chiefs like Molema were concerned about the BSAC's possession of the Bechuanaland strip, but they had also been the victims of incursions by the Boers and gave Jameson's troopers a wary welcome. Jameson did not recruit the promised number of 1,500 troopers but did start drilling with the 500 white men who volunteered, with an additional 70 troops who were African—he called them a "posse of K----rs" and "Cape Boys." Chamberlain instructed Robinson to release any troopers from the Bechuanaland Border Police who might wish to join. Jameson relied on his second-in-command, John Willoughby, to train the force in the hot summer weather. They foolishly drilled in the open, easily seen by Boer spies. Transvaal intelligence officers also cracked the code of telegrams sent back and forth between the plotters. In November, Jameson met with Rhodes in Kimberley, then proceeded to Johannesburg. The Reform Committee gave him an undated letter, which he put in his coat pocket, asking to be rescued from "great peril." Of course, the peril would have been created by Jameson and the Reform Committee, but no matter. His plan was to read it out loud to the troopers on the morning they rode for Johannesburg.[45]

Jameson was over-confident, partly owing to his personality, partly owing to his success in the war against the Ndebele kingdom. Over lunch with Fred Hamilton and Frank Rhodes, Hamilton told Jameson that the Boer fighters of the Transvaal would be hardy opponents. Jameson disagreed. "I shall get through as easily as a knife cuts butter," he declared. "You people do not know what the Maxim gun means. I have seen it at work."[46] Jameson returned to Pitsani to be with John Willoughby and the troopers. Meanwhile, conspirators shuttled back and forth between Hammond in Johannesburg and Rhodes at Groote Schuur. Hammond lost heart at the end of December, when the coup was supposed to happen. Too few weapons had arrived and besides, conditions in Johannesburg were good and few miners were interested in causing trouble. Hammond became anxious and asked for a postponement. Rhodes agreed.

All this was communicated to Jameson, either by telegraph or by messengers, but he chose to disregard his partners' hesitations. At 9:05 in the morning of Sunday, December 29, 1895, Jameson sent a telegram to the BSAC's Cape Town office for Rhodes, telling him that he would order his force to cross the border that evening. The message was delivered to Rhodes before noon. Rhodes had an hour to respond, because on Sundays, the telegraph offices closed at 1:30. He chose to wait until it was too late. After 1:30, he attempted to send a message to Jameson, telling him to halt, but it did not go through. Over the next few days, as Jameson and his troopers rode toward Johannesburg and the word of the invasion got out, visitors reported that Rhodes looked ashen. To Fred Hamilton, he commented that this was "the end" and that "the Dutch will never forgive me." To Will Schreiner, he repeated the words, over and over, "It is all true." Rhodes went on. "Poor old Jameson, twenty years we have been friends and how he goes and ruins me."[47]

Rhodes kept a commonplace book, a small notebook for jotting down thoughts and notes on readings. There is one entry labeled, "Written just before the raid." It reflects in a mindful, Stoic way on humanity, the sublime, and the empire:

> If you are in a difficulty go up a mountain and overlook humanity. Compare the vastness of nature and the pettiness of the human atom. The thoughts arising will probably give you a right decision.

> The dons of a college should tell the students once a year that England is not the British Isles but the world, that our strength lies in keeping the markets of the world open, that we are a small spot on the world's surface but the greatest power so long as we maintain our markets, that our politics are in a nutshell that as our whole business is the receipt of the raw material, working it up into the manufactured and its ultimate distribution over the world. We shall be great only as long as we keep our Empire.[48]

Rhodes watched from the sidelines as his network failed. Hammond, for all his swagger, became anxious at the last minute, just as he had done in confrontations in Idaho and Mexico, and decided that he was not ready to start an uprising. Jameson had no such hesitations and ordered the raid to begin anyway. The plan was to ensure surprise by cutting the telegraph lines to Cape Town and Pretoria. A BSAC trooper cut the cable to Cape Town, but instead of cutting the cable to Pretoria, he cut a wire fence. A small technical mistake by an obscure participant resulted in larger problems for the entire scheme, much in the same way that, seven years earlier, an African miner lighting a match in the De Beers Mine resulted in a fire that threatened Rhodes's broader interests. This time, Rhodes's vision was in deeper trouble. When the BSAC column crossed the border, they were scouted by Transvaal commandos, who easily communicated over the uncut wires with Pretoria, even as Jameson could no longer send messages to Rhodes on the telegraph line to Cape Town. Chamberlain learned of the raid and instructed Robinson to disavow it. Robinson instructed British subjects in the Transvaal not to get involved.

On January 1, 1896, when BSAC troopers approached Johannesburg, they began to encounter Boer skirmishers. Then, twenty miles northeast of Johannesburg at Krugersdorp, Jameson and Willoughby found the road blocked. To swing around Boer positions, the 600 troopers rode to Doornkop, which is today on the western edge of Soweto. Doornkop turned out to be a trap. Boer fighters occupied nearby ridges and fired down on the BSAC troopers, killing a dozen and wounding several dozen more. Jameson's Maxim guns were no use against trained marksmen, concealed behind rocks and trees, firing from elevated positions. The Boer fighters had figured out how to use topography and tactics to resist and defeat the BSAC's superior weaponry. Jameson decided to surrender. He and his troopers were marched to Pretoria and put in jail. In his pockets, Jameson foolishly carried letters from members of the Reform Committee, who were soon rounded up. More plotters were compromised after one of the BSAC captains, Robert White, was caught with the code book. Over the course of the next days, the members of the Reform Committee were put in jail.[49]

Initially Kruger was inclined to treat Jameson, Hammond, and the other coup plotters harshly, but after the initial violence and anger subsided, he decided that there were benefits to getting the gold-mining industry back on a normal, productive footing. Robinson negotiated for leniency, and by and large the plotters received it. Instead of retribution, Kruger settled for cash payments. Kruger released Jameson and Willoughby, who were sent to London to be tried for violating the Foreign Enlistment Act of 1870, which prohibited British subjects from participating in a war against a country that was at peace with Britain. The members of the Reform Committee were put on trial in the Transvaal, and all pleaded guilty. The low-ranking conspirators were punished with two years in prison, three years of banishment, and fines of £2,000 each. In May 1896, Rhodes paid the fines, and they were released from prison. Jack Hammond, Frank Rhodes, Lionel Phillips, and George Farrar pleaded guilty to high treason and were sentenced to death. Kruger then turned to Rhodes, who agreed to pay £25,000 to obtain the release of each man. Rhodes's total payments to the Transvaal amounted to £400,000, worth $60,000,000 in today's currency.[50]

Rhodes's vision of a unified South Africa, stretching from Cape Town to the Great Lakes, appeared to be ruined. So was his reputation. The failure of the raid seriously embarrassed the British government. Rhodes would no longer be welcome at Windsor. He was forced to resign as Cape prime minister, although he retained his seat in the House of Assembly. As for political unity in South Africa, it now seemed less likely than ever. Kruger remained in power. Rhodes and Beit were asked to step down as directors of the BSAC. The charter itself was called into question.

The raid was particularly damaging to Rhodes's carefully orchestrated relationships with Afrikaners. The Afrikaner Bond was willing to play along with Rhodes's northern schemes and to back Rhodes in his rivalry with Kruger. In exchange, the Bond expected Rhodes to help them maintain dominance in the Western Cape. After the raid, Hofmeyr, no longer a member of parliament but still influential, wrote to Kruger, congratulating him on the capture of Jameson and the plotters. Bower tried to bridge the gap between Rhodes and Hofmeyr by inviting them to meet. When they spoke, Hofmeyr revealed the extent of his disappointment.

> I could explain better if you had ever been a married man. You were never married. I have not yet forgotten the relation of perfect trust and

intimacy which a man has with his wife. We have often disagreed, you and I, but I would no more have thought of distrusting you than a man and his wife think of distrusting each other in any joint undertaking. So it was till now; and now you have let me go on being apparently intimate while you knew that this was preparing, and said nothing.[51]

Rhodes's plan for expanding colonial settlement depended on an elaborate network of people, places, and things. All aspects of the network needed to be built and then maintained with care. The 1888 De Beers Mine Fire showed that disaster could strike one part of the network and threaten related parts. The causes of the fire were downplayed, and the disaster was largely forgotten. By contrast, Jameson's attack on the Transvaal became an international sensation that most people blamed on Rhodes.

18

Defending the Vision

WHILE RHODES WAS managing the damage from the failed raid, his top priority was defending the colonialism of the BSAC. Just one week after the plotters were rounded up, and with controversy swirling all around him, Rhodes boarded a ship for England, intending to save the charter. On arriving in London, Rhodes met with his attorney, Bourchier Hawksley, to discuss two related problems: the upcoming trial of Jameson and Willoughby and the political pressure on Chamberlain to revoke the charter. At the end of January 1896, Rhodes and Hawksley received some ominous news. The decision allowing the BSAC to control the Bechuanaland Protectorate was overturned, and the territory reverted to the protection of the British government.

Britain had the authority to revoke the charter in other territories, too, but Rhodes and Hawksley had one point of leverage. They had fifty-four telegrams that had been exchanged between the London and Cape Town offices of the BSAC. The messages implicated Chamberlain and his colleagues at the Colonial Office in the attempted coup. Hawksley was going to be acting as the attorney for Jameson and Willoughby, and he wanted to use the telegrams as exculpatory evidence. Rhodes had a different idea. He used his friend, the courtier Reginald Brett, the future Lord Esher, as a go-between to schedule a meeting with Chamberlain and the undersecretary, Selborne. Before the meeting took place on February 6, 1896, Hawksley let Chamberlain know that Rhodes possessed damaging telegrams. Rhodes met privately with Chamberlain and Selborne at the Colonial Office and offered to take responsibility for the raid. He also informed them that he would remain silent about the telegrams if the BSAC's powers were preserved. If Chamberlain and Selborne revoked the charter of the BSAC, he would release the telegrams. Chamberlain and Selborne would then be finished.[1]

Not only did Rhodes blackmail Chamberlain, one of the most powerful politicians in Britain, and Selborne, the son-in-law of the prime minister, but by hiding the telegrams he made it more difficult for John Willoughby and his old friend, Dr. Jameson, to defend themselves in court. Chamberlain and Selborne agreed to the deal, and, in doing so, were able to remain influential in imperial and South African politics. Rhodes and Beit still had to relinquish their directorships, and during the summer of 1896, Jameson and Willoughby were tried in London and sentenced to prison for fifteen and ten months, respectively. It was better than facing a firing squad in Pretoria, but they still had been sold out by Rhodes.

Even with all the accumulating difficulties facing the BSAC, Rhodes still advocated for a white settler society in Rhodesia. The all-male veterans of the Pioneer Column had been given claims to farms, as promised, while almost two hundred mining companies were operating. Telegraph lines connected the main colonial settlements to Mafeking and Cape Town. Several thousand settlers were attracted to the area, but there were many obstacles. Rhodes had once hoped for colonization to proceed rapidly, but the realities on the ground slowed down the company. It was still very difficult to traverse the geographical spaces of Rhodesia with the available infrastructure. By the start of 1896, the railroad track from Kimberley still did not go farther than Mafeking, while construction of the "eastern" railroad from Beira had only made it to Chimoio, in Mozambique, one-third of the way to Harare. The overland journey from the Cape or from Mozambique remained difficult and expensive, keeping prices for ordinary goods at extraordinary levels. Mining in Rhodesia was disappointing. There were almost two hundred gold-mining companies operating, with several employing up-to-date and expensive stamp mills to process the reef, but the results were minimal. There was some development in Bulawayo, where settlers built a town on the outlines of the Ndebele capital, and in Salisbury, where a town grew from nothing.

After the Jameson Raid, changes were made in the administration of the BSAC. Jameson had to resign. He was replaced by Albert Grey, who had served on the board of the BSAC since its inception. He had just been invested as Earl Grey, which entitled him to a seat in the House of Lords. Grey's status reassured investors. The British government provided further reassurances. The Jameson Raid showed that BSAC armed forces needed to be controlled by the British governor-general and high commissioner. A cavalry colonel from the British Army, Richard Martin, was appointed to be Rhodesia's deputy commissioner. He ordered a fellow cavalry officer, Major Herbert Plumer, to disarm the BSAC Police. The disarming would not last long, but from this point forward the force would be under imperial control and known as the BSA Police, their letter "C" discarded with their ties to the company.[2]

Defending the Vision

Before 1893, the company's settlers engaged in a limited quest for riches. After the war of 1893, white settlers became more deeply rooted in Rhodesia. Colonists who fought for the BSAC Police against the Ndebele kingdom were each given 3,000 morgen of land, equivalent to 6,351 acres. After the war was over, police veterans rode quickly to the countryside, pegging off their claims. The settlers felt justified in doing so, maintaining the convenient belief that Ndebele people had not legally owned the land. Ndebele people drifted back to their ruined villages to find their land occupied by land-grabbing colonist rent-seekers. Many Ndebele families remained and worked on their own lands, resenting their new roles as tenants and laborers for white settlers. By 1895 there were one thousand settler farms in Ndebele territory. They occupied 10,000 square miles. From the perspective of Ndebele people, renting from colonists may have been a better option than living on one of the two large "native reserves" that were marked off. These were generally thought to be poorly suited to farming and cattle-keeping. Mission churches were given grants of land so that they could better establish Christianity among African people, some of whom were driven to live near the missionaries after settlers took Ndebele and Shona lands. In the midst of the rapid imposition of colonial domination, recognizable Ndebele and Shona political and military structures were still in place.[3]

BSAC officials imposed further harsh policies. In May 1893, the chartered company announced a hut tax on Ndebele and Shona people. The Colonial Office, which still had some scruples, found the hut tax to be illegal, on the grounds that the charter did not give authority to levy taxes. The decision was reversed in 1894, and the BSAC was given permission to collect the taxes. Taxes on polygamists and dog owners were announced, too. The tax collectors were African mercenaries known as "levies" who were managed by BSAC officials and pressured by white settlers. The tax collectors became known for predatory, rough behavior. When Ndebele or Shona communities were unable to pay taxes in cash, people were marched off for labor on public works, or even to work on mines and farms. People who resisted—even chiefs—were flogged in public. There were also accusations of rape.[4]

After the 1893 war, the BSAC authorized the seizure of cattle, a heavy blow. Ndebele and Shona people were not just raising cattle for meat and for milk. In many Southern African societies, cattle represented wealth and status. In the early years of contact with Transvaal traders, Ndebele people were victimized by cattle rustlers. The BSAC did not make things better. From October 1893 to March 1896, settlers took upwards of 200,000 cattle. In 1895, all Ndebele cattle were proclaimed to be the property of the BSAC. Unlike

Ndebele people, Shona people had not been defeated in war but were still subject to confiscation for owing taxes. Not only were tens of thousands of cattle taken, but sheep and goats were taken, too. In any event, livestock turned out to be a wasting asset. In March 1896, the cattle rinderpest, a viral infection that had become widespread in East Africa, crossed the Zambezi River. Over the course of 1896 and 1897, approximately 90 percent of Southern Africa's cattle died, together with substantial numbers of wild and domesticated animals. The confiscations, the rinderpest, and, at the same time, a plague of locusts, devastated Southern African societies that were already subject to the BSAC and Rhodes.[5]

Although the region's societies were experiencing terrible environmental and economic stress, they retained sufficient cohesion for people to fight back against colonialism. The failure of the BSAC's Jameson Raid presented an opportunity. One of Jameson's many mistakes was to remove the vast majority of the BSAC Police troopers from Rhodesia and send them to the Transvaal. When Jameson and his troopers were captured at Doornkop, only sixty troopers remained north of the Limpopo. Any advantages from modern weaponry were now gone. News of the raid's failure inspired a revolt.

In March 1896, Ndebele fighters struck against the BSAC and its settlers. The oldest accounts attributed leadership of the rebellion to a figure known as "the Mlimu," the head of a cult, although this account has been challenged. Ndebele soldiers were still organized in much the same way as they were in 1893 but were using new tactics. Instead of attacking BSA Police troopers holding defensive positions with modern weaponry, Ndebele fighters attacked isolated white farmers, miners, and administrators, as well as their African employees and converts to Christianity. After 200 settlers were killed, Ndebele forces made their next move against Bulawayo, surrounding the town and its 1,500 white inhabitants while still avoiding a pitched battle. The settlers at Bulawayo formed a defensive laager, taking fullest advantage of their breechloaders and machine guns. Ndebele soldiers now knew to avoid an all-out frontal assault. They did not cut the line from Bulawayo to Mafeking, where a relief force began to muster, but they did disrupt settler communication by cutting the line from Bulawayo to Salisbury, near the Shangani River.[6]

When the fighting broke out, Rhodes was already on his way to Rhodesia together with the railroad engineer, Charles Metcalfe. They disembarked in Beira and followed the planned line of railway construction to Salisbury. Rhodes and Metcalfe completed the arduous journey and arrived in Salisbury, where Rhodes organized a mounted squadron of 150 settlers. The telegraph to

Bulawayo was still open, and the officer in charge of the town's defense, Maurice Gifford, advised him that Rhodes needed more troopers. Rhodes disregarded the advice and led the squadron on the old Road to the North in the direction of Bulawayo. Arriving at Gweru, then called Gwelo, one hundred miles to the northeast of Bulawayo, Rhodes appointed himself to be a colonel, even though, strictly speaking, commissioning oneself as an officer was against law and custom. The new administrator of the BSAC, Albert Grey, was supposed to be in charge, but he was assembling another force in Mafeking. Actual leadership in the field fell to Rhodes.

It soon became evident to Rhodes and the settler forces that Ndebele soldiers had improved their tactics since the war of 1893. Ndebele soldiers were now using rifles to better effect this time, sniping at BSAC defenses. When armed troopers rode out into the countryside, they were vulnerable to ambush. When ambushes occurred, the colonists fought against the "savages" with "merciless ferocity," to quote Rhodes's friend, Frederick Courteney Selous, who commanded a section of two dozen militia cavalry and wrote about the experience in a book. The volunteers were instructed by Selous to take "prompt action to strike terror into the hearts of some of the rebels" and "to reassure those who were content with the white man's rule." Selous had further instructions: "I told them that any K----rs we might find with arms in their hands, who had left their kraals and gone off into the hills with stolen cattle, ought to be shot without question and without mercy, as they were every one of them more or less responsible for the cruel murders of white men that had already been committed." Selous reported that he took this approach with one group of Ndebele, discovered with 150 cattle in a hilly area. Selous described how his militia immediately opened fire and gave chase. Sensing that readers might perceive this action to be unjust, he wrote that "this action may possibly be cited as an example of the brutality and inhumanity of the Englishmen in Rhodesia," but he justified the attack by reminding his audience that "the K----rs whom we sought to destroy" were no more than "a pack of wild dogs."[7]

Despite suffering from a case of malaria acquired on the way from Beira, Rhodes still appeared on the battlefield with a riding crop in his hand, directing his followers in the hands-on work of fighting and pillaging. His companion and secretary, Gordon Le Sueur, described Rhodes's participation in a raid on a hilltop Ndebele village. Climbing the hill in the wee hours of the morning, Rhodes went "puffing along in his white flannel trousers with the best of them, a little riding switch in his hand." At dawn, the party "attacked the unsuspecting natives, who were shot as they ran from their huts." Seventy were killed. Rhodes insisted on a precise count. Le Sueur described another incident, in which Rhodes met a BSA Police officer, just returning from a skirmish with Ndebele fighters. Rhodes asked how many were killed, and the officer replied, "Very few, as the natives threw down their arms, went on their knees, and begged for mercy." Le Sueur recorded the response: "Well," said Rhodes, "you should not spare them. You should kill all you can, as it serves a lesson to them when they talk things over at their fires at night."[8]

According to Jameson's Oxford-educated private secretary, Marshall Hole, Rhodes "took part in several small actions, exposing himself in a manner which caused great anxiety to his friends." When one unit of volunteers was attacked by Ndebele sharpshooters and separated from their wagon train, Rhodes took charge of a group of African auxiliaries armed only with assegais. He led them into "the bush" against the advice of Metcalfe and other friends. In Hole's account, the man known as "The Great White Chief" inspired the African troops. They "plucked up courage and followed, beating the bush and yelling some sort of war-cry. The Matabele skirmishers fired a few more shots, but were evidently misled by the hullaballoo into thinking that the whole patrol was turning back on them; they wavered, crept from their positions, and were soon in full retreat."[9]

Ndebele resistance was not well coordinated. Fighters faded away into remote areas, making it possible for Rhodes's force to link up with settler units from Bulawayo on June 1, one day before the arrival of the British units under Major-General Frederick Carrington, commander of the Bechuanaland Border Police. Carrington was an old acquaintance of Rhodes from the Frontier Light Horse and the Warren Expedition who was unlikely to keep a friend on a tight leash. Carrington brought with him several men who would later become influential public figures. There was Carrington's second-in-command, Colonel Robert Baden-Powell, future founder of the Boy Scouts, and Lieutenant-Colonel Herbert Plumer, future commander of the British Second Army on the Western Front, as well as Frederick Russell Burnham, who would become one of the United States' best-known outdoorsmen. A veteran of Arizona's range wars and of warfare against the Apache people, he arrived in Rhodesia in 1893, just in time for the campaign against Lobengula. In 1895, Burnham led the BSAC's "Northern Territories Expedition" as far as the border with Katanga. He was now once again scouting together with Selous in their second war against Ndebele people. Led by Carrington, Baden-Powell, Plumer, Burnham, and Selous, the British and settler forces staged a brutal campaign in Ndebele country. Plumer directed one pitched battle against Ndebele fighters at Ntaba zika Mambo that resulted in two

Defending the Vision

hundred Ndebele deaths. The ruthlessness of the British and the determination of the resistance worsened and prolonged the war. In the words of historian William Beinart, British Army and company forces engaged in "extreme violence," including massacres, starvation, mistreatment of prisoners and extralegal courts-martial that resulted in executions.[10]

Following the outbreak of war between the BSAC and Ndebele people, Shona people rose up as well. Their resistance took shape mainly in districts that had experienced the greatest impact from the BSAC and where chiefs had prior tributary relationships with the Ndebele leadership. Some British settlers were taken by surprise when Shona people began to attack them. One of the stereotypes that white settlers held was that Shona people were not warlike. They also believed that Shona people hated Ndebele people. Both notions turned out not to be true. Shona people felt aggrieved over the disrespectful treatment by the BSAC and its settlers, including the seizure of land, the imposition of taxes, the coercion of labor, and the taking of hostages, as well as the disruption of trade networks. Just like every other region in Southern Africa, Mashonaland was stressed by colonialism at the same time as the area was experiencing rinderpest, locust swarms, and drought.

The war that unfolded in Mashonaland resembled the one in Matabeleland, with attacks on settlers followed by reprisals. Shona fighters attacked telegraphs and killed several telegraph workers. Rhodes helped direct the counterinsurgency. Villages were bombarded by artillery and food plots were torched. The rebellion sputtered on, with more guerrilla attacks followed by more reprisals. Shona guerrillas were driven into hiding but were very difficult to root out. Some took to the caves of the region, where British and settler forces trapped them and blasted them to death with dynamite.[11]

British officers were confident that they could defeat Shona and Ndebele insurgents but openly discussed how they needed more time, troops, and resources. The rainy season was approaching, which would force a postponement of the final campaign until the following year. Rhodes had spent months on the front lines, gaining familiarity with the terrain and the fighting. He knew that as one of the biggest shareholders in the BSAC, he would wind up paying the extra expense of another year of warfare. The British government insisted that the BSAC pay for the intervention of British troops. Funds were scarce. Rhodes knew from Hammond's report that major yields would not be produced by gold mining. He knew that European-style agriculture was still not on solid footing, especially with limited infrastructure and warfare in much of the countryside. In August 1896, Rhodes decided to negotiate with the Ndebele leadership and to make peace. The peace-making is best understood as a gesture of pragmatism by the head of a struggling company. Footing the bill for the war was highly costly, while casualties are not good for share values: 450 settlers were dead and almost 200 were wounded. Ndebele and Shona deaths from fighting and starvation ranged from 15,000 to 20,000, out of a total population estimated to be 500,000 to 700,000.[12]

Rhodes set aside the grim toll of his wars, much like the people who later built his memorials and statues. Rhodes had negotiated deals with rivals before. Now he would have to take a great leap and negotiate a deal with African people whom he held in contempt. For a short time, he was willing to put aside his racism to save his colonialist aspirations. On August 21, 1896, Rhodes went to a small valley in the Matopos for his first conference with the Ndebele leadership. The meeting was set up thanks to the capture and release of a senior Ndebele woman, Nyambezane, who delivered a message from Rhodes across the lines. Two Mpondo guides opened the talks by speaking at a distance with several Ndebele soldiers. They indicated that their generals were ready to confer with "Ulodzi." Rhodes was joined by Colenbrander, who could translate, as well as by his friend Hans Sauer, who had recently been released from jail in Pretoria. The fourth white person present, Vere Stent, was the journalist son of the architect, Sydney Stent, the designer of Kenilworth. Stent recorded how the four men rode up on horseback, dismounted, and approached the Ndebele leaders. Rhodes addressed them with a few words in their own language, with help from Colenbrander. Rhodes indicated that he wanted peace. One of the chiefs, Somabhulana, agreed that he too wanted peace but was reluctant, given the BSAC's mistreatment of his people. In the end, Somabhulana conceded to Rhodes conditionally, saying "You came, you conquered. The strongest takes the land. We accepted your rule. We lived under you. But not as dogs! If we are to be dogs it is better to be dead."

Rhodes handled the situation skillfully and encouraged Somabhulana to keep talking about his grievances against the BSAC. Stories were told of young women raped by BSAC officials and "native police." More stories were told about insults and injuries. At the end of the recitation, Rhodes said, "All that is over," and reaffirmed that he wanted peace. He spoke as a leader without revealing that he no longer had an official role as a BSAC director or as the Cape prime minister. Rhodes indicated that he was willing to change the BSAC administration, but Stent noted that these were merely his "personal assurances." As the meeting ended and the sun went down, Stent and Sauer received instructions from Rhodes to ride to the telegraph station in Bulawayo. They were instructed to buy BSAC shares before reporting the news about the peace. There was only a narrow window of time for some insider trading.[13]

A second, larger peace negotiation took place on August 28. This time, Rhodes, Stent, and several others were joined by Lt.-Col. Plumer. The Ndebele chiefs included the senior leaders Babayane, who had visited Queen Victoria, as well as Dliso. Rhodes again promised that the peace would include administrative reforms as well as land reservations. One young chief mocked him, "You will give us land in our own country! That's good of you." Rhodes responded with good-natured banter and even gifts of cash to demonstrate his good will. Rhodes, sometimes joined by Martin and Grey, led more meetings in September and October, all delivering commitments to peace and better administration. On October 13, 1896, all the Ndebele chiefs who fought colonialism made a formal surrender. They turned over their weapons to Rhodes, who promised to restore their authority and to pay them salaries in exchange for loyalty. The BSAC also paid them £50,000 worth of grain, much of it stolen to begin with. Skeptics noted that the chiefs were negotiating under pressure of starvation. Several Shona chiefs still held out and were attacked by company forces, sometimes led by Rhodes himself. White settlers in Matabaleland and Mashonaland received compensation worth £350,000.[14]

Rhodes was very proud of the settlement. He even kept a photograph of Nyambezane, the peace broker, in his bedroom at Groote Schuur. Ten days after concluding the negotiations with the Ndebele leadership, Rhodes went riding with Hans Sauer in the Matopos. Sauer took him to an attractive spot that he had visited earlier in the year. The path twisted and turned through the hills, passing granite walls and giant boulders. Sauer recalled that "Rhodes's attention was suddenly attracted to a formidable granite dome with some large boulders placed in circular form on the top." The two men dismounted and walked to the top of the hill. In the words of Sauer, they "were rewarded with a magnificent view over the rugged masses of the Matopos, with the deep twisting valleys and gigantic boulders heaped up in profusion wherever we looked. Rhodes was profoundly moved by the impressive panorama before us, and said: 'This is the World's View.'" He was so taken by the beauty of the spot that a few days later, he asked Sauer to lead him back. According to Sauer, "Rhodes spent an hour on the summit absorbed in his own thoughts," and made up his mind to be buried there. Rhodes and his BSAC colleagues knew that Lobengula's father, Mzilikazi, was buried nearby at a hill called Entumbane. The tomb was desecrated by British soldiers during the war; Rhodes had the tomb restored as a gesture of reconciliation. One historian, Terence Ranger, notes that Rhodes intended for his burial to convey a message: "Now he planned to replace the Ndebele king as master of the land."[15]

Rhodes at His Own Gravesite in the Matopos. Courtesy of the McGregor Museum, Kimberley, MMKP 932.

Rhodes was contemplating death even as he was trying to resurrect his reputation. The Cape Parliament investigated him for his involvement in the Transvaal coup and issued a reprimand. Rhodes still kept his seat as a member of the House of Assembly. Rhodes's English-speaking critics in the Cape Parliament, like Merriman, now supported him. Rhodes learned that another investigation was commencing at Westminster. In July, the British Parliament authorized a select committee to investigate the raid. Rhodes was the key figure yet kept the investigators waiting until the end of the war in Rhodesia, when he made his way to London. As he traveled through the Cape in December 1896, he was greeted by adoring crowds. It was expected that the war against the Ndebele and Shona people would play well among the English-speakers in Port Elizabeth and Cape Town, but he was even cheered in predominantly Afrikaner towns such as Worcester and Paarl.[16]

On December 15, 1896, while Rhodes was touring the Eastern Cape, a fire broke out at Groote Schuur. The traditional thatched roof burned rapidly, destroying the upper-story bedrooms. At the time of the blaze, Rhodes's sister Edith and his brother Elmhirst were guests at the house. They directed the servants to carry out as much of the downstairs furniture as possible. Rhodes's books, flags, and billiard table were saved from the library, but many of Rhodes's papers were burned to ashes. Rhodes returned home quickly and was quoted as saying, "the Raid, rebellion, famine, rinderpest, and now my house burnt, I feel like Job, all but the boils." Rhodes gathered his thoughts and instructed Baker to restore the house to its former condition. While Baker and his contractor were working on the project, they took the opportunity to introduce new amenities, including better plumbing, and they installed electricity generated by a steam engine. It took two and a half years to finish.[17]

Soon after instructing Baker to start the renovations, Rhodes resumed his efforts at political rehabilitation. One of Rhodes's most interesting speeches was given in Kimberley, on December 28, 1896, when he chaired the annual meeting of De Beers. He had arrived in Kimberley only two days earlier and admitted that "I feel like a boy who goes to school without having prepared his lesson as he should have done. You must take my statement with its defects and the knowledge of the fact that I have been away from Kimberley for a very long time." Striking a jovial tone, he blamed fellow directors for having insisted on his making a speech. Having lowered expectations, he went on to give a frank and thorough round-up of company business. Rhodes was proud that the company had always paid a dividend to shareholders, and he was happy, also, to be the head of a monopoly with a large reserve of consols, diamonds, and floors. He referred to the new diamond mines that had sprung up in South Africa and noted that even if they can initially produce more carats per load, De Beers "have it always in our power to produce double the amount which we do, but we regulate our production by the wants of the world. I think it is one of those cases where a monopoly is judicious and justified by the results."

In the speech, Rhodes indicated that he was pleased about an initiative that he took at the 1894 annual meeting to make a profit from selling food and goods to the workers in the compounds and to place those earnings in a chairman's fund for community philanthropy, with contributions to local schools and hospitals. The largest gifts went to open the Kimberley Sanatorium, "a bit of a hobby of mine," which he started because, as Rhodes said, "I have always thought that Kimberley would be an admirable place for people with chest complaints from Home." Over several years, Rhodes arranged for De Beers to set aside funds totaling £47,000 for the sanatorium.[18]

In the conclusion of the speech, Rhodes took stock of De Beers and his role more generally. "The only trouble with regard to the [diamond] industry is that it is becoming a matter of course and uninteresting (laughter). It goes like clockwork. There is a huge number of people at work, and with the administration of the local directors, everything goes smoothly." It was a "good steady industry" with an "element of certainty that was not there in the past." Given all that, he admitted that "to my mind the industry has not the interest it had in the past, when one had to use one's mind and brain to bring about that amalgamation." The profits were steady, coming close to long-term goals that Rhodes had set in the late 1880s. "One has made many prophecies in the past on many questions," he said rather grandly, "but when the amalgamation was made I said De Beers would reach £70." Since than the shares had split and were currently valued at £32, equivalent to £64 in the original shares. With the share values nearing the threshold of his "prophecy," he then said, "I shall be glad when my career with De Beers is closed, if I can say that with the philanthropic assistance of the outside world, my prophecy will have been fulfilled." Production at De Beers was no longer all that interesting, even though the profits were still essential.[19]

In January 1897, Rhodes arrived in London, where he was greeted by more cheering crowds. Albert Grey wrote to Rhodes with encouragement. Grey was still the consummate London insider and an ally of Chamberlain's. "If there is any statesmanship," wrote Grey, "either at Pretoria or London, the Enquiry into the Raid will be allowed by common consent to fizzle. An Enquiry cannot after your reception do any good."[20] The British Parliament's committee included Rhodes's Liberal critics, Henry Labouchère and William Harcourt, as well as his Liberal supporter, Sydney Buxton, plus John Ellis, a Quaker railway engineer, and the future prime minister, Henry Campbell-Bannerman. The members also included four formidable Conservative frontbenchers: Richard Webster, the former attorney-general and future lord chief justice; Michael Hicks Beach, the former secretary of state for the colonies and chancellor of the exchequer; George Wyndham, an ardent imperialist and former officer of the Coldstream Guards; and the chair, William Jackson, who had also been lord mayor of Leeds and chair of the Great Northern Railway. Joseph Chamberlain was also included as a member of the committee, even though he had played a role in the raid. In private, Chamberlain had admitted to the Conservative prime minister, Salisbury, that Rhodes held the damning telegrams in reserve, as blackmail. Salisbury indicated his support of Chamberlain by refusing to accept his resignation. As the committee prepared for the hearings, Chamberlain's friend, the Conservative committee member, George Wyndham, was sent to Rhodesia to interview Rhodes. The interview had two purposes: to make sure that Rhodes would return to Britain to face the enquiry, and that when he did, he would remain quiet about Chamberlain's telegrams. Rhodes agreed to both stipulations. Hercules

Robinson would stay quiet, too. Chamberlain ordered him to stay in Cape Town until the arrival of the next governor, Alfred Milner, who was sent after the conclusion of the investigation.

The Westminster hearings lasted for six days in February 1897 and received much attention from the press. Rhodes appeared confident while the parliamentary investigators questioned him. In one session, he was asked to hand over missing telegrams from Chamberlain to the BSAC. He replied that he did not have them in his possession, which was technically correct. They were, in fact, in the briefcase of his attorney, Bourchier Hawksley, readily available just in case Chamberlain stepped out of line.[21]

The final committee report was released in July 1897. Chamberlain's role was overlooked, and Rhodes was blamed for being the main instigator of the raid. The committee's report faulted the governor's secretary, Graham Bower, and Edward Fairfield, the senior staffer at the Colonial Office, for knowing about the plan for the raid and doing nothing to stop it. Bower was punished by being reassigned to Mauritius, then a malarial backwater with a declining sugar industry, where he was appointed colonial secretary. Fairfield died, reportedly of stress, knowing that his long career of public service was ruined. No punishment was recommended for Rhodes. He had already stepped down as Cape prime minister and as the managing director of the BSAC. Cawston and Gifford, Rhodes and Beit were both asked to leave the board of the BSAC, although they kept their shares and their influence. As a shareholder and influencer, Rhodes would continue to be a dominant influence over Rhodesia. He also kept his honorary seat on the Privy Council. By 1898, Rhodes and Beit would be back on the BSAC board and Maguire was elected, too. Cawston quietly resigned. So, too, did Fife and Farquhar.[22]

In the aftermath of the raid, Rhodes managed to patch up his relationship with Jameson. In 1896, while Rhodes was fighting against the Ndebele and Shona resistance, Jameson and Willoughby began serving their sentences in prison. They were initially dressed in ordinary prisoners' garb and sent to Wormwood Scrubs, a jail in London for common criminals. Not long after, they were reassigned to Holloway Prison, where outside clothing was permitted and conditions were better. Jameson was even visited occasionally by his longtime servant, Garlick. Jameson was still miserable despite his improved circumstances. To make matters worse, while in prison he was subjected to a lithotomy, a ghastly procedure performed to remove a bladder stone.[23]

In February 1897, Garlick learned that Rhodes had arrived in London to testify before the parliamentary commission. Garlick knew that Jameson would also testify and that he worried about losing Rhodes's friendship. During the second half of 1896, Rhodes had been involved in a war and had not corresponded with Jameson at all. The servant sent a message to Rhodes, who arrived at once. He entered Jameson's cell and said, "Both of us have had a rough time, but you have had a rougher time than I." Rhodes raised Jameson's spirits by making it clear to him that they were still friends. The two men even schemed together about Jameson's future employment on a survey for the telegraph line that would run through the Great Lakes region. Jameson was forgiven and was once again involved in Rhodes's plans.[24]

19

Recovering the Vision

DURING THE 1890S, Cecil Rhodes became one of the best-known celebrities in the British Empire. Thanks to images printed in the press, he was recognized on the streets of London by pedestrians and hansom cab drivers. From 1890 to his death in 1902, he was featured in 79,423 British newspaper stories, with 14,544 stories published in 1896 alone.[1] Hundreds of people bought one or two shares in the British South Africa Company, just to get a seat at the crowded shareholder meetings. Celebrity kept Rhodes busy. On any given day, he engaged in correspondence by letter and telegram about politics, mining, farming, and finance, as well as railroads and telegraphs. He traveled frequently back and forth between London, Cape Town, Kimberley, Bulawayo, and Salisbury, with trips to other destinations, to protect and extend what he now called "The Idea."

Rhodes, who boasted about being descended from cattle-keepers, became more and more interested in farming. Key decisions revolved around support for rural development. In the Western Cape, Rhodes's farms became sites of progressive agricultural, business, and social experimentation. In Rhodesia, he encouraged experiments with crops and livestock while also pushing for infrastructure development. At Kenilworth he displayed an interest in experimental agriculture, cultivating fruit trees and vineyards to supply the employees of De Beers. The most interesting projects were undertaken in the Western Cape. Rhodes was partly inspired by jealousy. He watched his fierce critic, Percy Alport Molteno, get ahead of him in progressive, scientific farming. Percy was the younger brother of John Charles Molteno, Jr., who represented Tembuland in the House of Assembly and who resisted Rhodes's policies toward African people. (Their father, John Charles Molteno, Sr., had been the first prime minister of the Cape Colony.) Percy was educated at Cambridge and was called to the bar of the Inner Temple in London. Returning to Cape Town, he practiced law and traveled in the same orbit as Olive Schreiner, who had just skewered Rhodes in a blistering novel called *Trooper Peter Halket of Mashonaland*. Percy married the daughter of another critic of Rhodes, shipping magnate and De Beers partner Donald Currie. Percy joined his father-in-law's business and became one of the senior managers of the Union-Castle Shipping Line, which was experimenting with new refrigeration technologies. If fruit could be harvested in the southern hemisphere summer and shipped fresh to consumers in the northern hemisphere winter, a fortune could be made. The Union-Castle Line fitted a ship with a refrigerated hold, and in 1892, the first shipment arrived in England, accompanied by John X. Merriman. The fruit arrived in good condition and sold for a high price, inspiring several more farmers, including more members of the large Molteno family, to buy farms and plant fruit trees.[2]

When Rhodes returned from Rhodesia at the end of 1896—and just before leaving to testify in London—he began planning a farming enterprise to rival that of the Moltenos. Rhodes arranged a fateful meeting with an agricultural engineer named Harry Pickstone, an Englishman who had served in the Warren Expedition and who had subsequently worked in the orchards of California, where he learned how to raise fruit trees. In 1892, Pickstone returned to South Africa, where he became reacquainted with Rhodes and met Merriman. The two leaders of the Cape Colony were following the example of other European colonies in establishing a scientific department of agriculture. They hired Pickstone to work for their new department as an extension agent. Pickstone experimented with fruit trees and advised farmers. He also developed a side business as a nurseryman, partnering with Herbert Baker's brother, Lionel. In 1893, Rhodes and Rudd hired Pickstone as a private contractor to establish three nurseries in the Western Cape. Pickstone carried on as the Cape's fruit expert until late 1896, when Rhodes hired him as a part-time private consultant. Rhodes drew on his personal funds and persuaded Alfred Beit and De Beers to invest enough money so that Pickstone, as manager, could purchase twenty-nine farms in the Western Cape's wine region. Rhodes and Pickstone grouped these into thirteen units and invested in them heavily. From 1897 to 1901, Rhodes, Beit, and De Beers each chipped in £53,000.

Rhodes, Michell, and Pickstone were looking for properties that might be improved through capital investments. As many people knew, Rhodes tended to think in terms of large projects, but in the words of Herbert Baker, "'The foible of size' was here justified, as both realized, with their gift of the long view, that farming on a big scale was necessary to force the essential organization of transport and cold storage by the railway officials and the shipping companies without which it would have been impossible to establish the market in Europe." Pickstone's ideal farm managers were young, single men like himself, from England, California, and the Cape. The foremen and overseers were recruited from Cape Afrikaner families already familiar with local working conditions.[3]

Pickstone and Rhodes pushed for a progressive approach. Scientific methods were used to address many problems, including crop diseases. Pickstone used grafting to revive vineyards that were infested by the phylloxera louse. He also used ladybugs to kill off the scale insects that were damaging orange groves. They also hoped to improve the lot of the mixed-race or "Coloured" farmworkers of the Cape, who were historically disadvantaged. Baker recorded Rhodes's racially tinged thoughts on his new workers:

> Rhodes was much concerned at the state of decadence of the coloured population, Hottentot and European bastards, the descendants of the slaves. They were so different from the healthy barbarism of the natives, whom he knew and loved. I remember, on the day he first walked over his land at Groote Schuur with me, how he shuddered, on passing some debased specimens, and said that "They are hardly human."[4]

When Pickstone recruited young farm managers, he remarked that they would need "tact and patience & plenty of both" with the Western Cape's seemingly problematic farm workers. "This labour question is the one of the day," wrote Pickstone, "& is the thorny point in managing a large estate." He spoke critically of the wine region's tradition of managing workers by means of alcoholism and dependency. "The general run of farmers maintain their influence over their boys entirely through the wine bottle, a most pernicious system & one which they will learn to rue." Pickstone reported that he was experimenting with a better approach:

> On my Farm & on several others under my management no wine is given & I expect the managers to hold the respect of the boys by being able to do every branch of the work thoroughly. Coloured labour if sober is very intelligent & quickly sees if the baas understand his work & have a corresponding respect for him. This is what I shall endeavour to instill into the men [managers] that come out & I <u>know it will succeed</u>.[5]

Using paternalistic management and new techniques, it took years for the orchards to mature. Pickstone often asked for more authority to make decisions, which Michell resisted, on the grounds that the "obstinate" manager of the fruit business had limited abilities when it came to budgeting.[6] The Rhodes Papers document Pickstone's methods with photographs of workers using modern technologies like tree sprayers. Workers at Languedoc were shown collecting their wages in cash rather than cheap wine.[7]

Rhodes still liked to dabble in a range of entrepreneurial activities. His correspondence with his banker, Michell, indicates that they considered buying sugar estates in Natal but passed on the opportunity.[8] Rhodes and his associates decided to build several other new businesses, including one that involved refrigeration. The mines at Kimberley had 10,000 workers whose normal rations included meat, but the rinderpest epizootic had a terrible impact on Southern African livestock. Prices for meat were very high. and the market was dominated by a handful of refrigeration businesses that were importing frozen meat from overseas. Rhodes advocated for the construction of public refrigeration units. When that failed, he had De Beers construct its own cold storage facilities in Cape Town and Kimberley.[9]

Rhodes's new refrigeration business attracted little attention in the Western Cape, but his construction of a dynamite factory in Somerset West raised more than a few concerns. Dynamite was an important part of Rhodes's

Pay Day at Languedoc, Rhodes's Agricultural Village in the Western Cape. Courtesy of the Rhodes Trust and the Bodleian Library, Rhodes Papers, Rhodes Fruit Farm Album, MSS. Afr. S. 12/1.

mining operations. For years, De Beers, Gold Fields, and the BSAC were at the mercy of Transvaal's dynamite monopoly, managed by Lippert and his delegates and supplied by Nobel, which had opened a dynamite factory at Modderfontein on the East Rand. Nobel indicated its intention to stay by building a workers' village, complete with a manager's house that overlooked the settlement. Rhodes was frustrated by the expense of dynamite purchases, which were costing De Beers £60,000 per year. When Rhodes failed to get a better price, in 1898 he authorized De Beers to spend £500,000 to start a company, Cape Explosives, which built its own factory. Rhodes received advice from one of the managers of Nobel's Modderfontein factory, who considered himself a British patriot. He wrote to Rhodes secretly to offer his services in starting a dynamite company. Gardner Williams decided, instead, to hire an American manager, William Quinan, an energetic former officer in the US Army who had operated one of the most important explosives plants for the Hercules Company in California. Quinan and the five Americans who accompanied him to the Cape built an extensive physical plant in the Western Cape village of Helderberg, near Somerset West, during the war of 1899–1902. The De Beers board expressed concerns that Rhodes and Williams were operating outside of their oversight. Rhodes assured the board that they would be able to sell dynamite at a much lower price than their competitors. The first dynamite shipped to Kimberley in 1903.[10]

Rhodes's image of himself as a successful entrepreneur and progressive farmer in the Western Cape, with twenty-nine properties in the Afrikaner heartland of Franschhoek, Paarl, and Stellenbosch, was interesting given the fallout from the Jameson Raid. By the time Rhodes returned from his testimony in London, the majority of Afrikaner opinion had swung against him. Only a handful of prominent Afrikaners remained loyal, such as David Christiaan de Waal, who had been involved in Rhodes's northern projects. Rhodes sensed that his political future lay now with the pro-Empire "jingoes," a term that came into use at that time to describe vocal British patriots. Rhodes began to speak out in favor of the old idea of imperial federation, the combination of the British colonies of the Cape and Natal with the Boer republics of the Transvaal and the Orange Free State. In the service of anglophone patriotism, Rhodes even used progressive farming as a club for beating the Bond. In one speech given in Cape Town in March 1897, Rhodes attacked his former allies, saying that "the little gang in Camp Street," the site of Bond headquarters, were "terrorizing the country." He falsely claimed that the Bond represented a minority of Afrikaner opinion: "My own idea is that they are not the politics of the Dutch people, but that they are the politics of a very small coterie. Let us think what the politics are— non-education, drunken coloured labour, anti-Fleet vote, anti-the-North, favourable to the present policy in the Transvaal."[11] Better treatment of labor could be used in the service of patriotic politics.

Rhodes was able to establish a relatively high profile in the Western Cape's wine region. At one of his oldest vineyards, Boschendal, located in between Paarl and Stellenbosch, Rhodes had Baker design a cottage that could be used as a retreat from Groote Schuur. The small home was built in the Arts and Crafts style and was nestled at the foot of a mountain. Rhodes instructed Baker to create a structure that was "a record of simplicity and cheapness." According to Baker, "Though it was indeed a bare-walled, bare-boarded little building... he was quite content with it." From the front door, the view swept over the old vineyards. The existing settlements for the Coloured farm workers were not to Rhodes's taste, so a short distance from his cottage, Rhodes instructed Baker to build a model village for the workers. They named it Languedoc. It was intended to be a Western Cape version of Kenilworth, without alcohol. The cottages were simple but sturdy, designed in the Arts and Crafts style. Baker also built a school and a church.[12] Rhodes then paid the Coloured workers just enough cash that they would be eligible to vote in the Paarl electoral district. Rhodes had never been much of a supporter of voting rights for non-white South Africans, but in this case, he could set aside his racist principles to gain an electoral advantage over his neighbors from the Afrikaner Bond.

Rhodes saw his farms in the Western Cape and Rhodesia as the places where he would enact "the idea," what one biographer, John Flint, has called his "inner mystical, imperialist and racial 'dreams,'" an obsession that was "interconnected with a frequent brooding upon death, his own in particular, and with a concern for a heroic and immortal place in history."[13] Rhodes was transforming his ideas into a legacy. Like his early days in Kimberley, he moved easily between the vision and the material details. With Groote Schuur rebuilt after the fire, Rhodes traveled to Rhodesia in June 1897 and spent the rest of the year working on his farms. He was soon joined by Jameson, who had been freed from prison and who resumed his involvement with the BSAC. Jameson had performed poorly as an administrator and officer, but he was relatively fearless when it came to difficult journeys and negotiations. He now sought to redeem himself at Inyanga.

Inyanga, today called Nyanga, is located in the Eastern Highlands north of Umtali, near the border with Mozambique. Rhodes may have first heard about the area's mountains and valleys from Selous, who had passed through the area as early as 1878. Fifteen years later, the area was divided into claims for BSAC veterans. As they began work on their farms, the settlers made the area accessible by persuading the BSAC commissioner of works, the engineer, George Pauling, to build a road to Umtali, with labor and funds supplied by settler farmers. In 1974, a settler historian commented that this "was an excellent example of self-help."[14] This version of self-help really meant "help yourself" to African land and labor. In the early years of BSAC rule, it was common for public works to be built with labor coerced from African people who lived nearby.

Rhodes loved the views at Inyanga. He also found the location ideal for his agricultural experiments. After the conclusion of the 1896 war, he bought Inyanga and nine adjacent farms, totaling 96,000 acres. Rhodes continued the experiments of the original owners with apple trees. He tried experiments with cattle and sheep ranching, too, punctuated by the rinderpest epizootic, while locusts damaged early efforts at grain cultivation. Rhodes built a home on another one of the Inyanga farms, called Fruitfield, hiring an Umtali mason named Dickie Marks to construct a homestead and barn out of sturdy stone, as well as several outbuildings.[15]

Rhodes spent most of the second half of 1897 at Inyanga. At an altitude of 6,000 feet, Inyanga had fresh air and mountain breezes. There were views of Pungwe Falls and remains of ancient structures, which together gave the area a romantic feel. Rhodes's enjoyment was cut short by bad health. On top of his chronic cardiovascular difficulties, Rhodes suffered from another bout of malaria. Jameson came to his assistance.

Shortly after Jameson had been released from prison, Rhodes and the BSAC had entrusted him with negotiations with the Portuguese over the telegraph line that would run from Umtali and Inyanga northeast to Tete, in Mozambique, and from there to Blantyre in Nyasaland. Jameson and his servant, Garlick, set out on foot from Umtali and walked the length of the prospective line to Inyanga and from there all the way to Tete, just under three hundred miles. Jameson concluded his mission, a kind of pilgrimage of penance, by riding on the Zambezi River in a dugout canoe from Tete to the sea. The river was dangerous, and at one point, Jameson averted a mutiny of his crew by attacking the leader with a paddle. Jameson told a companion, Seymour Fort, that "this was the first time he had ever struck a K----r." Treated thus, "The K----rs grinned and obeyed." When Jameson reached the sea at Chinde, he hopped a steamer to Beira, then rode the riverboats and railroad trains back to Umtali and from there to Inyanga.[16] On arriving at Inyanga, Jameson once again played doctor and nurse to Rhodes, helping him to recover his health. The two men then vacationed together, spending time exploring the vicinity and working on the farm and getting to know local colonists.

Their time together was interrupted by a meeting with Milner, the governor-general and high commissioner, who was touring the area. Milner and Rhodes had attended Oxford at the same time but did not know each other. They had been introduced in 1889 by W. T. Stead, the influential journalist.[17] Now, in Rhodesia, the two men had their first experience negotiating with each other. Rhodes pushed Milner for the Bechuanaland Protectorate to be given again to the BSAC. Rhodes was keen, but Milner made no commitments. Milner believed that Rhodes could be a key ally in the plan to unify South Africa. Milner also knew that Rhodes would best be kept in line by having the carrot of the Bechuanaland Protectorate dangled before his nose. After meeting with Rhodes, Milner wrote to Selborne at the Colonial Office about the way in which he hoped to control Rhodes by using the Colossus's appetite for land against him:

> [We] can keep a hold on him for the present to a great extent *by means of the Protectorate*. Here we have still, by the mercy of Providence, something which he dearly wishes to get hold of. It [Bechuanaland] is rubbish . . . and troublesome and expensive rubbish. But it is well worth the trouble and expense, if Rhodes wants it, for in order to get it he will behave himself as he never would, if there was not something which he wanted to get out of us. Men are ruled by their foibles, and Rhodes's foible is <u>size</u>. He really will be little or no better off for having the Protectorate. It does not materially affect the game. But he looks at that big map. He sees on the one side the Cape Colony, of which he once was master and hopes to be again, on the other side is Rhodesia, of which he is master. Between the two he sees that huge patch, which he all but got once and is still without. It makes his mouth water and he will do all he can to get it. . . . Let him wait for it and deserve it.[18]

Milner hoped to use Bechuanaland "as a card in the general game."[19] Without any regard for the African people who lived in those spaces, Milner showed some understanding of the appeal of territoriality to imperialists, even if he overestimated his ability to discipline Rhodes.

The meeting at Umtali had been friendly, and the two men parted company prepared to cooperate. Even so, Milner was correct that Rhodes would not relent in his pursuit of more territory for the BSAC. In January 1898,

Milner and Rhodes met again in Cape Town. Rhodes accepted that it was unlikely that the BSAC would acquire the entire Bechuanaland Protectorate but still pressed Milner to allow the BSAC to govern an eastern strip of land near the railway that could be settled by colonists. Milner described Rhodes's sales pitch with annoyance: "He came down here about a week ago *full of the subject*, and bothers my life out over it."[20]

While in Cape Town, Rhodes spent more money on Inyanga. To get the farm started, his 1898 account book at De Beers reveals correspondence related to plants and livestock being selected for trial and shipped to the north.[21] At Inyanga, Rhodes employed two of his young assistants as managers, John Norris and fun-loving, unreliable Johnny Grimmer. Rhodes chose Grimmer because he enjoyed his company and had formed a special attachment to him.[22] Grimmer corresponded with Rhodes about the initial land purchases, then supervised the estate. Norris managed the estate's farming operations. Rhodes became frustrated when the early experiments with farming did not go well. In May 1899, Norris reported that livestock died, crops failed, and fruit trees did not grow. Conditions were challenging, with heavy rains and a swarm of locusts. Rhodes grew frustrated, at one point writing sarcastically to Norris that he feared "extinction by pecuniary exhaustion."[23]

With Inyanga struggling to launch, in 1898 the correspondence with Grimmer grew contentious. Grimmer claimed that when Rhodes left Inyanga, he did so precipitately. He informed Grimmer that he would correspond with him through the local magistrate, Scott Turner. Grimmer let Rhodes know that he was hurt. "You will know of course why I have never written, the one reason is your last sentence to me was 'let all your correspondence be done through Capt. Turner' and then you rode off without even saying goodbye. I have a heart and feelings and naturally was cut by such treatment." Grimmer reported to Rhodes about the details of their experiments with cattle, adding "You say you think the time has come when the farm should be paying for itself. If when starting the farm the idea had been given me that I have to make things pay after the first year I should have started things very differently to what they were. What I understood from you was that 'money was no object' and what you wanted was a place a la Groote Schuur and that the thing was to be done on a large scale and to be worked to pay after things were ship shape."[24] To add fuel to the fire, Rhodes also took issue with the laborers recruited from local African communities, requesting that the farm find several dozen Ndebele men instead.

Rhodes and his managers persevered through their agricultural and personal challenges, with Rhodes visiting again in July and August of 1900. By

1901, the farm was becoming successful. The orchards were thriving, with 1,400 trees about to bear fruit. Experiments with merino sheep had not worked out, but crosses of Cape sheep with Persian rams showed promise. A herd of several hundred cattle was starting to show success with Herefords, and Devons, and mixed breeds. Acorns were brought up from the Cape so that oak trees, symbols of royal power, could be grown by the entrance to the house.[25]

Inyanga was not Rhodes's only estate in Rhodesia. Near Bulawayo, Rhodes bought a farm that was originally owned by Hans Sauer. The doctor and conservationist had given up his lucrative practice as the district surgeon of Johannesburg to train in London as an attorney, then returned to Bulawayo, where he settled with his family at a location later called Sauer Township. After the 1893 war, the BSAC dispossessed Ndebele people and distributed their lands to white troopers in 3,000-acre parcels. Sauer owned a company that bought those parcels as investments and resold them. Sauer spent £500 on a block of properties totaling 62,000 acres on the southern edge of Bulawayo. He named the farm Sauerdale and three months later sold it to his friend, Cecil Rhodes, for £20,000.[26] The transaction was likely to have been a way for Rhodes to pay for Sauer's support. Rhodes hired farm managers to run Sauerdale, but judging by his correspondence, he took a personal interest in experiments with grain crops like maize, as well as efforts to grow alfalfa and potatoes. Experiments were made with different cattle breeds, as well as with the Angora goats descended from the ones that he acquired during his visit to the Ottoman sultan. The experimental animals, plants, and tools were paid for out of Rhodes's account at De Beers.[27]

At Sauerdale, McDonald introduced ostriches as well as new breeds of goats, sheep, and cattle. Rhodes's agronomist from the Western Cape, Harry Pickstone, advised McDonald and Rhodes about planting fruit trees and decorative trees. New crops were tried, while new plows and tools were delivered. Wells, dams, and irrigation systems were constructed. All manner of efforts by McDonald crossed Rhodes's desk, ranging from reports about the economic potential of remote districts, the Bulawayo Turf Club, and shopping for dining room furniture. Mining, railroads, and disputes about claims to land were all discussed. The letters show that Rhodes was involved with various experiments and even derived enjoyment from them. "A division is being made in the Ostrich Camp," wrote McDonald, "for breeding birds, as you suggested." McDonald continued: "In the new arrangement Huntley's sister will be the means of the cows being looked after & also the ostriches when they come. I told [Percy] Ross [a white tenant] you wanted to bet he'd only have a pair of trousers left in 2 years. 'Tell Mr. Rhodes,' he said in reply, 'that I'll have enough out of profits to buy him a pair,' which was rather a good answer."[28]

In 1899, McDonald forwarded a letter to Rhodes by one of the main white tenants, Huntley, who suggested that "I think the time has now arrived when your farms here should be put on a sound business basis so that they will prove profitable & be a lesson to South Africa." Huntley tried to persuade Rhodes that "cattle ranching must be the main industry, as it is the best means of turning to profit the existing advantages." Rhodes's white tenant advised him to practice the same kind of ranching that had been practiced by Ndebele people whose land and cattle were stolen by the BSAC. Huntley was not indicating that the Ndebele people deserved respect. On the contrary, with African tenants occupying fifty kraals near Sauerdale, Huntley advised Rhodes that he needed to demonstrate "complete control of native labour."[29]

Rhodes visited Sauerdale when it was necessary. One important occasion was the celebration of Queen Victoria's diamond jubilee, when Rhodes invited 150 indunas to a gathering. The indunas asked for Rhodes to address their complaints. They were concerned that the BSAC and even Rhodes himself were placing restrictions on what could, and could not, be grown on their land. They also voiced complaints about *lobola*, or bride price. *Lobola* was traditionally paid in cattle, but the BSAC's confiscations and the rinderpest made the practice difficult. Rhodes responded in his characteristic manner: "the best thing for them is to teach their young men to go out and work." Such a haughty comment might justifiably have provoked a riot. Instead, the *Bulawayo Chronicle* reported that Rhodes's confident approach with the aggrieved indunas carried the day:

> The changes of manner too as he put the different answers were remarkable, there was a touch of masterfulness when he said, "Tell Somabulana [an absent induna] that he had better come and see me." But coming to speak to the indunas individually Mr. Rhodes's manner underwent a startling change, it assumed a boyish exuberance and aspect of pleasure, which was immensely gratifying to the indunas personally known to him, and though the remarks might be the same, still, there was a suggestion conveyed to each of the circumstances under which they had last met, which indicated an extraordinarily capable memory.[30]

The newspaper recorded that the indunas responded with a chorus of "Nkos! Nkos!" which means "Lord." Rhodes continued to play the lord ten days later, when he hosted a crowd of more than a thousand Ndebele people as well as colonial settlers for his forty-fourth birthday party. Two hundred sheep were given away, together with gifts of tobacco and blankets. The beneficent Rhodes held court, too, resolving conflicts in the style of an African chief or an English lord of the manor.[31] After the Jameson Raid and the 1896 war, the British government was insisting that the BSAC take a more organized approach to "native administration." Rhodesia was to be governed by a BSAC administrator-in-council. Matabeleland and Mashonaland were then divided into districts and subdistricts, run by "native commissioners" and "assistant native commissioners." The informality and improvisation of Jameson's days were finished. Chiefs were appointed by the administrator-in-council and were turned into paid functionaries, subject to dismissal. One of their jobs was to administer the hut tax, using "native police." The administration laid out strict, written "Native Regulations" that were complained about extensively.[32] White settlers also complained bitterly about African laborers. After the end of the 1896 war, the editor of Salisbury's *Rhodesia Herald* newspaper opined:

> We have a worse class of [Shona] native to deal with than can be found throughout the whole length and breadth of South Africa. They are cowardly, cruel, treacherous and without an atom of gratitude in their nature. The Matabele are not much better. The vice of cowardice, however, cannot with equal truth be attributed to them.... The natives are children in everything but vice and therefore ought to be treated accordingly. We should treat them with firmness but justice, always impressing on them the wholesome fact that they are our inferiors, morally, socially, and mentally, and can never hope to be otherwise. If we try to do that which has been attempted in the past, viz.: to civilize them in as many years as it has taken centuries to civilize us, we shall not only ignominiously fail but hand this vexed question down to posterity, far more involved and complicated than we found it.[33]

White settlers and the BSAC administration pushed for forced labor on public works and even on private farms. Their views were so extreme that they could not get the approval of the high commissioner, Milner, who turned down colonist requests for forced labor, knowing that humanitarians in Britain would mobilize against such measures and defeat them. Under BSAC rule, African laborers were coerced to earn cash by having to pay taxes. By the time of Rhodes's death in 1902, rural African people were having their mobility constrained by a pass law, while their obligations under contracts were spelled out in a "masters and servants ordinance." Both sorts of laws were familiar to Black people living in South Africa. In Rhodesia, mine owners also started to restrict mobility by importing the closed compound system from Kimberley. The company followed empire-wide trends and made a stronger effort to support estate management, crop loans, and scientific agriculture.[34]

BSAC promoters still did not relent in their efforts to promote Rhodesia as a site for gold mining. In 1898, the BSAC sent teams under Francis Oats and Percy Tarbutt to explore gold prospects in Rhodesia. Oats found abandoned mines that he believed were not worth resuscitating; Tarbutt recommended modest investments in one mine. The hesitations of the engineers were balanced by Rhodes's friends Robert Williams and John Willoughby, who sent optimistic reports from Rhodesia in 1898 and from BSAC territories to the north in 1900. As late as 1900, the company displayed gold nuggets in London in an attempt to prove that Rhodesia had potential for mining. The London office sent newspaper clippings to Rhodes, with headlines such as "A Wonderful Strike" and "Marvels from Rhodesia." One paper reported "undeniable proof of the mineral riches of Rhodesia . . . more than anything before seen in this city [since] the rich finds of the Klondike," which occurred in northwestern Canada in 1896. Another paper ran a story called "A Rich Gold Discovery in Rhodesia," about the "solid masses of gold" that "weigh about 200 ozs., and represent only a small portion of the prospectors' find," although even that glowing report added an equivocation: "It is not maintained, of course, that these rich samples fairly represent the character of the reef from which they are taken." By then it was widely recognized that Rhodesia was not going to be El Dorado.[35]

White colonists were constantly reminded of the need for railroad construction, the key element of infrastructure for Rhodes's colonial plan. When rinderpest spread south of the Zambezi River in 1896, most of the region's transport oxen were killed. Not only did the epizootic cause famine and strife—it also drove up the cost of shipping freight by wagon. Without railroads, Rhodesia's farm products would be too expensive to compete on world markets. Although the failure of the Jameson Raid undermined the BSAC plan to administer the Bechuanaland Protectorate, the company still sought to build the railway along the eastern strip that bordered the Transvaal. In early 1896, Charles Metcalfe supervised the surveys of the proposed 500-mile line from Mafeking to Bulawayo. The placement of the line required negotiations with Chamberlain and Khama. In May 1896, Khama accepted payment for a narrow strip of land through his territory, allowing construction to begin. The line was built by the rail contractor, George Pauling, who was also the commissioner of public works in Rhodesia. To pay for all this, the BSAC used its subsidiary, the Bechuanaland Railway Company, to issue more debenture stocks in 1895 and again in 1897. The additional debentures were valued at £2,000,000, with the interest guaranteed by the BSAC. The British government contributed a subsidy of £200,000, while the Cape government offered to manage and maintain the line. The economic commitment to this undertaking was enormous by the standards of the day.[36]

The BSAC and its settlers believed that large financial commitments were crucial for the railways to be built so that produce would reach markets. Rhodes began to put in place the infrastructure that would make Rhodesia seem like a colony with good prospects. Metcalfe pushed railroad construction hard and fast, even cutting corners to get there on time. At the start of 1896, the rail reached as far as Mafeking, with lines connected to East London and Port Elizabeth as well as Cape Town. Trains ran nearly every day from Cape Town to Mafeking, a 54-hour journey. Passengers could continue on the Road to the North by stagecoach to Bulawayo, a 525-mile journey that lasted five or six days. Ox-wagons carried passengers and freight, too, taking longer on account of the slower pace. Railway construction was pushed along by the rinderpest and the revolt. Helen Townsend, spouse of railway engineer Stephen Townsend, recalled: "When rinderpest was so bad Mr. Rhodes urged everyone to get on with the railway to Bulawayo as quickly as possible, 'Even if you have to lay the tracks on the veld and not worry about embankments.'" By July of 1896, Metcalfe stretched the line from Mafeking to Gaborone in Bechuanaland. After Gaborone, Metcalfe built a temporary light rail to get from Gaborone to Palapye and from there all the way to Bulawayo.[37]

By May 1897 the railway line to Palapye was open, and in a final burst of construction, the line reached Bulawayo in October 1897. To mark the event, special trains brought dignitaries and guests from Cape Town to Bulawayo, including Milner, whose dedication speech kicked off a week of festivities. The Bulawayo railroad station was decorated with banners that read "Our Two Roads to Progress," "Railroads and Cecil Rhodes," and "Change Here for Zambezi." Two more banners read "Pro Bono Publico" [For the Public Good] and "Cui Bono" ["What Party Benefits?"]. Perhaps the sign-makers intended irony. Rhodes, feeling ill, did not attend.[38]

Not to be outdone by their comrades in Bulawayo, settlers in Salisbury pressed for the completion of the line from their home to Beira on the Mozambique coast. In November 1896, Rhodes attended a public meeting at which settlers complained and even asked for representation on the BSAC board. Rhodes exchanged messages with Metcalfe and Beit about rail construction, then wrote to the BSAC offices in London and Cape Town, instructing them to "act promptly." He sympathized with the settlers: "Owing to rinderpest there is no transport; cost of living is prohibitive and there is no hope for the future without immediate railway extension."[39] The construction of that route was technically challenging and very expensive. In spite of Rhodes's promises, the line from Beira to Salisbury was not completed until 1899.

The financing and organization of railway construction raised questions in South Africa and London. Investors in the City still regarded Rhodes as a middle-class upstart. Even Natty Rothschild was less than enthusiastic about investing in Rhodes's railway schemes. Metcalfe worked for the established engineering firm of John Fox and Sons, which helped to attract other investors. The contractor was George Pauling, the builder of the railway from Beira to Umtali who oversaw himself as the BSAC commissioner of public works. The actual construction was the responsibility of George Pauling's cousin, Harold Pauling, who had also supervised the construction of the line from Vryburg to Mafeking as an employee of the Cape Colony. The Bechuanaland Railway Company looked like a risky investment to the top-tier banks in the City of London. The railway was financed by a lower-profile firm, Baron d'Erlangers, which had experience in railroad development. The Paulings received a monopoly on railway construction in Rhodesia.

Together the Paulings Company, the BSAC, and Baron d'Erlangers engaged in dodgy financial practices. One historian who investigated the collaboration, Jon Lunn, calls it an "informal banking system," with the BSAC as the "central banker." The company, in turn, was bankrolled by its "friends" at De Beers and Gold Fields. Rhodes was using the BSAC to distance himself from the risks involved in building and maintaining the railroads, while positioning himself to reap the profits. Rhodes refused to pay extra when the construction ran into new problems, meaning that the contractors would be saddled with the expenses. One case illustrates the way in which the three companies resolved these tensions. In 1895, the Beira Railway Company was struggling as construction encountered problems. It sold its rights to part of the construction to another company, the London and Paris Exploitation Company, which was actually controlled by Baron d'Erlangers and Paulings. That company in turn set up another company to manage the construction, the Beira Junction Railway Company. Baron d'Erlangers called this deal "the craziest piece of finance with which I have ever been associated."[40]

The construction process involved passing risks from the BSAC to financiers and contractors. From there, risk was passed to subcontractors and laborers. There were two kinds of subcontractors. Some supervised technical work, such as plate-laying. Most of these subcontractors had regular, steady work with Paulings. There were also unskilled subcontractors who were typically British settlers. Often their mining and farming operations had not worked out, so they sought opportunities in construction. Some were regular followers of the Paulings. The unskilled subcontractors supervised all aspects of earthworks, including the heavy work of making cuttings through hills and building embankments. Paulings recruited their unskilled African workers through BSAC administrators called "native commissioners." In the 1890s, native commissioners and their armed assistants simply walked into villages and seized laborers to work on the railroad. The working conditions were often terrible, involving digging and hauling dirt in low-lying country that was infested by mosquitos. Many workers became ill and died. Physical violence was common.[41]

The contractors who built the Beira Railway faced significant challenges from Mozambican geography. The tracks from Beira to Umtali were made only two feet wide, so that they could be built around the contours of the landscape. This allowed the company to avoid digging straight tracks through hills, but it also meant that trains would have to run at slower speeds. The segment from Umtali to Salisbury was constructed to the normal South African gauge of three feet, six inches, which was significantly faster. Goods were unloaded from two-foot wagons and put on the 3-foot, 6-inch wagons until 1900, when the Umtali to Beira segment was upgraded to the 3-foot, 6-inch gauge. Floods along the Pungwe River slowed construction on the eastern side of the track. The tracks rose in elevation from 650 feet to 2,029 feet above sea level over the course of the third 25-mile segment from Beira. Europeans died from malaria, while oxen died from trypanosomiasis. Local African laborers were not attracted by the relatively low wage of one shilling a day, plus food. The company made up the labor shortfall by importing workers from India, but many of these men became sick and some of them died.

Rhodes knew that when it came to rail construction, it was best to get the basics done first, aiming for a quick connection to Salisbury that would satisfy the settlers. Rhodesia's settlers described what it was like to travel to Salisbury from Beira. One passenger, Percy Shinn, described arriving at Beira in a tug, whose captain first deliberately ran his boat aground "on a sandbank where," Shinn observed, "we remained until the stock of liquor was sold out, then he managed to get off and proceed on his journey." The railway began at nearby Fontesvilla, which Shinn described as a "city consisting of a few mud huts, each hut fitted up with six canvas stretcher beds, and a kind of eating house where we got some sort of meal." Another traveler, Edith Campbell, described the train itself, "a queer-looking concern, very narrow and only a couple of carriages and about three engines. The carriages are long narrow things with hard seats and 10 inches wide. The train conveniently slackened off for hunters to shoot at each herd of game." At one point, the train slipped off the tracks. While the crew and passengers waited for another engine to arrive, "a man came along on a trolley with a basket of meat, some gin and beer." The journey continued along an uphill line that was "comical." It was "a zigzag on the side of a hill and the train is pushed backwards and forwards to get to the top of the hill." The bridges were especially hair-raising. In the words of a staffer, Duncan Bailey, "When the Siluvu hills are reached, right up 4,000 ft. to Umtali the scenery is magnificent, the little railway winding over gorges and through lovely valleys. There were few bridges, but one I noticed was of timber, the sleepers being about 3 ft. apart with nothing between them, and the rails held on with nails in places."[42]

Pauling wrote a memoir about railway construction and commented on what it was like to work with Rhodes. In one story, Rhodes and Pauling were in Mozambique, where the Colossus took advantage of his executive position to bully his subcontractors and foremen. The tracks had not yet reached Umtali when Rhodes and Jameson arranged for a special train to take them from Chimoio, then at the railhead, to the coast. The train arrived and the subcontractor, Arthur Lawley, had to stop work and wait for Rhodes and Jameson to arrive. Pauling wrote that when the BSAC chiefs' stagecoach finally pulled up to the campsite, Rhodes disembarked and asked: "Are you Lawley?"

> Lawley replied that he was, whereupon Mr. Rhodes commenced to swear and to abuse him in the presence not only of the visiting party, but of everyone, including about a thousand natives engaged at the platelaying camp. As was usual with Mr. Rhodes when he became excited or lost his temper his remarks were characterised by a gradual crescendo of unparliamentary language until he attained a high falsetto tone. As Lawley's instructions had been carried out to the letter, he was completely astounded, and for some time he listened in the hope of ascertaining the cause of the trouble. No explanation, however, was forthcoming, and, realising that he was being stultified in the presence of his subordinates, he lost his temper and opened fire by saying to Mr. Rhodes: "Who the H--- are you, and who do you think you are talking to, squealing at me like a damned rabbit. Damn your eyes;

I won't allow any man on earth to speak to me like that. Are you mad?" There followed such a flood of railway vernacular as was the admiration of the assembly with the exception, perhaps, of Mr. Rhodes who was so astonished at Lawley's unexpected daring that he turned on his heels and walked away to a clump of trees about a hundred yards from the train.[43]

Lawley then directed the laborers to put Rhodes's and Jameson's baggage on the train and told the two men they had five minutes before the train left. Later, on board the train, Rhodes made peace with Lawley. White working men could be the subject of Rhodes's ire, but generally he treated them with paternalism, as was expected of an English gentleman. Special cases received charity, including wounded BSAC troopers and the widows of miners. African workers were generally ignored.

The construction of the railroad to Rhodesia encouraged plans for imperial expansion farther north. What was to become Northern Rhodesia, later known as Zambia, was officially under the administration of the BSAC, while the British government had been responsible for Nyasaland, later known as Malawi, since 1894. Harry Johnston remained in Nyasaland as the commissioner. Like Rhodes, he had a plan to transform his territory through colonial settlement and railways, which were important for Northern Rhodesia. Nyasaland's Shire highlands were thought to be suitable for European-style agriculture. Johnston even believed that the protectorate could become "as valuable as Ceylon." The key to success involved funneling African workers toward the white-owned farms and away from labor as porters. Porters had been needed to carry goods back and forth between the Shire Highlands and Quelimane on the central coast of Mozambique. In 1895, Johnston began to advocate for a railroad to be built from Blantyre to Quelimane. This would have been the most direct and sensible colonial infrastructure project, but decisions about trade by the colonial powers hobbled the colony's development. Goods sent from British Blantyre by rail to Portuguese Quelimane would be charged a customs duty. One settler, Eugene Sharrer, proposed an alternative plan which was later accepted: to leave the Zambezi River and its tributaries open to free trade. Sharrer proposed that the railway run from Blantyre to the Shire River. Goods could be unloaded and then sent downriver to the Zambezi River and out to sea. Sharrer's plan attracted prominent British investors, but the plan failed to earn the traditional support that rail projects received from the imperial government, the guarantee on the payment of interest. The project was not taken up during Rhodes's lifetime but remained under consideration for decades until an alternative plan was ultimately chosen, financed by the impoverished colony of Nyasaland.[44]

The international diplomacy related to the new colonies became complex. In 1899, the British government reached a secret agreement with the German government to partition Mozambique, if a conflict with Portugal ever presented the opportunity for conquest. The British would take the area south of the Zambezi River, including the territories of the Zambezi Company and the Mozambique Company, while the Germans would take the northern part that came under the Nyassa Company. Conflict, occupation, and partition never happened, but the agreement is instructive in that it shows the extent to which imperialist aggression was contemplated by both the British and German governments.[45]

20

Falling Short

WITH HIS HEALTH failing and his influence waning, Rhodes had some success in agriculture and railway construction. His mining companies continued to be productive and profitable. And even his efforts to re-enter Cape politics met with a degree of success. He remained a member of the Cape House of Assembly and in 1898 came close to becoming prime minister again. It was in promoting new, imperialist projects that Rhodes's reach exceeded his grasp.

On the way home from England in 1893, he passed through Cairo, where he met Herbert Horatio Kitchener, the irascible British general in charge of Egypt's armed forces.[1] Rhodes and Kitchener had personal connections. Both men were Freemasons, and Kitchener knew Rhodes's brother Frank, who had served together with him in the 1885 campaign to rescue Charles Gordon at Khartoum. Cecil Rhodes kept in touch with Kitchener during the British conquest of the Sudan, which began in 1896 and which involved the construction of the famous Sudan Military Railway by the Canadian engineer Percy Girouard. After the attempted coup in the Transvaal, Kitchener allowed the disgraced Frank Rhodes to follow the army back to the Sudan as a journalist. On September 6, 1898, Rhodes congratulated Kitchener on winning the Battle of Omdurman. "Glad you beat the Khalifa," Rhodes wrote in a telegram. "We have just finished our elections and result promises to be a tie. [Rhodes eventually lost.] I hear Frank is wounded. They certainly should now restore his commission. His heart is set on it." Next Rhodes reminded Kitchener of his broader ambitions: "My telegraph will shortly be at south side of [Lake] Tanganyika. If you don't look sharp, in spite of your victory I shall reach Uganda before you."[2] Kitchener insisted that the Sudan railway be built with the Cape gauge of three and a half feet, imagining, like Rhodes, that a connection was feasible. Rhodes was so impressed that when three BSAC locomotives were being shipped from England via Suez, he allowed Kitchener to borrow them.

Kitchener and Rhodes both supported the Cape-to-Cairo scheme, but the idea was impractical. It was more economical for people and goods to take ships up and down the east coast of Africa, where the interior of the continent could be accessed by shorter rail lines running from the coasts to the center. However, Rhodes still argued that the Cape-to-Cairo scheme, built in segments by the Bechuanaland Railway, would provide access for future mining companies. Rhodes advertised another possible benefit of a rail line from Central Africa: cheap labor. "The enormous demand for labour for the Mines at Kimberley, Johannesburg, and in Rhodesia, have caused the wages for unskilled labour to reach an unduly high figure," he wrote to Chamberlain, adding, "At the De Beers Mine, wages at the rate of £1 per week are being paid for labour which can be readily obtained North of the Zambesi for 2d. per diem." The railway would help solve the problem of high wages in South Africa's mines. He continued: "The Natives in these Northern Districts are anxious to obtain work, but, so far, the great distances which they have had to cover on foot have prevented extensive employment of their services." Rhodes imagined long-term benefit to the mines: "On the completion of the projected railway there is every possibility of large numbers of labourers being constantly carried to and from the Mining Districts, of a highly remunerative traffic being thus established, and of a considerable benefit being at the same time conferred upon the most important industry of South Africa." Seeing a connection between private and public good, Rhodes proposed to Chamberlain that the railway be financed by the Cape Colony, with the collateral provided by the existing tracks of the Bechuanaland Railway, a public-private partnership. Rhodes hoped that the railway and the state would be closely intertwined. A "strong administration" would be needed. Rhodes reflected on the past and urged authoritative rule. "Experience has conclusively shown," wrote Rhodes, "that the contact of European civilisation with barbarism will always result in Native wars and disturbances unless authority can be effectively exercised."[3]

Rhodes dispatched an exploration party to gather information about the geography and politics along the railroad's proposed route north to Lake Tanganyika. The reports featured references to the detrimental effects of slave-raiding. Rhodes emphasized the importance of the line to civilization and to trade, especially when the main north-south line would be connected to east-west lines that were expected to run to the coast. The discussions with Chamberlain and the Colonial Office bogged down over finances. The notion of laborers shuttling from Central Africa to Kimberley and the Witwatersrand was appealing from the standpoint of colonial development, but it was widely known that the BSAC, a central party to the scheme, had not yet paid a dividend.[4]

Practical people were becoming wary of backing another one of Rhodes's schemes. In 1899, a critique appeared in *Munsey's*, a prominent magazine published in New York. The author, an American colonel named Henry G. Prout, had served in the Egyptian administration of the Sudan as a surveyor, engineer, and governor and was currently the editor of a trade publication, *Railroad Gazette*. Prout wrote in *Munsey's* that Rhodes's "scheme is so grand and brilliant that it captures the swift imagination, and the laggard judgment cannot catch up." But catching up was necessary. Using estimates from British army engineers, he calculated the expense of the Cape-to-Cairo line would be double Rhodes's estimate of £10,000,000 and that the line would never pay enough "to compete with the ocean routes." Prout proposed instead that the freight could be unloaded onto steamboats that ran up and down the Great Lakes but that it would be preferable for rail lines to run from the interior to the coast. Prout believed that "the world seems to have taken Mr. Rhodes's plan for granted—it is so brilliant and so 'imperial.'" It was also unworkable.[5]

Rhodes and Sivewright hoped that a Cape-to-Cairo telegraph might be easier to achieve than a railway, but it, too, was never completed. The telegraph from Vryburg to Salisbury belonged to the BSAC, although Rhodes had to pay for it out of his own pocket. Rhodes planned for the next major telegraph line to be built northeast from Salisbury to Blantyre, in the Shire Highlands of Nyasaland. It was his overall hope that the line builders would overcome challenging geography and run the line as far as Khartoum, the endpoint of Egypt's system. From there the line would connect to Wadi Halfa and then to Cairo and Alexandria. The Rhodes Papers in Oxford contain detailed letters from surveyors, including reports on the local geography and the people who were encountered. The collection contains detailed maps, too, depicting the proposed lines of the telegraph as it ran from station to station across the length of the continent.[6]

To promote the transcontinental telegraph, Rhodes engaged in high-level diplomacy. In 1898, a standoff occurred between British and French troops at Fashoda, in the South Sudan, the exact point where Rhodes hoped that the Africa Trans-Continental Telegraph Company (ATT) line would enter Sudan. Meanwhile the Germans were siding with the Boer republics in their conflicts with Rhodes and the British Empire. The outcome of Rhodes's negotiations would determine whether the line would run along the eastern shore of Lake Tanganyika, in German East Africa, or along the western shore, in Leopold's private colony, the Congo Free State. At an 1899 luncheon with King Leopold II of Belgium, Rhodes proposed a merger of the BSAC and the Congo Free State, an idea that Leopold found unappealing. Rhodes failed to find common ground and wrote that Leopold haggled "like a Jew" to regain access to territory along the Upper Nile. Walking out of the room, Rhodes whispered to the British military attaché: "Satan, I tell you that man is Satan."[7]

The failed lunch with Leopold meant that the future of the transcontinental telegraph and railway was riding on the negotiations with the Germans. Luckily for Rhodes, the erratic Kaiser Wilhelm II was impressed with him. The Kaiser, who had congratulated Kruger on the roundup of Jameson and the BSAC at Doornkop, took a liking to Rhodes and said to the British ambassador, Frank Lascelles, "What a man he is. Why is he not my Minister? With him I could do anything." Rhodes was allowed to build his telegraph and railway in German territory, along the eastern shore of Lake Tanganyika, in exchange for Rhodes promising to put in a good word with the British government over the Berlin-to-Baghdad railway, the Kaiser's own imperialist technopolitical ambition.[8] Formal permission from the German government proceeded in stages. In March of 1899, the ATT line reached Abercorn (Mbala), on the south end of Lake Tanganyika near the border between BSAC territory and German East Africa. Rhodes wanted to continue construction in order to keep his crews together. He asked for the intervention of the British Foreign Office in support of the construction. "What about my telegraph," he demanded in a telegram. "Should not like enter German Territory without authority. The only alternative dismissing whole staff."[9] Rhodes got what he wanted. The ATT crews continued to work, pending a final agreement, which came in November 1899. Rhodes and the German government reached understandings over the details of access and pricing as well as the mobility of crews working on the line.

Rhodes reported to his partners that the agreement he signed with the German foreign ministry left the door open for the "contemplated railway which is to cross German East Africa from Rhodesia to British East Africa."[10] In the conversations with the Germans, Rhodes was assisted by a diplomat, Edmund Davis, who wrote to Rhodes's partner, Beit, that "I have had a great deal of trouble to get this conceded, and the Government was most anxious to absolutely debar the Chartered Company from connecting its railway system with the coast in any other manner than through the German Protectorate." Davis was not just talking about German East Africa. He suspected that "it is quite probable that the German Government will eventually take possession of Angola," the Portuguese colony on the west coast. Davis concluded that "the whole of this railway agreement really amounts to an obligation for the Rhodesian Railway system to be connected with the West African Coast."[11]

Rhodes continued to push strongly for the transcontinental telegraph. In characteristic fashion, he was engaged in high-level planning while keeping up with technical details. One example of Rhodes's technical interests involved telegraph poles. For the most part telegraph components were imported from England. Correspondence kept in his papers indicates that Rhodes was consulted about problems that were unique to Africa, including the type of wood, the chemical treatment of wood, the methods of transportation, and the tools used for installation.[12] Rhodes and his colleagues devoted much correspondence to modifying poles for the local environment. The wooden poles were knocked over by elephants, and they were also eaten by termites. The solution was to purchase poles made of iron, but these were heavy. Draught animals could not be easily used between Salisbury, Blantyre, and Ujiji because of tsetse flies. Porters had to carry the poles from the nearest port or railhead, so Rhodes and his technical advisers devised an ingenious solution. The cast-iron poles were custom manufactured in Yarrow, England, in three pieces: a circular base plate with a hole in the center; a four-foot-long tube that served as the base; and an upper tube that was capable of carrying the telegraph hardware and wires. The technical details, pricing, and manufacture absorbed Rhodes and required him to extend his network. To make an informed decision, Rhodes reviewed correspondence with officials in Australia, where steel poles were used in a transcontinental telegraph line. He also studied reports of experiments done in Dar es Salaam to evaluate whether treated wooden telephone poles withstood termites well.[13]

The challenges of constructing the African Transcontinental Telegraph were the subject of an appreciative article in *Scientific American*, which showed the extent to which Rhodes cultivated a positive public image. "It will be remembered," wrote the author, "that the idea of thus connecting the northern and southern extremities of this vast continent, and also providing a new trunk overland telegraph route to England, emanated from the Rt. Hon. Cecil Rhodes, and it is mainly through his energy and enterprise that the scheme is being realized." The project was described as a geographical triumph: "Certainly the construction of such a line, which when complete will measure approximately 5,600 miles in length, is a momentous achievement, especially when it is remembered that the greater part of the line extends through practically unknown country." The article followed the surveying party of three white engineers "and a sufficient army of blacks to carry their apparatus and necessities." According to the story, "Natives have to be requisitioned by the surveyors for the conveyance of their baggage." The exploration was dangerous, at various points passing "over extremely mountainous territory," with steep drops into lakes and wide ravine. The party had to pass "through one of the most obscure, inaccessible, and pestilential parts of the dark continent." The article featured one photograph of a special metal telephone pole, as well as a picture of one of the steamboats used to carry supplies along one of the lakes.[14]

The process of surveying and building the telegraph line resembled the way in which the railways were built in earlier decades. Once again, John Fox and Sons provided the engineering. The construction parties included ten white supervisors and a crew of a thousand African migrant workers. The dangers of labor unrest and external enemies was perceived to be so great, that one letter to Rhodes from the civil commissioner of Umtali, Scott Turner, recommended that the party be accompanied by a force of 100 Indian soldiers, armed with a Maxim gun and a six-pounder cannon.[15] To make matters worse, malaria, dysentery, and sleeping sickness were common, and in 1900 there was an outbreak of smallpox. Each day, the surveyors and two hundred laborers went ahead of the main party, selecting and clearing a route that was fifteen feet wide. Next, the second party widened the path to sixty feet across. Then teams followed to dig the holes, place the poles, and string the wires. The environment was challenging. The line crossed swamps, forests, and slopes. Workers were attacked by lions and crocodiles. On a good day, the laborers could finish two or three miles of the telegraph line.[16]

Rhodes's transcontinental telegraph was not completed in his lifetime. There were constant financial headaches. The first stretch of line was planned to run from Salisbury as far north as the mission station at Bandawe, in the central part of the western shore of Lake Nyasa. The estimated cost of construction was £140,000. Rhodes hoped to find subscribers and had some initial success, with a £10,000 stake taken by mining magnate Abe Bailey. The rest of the shares did not sell well, and Rhodes had to personally finance two-thirds of the construction. He persuaded the BSAC to pay for the rest. The attack on the original line from Salisbury to Mazoe and the decision to reroute via Umtali cost £40,000. Constructing the line from Abercorn to Ujiji was especially costly to the BSAC. Its total cost was £160,000. The ATT line was surveyed as far as Kisumu in eastern Kenya, on the shores of Lake Victoria. The Uganda Railway ended in Kisumu, so it was a logical location for connecting a telegraph, but the line from Salisbury was never completed. In 1903 it reached its farthest extent at Ujiji, on the north end of Lake Tanganyika, 700 miles to the southeast of Kisumu. The ATT was not a commercial success. Nine years after Rhodes's death, the company went out of business.[17]

Rhodes's telegraph extended as far as it was geographically possible. Although the line to Ujiji fell short of Khartoum by 2,000 miles, the achievement was still impressive. As far as the Cape-to-Cairo scheme was concerned, Rhodes had achieved more in telegraphy than he had in railroads, which had posed greater diplomatic problems. Imperial governments knew that railroads could be used for moving troops quickly through Africa, which raised the stakes considerably. After the Jameson Raid, the British government was of two minds over Rhodes's efforts to promote a continental railroad. Chamberlain still backed Rhodes's north-south proposal, possibly fearing French rivals, or he may have feared the release of the telegrams about the Jameson Raid. The Conservative Chancellor of the Exchequer, Michael Hicks Beach, put his foot down. The Treasury rejected Rhodes's request for guarantees of interest on the capital investment in the railroad, a traditional way for the government to back construction. Rhodes was furious, writing that Hicks Beach was "not fit to be treasurer to a village council and yet is in charge of an Empire." Hicks Beach refused to be manipulated.[18]

Rhodes pushed ahead with the construction of the railway north from Bulawayo. The board of De Beers refused to fund the construction. Rhodes threatened a fight among the shareholders and even resignation, but Natty Rothschild smoothed over the waters.[19] The banker arranged for separate financing from his own bank and from other investors, including Beit and the BSAC. Rhodes expressed the hope that the line would cross the Zambezi River at Victoria Falls. Rhodes would not live to see the breathtaking bridge opened in 1905. He knew, from Frederick Burnham's 1895 Northern Expedition, that there were African copper miners at work near the border with Katanga. Rhodes did live just long enough to have these early reports of copper deposits confirmed. Rhodes assigned the BSAC's rights to the Tanganyika Concessions Company, headed by his old friend from Kimberley, Robert Williams. Copper exploration and mining then began in earnest. By 1910, the railway stretched all the way north to Katanga. The railway to Cairo never came to pass.[20]

Rhodes's schemes for railways and telegraphs unfolded in the context of an attempted political comeback. In April 1897 he returned to Cape Town and once again took up his seat in the Cape House of Assembly, then being led by a caretaker ministry under Gordon Sprigg. Sprigg was forced to balance the demands of the Afrikaner Bond, which was now financed by Kruger, and those of a coalition of English-speakers that included Progressives. Merriman threatened Sprigg with a vote of no confidence, which Rhodes stymied by distributing money and calling in favors. Rhodes supported Sprigg at least in part because his government had promulgated a strict law in the Transkei that allowed police to arrest any African person who looked suspicious and lock them up for three months before they might appear before a magistrate. Years later, the apartheid government of South Africa would call this practice "detention without trial."[21]

Returning to the Cape Parliament for the session of 1898, Rhodes took over the leadership of the Progressives. Many of their members favored union and supported an aggressive stance against the Boer republics. To hold together the disparate Progressives, Rhodes even reconciled himself with the liberals, seeing that there might be some electoral advantage in supporting the expansion of the franchise for townspeople. Rhodes and his party even advocated for "Equal Rights for Civilized Men." To some Cape liberals, that meant extending the franchise to propertied African and Coloured men. Although he never advocated for racial equality, Rhodes, under electoral pressure, was open to considering some African and Coloured men as "civilized." His friend, banker, and biographer Lewis Michell explained what Rhodes meant by "Equal Rights for Civilized Men," a phrase that he deployed frequently in the last years of his life. According to Michell, Rhodes "adhered without flinching to his old formula that an educated coloured man should be permitted, if otherwise qualified, to exercise the franchise." Michell's explanation included a facsimile of a note that Rhodes penned on a scrap of paper. Rhodes scribbled, "My motto is / equal rights for every civilized man South of the Zambezi. / What is a civilized man / a man whether white or black who has / sufficient education to write his name, has some support, or works / in fact is not a slacker. C. J. Rhodes."[22]

In his quest to become prime minister again, Rhodes bankrolled the Progressives, placing stories in the newspapers and distributing contributions far and wide. In 1898, parliamentary maneuvering resulted in a vote of no confidence in Sprigg, which then prompted an election. With the election closely contested, Rhodes made stronger efforts to court the votes of African people. He funded a newspaper, *Izwi laBantu*, run by Allan Kirkland Soga, the son of the famous Xhosa missionary and translator Tiyo Soga. A follower of the African American scholar and priest Alexander Crummell and a graduate of Glasgow University, A. K. Soga supported Pan Africanism and the notion that African people on both sides of the Atlantic were responsible for their own "regeneration." A. K. Soga supported rights for African people— and in 1912 would be one of the founders of the South African Native National Congress, which became the African National Congress in 1923. It may seem odd that such a journalist would receive support from Rhodes. His thoughts on A. K. Soga are not recorded, but there may have been some common ground. Rhodes did believe that African societies could be pressured and dismantled to foster economic and political development. Rhodes may also have found Pan Africanism congenial to his thinking. The early Pan Africanists were socially conservative. They rejected colonialism, but they used terms like civilization and race in much the same way as white Victorians did. Hopes for racial improvement took for granted the idea that Black people had fallen behind white people.[23]

Rhodes followed through by speaking against the Parliamentary Registration Law Amendment Bill of 1899, which would have taken votes away from African and Coloured men. Rhodes argued that he had "always differentiated between the raw barbarians and the civilised natives" and reaffirmed that he believed in giving "equal rights to every civilised man south of the Zambezi." Again, there is little direct evidence about a positive shift in Rhodes's racial thinking. His statements about civilization, like the ones of the Pan Africanists, were still laden with racial and separatist assumptions. His statements can also be read in the context of political necessity.[24]

Rhodes used his account at De Beers to bankroll his political activities. Campaign spending did not go unnoticed by board members in Kimberley and London, some of whom objected to using company funds for partisan purposes. Fred Stow, who had fallen out with Rhodes years earlier over the issue of life governorships, was now secretary of the London board of De Beers. He wrote to the Kimberley board that "the Board of Directors should not launch the Company upon a political campaign in South Africa or elsewhere.... I more particularly object to the way in which the expenditure of considerable funds is intrusted to an individual Director ... under the pretext of promoting the welfare of the Shareholders in Mining Ventures in distant parts of Africa away from the Company's centre of action, and in metals or ores with which the Company has hitherto had nothing to do, and for which there is no real foundation or necessity."[25]

Rhodes soon learned that a full political comeback was not going to happen. The Progressives won the overall popular vote, but the Bond won a slight majority of seats. The Bond was generally antagonistic to Rhodes, so the new governor, Alfred Milner, could not appoint Rhodes to the premiership. Rhodes met with Milner and argued forcefully that the results were so close that Sprigg should be kept on again as a caretaker. Instead, Milner properly turned to the Bond's candidate, Will Schreiner.[26] Rhodes had little interest in leading the opposition, a role that required parliamentary tactics more than grandiose speeches. In the 1899 session, he spoke out against Will Schreiner and his old friend John Merriman, who was now on the side of the Bond. Rhodes became a strong backer of Alfred Milner, who moved aggressively against Kruger in the Transvaal.

White sentiment favored imperialism, but Rhodes still had plenty of detractors. An appearance at Oxford became controversial. Back in 1892, when Rhodes was at the height of his career, the university voted to confer on him a Doctor of Civil Laws. Traditionally, honorary degrees must be collected in person, but Rhodes had not had the time to accept this honor from his alma mater. Oxford contacts reminded him occasionally, and in 1899 he decided to attend the degree ceremony. Rhodes's fellow honorees included Victor Bruce, Lord Elgin, the viceroy of India; C. H. Parry, the composer best known for the patriotic hymn "Jerusalem"; the cultural anthropologist James Frazer of Cambridge; and Herbert Kitchener, the British general and Rhodes's friend. When word got out that Rhodes would collect his award, dozens of Oxford professors, including some of the university's most prominent leaders, protested in speeches and in writing.

The critical dons received their comeuppance from the British establishment when the Duke of York, the future King George V, made a public defense of Rhodes. Rhodes was also defended by Kitchener, who was riding a crest of popularity after winning the lopsided Battle of Omdurman. Kitchener informed the university that he would skip the ceremony if the degree were withheld from Rhodes. Under fire from Kitchener and the Duke of York, the university stuck to its original decision to present the award. The day before the ceremony, Kitchener and Rhodes went horseback riding together in Hyde Park. The next day they rode the train together from Paddington to Oxford, where the ceremony was held at the Sheldonian Theatre. When Rhodes collected his degree, the Latin citation compared him to Scipio Africanus and Scipio Aemilianus, who had laid waste to Carthage. Except for this classical reference, which could be read either as support or criticism, there were no protests. Rhodes was applauded when he collected his degree. His luncheon speech at Oriel College was uncharacteristic, in that he admitted mistakes. He had "done things which savoured rather of violence" but excused himself from any misdeeds, since the rules in South Africa were different from the rules in Britain.[27] Rhodes and Kitchener then left Oxford. The sword had proven mightier than the pen.

Triumph had to be balanced against failing health and looming war. To make matters even worse, Rhodes, whose plans for northern colonialism had originally unfolded as a confidence scheme, himself became the mark of a brilliant con artist. Yekaterina Rzewuska was the daughter of a Polish aristocrat. She was married to Prince Wilhelm Radziwill, with whom she had five children. As Catherine Radziwill, she flourished as a socialite at the Prussian court during the early 1880s. She was a gifted raconteur and linguist, fluent in Polish, German, Russian, French, and English. In 1885, at the age of thirty, she published a gossipy account of the Prussian court that got her family kicked out of Berlin. She settled in St. Petersburg but traveled often in Europe, especially after she became separated from her husband. In London, she became acquainted with Rhodes's good friend Stead, the journalist who shared Rhodes's mystical passion for "the idea" of extending British settlement to the far corners of the world. In 1894, more gossip, a collapsing marriage, and a new tsar got her kicked out of St. Petersburg. She turned up in London with only her cleverness to support her lifestyle. She used her talents to become a fixture of London society. Her network included journalists, aristocrats, and financiers, several of whom shared connections to Rhodes.

Catherine Radziwill met Rhodes at a dinner in 1896, but it was not until 1899 that she set her sights on him. Rhodes, Metcalfe, and Rhodes's private secretary, Philip Jourdan, were settling down for their first meal on board a

Princess Catherine Radziwill. Library of Congress, LC-DIG-ggbain-24265.

ship bound for Cape Town, when Radziwill sat down with them and hijacked the conversation. She charmed her way into Rhodes's company for the entire voyage, at one point even fainting into his arms outside by the ship's rail. Rhodes helped her to establish herself in Cape Town, where she spent several years networking with colonial politicians and visiting frequently at Groote Schuur. She may have been attracted to Rhodes. She even invented stories about their upcoming marriage. Rhodes was not attracted to her and vacillated about whether he should continue his friendship with her, until he learned that she was stealing his documents and forging his name. The police were notified and caught her faking an insurance claim for stolen jewelry. In 1902, she was tried and sentenced to two years in jail.[28]

Although the story of Catherine Radziwill is not central to understanding Rhodes, her presence in Rhodes's circle illustrates the decline of his social network in the wake of the Jameson Raid. The exception to the rule—and by far the most interesting figure to enter Rhodes's network at the end of his life— was Rudyard Kipling. Kipling was twelve years younger than Rhodes and had first met him in Cape Town in 1891, when the author was just starting to be recognized for early works such as *Plain Tales from the Hills* (1888) and *The City of Dreadful Night* (1890). Kipling spent the next few years traveling and, with his wife, Carrie, lived for several years in Vermont with her family before they moved to England. Kipling published *Barrack-Room Ballads* (1892) and the two parts of *The Jungle Books* (1894 and 1895), followed by *Captains Courageous* (1897). In the late 1890s he was one of the best-known authors in the English language, with a social network that included the likes of Andrew Carnegie, Henry James, and Theodore Roosevelt.

When Kipling, Carrie, and their three children arrived in Cape Town, the celebrity author was welcomed into Rhodes's circle. Kipling became such a frequent guest at Groote Schuur that Rhodes purchased a home nearby called The Woolsack and converted it into a guest house, where Kipling and his family stayed for ten summers. Similar likes and dislikes may explain why Rhodes and Kipling struck up a friendship that was based on their mutual interests. Both men were Freemasons and imperialists who were fond of the outdoors and conventional masculine pursuits. Both men believed in the importance of race for explaining the workings of the world.[29] Kipling and Rhodes also shared an interest in the United States, which Rhodes had never visited. Kipling published his famous poem "The White Man's Burden" while getting to know Rhodes. The poem summarized the ironies of imperialism for Americans just becoming acquainted with their "new-caught, sullen" Philippine Islands. While campaigning to expand the empire, Rhodes's

Rudyard Kipling. Wikimedia Commons.

personal style tended toward Stoic simplicity. Kipling had a soft spot for common soldiers and a reflexive dislike for high-ranking officers. He also disliked evangelicals, pacifists, liberals, and most literati, the sorts of people who were not invited to Groote Schuur. Kipling and Rhodes also had a layperson's appreciation of industrial technology. Kipling had written several short stories, such as "The Bridge-Builders" and "The Devil and the Deep Blue Sea," that, in the words of his biographer, David Gilmour, "contain such a mass of technical detail that they are not only irritating but often incomprehensible to readers who are less fascinated than the author by bridge construction and marine engineering." Kipling's ".007" and "The Ship that Found Herself" even personify engines and ships.[30]

It was Kipling's sense that the British Empire was diminishing. In 1897, he caused a stir when he published a poem in *The Times* called "Recessional." It was written to mark Queen Victoria's Diamond Jubilee, but the poem surprised readers with its chiding, solemn tone. A recessional is a hymn that is sung at the end of a service as the clergy are processing down the aisle to exit the church. Kipling wrote his "Recessional" so that it could be set to the solemn tune of "Melita" by John Bacchus Dykes. Dykes's tune is usually set to the words of the hymn "Eternal Father, Strong to Save," written in 1860 by William Whiting to be sung at navy funerals. Churchgoers of the 1890s would have recognized the song's funerary pomp. Victorian readers would have also recognized Kipling's Biblical and classical references, such as the refrain, "Lest we forget," from the translation of the book of Deuteronomy found in the King James Bible.

In "Recessional," Kipling urged the British people to be mindful of God, even as their empire slipped away. In the poem he writes: "The tumult and the shouting dies; / The captains and the kings depart: / Still stands Thine ancient sacrifice, / An humble and contrite heart." And while "navies melt away," critics with "wild tongues" are advised not to behave like "lesser breeds without the Law." The material legacies of the civilizing mission are fading, too: "For heathen heart that puts her trust / In reeking tube and iron shard, / All valiant dust that builds on dust." "Recessional" describes the moral and material failure of the empire. It is significant that just after publishing it, Kipling sought out Rhodes and became his companion and tenant.[31]

Kipling found it appealing that Rhodes supported the defense of the British Empire against the Boers. When war broke out in October 1899, Rhodes headed straight to the front lines near Kimberley. The city lay near the Cape's border with the Orange Free State, which still felt aggrieved, many years later, by the Cape Colony's acquisition of the diamond fields. Kimberley and its mines would be obvious targets of attack. Rhodes believed that Kimberley needed him to organize its defenses. He rode the train north from Cape Town, together with his secretary, Philip Jourdan; his doctor, Thomas Smartt; and Rochfort Maguire and his wife, Julia, daughter of Arthur Peel, speaker of the House of Commons from 1884 to 1895. Rochfort Maguire had lost his seat in Parliament and was working for the BSAC and Gold Fields. Julia Maguire was employed as a correspondent for *The Times*.

Rhodes and his party arrived in October 1899, a few days before Boer forces besieged the town. The siege lasted four months, and Rhodes found himself with little to do. Gardner Williams had to stop diamond-mining operations because the supply of coal ran low. Williams still had a stockpile of arms left over from the preparations for the Jameson Raid: six Maxim guns, 422 rifles, and 700,000 cartridges. Rhodes donated these to the defense of the town and allowed residents to shelter from Boer shelling in the mines. With food running low and with nerves getting frayed, Rhodes encouraged De Beers engineers to make contributions to the war effort. One of them, George Labram, used the company machine shop to craft a cannon, nicknamed "Long Cecil," which was used to shell the Boers. Rhodes was made an honorary lieutenant-colonel of the town militia, but the regular army officer who was commanding Kimberley's British forces, Lieutenant-Colonel Robert Kekewich, found Rhodes to be annoying. Rhodes routinely ignored orders to stop communicating with the outside world and undermining Kekewich's command. The overall progress of the war tended not to confirm the superiority of British military leadership. A British relief force under Lord Methuen approached Kimberley in December 1899 but was defeated by entrenched Boers in a bloody battle at nearby Magersfontein. Rhodes took up residence in the sanatorium and often found time to ride on horseback around the perimeter, dressed in his customary brown jacket and white flannel trousers. Somehow Boer sharpshooters did not kill him. A second British relief force liberated Kimberley in February 1900.

After the siege of Kimberley ended, Milner and Kitchener's war became a hard grind of counterinsurgency against Boer guerrillas. British and colonial soldiers burned Boer farms and rounded up civilians into concentration camps, where thousands died from disease and malnutrition. Rhodes himself was too sick to participate actively in politics, yet he still spoke excitedly about infrastructure, landscape, and unity. When Rhodes returned from Kimberley to Groote Schuur, he went riding with his architect, Herbert Baker. Baker's memoir summarizes Rhodes's words:

> On his first morning after his return from the siege of Kimberley I went with him along the new road which he had made on the mountain side. It was a beautiful morning, the flats a sea of mist, and the sun rising over the mountains, far beyond which the war still raged. After gazing and musing silently for a time, he said to me, "This will be all one country now; we must make this its beautiful capital."[32]

Rhodes gave his last presentation to a De Beers annual meeting on February 23, 1900, shortly after the end of the siege and just before diamond mining resumed. Rhodes seized the occasion as a moment to respond, once more, to critics of De Beers's contributions to the BSAC and to restate one of his core values, that money should not be made for its own sake but for some larger national purpose.

> Shareholders may be divided into two classes—those who are imaginative and those who are certainly unimaginative. To the latter class the fact of our connection with the Chartered Company has been for many years past a great trial. Human beings are very interesting. There

are those of the unimaginative type who pass their whole lives in filling money bags, and when they are called upon, perhaps more hurriedly than they desire, to retire from this world, what they leave behind is often dissipated by their offspring on wine, women, and horses. Of these purely unimaginative gentlemen, whose sole concern is the accumulation of wealth, I have a large number as my shareholders, and I now state for their consolation that the transactions with the Charter are closed.... And so I trust that my unimaginative shareholder will not continue to nag me about the transactions between the De Beers and the Charter, of which I was the author, and which were rendered possible by that change in the Trust Deed which enabled us, instead of dealing exclusively with diamonds, to embark upon other undertakings in various parts of the world, and which was devised in order that De Beers Company might lend its assistance to the work of Northern extension. We have also, I am glad to say, the imaginative shareholder. To him I would say, "it is pleasant for you to consider that undertakings which were embarked upon in the spirit of what I may call the doctrine of ransom have turned out so successfully. Had they failed I feel sure I should never have heard a word of reproach from you as to this trifle that we spent out of our great wealth to assist the work of opening up the North. We have now got the country developed far, far into the centre of Africa, largely through the means supplied by this commercial company." If I might go further and venture to draw a picture of the future, I would say that anyone visiting these mines 100 years hence, though he saw merely some disused pits, would, if he pushed his travels further into the interior, recognize the renewal of their life in the great European civilisation of the far North, and perhaps he would feel a glow of satisfaction at the thought that the immense riches which have been taken out of the soil have not been devoted merely to the decoration of the female sex. (Hear, hear.) And so, for my part, when the policy of this corporation is challenged, I always feel that it is no small thing to be able to say that it has devoted its wealth to other things besides the expansion of luxury.[33]

Rhodes played to the patriarchal beliefs of the audience when he joked about "the decoration of the female sex." This got some laughs and kept the audience's attention. The point of the speech was to foster "imagination" on the part of the stockholders and to encourage them to strive for a higher purpose. The reference to the "doctrine of ransom" was indicative. The concept originated in the thinking of an early Christian leader, Origen, who held that Christ sacrificed Himself to redeem the world from the Devil, a kind of ransom payment. Rhodes grew up in the Church and must have known what this meant. He was implying that he was like Christ and that his sacrifices of De Beers cash for the BSAC had redeemed Mashonaland and Matabeleland from the Devil.

After the end of the siege of Kimberley, the sickly Rhodes played little role in the management of De Beers, Gold Fields, or the BSAC. He did correspond with the directors of all these companies and occasionally contributed ideas. He spent most of the last two years of his life at Groote Schuur, conversing with visitors like Kipling or traveling in high style with his favorite companions to Rhodesia, England, Scotland, Europe, and Egypt. Rhodes often gasped for breath but still managed to spend five months riding in a cart throughout Rhodesia with his secretary, Philip Jourdan, his farm manager, Johnny Grimmer, and his servant, Tony de la Cruz. Rhodes was quite ill but still loved to be outdoors. In the late summer of 1901, he joined Jameson, Beit, and Metcalfe for grouse-shooting and trout-fishing in Scotland, but during the holiday his heart and lungs wavered. Ever pushing on, the group took a sightseeing trip, stopping at Paris, Lucerne, Venice, and Brindisi. The four men then crossed the Mediterranean and embarked on a voyage up the Nile. Rhodes appreciated the ancient ruins of Egypt and was curious about British efforts at development. He continued to envision the Cape-to-Cairo railway and urged his companions to travel with him as far as Khartoum, but he was obviously in failing health. At Wadi Halfa, on the border between Egypt and Sudan, Jameson insisted that they return home.[34]

Back in England at the start of 1902, he continued to dabble in property acquisitions by purchasing Dalham Hall, an estate near Newmarket in the horse country of West Suffolk. He then decided to travel to Cape Town in time for the forgery trial of Catherine Radziwill. Rhodes was concerned about her threats to reveal certain incriminating telegrams about imperial officials that she may have come across while visiting Groote Schuur, but no such revelations were made. While en route to Cape Town, Rhodes caught a cold and injured himself in a fall. He was not strong enough to appear in court. Rhodes made a deposition.

Rhodes's friends rented him a cottage nearby in Muizenberg, by False Bay. Rhodes hoped that the sea air would help his breathing, so he spent the nights in Muizenberg and the days at Groote Schuur. Rhodes and Baker began to make plans to construct a larger house at Muizenberg, but the plans never came to fruition. In early March of 1902, it became clear that Rhodes was

Rhodes in the Last Year of His Life, by Mortimer Menpes. Wikimedia

dying. He stayed in Muizenberg and took to his bed. Outside the house, people gathered quietly, waiting for news. Inside, Rhodes was attended around the clock by Jameson, who slept on a cot in the bedroom. Jourdan, Le Sueur, and Metcalfe were there, too, along with Rhodes's brother Elmhirst. The men admitted a handful of regular visitors, including Rhodes's friend Rudyard Kipling; Rhodes's banker, Lewis Michell; Johnny Grimmer, the manager of Inyanga; and "Mac" McDonald, who was still managing Sauerdale as well as Gold Fields interests in Rhodesia.

McDonald reported that at the end of his life, Rhodes gave detailed instructions about tree planting. He was particularly keen to finish the three-mile, tree-lined avenue that led up to Bulawayo's new Government House. The one-story headquarters of the BSAC was constructed on the site formerly occupied by Lobengula's kraal. Government House was built in the Cape Dutch style, featuring a verandah with neoclassical columns. The colonial structure was approached on a long avenue lined with oaks, symbolizing English royal power growing out of the ash-heap of Ndebele chiefship. Rhodes quoted a story from his childhood, told to him by an old naval officer who was fond of planting oaks, from which the ships of the Royal Navy were once constructed. " 'Trees, trees,—plant trees,' he said, 'help Nature in her efforts; do not strangle her desire to cover the nakedness of the earth.' " Rhodes had designs, as ever, and hoped that he would recover. It was not to be. He died on March 26, 1902, at the age of forty-eight. He whispered these final words to his banker, Lewis Michell: "So little done, so much to do." Or so people were told. He may have simply asked a servant, "Turn me over, Jack." In death, as in life, accounts of Rhodes were varied.[35]

Conclusion

PERPETUATING THE VISION

SIX AND A half hours after Rhodes died, Drs. Jameson, Smartt, and Stevenson gathered in Muizenberg to watch Dr. Stephen Syfret, the brother of Rhodes's attorney, perform an autopsy. Normally an autopsy is performed at a hospital or mortuary equipped for the cutting and draining. In the case of Rhodes, the dissection was performed in the Muizenberg house. Rhodes was stripped, examined, and measured and found to be in early stage of rigor mortis. The notes show that the head measured 11 ¾ inches frontally from ear to ear; 9 ½ inches from the root of the nose to the occipital protuberance; and 22 ½ inches in circumference. Syfret made an incision across the back of Rhodes's head and removed the top of the skull. Then the brain was cut out and weighed on a scale before being put back. Syfret noted that it was "49 ounces—Normal in all respects."

Next the post-mortem examination focused on the thoracic cavity. Incisions were made on the chest to pull back the skin, then the breastplate was cut out, rib by rib, by using saws, knives, or shears. The membrane covering the heart, known as the pericardium, was found to be "enormously thickened." The heart was cut open to reveal a clot in the right atrium. The aorta was found to be badly dilated. The membrane covering the lungs, called the pleura, was found to be thickened. The lungs were observed to be filled with fluid: "oedematous, congested and compressed." Rhodes died of heart failure, although the underlying diagnosis has never been established.[1]

Rhodes, the disassembler of rocks and societies, was himself taken apart by his medical friends. When they were done with the autopsy, they put the body back together and made a plaster cast of his face, so that a death mask sculpture could be created. Rhodes's brother Elmhirst, together with Jameson, Grimmer, and several other friends, had the body placed in a temporary coffin and rode with it on a special early morning train to Rondebosch. At the station, the body was removed from the train and lifted onto a horse-drawn hearse for a final ride up the hill to Groote Schuur. It was four o'clock in the morning on Maundy Thursday. Rhodes's secretary, Gordon Le Sueur, met the party at Groote Schuur. Years later he described the scene:

> The effect was weird in the extreme—the semi-darkened house with the little group of servants standing with bared heads waiting for the procession which slowly made its way between the great oaks which line the gravelled drive—waiting for the master who was coming home for the last time.
>
> There was a brilliant full moon that Thursday morning before Good Friday, and its rays shining through the oak leaves cast a pattern of patches of gold and black darkness upon the drive.
>
> Slowly the hearse approached, no sound being heard but the scrunching of the gravel beneath the horses' hoofs and the measured tread of the little band of mourners.... Then it stopped before the door, and the coffin was borne in and placed upon the table in the hall.[2]

Rhodes was placed in a coffin carved from Matabeleland teak. The coffin was left open on Thursday so that a small number of friends could gather around for a prayer service. Rhodes's friend and fellow Mason, Rudyard Kipling, joined the circle of mourners, together with the Grand Master of the Grand Lodge of South Africa, Conrad Christian Silberbauer. Rhodes's masonic regalia was placed inside the coffin before it was sealed up.[3] Then Kipling read a poem that he had written about Rhodes. The verses captured Rhodes's spirit as well as his shortcomings:

> When that great Kings return to clay,
>   Or Emperors in their pride,
> Grief of a day shall fill a day,
>   Because its creature died.
> But we—we reckon not with those
>   Whom the mere Fates ordain,
> This Power that wrought on us and goes
>   Back to the Power again.

Kipling's tone is stately and measured, yet he manages a typical jab at the origins of the aristocracy, who were frequent targets of his pen during the South African War. The poet observes that Rhodes was more than a king or emperor ordained by "mere Fates." Rhodes's power, suggests Kipling, originated with some greater "Power."

> Dreamer devout, by vision led
>   Beyond our guess or reach,
> The travail of his spirit bred
>   Cities in place of speech.
> So huge the all-mastering thought that drove—
>   So brief the term allowed—
> Nations, not words, he linked to prove
>   His faith before the crowd.

Kipling observes that Rhodes, who was not known to be a devout Christian, was instead devoted to his own dreams and led by a vision that was spiritual and inscrutable. Rhodes, who did not have a wife and children, had spiritual "travail"—the old word for childbirth—that resulted in cities, presumably Kimberley, Johannesburg, Bulawayo, and Salisbury, none of which he actually birthed. These cities were made "in place of speech," an acknowledgment of Rhodes's limited talent as a public speaker. Not only did his "all-mastering thought" produce cities; it produced unity among nations, a reference to the geographical sweep of Rhodes's thinking as well as the influence of "The Founder" on urban development. Kipling continued to highlight the geographical dimensions of Rhodes's vision:

> It is his will that he look forth
>   Across the world he won—
> The granite of the ancient North—
>   Great spaces washed with sun.

Kipling depicts Rhodes looking out over the entire world, especially the "North," where the mining baron would be entombed in granite. Those "great spaces washed with sun" are depicted without people who might have other ideas. In death, Rhodes would rule the "North":

> There shall he patient take his seat
>   (As when the Death he dared),
> And there await a people's feet
>   In the paths that he prepared.
> There, till the vision he foresaw
>   Splendid and whole arise,
> And unimagined Empires draw
>   To council 'neath his skies,

> The immense and brooding Spirit still
> Shall quicken and control.
> Living he was the land, and dead,
> His soul shall be her soul!

The mythic infrastructure of "the paths" had been laid out by Rhodes, to be followed by others. Rhodes received a sendoff that highlighted his ideas about conquest and mobility. First his body lay in state. Le Sueur estimated that on Saturday and Monday, 35,000 visitors filed past. On Wednesday, with Frank and Arthur Rhodes present at Groote Schuur, a private funeral was held. The body was transferred to the Houses of Parliament for an official lying in state, followed by a state funeral nearby at St. George's Cathedral. The coffin was draped in the Union Jack that usually hung in the billiard room at Groote Schuur. It was the flag carried by the explorer Ewart Grogan on his 1898–1900 walk from Cairo to Cape Town.

A funeral procession followed Rhodes's hearse to the train station, where the body was placed in the De Beers private railway car, pulled by the new, deluxe train for a final journey on the Road to the North. At station stops in the war-torn country, mourners and soldiers stood respectfully at attention. When the train reached Kimberley, a long line of townspeople paid their respects, filing past Rhodes for seven hours. When the train left the station for the rest of the journey north, there were concerns about a possible Boer attack. On March 7, not far away in the western Transvaal, a Boer force led by Koos de la Rey had defeated a thousand British troopers and captured its commanding general, Paul Methuen. The British army under Kitchener decided not to take any chances with Rhodes's body. Rhodes's train was preceded by an armored train that swept the veld with a searchlight. When Rhodes's train arrived in Vryburg, the passengers saw the British soldiers who had just escaped De la Rey; in Mafeking, the situation seemed safe, and the train was greeted by a throng of townspeople gathered on the platform. From Palapye, the train proceeded to the station at Bulawayo. There, Rhodes's coffin was taken off the train and carried on an artillery gun carriage pulled by eight mules. The body lay in state overnight at the Drill Hall, then the next day was brought twenty miles south to Rhodes's favorite campsite on a property called Westacre. Rhodes used to enjoy staying there with friends, sleeping in one of several rondavel huts, and dining al fresco under a large shelter, taking in the views. It was there, under the shelter, that he lay in state for one more night. On the next morning, he was taken to his final resting place.[4]

The man who envisioned an industrial, mobile, white-ruled country wanted to be buried in the remote, elevated Malindidzumu, renamed World's View, which required a nine-mile ride south. To deliver the body, McDonald and a team of African laborers had to pull off Rhodes's final infrastructure project. "Large gangs of natives were organized to cut a road," reported McDonald, "for there was none—from Rhodes's huts at the Matopo farm up to the mountain height he had chosen for his resting-place." The work had to be done quickly, so "preparations were carried on night and day." At the end, "on the summit of 'The World's View,' excavation was made for the tomb—a cavity hollowed in the solid granite and so that the outlook would be towards the north." At the base of World's View, the mules were exchanged for a more powerful team of oxen. The strong beasts drew the gun carriage and the coffin up the hill, with troopers standing at the ready with ropes, just in case more power was needed.[5]

At the top of the hill, the final rites followed a script written by Rhodes himself. McDonald, Le Sueur, Jameson, and other guests were present, together with an honor guard of the BSA Police. There were reports of thousands of Ndebele people attending, including Lobengula's son, Njube, who had been sent with Rhodes to Cape Town. William Gaul, the Anglican bishop of Mashonaland, led the service. Gaul knew Rhodes from Kimberley, where, in his earlier posting as the rector of St. Cyprian's Church, he had presided over the funerals of miners who died in the De Beers Mine fire. Gaul began with prayers, then read the poem that Kipling had recited at Groote Schuur and that had just been published in newspapers around the English-speaking world.

When Bishop Gaul finished the service, Rhodes's coffin was lowered into the tomb. Mourners lowered wreaths given by Queen Victoria, Jameson, and the Rhodes family. A "massive stone slab," in the words of Le Sueur, "upon which was riveted the plain brass plate bearing the inscription, 'Here lie the remains of Cecil John Rhodes,' was gently settled upon the grave." At the end of the service, Rhodes had a musical send-off with lyrics that highlighted work, war, and mobility. Gaul led the group in singing the familiar Victorian funeral hymn "Now the Laborer's Task Is O'er," with music by John Bacchus Dykes and words by John Ellerton.

> Now the laborer's task is o'er;
> Now the battle day is past;
> Now upon the farther shore
> Lands the voyager at last.

> Father, in thy gracious keeping,
> Leave we now thy servant sleeping.

At the same time, political and financial leaders were attending a memorial service for Rhodes in London's St. Paul's Cathedral, over the crypt that held the remains of Nelson, Wellington, and other heroes of the British Empire. In synchronizing the services, Rhodes's supporters emphasized the connections Rhodes built between the City of London and Southern Africa.

At the top of World's View, the burial did not conclude with the traditional salute by a firing party. Ndebele leaders objected to the idea of such a noise, on the grounds that rifle shots might disturb the spirits of the nearby hills, where burial sites were located. Ndebele men were given the last word on Rhodes: they closed the ceremony with the royal tribute shout of "Bayete!" It was a recognition of the steps that Rhodes had taken to end the BSAC's second war of conquest, when Rhodes, under financial pressure, made peace with the indunas whose followers had died by the thousands.[6]

After the funeral, Frank Rhodes met with Ndebele leaders and asked them to guard World's View as a gesture of reconciliation. To the former enemies, Frank Rhodes stated that "I know that the white man and the Matabele will be brothers and friends for ever. I will leave my brother's grave in your hands. I charge you to hand down this sacred trust from generation to generation and I know that if you do this my brother will be well pleased."[7] With Ndebele guards keeping watch, the site became a shrine for white heroes. In 1904, Allan Wilson and the BSAC troopers of the Shangani Patrol were reinterred in a special hilltop monument. In 1920, Jameson was buried near Rhodes. In 1930, the buried men were joined by Charles Coghlan, the first prime minister of Southern Rhodesia. The site was even referred to as a white man's Valhalla. In 1953, the Queen Mother and Princess Margaret visited the site, to mark the 100th anniversary of Rhodes's birth. When white Rhodesia faced anticolonial rebellion in the 1960s, World's View became contested by independence fighters and by Africanist politicians. After independence in 1980, Zimbabwe's dictator, Robert Mugabe, contemplated sending Rhodes's remains back to England, on the grounds that colonialism caused many of his nation's problems. The charge was not without merit, and by climbing on the high horse of anticolonialism, Mugabe distracted attention from his own ground-level failings. Statues of Rhodes were taken down and streets were renamed, yet Rhodes remains in his grave, at least in part because income from tourists is needed in the Matopos.[8]

Over the course of his life, Rhodes had given money to needy white people, especially in Kimberley and Rhodesia. Stories abounded of Rhodes encountering a white settler or miner who was down on his or her luck and dashing off a personal check to help them meet expenses, impromptu gestures of noblesse oblige. In his final years, Rhodes made plans to make his giving more strategic. His ideas may be understood by recalling the context of Andrew Carnegie's well-known 1889 essay "Wealth," also known as "The Gospel of Wealth," which was first published in the *North American Review* and then republished, at the urging of Gladstone, in Stead's *Pall Mall Gazette*. At that time, Stead was a member of Rhodes's inner circle. It seems likely that Rhodes was aware of the famous essay. Rhodes was certainly aware of Carnegie—the strike against Carnegie's Homestead steel mill was discussed in the 1892 session of the Cape Parliament. Rhodes may have found the ideas of this fellow monopolist appealing. Carnegie, also a keen follower of Herbert Spencer, believed that wealth was a measure of merit. Carnegie also argued that it was wrong to pass down wealth to one's family members. They would only become lazy and unhappy. Wealth should not be wasted; it should serve a civic purpose.[9]

Rhodes wrote multiple wills over the course of his adult life. As he grew more mature, so did his thinking about contributing private wealth to the public good. He penned the first will at age nineteen. It placed his funds in the hands of the secretary of state for the colonies, to be used for the extension of the British Empire. The 1877 "Confession of Faith" and the second will that went along with it proposed to give money to the secretary of state for the colonies and Sidney Shippard so that they would create a secret society of young men, modeled on the Jesuits, who would support the British domination of the world. In the third will, 1882, Rhodes left his fortune to Neville Pickering, while the fourth will, written soon after Pickering's death, and also the fifth will, left the money to Natty Rothschild. Rhodes reminded Rothschild to follow through on the plans to create a secret society. In a postscript to a letter, Rhodes told Rothschild, "In considering question suggested take Constitution [of] Jesuits if obtainable and insert 'English Empire' for 'Roman Catholic religion.'"[10]

In the 1890s, as even more money accumulated from De Beers and Gold Fields, Rhodes revised his wills so that they included funds for educational institutions that would shape future leaders of South Africa and the British Empire. Rhodes was not the only one to propose scholarships for young, white colonial men with the purpose of uniting the British Empire. One of Rhodes's contacts in London, journalist and activist John Astley Cooper, aimed to unify the Empire by staging athletic contests, but in a letter to the *Times*, published in 1891, he also advocated for an imperial scholarship scheme. The educational philanthropy of the American monopolists was well known. They endowed universities such as Vanderbilt (1873); Stanford (1885); Chicago (1890); and Carnegie Mellon (1900). The later wills of Cecil Rhodes proposed to support an English-speaking college for South Africa's settlers, to rival the Dutch-speaking college at Stellenbosch. Rhodes hoped to nurture a home-grown Anglophone elite. He recognized the material origins of this vision. He knew that the college endowment would come, in part, from the profits he made by putting African workers in closed compounds. According to his architect, Herbert Baker, Rhodes "used to repeat jokingly that 'he meant to build the University out of the K----rs' stomach.'"[11]

Rhodes signed his final will in July of 1899. On his death, a trust would have the authority to disperse his funds, subject to special guidelines. Rhodes named the first trustees: Lord Rosebery, Alfred Beit, Albert Grey, William T. Stead, Lewis Michell, and Bourchier Hawksley. In January 1901, Rhodes cut Stead from the list because he supported the Boers during the war. He was replaced by Milner. All trustees were reliable supporters of colonialism. None had much experience in academia. Neither did Jameson, who joined the original board soon after Rhodes's death. As Jameson had been Rhodes's friend for many years, having been forgiven for botching the Raid and having attended Rhodes during his final illness, the other board members were somewhat taken aback to hear Jameson wisecrack at an early meeting that Rhodes "was a nice old lady but not a genius."[12]

The Rhodes Trust carried out Rhodes's will immediately. The South African College still received support and would eventually become the University of Cape Town, located on Rhodes's property near Groote Schuur. The mansion and its immediate surroundings were given to the country, in the hope that it would be used as the home of the prime minister of a future union of the colonies and republics of South Africa. A special fund was set aside for the horses, servants, and gardens. Rhodes left his London properties to the trust, instructing the trustees to pay the income in equal shares to his siblings. Rhodes set aside annuities for his servants and a gift of £6,000 to the Parisian banker Albert Kahn, who had recently established "Les Jardins du Monde," an outdoor display of different styles of landscape design. Rhodes's will also endowed the monuments at World's View. Projects for a garden, dam, and railway would be continued at Sauerdale, his property near Bulawayo, so that colonial settlers could enjoy instructive weekend outings. The trust would administer Sauerdale and Inyanga, in Mashonaland, although in 1901 Rhodes attached a codicil giving

Johnny Grimmer ten thousand pounds and the use of Inyanga for life. Grimmer died from an illness a few months after the death of Rhodes, at which point the estate reverted to the trust.[13]

These aspects of his final will are not so famous as his support for the University of Oxford, which awarded him the honorary degree while he was actively considering the details of his bequest. He left £100,000 pounds to Oriel College, to be used for the construction of a new building on High Street, across from the University Church of St. Mary the Virgin. The money was also intended to support the college's affiliated faculty and their meals at the high table. The gift includes a breakdown of costs for the construction of what would be called the Rhodes Building. Rhodes hoped that when the building entered the planning phase, the experienced administrators of the trust would be consulted by the fellows, because "the College authorities live secluded from the world and so are like children as to commercial matters."[14] Usually it was only "the natives" who were called children.

In the most famous part of his will, Cecil Rhodes created the Rhodes Scholarships. Rhodes's earliest wills expressed a wish to create a secret society of men, modeled on the Jesuits, to govern and extend the British Empire, an idea that was not very practical. The revised will of 1899 directed the trustees to give scholarships to Americans and colonial settlers so that they could study at Oxford. There would be thirty-two scholarships for Americans, with a maximum of two given to students from any state. Twenty scholarships were allocated to British colonies, mainly colonies of white settlement. He directed that the scholars should be academically successful but "shall not be merely bookworms." Rhodes enjoyed horseback riding and as a young man participated in sports, so he directed the trust to choose scholars who had "fondness of and success in manly outdoor sports such as cricket football and the like." They would have to demonstrate qualities of leadership, which he described in a kind of stream of consciousness:

> his qualities of manhood truth courage devotion to duty sympathy for and protection of the weak kindliness unselfishness and fellowship and . . . his exhibition during school days of moral force of character and of instincts to lead and to take an interest in his schoolmates for those latter attributes will be likely in afterlife to guide him to esteem the performance of public duties as his highest aim.[15]

Then he divided these attributes into precise fractions. Applicants would be judged on the following basis: four-tenths academic; two-tenths athletic;

two-tenths manliness; and two-tenths leadership. He offered rules for the scholars. Some may seem surprising, such as the twenty-fourth rule: "No student shall be disqualified for election to a Scholarship on account of his race or religious opinions." It is not clear what, exactly, Rhodes meant in this case by "race." In those days, race could mean African, "Caucasian," Asian, and so forth, and race was often used as a term when describing the differences between English, Dutch, Irish, and German. In a codicil to the will written in January 1901, Rhodes added five scholarships for German students, a decision that is attributed to his enjoyable meeting with Kaiser Wilhelm II. Rhodes also tinkered with the fractions of the qualifications, dropping the academic qualification from four-tenths to three-tenths and raising the manliness qualification to equal status at three-tenths.

Rhodes sketched his early ideas for the scholars in correspondence with the BSAC's attorney, Bourchier Hawksley. In 1899, Rhodes wrote, "You should also select the best of the students and send them to different parts of the world. To maintain the Imperial thought in the colonies they would be better unmarried as the consideration of babies and other domestic agenda generally destroys higher thought. Please understand I am in no sense a woman hater but this particular business is better untrammeled with material thought."[16]

The trustees put Rhodes's ideas into action. The Rhodes Trust hired its first organizing secretary, Canadian historian and college administrator George Parkin, who traveled widely to set up the selection committees in the relevant countries. The first Rhodes Scholars arrived at Oxford in 1904. Many struggled to pass the entrance exams in Greek and Latin. At first, Oxford's faculty and students looked down their noses at colonials who struggled with classical languages, but over the years the requirements were modified, and the scholarship program became successful. Part of this success had to do with the trustees' willingness to adjust to the times. Scholarships were eventually offered to women and to students who were not white. On the centenary of the scholarships, the Rhodes Trust spun off a Mandela–Rhodes Foundation, whose title linked the names of the two rather different visionaries. The foundation provided funding for students to pursue one or two years of postgraduate study at a South African university, plus training in leadership.

Rhodes did not intend that the cultivation of student leaders be a way of whitewashing his reputation, although it has certainly had that effect. Many people today know about the Rhodes Scholarships but lack awareness of Rhodes's more problematic accomplishments. Ever since the days of the robber barons, when Rhodes, Beit, Barnato, and Robinson were overshadowed by Carnegie, Morgan, Rockefeller, and Vanderbilt, questions have been raised about big acts of philanthropy. In 1891, Rhodes's acquaintance from his Oxford days, Oscar Wilde, put his finger on the problem in an essay titled "The Soul of Man under Socialism," published in the *Fortnightly Review* two years after Carnegie published "The Gospel of Wealth." Wilde wrote that when philanthropists alleviate poverty by donating food or giving scholarships, they are only making "an aggravation of the difficulty." According to Wilde:

> *The proper aim is to try and re-construct society on such a basis that poverty will be impossible.* And the altruistic virtues have really prevented the carrying out of this aim. Just as the worst slave-owners were those who were kind to their slaves, and so prevented the horror of the system being realized by those who suffered from it, and understood by those who contemplated it, so, in the present state of things in England, the people who do most harm are the people who try to do most good.... Charity creates a multitude of sins.[17]

What could this mean if applied to Rhodes in the years since 1902, the year when the provisions of his will were announced? Few people dispute that it is a good thing to donate scholarships and buildings to a university. Wilde pointed out that if the money had been earned through deconstructing society, maybe it should be spent on reconstructing society rather than on allowing "the system" to grind on quietly. A silence develops around the means of earning great fortunes when the fortunes are spent on charity.[18]

Even scholars who study about Rhodes at Oxford are implicated in the world that Rhodes made. The Rhodes Papers form the backbone of any study of Rhodes, such as this one. The papers were first collected and curated by Rhodes himself; today they are the property of the Rhodes Trust. Some historians have even suspected that the Groote Schuur fire of 1896 that destroyed many documents in Rhodes's study was the result of a deliberate act, but there is no evidence to support the inference that the study contained incriminating evidence. The papers that survived, and the papers that were produced after the fire, were curated again by Rhodes's associates after his death. It is impossible to know what documents were discarded. Today the Rhodes Trust is generous with access to the documents. The papers must be read critically, with an awareness of possible omissions.

The Rhodes Papers are now housed in the Bodleian Library's Weston Building, but until 2014 they were kept in Oxford's Rhodes House, the headquarters of the Rhodes Trust. Designed by Herbert Baker as a memorial to Rhodes and opened in 1928, the building has a Roman, imperial portico and dome, in the style of the Pantheon, topped with a replica of a Zimbabwe bird. Visitors enter through the portico and walk under the dome. Looking up, they see a bust of Rhodes, ensconced in the wall, and an inscription to the Rhodes Scholars who died in the First and Second World Wars.

The dome is ringed with one of Rhodes's favorite quotations from Aristotle's *Nicomachean Ethics*. The quotation is written in classical Greek, in large capital letters: ΤΟ ΑΝΘΡΩΠΙΝΟΝ ΑΓΑΘΟΝ ΨΥΧΗΣ ΕΝΕΡΓΕΙΑ ΓΙΝΕΤΑΙ ΚΑΤ ΑΡΕΤΗΝ ΕΙ ΔΕ ΠΛΕΙΟΥΣ ΑΙ ΑΡΕΤΑΙ ΚΑΤΑ ΤΗΝ ΑΡΙΣΤΗΝ ΚΑΙ ΤΕΛΕΙΟΤΑΤΗΝ ΕΤΙ Δ ΕΝ ΒΙΩΙ ΤΕΛΕΙΩΙ. Translated into English, the passage means: "The human [or manly] good is born from activity of the soul in accordance with virtue, and if the virtues [are] many, in accordance with the best and the most complete [or perfect]. And still in a complete [or perfect] life." The next line of Aristotle's quotation has been cut. It advises that "one swallow does not make spring." Did Baker remove that part of the quotation, thinking that in Rhodes's case, one swallow did make spring? Or did he not want to draw a contrast between Aristotle's swallow and the replica of the looted Zimbabwe bird that is placed, directly above, on the top of the dome?[19]

When designing Rhodes House, Baker found his inspiration in the classical Greek and Roman past as well as the Arts and Crafts movement and the rustic Cape Dutch style of Groote Schuur. The Arts and Crafts style pervades the building, from the stout wooden beams and stairways, to the memorial inscriptions in Perpetua font, to the interior with its grand rooms. On the ground floor, the large, open Milner Hall can take on two appearances, depending on the arrangement of the seating. When the chairs are placed row on row for a large gathering, the hall looks like a chapel, with a portrait of Rhodes hanging in the place of the crucifix. (This is the portrait that the Rhodes Trust has kindly allowed the press to use for the jacket of this book.) When tables and chairs are arranged for a supper, the room looks like an Oxford college dining hall, with the Rhodes portrait in the center, above the high table, the traditional place for honoring great academic leaders. Upstairs, Rosebery Hall is a large, Arts and Crafts study space. It was originally used to house several hundred thousand volumes of the Bodleian Library's collection of books about the British Empire, the Commonwealth, and the United States.

Initially, some of the papers of the British South Africa Company were kept at Rhodes House; other papers were kept in a vault in the City of

London. During the Second World War, bomb damage to water mains caused the collection to be flooded and destroyed. Yet even after fires and bombs, plenty of government documents, personal papers, personal memoirs, newspaper reports, and company documents remained available. Many of these sources have been used before in political and social histories of late-nineteenth-century South Africa. The sources reveal mainly the views of white colonizers and administrators. Historians have struggled to find documentation of the views of African people about Rhodes. African farmers and miners were the very people who gave up their land, their labor, and their lives so that Rhodes could become wealthy and powerful. For the most part, the views of the African people in Rhodes's papers must be inferred from second-hand sources. Occasionally they are filtered through the accounts of the Europeans they encountered.

Reframing a Rhodes biography along the lines of material history—from buildings and archives to geography and infrastructure—and linking Rhodes's influence in those areas to the problems of contemporary South Africa, raises a thought about agency. If an individual and his network can play such an important role in setting up these structures of discrimination, then surely individuals and their networks can play a role in taking them down. For every Rhodes there can be a Mandela—and many more individuals and networks to follow. Visions are iterative, requiring reflection on results, then modification and fine-tuning. Decisions about the developing vision were based on the unfolding material, social, and ideological surroundings. As such they were always changing.[20]

Rhodes believed that his contributions would last. In 1893, when he wrote to Stead, entrusting him and Rothschild with the next-to-last will and testament, he quoted in Latin from Horace's *Ode* III.30, known as "The Poet's Monument." It begins with the line *"Exegi monumentum aere perennius / regalique situ pyramidum Altius."* Educated Victorians were familiar with the poem, which Rhodes quoted to show how he thought about his legacy:

> I have finished a monument more lasting than bronze, more lofty than the regal structure of the pyramids, one which neither corroding rain nor the ungovernable North Wind can ever destroy, nor the countless series of the years, nor the flight of time.
>
> I shall not wholly die, and a large part of me will elude the Goddess of Death. I shall continue to grow, fresh with the praise of posterity.[21]

Rhodes admitted to Stead that he had been quite taken with this poem ever since he was a "boy at school." Part of it, *"Non omnis moriar"*—"I shall not wholly die"—is inscribed around an image of the Matopos that is placed above the entryway of Oxford's Rhodes House.

Rhodes's most lasting legacy was not the British Empire, which faded in the twentieth century. Nor did it turn out to be the extension of white rule, which was highly contested and finally fell by the wayside in the early 1990s. The principal legacies of Rhodes's vision are the material and geographical constraints placed on freedoms. These range from the monuments and buildings of imperialism, to the selections and silences of archival sources, to the borders and infrastructures of Southern Africa, which exist above and below the ground. The constraints originated in the taking of land, the crushing of rocks, and the raising of capital, which fed the social and material disassembly line that drove Southern Africa under white rule. Many of the social and material impositions still exist and shape efforts to overcome them. It will be much easier to remove a few statues than to reverse the legacy of Cecil Rhodes. Understanding what he did is a first step to freedom.

Acknowledgments

THIS BOOK BUILDS on many works of scholarship related to Britain and Africa, including more than two dozen previous biographical studies of Cecil Rhodes. Some of the biographies were written by Rhodes's friends and associates, such as Herbert Baker, Thomas Fuller, Philip Jourdan, Gordon Le Sueur, Lewis Michell, Catherine Radziwill, and John Verschoyle, who wrote under the pseudonym of "Vindex." Their studies are generally adulatory or, in the case of Radziwill, have a particular bias. They still provide much useful material for the modern biographer. Verschoyle's book is especially helpful. More than 800 pages long, it is a biography with a supplementary collection of Rhodes's speeches.

The 1910 biography by Michell, Rhodes's friend and personal banker, is a long, two-volume study that established the standard interpretation of Rhodes's life. The narrative focuses on his business and political activities, culminating in what was perceived as his tragic overreaching during the Jameson Raid and his strenuous efforts to preserve colonialism in Rhodesia, later known as Zimbabwe, in the face of rebellion. The problems of colonialism were not addressed, even though they were apparent to many contemporaries. Michell's standard interpretation is generally followed by the first scholarly biography, by Basil Williams. Williams had met Rhodes and knew many of his associates who, as board members of the Rhodes Trust, granted access to most of the Rhodes Papers. Williams's study was interrupted by the First World War and was published in 1921. In addition to setting down the basic narrative of Rhodes's life, Michell and Williams also left traces in the archival record that need to be consulted by serious students of Rhodes. Both authors donated research notes and manuscripts to key collections. Michell's papers are in the Cape Town Archives Repository, and Williams's papers are in the Bodleian Library.

Michell and Williams admired Rhodes and wrote in the "great man" tradition of biography. So, too, did two generations of biographers, culminating with John Gilbert Lockhart and C. M. "Monty" Woodhouse's 1963 biography. Lockhart and Woodhouse were the first scholars granted full access to the Rhodes Papers, perhaps earned because both men were well-known authors, veterans, and politicians, the sort of men admired by Rhodes. Unlike Rhodes, in their own lifetimes they experienced the "Recessional" of the British Empire. While the book was being written, in 1960, British Prime Minister Harold Macmillan addressed the South African Parliament in Cape Town, announcing that "the wind of change is blowing through this continent. Whether we like it or not, this growth of national consciousness is a political fact." Macmillan's late recognition of African aspirations strikes modern ears as a rather mild rebuke to white South Africans, yet it stirred great resentment. The dominant National Party, led by apartheid's architect, Prime Minister Hendrik Verwoerd, leaned into the wind of change and pushed for a fully independent republic, free of the British monarchy and committed to apartheid, goals that were achieved in 1961.

After this turn of events, scholarly biographies of Rhodes took a more critical stance toward colonialism, even while preserving the standard narrative of Michell and Williams. John Flint's concise, 268-page biography appeared in 1974. The book recognized the criticisms made against Rhodes during his own lifetime, as well as critical studies of colonial history that were published in the 1950s and 1960s. Flint's book is a scholarly study, well written yet lacking footnotes. Sources are documented in a "Further Reading" section at the back of the book. Scholars who are familiar with the key primary and secondary sources about Rhodes will still recognize the imprint of Michell and Williams in the construction of Flint's critical narrative. Yet by the early 1970s, the critique of colonialism was not new, either.

A pathbreaking biography of Rhodes was written by a political scientist, Robert Rotberg, with the assistance of a psychiatrist, Miles Shore. The book was published in 1988 and looms large in the historiography. Weighing in at 800 pages, Rotberg's book is based on copious archival research that went well beyond the efforts of predecessors. While previous studies drew mainly on the Rhodes Papers, "Vindex," and published sources, Rotberg added research in archives throughout Britain and Southern Africa. With a stronger basis in primary and secondary sources, this biography supplements and extends the basic narration of Michell and Williams, as well as Lockhart, Woodhouse, and Flint. Like Flint, Rotberg takes a critical stance toward colonialism, with a brave effort at analysis that sets this book apart from all other

Rhodes biographies. Layered on top of the story of business and politics is a psychological interpretation, the product of Rotberg's interdisciplinary interests and Shore's professional expertise. Rhodes is shown to have tendencies toward narcissism. In addition, Rhodes's conflicts with strong, masculine figures such as Paul Kruger and Henry Loch, and Rhodes's attraction to personalities like those of Jameson and Pickering, are cast in the light of Rhodes's relationship with his father. His relationship with his mother and his place in his family's birth order are also used to help understand his complexities. Rotberg also broaches the subject of Rhodes's likely homosexuality in a thoughtful manner.

Most reviewers criticized Rotberg's efforts to supplement the standard Rhodes narrative with something new and interdisciplinary. My personal assessment, having read Rotberg's meticulous book and having also read many of the same primary and secondary sources, is that the psychological insights are difficult to prove yet still have much to offer. I also think that Rhodes had narcissistic tendencies, and I note his attractions to weaker men and his conflicts with stronger men. I first made contact with Rotberg in 2021, when the research for this book was complete. When we exchanged emails, I was delighted to learn that he is following the example of Michell and Williams in donating his research papers to an archive, in his case to the Harvard University Archives, so that future scholars might consult them. This knowledge came to me too late in the process of writing for a visit to Cambridge. I leave that to the next Rhodes biographers.

Other secondary sources were important for the present study. The history of the diamond fields has been narrated by Steve Lunderstedt, Colin Newbury, Brian Roberts, Robert Turrell, and William Worger. Late-nineteenth-century Cape politics, particularly the relationship between Rhodes and the Afrikaner Bond, has been recounted by Rodney Davenport and Mordechai Tamarkin. The history of the BSAC has been told by John Galbraith, Arthur Keppel-Jones, and Terence Ranger, while Rhodes's related efforts in Bechuanaland, later called Botswana, have been described by Paul Maylam, Neil Parsons, and Kevin Shillington. The Jameson Raid has been described by many historians and recently was the subject of a detailed investigation by Charles van Onselen. These secondary sources, plus many other articles and books, are referenced in the notes and in the bibliography. Here I wish to express my deep gratitude to the historians who have gone before me on many of the same paths.

The present study aims to push past the conventional narrative, as originally constructed by Michell and Williams, to include more information about Rhodes's efforts at agriculture, mining, railroads, and telegraphy, by way of showing the material constraints of his vision on the region's infrastructure. In doing so, this biography includes in its narrative topics that have not been emphasized before, such as the De Beers Mine Fire of 1888, as well as Rhodes's interest in experimental agriculture and urban development. I have also chosen to limit the amount of space devoted to political history. This book has more discussion of material aspects of Rhodes's career, with emphasis on the ways in which his network included the simultaneous manipulation of human and natural resources.

This focus on materiality and networks has been influenced by works in environmental history, particularly by Thomas Andrews, William Cronon, and Timothy LeCain. Works in science and technology studies have also been inspirational. Starting with my books about sugarcane in Mauritius and guns in South Africa, I have had productive engagement with Sheila Jasanoff and her ideas about the idiom of coproduction. When I first began to write about Rhodes, she commented on an early draft of a chapter that was published by the University of Chicago Press in a collection of essays she co-edited with Sang-Hyun Kim, titled *Dreamscapes of Modernity: Sociotechnical Imaginaries and the Fabrication of Power*. Scholars in science and technology studies will also recognize the influence of Bruno Latour's actor-network theory and the approach known as the social construction of technology, or SCOT, first elaborated by Wiebe Bijker, Thomas Hughes, and Trevor Pinch.

It has taken fifteen years to research and write this book. I wish to acknowledge the help of many librarians and archivists in South Africa, the United Kingdom, and the United States. Two archivists stand out for providing extensive help and hospitality: Vida Allen of the McGregor Museum in Kimberley and Lucy McCann of the University of Oxford's Bodleian Library. The research and writing also received support from my home institution, Millsaps College, which provided sabbatical time, travel funds, and library resources. Overall institutional support was given by our provost, Keith Dunn. My librarian colleagues, Tom Henderson, Jamie Wilson, and Wyatt Winnie, helped with Interlibrary Loan. Our division administrator, Suzette Jennings, helped me to manage time and space. I also wish to acknowledge the support of my history department colleagues David Davis, Amy Forbes, Bob McElvaine, and Stephanie Rolph. A classicist colleague, Dave Yates, assisted with key translations. Three students worked as research assistants: Alicia Anderson, Kate Sundell, and Lane Tillner. In the summer of 2013, my colleague at Rhodes College, Mike Leslie, welcomed me and my family to the British Studies at Oxford program at St. John's College, whose back gate is across Parks Road from Rhodes House, where I spent many afternoons reading through the bound volumes of the Rhodes Papers.

While I was drafting chapters, I benefited from the comments of colleagues in many different places. I was invited to give presentations at the McGregor Museum, Harvard, MIT, the University of Minnesota, and the University of Houston, where I had memorable interactions with Jennifer Alexander, Karl Ittmann, Sheila Jasanoff, Marty Melosi, and Rosalind Williams. I also had helpful comments from colleagues who attended presentations at the North American Conference on British Studies and the Society for the History of Technology, especially Keith Breckenridge, John Krige, and Richard Price. Bucky Stanton arranged for an engaging virtual presentation online at "Technology's Storytellers."

As the manuscript took shape, I shared ideas, proposals, and drafts with many colleagues. For their comments, I am grateful to William Beinart, Jan-Bart Gewald, Gabrielle Hecht, Karl Ittmann, Nancy Jacobs, Dane Kennedy, Giacomo Macola, John McNeill, Suzanne Moon, Christopher Saunders, and Sandra Swart. When the manuscript reached a third draft, I had the benefit of comments from three anonymous reviewers and from Susan Ferber, executive editor at Oxford University Press, who has shepherded this project from start to finish.

Family members provided insight and support. Over the years it has been a delight to visit with my paternal grandmother's relatives in Oxford, including members of an older generation, Cecil Walker, Denis Walker, and Joan Walker, as well as my contemporaries, Andy and Gill Walker, and Nick and Caroline Walker. When I walked down the steps of Rhodes House, I was mindful that across the street, at the Radcliffe Science Library, my great-great-grandfather, Joseph Walker, spent his career working as the assistant to the well-known head librarian, Henry Acland. In the course of his duties, my ancestor probably met two of the characters who are mentioned in this book, William Gladstone and the Duke of Marlborough, who were library trustees. More than a century later, my oldest son, Ian, the only family member to earn a degree at Oxford, was enrolled in the Byzantine Studies program when I needed help translating inscriptions and passages in classical Greek and Latin.

Immediate family members helped a lot while I was writing the book. Ian and his siblings, Andrew, Neil, Graham, and Robin, joined me on two head-clearing backpacking trips in remote parts of Yellowstone, plus two driving and hiking adventures along Ireland's Wild Atlantic Way. During a sabbatical in the midst of the Covid-19 pandemic, Graham went the extra distance and "podded" with his scribbling father for six months on Hilton Head Island. And back home in Madison, Mississippi, my wife, Joanna, is my Reviewer Z. She, too, read the manuscript and made comments on it. Somehow, she understands my fascination with the past and my traveling proclivities. She supports it all with patience and love.

Notes

INTRODUCTION

1. Junior Bester, "Protesters Throw Poo on Rhodes Statue," *IOL News*, March 10, 2015; Eve Fairbanks, "The Birth of Rhodes Must Fall," *The Guardian*, November 18, 2015.
2. Initially the building was unpopular for replacing picturesque storefronts with its bold design. Evelyn Waugh suggested it be dynamited, but in the 1960s, Jan Morris noted that Oxonians were getting used to it. Edward Impey, "The Rhodes Building at Oriel, 1904–2011: Dynamite or Designate?" *Oxoniensia* 76 (2011): 95–104.
3. *Rhodes Must Fall: The Struggle to Decolonize the Racist Heart of Empire*, ed. Roseanne Chantiluke, Brian Kwoba, and Athinangamso Nkopo (London: Zed Books, 2018); Richard Drayton, "Rhodes Must Not Fall? Statues, Postcolonial 'Heritage' and Temporality," *Third Text* 33, nos. 4–5 (2019): 662–664.
4. Oxford Union, "Must Rhodes Fall? Full Debate," January 19, 2016, https://www.youtube.com/watch?v=y3aBDBdDIgU, accessed December 16, 2023; Mark Twain (Samuel L. Clemens), *Following the Equator: A Journey around the World* (Hartford, CT: American Publishing, 1898), 710. Twain, an anti-imperialist, wrote these words about Rhodes after making an extensive tour of South Africa. Afterwards Beinart conducted more research and called for moving the statue.
5. Caroline Elkins, *Legacy of Violence: A History of the British Empire* (New York: Knopf, 2022), 658–659; Dane Kennedy, *The Imperial History Wars: Debating the British Empire* (London: Bloomsbury, 2018), 138–147; Richard Drayton, "Where Does the World Historian Write From? Objectivity, Moral Conscience and the Past and Present of Imperialism," *Journal of Contemporary History* 46, no. 3 (2011): 671–685.
6. For documents related to the controversy, see Oriel College, "The Rhodes Legacy: Context and History," https://www.oriel.ox.ac.uk/about/the-rhodes-legacy, consulted November 24, 2023. The position of the Rhodes apologists is fleshed out

most fully in Robert Calderisi, *Cecil Rhodes and Other Statues: Dealing Plainly with the Past* (Columbus, OH: Gatekeeper Press, 2021).

7. Peter Redfield and Steven Robins, "An Index of Waste: Humanitarian Design, 'Dignified Living' and the Politics of Infrastructure in Cape Town," *Anthropology Southern Africa* 39, no. 2 (2016): 145–162; Colin McFarlane and Jonathan Silver, "The Poolitical City: 'Seeing Sanitation' and Making the Urban Political in Cape Town," *Antipode* 49, no. 1 (2017): 125–148. On the relationship between hygiene and segregation, see Carl H. Nightingale, *Segregation: A Global History of Divided Cities* (Chicago: University of Chicago Press, 2012).

8. "The Freedom Charter," June 26, 1955, African National Congress, www.anc1912.org.za/the-freedom-charter-2/, consulted March 23, 2024.

9. William Cronon, *Nature's Metropolis: Chicago and the Great West* (New York: Norton, 1991), 210–211; Timothy LeCain, *Mass Destruction: The Men and the Giant Mines that Wired America and Scarred the Planet* (New Brunswick, NJ: Rutgers University Press, 2009), 131–133.

10. Thomas P. Hughes, *Networks of Power: Electrification in Western Society, 1880–1930* (Baltimore: Johns Hopkins University Press, 1983; Paul Israel, *Edison: A Life of Invention* (New York: John Wiley, 1998); Steven Watts, *The People's Tycoon: Henry Ford and the American Century* (New York: Vintage, 2005).

11. H. W. Brands, *American Colossus: The Triumph of Capitalism, 1865–1900* (New York: Doubleday, 2010); Ron Chernow, *Titan: The Life of John D. Rockefeller* (New York: Vintage, 1998); David Nasaw, *Andrew Carnegie* (New York: Penguin, 2006); T. J. Stiles, *The First Tycoon: The Epic Life of Cornelius Vanderbilt* (New York: Vintage, 2009); Richard White, *The Republic for Which It Stands: The United States during Reconstruction and the Gilded Age, 1865–1896* (New York: Oxford University Press, 2017).

12. Clapperton Chakanetsa Mavhunga, *Transient Workspaces: Technologies of Everyday Innovation in Zimbabwe* (Cambridge, MA: MIT Press, 2014), 14–17. See also Jean Comaroff and John Comaroff, *Of Revelation and Revolution*, vol. 1, *Christianity, Colonialism, and Consciousness in South Africa*; vol. 2, *The Dialectics of Modernity on a South African Frontier* (Chicago: University of Chicago Press, 1991, 1997); Jeremy Foster, *Washed with Sun: Landscape and the Making of White South Africa* (Pittsburgh: University of Pittsburgh Press, 2008); Keith Breckenridge, *Biometric State: The Global Politics of Identification and Surveillance in South Africa, 1850 to the Present* (Cambridge: Cambridge University Press, 2014); Gabrielle Hecht, *Being Nuclear: Africans and the Global Uranium Trade* (Cambridge, MA: MIT Press, 2012).

CHAPTER 1

1. Tony Crosby, "The Impact of Industry on the Market Towns of East Hertfordshire," in *A Country of Small Towns: The Development of Hertfordshire's Urban Landscape*

to 1800, ed. Terry Slater and Nigel Goose (Hatfield: University of Hertfordshire Press, 2008), 362–366.

2. Today scholars of ancient and medieval Britain tend to think that all these conquests led as much to acculturation and assimilation as they did to extermination and enslavement. See Francis Pryor, *Britain A.D.: A Quest for Arthur, England, and the Anglo-Saxons* (London: HarperCollins, 2004). See also Barry Cunliffe, *Britain Begins* (Oxford: Oxford University Press, 2013).

3. Christine Clark, *The British Malting Industry since 1830* (London: Hambledon Press, 1998), 14–15.

4. Jo Guldi, *Roads to Power: Britain Invents the Infrastructure State* (Cambridge, MA: Harvard University Press, 2012).

5. Lewis Michell, *The Life and Times of the Right Honourable Cecil Rhodes, 1853–1902*. 2 vols. (London: Mitchell Kennerley, 1910), 1:10–11.

6. Michell, *Life and Times*, 1:12–14; Rotberg, *Founder*, 14–17.

7. Ideas about God-sanctioned dominion may have been tempered by Victorian notions of good stewardship and right relations between landlords and tenants. See Erin Drew, *The Usufructuary Ethos: Power, Politics, and Environment in the Long Eighteenth Century* (Charlottesville: University of Virginia Press, 2021).

8. Michell, *Life and Times*, 1:13–15. On Victorian households, see Lucy Lethbridge, *Servants: A Downstairs History of Britain from the Nineteenth Century to Modern Times* (New York: Norton, 2013).

9. Michell, *Life and Times*, 1:18–19; Rotberg, *Founder*, 16–17. The reminiscences of the servants may be found in documents called "Fragments," "Ideas," and "Says." The compiler is unknown but is thought to have been the earlier Rhodes biographer Lewis Michell. See Rotberg's fn. 2, p. 694, for a description. The documents are held at the Bodleian Library, Rhodes Papers, MSS. Afr. s. 641.

10. Flint, *Cecil Rhodes*, 5–7; McDonald, *Rhodes*, 5; Michell, *Life and Times*, 1:18–22.

11. Gibbon, *Decline and Fall*, 1:94–95.

12. On Rhodes's early interest in Edward Gibbon and Marcus Aurelius, see Gordon Le Sueur, *Cecil Rhodes: The Man and His Work* (New York: McBride, Nast, 1914), 36, 47–48. For classical background, see Nancy Sherman, *Stoic Warriors: The Ancient Philosophy behind the Military Mind* (New York: Oxford University Press, 2005) and *Stoic Wisdom: Ancient Lessons of Modern Resilience* (New York: Oxford University Press, 2021). See also Michael Grant, *The Antonines: The Roman Empire in Transition* (London: Routledge, 1994).

13. Elkins, *Legacy of Violence*, chap. 1: "Liberal Imperialism."

14. John Darwin, *Unfinished Empire: The Global Expansion of Britain* (London: Bloomsbury, 2012); David Cannadine, *Victorious Century: The United Kingdom, 1800–1906* (London: Allen Lane, 2017).

15. Tyler Stovall, *White Freedom: The History of an Idea* (Princeton, NJ: Princeton University Press, 2021).

16. *Natal Witness*, April 28, 1868, 2.

17. Norman Etherington, Patrick Harries, and Bernard K. Mbenga, "From Colonial Hegemonies to Imperial Conquest, 1840–1880," in *The Cambridge History of South Africa*, vol. 1, *From Early Times to 1885*, ed. Carolyn Hamilton, Bernard K. Mbenga, and Robert Ross (Cambridge: Cambridge University Press, 2010), 358–359.
18. Thomas McClendon, chap. 2: "The Man Who Would Be *Inkosi*," in *White Chief, Black Lords: Shepstone and the Colonial State in Natal, South Africa, 1845–1878* (Rochester, NY: University of Rochester Press, 2010), 21–46; Etherington, Harries, and Mbenga, "From Colonial Hegemonies to Imperial Conquest," 358–365; Henry Slater, "Land, Labor and Capital in Natal: The Natal Land and Colonisation Company, 1860–1948," *Journal of African History* 16, no. 2 (1975): 257–283.
19. Jeff Guy, *Theophilus Shepstone and the Forging of Natal* (Pietermaritzburg: University of KwaZulu-Natal Press, 2013), 333–342.
20. Bodleian Library, Rhodes Papers, MSS. Afr. s. 1647, Hildersham Hall Papers (Rhodes Family), Box 1: Rhodes to his mother, April 11, 1871; Joseph Lyman, *Cotton Culture* (New York: Orange Judd, 1868).
21. For context, see John Tosh, "Home and Away: The Flight from Domesticity in Late-Nineteenth-Century England Re-visited," *Gender and History* 27, no. 3 (November 2015): 561–575.
22. Michell, *Life and Times*, 1:29–30, 33.
23. For details, see Martin Legassick, *The Politics of a South African Frontier: The Griqua, the Sotho-Tswana, and the Missionaries, 1780–1840* (Basel: Basler Afrika Bibliographien, 2010).
24. On Arnot, see Thelma Gutsche, *The Microcosm* (Cape Town: Howard Timmins, 1968), 66–68, 74, 91–92, 126–130, 149.
25. Gardner F. Williams, *The Diamond Mines of South Africa*, 2 vols. (New York: Buck & Co., 1905), 1:120–21; Brian Roberts, *Kimberley: The Turbulent City* (Cape Town: David Philip, 1976), 6–8.
26. Reunert, *Diamonds and Gold*, 6–7; Williams, *Diamond Mines of South Africa*, 1:123; Roberts, *Kimberley*, 12–14.
27. Kevin Shillington, *The Colonisation of the Southern Tswana, 1870–1900* (Johannesburg: Ravan Press, 1985), 25, 35–38.
28. Roberts, *Kimberley*, 16–20; Steve Lunderstedt, *The Big Five Mines of Kimberley* (Kimberley: Africana Library, 2008), 11–21.
29. Roberts, *Kimberley*, 44–46; Darren Reid, "Dispossession and Legal Mentalité in Nineteenth-Century South Africa: Grotian and Lockean Theories of Property Acquisition in the Annexations of British Kaffraria and Natalia," *Settler Colonial Studies* 11, no. 1 (2021): 69–85.
30. Charles Payton, *The Diamond Diggings of South Africa: A Personal and Practical Account* (London: Horace Cox, 1872), 8–9; Morley Nkosi, *Mining Deep: The Origins of the Labour Structure in South Africa* (Cape Town: David Philip, 2011), 42–47.
31. Nkosi, *Mining Deep*, chap. 2: "Copper Extends the Cape Colony," and chap. 3: "Diamonds Set the Foundations."
32. Michell, *Life and Times*, 1:31; Williams, *Cecil Rhodes*, 12.

33. The *Natal Witness* reported local cricket scores involving Herbert Rhodes on November 10 and 17, 1868; October 12 and 22, 1869; December 23, 1870. The newspaper also reported a Kimberley (Dutoitspan) match played by Herbert on July 21, 1871. Theophilus Shepstone himself, the secretary of native affairs, once played for Bishop's in Cape Town. For background on colonial cricket, see André Odendaal, Krish Reddy, Christopher Merrett, and Jonty Winch, *Cricket and Conquest: The History of South African Cricket Retold*, vol. 1, *1795–1914* (Cape Town: BestRed, 2016). For cricket's links to imperial history more generally, see Denis Judd, *Empire: The British Imperial Experience from 1765 to the Present* (New York: Basic Books, 1996), 301–303.
34. Bodleian Library, Rhodes Papers, Mss. Afr. s. 1647, Box 1, Hildersham Hall Letters, Rhodes to Mrs. Louisa Rhodes, December 16, 1870, 36.
35. Bodleian Library, Rhodes Papers, MSS. Afr. s. 1647, Hildersham Hall Papers (Rhodes Family), Box 1, 1868–1902, October 18, 1870, 24–25.
36. Bodleian Library, Rhodes Papers, MSS. Afr. s. 1647, Hildersham Hall Papers (Rhodes Family), Box 1, 1868–1902, March 17, 1871, 61–62.
37. Bodleian Library, Rhodes Papers, Mss. Afr. s. 1647, Hildersham Hall Papers (Rhodes Family), Box 1, 1868–1902, Rhodes to Mrs. Louisa Rhodes, September 11, 1870, quotations from 4, 11.
38. Williams, *Cecil Rhodes*, 13.
39. Michell, *Life and Times*, 1:37; *The Natal Witness*, May 31, 1871, 3. The newspaper reports that the toast was given by "Rhodes," so it is possible that this was Herbert, not Cecil, although it does appear that Herbert was in Kimberley at the time.

CHAPTER 2

1. Shillington in *The Colonisation of the Southern Tswana*, chap. 2: "Diamonds, the Tlhaping, and British Annexation, 1867–1871." See also Marian Robertson, *Diamond Fever: South African Diamond History 1866–9 from Primary Sources* (Cape Town: Oxford University Press, 1974); Reunert, *Diamonds and Gold*, 7–8; John Angove, *In the Early Days: The Reminiscences of Pioneer Life on the South African Diamond Fields* (Kimberley: Handel House, 1910), 6–8.
2. Lunderstedt, *Big Five Mines*, 21–39; Colin Newbury, *The Diamond Ring: Business, Politics, and Precious Stones in South Africa, 1867–1947* (Oxford: Clarendon Press, 1989), 9–14.
3. For an overview, see Paul S. Landau, *Popular Politics in the History of South Africa, 1400–1948* (Cambridge: Cambridge University Press, 2010).
4. Shillington, *Colonisation of the Southern Tswana*, chap. 2: "Diamonds, the Tlhaping, and British Annexation, 1867–1871."
5. Ibid.
6. Cornelis W. de Kiewiet, "The Establishment of Responsible Government in Cape Colony, 1870–1872," *Cambridge History of the British Empire*, vol. 8, *South Africa*, 2nd ed. (Cambridge: Cambridge University Press, 1963), 439–458.

7. De Kiewiet, "Establishment of Responsible Government," 457; Shillington, *Colonisation of the Southern Tswana*, 52–55.
8. Skepticism was voiced within the Colonial Office about the details. See Edward Fairfield, "Memorandum on South African Affairs," NA CO 879/9, Conf. Pr. Africa No. 84, 3.
9. Roberts, *Kimberley*, 68–69.
10. *Natal Witness*, September 1, 1871, 2.
11. Michell, *Life and Times*, 1:37–38; Williams, *Cecil Rhodes*, 25.
12. Williams, *Cecil Rhodes*, 25–26. For analysis of settler ideology as it relates to landscape, see Foster, *Washed with Sun*.
13. Bodleian Library, Rhodes Papers, MSS. Afr. s. 134, Basil Williams Papers, Box 1, Letter from Rhodes to Mrs. Louisa Rhodes, January 4, 1872, 1–4, inserted in Notebook VI. On the sublime in mines and industry, see Rosalind Williams, *Notes on the Underground: An Essay on Technology, Society, and the Imagination* (Cambridge, MA: MIT Press, 2008), 88–89. See also David Nye, *American Technological Sublime* (Cambridge, MA: MIT Press, 1994), 34–35, 64.
14. Bodleian Library, Rhodes Papers, MSS. Afr. s. 134, Basil Williams Papers, Box 1, Letter from Rhodes to Mrs. Louisa Rhodes, January 4, 1872, 3, inserted in Notebook VI.
15. Bodleian Library, Rhodes Papers, MSS. Afr. s. 134, Basil Williams Papers, Box 1, Letter from Rhodes to Mrs. Louisa Rhodes, January 4, 1872, 2–3, inserted in Notebook VI.
16. Nkosi, *Mining Deep*, 47–48, 54.
17. On the "Twelve Apostles," see Michell, *Life and Times*, 1:65. On Merriman's early years in Kimberley, see *Selections from the Correspondence of J. X. Merriman*, ed. Phyllis Lewsen (Cape Town: Van Rieebeck Society, 1963), vol. 1, chap. 1.
18. Flint, *Cecil Rhodes*, 18–19; Michell, *Life and Times*, 1:42–45; Rotberg, *Founder*, 76–78; Williams, *Cecil Rhodes*, 30–31.
19. Michell, *Life and Times*, 1:45.
20. William Charles Scully, *Reminiscences of a South African Pioneer* (London: T. Fisher Unwin, 1913), 128–129.
21. Roberts, *Kimberley*, chap. 5: "Dust, Drought, and Flies."
22. Williams, *Diamond Mines of South Africa*, 1:206; Charles A. Payton, *The Diamond Diggings of South Africa: A Personal and Practical Account* (London: Horace Cox, 1872), 8–9; Theodore Reunert, *Diamonds and Gold in South Africa* (Cape Town: Juta, 1893), 7–9.
23. Saskia Coenen Snyder, *A Brilliant Commodity: Diamonds and Jews in a Modern Setting* (New York: Oxford University Press, 2023), chap. 1: "Like Dewdrops in the Waving Grass: Diamonds in South Africa"; Newbury, *Diamond Ring*, 24–25; Williams, *Diamond Mines of South Africa*, 2:152–153.
24. Rotberg, *Founder*, 74.
25. J. G. Lockhart and C. M. Woodhouse, *Rhodes* (London: Hodder and Stoughton, 1963), 59; Michell, *Life and Times*, 1:51; Rotberg, *Founder*, 75. Quotation is from

Bodleian Library, Rhodes Papers, MSS. Afr. t.5, Miscellaneous Papers, Rhodes to Sutherland, n.d., ca. August 1873, 468ff.
26. Rotberg, *Founder*, 65–66; Roger T. Stearn, "Rudd, Charles Dunell," *Oxford Dictionary of National Biography* (2006), accessed online, February 4, 2024.
27. Worger, *South Africa's City of Diamonds*, 115–117.
28. Newbury, *Diamond Ring*, 17–26.
29. Fossor (pseud.), *Twelve Months at the South African Diamond Fields* (London: Edward Stanford, 1872), 43.
30. E. J. Dunn, *Notes on the Diamond-Fields* (Cape Town: Saul Solomon, 1871); E. Héritte, *The Diamond and Other Precious Stones* (Cape Town: Saul Solomon, 1867); George W. Stow, *Geological Notes upon Griqualand West* (London: Taylor and Francis, 1875).
31. Saul Dubow, *A Commonwealth of Knowledge: Science, Sensibility, and White South Africa, 1820–2000* (Oxford: Oxford University Press, 2006).
32. *Cape Monthly Magazine* 1, no. 3 (September 1870): 129–133; 1, no. 4 (October 1870): 249–253; 2, no. 12 (June 1871): 358–64.
33. *Cape Monthly Magazine* 9, no. 52 (October 1874): 254–256; 10, no. 55 (January 1875): 62–63; 10, no. 57 (March 1875): 191–193.
34. Jose Burman, *So High the Road: Mountain Passes of the Western Cape* (Cape Town: Human & Rousseau, 1963), quotation from 5. For a detailed and well-illustrated technical history of each mountain pass, see Graham Ross, *The Romance of Cape Mountain Passes* (Cape Town: David Philip, 2002). An economic and social history of roads and passes still needs to be written. See also Gordon Richings, *The Life and Work of Charles Michell* (Simonstown: Fernwood Press, 2006), chap. 9: "Architect & Civil Engineer" and chap. 10: "Lighthouses and Harbours"; Nigel Penn, "Close and Merciful Watchfulness: John Montagu's Convict System in the Mid-Nineteenth-Century Cape Colony," *Cultural and Social History* 5, no. 4 (2008): 465–480.
35. Burman, *So High the Road*, 133.
36. Wilson and Thompson, *Oxford History of South Africa*, 1:319–325.
37. Purkis, "Railway-Building," chap. 3: "Railway Agitations and the Constitution, 1870–1872."
38. See the following social scientific works about the politics of infrastructure. Brian Larkin, "The Politics and Poetics of Infrastructure," *Annual Review of Anthropology* 42 (2013): 327–343; Ashley Carse, "Keyword Infrastructure: How a Humble French Engineering Term Shaped the Modern World," in Penny Harvey, Casper Bruun Jensen, and Atsuro Morita, *Infrastructures and Social Complexity: A Companion* (London: Routledge, 2019), 27–39; Dennis Rodgers and Bruce O'Neill, "Introduction: Infrastructural Violence: Introduction to the Special Issue," *Ethnography* 13, no. 4 (December 2012): 401–412; James Ferguson, "Structures of Responsibility," *Ethnography* 13, no. 4 (December 2012): 558–562; Carl H. Nightingale, *Segregation: A Global History of Divided Cities* (Chicago: University of Chicago Press, 2012).

CHAPTER 3

1. Rotberg, *Founder*, 69, 72.
2. Michell, *Life and Times*, 1:81.
3. The most famous of these was John Henry Newman, founder of the Oxford Movement. See K. C. Turpin, "The Ascendancy of Oriel," in *The History of the University of Oxford*, vol. 6, *The Nineteenth Century*, part I (Oxford: Oxford University Press, 1997), 183–192; Patrick Allitt, *Catholic Converts: British and American Intellectuals Turn to Rome* (Ithaca, NY: Cornell University Press, 1997), 52–57.
4. Rotberg, *Founder*, 86–87.
5. Percy Alport Molteno, *The Life and Times of Sir John Charles Molteno* (London: Smith, Elder & Co., 1900), 1:203–204, 220.
6. Purkis, "Railway-Building," 158–160.
7. Molteno, *Life and Times*, 1:239.
8. Purkis, "Railway-Building," 337.
9. Ibid., 368.
10. Williams, *Diamond Mines of South Africa*, 227–229.
11. Michell, *Life and Times*, 1:68–70.
12. Robert Vicat Turrell, *Capital and Labour on the Kimberley Diamond Fields, 1871–1890* (Cambridge: Cambridge University Press, 1987), 83; McGregor Museum, Rhodes-Rudd Correspondence, October 9, 1874, no. 1; April 11, 1876, no. 5.
13. Shillington, *Colonisation of the Southern Tswana*, 68–69.
14. Rhodes to Rudd, October 9, 1874, Rudd-Rhodes Correspondence, McGregor Museum, no. 1. See also Michell, *Life and Times*, 1:68–70; Turrell, *Capital and Labour at the Kimberley Diamond Fields*, 84–85.
15. Nkosi, *Mining Deep*, 55–57; Williams, *Diamond Mines of South Africa*, vol. 1, chap. 8: "Opening the Craters"; Theodore Reunert, *Diamonds and Gold in South Africa* (Cape Town: Juta, 1893), 26–30.
16. Worger, *South Africa's City of Diamonds*, 27–28.
17. On entanglement, see On Barak, *Powering Empire: How Coal Made the Middle East and Sparked Global Carbonization* (Berkeley: University of California Press, 2020), 225–231.
18. Newbury, *Diamond Ring*, 38, 41.
19. Shillington, *The Colonization of the Southern Tswana*, 70–72. The connection between the earlier compounds and the later apartheid-era townships is made by Alan Mabin, "Labour, Capital, Class Struggle, and the Origins of Residential Segregation in Kimberley, 1880–1920," *Journal of Historical Geography* 12 (1986): 4–26.
20. Worger, *South Africa's City of Diamonds*, 28–29; "Report of Lieut.-Colonel Crossman, R.E., on the Affairs of Griqua-Land West," NA CO 879/9 Conf. Pr. Africa No. 96, 4.
21. Newbury, *Diamond Ring*, 14–17.
22. Turrell, *Capital and Labour on the Kimberley Diamond Fields*, 34–36.

23. Roberts, *Kimberley*, 131–133; Turrell, *Capital and Labour on the Kimberley Diamond Fields*, 36–45.
24. Bodleian Library, Rhodes Papers, MSS. Afr. s. 1647, Hildersham Hall, Box 1, Rhodes to Frank Rhodes, August 19, 1875, 98–99.
25. Turrell, *Capital and Labour on the Kimberley Diamond Fields*, 51–56.
26. Priya Satia, *Time's Monster: How History Makes History* (Cambridge, MA: Harvard University Press, 2020), chap. 3: "Progress of Elimination."
27. James A. Froude, *Two Lectures on South Africa* (London: Longmans, Green, 1880), 20, 41.
28. Ciaran Brady, *James Anthony Froude: An Intellectual Biography of a Victorian Prophet* (Oxford: Oxford University Press, 2013), 312–313. See also "Correspondence Relating to the Affairs of South Africa," June 1876, NA CO 879/9, Conf. Pr. Africa No. 99.
29. UK National Archives, CO 879/9, Confidential Print, Africa No. 96, "Colonel Crossman's Report, May 1, 1876," 43.
30. Ibid.
31. Ibid., 46–47.
32. Bodleian Library, Rhodes Papers, MSS. Afr. s. 134, Basil Williams Papers, Notebook 1, Letter of Rhodes to an anonymous recipient, n.d. 1876, 13–15. Republished in the *Diamond Fields Advertiser* Christmas Number, 1906. Clipping sent to Williams by J. X. Merriman.
33. Claire Leith, *Tin and Diamonds, A Fortune in the Making: The Life and Times of Francis Oats* (Penryn: Trevithick Society, 2009), 10–20.
34. UK National Archives, CO 879/9, Confidential Print, Africa No. 96, "Report of Lieut.-Col. Crossman," Encl. No. 6, Oats to Crossman, December 10, 1875, 62–64.
35. For background on pumping engines and winding engines, see Richard L. Hills, *Power from Steam: A History of the Stationary Steam Engine* (Cambridge: Cambridge University Press, 1989), 96–106, 141–144.
36. UK National Archives, CO 879/9, Confidential Print, Africa No. 96, "Report of Lieut.-Col. Crossman," Encl. No. 12, "Report of the Provincial Engineer," 76–84; Rhodes is referenced on 82.
37. UK National Archives, CO 879/9, Confidential Print, Africa No. 96, "Report of Lieut.-Col. Crossman," 14–16.
38. T. C. Kitto, *Report on the Diamond Mines of Griqualand West by the Order of H. E. Col. C. Warren, Administrator*, 59–60. As quoted by Mabin, "Residential Segregation in Kimberley," 12.
39. Daron Acemoglu and James A. Robinson, *Why Nations Fail: The Origins of Power, Prosperity, and Poverty* (New York: Currency, 2012), 91–95.

CHAPTER 4

1. Bodleian Library, Rhodes Papers, MSS. Afr. t. 14, Rhodes to Rudd, June 1, 1876, original with corrected transcription by R. V. Turrell, 214–228, quotations are from

214–221. Several more letters written in the spring of 1876 are contained in MSS. Afr. t. 14 and also indicate technical understanding, see 10–21.
2. Michell, *Life and Times*, 1:82–86; Rotberg, *Founder*, 90–92.
3. L. W. B. Brockliss, *The University of Oxford: A History* (Oxford: Oxford University Press, 2016), pt. 3, "Introduction: Reform and Resurrection"; Reba N. Soffer, *Discipline and Power: The University, History, and the Making of the English Elite, 1870–1930* (Stanford, CA: Stanford University Press, 1994), chap. 2: "Consensus and Tradition."
4. Jan Morris, *Oxford*, 3rd ed. (Oxford: Oxford University Press, 1987), 184–186; Peter Mitchell, *Imperial Nostalgia: How the British Conquered Themselves* (Manchester: Manchester University Press, 2021), 104.
5. Mary Beard, *Confronting the Classics: Traditions, Adventures, and Innovations* (New York: Norton, 2013). For the debate about White supremacist ideology in classical studies, see Solveig Lucia Gold, "The Colorblind Bard," July 13, 2017, and Dan-El Padilla Peralta and Solveig Lucia Gold, "The Colorblind Bard: An Exchange," August 31, 2017," in *The New Criterion*, newcriterion.com, accessed February 4, 2021. See also Rachel Poser, "He Wants to Save the Field of Classics from Whiteness. Can the Field Survive?" in *New York Times Magazine*, February 2, 2021.
6. Aristotle, *Politics*, trans. Benjamin Jowett (Oxford: Clarendon Press, 1885), bk. 1, chap. 5, p. 8.
7. Princess Catherine Radziwill, *Cecil Rhodes: Man and Empire-Maker* (New York: Funk & Wagnalls, 1918), 126–127. Radziwill was not an entirely reliable source of information, but unlike other stories she told about Rhodes, she did not have a reason to invent this one. On Reade, see Felix Driver, *Geography Militant: Cultures of Exploration and Empire* (Oxford: Blackwell, 2001), chap. 5: "Becoming an Explorer: The Martyrdom of Winwood Reade," 90–116. See the discussion of Reade's influence on Rhodes in Flint, *Cecil Rhodes*, 24–26. See also Dane Kennedy, *The Highly Civilized Man: Richard Burton and the Victorian World* (Cambridge, MA: Harvard University Press, 2005), 160–163.
8. Reade, *Martyrdom of Man*, 7.
9. Ibid., 405.
10. Ibid., 97.
11. *The Dialogues of Plato*, 4 vols., trans. Benjamin Jowett (Oxford: Oxford University Press, 1871).
12. Bodleian Library, Rhodes Papers, MSS. Afr. s. 134, Basil Williams Papers, Notebook 1, Letter of Rhodes to an anonymous recipient, n.d. 1876, 13–15. Republished in the *Diamond Fields Advertiser* Christmas Number, 1906. The clipping was sent to Williams by J. X. Merriman. For discussion of the wider context of male "flight from domesticity," see Tosh, "Home and Away," 561–575, with examples taken from the life of Rhodes on 566–567.
13. Linda Dowling, *Hellenism and Homosexuality in Victorian Oxford* (Ithaca, NY: Cornell University Press, 1998), 35–36.

14. Patrick M. Geoghegan, "James Rochfort Maguire," *Dictionary of Irish Biography* (2009), https://www.dib.ie/biography/maguire-james-rochfort-a5359.
15. "Obituary: Sir Charles Herbert Theophilus Metcalfe," *PICE (Proceedings of the Institution of Civil Engineers)* 228 (1928): 350–352.
16. Eric Hobsbawm, *Industry and Empire: The Making of Modern English Society*, vol. 2, *1750 to the Present Day* (New York: Pantheon, 1968), 152–153; Peter Mathias, *The First Industrial Nation: An Economic History of Britain, 1700–1914*, 2nd ed. (London: Methuen, 1983), 389–391.
17. George R. Parkin, *Imperial Federation: The Problem of National Unity* (London: Macmillan, 1892), 31, 48–49.
18. He was the uncle of another famous historian, Arnold J. Toynbee. The elder Toynbee's biographer was a later, important contact for Rhodes, who had also been at Oxford in the 1870s: Alfred Milner, *Reminiscences of Arnold Toynbee* (London: Edward Arnold, 1901), 28; John Marlowe, *Milner: Apostle of Empire* (London: Hamish Hamilton, 1976).
19. T. H. Green, *Prolegomena to Ethics*, ed. A. C. Bradley (Oxford: Clarendon Press, 1890).
20. Milner, *Reminiscences of Arnold Toynbee*, 49–56.
21. David Gilmour, *Curzon: Imperial Statesman* (New York: Farrar, Straus and Giroux, 1994), 23–39; Roy Jenkins, *Asquith: Portrait of a Man and an Era* (New York: Chilmark Press, 1964), 20–23.
22. John Ruskin, *Lectures on Art: Delivered before the University of Oxford in Hilary Term, 1870* (New York: John Wiley, 1873), 28–32.
23. Herbert Baker and W. T. Stead, *Cecil Rhodes: The Man and His Dream* (Bulawayo: Books of Rhodesia, 1977), 11. This book is a reprint of Baker's book, *Cecil Rhodes: By His Architect* (Oxford: Oxford University Press, 1934), and Stead's book, *The Last Will and Testament of Cecil John Rhodes* (London: Review of Reviews Press, 1902).
24. Oscar Wilde, "Art and the Handicraftsman," in *Miscellanies*, ed. Robert Ross (London: Methuen, 1908), 291–308. Quotation from 306–307. Other students working in the swamp that winter included Alfred Milner, George Parkin, and Arnold Toynbee.
25. Alexander Langlands, *Craeft: An Inquiry into the Origins and True Meaning of Traditional Crafts* (New York: Norton, 2018), 27–31; Howard P. Segal, *Utopias: A Brief History from Ancient Writings to Virtual Communities* (Oxford: Wiley-Blackwell, 2012), 58–60, 237.
26. Rhodes biographers are at variance when it comes to Ruskin's influence on Rhodes. Williams and Flint believe that Ruskin was a major influence. See Williams, *Cecil Rhodes*, 41–42, and Flint, *Cecil Rhodes*, 27–28. Rotberg believes the opposite. See Rotberg, *Founder*, 89, 95.
27. Bodleian Library, Rhodes Papers, MSS. Afr. t. 14, Rhodes to Rudd, June 1, 1876, original with corrected transcription by R. V. Turrell, 214–228, quotation is from 219–220. On Rhodes studying law, see Michell, *Life and Times*, 1:88–91.

28. Richard Ellmann, *Oscar Wilde* (New York: Alfred A. Knopf, 1988), 40, 68.
29. Jessica Harland-Jacobs, *Builders of Empire: Freemasonry and British Imperialism, 1717–1927* (Chapel Hill: University of North Carolina Press, 2007), 10–14, quotation from 283–84. On Rhodes becoming captivated by the masonic world view, see Flint, *Cecil Rhodes*, 29–30.
30. The "Confession of 1877," also known as Rhodes's "Confession of Faith," has been faithfully reproduced in Flint, *Cecil Rhodes*, 248–252. The original manuscript is housed in the Bodleian Library, Rhodes Papers, MSS. Afr. t. 1. Flint's version records a classical Greek phrase, μεγα χοχεγις, or "mega chochegis." This is an error in transcription. "Chochegis" is not a word. The correct transcription should actually be one word, "megalopsuchia," meaning "magnanimity" or "greatness of soul." This is one of the key virtues that Aristotle described in the *Nicomachean Ethics* (4.3).
31. Flint, *Cecil Rhodes*, 30–33, 248–249.
32. Ibid., 30–33, 249–250.
33. W. E. Gladstone, "Aggression on Egypt and Freedom in the East," *The Nineteenth Century: A Monthly Review* (1877): 149–166, quotation from 158. Pamphlet reprinted in London by an unknown publisher in 1884; Dean Jaensch, "Henry Bull Templar Strangways," *Australian Dictionary of Biography*, accessed online, June 5, 2017.
34. H. B. T. Strangways, "African Overland Telegraph," *Proceedings of the Royal Geographical Society* 1, no. 3 (March 1879): 217–218; Kerry Nicholls, James Augustus Grant, and Edwin Arnold, *Remarks on a Proposed Line of Telegraph Overland from Egypt to the Cape of Good Hope* (London: n.p., 1876); Harry Johnston, "My Story of the Cape to Cairo Scheme," in Leo Weinthal, *The Story of the Cape to Cairo Railway and River Route from 1887 to 1922*, vol. 1, *The Record and Romance of an Imperial* Project (London: Pioneer, 1923), 65–93; quotation is from 68. Weinthal's five volumes on the Cape-to-Cairo railway is an odd combination of history, policy, travel, and fantasy. For an analysis, see Merrington, "Staggered Orientalism," 353–354. For an early overview, see Lois A. C. Raphael, *The Cape-to-Cairo Dream: A Study in British Imperialism* (New York: Columbia University Press, 1936; repr. New York: Octagon Books, 1973), chap. 1: "Paths into Africa."
35. Flint, *Cecil Rhodes*, 250–252.
36. Duncan S. A. Bell, "Dissolving Distance: Technology, Space, and Empire in British Political Thought, 1770–1900," *Journal of Modern History* 77, no. 3 (September 2005): 523–562. Quotations from 525–526.
37. Bell, "Dissolving Distance," 552–553.
38. Rhodes to Rudd, June 1, 1876, Bodleian Library, Rhodes Papers, MSS. Afr. t. 14 (214–228); Rotberg, *Founder*, 97.
39. Joseph Millerd Orpen, *Reminiscences of Life in South Africa from 1846 to the Present Day*, 2 vols. (1908 and 1916; repr. ed. Cape Town: C. Struik, 1964); Andrew Bank, *Bushmen in a Victorian World: The Remarkable Story of the Bleek-Lloyd Collection of Bushman Folklore* (Cape Town: Double Storey Press, 2006), 304–311; Dubow, *Commonwealth of Knowledge*, 109.

40. Ian Colvin, *The Life of Jameson* (London: Arnold, 1922), 1:52; Lockhart and Woodhouse, *Rhodes*, 68; Rotberg, *Founder*, 103.
41. Rotberg, *Founder*, 103–104.

CHAPTER 5

1. Le Sueur, *Cecil Rhodes*, 7; McDonald, *Rhodes*, 48–49; Rotberg, *Founder*, 104–105; Williams, *Cecil Rhodes*, 146.
2. J. W. Matthews, *Incwadi Yami: Or Twenty Years' Personal Experience in South Africa* (New York: Rogers & Sherwood, 1887), 307–309.
3. Shillington, *Colonisation of the Southern Tswana*, 74–82.
4. Charles Warren, "Cecil Rhodes's Early Days in South Africa," *Contemporary Review* 81 (1902): 643–654. The quotation is from 649.
5. Matthews, *Incwadi Yami*, 107–108; Roberts, *Kimberley*, 143–146.
6. Russel Viljoen, "The Smallpox War on the Kimberley Diamonds Fields in the mid-1880s," *African Historical Review* 35, no. 1 (2004): 5–18. See also Matthews, *Incwadi Yami*, 108–111; Rotberg, *Founder*, 187; Worger, *South Africa's City of Diamonds*, 103–104.
7. Patrick Harries, *Work, Culture, and Identity: Migrant Laborers in Mozambique and South Africa, c. 1860–1910* (Portsmouth, NH: Heinemann, 1994), 48–63.
8. Lockhart and Woodhouse, *Rhodes*, 76–77; Rotberg, *Founder*, 127; Charles van Onselen, *The Cowboy and the Capitalist: John Hays Hammond, the American West, and the Jameson Raid in South Africa* (Charlottesville: University of Virginia Press, 2017), 139–145.
9. Rotberg, *Founder*, 147–148; Williams, *Cecil Rhodes*, 53.
10. Flint, *Cecil Rhodes*, 48; Rotberg, *Founder*, 113–114; Snyder, *Brilliant Commodity*, 54–55.
11. Stow, "Memoir of the Formation of the De Beers Mining Company," 12–13.
12. Snyder, *Brilliant Commodity*, 69–70.
13. Rotberg, *Founder*, 116–117; Stow, "Memoir of the formation of the de Beers Mining Company Limited," 7–9.
14. Rotberg, *Founder*, 116–117; Stow, "Memoir of the formation of the de Beers Mining Company Limited," 7–9.
15. Snyder, *Brilliant Commodity*, 56–57.
16. Stow, "Memoir of the formation of the de Beers Mining Company Limited," 14–15.
17. Williams, *Diamond Mines of South Africa*, 1:236–245. For the financial context, see Newbury, *Diamond Ring*, 53–59.
18. A. P. Cartwright, *The Dynamite Company: The Story of African Explosives and Chemical Industries* Limited (Cape Town: Purnell, 1964), 37–41.
19. LeCain, *Mass Destruction*, 139–141; Newbury, *Diamond Ring*, 60; Stephen R. Bown, *A Most Damnable Invention: Dynamite, Nitrates, and the Making of the Modern World* (New York: St. Martin's, 2005), 80–83.

20. CPP 1885 G28, "Report of the Inspector of Mines, Kimberley, for the Year 1884," 10, 30; Williams, *Diamond Mines of South Africa*, 2:27.
21. CPP 1890 G11, "Report of the Inspector of Mines, Kimberley, for the Year 1889," 3.
22. Michell, *Life and Times*, 1:185–189; Rotberg, *Founder*, 116–117.
23. Flint, *Cecil Rhodes*, 51. For a more charitable view, see Weinthal, *Memories, Mines, and Millions*.
24. Jade Davenport, *Digging Deep: A History of Mining in South Africa* (Johannesburg: Jonathan Ball, 2013), 187–197.
25. Rotberg, *Founder*, 123–125; Rhodes to Merriman, May 16, 1880, in Lewsen, *Correspondence of J. X. Merriman*, 1:81–82.
26. Anthony J. Dachs, "Missionary Imperialism: The Case of Bechuanaland," *Journal of African History* 13, no. 4 (1972): 649; Rotberg, *Founder*, 151.
27. Trollope, *South Africa*, 2:165. The official language was Dutch until 1925.
28. Michell, *Life and Times*, 1:94; Williams, *Cecil Rhodes*, 57.
29. Michell, *Life and Times*, 1:96–101.
30. William Ewart Gladstone, *Political Speeches in Scotland, November and December 1879* (London: Ridgway, 1879), 92–94.
31. Pamela Scully, "Liquor and Labor in the Western Cape, 1870–1900," in *Liquor and Labor in Southern Africa*, ed. Jonathan Crush and Charles Ambler (Athens: Ohio University Press, 1992).
32. T. R. H. Davenport, *The Afrikaner Bond, 1880–1911* (Cape Town: Oxford University Press, 1966), chap. 5: "Assault on the Imperial Factor"; Rotberg, *Founder*, 132–133; Williams, *Cecil Rhodes*, 60–62.
33. Mordechai Tamarkin, *Cecil Rhodes and the Cape Afrikaners: The Imperial Colossus and the Colonial Parish Pump* (London: Frank Cass, 1996), 45–46.
34. Rotberg, *Founder*, 131–132. On Solomon, see the biography written by his son: William Ewart Gladstone Solomon, *Saul Solomon: The Member for Cape Town* (Cape Town: Oxford University Press, 1948).
35. Storey, *Guns, Race, and Power in Colonial South Africa*, chap. 10: "The Origins of the Cape-Sotho Gun War, 1879–1880."
36. Vindex, *Cecil Rhodes*, 34–35. For an interpretation from the perspective of a contemporary biographer partial to Rhodes, see Michell, *Life and Times*, 1:96–102.
37. Vindex, *Cecil Rhodes*, 38–40.
38. Flint, *Cecil Rhodes*, 56–57; Lockhart and Woodhouse, *Rhodes*, 88–89; Michell, *Life and Times*, 1:138–142; Rotberg, *Founder*, 139–145; Williams, *Cecil Rhodes*, 65–66. Williams quotes Rhodes on the death of Gordon, "I am sorry I was not with him." The quotation is undocumented.
39. Vindex, *Cecil Rhodes*, 52–53.
40. Rotberg, *Founder*, 137–139; Worger, *South Africa's City of Diamonds*, 166–167.
41. Newbury, *Diamond Ring*, 59–60.

CHAPTER 6

1. Neil Parsons, *King Khama, Emperor Joe, and the Great White Queen: Victorian Britain through African Eyes* (Chicago: University of Chicago Press, 1998), 34–45.
2. Vindex, *Cecil Rhodes*, 40–41.
3. Deryck M. Schreuder, *The Scramble for Southern Africa: The Politics of Partition Reappraised* (Cambridge: Cambridge University Press, 1981), chap. 4: "The German Factor, 1884–85," and chap. 5: "Denying Bechuanaland to the Boers and the Germans, 1884–86."
4. Flint, *Cecil Rhodes*, 62; Michell, *Life and Times*, 160–184.
5. Flint, *Cecil Rhodes*, 60–62; Michell, *Life and Times*, 182–183.
6. John Mackenzie, *Austral Africa: Losing It or Ruling It*, 2 vols. (London: Sampson Low, 1887), 1:155.
7. Mackenzie, *Austral Africa*, 1:118.
8. Vindex, *Cecil Rhodes*, 62–69.
9. Ibid.
10. Flint, *Cecil Rhodes*, 64–66.
11. Michell, *Life and Times*, 1:200–204.
12. Rotberg, *Founder*, 161–162; Francis "Matabele" Thompson, *An Autobiography*, ed. Nancy Rouillard (Bulawayo: Books of Rhodesia, 1936; repr. ed. 1977), chap. 3: "With Rhodes in Bechuanaland."
13. There are many accounts of the "Scramble for Africa." The best known is Ronald Robinson and John Gallagher with Alice Denny, *Africa and the Victorians: The Official Mind of Imperialism* (London: Macmillan, 1961; 2nd ed. 1981). For a review and critique, see Ronald Hyam, "The Partition of Africa," *Historical Journal* 7, no. 1 (1964): 154–169. For a focused treatment on Bechuanaland, see Schreuder, *Scramble for Southern Africa*, chap. 5: "Denying Bechuanaland to the Boers and the Germans, 1884–6," and for bibliography see 372–379.
14. Flint, *Cecil Rhodes*, 69–72: Lockhart and Woodhouse, *Rhodes*, 101–105; Rotberg, *Founder*, 170–173.
15. Paul Maylam, *Rhodes, the Tswana, and the British: Colonialism, Collaboration, and Conflict in the Bechuanaland Protectorate, 1885–1899* (Westport, CT: Greenwood Press, 1980), 18–20; Burman, *Early Cape Railways*, 93.
16. Parsons, "Victorian Internet," 98–99.
17. Michell, *Life and Times*, 1:208–215; Williams, *Cecil Rhodes*, 84–86.
18. Williams, *Cecil Rhodes*, 86–90.
19. Parsons, *King Khama, Emperor Joe*, 41–44.
20. Maylam, *Rhodes, the Tswana, and the British*, 20–21; Flint, *Cecil Rhodes*, 71; C. W. de Kiewiet, *The Imperial Factor in South Africa* (London: Frank Cass, 1937; repr. ed. 1965), 325.
21. Shillington, *Colonisation of the Southern Tswana*, chap. 8: "The Blessings of British Rule." Quote is from 207.

22. Galbraith, *Crown and Charter*, 39–41; Rotberg, *Founder*, 175–176.
23. On images of the Ndebele nation, see Sabelo J. Ndlovu-Gatsheni, *The Ndebele Nation: Reflections on Hegemony, Memory, and Historiography* (Pretoria: UNISA Press, 2009).
24. Alois Mlambo, *A History of Zimbabwe* (Cambridge: Cambridge University Press, 2014), 26–29; David Beach, *The Shona and Their Neighbors* (Oxford: Blackwell, 1994), chap. 4: "Two Centuries of Change, c. 1700–1890."
25. Bodleian Library, Rhodes Papers, MSS Afr. s. 134, Box 1, Notebook 6, Rhodes to Ralph Williams, July 12, 1885, copied by Basil Williams, 64–84, quotation is from 76.
26. Bodleian Library, Rhodes Papers, MSS Afr. s. 134, Box 1, Notebook 6, Rhodes to Ralph Williams, July 12, 1885, copied by Basil Williams, 64–84, quotations from 72, 78.
27. Bodleian Library, Rhodes Papers, MSS Afr. s. 134, Box 1, Notebook 6, Rhodes to Ralph Williams, July 12, 1885, copied by Basil Williams, 64–84, quotation from 6.
28. Cecil Headlam, "The Race for the Interior," in *The Cambridge History of the British Empire*, vol. 8 (Cambridge: Cambridge University Press, 1961), 526–536.
29. Charles S. Maier, *Once within Borders: Territories of Power, Wealth, and Belonging since 1500* (Cambridge, MA: Harvard University Press, 2016), 188–195.

CHAPTER 7

1. CPP 1882 G.27, Report of the Diamond Mine Inspector, 10–12.
2. On the dynamic human and material network of the mine, see Thomas Andrews, *Killing for Coal: America's Deadliest Labor War* (Cambridge, MA: Harvard University Press, 2008). See also LeCain, *Mass Destruction*.
3. CPP 1882 G.27, Report of the Diamond Mine Inspector, 9.
4. Annual Report, DBMCo, 1885, 9; Newbury, *Diamond Ring*, 79–80.
5. Annual Report, DBMCo, 1885, 9.
6. Williams, *Diamond Mines of South Africa*, 1:252.
7. Annual Report, DBMCo, 1886.
8. Rhodes to Rudd, February 1, 1881, no. 9, Rudd-Rhodes Correspondence, McGregor Museum; Williams, *Diamond Mines of South Africa*, 1:246.
9. Annual Report, DBMCo, 1886, 9.
10. Annual Report, DBMCo, 1884, 11.
11. Newbury, *Diamond Ring*, 87; Rotberg, *Founder*, 187–188; Turrell, *Capital and Labour at the Kimberley Diamond Fields*, 210–211; Worger, *South Africa's City of Diamonds*, 195–197.
12. Newbury, *Diamond Ring*, 88–89; Rotberg, *Founder*, 188–190; J. X. Merriman to A. Merriman, February 10, 1886, in Lewsen, *Correspondence of J. X. Merriman*, 1:208; Sauer, *Ex Africa*, 96.
13. Michell, *Life and Times*, 1:188.
14. Rotberg, *Founder*, 191–192; McGregor Museum, Box 1.1, Letters of Rhodes to Stow, July 12, 1886, 2.

15. McGregor Museum, Box 1.1, Letters of Rhodes to Stow, July 12, 1886, 2.
16. Ibid., 1–2.
17. Leith, *Tin and Diamonds*, 29–31; Rotberg, *Founder*, 198–199.
18. The restriction of mobility in twentieth-century South Africa has been explored in Gordon Pirie, "Railways and Labour Migration to the Rand Mines: Constraints and Significance," *Journal of Southern African Studies* 19, no. 4 (1993): 713–730. See also Jacob Dlamini, *Safari Nation: A Social History of the Kruger National Park* (Columbus: Ohio University Press, 2020), chap. 3: "New Africans"; chap. 4: "From Roots to Routes." Studies about freedom and mobility in the US are revelatory. See Mia Bay, *Traveling Black: A Story of Race and Resistance* (Cambridge, MA: Harvard University Press, 2021); W. Jeffrey Bolster, *Black Jacks: African American Seamen in the Age of Sail* (Cambridge, MA: Harvard University Press, 1997); Gretchen Sorin, *Driving while Black: African American Travel and the Road to Civil Rights* (New York: Liveright, 2020).
19. Worger, *South Africa's City of Diamonds*, chap. 3: "Workers as Criminals: The Rule of Law, 1870–86," quotation from 124.
20. The etymology of the word "compound" indicates the international origins of mining practices. The *Oxford English Dictionary* and the *Dictionary of South African English* note two origins for the word: from Middle English, it means the joining together of two or more things; from Southeast Asia, connected to South Africa via the Dutch East India Company, it derives from *kampong*, a fenced village.
21. CPP 1885, G.28, Report of the Diamond Mine Inspector, 11.
22. Annual Report, DBMCo, 1883.
23. Worger, *South Africa's City of Diamonds*, 129, 184–187.
24. Annual Report, DBMCo, 1884.
25. Newbury, *Diamond Ring*, 71–72.
26. Annual Report, DBMCo, 1886, 9.
27. Worger, *South Africa's City of Diamonds*, 141–146; CPP 1885, G.28, Report of the Diamond Mine Inspector, 9; Philip Payton, *The Cornish Overseas: A History of Cornwall's "Great Emigration"* (Exeter: University of Exeter Press, 2005), 357.
28. Annual Report, DBMCo, 1888.
29. Rotberg, *Founder*, 220.
30. Thompson, *Autobiography*, 81–85.
31. On the structure of the compounds, see Williams, *Diamond Mines of South Africa*, vol. 2, chap. 14: "The Workers in the Mines." On alcohol consumption by non-Europeans, see Satnam Sanghera, *Empireland: How Imperialism Has Shaped Modern Britain* (London: Penguin, 2021), 95.
32. Williams, *Diamond Mines of South Africa*, 2:81; see also 1:99.
33. Marcia Pointon, "De Beers's Diamond Mine in the 1880s: Robert Harris and the Kimberley Searching System," *History of Photography* 42, no. 1 (2018): 4–24.
34. Newbury, *Diamond Ring*, 125–127.
35. Annual Report, DBMCo, 1887, 4.

36. Harries, *Work, Culture, and Identity*, 66–71. For comparisons, see Arthur L. Bowley, *Wages in the United Kingdom in the Nineteenth Century* (Cambridge: Cambridge University Press, 1900), 107–109.
37. Harries, *Work, Culture, and Identity*, 66–71. Quotation is from 71.
38. Harries, *Work, Culture, and Identity*, 71–74.
39. Ibid., 75–77.
40. A. Williams, *Some Dreams Come True*, 513–514 and passim.
41. Ibid., 222–223.
42. McGregor Museum, Rhodes-Rudd Correspondence, January 8, 1886, no. 13.
43. Elaine Katz, "Outcrop and Deep Level Mining in South Africa before the Anglo-Boer War: Re-Examining the Blainey Thesis," *Economic History Review* 48, no. 2 (May 1995), 309; Robert Kubicek, *Economic Imperialism in Theory and Practice: The Case of South African Gold Mining Finance, 1886–1914* (Durham, NC: Duke University Press, 1979), 39–42.
44. Rhodes to Rudd, date of letter missing, no. 22, Rudd-Rhodes Correspondence, McGregor Museum.
45. Flint, *Cecil Rhodes*, 80.
46. Sauer, *Ex Africa*, 118–120.
47. Ibid.
48. J. Percy FitzPatrick, *South African Memories: Scraps of History*, ed. Deborah Lavin (Johannesburg: Donker, 1979), 75; Colvin, *Jameson*, 1:81; Lockhart and Woodhouse, *Rhodes*, 125–126; Rotberg, *Founder*, 194–195; Sauer, *Ex Africa*, 119.
49. McGregor Museum, Rhodes-Rudd Correspondence, December 12, 1886, no. 14.
50. Sauer, *Ex Africa*, 129; A. Williams, *Some Dreams Come True*, 542–555.
51. John Cooper, *The Unexpected Story of Nathaniel Rothschild* (London: Bloomsbury, 2015); Niall Ferguson, *The House of Rothschild: The World's Banker, 1849–1999* (New York: Penguin, 1999).
52. Kubicek, *Economic Imperialism*, 87–88.
53. Rhodes to Rudd, December 12, 1886, no. 14, Rudd-Rhodes Correspondence, McGregor Museum.
54. Lockhart and Woodhouse, *Rhodes*, 128.

CHAPTER 8

1. DBMCo Annual Report of 1887, 1–3.
2. Annual Report, DBMCo, 1887, 10.
3. Annual Report, DBMCo, 1888.
4. CPP 1890 G.11, "Government Mine Inspector Report," 42.
5. Annual Report, DBMCo, 1888, 11.
6. On mine-mapping in the USA, see Eric Nystrom, *Seeing Underground: Maps, Models, and Mining Engineering in America* (Reno: University of Nevada Press, 2014), 52.

7. Annual Reports, DBMCo, 1882–1887; Williams, *Diamond Mines of South Africa*, 2:15–17.
8. Annual Reports, DBMCo, 1886, 2; 1887, 3; 1888, 11.
9. Annual Reports, DBMCo, 1881, 1886–1888.
10. Rotberg, *Founder*, 200; Snyder, *Brilliant Commodity*, 34–38, 65–67, 161; Williams, *Cecil Rhodes*, 43–47.
11. Rotberg, *Founder*, 201; Williams, *Cecil Rhodes*, 99–100.
12. Alpheus Williams, *Some Dreams Come True* (Cape Town: Timmins, 1948), 229.
13. Ferguson, *House of Rothschild*, 356–360; Flint, *Cecil Rhodes*, 86–87; Newbury, *Diamond Ring*, 91–93; Rotberg, *Founder*, 202–205.
14. Flint, *Cecil Rhodes*, 86–87; Rotberg, *Founder*, 202–205.
15. McGregor Museum, Box 1.1, Letters of Rhodes to Stow, October 22, 1887, 35.
16. Stow, "Memoir of the formation of the de Beers Mining Company Limited," 65–91; Flint, *Cecil Rhodes*, 88–90; Lockhart and Woodhouse, *Rhodes*, 115–121; Rotberg, *Founder*, 207–209.
17. Newbury, *Diamond Ring*, 92–93.
18. Michell, *Life and Times*, 1:190–194; Rotberg, *Founder*, 207–210.
19. Annual Report, DBMC, 1888, 12.
20. Annual Report, DBMC, 1888, 13.
21. *Daily Independent*, July 17, 1888. For comparisons of responses, see Anthony F. C. Wallace, "The Disaster Syndrome," in Anthony F. C. Wallace, *Revitalizations and Mazeways: Essays on Culture Change*, vol. 1, ed. Robert S. Grumet (Lincoln: University of Nebraska Press, 2003): 149–163, especially 155–158.
22. *Diamond Fields Advertiser*, July 12 and July 13, 1888; *Daily Independent*, July 13, 1888.
23. *Diamond Fields Advertiser*, July 14, 1888.
24. *Daily Independent*, July 14, 1888.
25. Ibid., July 23, 1888.
26. *Diamond Fields Advertiser*, July 14, 1888; *Daily Independent*, July 14, 1888.
27. W. Pickering to Morrogh, Cape Town, ca. July 14–15, 1888, DBMC Letterbook 6, 207–208.
28. W. Pickering to Secretary, De Beers Mining Co., London, ca. July 15, 1888, DBMC Letterbook 6, 241.
29. W. Pickering to Capt. Penfold, Cape Town, July 17, 1888, DBMC Letterbook 6, 246–248.
30. W. Pickering to Morrogh, International Hotel, Cape Town, ca. July 18, 1888, DBMC Letterbook 6, 270.
31. *Diamond Fields Advertiser*, July 13, 1888. The *Diamond Fields Advertiser* usually supported Rhodes, while the *Independent* was owned by Rhodes's rival, Joseph B. Robinson. Robinson relished stirring controversy among the mine owners, and the *D.F.A.*'s editor, Robert Fisher Wilson, had a reputation for independence. Roberts, *Kimberley*, 172, 299; Steve Lunderstedt, "Today in Kimberley's

History: Newspaper Editors," March 23, 2018, online publication: www.kimberley.org.za.
32. Jamie L. Bronstein, *Caught in the Machinery: Workplace Accidents and Injured Workers in Nineteenth-Century Britain* (Stanford, CA: Stanford University Press, 2008), 20.
33. Bronstein, *Caught in the Machinery*, 14; Anthony F. C. Wallace, *St. Clair: A Nineteenth-Century Town's Experience with a Disaster-Prone Industry* (New York: Knopf, 1987), 260–261.
34. Payton, *The Cornish Overseas*, 350–358. See also Richard Dawe, *Cornish Pioneers in South Africa* (St. Austell: Cornish Hillside Publications, 1998).
35. Catherine Mills, *Regulating Health and Safety in the British Mining Industries, 1800–1914* (Farnham: Ashgate, 2010), 85, 241.
36. *Diamond Fields Advertiser*, July 16, 1888.
37. Edward "E. A." Judge had a long career in government service but was best known for a youthful accomplishment: in 1859, he scored a 49 for Bishops Cricket at a time when that was considered a very high score. See Odendaal et al., *Cricket and Conquest*, 1:28.
38. *Diamond Fields Advertiser*, July 20, 1888. On public mistrust of mine enquiries, see Bronstein, *Caught in the Machinery*, 128–168. See also Whiteside, *Regulating Danger*, 22–23 and 84–85.
39. *Diamond Fields Advertiser*, July 26, 1888; *Daily Independent*, July 26, 1888.
40. *Daily Independent*, July 27, 1888. The story was largely the same as the one that Williams told years later in his book.
41. *Daily Independent*, Saturday, July 28, 1888. On the sociology of scapegoating, see Tom Douglas, *Scapegoats: Transferring Blame* (London: Routledge, 1995), especially 138 and 157. See also René Girard, *The Scapegoat*, trans. Yvonne Freccero (Baltimore: Johns Hopkins University Press, 1986), 8–11.
42. *Daily Independent*, Friday, July 27, 1888.
43. Ibid.
44. Ibid. On Hambly and his subsequent career in the US West and Australia, see *South Australian Register* (Adelaide), April 3, 1896.
45. *Daily Independent*, Friday, July 27, 1888, Supplement.
46. *Daily Independent*, Saturday, July 28, 1888.
47. Ibid.
48. Ibid., Friday, July 27, 1888.
49. *Diamond Fields Advertiser*, July 30, 1886.
50. *Daily Independent*, Friday, July 27, 1888, Supplement.
51. Ibid.
52. *Daily Independent*, Monday, July 30, 1888.
53. Ibid. Vingoe's testimony was reproduced in the *Daily Independent*, Saturday, August 4, 1888.
54. *Daily Independent*, Monday, July 30, 1888.

55. Ibid., Tuesday, July 31, 1888.
56. *Diamond Fields Advertiser*, Wednesday, August 1, 1888; *Daily Independent*, Thursday, August 2, 1888.
57. *Daily Independent*, Monday, July 30, 1888.
58. Ibid., Thursday, August 9, 1888.
59. "The DeBeer's Catastrophe: The Report of the Commission of Enquiry," *Diamond Fields Advertiser*, August 15, 1888.
60. *Daily Independent*, August 15, 1888.
61. Ibid.
62. T. Dunbar Moodie, with Vivian Ndatshe, *Going for Gold: Men, Mines, and Migration* (Berkeley: University of California Press, 1994), 75. See also Carter Goodrich, *The Miner's Freedom: A Study of the Working Life in a Changing Industry* (Boston: Marshall Jones, 1925), 19. Goodrich's insight is confirmed by Moodie and by Whiteside, *Regulating Danger*, 42–43.
63. On the agency of African miners within larger technopolitical systems, see Hecht, *Being Nuclear*, 21–22. On the many ways in which imperialism is resisted, in history and historiography, see Priyamada Gopal, *Insurgent Empire: Anticolonial Resistance and British Dissent* (London: Verso, 2019). For an older work that takes up the issue of the variety of resistance, see Edward Said, *Culture and Imperialism* (New York: Knopf, 1993), especially chap. 3, "Resistance and Opposition."
64. DBCMC, *First Annual Report*, July 1889. Barnato's speech is reported in a reprint from the *Daily Independent*, 2.
65. Ted Steinberg, *Acts of God: The Unnatural History of Natural Disaster in America* (New York: Oxford University Press, 2000), 5–20, 38, 64, 155, 192–193.
66. Williams, *Diamond Mines*, 2:29.
67. Williams, *Diamond Mines*, 1:325–6.
68. Annual Report, DBMC, 1888, 11.

CHAPTER 9

1. Rhodes's final will gave the Dalston properties to the Rhodes Trust Estate, not to be confused with the Rhodes Trust at Oxford. In 1959 the Dalston properties were purchased by the Hackney Borough Council. The Rhodes Estate in Dalston, with 296 properties, was built in the 1970s. "Hackney: Rhodes Information Sheet," ca. 2022, https://consultation.hackney.gov.uk/communications-engagement/rhodes-estate-survey/supporting_documents/Rhodes%20Information%20leaflet.pdf. See also "Hackney: Dalston and Kingsland Road," British History Online, https://www.british-history.ac.uk/vch/middx/vol10/pp28-33, consulted September 13, 2023.
2. Rotberg, *Founder*, 215; Williams, *Cecil Rhodes*, 111.
3. T. R. H. Davenport, "The Cape Liberal Tradition to 1910," in *Democratic Liberalism in South Africa: Its History and Prospect*, ed. Jeffrey Butler, Richard Elphick, and David Welsh (Middletown, CT: Wesleyan University Press, 1987), 21–34.

4. Merriman to Currey, March 24 and June 14, 1886, in Lewsen, *Correspondence of J. X. Merriman*, 209–214; Davenport, *The Afrikaner Bond*, 119–123; Rotberg, *Founder*, 222–223.
5. James Rose Innes, *James Rose Innes: Chief Justice of South Africa: Autobiography*, ed. B. A. Tindall (Cape Town: Oxford University Press, 1949), 74–75; Rotberg, *Founder*, 223–224.
6. Davidson Don Tengo Jabavu, *The Life of John Tengo Jabavu* (Lovedale: Lovedale Institution Press, 1922), 28–37; Rotberg, *Founder*, 224.
7. Vindex, *Cecil Rhodes*, 158–163. The term "class legislation" meant legislation that discriminated among different groups of people, including ethnic and national groups. That kind of legislation was prohibited by the Cape's constitution. For the reactions of a future chief justice, see Innes, *Autobiography*, 75.
8. Farai Nyika and Johan Fourie, "Black Disenfranchisement in the Cape Colony, c. 1887–1909: Challenging the Numbers," *Journal of Southern African Studies* 46, no. 3 (2020): 455–469. Further restrictions were legislated in the 1890s. The Cape franchise for African people was eliminated in 1936. Mixed-race, "Coloured" people lost their voting rights in 1956.
9. Robinson and Gallagher, *Africa and the Victorians*, 218.
10. Vindex, *Cecil Rhodes*, 133.
11. Schreuder, *Scramble for Southern Africa*, 193–197. For an overview, see Jean van der Poel, *Railway and Custom Policies in South Africa, 1885–1910* (London: Longmans, Green, 1933).
12. Schreuder, *Scramble for Southern Africa*, 194.
13. Vindex, *Cecil Rhodes*, 173–174.
14. Burman, *Early Railways at the Cape*, 138–140.
15. Kenneth Wilburn, *The Life of Statesman and Industrialist Sir James Sivewright of South Africa, 1848–1916* (Lewiston, NY: Mellen Press, 2010). For background, see Bruce J. Hunt, *Imperial Science: Cable Telegraphy and Electrical Physics in the Victorian British Empire* (Cambridge: Cambridge University Press, 2021).
16. Wilburn, *Sivewright*, 132.
17. Ibid., 131.
18. Bodleian Library, Rhodes Papers, MSS. Afr. s. 228, C2A "Cape," no. 35, Sivewright to Rhodes, December 8, 1891.
19. Bodleian Library, Rhodes Papers, MSS. Afr. s. 228, C 16 "Miscellaneous," no. 14, Report of Carrington Wilmer, January 12, 1891.
20. Robinson and Gallagher, *Africa and the Victorians*, 222–229.
21. Rotberg, *Founder*, 245–246.
22. *The Times*, November 11, 1885, 8. The style of the letter is more formal than Rhodes's usual prose. This is because the first letter was dictated to Rhodes's friend and Maund's companion Ralph Williams, who coached Rhodes. It was then edited by Rochfort Maguire. See Williams, *Cecil Rhodes*, 90.

23. *The Times*, November 11, 1885, 8.
24. Ibid.
25. Ibid,
26. *A Selection from the Diaries of Edward Henry Stanley, 15th Earl of Derby (1826–93) between September 1869 and March 1878*, ed. John Vincent (London: The Royal Historical Society, 1994), 523.
27. John Gordon Swift MacNeill, *What I Have Seen and Heard* (Boston: Little Brown, 1925), 264–266; Flint, *Cecil Rhodes*, 101–102; Rotberg, *Founder*, 229–230; Williams, *Cecil Rhodes*, 133–134.
28. Flint, *Cecil Rhodes*, 102–103; MacNeill, *Seen and Heard*, 264–266; Michell, *Life and Times*, 1:259–262; Rotberg, *Founder*, 230–233; Williams, *Cecil Rhodes*, 133–134.
29. Frank Johnson, *Great Days: The Autobiography of an Empire Pioneer* (London: G. Bell, 1940), chap. 2: "At the Court of Lo Bengula"; Shippard to Robinson, May 21, 1887, cited in J. I. Rademeyer, *Die Land Noord van die Limpopo in die Ekspansie-Belied van di Suid-Afrikaanse Republiek* (Cape Town: Balkema, 1949), 58–59; Rotberg, *Founder*, 247–248.
30. Arthur Keppel-Jones, *Rhodes and Rhodesia: The White Conquest of Zimbabwe, 1884–1902* (Kingston: McGill-Queen's University Press, 1984), 34–36. The legitimacy of the treaty has been called into question by other historians, but Keppel-Jones verifies it. See also John S. Galbraith, *Crown and Charter: The Early Years of the British South Africa Company* (Berkeley: University of California Press, 1974), 68. See also Flint, *Cecil Rhodes*, 95, and Rotberg, *Founder*, 248–249.
31. Robert Unwin Moffat, *John Smith Moffat, C.M.G. Missionary: A Memoir* (London: 1921), 214–220.
32. Steven Press, *Rogue Empires: Contracts and Conmen in Europe's Scramble for Africa* (Cambridge, MA: Harvard University Press, 2017), 4–9, 18–24, 229–230.
33. Flint, *Cecil Rhodes*, 95; Keppel-Jones, *Rhodes and Rhodesia*, 59–61; Rotberg, *Founder*, 250.
34. Rotberg, *Founder*, 252.
35. Paul Maylam, "The Making of the Kimberley-Bulawayo Railway: A Study in the Operations of the British South Africa Company," *Rhodesian History* 8 (1977): 13–33, citation to 13; Charles Metcalfe, "My Story of the Scheme," in Leo Weinthal, *The Story of the Cape to Cairo Railway and River Route from 1887 to 1922*, vol. 1, *The Record and Romance of an Imperial Project* (London: Pioneer, 1923), 95–103, citation to 97; "Charles Herbert Theophilus Metcalfe," *Grace's Guide to British Industrial History*, https://www.gracesguide.co.uk/Charles_Herbert_Theophilus_Metcalfe, consulted August 30, 2020.
36. Rotberg, *Founder*, 252.
37. On nineteenth-century chartered companies, see Press, *Rogue Empires*.
38. Rotberg, *Founder*, 252–255; Schreuder, *Scramble for Southern Africa*, 234.

CHAPTER 10

1. Bodleian Library, Rhodes Papers, MSS. Afr. t. 5, "Miscellaneous Papers," Rhodes to Shippard, August 1, 1888.
2. Bodleian Library, Rhodes Papers, MSS. Afr. t.5, "Miscellaneous Papers," Rhodes to Shippard, August 14, 1888.
3. Maylam, "Making of the Kimberley-Bulawayo Railway," 16; Metcalfe, "My Story of the Scheme," 97; Williams, *Cecil Rhodes*, 130.
4. Vindex, *Cecil Rhodes*, 224. "Advocating a Barkly pump" is from an old expression in British politics, "the parish pump," a mildly derisive reference to advocating for local needs.
5. Vindex, *Cecil Rhodes*, 225. In 1893, Frederick Jackson Turner presented his thesis as an academic paper, "The Significance of the Frontier in American History," at a special meeting of the American Historical Association held during Chicago's Columbian Exposition.
6. Bodleian Library, Rhodes Papers, MSS. Afr. t. 5, "Miscellaneous Papers," Rhodes to Shippard, August 14, 1888; Rotberg, *Founder*, 257.
7. Flint, *Cecil Rhodes*, 103; Michell, *Life and Times*, 1:253; Rotberg, *Founder*, 90–91; Williams, *Cecil Rhodes*, 39–53. Two years later, with Rhodes's support, Maguire did win a seat in the British Parliament, representing North Donegal, adjacent to MacNeill's district in South Donegal.
8. Rotberg, *Founder*, 259–260.
9. Thompson, *Autobiography*, 127.
10. Galbraith, *Crown and Charter*, 68.
11. Maylam, *Rhodes, the Tswana, and the British*, 52–53.
12. Galbraith, *Crown and Charter*, 68.
13. Rhodes to Rudd, September 10, 1888, Ms. 110/10, Brenthurst Library, Johannesburg. As cited by Rotberg, *Founder*, 260–261.
14. Galbraith, *Crown and Charter*, 69–72. A more detailed account may be found in Keppel-Jones, *Rhodes and Rhodesia*, chap. 2: "The Rudd Concession and Its Enemies." The Rudd Concession is discussed in all other biographies of Rhodes.
15. Michell, *Life and Times*, 1:255–257; Williams, *Cecil Rhodes*, 126–127.
16. Rhodes to Rudd, September 19, 1888, no. 20, Rudd-Rhodes Correspondence, McGregor Museum.
17. Beach, *Shona and Their Neighbours*, 134–137.
18. Galbraith, *Crown and Charter*, 74–75; Rotberg, *Founder*, 264.
19. Julian Cobbing, "Lobengula, Jameson and the Occupation of Mashonaland, 1890," *Rhodesian History* 4 (1973): 39; Galbraith, *Crown and Charter*, 70–74; Lockhart and Woodhouse, *Rhodes*, 146–147; Rotberg, *Founder*, 262–263.
20. Galbraith, *Crown and Charter*, 77; Maylam, *Rhodes, the Tswana, and the British*, 55–56; Rotberg, *Founder*, 265. On the politicization of skill descriptions, see Storey, *Guns, Race, and Power*, chap. 6: "Risk, Skill, and Citizenship in the Eastern Cape, 1876–9."

21. McGregor Museum, Rudd Papers, 11023/10, Maguire to Rudd, March 1, 1889.
22. McGregor Museum, Rudd Papers, 11023/11, Maguire to Rudd, March 7, 1889.
23. McGregor Museum, Rudd-Rhodes Correspondence, Rhodes to Rudd, no. 27, undated, December 1888.
24. Keppel-Jones, *Rhodes and Rhodesia*, 87.
25. Ibid., 104–105; Rotberg, *Founder*, 268–276.
26. Keppel-Jones, *Rhodes and Rhodesia*, 105–106.
27. Ibid., 106; Jennifer Davey, "Cavendish, Lucy Caroline," *Oxford Dictionary of National Biography* (2023), accessed online, February 4, 2024.
28. Keppel-Jones, *Rhodes and Rhodesia*, 106.
29. Lockhart and Woodhouse, *Rhodes*, 109–110; Rotberg, *Founder*, 271–272; Williams, *Cecil Rhodes*, 130–131.
30. *Hansards*, House of Commons Debates, March 11, 1889, vol. 333, cc.1401–2.
31. *Hansards*, House of Commons Debates, March 26, 1889, vol. 334, cc. 837–39.
32. Keppel-Jones, *Rhodes and Rhodesia*, 109.
33. Ibid., 110.
34. Ibid., 89–90.
35. Rotberg, *Founder*, 253, 265–266; Storey, *Guns, Race, and Power*, 323.
36. Storey, *Guns, Race, and Power*, 323–324.
37. Galbraith, *Crown and Charter*, 82–83; Rotberg, *Founder*, 269–270.

CHAPTER 11

1. Galbraith, *Crown and Charter*, 84–85.
2. Bodleian Library, Rhodes Papers, MSS. Afr. s. 229, IV: Papers of E. A. Maund, 1923–1929, "Reminiscences of Cecil Rhodes, Box One, September 26, 1923, 13ff.
3. Bodleian Library, Rhodes Papers, MSS. Afr. s. 229, IV: Papers of E. A. Maund, 1923–1929, "Reminiscences of Cecil Rhodes, Box One, September 26, 1923, 15ff. See also Galbraith, *Crown and Charter*, 84–85, and Rotberg, *Founder*, 276–277.
4. Galbraith, *Crown and Charter*, 83–84.
5. Rose Innes, *Autobiography*, 87; Schreuder, *Scramble for Southern Africa*, 243–244.
6. Cannadine, *Victorious Century*, 358–359; Edna Healey, "Coutts, Angelina Georgina Burdett-," *Oxford Dictionary of National Biography* (2012), accessed online, February 4, 2024. In Cape Town's St. George's Cathedral, which was begun in 1901 by Herbert Baker, Burdett-Coutts is depicted on a stained-glass window.
7. Galbraith, *Crown and Charter*, 113–115; Alvin Jackson, "Hamilton, James, second duke of Abercorn," *Oxford Dictionary of National Biography* (2023), accessed online, February 4, 2024; Lockhart and Woodhouse, *Rhodes*, 170–171.
8. Galbraith, *Crown and Charter*, 115–117; Lockhart and Woodhouse, *Rhodes*, 170–171.
9. Cannadine, *Victorious Century*, 318–322, 392–397.
10. This combination of aristocrats and bankers has been described as "gentlemanly capitalism." See Cain and Hopkins, *British Imperialism: Innovation and Expansion*,

1688–1914. See also Raymond E. Dumett, *Gentlemanly Capitalism and British Imperialism: The New Debate on Empire* (London: Longman, 1999).

11. Galbraith, *Crown and Charter*, 116; Carman Miller, "Grey, Albert Henry George," *Oxford Dictionary of National Biography* (2008), accessed online, February 4, 2024.
12. Robert Cecil went on to a distinguished career in politics. For his role in founding and helping to lead the League of Nations, he won the 1937 Nobel Peace Prize.
13. Galbraith, *Crown and Charter*, 91–93; Keppel-Jones, *Rhodes and Rhodesia*, 125; Rotberg, *Founder*, 278.
14. Roland Oliver, *Sir Harry Johnston and the Scramble for Africa* (London: 1957), 143; David Birmingham, *Portugal and Africa* (Athens: Ohio University Press, 1999), 114.
15. Roland Oliver, *Harry Johnston*, 148–153; Birmingham, *Portugal and Africa*, 113–115, 119.
16. Galbraith, *Crown and Charter*, 97–99; Keppel-Jones, *Rhodes and Rhodesia*, 122–126; Rotberg, *Founder*, 278.
17. On the way in which investment decisions are part of social and technical networks, see Donald Mackenzie, *Material Markets: How Economic Agents Are Constructed* (Oxford: Oxford University Press, 2009), chap. 2: "Ten Precepts for the Social Studies of Finance." On "gentlemanly capitalism," see P. J. Cain and Anthony J. Hopkins, *British Imperialism: Innovation and Expansion, 1688–1914* (London: Longman, 1993).
18. Maylam, *Rhodes, the Tswana, and the British*, 58.
19. On the psychological ploys of con artists, see Maria Konnikova, *The Confidence Game: Why We Fall for It Every Time* (New York: Penguin, 2017). On the functionality of belief in things that are known to be wrong, see Shankar Vedantam and Bill Mesler, *Useful Delusions: The Power and Paradox of the Self-Deceiving Brain* (New York: Norton, 2021).
20. Francisco I. Ricarde-Seaver and Charles Metcalfe, "The British Sphere of Influence in South Africa," *Fortnightly Review* 51 (March 1889): 349–362. Quotations from 352 and 361.
21. Keppel-Jones, *Rhodes and Rhodesia*, 118–121.
22. Ibid., 126–127.
23. Ibid., 139–140.
24. Ibid., 140.
25. Thompson, *Autobiography*, 175–183.
26. Cobbing, "Lobengula, Jameson," 41–42; Rotberg, *Founder*, 292.
27. Keppel-Jones, *Rhodes and Rhodesia*, 143.
28. Maylam, "Making of the Kimberley-Bulawayo Railway," 17–18.
29. Rotberg, *Founder*, 285–286.
30. Keppel-Jones, *Rhodes and Rhodesia*, 129–130.
31. Galbraith, *Crown and Charter*, 84–86.
32. Keppel-Jones, *Rhodes and Rhodesia*, 131; Metcalfe, "My Story of the Scheme," 100.
33. Davenport, *Afrikaner Bond*, 128–129.
34. Maylam, "Making of the Kimberley-Bulawayo Railway," 20, 27.

35. Keppel-Jones, *Rhodes and Rhodesia*, 143.
36. Cobbing, "Lobengula, Jameson," 41–42; Rotberg, *Founder*, 292–293.
37. Flint, *Cecil Rhodes*, 128–129; Rotberg, *Founder*, 294–295. The plan to stage a coup is glossed more favorably by earlier biographers. See Michell, *Life and Times*, 1:308–309, and Williams, *Cecil Rhodes*, 144–145.
38. Keppel-Jones, *Rhodes and Rhodesia*, 143–145.

CHAPTER 12

1. Maylam, "Making of the Kimberley-Bulawayo Railway," 15.
2. Maylam, *Rhodes, the Tswana, and the British*, 32–33.
3. Vindex, *Cecil Rhodes*, 238–240.
4. Davenport, *Afrikaner Bond*, 132–133; Rotberg, *Founder*, 340–341; Tamarkin, *Cecil Rhodes and the Cape Afrikaners*, 121–123; Williams, *Cecil Rhodes*, 183–186.
5. Wilburn, *Sivewright*, 154–156. Sivewright's initial appointment was complicated by travel and by a constitutional technicality. Traditionally Cape prime ministers held one of the Cabinet portfolios. Rhodes chose to hold the portfolio of the commissioner of crown lands and public works, with Sivewright running the office in his name, until two months later, when the chief justice decided to let Rhodes serve as prime minister without having to hold another office.
6. Rotberg, *Founder*, 345–347; Williams, *Cecil Rhodes*, 186.
7. Gutsche, *Microcosm*, 189.
8. Flint, *Cecil Rhodes*, 160.
9. Vindex, *Cecil Rhodes*, 242–243.
10. Headlam, "Race for the Interior," 535; Bodleian Library, Rhodes Papers, MSS. Afr. s. 228, C.25 "Delagoa Bay," nos. 1, 9, 19–21. Item no. 21 is Rhodes's account of the attempted purchase, written in March of 1894; Bodleian Library, Rhodes Papers, MSS. Afr. s. 1826, "Letters to Various Recipients," Rhodes to Rosebery, June 22, 1893, 7–9, 14.
11. Vindex, *Cecil Rhodes*, 243–244.
12. Bodleian Library, Rhodes Papers, MSS. Afr. s. 228, C.27 "Personal," no. 12 (but placed out of order near the back of the volume), Schreiner to Rhodes, undated letter ca. 1890.
13. Flint, *Cecil Rhodes*, 264; Rotberg, *Founder*, 397–404.
14. Rotberg, *Founder*, 360–367. On Kimberley, see Bodleian Library, Rhodes Papers, MSS. Afr. s. 228, C2A, Cape Colony, Item 40, J. H. Lange to Rhodes, December 22, 1891.
15. Davenport, *Afrikaner Bond*, 142–146; Rotberg, *Founder*, 360–369; Tamarkin, *Cecil Rhodes and the Cape Afrikaners*, 175–176. On the less-than-intended statistical impact, see the fascinating study by Farai and Nyika, "Black Disenfranchisement."
16. Wilburn, *Sivewright*, chap. 6: "Ministry of All the Talents"; chap. 7: "The Sivewright Agreement."

17. Wilburn, *Sivewright*, chap. 8: "Abroad"; chap. 9: "In Country."
18. Tamarkin, *Cecil Rhodes and the Cape Afrikaners*, 186–187.
19. Rotberg, *Founder*, 460–463; Tamarkin, *Cecil Rhodes and the Cape Afrikaners*, 198. For background, see William Beinart, *The Political Economy of Pondoland, 1860–1930* (Cambridge: Cambridge University Press, 1982), chap. 1: "The Political Economy of Pondoland in the Nineteenth Century," and chap. 2: "Crops, Cattle, and the Origins of Labour Migrancy, 1894–1911." Various biographies claim that Rhodes intimidated the Pondo leadership by demonstrating the effects of a machine gun on a field of maize. The story cannot be corroborated.
20. Clifton Crais, *Poverty, War, and Violence in South Africa* (Cambridge: Cambridge University Press, 2011), 110–121.
21. Shula Marks, "Class, Culture, and Consciousness in South Africa, 1880–1899," *The Cambridge History of South Africa*, vol. 2, *1885–1994* (Cambridge: Cambridge University Press, 2011), 120–122.
22. Richard Bouch, "Glen Grey before Cecil Rhodes: How a Crisis of Local Colonial Authority Led to the Glen Grey Act of 1894," *Canadian Journal of African Studies* 27, no. 1 (1993): 1–24.
23. See the discussion of the historiography in Crais, *Poverty, War, and Violence*, 12–29.
24. Davenport, *Afrikaner Bond*, 148–149, 154–155, 361–362. Sampson became an influential jurist. For background (without discussion of Glen Grey) see Victor Sampson, *My Reminiscences* (London: Longmans, 1926). Milton was an athlete who led efforts to segregate sports, then became administrator of Rhodesia. Odendaal et al., *Cricket and Conquest*, 1:171, 246–249, 256–257; Pelham Warner, *Long Innings* (London: George G. Harrap, 1951), 36–37; Jonty Winch and Richard Parry, *Too Black to Wear Whites: The Remarkable Story of Krom Hendricks, a Cricket Hero Who Was Rejected by Cecil John Rhodes's Empire* (Cape Town: Penguin, 2020).
25. Flint, *Cecil Rhodes*, 167–169; Michell, *Life and Times*, 1:117–121; Rotberg, *Founder*, 472–473; Williams, *Cecil Rhodes*, 211–212.
26. Konnikova, *Confidence Game*, 58–59.
27. Davenport, *Afrikaner Bond*, 154–155; Flint, *Cecil Rhodes*, 167–169; Michell, *Life and Times*, 1:117–121; Rotberg, *Founder*, 472–473; Williams, *Cecil Rhodes*, 211–212. For a history of legal thinking by white settlers about dispossession, see Darren Reid, "Dispossession and Legal Mentalité in Nineteenth-Century South Africa: Grotian and Lockean Theories of Property Acquisition in the Annexations of British Kaffraria and Natalia," *Settler Colonial Studies* 11, no. 1 (2021): 69–85.
28. *Imvo Zabantsundu*, April 11, 1894, 3.
29. Ibid., April 18, 1894, 3.
30. Ibid., May 2, 1894, 3. Asquith was speaking in defense of the Mpondo chief, Sigcawu, who was illegally arrested by Rhodes. The arrest was overturned by Cape courts and counter appealed to London.
31. Vindex, *Cecil Rhodes*, 371–372.
32. Ibid., 372.

33. Ibid., 373.
34. Ibid., 374–375.
35. Ibid., 389.
36. *Imvo Zabantsundu,* July 7, 1892, 3.
37. Vindex, *Cecil Rhodes,* 381–382.
38. Ibid., 382.
39. Ibid., 388–390.
40. *Imvo Zabantsundu,* July 18, 1894.
41. Rotberg, *Founder,* 473–475; *Imvo Zabantsundu,* August 22, 1894.
42. Rotberg, *Founder,* 473–475; *Imvo Zabantsundu,* August 22, 1894; Bodleian Library, Rhodes Papers, MSS. Afr. s. 228, C2A "Cape," nos. 96, 97, 108. These letters are practically the only examples of legislative fan mail in the entire collection.
43. Colin Bundy, "Mr. Rhodes and the Poisoned Goods: Popular Opposition to the Glen Grey Council System, 1894–1906," in *Hidden Struggles in Rural South Africa,* ed. William Beinart and Colin Bundy (Berkeley: University of California Press, 1987): 138–165. Quotation is from 138.
44. *Imvo Zabantsundu,* October 17, 1894, 3. Jabavu's biography was written by his son, Don, who reported that his father made his peace with the Glen Grey Act. Jabavu apparently became resigned to his fate and urged people to overlook the act's "imperfections" and to work within the separate system of representation to advocate for their communities. Jabavu, *The Life of John Tengo Jabavu,* 38.
45. *Imvo Zabantsundu,* August 29, 1894, 3.
46. A dual economy, with different rules for different groups of people, is a recipe for poverty according to Acemoglu and Robinson, *Why Nations Fail,* 258–271.
47. Davenport, *Afrikaner Bond,* 155–159; Tamarkin, *Cecil Rhodes and the Cape Afrikaners,* 200–210.
48. Michell, *Life and Times,* 2:154–155; Rotberg, *Founder,* 513.
49. Tamarkin, *Cecil Rhodes and the Cape Afrikaners,* 199–210; Mordechai Tamarkin, *Volk and Flock: Ecology, Culture, Identity, and Politics among Cape Afrikaner Sheep Farmers in the Late Nineteenth Century* (Pretoria: UNISA Press, 2009).
50. Lockhart and Woodhouse, *Rhodes,* 203; Rotberg, *Founder,* 379; Williams, *Cecil Rhodes,* 59, 233.
51. For background on Baker, see Norman Etherington, *Imperium of the Soul: The Political and Aesthetic Imagination of Edwardian Imperialists* (Manchester: Manchester University Press, 2017), chap. 3: "How Herbert Baker Created an Architecture of Imperial Power"; Foster, *Washed with Sun,* 157–166.
52. Phillida Brooke Simons, *Groote Schuur: Great Granary to Stately Home* (Vlaeberg: Fernwood Press, 1996), 16–22, 94–95, 138–139; Lockhart and Woodhouse, *Rhodes,* 203–204, 208; Rotberg, *Founder,* 378–387; Sauer, *Ex Africa,* 202; Williams, *Cecil Rhodes,* 219–227.
53. Flint, *Cecil Rhodes,* 162–163; Rotberg, *Founder,* 348–350.

CHAPTER 13

1. Michell, *Cecil John Rhodes*, 1:306–307.
2. Ndlovu-Gatsheni, *Ndebele Nation*, 62–67, 86–89, 105–108.
3. On camels, see Bodleian Library, Rhodes Papers, MSS. Afr. s. 228, C3A "Charter" 1889–90, no. 5, Capt. Tomkins to BSAC Board, July 8, 1890.
4. Flint, *Cecil Rhodes*, 129–131; Michell, *Life and Times*, 1:308–311; Rotberg, *Founder*, 294–296; Williams, *Cecil Rhodes*, 145–147.
5. Keppel-Jones, *Rhodes and Rhodesia*, 158–159.
6. Ibid., 161–162. See also Galbraith, *Crown and Charter*, 148–150.
7. Michell, *Cecil John Rhodes*, 1:310.
8. Cobbing, "Lobengula, Jameson," 48–49; Keppel-Jones, *Rhodes and Rhodesia*, 159–160. The regiments have been called *amabutho,* implying a resemblance to the Zulu system of celibate, age-based regiments of professionals, but the Ndebele fighters were part-timers. See Beach, *Shona and Their Neighbours*, 135.
9. Maylam, *Rhodes, the Tswana, and the British*, 60–61.
10. Frank Johnson, *Great Days* (London: Bell & Sons, 1940), 109.
11. Williams, *Cecil Rhodes*, 148–149.
12. Flint, *Cecil Rhodes*, 130–131; Michell, *Life and Times*, 1:148–149; Rotberg, *Founder*, 298–299.
13. Keppel-Jones, *Rhodes and Rhodesia*, 7. Storey, *Guns, Race, and Power*.
14. Ian James Cross, "The Ordnance and Machine Guns of the British South Africa Company, 1889–1896; Part One: 1889–1891," *Military History Journal: South African Military History Society* 16, no. 2 (December 2013), online publication, samilitaryhistory.org/vol162ic.html.
15. Trevor N. Dupuy, *The Evolution of Weapons and Warfare* (Indianapolis, IN: Bobbs-Merrill, 1980), 201–202, 326–327.
16. Keppel-Jones, *Rhodes and Rhodesia*, 151–153.
17. Williams, *Cecil Rhodes*, 149.
18. Ibid., 149–150.
19. Keppel-Jones, *Rhodes and Rhodesia*, 163–172; Michell, *Cecil John Rhodes*, 1:314–317.
20. Rotberg, *Founder*, 309.
21. Birmingham, *Portugal and Africa*, chap. 10: "Britain and the Ultimatum of 1890."
22. Galbraith, *Crown and Charter*, 182–186.
23. Rotberg, *Founder*, 311.
24. Galbraith, *Crown and Charter*, 170–176; Lockhart and Woodhouse, *Rhodes*, 222–225; Rotberg, *Founder*, 313–315.
25. "The Duke of Marlborough Found Dead," *New York Times*, November 10, 1892.
26. Galbraith, *Crown and Charter*, 178–182; Lockhart and Woodhouse, *Rhodes*, 228–229; Rotberg, *Founder*, 315.
27. Lockhart and Woodhouse, *Rhodes*, 225–227; Galbraith, *Crown and Charter*, 191–193.

28. Galbraith, *Crown and Charter*, 195–196; Rotberg, *Founder*, 317. On the policy of protecting British subjects, see Cannadine, *Victorious Century*, 246–248.
29. Galbraith, *Crown and Charter*, 196–202.
30. Bodleian Library, Rhodes Papers, MSS. Afr. s. 228, C3A "Charter," no. 187, Selous to Rhodes, August 26, 1891, 2–3.
31. Bodleian Library, Rhodes Papers, MSS. Afr. s. 228, C3A "Charter," no. 189, Currie to Rhodes, October 29, 1891. See also Leroy Vail, "The Making of an Imperial Slum: Nyasaland and Its Railways, 1895–1935," *Journal of African History* 16, no. 1 (1975): 89–112, citation to 94.
32. Pauling, *Chronicles of a Contractor*, 133–134; Jon Lunn, *Capital and Labour on the Rhodesian Railway System, 1888–1947* (London: Macmillan, 1997), 19–20.
33. Mutumba Mainga Bull, *Bulozi under the Luyana Kings: Political Evolution and State Formation in Pre-colonial Zambia* (Lusaka: Gadsden Books, 1973; repr. e-book ed. 2010), chap. 6: "The Restored Lozi Kingdom, 1864–85"; chap. 7: "Lewanika and the Survival of the Monarchy, 1885–1900."
34. Gerald L. Caplan, "Barotseland's Scramble for Protection," *Journal of African History* 10, no. 2 (1969): 277–294; Galbraith, *Crown and Charter*, 100–101, 217–222; Lockhart and Woodhouse, *Rhodes*, 238–241; Michell, *Cecil John Rhodes*, 1:339–341; Rotberg, *Founder*, 323–327.
35. Galbraith, *Crown and Charter*, 222–240; Rotberg, *Founder*, 333–335.
36. Galbraith, *Crown and Charter*, 240–246; Lockhart and Woodhouse, *Rhodes*, 175–176.
37. Galbraith, *Crown and Charter*, 246–249; Lockhart and Woodhouse, *Rhodes*, 241–244; Rotberg, *Founder*, 330–333.
38. Galbraith, *Crown and Charter*, 249–251; Lockhart and Woodhouse, *Rhodes*, 243–244; Rotberg, *Founder*, 330–333.

CHAPTER 14

1. Williams, *Cecil Rhodes*, 172–173.
2. Flint, *Cecil Rhodes*, 148–149; Michell, *Cecil John Rhodes*, 1:335–337; Rotberg, *Founder*, 336–337; Williams, *Cecil Rhodes*, 171–172. In 1918, a court case brought by settlers resulted in the Privy Council nullifying the Lippert Concession. The decision did not also nullify the titles that had been assigned by the BSAC.
3. Flint, *Cecil Rhodes*, 149; Rotberg, *Founder*, 336–337.
4. Rotberg, *Founder*, 424–425, 675–677.
5. Bodleian Library, Rhodes Papers, MSS. Afr. t. 1, Item 19, Rhodes to Stead, August 19, 1891, insert of September 3, 1891, 8–11.
6. Roland Quinault, "Churchill, Lord Randolph Henry Spencer," *Oxford Dictionary of National Biography* (2004), accessed online, February 11, 2024. See also two fine biographies of Winston Churchill that provide background on his father: Roy Jenkins, *Churchill: A Biography* (New York: Farrar, Straus and Giroux, 2001), 3–8;

and Andrew Roberts, *Churchill: Walking with Destiny* (New York: Viking, 2018), 12–31.

7. Parsons, "Victorian Internet," 102–103; Hylda Richards, *False Dawn: The Story of Dan Judson, Pioneer* (Bulawayo: Rhodesia Reprints, 1974), 25–26, 91, 211.

8. Bodleian Library, Rhodes Papers, MSS. Afr. t. 1, Item 19, Rhodes to Stead, August 19, 1891, insert of September 3, 1891, 8.

9. Ibid.

10. J. Theodore Bent, *The Ruined Cities of Mashonaland* (London: Longmans, Green, 1892; 3rd ed. 1896), 117, 185, 188. See also David Christiaan de Waal, *With Rhodes in Mashonaland* (Cape Town: Juta, 1896), chaps. 22–23. On research at the Vatican, see Bodleian Library, Rhodes Papers, MSS. Afr. s. 228, C3B, "Charter," no. 267, Wilmot to Rhodes, November 12 and 20, 1895. For an overview of the history of Great Zimbabwe archaeology, see Shadreck Chirikure, *Great Zimbabwe: Reclaiming a "Confiscated" Past* (London: Routledge, 2021). For an earlier analysis, see Henrika Kuklick, "Contested Monuments: The Politics of Archeology in Southern Africa," in *Colonial Situations: Essays on the Contextualization of Ethnographic Knowledge*, ed. George W. Stocking (Madison: University of Wisconsin Press, 1991): 135–169. On archaeology and looting, see Sanghera, *Empireland*, chap. 4: "Emotional Loot."

11. The reports were published serially over the last half of 1891 and were then put together in a book that was published in early 1892 and reissued in 1897. Randolph Churchill, *Men, Mines, and Animals in South Africa*, 2nd ed. (London: Sampson Low, Marston, 1897), 198.

12. Churchill, *Men, Mines, and Animals in South Africa*, 206–207.

13. Ibid., 208–209.

14. Galbraith, *Crown and Charter*, 266–267. Galbraith assigns even more weight to Churchill's reports. See also Williams, *Cecil Rhodes*, 159–161.

15. Galbraith, *Crown and Charter*, 268.

16. Bodleian Library, Rhodes Papers, C3B, "Charter," no. 201 (b) Farquhar to Rhodes, January 20, 1892; no. 201 (c) Merriman to Rhodes, January 22, 1892.

17. Richard Scully, "Constructing the Colossus: The Origins of Linley Sambourne's Greatest *Punch* Cartoon," *International Journal of Comic Art* 14, no. 2 (Fall 2012): 120–142.

18. Bodleian Library, Rhodes Papers, MSS. Afr. s. 228, C3B, Charter, no. 201, Johnson to Rhodes, January 7, 1892.

19. Bodleian Library, Rhodes Papers, MSS. Afr. s. 228, C3B, "Charter," no. 201 (a), Rothschild to Rhodes, January 15, 1892.

20. Ibid.

21. Ferguson, *House of Rothschild*, 361.

22. Ranger, *Revolt in Southern Rhodesia*, 65–66.

23. Maylam, "Making of the Kimberley-Bulawayo Railway," 28–30.

24. Bodleian Library, Rhodes Papers, MSS. Afr. s. 1826, "Letters to Various Recipients," typed copy of letter from Harry Johnston to Rhodes, January 28, 1893, enclosed in Rhodes to Rosebery, June 22, 1893, quotations from 30–31.

25. Bodleian Library, Rhodes Papers, MSS Afr. s 228, C3B, "Charter," no. 246, Forbes to Rhodes, June 10, 1895.
26. Richards, *False Dawn*, 25–26, 91, 211; C. D. Twynam, "The Telegraph in British Central Africa," *Nyasaland Journal* 6, no. 2 (July 1953): 52–55.
27. Rotberg, *Founder*, 511–512.
28. Ibid., 512–513.
29. Bodleian Library, Rhodes Papers, MSS Afr. s228, C3B Charter, no. 212, Rosebery to Rhodes, March 29, 1893, enclosed in Bower to Rhodes, May 12, 1893.
30. Bodleian Library, "Letters to Various Recipients," MSS. Afr. s. 1826, Rhodes to Rosebery, April 16, 1893, 55–64.
31. Bodleian Library, Rhodes Papers, MSS Afr. s 1826, "Letters to Various Recipients," Rhodes to Rosebery, June 22, 1893, 13. Proportional tithing is described in Luke 21:1–4 and in 1 Corinthians 16:2.

CHAPTER 15

1. Keppel-Jones, *Rhodes and Rhodesia*, 234–235; Parsons, "Victorian Internet," 105–106.
2. Galbraith, *Crown and Charter*, 296–297; Keppel-Jones, *Rhodes and Rhodesia*, 242–244.
3. Flint, *Cecil Rhodes*, 151; Michell, *Cecil John Rhodes*, 2:87–89; Rotberg, *Founder*, 486; Williams, *Cecil Rhodes*, 174–175.
4. Churchill, *Men, Mines, and Animals*, 202.
5. Keppel-Jones, *Rhodes and Rhodesia*, 259–260; Lockhart and Woodhouse, *Rhodes*, 259.
6. Ian Phimister, "Rhodesia and the Rand," *Journal of Southern African Studies* 1, no. 1 (October 1974): 81.
7. Galbraith, *Crown and Charter*, 305–307; Rotberg, *Founder*, 440.
8. Keppel-Jones, *Rhodes and Rhodesia*, 265–266.
9. University of Cape Town Library, Special Collections, Papers of E. A. Judge, BC 500/B 53, C. E. Judge to Mrs. Judge, October 24, 1893, 5. Sadly the UCT Special Collections Library was destroyed by fire in April of 2021.
10. Cross, "Ordnance and Machine Guns of the BSAC, 1889–91."
11. Galbraith, *Crown and Charter*, 68.
12. University of Cape Town Library, Special Collections, Papers of E. A. Judge, BC 500/B 53, C. E. Judge to Mrs. Judge, October 24, 1893, 4–5. The battle is recounted in Keppel-Jones, *Rhodes and Rhodesia*, 269–274.
13. Keppel-Jones, *Rhodes and Rhodesia*, 273–274.
14. George Knight-Bruce, *Memories of Mashonaland* (London: Edward Arnold, 1895), 230–232.
15. Keppel-Jones, *Rhodes and Rhodesia*, 276–277.
16. Ferguson, *House of Rothschild*, 361.
17. Herbert Sidebotham, revised by H. C. G. Matthew, "Labouchère, Henry Du Pré," *Oxford Dictionary of National Biography* (2009), accessed February 11, 2024.

18. *Hansards* HC Debate, November 9, 1893, vol. 18, cc. 544–64. See also Flint, *Cecil Rhodes*, 155.
19. *Hansards* HC Debate, November 9, 1893, vol. 18, cc. 568–79.
20. *Hansards* HC Debate, November 9, 1893, vol. 18, cc. 581–601.
21. *Truth*, November 30, 1893, 1154–1156.
22. *Truth*, November 30, 1893, 1156.
23. Merriman to Currey, December 14, 1894, in Lewsen, *Correspondence of J. X. Merriman*, 2:168.
24. Keppel-Jones, *Rhodes and Rhodesia*, 284–286.
25. Rotberg, *Founder*, 446–448.
26. The BSAC dispossession of Ndebele people is summarized in William Beinart, "Cecil Rhodes: Racial Segregation in the Cape Colony and Violence in Zimbabwe," *Journal of Southern African Studies* 48, no. 3 (2022): 587–590. See also William Beinart, "Appendix A," *Report of a Commission of Enquiry Established by Oriel College, Oxford, into Issues Associated with Memorials to Cecil Rhodes*, April 2021, 108–109. For an early comprehensive interpretation, see Keppel-Jones, *Rhodes and Rhodesia*, chap. 10: "The Black Experience, 1890–1896"; for a more recent interpretation, see Ndlovu-Gatsheni, *Ndebele Nation*, chap. 6: "Imperial Violence and Loss of Sovereignty."
27. Keppel-Jones, *Rhodes and Rhodesia*, 398–399; Bodleian Library, Rhodes Papers, MSS Afr. s 228, C3B "Charter," no. 229, "Report of the Land Commission."
28. BSAC policies amounted to "rent-seeking behavior." See Joseph E. Stiglitz, *The Price of Inequality: How Today's Divided Society Endangers Our Future* (New York: Norton, 2012), chap. 2: "Rent-Seeking and the Making of an Unequal Society."
29. Bodleian Library, Rhodes Papers, MSS. Afr. s. 228, C.27 "Personal," no. 11, bound out of order before no. 7, "Scrap" of Nguboyenja's writing, undated. The story of Lobengula's sons has never been fully researched and written.
30. Hammond, *Autobiography*, 277–278.
31. Ibid., 278.

CHAPTER 16

1. Rhodes to De Beers London Office, April 6, 1893, from Stow Papers, Box 1.1, McGregor Museum, Kimberley.
2. Lee Vinsel and Andrew Russell, *The Innovation Delusion: How Our Obsession with the New Has Disrupted the Work that Matters Most* (New York: Currency, 2020).
3. Williams, *Diamond Mines of South Africa*, 1:307–311; DBCMC Annual Report, 1890, 8.
4. DBCM Annual Report 1894, 4–5; Williams, *Diamond Mines of South Africa*, 2.40–44.
5. Newbury, *Diamond Ring*, 95–96.
6. Ibid., 103–104; Worger, *South Africa's City of Diamonds*, 260; Roberts, *Kimberley*, 280–281.

7. McGregor Museum, Box 1.1, Letters of Rhodes to Stow, November 29, 1891, 129–133. Wesselton's early years are traced in Lunderstedt, *Big Five Mines*, 40–48.
8. Snyder, *Brilliant Commodity*, 73–74.
9. Worger, *South Africa's City of Diamonds*, 262; Bodleian Library, Rhodes Papers, C 7 A "De Beers Mines, 1890–96," Item 5, Stow to Rhodes, September 17, 1890; Item 14, Stow to Rhodes, November 15, 1890; Item 30, Stow to Rhodes, March 13, 1891; Item 37, April 24, 1891; Item 48, May 22, 1891.
10. DBCM Annual Report of 1893, 25.
11. DBCM Annual Report for 1894, 26–27.
12. Williams, *Diamond Mines of South Africa*, 2:14.
13. Ibid., 2:2–10.
14. DBCM Annual Report 1894, 9; Williams, *Diamond Mines of South Africa*, 2:11–23.
15. CPP 1894 G.38, Reports of the Inspector of Mines, Kimberley, 6; CPP 1898 G.43, Reports of the Inspector of Mines, Kimberley, 6.
16. DBCM Annual Report, 1894, 3–6; Williams, *Diamond Mines of South Africa*, 2:16.
17. DBCM Annual Report, 1893, 6; 1894, 8; Pat Gibbs, "Coal, Rail, and Victorians in the South African Veld: The Convergence of Colonial Elites and Finance Capital in the Stormberg Mountains of the Eastern Cape, 1880–1910," *Britain and the World* 11, no. 2 (2018): 173–194, references to 180–183.
18. Williams, *Diamond Mines of South Africa*, 2:151–158, 165; Steven Press, *Blood and Diamonds: Germany's Imperial Ambitions in Africa* (Cambridge, MA: Harvard University Press, 2021), 93–94.
19. "Report of the Diamond Mine Inspector," CPP 1885, G.28, 12.
20. *Diamond Fields Advertiser*, January 4, 1899; Roberts, *Kimberley*, 271.
21. *Daily Independent*, March 12, 1890, 3.
22. DBCM Annual Report 1894, 8.
23. Williams, *Diamond Mines*, 2:81.
24. Bryce, *Impressions of South Africa*, 200.
25. Ibid., 360. For Bryce's analysis of the US, see James Bryce, *The American Commonwealth*, 3 vols. (London: Macmillan, 1888), and an interesting review, Woodrow Wilson, "Bryce's American Commonwealth," *Political Science Quarterly* 4, no. 1 (March 1889): 153–169. Bryce served as British ambassador to the United States, 1907–13.
26. *Imvo Zabantsundu*, December 29, 1892.
27. CTAR, NA 231, G. W. Barnes, Protector of Natives, monthly report of January 31, 1895.
28. Rotberg, *Founder*, 499–500.
29. Randolph Churchill, *Men, Mines, and Animals in South Africa*, 2nd ed. (London: Sampson, Low, & Marston, 1897), 71–72.
30. Davenport, *Digging Deep*, 175–177.
31. Ibid., 178–181.

32. Nkosi, *Mining Deep*, 116–122.
33. Paul Johnson, *Consolidated Gold Fields: A Centenary Portrait* (New York: St. Martin's, 1987), 23–29; Davenport, *Digging Deep*, 179–182; Rotberg, *Founder*, 502–505.
34. Garth Tai-shen Ahnie, "Ik Weet Niets van de Ontploffing: An Examination of the Braamfontein Explosion of 1896" (master's thesis, Stellenbosch University, 2017), 13–17; Cartwright, *Dynamite Company*, chap. 4: "Monopoly"; G. Blainey, "Lost Causes of the Jameson Raid," *Economic History Review* 18, no. 2 (1965): 350–366; Katz, "Outcrop and Deep Level Mining in South Africa," 317–318.
35. Nkosi, *Mining Deep*, 140–161.
36. For a social and political history of the impact of low wages in the twentieth century, see Francis Wilson, "Minerals and Migrants: How the Mining Industry Has Shaped South Africa," *Daedalus* 230, no. 1 (Winter 2001): 99–121.
37. Davenport, *Digging Deep*, 198–202.
38. Fredric Quivik, "Nuisance, Source of Wealth, or Potentially Practical Material: Visions of Tailings in Idaho's Coeur d'Alene Mining District, 1888–2001," *Journal of the Society for Industrial Archaeology* 39, no. 1/2, Special Issue: "Industrial Waste" (2013): 41–64; Fredric Quivik, "Of Tailings, Superfund Litigation, and Historians as Experts: U.S. v. Asarco, et al. (the Bunker Hill Case in Idaho)," *Public Historian* 26, no. 1 (Winter 2004): 81–104.
39. Thorsten Rösner, "The Environmental Impact of Seepage from Gold Mine Tailings Dams near Johannesburg, South Africa" (PhD diss., Dept. of Earth Sciences, University of Pretoria, 1999).
40. On toxic mining practices in more recent times, see Gabrielle Hecht, *Residual Governance: How South Africa Foretells Planetary Futures* (Durham, NC: Duke University Press, 2023).
41. J. F. Durand, "The Impact of Gold Mining on the Witwatersrand on the Rivers and Karst System of Gauteng and North West Province, South Africa," *Journal of African Earth Sciences* 68 (2012): 24–43; Rebecca Adler, Marius Claasen, Linda Godfrey, and Anthony Turton, "Water, Mining, and Waste: An Historical and Economic Perspective on Conflict Management in South Africa," *Economics of Peace and Security Journal* 2, no. 7 (2007): 33–41; Terence McCarthy, "The Impact of Acid Mine Drainage in South Africa," *South African Journal of Science* 107, no. 5/6 (2011): 1–7.

CHAPTER 17

1. Tamarkin, *Cecil Rhodes and the Cape Afrikaners*, 194.
2. *The Times*, January 8, 1894, 5; January 29, 1894, 5.
3. Ibid.
4. Ibid.
5. Charles van Onselen, *The Cowboy and the Capitalist: John Hays Hammond, the American West, and the Jameson Raid* (Charlottesville: University of Virginia Press, 2017).

6. Hammond, *Autobiography*, 1:211–214.
7. Flint, *Cecil Rhodes*, 175–176; Williams, *Cecil Rhodes*, 246–249.
8. Charles van Onselen, *Studies in the Social and Economic History of the Witwatersrand*, vol. 1, *New Babylon* (London: Longmans, 1982), 12; Blainey, "Lost Causes of the Jameson Raid," 357–358.
9. Michell, *Life and Times*, 2:63.
10. Blainey, "Lost Causes of the Jameson Raid," 362. Blainey's article strongly correlated the ownership of the deep-level mines with the leadership of the Jameson Raid, a useful thesis that was complicated by subsequent research. Robert Kubicek, "The Randlords in 1895: A Reassessment," *Journal of British Studies* 11, no. 2 (May 1972): 84–103; Richard Mendelsohn, "Blainey and the Jameson Raid: The Debate Renewed," *Journal of Southern African Studies* 6, no. 2 (April 1980): 157–170; Elaine Katz, "Outcrop and Deep Level Mining in South Africa before the Anglo-Boer War: Re-Examining the Blainey Thesis," *Economic History Review* 48, no. 2 (May 1995): 304–328.
11. Flint, *Cecil Rhodes*, 177–178; Rotberg, *Founder*, 526.
12. *The Times*, January 29, 1895, 10.
13. Bodleian Library, Rhodes Papers, MSS Afr. s 228, C3B, "Charter," no. 232, "Confidential: Correspondence Related to Bechuanaland Protectorate," Loch-Rhodes Correspondence, Cape Town, July 17, 1894, 29–31.
14. M. D. Burgess, "Lord Rosebery and the Imperial Federation League, 1884–1893," *New Zealand Journal of History* 13, no. 2 (1979): 165–181.
15. Ellman, *Oscar Wilde*, 404–405, 450–451; John Davis, "Primrose, Archibald Philip, fifth earl of Rosebery," *Oxford Dictionary of National Biography* (2015), accessed online, February 13, 2024.
16. *The Times*, January 1, 1895, 7.
17. Williams, *Cecil Rhodes*, 234.
18. Flint, *Cecil Rhodes*, 180–183; Michell, *Cecil John Rhodes*, 2:135; Rotberg, *Founder*, 527; Williams, *Cecil Rhodes*, 252–253. Michell and Williams have a more positive assessment of Robinson's reappointment than Flint and Rotberg.
19. Parsons, *King Khama, Emperor Joe*, 49–50.
20. Maylam, "Making of the Kimberley-Bulawayo Railway," 17–18; Rotberg, *Founder*, 301–304.
21. Bodleian Library, Rhodes Papers, MSS Afr. s 228, C3B, "Charter," no. 232, "Confidential: Correspondence Related to Bechuanaland Protectorate," 25.
22. Bodleian Library, Rhodes Papers, MSS Afr. s 228, C3B, "Charter," no. 232, "Confidential: Correspondence Related to Bechuanaland Protectorate," enclosures, Rhodes to Ripon, November 28, 1894, and Ripon to Rhodes, November 30, 1894.
23. Maylam, *Rhodes, the Tswana, and the British*, 149–150.
24. Bodleian Library, Rhodes Papers, MSS Afr. s 228, C3B, "Charter," no. 232, "Confidential: Correspondence Related to Bechuanaland Protectorate," Ripon to Rhodes, November 30, 1894, 36–37; Wingfield to Rhodes, December 11, 1894, 44.

25. Parsons, *King Khama, Emperor Joe*, 52–57.
26. Maylam, *Rhodes, the Tswana, and the British*, 144–149; Louis W. Truschel, "The Tawana and the Ngamiland Trek," *Botswana Notes and Records* 6 (1974): 47–55; Bodleian Library, Rhodes Papers, MSS. Afr. s. 228, C3B, "Charter," no. 232, "Confidential: Correspondence Related to Bechuanaland Protectorate," 75; no. 233, J. L. Hofmeyr to Rhodes, February 18, 1895. In 1898 a follow-up scheme also failed. See MSS. Afr. s. 228, C17 "Ngami Trek." J. L. Hofmeyr was the cousin of J. H. Hofmeyr.
27. Bodleian Library, Rhodes Papers, MSS Afr. s 228, C3B, "Charter," no. 249, Grey to Rhodes, June 22, 1895.
28. Shillington, *Colonisation of the Southern Tswana*, chap. 8: "The Blessings of British Rule." Quote is from 207.
29. Parsons, *King Khama, Emperor Joe*, 33–34, 57–58.
30. Peter T. Marsh, "Chamberlain, Joseph," *Oxford Dictionary of National Biography* (2013), accessed online, February 16, 2024.
31. Bodleian Library, Rhodes Papers, MSS Afr. s 228, C3B, "Charter," no. 255, Canning to Rhodes, handwritten copy of a telegram, August 2, 1895.
32. Ibid.
33. Ibid.
34. Maylam, *Rhodes, the Tswana, and the British*, 162–164.
35. The full story of the chiefs' visit to Britain is recounted in Parsons, *King Khama, Emperor Joe, and the Great White Queen*.
36. UK National Archives, CO 879/44/498, 128, Khama, Sebele, and Bathoen to CO, November 4, 1895. As quoted by Maylam, *Rhodes, the Tswana, and the British*, 182.
37. Parsons, *King Khama, Emperor Joe*, 206–211; Rotberg, *Founder*, 486–487.
38. Parsons, *King Khama, Emperor Joe*, 224–236.
39. Ibid., 199–200.
40. Bodleian Library, Rhodes Papers, MSS Afr. s 228, C3B, "Charter," no. 274, Rhodes to Fife, [n.d.] December 1895.
41. Flint, *Cecil Rhodes*, 179–183; Lockhart and Woodhouse, *Rhodes*, 193–194; Michell, *Cecil John Rhodes*, 2:140–141; Rotberg, *Founder*, 484, 533–534; Williams, *Cecil Rhodes*, 258–260.
42. Flint, *Cecil Rhodes*, 185–189; Rotberg, *Founder*, 535.
43. Van Onselen, *Cowboy and the Capitalist*, 162–166.
44. Flint, *Cecil Rhodes*, 188–189; Williams, *Cecil Rhodes*, 265–266.
45. Flint, *Cecil Rhodes*, 189–191; Van Onselen, *Cowboy and the Capitalist*, 170.
46. Flint, *Cecil Rhodes*, 194; Rotberg, *Founder*, 535.
47. Quotation from Williams, *Cecil Rhodes*, 271. On the details of the raid, the old standard account is from Williams, with updated versions in Flint, *Cecil Rhodes*, 192–197, and Rotberg, *Founder*, 537–545. All are superseded by the extensive account presented by Van Onselen in *Cowboy and the Capitalist*.

48. Bodleian Library, Rhodes Papers, MSS. Afr. s. 1647, Hildersham Hall Papers (Rhodes Family), Box 1, Item 6, Commonplace Book, 29–31.
49. Flint, *Cecil Rhodes*, 193–197; Rotberg, *Founder*, 543–546; Williams, *Cecil Rhodes*, 272–275.
50. Flint, *Cecil Rhodes*, 198–200; Rotberg, *Founder*, 547; Williams, *Cecil Rhodes*, 277.
51. Tamarkin, *Cecil Rhodes and the Cape Afrikaners*, 239; Williams, *Cecil Rhodes*, 272–273.

CHAPTER 18

1. Flint, *Cecil Rhodes*, 201–203; Rotberg, *Founder*, 547. For a detailed history of the investigations into Rhodes, see Jeffrey Butler, *The Liberal Party and the Jameson Raid* (Oxford: Clarendon Press, 1968).
2. Keppel-Jones, *Rhodes and Rhodesia*, 365, 431–432.
3. Mlambo, *History of Zimbabwe*, 46–50; Julian Cobbing, "The Absent Priesthood: Another Look at the Rhodesian Risings of 1896–1897," *Journal of African History* 18, no. 1 (1977): 61–84.
4. Mlambo, *History of Zimbabwe*, 46–50.
5. Keppel-Jones, *Rhodes and Rhodesia*, chap. 10: "The Black Experience."
6. Mlambo, *History of Zimbabwe*, 45–46; Parsons, "Victorian Internet," 106.
7. Selous, *Sunshine and Storm*, 29–32, 61–64; Oriel Rhodes Commission Report, 111.
8. Le Sueur, *Cecil Rhodes*, 128, 159. For more on Rhodes's campaigning, see Flint, *Cecil Rhodes*, 204–205; Rotberg, *Founder*, 556–563.
9. Bodleian Library, MSS. Afr. t.5, ff.272, H. Marshall Hole, "The Courage of Cecil Rhodes," 2–3.
10. Beinart, "Cecil Rhodes," 586, 593–596. The details of the campaign may be found in Keppel-Jones, *Rhodes and Rhodesia*, chaps. 11–12.
11. Mlambo, *History of Zimbabwe*, 46–50. Beinart, "Cecil Rhodes," 596–600.
12. Beinart, "Cecil Rhodes," 600–602.
13. Vere Stent, *A Personal Record of Some Incidents in the Life of Cecil Rhodes* (Bulawayo: Books of Rhodesia, 1925; reprint ed. 1974), 35–61. See also Sauer, *Ex Africa*, 313–323.
14. As quoted by Rotberg, *Founder*, 570–571.
15. Sauer, *Ex Africa*, 323–324; Terence Ranger, *Voices from the Rocks: Nature, Culture, and History in the Matopos Hills of Zimbabwe* (Bloomington: Indiana University Press, 1999), 30. See also Donal Lowry, "The Granite of the Ancient North: Race, Nation, and Empire at Cecil Rhodes's Mountain Mausoleum and Rhodes House, Oxford," in *Pantheons: Transformations of a Monumental Idea*, ed. Richard Wrigley and Matthew Craske (London: Ashgate, 2004): 193–219.
16. Tamarkin, *Cecil Rhodes and the Cape Afrikaners*, 259–261.
17. Simons, *Groote Schuur*, 22–27. The quotation is from Sarah Gertrude Millin, *Cecil Rhodes* (New York: Harper and Brothers, 1933), 362.

18. DBCM Annual Report of 1896, 10–13. The old sanatorium building now houses the McGregor Museum.
19. DBCM Annual Report of 1896, 14.
20. Bodleian Library, Rhodes Papers, MSS Afr. s 228, C1, v.1, "Administrators," no. 3, Grey to Rhodes, January 11, 1897.
21. All Rhodes biographies have an account of the hearings, as do the many books that address the Jameson Raid. Flint, *Cecil Rhodes*, 208–211; Lockhart and Woodhouse, *Rhodes*, 357–385; Michell, *Cecil John Rhodes*, 2:203–207; Rotberg, *Founder*, 547–550; Williams, *Cecil Rhodes*, 276–285. The best account of the hearings may be found in Butler's monograph, *The Liberal Party and the Jameson Raid*.
22. J. S. Galbraith, "The British South Africa Company and the Jameson Raid," *Journal of British Studies* 10, no. 1 (November 1970): 145–161.
23. Colvin, *Life of Jameson*, 2:157.
24. Ibid., 2:158–160.

CHAPTER 19

1. Search results are from britishnewspaperarchive.co.uk. Search conducted on October 1, 2021.
2. Gerhard de Beer, Annemarie Paterson, Hennie Olivier, *160 Years of Export: The History of the Perishable Products Export Control Board* (Parow: PPECB, 2003), 22–27.
3. Baker and Stead, *Cecil Rhodes*, 61–63.
4. Ibid., 66.
5. Bodleian Library, Rhodes Papers, MSS Afr. s 228, C15 "Michell," no. 16, Pickstone to Michell, September 25, 1897, 3.
6. Bodleian Library, Rhodes Papers, MSS Afr. s 228, C15 "Michell," no. 56, Michell to Rhodes, September 1, 1901.
7. On the legacy of Rhodes's and Molteno's fruit farming and their different approaches, see Simons, *Apples of the Sun*, chaps. 3–4.
8. Bodleian Library, Rhodes Papers, MSS Afr. s 228, C15 "Michell," no. 32, Michell to Rhodes, July 5, 1900.
9. Rotberg, *Founder*, 643–644.
10. Bodleian Library, Rhodes Papers, MSS. Afr. s. 228, C16 "Miscellaneous," no. 54, Sigmund Haagner to Rhodes, April 18, 1898; De Beers Archive, Board 4/1/1, Private Letters of C. J. Rhodes, Jourdan to Grimmer, November 12, 1900; Cartwright, *Dynamite Company*, chap. 8: "Quinan's Plans"; Newbury, *Diamond Ring*, 162–167; Rotberg, *Founder*, 641–643.
11. Tamarkin, *Cecil Rhodes and the Cape Afrikaners*, 278–279. "Anti-Fleet" refers to the objections of Afrikaner Bond members to Prime Minister Sprigg's decision to subscribe Cape Colony funds for the construction of vessels for the Royal Navy.

12. Baker and Stead, *Cecil Rhodes*, 66–67.
13. Flint, *Cecil Rhodes*, 212.
14. Richard W. Petheram, "Inyanga: With Special Reference to the Rhodes Inyanga Estate," *Rhodesiana* 31 (1974): 36–50. Quotation from 39.
15. Petheram, "Inyanga," 39.
16. Colvin, *Life of Jameson*, 2:174–175.
17. Milner was enrolled at Balliol College from 1872 to 1876 and earned a position at New College, where he remained until 1879. See J. Lee Thompson, *Forgotten Patriot: A Life of Alfred, Viscount Milner of St. James's and Cape Town, 1854–1925* (Madison, NJ: Fairleigh Dickinson University Press, 2007), 75.
18. *The Milner Papers: South Africa, 1897–1899*, ed. Cecil Headlam (London: Cassell, 1931), Milner to Selborne, June 2, 1897, 106–107.
19. *Milner Papers: 1897–1899*, Milner to Selborne, June 2, 1897, 107–108.
20. *Milner Papers: 1897–1899*, Milner to Selborne, January 26, 1898, 150.
21. De Beers Archive, Rhodes Private Letters, Board 1/1/1.
22. It is interesting to note that Johnny Grimmer was the son of Dr. William Grimmer of Colesberg. Thirty years earlier, William Grimmer had been David Arnot's partner in the mineral concession granted by Andries Waterboer at the diamond fields. Perhaps it gave Rhodes some enjoyment to think that if things had gone differently at the diamond fields, Johnny Grimmer might have inherited a diamond empire.
23. Bodleian Library, Rhodes Papers, MSS. Afr. t. 5, "Miscellaneous Papers," Rhodes to Norris, undated draft of a letter or telegram, 138.
24. Bodleian Library, Rhodes Papers, MSS. Afr. s. 228, C13 "Inyanga," no. 16, Grimmer to Rhodes, October 31, 1898.
25. Petheram, "Inyanga," 42–43. See also Bodleian Library, Rhodes Papers, MSS. Afr. s. 228, C13 "Inyanga," Norris to Rhodes, November 14, 1898; much of the subsequent correspondence in C13 "Inyanga" shows Norris and Grimmer reporting to Rhodes about details of land purchases, employees, contractors, and experiments with animal husbandry.
26. J. Charles Shee, "Rhodes and the Doctors (4): Hans Sauer," *Central African Journal of Medicine* (August 1963): 328–331.
27. De Beers Archive, Board 4/1/1: Private Letters of C. J. Rhodes, January 1894 to December 1901.
28. Bodleian Library, Rhodes Papers, MSS Afr. s 228, C14 "McDonald," no. 18, McDonald to Rhodes, October 29, 1898, 3. There are 87 detailed letters by McDonald, many of them similar to this one.
29. Bodleian Library, Rhodes Papers, MSS Afr. s 228, C14 "McDonald," no. 30, McDonald to Rhodes, August 24, 1899, 1.
30. *Bulawayo Chronicle*, June 26, 1897. With thanks to Matthew Kidd for help in locating this citation.

31. When Rhodes was besieged in Kimberley from October 1899 to February 1900, details of the plans for Sauerdale were discussed in correspondence with Lewis Michell, Rhodes's banker in Cape Town. Bodleian Library, Rhodes Papers, MSS Afr. s 228, C15 "Michell," no. 35.
32. Keppel-Jones, *Rhodes and Rhodesia*, 528–529.
33. *Rhodesia Herald*, December 2, 1896, as cited by Keppel-Jones, *Rhodes and Rhodesia*, 533.
34. Mlambo, *History of Zimbabwe*, 54–77.
35. Galbraith, *Crown and Charter*, 278–286. Keppel-Jones, *Rhodes and Rhodesia*, 365. On the reports by Oats, Tarbutt, Williams, Willoughby, and others, see Bodleian Library, Rhodes Papers, MSS. Afr. s. 228, C19 "Rhodesian Goldreefs," nos. 1–10, 14–18. On the 1900 marketing campaign, see Bodleian Library, Rhodes Papers, MSS. Afr. s. 228, C4, "Charter (Home Board)," no. 40, Jones to Jourdan, July 14, 1900.
36. Maylam, *Rhodes, the Tswana, and the British*, 194–196.
37. Bodleian Library, Rhodes Papers, MSS. Afr. t. 5, ff.263, Reminiscences of Helen Townsend, ca. 1951, 4. Pauling completed work on the railway from Mafeking to Bulawayo in 1897. Salisbury and Bulawayo were eventually connected in 1902.
38. Anthony H. Croxton, *Railways of Zimbabwe: The Story of the Beira, Mashonaland, and Rhodesia Railways* (Newton Abbot: David and Charles, 1973; 2nd ed. 1982), 50; Louis W. Bolze, "The Railway Comes to Bulawayo," *Rhodesiana* 18 (July 1968): 47–84, citation to 56–58.
39. Bodleian Library, Rhodes Papers, MSS. Afr. s. 228, C3B, "Charter," no. 287, Canning's copy of telegrams exchanged with Rhodes and Beit, November 14, 1896.
40. Lunn, *Capital and Labour*, 31–32.
41. Ibid., 108–112.
42. Croxton, *Railways of Zimbabwe*, 24–25, 35–36.
43. Pauling, *Chronicles of a Contractor*, 254–255.
44. Vail, "Making of an Imperial Slum," 91–93.
45. Robinson and Gallagher, *Africa and the Victorians*, 446–448.

CHAPTER 20

1. Flint, *Cecil Rhodes*, 170, 212; Williams, *Cecil Rhodes*, 233.
2. De Beers Archive, Rhodes Private Letter Book, Board 4/1/2, Rhodes to Kitchener, September 6, 1898.
3. Bodleian Library, Rhodes Papers, MSS. Afr. s. 228, C18 "Northern Rhodesia," part 1, no. 4, Rhodes to Chamberlain, April 28, 1898, 4–5, 9. The expenses of railroad maintenance are made clear in annual reports; for example, see Bodleian Library, Rhodes Papers, MSS. Afr. s. 228, C20 "Rhodesia Railways," no. 91.
4. Bodleian Library, Rhodes Papers, MSS. Afr. s. 228, C18 "Northern Rhodesia," part 2.

5. Henry G. Prout, "The Cape to Cairo Railroad," *Munsey's Magazine* 21 (April 1899): 113–117.
6. R. Cherer Smith, "The Africa Trans-Continental Telegraph Line," *Rhodesiana* 33 (September 1975): 1–18. For surveyor reports, see Bodleian Library, Rhodes Papers, MSS Afr. s 228, C22 "Telegraph," no. 32, Enclosed in Administrator, N. E. Rhodesia, to Rhodes, March 16, 1901.
7. Rotberg, *Founder*, 596; Williams, *Cecil Rhodes*, 309–310.
8. Michell, *Life and Times*, 2:256–259; Rotberg, *Founder*, 596–597.
9. Williams, *Cecil Rhodes*, 310.
10. Bodleian Library, Rhodes Papers, MSS Afr. s.228, C22 "Telegraph," no. 15, Correspondence of Rhodes with British and German diplomats, January–March 1899; no. 24, Jones to Rhodes, September 2 and November 11, 1899.
11. Bodleian Library, Rhodes Papers, MSS Afr. s.228, C22 "Telegraph," no. 12, Davis to Beit, October 2, 1899, 2.
12. Gloria Calhoun, "Holding up the Line: The Telegraph Pole as a System Component," paper presented to the annual meeting of the Society for the History of Technology, November 12, 2022. See also Gloria Calhoun, "Why Wire Mattered: Building U.S. Networked Infrastructures, 1845–1910," *Technology and Culture* 62, no. 1 (2021): 156–184.
13. Bodleian Library, Rhodes Papers, MSS Afr. s.228, C22 "Telegraph," no. 12, Correspondence of Rhodes with Postmasters-General of Cape Colony, Cape Town, and South Australia, Adelaide, December 1, 1898, to January 19, 1899; no. 15, Correspondence of Rhodes with British and German diplomats, January–March 1899.
14. "The Cape to Cairo Telegraph," *Scientific American*, November 30, 1901, 343.
15. Bodleian Library, Rhodes Papers, MSS Afr. s 228, C22 "Telegraph," no. 5, Turner to Rhodes, March 16, 1898.
16. S. R. Denny, "The Cape to Cairo Telegraph," *Northern Rhodesia Journal* 5, no. 1 (1962): 39–43.
17. Denny, "Cape to Cairo Telegraph," 39–43.
18. Flint, *Cecil Rhodes*, 212–213; Williams, *Cecil Rhodes*, 308–309.
19. De Beers Archive, Board 4/1/1, Private Letters of Rhodes, Rhodes to London Board, April 19, 1899.
20. Frederick Russell Burnham, "Northern Rhodesia," in *Bulawayo up to Date: Being a General Sketch of Rhodesia*, ed. Walter H. Wills et al. (London: Simpkin, Marshall, Hamilton, Kent, 1898); Rotberg, *Founder*, 595.
21. Rotberg, *Founder*, 602. See also Davenport, *Afrikaner Bond*, 181.
22. Michell, *Life and Times*, 2:282–283. The speech was given on February 23, 1900, but is characteristic of speeches given by Rhodes from 1898 to 1901. For discussion of what Rhodes meant by "civilized men," see Flint, *Cecil Rhodes*, 82–83, and Rotberg, *Founder*, 611, 618.
23. On early Pan Africanism, see Kwame Anthony Appiah, *In My Father's House: Africa in the Philosophy of Culture* (New York: Oxford University Press, 1992),

chap. 1: "The Invention of Africa." On the early ANC, see Saul Dubow, *The African National Congress* (Thrupp, Gloucs.: Sutton, 2000), 1–7.

24. For a more favorable analysis of Rhodes's statements, see Nigel Biggar, "A Critical Response," Appendix A to the *Report of the Oriel College Commission* (Oxford: Oriel College, 2021), 1–2, https://www.oriel.ox.ac.uk/wp-content/uploads/2022/08/beinart_appendix_a_response_by_nigel_biggar.pdf, consulted on November 29, 2023.

25. De Beers Archive, Board 4/1/1, Private Letters of C. J. Rhodes, Stow to Chairman, with "Original sent to Mr Rhodes at Salisbury," January 29, 1898. The same file records many cash disbursements, mainly to Willie Pickering, which may have been used for buying votes.

26. Davenport, *Afrikaner Bond*, 183–188; Tamarkin, *Cecil Rhodes and the Cape Afrikaners*, 284–290.

27. Rotberg, *Founder*, 651–652; Williams, *Rhodes*, 313–314; Ziegler, *Legacy*, 16.

28. Flint, *Cecil Rhodes*, 218–222; Rotberg, *Founder*, 652–656. The Radziwill affair is narrated extensively by Rhodes's private secretary: Le Sueur, *Cecil Rhodes*, chap. 14: "Rhodes's Last Days and the Princess Radziwill." Rhodes's banker and biographer, Michell, references his own extensive involvement but does not mention Radziwill by name. See Michell, *Life and Times*, 2:309.

29. Etherington, *Imperium of the Soul*, chap. 2: "Love and Loathing: Rudyard Kipling's India."

30. David Gilmour, *The Long Recessional: The Imperial Life of Rudyard Kipling* (New York: Farrar, Straus, and Giroux, 2003), 107.

31. Gilmour, *Long Recessional*, chap. 8: "The Prophet's Burden"; chap. 9: "Rhodes and Milner"; chap. 10: "Lessons from the Boers."

32. Baker and Stead, *Cecil Rhodes*, 54–55.

33. DBCM Annual Report, 1899, 17.

34. Colvin, *Life of Jameson*, 2:204–206.

35. The two different accounts are from McDonald, *Rhodes: A Life*, 365–366, and from Millin, *Cecil Rhodes* (London: 1933), 403.

CONCLUSION

1. There are two autopsy reports that vary in some of their details: Bodleian Library, MSS. Afr. t.5, 491 a-b, and CTAR, A540/37, Stevenson to Fowler (telegram), March 27, 1902. The autopsy techniques were not recorded but are inferred from a textbook then in use: Rudolph Virchow, *Description and Explanation of the Method of Performing Post-Mortem Examinations* (London: J. & A. Churchill, 1876). Robert Rotberg and his collaborator, Dr. Miles Shore, reviewed the autopsy reports and attempted a differential diagnosis. They decided that they lacked sufficient evidence to make a diagnosis that is firm. It is thought that a second page of examination notes is missing. See Rotberg, *Founder*, 675–677.

2. Le Sueur, *Cecil Rhodes*, 326–327.
3. Ibid., 327–328.
4. Jourdan, *Cecil Rhodes*, 275–279; Le Sueur, *Cecil Rhodes*, 329–331.
5. McDonald, *Rhodes: A Life*, 368–369. For a description and analysis of the burial service, see Lowry, "Granite of the Ancient North," 193–196.
6. For insight into the participation of these Ndebele men, see Jacob Dlamini, *Askari: A Story of Collaboration and Betrayal in the Anti-Apartheid Struggle* (Auckland Park: Jacana, 2014), 8–17.
7. Lowry, "Granite of the Ancient North," 196.
8. Paul Maylam, *The Cult of Rhodes: Remembering an Imperialist in Africa* (Cape Town: David Philip, 2005), 32–46. See also Ranger, *Voices from the Rocks*, chap. 1: "Seeing the Matopos."
9. Nasaw, *Andrew Carnegie*, chap. 20: "The Gospels of Andrew Carnegie."
10. Bodleian Library, Rhodes Papers, MSS. Afr. t. 1, Item 24, Rhodes to Rothschild, June 20, 1888.
11. Baker and Stead, *Cecil Rhodes*, 48; Ziegler, *Legacy*, 15–16.
12. Ziegler, *Legacy*, 23. Jameson once made the same remark about Grey, when he was appointed as the governor-general of Canada.
13. Philip Ziegler, *Legacy: Cecil Rhodes, the Rhodes Trust and Rhodes Scholarships* (New Haven, CT: Yale University Press, 2008), Appendix One, "Rhodes's Will," 335–347.
14. Ziegler, *Legacy*, 337–338.
15. Ibid., 341.
16. Bodleian Library, Rhodes Papers, MSS. Afr. t. 1, Item 20, Rhodes to Hawksley, undated ca. July 1899.
17. Wilde, "The Soul of Man under Socialism," *Fortnightly Review* 55 (1891): 292–319; quotation from 292–293. The italics are in the original.
18. Wilde's argument has been embraced and extended by contemporary critics of philanthropy. See Anand Giridharadas, *Winners Take All: The Elite Charade of Changing the World* (New York: Knopf, 2018), 8–9.
19. Aristotle, *Nicomachean Ethics*, trans. Harris Rackham, Loeb Classical Library 73 (Cambridge, MA: Harvard University Press, 1926), 32–33. The literal translation in brackets and the contextual advice were provided by Ian Storey.
20. The long view of colonial technopolitical legacies is taken by Suzanne Moon in *Technology in Southeast Asian History* (Baltimore: Johns Hopkins University Press, 2023), 215. These findings about Rhodes tend to confirm previously written studies of material culture. Daniel Miller, *Stuff* (Cambridge: Polity Press, 2010); David Harvey, *Spaces of Global Capitalism: Towards a Theory of Uneven Geographical Development* (London: Verso, 2006); Foster, *Washed with Sun*, 185, 246; Gillian Hart, *Disabling Globalization: Places of Power in Post-Apartheid South Africa* (Berkeley: University of California Press, 2002), 13.

21. Horace, *Odes and Epodes*, Loeb Classical Library 33, ed. and trans. Niall Rudd (Cambridge, MA: Harvard University Press, 2004), 216–217. Rhodes's quotation of the poem is in the Bodleian Library, Rhodes Papers, MSS Afr. t.1, Item 13. This note is in Rhodes's handwriting and is enclosed with Item 12, which is the will of September 8, 1893, that was sent to W. T. Stead.

Select Bibliography

ARCHIVAL SOURCES

University of Oxford, Bodleian Library

Rhodes Papers
MSS Afr. s 8   Miscellaneous Papers.
MSS Afr. s 12   Rhodes Fruit Farms: Photograph Album.
MSS Afr. s 69   Reminiscences of C. J. Rhodes. 1923–1963.
MSS Afr. s 115 Letters from C. J. Rhodes to his family.
MSS Afr. s 134 Basil Williams Papers. 1914–1921.
MSS Afr. s 228 C 1. Administrators. Rhodesia. Vol. 1, 1897–99.
C 1. Administrators. Rhodesia. Vol. 2, 1900–1902.
C 2. Cape Colony. Vol. 2 A, 1890–93.
C 2. Cape Colony. Vol. 2 A, 1894–95.
C 2. Cape Colony. Vol. 2 B, 1896–1900.
C 3. Charter. Matabeleland and Mashonaland. Vol. 3 A, 1889–1890.
C 3. Charter. Matabeleland and Mashonaland. Vol. 3 A, 1891.
C 3. Charter. Matabeleland and Mashonaland. Vol. 3 B, 1892–96.
C 4. Charter. Home Board. 1897–1902.
C 5. Charter. Cape. 1898–1901.
C 6. Cold Storage. 1899–1902.
C 7. De Beers. Vol. 7 A, 1890–96.
C 7. De Beers. Vol. 7 B, 1897–99.
C 7. De Beers. Vol. 7 B, 1900–1902.
C 8. Farms. 1897–1901.
C 9. Finance. 1888–95.
C 10. Gold Fields. Vol. 1, 1890–94.
C 10. Gold Fields. Vol. 2, 1895–1902.
C 11. Hawkesley. 1897–1908.
C 12. Immigration. 1902.

C 13. Inyanga. 1896–1901.
C 14. McDonald. 1897–1902.
C 15. Michell. 1897–1902.
C 16. Miscellaneous. 1890–1902.
C 17. Ngami Trek. 1897–1902.
C 18. Northern Rhodesia. 1897–1901.
C 19. Rhodesian Goldreefs. 1898–1902.
C 20. Rhodesian Railways. 1897–1901.
C 21. Syfret. 1897–1902.
C 22. Transcontinental telegraph. 1897–1902.
C 23. Transvaal. 1900–1902.
C 24. Wernher, Beit & Co. 1890–91.
C 25. Delagoa Bay. 1892–1895.
C 26. Papers Saved from Groote Schuur Fire. 1875–96.
C 27. Personal. 1888–1902.
C 28. Personal. 1884–1902.

MSS Afr. s 229   III. Papers of Gordon Le Sueur.
IV. Papers of E. A. Maund.
V. Papers of Sir Lewis Michell.
VI. Papers relating to the Princess Radziwill.

MSS Afr. s 1647   Hildersham Hall Papers. (Rhodes family letters and papers.)
MSS Afr. t 1   Wills and related papers. 1871–1899.
MSS Afr. t 5   Miscellaneous papers. 1869–1955.
MSS Afr. t 6   Correspondence between C. J. Rhodes and the 4th Earl Grey. 1889–1900.
MSS Afr. t 14   Miscellaneous papers. 1868–1902.

U.K. National Archives, Kew

NA CO 879/9, Confidential Print, Africa, No. 84. Edward Fairfield, "Memorandum on South African Affairs." January 1876.
NA CO 879/9, Conf. Pr. Africa No. 86, Edward Fairfield, "Memorandum on the Native Question in South Africa."
NA CO 879/9 Conf. Pr. Africa No. 96.
NA CO 879/9, Conf. Pr. Africa No. 99.

McGregor Museum, Kimberley

Rhodes-Rudd Correspondence.
Stow, Frederick S. "Memoir of the formation of the de Beers Mining Company."

National Library of South Africa, Cape Town

Cape Parliamentary Papers

Report of the Commissioners Appointed to Inquire and Report upon the Diamond Trade Acts, the Detective or Searching Department, the Compound System, and Other Matters Connected with the Diamond Industry of Griqualand West, 1887. [G. 3] 1888.

Report of the Commissioners Appointed to Inquire and Report upon the Working and Management of the Diamond Mines of Griqualand West, 1881–1882. [G. 86] 1882.

Reports by the Inspectors of Diamond Mines, 1882–1902.

G. 27, 1882
G. 34, 1883
G. 40, 1884
G. 28, 1885
G. 26, 1886
G. 28, 1888
G. 11, 1890
G. 24, 1891
G. 27, 1892
G. 26, 1893
G. 38, 1894
G. 25, 1895
G. 49, 1896
G. 37, 1897
G. 43, 1898
G. 32, 1899
G. 61, 1900
G. 41, 1901
G. 76, 1902

Churchill Archive [Online resource]

Letters of Lady Jennie Churchill.
Letters of Lord Randolph Churchill.
Letters of Sir Winston S. Churchill.

University of Cape Town, Jagger Library Special Collections

E. A. Judge Papers, BC 500.
J. M. Smalberger Collection, BC 635.

De Beers Archive, Kimberley

Annual Reports, De Beers Mining Company.
Annual Reports, De Beers Consolidated Mining Company.
Letterbooks, De Beers Mining Company.
Private Letters of C. J. Rhodes, Board 4/1/1.

Cape Town Archives Repository

Papers of Lewis Michell, "Typescript of a Personal Memoir," A 540/29.
Reports of the Protector of Natives, NA 231.

PERIODICALS

Cape Argus. National Library of South Africa.
Cape Monthly Magazine. National Library of South Africa.
Daily Independent (Kimberley). Africana Library, Kimberley, and National Library of South Africa.
Diamond Fields Advertiser. Africana Library, Kimberley, and National Library of South Africa.
Hansards, House of Commons Debates. Online archive.
Imvo Zabantsundu. African Newspapers Online.
Natal Witness. African Newspapers Online.
The Grahamstown Journal. African Newspapers Online.
The Times (London). Online archive.

PUBLISHED PRIMARY SOURCES

Angove, John. *In the Early Days: The Reminiscences of Pioneer Life on the South African Diamond Fields*. Handel House, 1911.
Aristotle. *Nicomachean Ethics*. Translated by Harris Rackham. Loeb Classical Library 73. Harvard University Press, 1926.
Aristotle. *Politics*. Translated by Benjamin Jowett. 2 vols. Clarendon Press, 1885.
Bent, Theodore. *The Ruined Cities of Mashonaland*. Longmans, Green, 1892; 3rd ed. 1896.
Boswell, James. *The Life of Johnson*. 3 vols. Heritage Press, 1963.
Bryce, James. *The American Commonwealth*. 3 vols. Macmillan, 1888.
Bryce, James. *Impressions of South Africa*. Richard Clay, 1897; 3rd ed. 1899.
Churchill, Randolph. *Men, Mines, and Animals in South Africa*. 2nd ed. Sampson Low, Marston, 1897.
De Waal, David Christiaan. *With Rhodes in Mashonaland*. Juta, 1896.
Dunn, E. J. *Notes on the Diamond-Fields*. Saul Solomon, 1871.

FitzPatrick, J. Percy. *South African Memories: Scraps of History*. Edited by Deborah Lavin. Donker, 1979.

Fossor (pseud.). *Twelve Months at the South African Diamond Fields*. Edward Stanford, 1872.

Gibbon, Edward. *The History of the Decline and Fall of the Roman Empire*. Claxton, 1875.

Gladstone, William Ewart. "Aggression on Egypt and Freedom in the East." *The Nineteenth Century: A Monthly Review* (1877): 149–166. Reprinted in London by an unknown publisher in 1884.

Gladstone, William Ewart. *Political Speeches in Scotland, November and December 1879*. Ridgway, 1879.

Green, T. H. *Prolegomena to Ethics*. Edited by A. C. Bradley. 3rd ed. Clarendon Press, 1890.

Héritte, E. *The Diamond and Other Precious Stones*. Saul Solomon, 1867.

Horace. *Odes and Epodes*. Translated by Niall Rudd. Loeb Classical Library 33. Harvard University Press, 2004.

Jabavu, Davidson Don Tengo. *The Life of John Tengo Jabavu*. Lovedale Institution Press, 1922.

Johnson, Frank. *Frank Johnson, Great Days: The Autobiography of an Empire Pioneer*. G. Bell, 1940.

Johnston, Harry. "My Story of the Cape to Cairo Scheme." In *The Story of the Cape to Cairo Railway and River Route from 1887 to 1922*, edited by Leo Weinthal. Vol. 1, *The Record and Romance of an Imperial Project*. Pioneer, 1923.

Lewis, William P. *Lectionaries: English and Irish*. Claxton, Remsen, and Haffelfinger, 1878.

Lyman, Joseph. *Cotton Culture*. Orange Judd, 1868.

Mackenzie, John. *Austral Africa: Losing It or Ruling It*. 2 vols. Sampson Low, Marston, Searle & Rivington, 1887.

MacNeill, John Gordon Swift. *What I Have Seen and Heard*. Little Brown, 1925.

Matthews, J. W. *Incwadi Yami: Or Twenty Years' Personal Experience in South Africa*. Rogers & Sherwood, 1887.

Merriman, John X. *Selections from the Correspondence of J. X. Merriman*. Edited by Phyllis Lewsen. 4 vols. Van Rieebeck Society, 1960–69.

Metcalfe, Charles. "My Story of the Scheme." In *The Story of the Cape to Cairo Railway and River Route from 1887 to 1922*, edited by Leo Weinthal. Vol. 1, *The Record and Romance of an Imperial Project*. Pioneer, 1923.

Michell, Lewis. *The Life and Times of the Honourable Cecil John Rhodes, 1853–1902*. 2 vols. Mitchell Kennerley, 1910.

Nichols, Kerry, James Augustus Grant, and Edwin Arnold. *Remarks on a Proposed Line of Telegraph Overland from Egypt to the Cape of Good Hope*. London, 1876.

Orpen, Joseph Millerd. *Reminiscences of Life in South Africa from 1846 to the Present Day*. 2 vols., 1908 and 1916. Reprint, C. Struik, 1964.

Parkin, George R. *Imperial Federation: The Problem of National Unity*. Macmillan, 1892.
Pauling, George. *Chronicles of a Contractor*. Books of Rhodesia, 1969.
Payton, Charles A. *The Diamond Diggings of South Africa: A Personal and Practical Account*. Horace Cox, 1872.
Plato. *The Dialogues of Plato*. Translated by Benjamin Jowett. 4 vols. Oxford University Press, 1871.
Prout, Henry G. "The Cape to Cairo Railroad." *Munsey's Magazine* 21 (April 1899): 113–117.
Radziwill, Catherine. *Cecil Rhodes: Man and Empire-Maker*. Funk & Wagnalls, 1918.
Reunert, Theodore. *Diamonds and Gold in South Africa*. Juta, 1893.
Ricarde-Seaver, Francisco I., and Charles Metcalfe. "The British Sphere of Influence in South Africa." *Fortnightly Review* 51 (March 1889): 349–362.
Rose Innes, James. *James Rose Innes: Chief Justice of South Africa: Autobiography*. Edited by B. A. Tindall. Oxford University Press, 1949.
Ruskin, John. *Lectures on Art: Delivered before the University of Oxford in Hilary Term, 1870*. John Wiley, 1873.
Sampson, Victor. *My Reminiscences*. Longmans, 1926.
Sauer, Hans. *Ex Africa*. London, 1937; reprint, Books of Rhodesia, 1973.
Schreiner, Olive. *The Story of an African Farm*. Oxford University Press, 1992.
Scully, William Charles. *Reminiscences of a South African Pioneer*. T. Fisher Unwin, 1913.
Stent, Vere. *A Personal Record of Some Incidents in the Life of Cecil Rhodes*. Books of Rhodesia, 1925; reprint 1974.
Stow, George W. *Geological Notes upon Griqualand West*. Taylor and Francis, 1875.
Strangways, H. B. T. "African Overland Telegraph." *Proceedings of the Royal Geographical Society* 1, no. 3 (March 1879): 217–218.
Thompson, Francis "Matabele." *An Autobiography*. Edited by Nancy Rouillard. Books of Rhodesia, 1936; reprint 1977.
Trollope, Anthony. *South Africa*. 3rd ed. 2 vols. Chapman and Hall, 1878.
Twain, Mark [Samuel Clemens]. *Following the Equator: A Journey around the World*. American Publishing, 1898.
Vindex [John Verschoyle]. *Cecil Rhodes: His Political Life and Speeches, 1881–1900*. Chapman and Hall, 1900.
Warren, Charles. "Cecil Rhodes's Early Days in South Africa." *Contemporary Review* 81 (1902): 643–654.
Wilde, Oscar. "Art and the Handicraftsman." In *Miscellanies*, edited by Robert Ross. Methuen, 1908.
Wilde, Oscar. "The Soul of Man under Socialism." *Fortnightly Review* 55 (1891): 292–319.
Wilson, Woodrow. "Bryce's American Commonwealth." *Political Science Quarterly* 4, no. 1 (March 1889): 153–169.

SECONDARY SOURCES

Acemoglu, Daron, and James A. Robinson. *Why Nations Fail: The Origins of Power, Prosperity, and Poverty*. Currency Press, 2012.

Adler, Rebecca, Marius Claassen, Linda Godfrey, and Anthony Turton. "Water, Mining, and Waste: An Historical and Economic Perspective on Conflict Management in South Africa." *Economics of Peace and Security Journal* 2, no. 7 (2007): 33–41.

Ahnie, Garth Tai-shen. "Ik Weet Niets van de Ontploffing: An Examination of the Braamfontein Explosion of 1896." Master's thesis, Stellenbosch University, 2017.

Ahuja, Ravi. *Pathways of Empire: Circulation, "Public Works," and Social Space in Colonial Orissa, c.1780–1914*. Orient Blackswan, 2009.

Aldrich, Mark. *Safety First: Technology, Labor, and Business in the Building of American Work Safety, 1870–1939*. Johns Hopkins University Press, 1997.

Aldrich, Robert. *Colonialism and Homosexuality*. Routledge, 2003.

Allitt, Patrick. *Catholic Converts: British and American Intellectuals Turn to Rome*. Cornell University Press, 1997.

Andrews, Thomas. *Killing for Coal: America's Deadliest Labor War*. Harvard University Press, 2008.

Appiah, Kwame Anthony. *In My Father's House: Africa in the Philosophy of Culture*. Oxford University Press, 1992.

Baker, Herbert. *Cecil Rhodes: By His Architect*. Oxford University Press, 1934.

Baker, Herbert, and W. T. Stead. *Cecil Rhodes: The Man and His Dream*. Books of Rhodesia, 1977.

Bank, Andrew. *Bushmen in a Victorian World: The Remarkable Story of the Bleek-Lloyd Collection of Bushman Folklore*. Double Storey Press, 2006.

Barak, On. *Powering Empire: How Coal Made the Middle East and Sparked Global Carbonization*. University of California Press, 2020.

Barczewski, Stephanie. *Country Houses and the British Empire*. Manchester University Press, 2014.

Bay, Mia. *Traveling Black: A Story of Race and Resistance*. Harvard University Press, 2021.

Beach, David. *The Shona and Their Neighbors*. Blackwell, 1994.

Beard, Mary. *Confronting the Classics: Traditions, Adventures, and Innovations*. Norton, 2013.

Beinart, William. "Appendix A." In *Report of a Commission of Enquiry Established by Oriel College, Oxford, into Issues Associated with Memorials to Cecil Rhodes*, April 2021. Online publication accessed May 2021. https://www.oriel.ox.ac.uk/wp-content/uploads/2022/08/beinart_appendix_a_response_by_nigel_biggar.pdf.

Beinart, William. *The Political Economy of Pondoland, 1860–1930*. Cambridge University Press, 1982.

Belich, James. *Replenishing the Earth: The Settler Revolution and the Rise of the Anglo-World, 1783–1939*. Oxford University Press, 2009.

Bell, Duncan S. A. "Dissolving Distance: Technology, Space, and Empire in British Political Thought, 1770–1900." *Journal of Modern History* 77, no. 3 (September 2005): 523–562.

Birmingham, David. *Portugal and Africa*. Ohio University Press, 1999.

Blainey, G. "Lost Causes of the Jameson Raid." *Economic History Review* 18, no. 2 (1965): 350–366.

Bolster, W. Jeffrey. *Black Jacks: African American Seamen in the Age of Sail*. Harvard University Press, 1997.

Bolze, Louis W. "The Railway Comes to Bulawayo." *Rhodesiana* 18 (July 1968): 47–84.

Bouch, Richard. "Glen Grey before Cecil Rhodes: How a Crisis of Local Colonial Authority Led to the Glen Grey Act of 1894." *Canadian Journal of African Studies* 27, no. 1 (1993): 1–24.

Bowley, Arthur L. *Wages in the United Kingdom in the Nineteenth Century*. Cambridge University Press, 1900.

Bown, Stephen R. *A Most Damnable Invention: Dynamite, Nitrates, and the Making of the Modern World*. St. Martin's, 2005.

Brady, Ciaran. *James Anthony Froude: An Intellectual Biography of a Victorian Prophet*. Oxford University Press, 2013.

Brands, H. W. *American Colossus: The Triumph of Capitalism, 1865–1900*. Doubleday, 2010.

Breckenridge, Keith. *Biometric State: The Global Politics of Identification and Surveillance in South Africa, 1850 to the Present*. Cambridge University Press, 2014.

Brockliss, L. W. B. *The University of Oxford: A History*. Oxford University Press, 2016.

Bronstein, Jamie L. *Caught in the Machinery: Workplace Accidents and Injured Workers in Nineteenth-Century Britain*. Stanford University Press, 2008.

Bull, Mutumba Mainga. *Bulozi under the Luyana Kings: Political Evolution and State Formation in Pre-colonial Zambia*. Longmans, 1973. Reprint Gadsden Books (Lusaka), published in 2010 and made available on Project Muse.

Bundy, Colin. "Mr. Rhodes and the Poisoned Goods: Popular Opposition to the Glen Grey Council System, 1894–1906." In *Hidden Struggles in Rural South Africa*, edited by William Beinart and Colin Bundy. University of California Press, 1987.

Burchardt, Jeremy. *Paradise Lost: Rural Idyll and Social Change in England since 1800*. I. B. Tauris, 2002.

Burgess, M. D. "Lord Rosebery and the Imperial Federation League," 1884–1893." *New Zealand Journal of History* 13, no. 2 (1979): 165–181.

Burman, Jose. *Early Railways at the Cape*. Human & Rousseau, 1984.

Burman, Jose. *So High the Road: Mountain Passes of the Western Cape*. Human & Rousseau, 1963.

Burman, Jose. *Towards the Far Horizon: The Story of the Ox-Wagon in South Africa*. Human & Rousseau, 1988.

Butler, Jeffrey. *The Liberal Party and the Jameson Raid*. Clarendon Press, 1968.

Cain, P. J., and A. G. Hopkins, *British Imperialism: Innovation and Expansion, 1688–1914*. Longman, 1993.

Calderisi, Robert. *Cecil Rhodes and Other Statues: Dealing Plainly with the Past.* Gatekeeper Press, 2021.
Calhoun, Gloria. "Why Wire Mattered: Building U.S. Networked Infrastructures, 1845–1910." *Technology and Culture* 62, no. 1 (2021): 156–184.
Cannadine, David. *Victorious Century: The United Kingdom, 1800–1906.* Allen Lane, 2017.
Caplan, Gerald L. "Barotseland's Scramble for Protection." *Journal of African History* 10, no. 2 (1969): 277–294.
Carse, Ashley. "Keyword Infrastructure: How a Humble French Engineering Term Shaped the Modern World." In *Infrastructures and Social Complexity: A Companion*, edited by Penny Harvey, Casper Bruun Jensen, and Atsuro Morita. Routledge, 2019.
Cartwright, A. P. *The Dynamite Company: The Story of African Explosives and Chemical Industries Limited.* Purnell and Sons, 1964.
Chernow, Ron. *Titan: The Life of John D. Rockefeller.* Vintage, 1998.
Chirikure, Shadreck. *Great Zimbabwe: Reclaiming a "Confiscated" Past.* Routledge, 2021.
Cobbing, Julian. "The Absent Priesthood: Another Look at the Rhodesian Risings of 1896–1897." *Journal of African History* 18, no. 1 (1977): 61–84.
Cobbing, Julian. "Lobengula, Jameson and the Occupation of Mashonaland, 1890." *Rhodesian History* 4 (1973): 39–56.
Cobbing, Julian. "The Mfecane as Alibi: Thoughts on Dithakong and Mbolompo." *Journal of African History* 29, no. 3 (1988): 487–519.
Colvin, Ian. *The Life of Jameson.* Arnold, 1922.
Comaroff, Jean, and John Comaroff. *Of Revelation and Revolution.* Vol. 1, *Christianity, Colonialism, and Consciousness in South Africa*; Vol. 2, *The Dialectics of Modernity on a South African Frontier.* University of Chicago Press, 1991, 1997.
Cooper, John. *The Unexpected Story of Nathaniel Rothschild.* Bloomsbury, 2015.
Crais, Clifton. *Poverty, War, and Violence in South Africa.* Cambridge University Press, 2011.
Crais, Clifton. *White Supremacy and Black Resistance in Pre-Industrial South Africa: The Making of the Colonial Order in the Eastern Cape, 1770–1865.* Cambridge University Press, 1992.
Cronon, William. *Nature's Metropolis: Chicago and the Great West.* Norton, 1991.
Crosby, Tony. "The Impact of Industry on the Market Towns of East Hertfordshire." In *A Country of Small Towns: The Development of Hertfordshire's Urban Landscape to 1800*, edited by Terry Slater and Nigel Goose. University of Hertfordshire Press, 2008.
Cross, Ian James. "The Ordnance and Machine Guns of the British South Africa Company, 1889–1896; Part One: 1889–1891." *Military History Journal: South African Military History Society* 16, no. 2 (December 2013). Online publication. samilitaryhistory.org/vol162ic.html.
Croxton, Anthony H. *Railways of Zimbabwe: The Story of the Beira, Mashonaland, and Rhodesia Railways.* David and Charles, 1973; 2nd ed. 1982.

Cunliffe, Barry. *Britain Begins*. Oxford University Press, 2013.
Dachs, Anthony J. "Missionary Imperialism: The Case of Bechuanaland," *Journal of African History* 13, no. 4 (1972): 647–658.
Darwin, John. *Unfinished Empire: The Global Expansion of Britain*. Bloomsbury, 2012.
Davenport, Jade. *Digging Deep: A History of Mining in South Africa*. Jonathan Ball, 2013.
Davenport, T. R. H. *The Afrikaner Bond: The History of a South African Political Party, 1880–1911*. Oxford University Press, 1966.
Davenport, T. R. H. "The Cape Liberal Tradition to 1910." In *Democratic Liberalism in South Africa: Its History and Prospect*, edited by Jeffrey Butler, Richard Elphick, and David Welsh. Wesleyan University Press, 1987.
David, Gilmour. *The Long Recessional: The Imperial Life of Rudyard Kipling*. Farrar, Straus, and Giroux, 2003.
Dawe, Richard. *Cornish Pioneers in South Africa*. Cornish Hillside Publications, 1998.
De Kiewiet, Cornelis W. *The Imperial Factor in South Africa*. Frank Cass, 1937; reprint 1965.
Deaton, Angus. *The Great Escape: Health, Wealth, and the Origins of Inequality*. Princeton University Press, 2013.
Denny, S. R. "The Cape to Cairo Telegraph." *Northern Rhodesia Journal* 5, no. 1 (1962): 39–43.
Dlamini, Jacob. *Askari: A Story of Collaboration and Betrayal in the Anti-Apartheid Struggle*. Jacana, 2014.
Dlamini, Jacob. *Safari Nation: A Social History of the Kruger National Park*. Ohio University Press, 2020.
Douglas, Tom. *Scapegoats: Transferring Blame*. Routledge, 1995.
Dowling, Linda. *Hellenism and Homosexuality in Victorian Oxford*. Cornell University Press, 1998.
Drayton, Richard. "Rhodes Must Not Fall? Statues, Postcolonial 'Heritage' and Temporality." *Third Text* 33, nos. 4–5 (2019): 651–666.
Drayton, Richard. "Where Does the World Historian Write From? Objectivity, Moral Conscience and the Past and Present of Imperialism." *Journal of Contemporary History* 46, no. 3 (2011): 671–685.
Drew, Erin. *The Usufructuary Ethos: Power, Politics, and Environment in the Long Eighteenth Century*. University of Virginia Press, 2021.
Driver, Felix. *Geography Militant: Cultures of Exploration and Empire*. Blackwell, 2001.
Dubow, Saul. *The African National Congress*. Sutton, 2000.
Dubow, Saul. *A Commonwealth of Knowledge: Science, Sensibility, and White South Africa, 1820–2000*. Oxford University Press, 2006.
Dumett, Raymond E. *Gentlemanly Capitalism and British Imperialism: The New Debate on Empire*. Longman, 1999.
Dupuy, Trevor N. *The Evolution of Weapons and Warfare*. Bobbs-Merrill, 1980.
Durand, J. F. "The Impact of Gold Mining on the Witwatersrand on the Rivers and Karst System of Gauteng and North West Province, South Africa." *Journal of African Earth Sciences* 68 (2012): 24–43.

Edwards, Paul N. "Infrastructure and Modernity: Force, Time, and Social Organization in the History of Sociotechnical Systems." In *Modernity and Technology*, edited by Thomas J. Misa and Philip Brey. MIT Press, 2004.

Elkins, Caroline. *Legacy of Violence: A History of the British Empire*. Knopf, 2022.

Ellmann, Richard. *Oscar Wilde*. Knopf, 1988.

Etherington, Norman. *The Great Treks: The Transformation of Southern Africa, 1815–1854*. Longman, 2001.

Etherington, Norman. *Imperium of the Soul: The Political and Aesthetic Imagination of Edwardian Imperialists*. Manchester University Press, 2017.

Etherington, Norman, Patrick Harries, and Bernard K. Mbenga. "From Colonial Hegemonies to Imperial Conquest, 1840–1880." In *The Cambridge History of South Africa*. Vol. 1, *From Early Times to 1885*, edited by Carolyn Hamilton, Bernard Mbenga, and Robert Ross. Cambridge University Press, 2010.

Faber, Geoffrey. *Jowett: A Portrait with Background*. Faber & Faber, 1957.

Ferguson, James. "Structures of Responsibility." *Ethnography* 13, no. 4 (December 2012): 558–562.

Ferguson, Niall. *The House of Rothschild: The World's Banker, 1849–1999*. Penguin, 1999.

Flint, John. *Cecil Rhodes*. Little, Brown, 1974.

Fone, Byrne R. S. *The Columbia Anthology of Gay Literature: Readings from Western Antiquity to the Present Day*. Columbia University Press, 1998.

Foster, Jeremy. *Washed with Sun: Landscape and the Making of White South Africa*. University of Pittsburgh Press, 2008.

Freeman, Joshua B. *Behemoth: A History of the Factory and the Making of the Modern World*. Norton, 2018.

Froude, James A. *Two Lectures on South Africa*. Longmans, Green, 1880.

Galbraith, John S. "The British South Africa Company and the Jameson Raid." *Journal of British Studies* 10, no. 1 (November 1970): 145–161.

Galbraith, John S. *Crown and Charter: The Early Years of the British South Africa Company*. University of California Press, 1974.

Gibbs, Pat. "Coal, Rail, and Victorians in the South African Veld: The Convergence of Colonial Elites and Finance Capital in the Stormberg Mountains of the Eastern Cape, 1880–1910." *Britain and the World* 11, no. 2 (2018): 173–194.

Gilmour, David. *Curzon: Imperial Statesman*. Farrar, Straus and Giroux, 1994.

Girard, René. *The Scapegoat*. Translated by Yvonne Freccero. Johns Hopkins University Press, 1986.

Giridharadas, Anand. *Winners Take All: The Elite Charade of Changing the World*. Knopf, 2018.

Goodrich, Carter. *The Miner's Freedom: A Study of the Working Life in a Changing Industry*. Marshall Jones, 1925.

Gopal, Priyamvada. *Insurgent Empire: Anticolonial Resistance and British Dissent*. Verso, 2019.

Gordon, Robert B. "Custom and Consequence: Early Nineteenth-Century Origins of the Environmental and Social Costs of Mining Anthracite." In *Early American Technology: Making and Doing Things from the Colonial Era to 1850*, edited by Judith A. McGaw. University of North Carolina Press, 1994.

Grant, Michael. *The Antonines: The Roman Empire in Transition*. Routledge, 1994.

Guldi, Jo. *Roads to Power: Britain Invents the Infrastructure State*. Harvard University Press, 2012.

Gumede, William. *Restless Nation: Making Sense of Troubled Times*. Tafelberg, 2012.

Gutsche, Thelma. *The Microcosm*. Howard Timmins, 1968.

Guy, Jeff. *Theophilus Shepstone and the Forging of Natal*. University of KwaZulu-Natal Press, 2013.

Hamilton, Carolyn. *Terrific Majesty: The Powers of Shaka Zulu and the Limits of Historical Invention*. Harvard University Press, 1998.

Hamilton, Carolyn, Bernard Mbenga, and Robert Ross, eds. *Cambridge History of South Africa*. Vol. 1, *From Early Times to 1885*. Cambridge University Press, 2010.

Harland-Jacobs, Jessica. *Builders of Empire: Freemasonry and British Imperialism, 1717–1927*. University of North Carolina Press, 2007.

Harries, Patrick. *Work, Culture, and Identity: Migrant Laborers in Mozambique and South Africa, c. 1860–1910*. Heinemann, 1994.

Hart, Gillian. *Disabling Globalization: Places of Power in Post-Apartheid South Africa*. University of California Press, 2002.

Hart, Jennifer. *Ghana on the Go: African Mobility in the Age of Motor Transportation*. Indiana University Press, 2016.

Hartley, Robert E., and David Kenney. *Death Underground: The Centralia and West Frankfort Mine Disasters*. Southern Illinois University Press, 2006.

Harvey, David. *Spaces of Global Capitalism: Towards a Theory of Uneven Geographical Development*. Verso, 2006.

Headlam, Cecil. "The Race for the Interior." In *The Cambridge History of the British Empire*. Vol. 8. Cambridge University Press, 1961.

Headrick, Daniel. *The Tentacles of Progress: Technology Transfer in the Age of Imperialism, 1850–1940*. Oxford University Press, 1988.

Headrick, Daniel. *The Tools of Empire: Technology and European Imperialism in the Nineteenth Century*. Oxford University Press, 1981.

Hecht, Gabrielle. *Being Nuclear: Africans and the Global Uranium Trade*. MIT Press, 2012.

Hecht, Gabrielle. *Residual Governance: How South Africa Foretells Planetary Futures*. Duke University Press, 2023.

Hills, Richard L. *Power from Steam: A History of the Stationary Steam Engine*. Cambridge University Press, 1989.

Hobsbawm, Eric J. *Industry and Empire: The Making of Modern English Society*. Vol. 2, *1750 to the Present Day*. Pantheon, 1968.

Hughes, Thomas P. *Networks of Power: Electrification in Western Society, 1880–1930*. Johns Hopkins University Press, 1983.

Hunt, Bruce J. *Imperial Science: Cable Telegraphy and Electrical Physics in the Victorian British Empire*. Cambridge University Press, 2021.
Hyam, Ronald. *Empire and Sexuality: The British Experience*. Manchester University Press, 1990.
Hyam, Ronald. "The Partition of Africa." *Historical Journal* 7, no. 1 (1964): 154–169.
Impey, Edward. "The Rhodes Building at Oriel, 1904–2011: Dynamite or Designate?" *Oxoniensia* 76 (2011): 95–104.
Israel, Paul. *Edison: A Life of Invention*. John Wiley, 1998.
Jasanoff, Sheila, and Sang-Hyun Kim. *Dreamscapes of Modernity: Sociotechnical Imaginaries and the Fabrication of Power*. University of Chicago Press, 2015.
Jenkins, Roy. *Asquith: Portrait of a Man and an Era*. Chilmark Press, 1964.
Jenkins, Roy. *Churchill: A Biography*. Farrar, Straus and Giroux, 2001.
Jenkins, Roy. *Gladstone: A Biography*. Random House, 2002.
Jensen, Casper Bruun, and Atsuro Morita. "Introduction: Infrastructures as Ontological Experiments." *Ethnos* 82, no. 4 (2017): 615–626.
Johnson, Paul. *Consolidated Gold Fields: A Centenary Portrait*. St. Martin's, 1987.
Jones, S. R. H., and Simon P. Ville. "Efficient Transactors of Rent-Seeking Monopolists? The Rationale for Early Chartered Companies." *Journal of Economic History* 56, no. 4 (December 1996): 898–915.
Judd, Denis. *Empire: The British Imperial Experience from 1765 to the Present*. Basic Books, 1996.
Kanger, Laur, and Johan Schot. "Deep Transitions: Theorizing the Long-Term Patterns of Socio-Technical Change." *Environmental Innovation and Societal Transitions* 32 (2019): 7–21.
Katz, Elaine. "Outcrop and Deep Level Mining in South Africa before the Anglo-Boer War." *Economic History Review* 48, no. 2 (May 1995): 304–328.
Keegan, Timothy. *Colonial South Africa and the Origins of the Racial Order*. University of Virginia Press, 1997.
Kennedy, Dane. *The Highly Civilized Man: Richard Burton and the Victorian World*. Harvard University Press, 2005.
Keppel-Jones, Arthur. *Rhodes and Rhodesia: The White Conquest of Zimbabwe, 1884–1902*. McGill-Queen's University Press, 1984.
Kline, Ronald J. *Steinmetz: Engineer and Socialist*. Johns Hopkins University Press, 1992.
Knowles, Scott Gabriel. *The Disaster Experts: Mastering Risk in Modern America*. University of Pennsylvania Press, 2011.
Konnikova, Maria. *The Confidence Game: Why We Fall for It Every Time*. Penguin, 2017.
Kubicek, Robert. *Economic Imperialism in Theory and Practice: The Case of South African Gold Mining Finance, 1886–1914*. Duke University Press, 1979.
Kubicek, Robert. "The Randlords in 1895: A Reassessment." *Journal of British Studies* 11, no. 2 (May 1972): 84–103.

Kuklick, Henrika. "Contested Monuments: The Politics of Archeology in Southern Africa." In *Colonial Situations: Essays on the Contextualization of Ethnographic Knowledge*, edited by George W. Stocking. University of Wisconsin Press, 1991.

Landau, Paul S. *Popular Politics in the History of South Africa, 1400–1948*. Cambridge University Press, 2010.

Langlands, Alexander. *Cræft: An Inquiry into the Origins and True Meaning of Traditional Crafts*. Norton, 2018.

Larkin, Brian. "The Politics and Poetics of Infrastructure." *Annual Review of Anthropology* 42 (2013): 327–343.

Latour, Bruno. *Reassembling the Social: An Introduction to Actor-Network Theory*. Oxford University Press, 2005.

Latour, Bruno. *Science in Action*. Open University Press, 1985.

Layton, Edward. *The Revolt of the Engineers: Social Responsibility and the American Engineering Profession*. Case Western University Press, 1971. Revised ed. Johns Hopkins University Press, 1986.

LeCain, Timothy. *Mass Destruction: The Men and the Giant Mines that Wired America and Scarred the Planet*. Rutgers University Press, 2009.

Legassick, Martin. *The Politics of a South African Frontier: The Griqua, the Sotho-Tswana, and the Missionaries, 1780–1840*. Basler Afrika Bibliographien, 2010.

Legassick, Martin, and Robert Ross. "From Slave Economy to Settler Capitalism: The Cape Colony and Its Extensions, 1800–54." In *The Cambridge History of South Africa*. Vol. 1, *From Early Times to 1885*, edited by Carolyn Hamilton, Bernard Mbenga, and Robert Ross. Cambridge University Press, 2010.

Leith, Claire. *Tin and Diamonds, A Fortune in the Making: The Life and Times of Francis Oats*. Trevithick Society, 2009.

Le Sueur, Gordon. *Cecil Rhodes: The Man and His Work*. New York: McBride, Nast, 1914.

Lethbridge, Lucy. *Servants: A Downstairs History of Britain from the Nineteenth Century to Modern Times*. Norton, 2013.

Levine, Philippa, ed. *Gender and Empire*. Oxford History of the British Empire Companion Series, edited by William Roger Louis. Oxford University Press, 2004.

Levine, Philippa. *Prostitution, Race, and Politics: Policing Venereal Disease in the British Empire*. Routledge, 2003.

Lockhart, John Gilbert, and Christopher Montague Woodhouse. *Cecil Rhodes: The Colossus of Southern Africa*. Hodder & Stoughton, 1963.

Lowry, Donal. "The Granite of the Ancient North: Race, Nation, and Empire at Cecil Rhodes's Mountain Mausoleum and Rhodes House, Oxford." In *Pantheons: Transformations of a Monumental Idea*, edited by Richard Wrigley and Matthew Craske. Ashgate, 2004.

Lunderstedt, Steve. *The Big Five Mines of Kimberley*. Africana Library, 2008.

Lunn, Jon. *Capital and Labour on the Rhodesian Railway System, 1888–1947*. Macmillan, 1997.

Mabin, Alan. "Labour, Capital, Class Struggle, and the Origins of Residential Segregation in Kimberley, 1880–1920." *Journal of Historical Geography* 12 (1986): 4–26.

Mackenzie, Donald. *Material Markets: How Economic Agents are Constructed.* Oxford University Press, 2009.

Mackinnon, Aran. *The Making of South Africa: Culture and Politics.* 2nd ed. Pearson, 2012.

Maier, Charles. *Once within Borders: Territories of Power, Wealth, and Belonging since 1500.* Harvard University Press, 2016.

Marks, Shula. "Class, Culture, and Consciousness in South Africa, 1880–1899." In *The Cambridge History of South Africa.* Vol. 2, *1885–1994*, edited by Robert Ross, Anne Kelk Mager, and Bill Nasson. Cambridge University Press, 2010.

Marlowe, John. *Milner: Apostle of Empire.* Hamish Hamilton, 1976.

Mathias, Peter. *The First Industrial Nation: An Economic History of Britain, 1700–1914.* 2nd ed. Methuen, 1983.

Mavhunga, Clapperton Chakanetsa. *Transient Workspaces: Technologies of Everyday Innovation in Zimbabwe.* MIT Press, 2014.

Maylam, Paul. *The Cult of Rhodes: Remembering an Imperialist in Africa.* David Philip, 2005.

Maylam, Paul. "The Making of the Kimberley-Bulawayo Railway: A Study in the Operations of the British South Africa Company." *Rhodesian History* 8 (1977): 13–33.

Maylam, Paul. *Rhodes, the Tswana, and the British: Colonialism, Collaboration, and Conflict in the Bechuanaland Protectorate, 1885–1899.* Greenwood Press, 1980.

McCarthy, Terence. "The Impact of Acid Mine Drainage in South Africa." *South African Journal of Science* 107, no. 5/6 (2011): 1–7.

McClendon, Thomas. *White Chief, Black Lords: Shepstone and the Colonial State in Natal, South Africa, 1845–1878.* University of Rochester Press, 2010.

McCray, W. Patrick. *The Visioneers: How a Group of Elite Scientists Pursued Space Colonies, Nanotechnologies, and a Limitless Future.* Princeton University Press, 2013.

McDonald, James G. *Rhodes: A Life.* Philip Allan, 1927; 3rd ed. 1929.

McFarlane, Colin, and Jonathan Silver. "The Poolitical City: 'Seeing Sanitation' and Making the Urban Political in Cape Town." *Antipode* 49, no. 1 (2017): 125–148.

Mendelsohn, Richard. "Blainey and the Jameson Raid: The Debate Renewed." *Journal of Southern African Studies* 6, no. 2 (April 1980): 157–170.

Merrington, Peter. "A Staggered Orientalism: The Cape-to-Cairo Imaginary." *Poetics Today* 22, no. 2 (Summer 2001): 323–364.

Midgley, Claire, ed. *Gender and Imperialism.* Manchester University Press, 1998.

Miller, Daniel. *Stuff.* Polity Press, 2010.

Millin, Sarah Gertrude. *Cecil Rhodes.* Harper and Brothers, 1933.

Mills, Catherine. *Regulating Health and Safety in the British Mining Industries, 1800–1914.* Ashgate, 2010.

Mills, Charles W. *Black Rights/White Wrongs: The Critique of Racial Liberalism.* Oxford University Press, 2017.

Milner, Alfred. *The Milner Papers: South Africa, 1897–1899*. Edited by Cecil Headlam. Cassell, 1931.

Milner, Alfred. *Reminiscences of Arnold Toynbee*. Edward Arnold, 1901.

Mitchell, Peter. *Imperial Nostalgia: How the British Conquered Themselves*. Manchester University Press, 2021.

Mitchell, Timothy. *Carbon Democracy: Political Power in the Age of Oil*. Verso, 2011.

Mkhize, Nomalanga. "In Search of Native Dissidence: R.T. Kawa's *Mfecane* Historiography in *Ibali lamaMfengu* (1929)." *International Journal of African Renaissance Studies* 13, no. 2 (2018): 92–111.

Mlambo, Alois. *A History of Zimbabwe*. Cambridge University Press, 2014.

Moffat, Robert Unwin. *John Smith Moffat, C.M.G. Missionary: A Memoir*. John Murray, 1921.

Molteno, Percy Alport. *The Life and Times of Sir John Charles Molteno*. Smith, Elder, 1900.

Moodie, T. Dunbar, with Vivian Ndatshe. *Going for Gold: Men, Mines, and Migration*. University of California Press, 1994.

Moon, Suzanne. *Technology in Southeast Asian History*. Johns Hopkins University Press, 2023.

Morris, Jan. *Oxford*. 3rd ed. Oxford University Press, 1987.

Mostert, Noel. *Frontiers: The Epic of South Africa's Creation and the Tragedy of the Xhosa People*. Knopf, 1992.

Murray, John E., and Javier Silvestre. "How Do Mines Explode? Understanding Risk in European Mining Doctrine, 1803–1906." *Technology and Culture* 62, no. 3 (July 2021): 780–811.

Nasaw, David. *Andrew Carnegie*. Penguin, 2006.

Ndlovu-Gatsheni, Sabelo J. *The Ndebele Nation: Reflections on Hegemony, Memory, and Historiography*. UNISA Press, 2009.

Newbury, Colin. *The Diamond Ring: Business, Politics, and Precious Stones in South Africa, 1867–1947*. Clarendon Press, 1990.

Nightingale, Carl H. *Segregation: A Global History of Divided Cities*. University of Chicago Press, 2012.

Nkosi, Morley. *Mining Deep: The Origins of the Labour Structure in South Africa*. David Philip, 2011.

Nye, David. *American Technological Sublime*. MIT Press, 1994.

Nyika, Farai, and Johan Fourie. "Black Disenfranchisement in the Cape Colony, c. 1887–1909: Challenging the Numbers." *Journal of Southern African Studies* 46, no. 3 (2020): 455–469.

Nystrom, Eric. *Seeing Underground: Maps, Models, and Mining Engineering in America*. University of Nevada Press, 2014.

Odendaal, André, Krish Reddy, Christopher Merrett, and Jonty Winch. *Cricket and Conquest: The History of South African Cricket Retold*. Vol. 1, *1795–1914*. BestRed, 2016.

Oldenziel, Ruth. *Making Technology Masculine: Men, Women, and Modern Machines in America, 1870–1945*. Amsterdam University Press, 1999.

Oliver, Roland. *Sir Harry Johnston and the Scramble for Africa*. St. Martin's, 1957.

Parsons, Neil. *King Khama, Emperor Joe, and the Great White Queen: Victorian Britain through African Eyes*. University of Chicago Press, 1998.

Parsons, Neil. "The Victorian Internet Reaches Halfway to Cairo: Cape Tanganyika Telegraphs, 1875–1926." In *The Social Life of Connectivity in Africa*, edited by Mirjam de Bruijn and Rijk van Dijk. Palgrave Macmillan, 2012.

Payton, Philip. *The Cornish Overseas: A History of Cornwall's "Great Emigration."* University of Exeter Press, 2005.

Penn, Nigel. "Close and Merciful Watchfulness: John Montagu's Convict System in the Mid-Nineteenth-Century Cape Colony." *Cultural and Social History* 5, no. 4 (2008): 465–480.

Perrow, Charles. *Normal Accidents: Living with High-Risk Technologies*. Basic Books, 1984. Reprint Princeton University Press, 1999.

Petheram, Richard W. "Inyanga: With Special Reference to the Rhodes Inyanga Estate." *Rhodesiana* 31 (1974): 36–50.

Phimister, Ian. "Rhodes, Rhodesia, and the Rand." *Journal of Southern African Studies* 1, no. 1 (October 1974): 74–90.

Pirie, Gordon. "Railways and Labour Migration to the Rand Mines: Constraints and Significance." *Journal of Southern African Studies* 19, no. 4 (1993): 713–730.

Plant, Arnold. "Economic Development, 1795–1921." In *Cambridge History of the British Empire*. Vol. 8, *South Africa*. 2nd ed. Cambridge University Press, 1963.

Pointon, Marcia. "De Beers's Diamond Mine in the 1880s: Robert Harris and the Kimberley Searching System." *History of Photography* 42, no. 1 (2018): 4–24.

Press, Steven. *Blood and Diamonds: Germany's Imperial Ambitions in Africa*. Harvard University Press, 2021.

Press, Steven. *Rogue Empires: Contracts and Conmen in Europe's Scramble for Africa*. Harvard University Press, 2017.

Pritchard, Sara B. "An Environmental Disaster: Nature, Technology, and Politics at Fukushima." *Environmental History* 17 (April 2012): 219–243.

Pryor, Francis. *Britain A.D.: A Quest for Arthur, England, and the Anglo-Saxons*. HarperCollins, 2004.

Purkis, Andrew J. "The Politics, Capital, and Labour of Railway-Building in the Cape Colony, 1870–1885." PhD diss., St. Antony's College, Oxford University, 1979.

Quivik, Fredric. "Nuisance, Source of Wealth, or Potentially Practical Material: Visions of Tailings in Idaho's Coeur d'Alene Mining District, 1888–2001." *Journal of the Society for Industrial Archaeology* 39, no. 1/2, Special Issue: "Industrial Waste" (2013): 41–64.

Quivik, Fredric. "Of Tailings, Superfund Litigation, and Historians as Experts: U.S. v. Asarco, et al. (the Bunker Hill Case in Idaho)." *Public Historian* 26, no. 1 (Winter 2004): 81–104.

Rademeyer, J. I. *Die Land Noord van di Limpopo in die Ekspansie-Belied van di Suid-Afrikaanse Republiek.* Balkema, 1949.

Ranger, Terence. *Voices from the Rocks: Nature, Culture, and History in the Matopos Hills of Zimbabwe.* Indiana University Press, 1999.

Raphael, Lois A. C. *The Cape-to-Cairo Dream: A Study in British Imperialism.* Columbia University Press, 1936; reprint, Octagon Books, 1973.

Redfield, Peter, and Steven Robins. "An Index of Waste: Humanitarian Design, 'Dignified Living' and the Politics of Infrastructure in Cape Town." *Anthropology Southern Africa* 39, no. 2 (2016): 145–162.

Reid, Darren. "Dispossession and Legal Mentalité in Nineteenth-Century South Africa: Grotian and Lockean Theories of Property Acquisition in the Annexations of British Kaffraria and Natalia." *Settler Colonial Studies* 11, no. 1 (2021): 69–85.

Richards, Hylda. *False Dawn: The Story of Dan Judson, Pioneer.* Rhodesia Reprints, 1974.

Richings, Gordon. *The Life and Work of Charles Michell.* Fernwood Press, 2006.

Roberts, Andrew. *Churchill: Walking with Destiny.* Viking, 2018.

Roberts, Brian. *Kimberley: Turbulent City.* David Philip, 1976.

Robertson, Marian. *Diamond Fever: South African Diamond History 1866–9 from Primary Sources.* Oxford University Press, 1974.

Robinson, Ronald, and John Gallagher, with Alice Denny. *Africa and the Victorians: The Official Mind of Imperialism.* Macmillan, 1961; 2nd ed. 1981.

Rodgers, Dennis, and Bruce O'Neill. "Introduction: Infrastructural Violence: Introduction to the Special Issue." *Ethnography* 13, no. 4 (December 2012): 401–412.

Rösner, Thorsten. "The Environmental Impact of Seepage from Gold Mine Tailings Dams near Johannesburg, South Africa." PhD diss., University of Pretoria, 1999.

Ross, Graham. *The Romance of Cape Mountain Passes.* David Philip, 2002.

Ross, Robert. *A Concise History of South Africa.* Cambridge University Press, 2008.

Ross, Robert, Anne Kelk Mager, and Bill Nasson, eds. *Cambridge History of South Africa.* Vol. 2, *1885–1994.* Cambridge University Press, 2010.

Rotberg, Robert, with Miles F. Shore. *The Founder: Cecil Rhodes and the Pursuit of Power.* Oxford University Press, 1988.

Said, Edward. *Culture and Imperialism.* Knopf, 1993.

Said, Edward. *Orientalism.* Pantheon, 1978.

Sanghera, Satnam. *Empireland: How Imperialism Has Shaped Modern Britain.* Penguin, 2021.

Satia, Priya. *Time's Monster: How History Makes History.* Harvard University Press, 2020.

Schreuder, Deryck M. *The Scramble for Southern Africa: The Politics of Partition Reappraised.* Cambridge University Press, 1981.

Scott, James. *Seeing Like a State: How Certain Schemes to Improve the Human Condition Have Failed.* Yale University Press, 1998.

Scully, Pamela. "Liquor and Labor in the Western Cape, 1870–1900." In *Liquor and Labor in Southern Africa,* edited by Jonathan Crush and Charles Ambler. Ohio University Press, 1992.

Scully, Richard. "Constructing the Colossus: The Origins of Linley Sambourne's Greatest Punch Cartoon." *International Journal of Comic Art* 14, no. 2 (Fall 2012): 120–142.

Segal, Howard P. *Utopias: A Brief History from Ancient Writings to Virtual Communities*. Wiley-Blackwell, 2012.

Shee, J. Charles. "Rhodes and the Doctors (4): Hans Sauer." *Central African Journal of Medicine* 9, no. 8 (August 1963): 328–331.

Sherman, Nancy. *Stoic Warriors: The Ancient Philosophy behind the Military Mind*. Oxford University Press, 2005.

Sherman, Nancy. *Stoic Wisdom: Ancient Lessons of Modern Resilience*. Oxford University Press, 2021.

Shillington, Kevin. *The Colonisation of the Southern Tswana, 1870–1900*. Ravan Press, 1985.

Simons, Phillida Brooke. *Apples of the Sun, Being an Account of the Lives, Vision and Achievements of the Molteno Brothers, Edward Bartle Frere and Henry Anderson*. Fernwood Press, 1999.

Simons, Phillida Brooke. *Groote Schuur: Great Granary to Stately Home*. Fernwood Press, 1996.

Slater, Henry. "Land, Labor and Capital in Natal: The Natal Land and Colonisation Company, 1860–1948." *Journal of African History* 16, no. 2 (1975): 257–283.

Slayton, Rebecca, and Richard Clarke. "Trusting Infrastructure: The Emergence of Computer Security Incident Response, 1989–2005." *Technology and Culture* 61, no. 1 (January 2020): 173–206.

Smith, Adam. *The Essential Adam Smith*. Edited by Robert Heilbroner. Norton, 1986.

Smith, R. Cherer. "The Africa Trans-Continental Telegraph Line." *Rhodesiana* 33 (September 1975): 1–18.

Snyder, Saskia Coenen. *A Brilliant Commodity: Diamonds and Jews in a Modern Setting*. Oxford University Press, 2023.

Soffer, Reba N. *Discipline and Power: The University, History, and the Making of the English Elite, 1870–1930*. Stanford University Press, 1994.

Solomon, William Ewart Gladstone. *Saul Solomon: The Member for Cape Town*. Oxford University Press, 1948.

Sorin, Gretchen. *Driving while Black: African American Travel and the Road to Civil Rights*. Liveright, 2020.

Spence, Clark C. *British Investments and the American Mining Frontier, 1860–1901*. Cornell University Press, 1958.

Stanley, Edward Henry. *A Selection from the Diaries of Edward Henry Stanley, 15th Earl of Derby (1826–93) between September 1869 and March 1878*. Edited by John Vincent. The Royal Historical Society, 1994.

Stapleton, Timothy. *Maqoma: The Legend of a Great Xhosa Warrior*. Amava Heritage Publishing, 2016.

Stead, W. T. *The Last Will and Testament of Cecil John Rhodes*. Review of Reviews Press, 1902.

Steinberg, Ted. *Acts of God: The Unnatural History of Natural Disaster in America*. Oxford University Press, 2000.

Stiglitz, Joseph E. *The Price of Inequality: How Today's Divided Society Endangers Our Future*. Norton, 2012.

Stiles, T. J. *The First Tycoon: The Epic Life of Cornelius Vanderbilt*. Vintage, 2009.

Stoler, Ann Laura. "Imperial Debris and Ruination." In *Duress: Imperial Durabilities in Our Times*. Duke University Press, 2016.

Storey, William Kelleher. *Guns, Race, and Power in Colonial South Africa*. Cambridge University Press, 2008.

Stovall, Tyler. *White Freedom: The History of an Idea*. Princeton University Press, 2021.

Swart, Sandra. *Riding High: Horses, Humans, and History in South Africa*. Wits University Press, 2010.

Symonds, Richard. "Oxford and the Empire." In *The History of the University of Oxford*. Vol. 7, Pt. 2, *Nineteenth-Century Oxford*. Clarendon Press, 2000.

Tamarkin, Mordechai. *Volk and Flock: Ecology, Culture, Identity, and Politics among Cape Afrikaner Sheep Farmers in the Late Nineteenth Century*. UNISA Press, 2009.

Taylor, Dorceta E. *Toxic Communities: Environmental Racism, Industrial Pollution, and Residential Mobility*. New York University Press, 2014.

Thomas, Pradip Ninan. *Empire and Post-Empire Telecommunications in India: A History*. Oxford University Press, 2019.

Thompson, J. Lee. *Forgotten Patriot: A Life of Alfred, Viscount Milner of St. James's and Cape Town, 1854–1925*. Fairleigh Dickinson University Press, 2007.

Tosh, John. "Home and Away: The Flight from Domesticity in Late-Nineteenth-Century England Re-visited." *Gender & History* 27, no. 3 (November 2015): 561–575.

Turpin, K. C. "The Ascendancy of Oriel." In *The History of the University of Oxford*. Vol. 6, Pt. 1, *The Nineteenth Century*. Oxford University Press, 1997.

Turrell, Robert Vicat. *Capital and Labour on the Kimberley Diamond Fields, 1871–1890*. Cambridge University Press, 1987.

Twynam, C. D. "The Telegraph in British Central Africa." *Nyasaland Journal* 6, no. 2 (July 1953): 52–55.

Vail, Leroy. "The Making of an Imperial Slum: Nyasaland and Its Railways, 1895–1935." *Journal of African History* 16, no. 1 (1975): 89–112.

Van der Poel, Jean. *Railway and Custom Policies in South Africa, 1885–1910*. Longmans, Green, 1933.

Van der Vleuten, Erik. "History and Technology in an Age of Grand Challenges: Raising Questions." *Technology and Culture* 61, no. 1 (January 2020): 260–271.

Van Laak, Dirk. *Lifelines of Our Society: A Global History of Infrastructure*. Translated by Erik Butler. MIT Press, 2023.

Van Onselen, Charles. *The Cowboy and the Capitalist: John Hays Hammond, the American West, and the Jameson Raid in South Africa*. University of Virginia Press, 2017.

Van Onselen, Charles. *Studies in the Social and Economic History of the Witwatersrand*. Vol. 1, *New Babylon*; Vol. 2, *New Nineveh*. Longmans, 1982.

Vedantam, Shankar, and Bill Mesler. *Useful Delusions: The Power and Paradox of the Self-Deceiving Brain*. Norton, 2021.

Viljoen, Russel. "The Smallpox War on the Kimberley Diamonds Fields in the mid-1880s." *African Historical Review* 35, no. 1 (2004): 5–18.

Vinsel, Lee, and Andrew Russell. *The Innovation Delusion: How Our Obsession with the New Has Disrupted the Work that Matters Most*. Currency, 2020.

Wallace, Anthony F. C. "The Disaster Syndrome." In *Revitalizations and Mazeways: Essays on Culture Change*, edited by Robert S. Grumet. Vol. 1. University of Nebraska Press, 2003.

Wallace, Anthony F. C. *St. Clair: A Nineteenth-Century Town's Experience with a Disaster-Prone Industry*. Knopf, 1987.

Watts, Steven. *The People's Tycoon: Henry Ford and the American Century*. Vintage, 2005.

White, Richard. *The Republic for Which It Stands: The United States during Reconstruction and the Gilded Age, 1865–1896*. Oxford University Press, 2017.

Whiteside, James. *Regulating Danger: The Struggle for Mine Safety in the Rocky Mountain Coal Industry*. University of Nebraska Press, 1990.

Wilburn, Kenneth. *The Life of Statesman and Industrialist Sir James Sivewright of South Africa, 1848–1916*. Mellen Press, 2010.

Williams, Alpheus. *Some Dreams Come True*. Timmins, 1948.

Williams, Gardner F. *The Diamond Mines of South Africa*. 2 vols. Buck & Co., 1905.

Williams, Rosalind. *Notes on the Underground: An Essay on Technology, Society, and the Imagination*. MIT Press, 2008.

Wilson, A. N. *The Victorians*. Norton, 2003.

Wilson, Francis. "Minerals and Migrants: How the Mining Industry Has Shaped South Africa." *Daedalus* 230, no. 1 (Winter 2001): 99–121.

Wilson, Monica, and Leonard Thompson, eds. *The Oxford History of South Africa*. Vol. 1, *South Africa to 1870*; Vol. 2, *South Africa 1870–1966*. Oxford University Press, 1969.

Winch, Jonty, and Richard Parry. *Too Black to Wear Whites: The Remarkable Story of Krom Hendricks, a Cricket Hero Who Was Rejected by Cecil John Rhodes's Empire*. Penguin, 2020.

Woodham-Smith, Cecil. *The Great Hunger: Ireland, 1845–1849*. Hamish Hamilton, 1962.

Worden, Nigel. *The Making of Modern South Africa*. 5th ed. Wiley-Blackwell, 2012.

Worden, Nigel, Elizabeth van Heyningen, and Vivian Bickford-Smith. *Cape Town: The Making of a City*. David Philip, 1998.

Worger, William H. *South Africa's City of Diamonds: Mine Workers and Monopoly Capitalism in Kimberley, 1867–1895*. Yale University Press, 1987.

Wright, John. "Turbulent Times: Political Transformations in the North and East, 1760s–1830s." In *The Cambridge History of South Africa*. Vol. 1, *From Earliest Times to 1885*, edited by Carolyn Hamilton, Bernard K. Mbenga, and Robert Ross. Cambridge University Press, 2010.

Wyman, Mark. *Hard Rock Epic: Western Miners and the Industrial Revolution, 1860–1910*. University of California Press, 1979.

Index

For the benefit of digital users, indexed terms that span two pages (e.g., 52–53) may, on occasion, appear on only one of those pages.

Abdul Hamid II (sultan of Ottoman Empire), 242–243
Abercorn, Duke of (James Hamilton)
   biographical background of, 202–203
   British South Africa Company and, 202–204, 207–208, 213t, 278
   Labouchère's criticism of, 297
   Lobengula and, 218–219
   Marlborough and, 261
Aborigines Protection Society, 240
African Lakes Company, 204–206, 266
African National Congress (ANC), 4, 389–390
Africa Trans-Continental Telegraph Company (ATT), 283–284, 384–385, 387
Afrikaner Bond
   Boer nationalism promoted by, 108–109, 164
   British South Africa Company and, 224
   coal mining and, 170
   election of 1898 and, 390–391
   Farmers' Protection Society and, 90
   newspaper allies of, 90
   racial discrimination supported by, 168, 228–230

   railroads and, 169–170, 172, 216–217, 220–221
   Rhodes and, 91, 97, 163–164, 168–169, 226, 229, 238, 243, 246, 322, 367–368
   settler movement promoted by, 97
   sheep farming and, 241–243
   Sprigg and, 226, 388–389
   tariff legislation and, 168–169
   Transvaal and, 216–217, 347
   voting laws in Cape Colony and, 165–166, 228, 232
   wine taxes and, 90
Afrikaners. *See also* Boers; *specific territories*
   cultural nationalism among, 108–109, 163–164
   Hofmeyr's role as a political leader of, 87–88, 90
   religious conservatives among, 164
   Rhodes as a representative in Cape Colony parliament for, 87, 97–98
   Rhodes's political alliances with, 162–163
   vineyards owned by, 89–90
   Western Cape as self-identified homeland of, 89, 231
"Aggression on Egypt and Freedom in the East" (Gladstone), 68–69

Albert Edward, Prince of Wales, 202, 261, 329–332
Alexander, Fred, 131
Andrews, Thomas, 116–117, 156–157
Anglo-Zulu War (1879), 75–76
Apollo Lodge (Oxford University), 66
Aristotle, 60, 67–70
Arnold, Edwin, 69
Arnot, David, 17–18, 24–26, 224–225
Arnot, Frederick Stanley, 264–265
Arts and Crafts movement, 65, 245, 313, 368, 412
Asquith, H. H., 63–64, 235
Atherstone, William G., 18
Austral Africa Company, 199–200
Australian Gully Block Company, 119
Aylward, Alfred, 50

Babayane, 192–194, 196–197, 209–210, 357
Babe, Jerome, 20
Baden-Powell, Robert, 354–355
Bailey, Abe, 387
Bailey, Duncan, 378–379
Baker, Herbert, 7, 324, 368, 411–412
Baker, Lionel, 364
Balfour, Arthur, 296–297
Balfour of Burleigh, Lord, 202–204
Barberton reef, 130, 132
Baring Brothers bank, 304–305
Baring-Gould, Francis, 84, 118, 142–146, 307
Barkly, Henry, 25–26, 47–48, 173, 244
Barkly West mining camp, 19, 87, 104, 183, 229–230
Barnato, Barney
  biographical background and Jewish origins of, 141–142, 145–146
  British South Africa Company and, 213t, 216
  De Beers Consolidated Mining and, 144–146, 160, 306–307
  De Beers mine fire (1888) and, 160
  diamond trade and, 80, 306
  gold mining and, 162–163, 325–326
  Gould's alliance with, 143
  illicit diamond buying and, 141–142, 145–146
  Johannesburg water supply and, 327–328
  Kimberley mine and, 141–143
  Rhodes's business dealings with, 143–146
  Transvaal electoral politics and, 328
Barnato Mining, 141–142
Barnes, G. W., 316
Barotseland, 264–266, 268
Barry, Jacob, 30, 53
Bartle Frere, Henry, 75–76, 91, 163–164
Basutoland (Lesotho), 90–94, 230
Bateman, Lucinda, 183
Bathoen, 96, 333, 339–341
Bechuanaland. *See also* Bechuanaland Protectorate; British Bechuanaland Colony
  Boer settlement movement in, 100
  British suzerainty in, 100
  deforestation of, 311
  Goshen republic in, 97–98, 100–103, 333
  proposals to have Cape Colony annex, 104–105, 337
  Rhodes's expansionist plans and, 101–102, 104–105, 107–108, 175, 333–334, 342–343, 370–371
  Rhodes's skepticism regarding white settlement in, 108
  Road to the North and, 101–102, 108
  Stellaland republic in, 97–98, 100–102, 104–105
  Warren Expedition (1884–1885) and, 103–104
Bechuanaland Border Police, 105, 293–294, 329
Bechuanaland Exploration Company. *See* Exploring Company

Bechuanaland Protectorate
  British South Africa Company and,
    335–341, 349, 370–371
  Colonial Office and, 334–336
  establishment of, 102–105, 107, 322–323
  railroads and, 172, 283, 375–377
  Rhodes's proposal to expand, 173–174
  Tswana people and, 335, 339–340
Beinart, William, 3–4, 355–356
Beira Junction Railway Company, 377
Beira Railway Company, 263–264, 278, 377
Beit, Alfred
  agricultural endeavors with Rhodes
    and, 364
  British South Africa Company and,
    213*t*, 216, 251
  Corner House and, 318–320, 330
  De Beers Consolidated Mining and,
    120–121, 145, 160, 304, 306–307, 347
  De Beers mine claims of, 81
  diamond trade and, 79–80
  The French Company and, 80
  gold mining concessions in
    Matabeleland and, 200
  gold mining industry and, 131–132,
    134, 136, 162–163
  railroad development and, 388
  Rhodes's friendship and business
    dealings with, 79–80, 143
  Rhodes Trust and, 408
  Rothschild and, 143, 145
  Transvaal coup attempt (1895–1896)
    and, 330, 347, 349–350
Beit, Otto, 263–264, 278
Belgium, 96–97, 212. *See also* Leopold II
  (king of Belgium)
Bent, Theodore and Mabel, 276
Berlin Conference (1884–1885), 172–173,
  184, 204
Biggar, Nigel, 3–4
Bin Abdullah, Muhammad Ahmad (The
  Mahdi), 93, 287

Bishop's Stortford (England), 9–10
Blair, Tony, 3–4
Bloemfontein, 169–170, 225, 228–229,
  342–343
Blood River, battle (1838) of, 14–15
Boeren Beschirmings Vereeniging
  (Farmers' Protection Society), 90
Boers. *See also* Afrikaners; *specific territories*
  Black Africans' relations with, 17
  British Bechuanaland and, 100,
    105–107
  British purchase of land in Natal from,
    14–15
  diamond mining industry in Cape
    Colony and, 17–18, 25–26
  electoral politics in Cape Colony
    and, 87
  First Anglo-Boer War (1880–1881) and,
    88–89
  Germany and, 97–98, 384–385
  proposals for united South African
    colony and, 17
  racial discrimination practiced by, 51,
    163–164
  Road to the North and, 96–97
  settlement movement promoted by,
    97–99
  Transvaal coup attempt resisted by,
    346–347
  trekkers into Mashonaland and,
    250–251
  Zulu military conflicts with, 14–15
Boschendal vineyard, 7, 368
Bosman, Isaac John, 336–337
Botswana. *See* Bechuanaland
Bower, Graham
  British imperialism in Africa
    commended by, 323–324
  British South African Police criticized
    by, 282
  gold mining concessions in
    Matabeleland and, 190, 193, 201

Bower, Graham (*Continued*)
    imperial secretary appointment of, 221–222
    on Rhodes's relationship with Pickering, 79
    Road to the North and, 98
Boyes, Lorenzo, 18
Boyle, H. D., 213*t*, 216
Bramston, John, 209
Brand, Jan, 50
Brett, Reginald, 349
British Bechuanaland Colony, 104–107, 220–221, 333
British Company (mining), 141–142
British Empire. *See* Great Britain
British North Borneo Company, 181
British South Africa Company (BSAC)
    agriculture and, 324–325
    archives of, 412–413
    Barotseland and, 265–266, 268
    Bechuanaland Protectorate and, 335–341, 349, 370–371
    board of, 202–204, 206, 251, 307
    cattle seizures by, 351–352, 373
    charter of, 349–350
    Colonial Office (Great Britain) and, 209, 269–270, 334–335
    De Beers Consolidated Mining and funding for, 213*t*, 216, 281, 305–308, 316, 318–319, 377
    forced labor proposals in Rhodesia by, 374–375
    Gazaland and, 262
    gold surveys in Rhodesia and, 375
    headquarters of, 399–400
    hut taxes and, 351, 373–374
    Katanga and, 266–267
    Manicaland and, 259–261
    Mashonaland and, 247–250, 269, 271
    Matabeleland and, 271
    Matabele War and, 290–294, 296, 300, 323–324
    Nyasaland and, 205, 269
    Panic of 1893 and, 279
    police force of, 252–256, 278–279, 282, 288–293, 330, 350–351, 353
    Portuguese attack on the forces of, 263
    profitability of, 247, 269–270, 278–282, 290
    railroads and, 211, 216–217, 283–284, 308, 336, 340–341
    Rhodes's ownership stake and management of, 6, 56–57, 206, 210, 212–216, 213*t*, 221, 224, 242, 259–260, 269, 278–279, 287, 347, 349
    Rudd Concession and, 207, 211, 216, 269–270
    stock distribution at, 202, 212–216, 213*t*, 224, 246, 251
    telegraph development and, 287–288
    Transvaal coup (1895–1896) and, 330, 333, 344, 346–347, 352
    white settlement promoted by, 278–279
Bruce, Alexander Livingstone, 204, 213*t*
Bruce, Victor (Lord Elgin), 391
Bryce, James, 314–315
Bulawayo
    as capital of Matabeleland, 107
    diamond mining in, 17–18
    Government House at, 399–400
    Matabele War and, 293–294, 299
    Ndebele attacks on white settlers in, 352
    railroads in, 86, 220–221, 283, 334, 340, 375–376
    telegraph lines and, 352–353
Bultfontein mine, 19–20, 23–24, 40, 304–305, 312–313
Burdett-Coutts, Angela, 202
Burgers, Thomas, 88–89
Burnham, Frederick Russell, 354–355, 388
Bush, George W., 3–4
Buxton, Sydney, 296, 360–361
Buxton, Thomas Fowell, 194–195, 213*t*, 216

Index 493

Cadbury, John, 313
Caisse des Mines de Paris, 179
Caldecott, Harry, 77, 131–133, 136
Campbell, Edith, 378–379
Campbell-Bannerman, Henry, 360–361
Canning, Herbert, 338–339
Cannon, Sophia, 3
Cape Argus newspaper, 90, 92, 235
Cape Colony
    Basutoland War (1880–1881) and, 90–93
    Bechuanaland annexation proposal and, 104–105, 337
    British government's administration of, 25–26, 37, 42, 50
    British South Africa Company and, 211
    customs union in southern Africa and, 109, 169–170, 221–222
    diamond discoveries in, 17–20, 23–25
    Griqualand West colony incorporated (1880) into, 56–57, 84–85, 87
    land claims by Black Africans in, 24–26
    Lesotho established as a separate colony (1883) from, 93–94
    proposals for unified South African colony and, 17, 72, 86–87, 93–94, 108–109, 329
    race relations and racial discrimination laws in, 38, 50–51, 56–57, 91, 163, 166, 217
    railroads in, 40–42, 85–86, 164, 169–170, 181, 211, 223, 376
    Rhodes as prime minister of, 1, 7, 220, 223–224, 229, 302
    Road to the North and, 97–98
    Transvaal annexed (1877) by, 72
    voting laws in, 164–168, 228, 232–239, 389–390
Cape Explosives company, 366–367
Cape Government Railways, 41–42, 211, 308, 334, 342–343
Cape Monthly Magazine, 36
Cape of Good Hope Bank, 142
Cape Parliament. *See also* House of Assembly (Cape Colony)
    Diamond Trade Act of 1882 and, 94
    election (1898) and, 389–390
    establishment (1853) of, 37
    Griqualand West established (1871) by, 26
    Peace Preservation Act of 1878 and, 91
    photo of buildings of, 165*f*
    Precious Stones and Minerals Act of 1883 and, 95
    Rhodes as member of, 56–57, 87, 89, 97–98, 183, 220, 382, 389
    Road to the North and, 97
Cape-to-Cairo connections. *See also* Road to the North
    critiques of, 384
    German East Africa and, 257
    railroads and, 208, 388
    Rhodes's promotion of, 1, 7–8, 17–18, 180, 382–383
    Strangways's promotion of, 69
    telegraph lines and, 69, 171, 279, 287, 382–383, 386–388
Cape Town
    railroads and, 37–38, 41, 85, 169, 228–229, 334, 376
    scientific institutions during nineteenth century in, 36
    telegraph lines and, 350
Carlyle, Thomas, 51, 237
Carnarvon, Lord (Henry Herbert), 51–52, 180–181
Carnegie, Andrew, 6–7, 407–408, 410–411
Carrington, Frederick, 249, 354–355
Castle Shipping Line, 367–368
Cavendish, Frederick, 193–194
Cavendish, Lucy, 193–194
Cawston, George
    biographical background of, 180
    British South Africa Company and, 206, 211, 213*t*, 216, 251, 259–260, 278

Cawston, George (*Continued*)
  Exploring Company and, 179–181
  gold mining concessions in
    Matabeleland and, 192–193, 196–197,
    199–200
  railroads and, 181–183, 211
Cecil, Robert. *See* Salisbury, Lord
Central Company
  Baring Gould as founder of, 84
  compound housing for African
    workers and, 123–124
  De Beers Consolidated Mining's
    amalgamation and, 143–145, 160
  Kimberley Central Company's
    absorption (1887) of, 143
  Kimberley mine and, 112, 114, 142
  mining innovations introduced by, 114
Central Search Association, 199–203, 207
Chamberlain, Joseph
  appointment as secretary of state for
    colonies of, 338
  Bechuanaland and, 338–339
  biographical background of, 338
  British South Africa Company and, 338
  imperialism promoted by, 135–136
  Irish home rule opposed by, 338
  Khama's meeting with, 340
  railroad development and, 375–376,
    382–383, 388
  Rothschild and, 135–136
  Rudd Concession and, 194–196
  Transvaal coup attempt and, 338–339,
    344–345, 349–350, 360–361
Charles Fox and Sons, 62–63, 180
Chartered Company, 281, 294–295, 297,
  302, 307–308, 335, 385, 396–397
Churchill, Randolph
  British imperialism supported by, 273
  British South Africa Company and,
    273–275, 288–289, 301
  Conservative Party and, 273
  Gladstone and, 273

on gold mining in South Africa, 316
Mashonaland travels of, 273–275,
  277–278, 281–282
photo of, 274*f*
Rhodes's interactions with, 274–275
Churchill, George Spencer, 261
Churchill, Randolph Spencer, 261
Clement, Victor, 325–326, 330
Coghlan, Charles, 406
Cohen, E., 36
Coillard, François, 265–266
Colenbrander, Johan, 192–194, 209–210,
  213*t*, 356
Colesberg Kopje mine, 23–24, 27–29,
  31–32. *See also* Kimberley mine
Colonial Office (Great Britain)
  Barotseland and, 265
  Bechuanaland Protectorate and,
    334–336
  Boer republics of Stellaland and
    Goshen opposed by, 97–98
  British Bechuanaland Colony and, 105
  British South Africa Company and,
    209, 269–270, 334–335
  hut taxes and, 351
  Matabeleland mining concessions and,
    184, 189–190, 197, 207, 209–210
  Matabele War and, 298–299
  Pioneer Column and, 249, 251–252
  railroads and, 179–181
  restrictions on punishments for
    diamond workers and, 121
  Road to the North promoted by,
    97–98
  Transvaal and, 329–331, 349
  voting rights in Cape Colony and, 167
Colquhoun, Archibald, 213*t*, 255–256,
  260–261, 266–267, 269–271, 278–279
Compagnie Française des Mines de
  Diamants du Cap de Bonne-
  Espérance. *See* The French Company
Compton, George, 81–82

Compton, Stow, and English, 116
"Confession of 1877" (Rhodes), 67–72, 162, 407
Congo Free State, 172–173, 264, 267–268, 384–385
Consolidated Gold Fields, 290, 294, 318–319, 326, 330
Cooke, Jay, 35
Cooper, John Astley, 407–408
Corner House, 318–320, 330
Corn Laws (Great Britain), 13–14, 203
Cromer, Lord (Evelyn Baring), 284–285
Cronon, William, 6
Crosby, J. M., 151–156, 159–160
Crossman, William, 51–56
Crossman Report, 54, 56–57, 80–81, 84–85, 122
Crummell, Alexander, 389–390
Cruz, Antonio "Tony" de la, 273, 275–276, 290, 398
Curgenven, Bernard, 157
Currey, Harry, 103, 118
Currey, John Blades, 30, 32, 48–49, 51–52, 298
Currie, Donald, 142, 202–203, 213*t*, 304, 307, 363–364
Curtis, Joseph Storey, 317–318
Curzon, George, 63–64

Darwin, Charles, 51
Davies, Herbert, 318–319
Davis, Edmund, 385
Dawson, James, 289–290
De Beers Consolidated Mining
  British imperial goals promoted by funds from, 182, 396–397
  British South Africa Company funded by profits from, 213*t*, 216, 281, 305–308, 316, 318–319, 377
  coal supplies for, 311
  corporate structure of, 145–147
  De Beers mine fire (1888) and, 158–161
  diamond trade and, 306
  donations to Rhodes's political campaigns by, 390
  dynamite supply for,
  establishment (1888) of, 138–139, 143–147
  falsification of mining data by, 306–307
  Matabeleland and, 182
  monopoly held by, 146–147, 305–306
  Pioneer Columns and, 249
  processing of diamonds at, 309–313
  profitability of, 269, 303, 306, 308, 313, 359–360
  Rhodes's ownership stake in and management of, 143–147, 150, 158, 160, 179, 224, 269, 287, 302, 304, 306–307, 322, 359–360
  Rudd Concessions and, 207
  Transvaal coup (1895–1896) and, 330
  Williams as general manager of, 135–136, 138, 144–145, 160, 324
  workplace safety at mines of, 303–304
De Beers family, 19–20
De Beers mine
  Crossman's investigation (1876) of, 51–53
  diggers' committees and early governance of, 24
  discovery of diamond deposits (1871) at, 23
  environmental impact of operations at, 310–311
  fire (1888) at, 147–160, 148*f*, 153*f*, 182, 184, 348
  Friggens Shaft at, 152–157, 159–161
  innovations in mining at, 40, 44–46, 111–112, 138–141
  labor costs at, 382–383
  mining oversight board at, 49, 51–53
  photos of, 34*f*, 311*f*
  private ownership of, 47–48

De Beers mine (*Continued*)
  Rhodes and, 33–34, 51–53, 133
  workplace safety and accidents at, 82–83, 112, 139–140, 147–161, 148*f*, 153*f*, 304
De Beers Mining Company
  British imperialism promoted by, 144–145
  buyout attempt thwarted (1886) at, 117–118
  compound housing for African workers and, 123–129, 124*f*, 138–139
  convict labor and, 124–125
  corporate amalgamation into De Beers Consolidated Mining and, 138–139, 143–147
  De Beers mine claims purchased by, 80–81, 84, 119
  illicit diamond buying and, 122–123
  innovations in mining promoted by, 113–116, 121, 128–129, 138–141, 304, 308–309
  mining companies acquired after 1880 by, 82, 84, 119–121
  profitability of, 139
  Rhodes's ownership stake and management of, 56–57, 80–82, 84, 113–114, 116–121, 123, 136, 138–139, 143
  Rudd's ownership stake and management of, 80–81, 113–114, 116–117, 120, 136, 144–145
  strike (1884) at, 123
  white settler colonialism and, 111
de Crano, Edmund, 130–131, 134–135, 143
Delagoa Bay (Portuguese Mozambique)
  British imperial plans and, 176–177
  deepwater port at, 216–217
  as harbor of Lourenço Marques, 96–97
  railroads and, 109, 169–170, 216–217, 225–226, 328
  Rhodes's attempt to purchase, 225–226

de la Rey, Koos, 404
Derby, Lord, 98, 101–103
d'Erlangers, Baron, 377
de Souza, Manuel António ("Gouveia"), 258–259, 261
Dever, Martin, 157
de Villiers, John Henry, 213*t*, 216, 229
de Waal, David Christiaan, 213*t*, 223, 273–276, 322, 367–368
de Worms, Henry, 195–196
Diamond Fields Commission, 49–50
Diamond Fields Horse militia, 74–76, 103
Diamond Mining Protection Society, 94
Diamond Trade Act of 1882 (Cape Colony), 94
Dikgatlong, 18–19
Dingane, 14–15
Disraeli, Benjamin, 88–89, 91, 163–164, 180–181
Dliso, 357
Dorstfontein mine, 19–20, 23–24. *See also* Dutoitspan mine
Douglas, Alfred, 331–332
Douglas, Francis, 331–332
Douglas, John (Marquess of Queensberry), 331–332
Dowden, Oliver, 3–4
Drayton, Richard, 3
Dreyfus, Paul, 146
Drifts Crisis (1895), 342–343
Drumlanrig, Viscount (Francis Douglas), 331–332
Duff, Alexander. *See* Fife, Duke of
Duke of York, 391
Dünkelsbühler company, 306
Dunn, E. J., 36
Dunn, John, 33
Durban, 109, 328
Dutoitspan mine, 19, 23, 40, 44–46, 114, 117–118, 304, 312–313, 318
Dykes, John Bacchus, 394–395, 405
dynamite, 82–83, 366–367

Eagle Company, 119
Eastern Cape
  agriculture in, 108–109, 241–242
  Black African voters and voting laws in, 164–166
  boundaries of, 164–165
  coal mining in, 85, 170, 311
  railroads and, 41, 108–109
  separatist movement in, 87–88
East India Company, 181, 207–208
East London, 41, 235, 376
Eckstein, Hermann, 134, 162–163, 213t, 318–319
Edison, Thomas, 6
Egypt, 68–69, 284–285, 382
Ellerton, John, 405
Ellis, John, 360–361
Elma Company, 119
English, Robert, 81–82, 116, 123
Erskine, William
  compound housing for African workers in diamond mines and, 122
  convict labor in diamond mines supported by, 124–125
  De Beers mine explosion (1884) and, 83
  De Beers mine fire (1888) and, 149–150, 152, 155
  on increasing number of diamond mining accidents during 1880s, 139–140
  Kenilworth workers' compound and, 313
  workers blamed for diamond mine accidents by, 112
Exploring Company
  British South Africa Company and, 213t
  charter company proposal and, 181
  establishment of, 179–180
  gold mining concessions in Matabeleland and, 185–186, 199–200
  Lobengula and, 180, 182
  Ndebele people and, 173
  railroads and, 181–183, 211, 216–217, 220–221
Eyre, Edward, 13–14

Fairfield, Edward, 189, 196, 209, 249, 338, 340–341, 361
Farmers' Protection Society, 90
Farquhar, Horace, 203, 213t, 278, 361
Farrar, George, 328, 347
Faure, Pieter, 223–224
Feltham, H. J., 71, 120
Fife, Duke of (Alexander Duff), 203–204, 207–208, 213t, 262, 278, 297
Fillmore, James Henry, 183
First Anglo-Boer War (1880–1881), 88–89
First World War, 254–255, 293
FitzPatrick, Percy, 328
Flint, John, 84, 368
Forbes, Patrick, 261, 283–284, 291, 298
Ford, Henry, 6
Forster, W. E., 70–71
Fort Salisbury
  Churchill's description of, 277
  establishment of, 256–257
  railroads and, 258, 278, 352–353, 376–378
  Rhodes's visit to, 273
  telegraph lines and, 283–284, 384, 386–387
Fort Victoria, 256–257
Fourie, Johan, 168
Frazer, James, 391
Freedom Charter (African National Congress, 1955), 4–5
Freemasons
  international brotherhood ideology of, 66–67
  legislative politics in Cape Colony and, 87–88
  at Oxford University, 66, 73
  Rhodes's membership in and inspiration from, 66–70, 73, 402

Free State. *See* Orange Free State
The French Company, 80, 112, 114, 123–124, 142–144
Froude, James Anthony, 51, 163–164
Fruitfield farm, 369
Fry, Ivon, 184
Fuller, J. W., 336–337

Gaborone, 220, 338–339, 376–377
Gambo, 192
Garanganze kingdom, 267
Garlick (servant of Leander Starr Jameson), 361–362, 369–370
Garstin, Norman, 30
Gaseitsiwe, 96, 104–105, 333
Gaul, William, 405
Gaza territory, 258–260, 263
Gem Company, 119–120, 138–139, 141
George V (king of England), 391
Germany
　Boer population in southern Africa and, 97–98, 384–385
　German East Africa and, 257, 269–270, 384–385
　German South-West Africa (Namibia) and, 96–98, 103, 172–173, 242, 257, 336–337
　Mpondo chiefdom and, 97–98
　potential for expansion of colonies in Africa by, 107–108, 172–174, 208
　telegraph development in Africa and, 285
　unification (1871) of, 35, 172
Gibbon, Edward, 13
Gifford, Edric
　biographical background of, 180
　British South Africa Company and, 206, 211, 213*t*, 216
　Exploring Company and, 180–183
　gold mining concessions in Matabeleland and, 179–180, 192–193, 196–197, 199–200
　railroads and, 181, 211

Gifford, Maurice, 352–353
Girouard, Percy, 382
Gladstone, William
　Bechuanaland and, 103
　British imperial expansion opposed by, 68–69, 88–89, 282–283
　Cape Colony political administration and, 91
　Carnegie and, 407
　Churchill and, 273
　First Anglo-Boer War and, 88–89
　Irish home rule and, 175–176, 286
　Lesotho's establishment as a separate colony (1883) under, 93
　Matabele War and, 296–297
　Nyasaland and, 172–173
　resignation as prime minister (1886) of, 175–176
Glen Grey district (Cape Colony), 231–233, 235, 238
Gold Fields of South Africa
　British imperial goals promoted by funds from, 182
　British South Africa Company and, 213*t*, 377
　establishment (1887) of, 136
　Pioneer Column and, 249
　profitability of, 269, 290, 316, 324–325
　Rhodes's ownership stake and management of, 56–57, 136–137, 162–163, 224, 269, 287, 302, 316, 322
　Rudd Concession and, 199–200, 207
　Rudd's ownership stake and management of, 136, 162–163, 316
　Transvaal coup (1895–1896) and, 330, 344
Goold-Adams, Hamilton John, 186–187, 213*t*
Goold-Adams, Kenneth, 289–291
Gordon, Charles, 92–93
Goshen, 97–98, 100–103, 333
Gouldie, Joseph, 153–154

Gouveia, 258–259, 261
Graham, Frederick, 197
Graham, Robert Dundas, 80–81
Grahamstown, 41, 102, 169
Grant, Junior, James Augustus, 69, 266–267
Grant, Senior, James Augustus, 266–267
Great Britain
　abolition of slavery (1833) in, 13–14
　agricultural depression (1873-1896) in, 203
　Black Africans' legal rights as subjects of, 50–51
　Cape Colony administration and, 25–26, 37, 42, 50
　Corn Laws in, 13–14, 203
　First Anglo-Boer War and opinion regarding imperialism in, 89
　Panic of 1873 and, 35
　parliamentary reforms (1832) in, 13–14
　Portugal's alliance with, 257–258
　Transvaal coup attempt investigated in, 358, 360–361
Great Zimbabwe ruins, 256–257, 275–276, 301–302
Green, Thomas Hill, 63–65
Gregory, J. R., 18
Grey, Albert
　Bechuanaland and, 337–338, 340
　British South Africa Company and, 203–204, 207–208, 213*t*, 251, 278, 350, 352–353, 357
　Rhodes Trust and, 408
　Transvaal coup attempt and, 338–339
Grey, E., 80–81
Grier, W. M., 151–154
Grimmer, Johnny, 371, 398–399, 401–402, 408–409
Griqualand East, 74–75, 230
Griqualand West
　boundary disputes regarding, 98
　Cape Colony's incorporation (1880) of, 56–57, 84–85, 87
　Crossman's recommendations regarding, 55
　diamond mining industry in, 35–36
　diggers' committees in, 49
　establishment (1871) of, 26
　militia forces in, 74–75
　multiple claim problem within mining industry in, 46–47
　race relations in, 50–51
　rebellion (1878) in, 74–75
Griqua people, 17–19, 24–26
Grobler, Pieter J., 177–179
Groote Schuur
　Baker's role in designing, 7, 324
　Cape Dutch style and, 412
　decor at, 245–246
　donation from Rhodes to Cape Colony by, 408–409
　fire (1896) at, 358–359, 411
　Kipling's stay at, 393–394
　photo of, 244*f*
　political negotiations conducted at, 245–246
　rebuilding after fire at, 368
　Rhodes's final years at, 398–399
　Rhodes's funeral services and, 404
　Rhodes's purchase (1892) of, 244
　Rhodes's renovations at, 245
　staff at, 245–246
Gungunyana, 258, 260, 262

Haggard, Alfred, 199–200, 213*t*
Haggard, Rider, 196, 213*t*
Hall, William "Tramway," 45–46
Hambly, William, 152, 154, 158–159
Hamilton, James. *See* Abercorn, Duke of
Hammond, John Hays
　biographical background of, 325
　as engineer in Rhodes's operations, 6–7, 324–326

Hammond, John Hays (*Continued*)
    gold mining work in United States by, 321, 325
    innovations in gold mining introduced by, 326
    photo of, 301*f*
    Rhodesia gold surveys by, 301, 355–356
    Transvaal coup attempt (1895–1896) and, 329–330, 343–345
    Transvaal National Union and, 328
Hammond, Natalie, 325
Harcourt, William, 333, 360–361
Harland-Jacobs, Jessica, 66–67
Harris, David, 134
Harris, Robert, 126–127
Hatton Garden diamond market (London), 32, 58, 306
Hawksley, Bourchier, 210, 213*t*, 349, 361, 408
Heany, Maurice, 179, 213*t*, 218
Helm, Charles, 188–190, 192
Herbert, Henry. *See* Knutsford, Lord
Herbert, Robert, 180–181, 184, 189, 209, 217
Hicks Beach, Michael, 360–361, 388
Hofmeyr, Jan Hendrik
    Afrikaner political constituencies represented by, 87–88, 90
    agriculture and, 163
    Farmers' Protection Society and, 90
    Freemasonry and, 87–88
    Imperial Preference System and, 246
    Lesotho and, 93–94
    as member of Scanlen's cabinet, 91–92
    photo of, 88*f*
    railroads and, 217, 223
    resignation from parliament (1895) by, 242
    Rhodesia settlement promoted by, 322
    Rhodes's political alliance with, 87–88, 90, 163–165, 229–230
    Transvaal coup attempt and, 347–348

    voting laws in Cape Colony and, 164–166, 228
Hofmeyr, Tielman, 213*t*, 223
Hole, Marshall, 354
Holland, Henry, 180–181
Horace, 413–414
House of Assembly (Cape Colony). *See also* Cape Parliament
    apportionment of seats in, 87, 165–166
    coalition politics in, 87–88
    compound housing at diamond mines and, 125
    elections (1884) for, 229–230
    elections (1888) for, 183
    establishment (1853) of, 37
    prime ministers chosen by, 37
    Rhodes as member of, 56–57, 87, 89, 97–98, 183, 220, 382, 389
House of Rothschild. *See* Rothschild family
Hudson's Bay Company, 181
Huteau, E., 51–53

IDB (illicit diamond buying)
    De Beers Mining Company and, 122–123
    Diamond Trade Act of 1882 and, 94
    punishments for, 121–122
    race relations in Cape Colony and, 50–51, 121
    searches of miners and compound housing as means of preventing, 122–123, 125–127, 127*f*, 313–314
Imperial Preference tariff system, 246
India rebellion (1857), 13–14, 51
Ingubo, 289–290
Ingubogubo, 289–290
Inner Temple (London barrister organization), 66
Innes, James Rose, 166–167, 201–202, 224, 229, 238–239
Inniskilling Dragoons regiment, 103, 275
Inyanga, 368–371, 408–409

Irish home rule, 175–176, 286, 332–333, 338
Isaacs, Barnet. *See* Barnato, Barney
Ismail Pasha (ruler of Egypt), 284–285

Jabavu, Davidson Don, 234*f*
Jabavu, John Tengo
    De Beers housing facilities described favorably by, 315
    Native Land Act of 1913 and, 240
    photo of, 234*f*
    voting laws in Cape Colony and, 166–167, 233–240
Jackson, William, 360–361
Jagersfontein mine, 305
Jamaica rebellion (1865), 13–14, 51
James, Henry, 393
Jameson, Leander Starr
    autopsy of Rhodes and, 401
    British South Africa Company and, 213*t*, 217, 278–279, 288–290, 299, 350
    funeral services for Rhodes and, 405
    gold mining concessions in Matabeleland and, 190–193, 198, 211, 218
    Great Zimbabwe ruins and, 275–276
    imprisonment in Great Britain of, 349–350
    Lobengula and, 211–212, 217–219, 250–251, 288
    Mashonaland and, 250
    Matabele War and, 290–291, 298
    Ndebele people and, 288, 290–291
    photo of, 78*f*
    Pickering and, 133–134
    Pioneer Column and, 251–252, 255–256
    Portuguese forces' capture of, 262
    Rhodes's friendship with, 77–79
    Rhodes's housing in Kimberley with, 243–244
    Rhodes's trust and, 408
    sexuality of, 78–79

    smallpox outbreaks in Kimberley and, 77
    Transvaal coup attempt (1895–1896) and, 329–330, 333, 344–350, 352
    United Concession Company and, 216
Jantjie Mothibi, 18–19, 24–26, 75
Jenkins, John Edward, 70–71
Jesuits, 67–68, 407, 409
Joel, Solomon, 80
Joel, Woolf, 80, 305
Johannesburg
    Black African laborers and communities in, 108–109
    gold mining industry in, 4–5, 108–109
    railroads and, 169–171, 220–221, 225–226
    water supply of, 327–328
John Fox and Sons, 377, 387
Johnson, Frank
    British South Africa Company and, 213*t*, 251–252, 259–260, 279–281
    gold industry and, 176–177
    Lobengula assassination plot (1889) and, 218
    mining concession negotiations and, 179
    Nyasaland and, 257–258, 266
    Pioneer Column and, 255–256
Johnston, Harry
    Cape-to-Cairo railway and, 180, 204–205
    Nyasaland and, 204–205, 380–381
    Road to the North and, 108–109
    telegraph lines and, 283–284, 286
Jones, Edward, 115, 133, 138–139, 141
Jones, Joseph, 155
Joubert, Piet, 177
Jourdan, Philip, 392–393, 395, 398–399
Jowett, Benjamin, 59–62
Judge, C. E., 291–292
Judge, Edward, 124–125, 151–152, 155, 231–232

Kahn, Albert, 408–409
Kalanga people, 288
Karim, Abdul, 341

Katanga, 7–8, 212, 264, 266–268, 388
Keate, Robert, 25–26, 48–49
Kekewich, Robert, 395–396
Kenilworth
  agricultural practices at, 363–364
  De Beers Mining Company's purchase of, 113
  international visitors at, 314–315
  photo of, 314f
  reservoir at, 141, 310–311
  Rhodes's role in designing, 7
  workers' village at, 7, 313–315
Keppel-Jones, Arthur, 217
Kerr, Schomberg Henry, 194
Khama
  Barotseland and, 265
  Bechuanaland and, 105, 175
  British South Africa Company and, 339–340
  gold mining concessions in Matabeleland and, 179, 185–186, 197–198
  Great Britain's relationship with, 104–105
  Great Zimbabwe ruins and, 276
  Grobler's killing and, 178–179
  Lobengula's rivalry with, 104–105
  Matabele War and, 290–291, 293–294
  Ngwato chiefdom and, 96
  photo of, 106f
  Pioneer Column and, 249
  railroad development and, 375–376
  rifles obtained by, 197–198
  visit to London (1895) by, 339–340
  white settlement in Tswana lands and, 104–105
Khayelitsha, 1, 4
Khoisan people, 89
Khumalo, Mtshane, 292
Kimberley. *See also* Kimberley mine
  Black African laborers and communities in, 31, 47, 55–56, 77–78, 105–109, 121
  capital investment in, 47–48
  challenges and innovations in mining at, 35, 40, 42–44, 47, 54–55, 82–83
  diamond mining industry in, 4–8, 23, 31–32, 35–36, 39, 42–44, 47, 77–78, 105–107
  diamond trading networks in, 80
  diggers' committees and early governance in, 23–24
  geology at, 35–36
  infrastructure development at, 37–38
  migrant laborers in, 31, 47
  Panic of 1873 and economic instability in, 39–40
  railroads and, 41, 44–45, 85–86, 91–92, 108–109, 168–170, 179–180, 217, 220–222, 311, 331, 334, 342–343, 350
  restrictions placed on gambling and prostitution in, 76
  Rhodes's social life in, 30–31
  sanatorium in, 359
  sanitation facilities in, 76
  Second Boer War and, 395–396
  smallpox outbreaks in, 77
  telegraph lines and, 171
  telegraph services in, 76
  white migrant laborers and communities in, 151
Kimberley Central Company, 123, 143–146
Kimberley Club, 145–146
Kimberley mine. *See also* Colesberg Kopje mine
  Barnato's holdings in, 141–143
  Black African workers at, 46, 123–124
  compound housing at, 123–124
  consolidation of claims during 1880s at, 84
  diggers' committees and early governance of, 24
  environmental impact of operations at, 310–311

innovations in mining at, 40, 45–47,
  112, 114, 304, 308
migrant laborers in, 29
mining oversight board and
  governance of, 49, 52–53, 82
multiple claim problem at, 46–47, 49
photos of, 48f, 312f
private ownership of, 47–48
processing of diamonds at, 312–313
Rhodes's attempt to buy stakes in, 142
workplace safety and accidents at, 82,
  112, 139–140, 304
Kimberley Mining Company, 80
Kipling, Carrie, 393–394
Kipling, Rudyard
  British imperialism supported by,
    394–395
  Freemasons and, 393–394
  international success of books by, 393
  photo of, 394f
  racial views of, 393–394
  Rhodes as subject of poem by, 402–403
  Rhodes statue at University of Cape
    Town and, 1–2
Kisumu, 387
Kitchener, Herbert Horatio, 382–383,
  391, 396, 404
Kitto, Thomas C., 55–56, 122
Knight-Bruce, George, 190, 263,
  292–293
Knutsford, Lord (Henry Holland)
  British South Africa Company and,
    209, 263, 282
  Exploring Company and, 180–181
  gold mining concessions in
    Matabeleland and, 192–194,
    196–197, 295–296
  Lobengula and, 218–219
Koffiefontein mine, 305
Kok, Adam, 26
Koranna people, 75–76, 97
Kora people, 17

Kruger, Paul
  Afrikaner Bond and, 388–389
  Bechuanaland and, 104
  coup attempt (1895–1896) against,
    329–331, 344, 347
  governing style of, 326–327
  Mozambique and, 109
  railroads and, 96–97, 109, 169–170,
    220–221, 223, 225–226, 228–229
  Road to the North and, 96–97
  Swaziland and, 249–250
  tariffs on Cape Colony and, 101–102,
    223
  Transvaal National Union and, 328
  uitlanders and, 329
  Warren's meeting (1885) with, 104
Kumi, Yasmin, 3
Kwena chiefdom, 96, 105, 333

L. & A. Abrahams, 306
Labouchère, Henry
  Rhodes and British South Africa
    Company criticized by, 294–298
  Rudd Concession and, 195–196,
    294–295
  Transvaal coup attempt investigation
    and, 360–361
Labram, George, 395–396
Laing, John, 224, 229
Lake Nyasa (Lake Malawi), 104, 283–285,
  387
Lake Tanganyika, 107, 283–284, 382, 385
Languedoc, 7, 365–366, 366f, 368
Lanyon, Owen, 48–49, 51–52, 74–76, 121
Lascelles, Frank, 385
Lawley, Arthur, 379–380
Lawson, Harrison, 154–155
LeCain, Timothy, 6
Legislative Council (Cape Colony), 37
LeJeune, Jules, 58
Lendy, Graham, 282, 288–289
Leonard, Charles, 330, 343–344

Leopold II (king of Belgium)
  Gordon and, 93
  Katanga and, 264, 268
  Rhodes's meetings with, 384–385
  telegraph lines and, 285, 384–385
  treaties with African chiefs and, 178
Lesotho (Basutoland), 90–94, 163–164
Le Sueur, Gordon, 290, 353–354, 398–399, 401–402, 404–405
Lewanika, 264–266
Lewis, Barnet, 80
Lewis, Isaac, 80
Lewis, Thomas, 154–156
Lilienfeld Brothers, 18
Lilienthal Brothers, 32
Lincoln, Abraham, 14
Lippert, Edouard
  British South Africa Company and, 213*t*
  dynamite concession held by, 270–271, 282, 294–295, 319–320, 327–328, 366–367
  gold mining negotiations in Matabeleland and, 192
Livingstone, David, 86, 266
Lloyd, Edwin, 341
Lobengula
  Bechuanaland Protectorate and, 107
  British South Africa Company and, 206–207, 218–219, 288, 290, 339–340
  cattle and, 288–289
  gold mining concessions in Matabeleland and, 179–180, 184–197, 207, 209–211, 294–295
  Khama's rivalry with, 104–105
  Mashonaland and, 174, 209–210
  Matabele War and, 292–296, 298
  photo of, 186*f*
  Pioneer Column and, 249–253, 255
  Rhodes's assassination plot (1889) against, 218
  Road to the North and, 249
  Shona people and, 189, 282
  sons of, 300
  southern Africa gold rush and, 176–177
  suicide of, 298
  telegraph lines and, 288
  Transvaal and, 177–179
  visitors to the court of, 176–177
  weapons acquired by, 190, 197–199, 253
Loch, Henry Brougham
  appointment as governor of Cape Colony of, 221
  Bechuanaland and, 283, 335
  biographical background of, 221
  British South Africa Company and, 263, 270–271, 290, 294, 336
  Colonial Office and, 221
  Lobengula assassination plot (1889) and, 218
  Manicaland and, 262
  Matabele War and, 290–291
  Ndebele kingdom and, 286, 288–291
  photo of, 222*f*
  Pioneer Column and, 249–250
  Rhodes's political maneuvers against, 331
  Swaziland and, 249–250
  Transvaal and, 329–330
Lochner, Frank, 265–266
Logan, James, 229
London and Paris Exploitation Company, 377
Lotshe, 188, 210
Louise (princess of England), 203
Lourenço Marques, 96–97, 109, 169, 176–177
Lozi kingdom, 264–266
Lyman, Joseph, 16

MacArthur-Forrest process (gold cyanidation), 318, 321
Mackenzie, John
  Bechuanaland deputy commissioner appointment of, 100, 102

Black Africans' civil and political
    rights promoted by, 98–99, 104–105
  British protectorate in Bechuanaland
    and, 102, 104
  gold mining concessions in
    Matabeleland and, 194–195
  Lobengula assassination plot (1889)
    and, 218
  photo of, 100f
  on racial discrimination in Transvaal,
    99
  Rhodes's efforts to marginalize, 102–104
  Road to the North and, 98–99
  Tswana chiefdoms' negotiations with,
    104–105
  Warren Expedition in Bechuanaland
    (1884–1885) and, 103
Mackinnon, William, 202–203
MacNeill, John Gordon Swift, 175–176
Mafeking
  railroads and, 179–180, 283, 323–324,
    331, 334, 339–340, 375–376
  Rhodes's funeral train and, 404
  Road to the North and, 104
  telegraph lines and, 350
  Warren Expedition and, 103–104
Maguire, James Rochfort
  Bechuanaland and, 339
  British South Africa Company and,
    213t, 251, 295–296
  Delagoa Bay purchase attempt and,
    225–226
  gold mining concessions in
    Matabeleland and, 185–186, 188,
    190–193, 198
  as House of Commons member, 62
  as Oxford University student, 62, 185
  Rhodes's friendship with, 62
Maguire, Julia, 395
The Mahdi (Muhammad Ahmad Bin
    Abdullah), 93, 287
Majuba, battle (1881) of, 88–89

Malawi. *See* Nyasaland
Mandela-Rhodes Foundation, 410
Manet, Elizabeth Sophia, 11
Manicaland
  British South Africa Company and,
    259–261
  gold mining in, 258
  Portugal and, 257–258, 260–263, 278
  railroads and, 259, 283–284
  Rhodes's plans in, 261
  telegraph lines and, 283–284
Manifest Destiny philosophy, 184
Mankurwane, 102, 337
Mantusi, 289–290
Maputo. *See* Lourenço Marques
Marcus Aurelius, 13, 61, 65–66
Marks, Dickie, 369
Marks, Samuel, 80
Martin, Richard, 350, 357
The Martyrdom of Man (Reade), 60–61, 67
Mashonaland. *See also* Zimbabwe
  agriculture in, 271
  Boer trekkers in, 250–251
  British suzerainty in, 271
  Churchill's travels in, 273–275, 277–278,
    281–282
  gold mining in, 17, 107, 271–272,
    277–279, 295
  Mozambique and, 247–248
  Pioneer Column and, 249–256
  Portugal's claims in, 209–210, 248–249,
    257–259
  railroads and, 86, 275
  Rhodes's expansionist plans and,
    107–108, 144–145, 174, 176, 181, 257,
    272, 279–281, 290, 331
  Rhodes's travels in, 273, 275–276
  Road to the North and, 107–108,
    247–248
  telegraph lines and, 275
Masters and Servants Amendment Bill of
    1890 (Strop Bill), 226–227, 236–237

Matabeleland. *See also* Zimbabwe
  British South Africa Company and, 281, 373–374
  British suzerainty in, 271
  Christian missionaries in, 185
  diamond mining in, 17–18
  gold mining concession negotiations in, 179–180, 184–201, 207, 209–211, 294–295
  gold mining in, 17
  Ndebele people and, 107
  Portugal and, 192–194
  Rhodes's expansionist plans and, 107–108, 144–145, 176, 181–182, 331
  Rhodes's skepticism regarding white settlement in, 108
  Road to the North and, 107–108
Matthews, Josiah, 74–75, 77, 87, 125
Mauch, Karl, 275–276
Maund, Edward
  British South Africa Company and, 213*t*
  Exploring Company and, 180–181, 184
  Freemasonry and, 107–108
  gold mining concessions in Matabeleland and, 185–189, 192–193, 200–201, 209–210
  Lobengula and, 173, 176–177
  railroads and, 181
  report on Ndebele territories (1885) by, 173
  Rhodes's friendship and political alliances with, 107–108
  Road to the North and, 107
Maund, John, 200, 213*t*
Maxwele, Chumani, 1–2, 4
McDonald, James "Mac," 64, 372–373, 398–400, 405
McKenzie, James, 45–47
McMurdo, Edward, 109, 225–226
Meade, Robert, 334–335, 338, 340–341
Merriman, John X.
  British South Africa Company and, 251, 278
  as Cape Parliament member, 29, 85–86
  capital investment in diamond industry and, 47–48
  compound housing at diamond mines and, 125
  De Beers Mining Company buyout attempt (1886) managed by, 117–118
  Delagoa Bay purchase attempt and, 225–226
  Diamond Trade Act of 1882, 94
  gold mining concessions in Matabeleland and, 191–192
  Labouchère's criticisms of Rhodes and, 298
  Logan corruption case and, 229
  as member of Rhodes's cabinet, 224, 229–230
  as member of Scanlen's cabinet, 91–92
  railroad development in Cape Colony and, 85–86
  Rhodes's friendship and business dealings with, 29, 85–86, 117–119
  voting laws in Cape Colony and, 165–167, 238–239
Metcalfe, Charles
  Bechuanaland railroad development and, 283, 376
  British South Africa Company and, 213*t*
  Cape to Cairo railway proposal and, 208
  Mashonaland railroad development and, 290
  as Oxford University student, 62–63, 180
  railroad to Fort Salisbury and, 352–353
  Rhodes's death and, 398–399
  Rhodes's military attacks against Ndebele people and, 354
  Road to the North and, 207–208
Methuen, Paul, 256, 395–396, 404
Mfengu people, 239
Michell, Lewis
  agricultural endeavors with Rhodes and, 364–366

on Rhodes's childhood, 12
Rhodes's death and, 398–399
on Rhodes's small number of intimate friends, 119
Rhodes Trust and, 408
Milner, Alfred
appointment as Cape Colony governor and, 370, 390–391
Bechuanaland Protectorate and, 370–371
forced labor in Rhodesia refused by, 374–375
Milner Hall at Rhodes House and, 412
as Oxford University student, 63–64, 370
railroad development and, 376
Rhodes Trust and, 408
Milton, William, 232
Mining Ordinance of 1874 (Cape Colony), 49–50
"The Mlimu," 352
Moffat, John Smith
appointment as assistant commissioner in Bechuanaland and, 177–178
biographical background of, 177–178
British South Africa Company and, 217, 271
Lobengula and, 177–179, 181, 209–210, 217–218
mining concession negotiations and, 185, 192
Pioneer Column and, 249–251
Moghabi, 282
Mohr, Edouard, 33
Moir, Fred, 266–267
Moir, John, 266–267
Molema, Silas, 344–345
Molopo River, 96, 105, 333
Molteno, John C., 37, 40–41, 51
Molteno, Percy Alport, 363–364
Molteno Plan, 40–42
Montshiwa, 102, 337, 341–342
Moore, Harry, 216

Morris, William, 65
Morrogh, John, 116, 307
Morse, Samuel, 6
Mosenthal, Harry, 305
Mosenthal Brothers, 32, 179–180
Moshoeshoe, 17
Mozambique. *See also* Mozambique Company
borders of, 257–258
German-British agreement (1899) on possible partition of, 381
Mashonaland and, 247–248
railroads in, 96–97, 109, 169–170, 376–377
Rhodes's plans in, 260–261
Rudd Concession and border of, 212
telegraph lines and, 283–284
Transvaal and, 109
Willoughby's incursion into, 251
Mozambique Company, 258–259, 261–264, 278, 381
Mpande, 14–15
Mpezeni, 300
Mpondo chiefdom, 97–98
Mshete, 192–194, 209–210, 250–251
Msiri, 267–268
Mugabe, Robert, 406
Murray, R. W., 182–183
Musa, Philip, 156
Mutasa, 258, 260–261, 263
Mzilikazi, 357

Namaqualand, 29
Namibia. *See* German South-West Africa (Namibia)
Natal
Black African residents of, 14–16
British annexation of Boer colony (1842) in, 14–15
British "indirect rule" of African residents of, 15
coal mining in, 85
cotton cultivation in, 15–17

Natal (*Continued*)
  European migrant residents of, 14–16
  indentured labor from India in, 15–16
  railroads in, 168–170, 328
  tariff policies and, 225
  telegraph lines and, 171
Natalia republic, 14–15
Natal Land and Colonisation Company, 15–16
Native Bill for Africa, 232–241
Native Recruiting Corporation, 320
Natives Land Act (1913), 240
Ncome, battle (1838) of, 14–15
Ndebele people
  Bechuanaland Border Police killing of leaders of, 289–290
  Bechuanaland Protectorate and, 173–174
  British South Africa Company and, 300, 353–357, 372
  cattle and, 299–300, 351–352
  Christianity and, 351
  hut taxes and, 351
  Kalanga people and, 288
  Matabeleland as home of, 107
  Matabele War (1893–1894) and, 290–294, 298–300, 323–324
  military attacks led by Rhodes against, 353–355
  Ngwato chiefdom and, 104–105
  Pioneer Column and, 250–256
  Rhodes's funeral and, 406
  Shona people and, 107, 189, 247, 282, 287–288
  weapons obtained by, 56–57, 87, 89, 97–98, 183, 188, 190–192, 195–199, 220, 253–254, 289, 382, 389
  white settlers in Bulawayo attacked by, 352
Ngami Trek, 336–337
Ngomo, 282
Nguboyenja, 300
Ngwaketse chiefdom, 96, 105, 333

Ngwato chiefdom
  gold mining concessions and, 179
  Grobler killing and, 178–179
  Khama as ruler of, 96
  Matabele War and, 290–291
  Ndebele people and, 104–105
  Pioneer Column and, 256
Nicholls, Kerry, 69–70
Njube, 300, 405
Nkopo, Athinangamso Esther, 3
Nobel, Alfred, 82–83, 319–320, 366–367
Norris, John, 371
Northern Rhodesia. *See also* Zambia
Nyambezane, 356–357
Nyasaland
  borders of, 257–260
  British suzerainty in, 172–173, 380–381
  Cape-to-Cairo connection and, 172–173
  Christian missionaries in, 204
  Portuguese expeditions into, 204, 257–258
  railroads in, 174
  Rhodes's expansionist designs in, 205
  telegraph lines and, 283–284, 384
Nyassa Company, 258–259, 381
Nyika, Farai, 168

Oats, Francis, 54–55, 119–122, 307–308, 375
Old Rush mine. *See* De Beers mine
Orange Free State
  Basutoland and, 90–91, 93–94
  Boer nationalism in, 108–109
  British suzerainty in, 17, 26
  coal mining in, 85, 221–222
  customs union in southern Africa and, 109, 169–170, 221–222
  diamond mining industry in Cape Colony and, 17, 23–26, 305
  diggers' committees and, 24, 49
  establishment of, 17

racial discrimination and
    discriminatory laws in, 26, 50–51,
    55–56
railroads in, 168–170, 220–223, 225
voting laws in, 167–168
Oriel College. *See* Oxford University
Oriental Company, 119–120
Origen, 397–398
Orpen, Francis Henry, 71–72
Orpen, Joseph Millerd, 71–72, 87
Ottoman Empire, 242–243
Oxford University
    classical curriculum at, 59–62, 73
    Freemasons at, 66, 73
    honorary degree conferred to Rhodes
        at, 391, 409
    protests against Rhodes at, 2–4
    Rhodes as benefactor of, 2–3,
        409–411
    Rhodes as student at, 2–3, 40, 58–67,
        72–73, 92–93
    Rhodes House at, 411–414
    Rhodes Scholarships at, 6–7, 61,
        409–412
    Rhodes statue at, 2–4
    social clubs at, 58–59

Padden, John, 71
Paiva de Andrada, Joaquim Carlos,
    258–259
Palmer, William. *See* Selborne, Earl of
Pan Africanism, 389–390
Panic of 1873, 35, 39–40, 47–48
Panic of 1893, 279
Parkin, George, 63, 410
Parliamentary Registration Law
    Amendment Bill of 1899, 390
Parnell, Charles Stewart, 175–176, 180–181,
    185, 193–194, 202–203, 206, 332–333
Parry, C. H., 391
Pauling, George, 260, 283, 290, 299,
    375–379

Paulings Company, 377–378
Paull, Harry, 149–150
Peace Preservation Act of 1878, 91–92,
    163–164, 166–168, 240–241
Peacock, Anthony Taylor, 11
Peacock, Sophy, 12, 16
Pedi people, 74–75, 88–89, 125–126
Peel, Arthur, 395
Penfold, M. H., 150, 243–244
Pennefather, Edward, 252, 255–256
Phillips, Lionel, 319–320, 328–330,
    343–344, 347
Phylloxera louse, 242–243, 365
Pickering, Neville
    death of, 133–134, 136
    as private secretary of Rhodes, 79
    Rhodes's friendship with, 79, 93, 134,
        136
    Rhodes's will and, 162, 407
Pickering, William, 134, 150
Pickstone, Harry, 364–366, 372–373
Pilgrim's Rest, 130, 132
Pinto, Serpa, 264–265
Pioneer Column
    arming and military strategies of,
        252–253, 255
    Colonial Office and, 249, 251–252
    De Beers Consolidated Mining and,
        249
    Lobengula and, 249–253, 255
    Ndebele people and, 250–256
    recruiting for, 252–253
Plato, 61–62
Plumer, Herbert, 350, 354–355
Porgès, Jules
    Corner House and, 318
    De Beers Consolidated Mining and,
        120–121, 145, 304
    The French Company ownership stake
        of, 80, 142
    gold mining industry and, 134, 136,
        162–163

Port Elizabeth, 18, 23–24, 37–38, 41, 85, 169–170, 376
Portugal
　Great Britain's alliance with, 257–258
　Manicaland and, 257–258, 260–263, 278
　Mashonaland and, 209–210, 248–249, 257–259
　Nyasaland and, 204, 257–258
　potential for expansion of colonies in Africa by, 172–173
Posno, Charles, 117–118
Precious Stones and Minerals Act of 1883, 95
Pretoria, 169–170, 328
Primrose, Archibald. *See* Rosebery, *Lord*
Progressives, 224, 226, 228–229, 389–391
Prout, Henry G., 384

Queensberry, Marquess of (John Douglas), 331–332
Quelimane, 380–381
Quinan, William, 366–367
Qwabe, Ntokozo, 3

Radziwill, Princess Catherine, 60, 391–393, 392*f*, 398
Radziwill, Prince Wilhelm, 391–392
Rand Mines Limited, 319
Randolph, Lord, 261, 281
Reade, Winwood, 60–61, 67
"Recessional" (Kipling), 394–395
Reform Committee, 330, 344–347
Renny-Tailyour, Edward, 213*t*, 250–251, 270–271
Rezende, Baron de, 258–259, 261–262
Rhodes, Arthur, 12, 404
Rhodes, Basil, 12
Rhodes, Bernard, 12
Rhodes, Cecil
　Afrikaner Bond and, 91, 97, 163–164, 168–169, 226, 229, 238, 243, 246, 322, 367–368

　agricultural endeavors of, 364, 368, 371–373
　Arts and Crafts movement and, 65–66
　autopsy of, 401–402
　Basutoland War (1880–1881) and, 91–93
　Bechuanaland and expansionist plans of, 101–102, 104–105, 107–108, 175, 333–334, 342–343, 370–371
　British imperialism promoted by, 64, 67–68, 72, 98, 101–102, 138, 144–145, 162, 164, 173–176, 181–184, 272, 322–324
　British South Africa Company ownership stake of and management by, 6, 56–57, 206, 210, 212–216, 213*t*, 221, 224, 242, 259–260, 269, 278–279, 287, 347, 349
　childhood of, 9–12, 14
　classical history and philosophy interests of, 12–13, 59, 67
　compound housing system for African workers in mining industry and, 56, 123–126, 139
　cricket and, 21
　death of, 398–400
　De Beers Consolidated Mining Company ownership stake and management by, 143–147, 150, 158, 160, 179, 224, 269, 287, 302, 304, 306–307, 322, 359–360
　De Beers Mining Company ownership stake and management by, 56–57, 80–82, 84, 113–114, 116–121, 123, 136, 138–139, 143
　Diamond Fields Horse militia membership of, 75–76
　diamond mine safety and accidents under, 150–151, 153–154
　Diamond Trade Act of 1882, 94
　discriminatory views regarding Black Africans and, 2–3, 5, 8, 22, 91–92, 95, 101, 129, 161, 163–164, 167–168,

226, 228–229, 236–239, 333–334, 342, 365
English real estate holdings of, 398
entry into diamond mining industry by, 27–30, 32–36
entry into gold mining industry by, 129–136
Freemasonry and, 66–70, 73, 402
Gold Fields of South Africa ownership stake and management by, 56–57, 136–137, 162–163, 224, 269, 287, 302, 316, 322
gold mining concessions in Matabeleland and, 187–193, 195, 199–201
grave site and funeral of, 357, 358f, 402–406
health challenges faced by, 32, 40, 228, 271–272, 369, 382, 391–392, 396, 398
as House of Assembly member in Cape Colony, 56–57, 87, 89, 97–98, 183, 220, 382, 389
innovations in diamond mining promoted by, 43–47, 55, 58, 111–113, 115–116, 121, 138–139
Irish nationalists' interaction with, 175–176
legal career briefly pursued by, 66
Mashonaland and expansionist plans of, 107–108, 144–145, 174, 176, 181, 257, 272, 279–281, 290, 331
Matabeleland and expansionist plans of, 107–108, 144–145, 176, 181–182, 331
military attacks against Ndebele led by, 353–355
modern-day protests against, 1–4
negotiations with Ndebele kingdom by, 355–357
as Oxford University student, 2–3, 40, 58–67, 72–73, 92–93
Peace Preservation Act of 1878, 91–92, 163–164

photo illustration of, 399f
primary and secondary education of, 12–13
as prime minister of Cape Colony, 1, 7, 220, 223–224, 229, 302
Privy Council appointment of, 332
railroads and, 7, 22, 39, 85–86, 91–92, 101, 121, 169–172, 174, 208, 211, 220–222, 225–226, 263–264, 378–379, 385, 388
refrigeration business of, 366–367
resignation as Cape Colony prime minister of, 347
Road to the North promoted by, 90, 96–98, 101–103, 107–109, 121, 144–145, 162–164, 180
Second Boer War and, 395
settlement and cotton farming in Natal (1870) by, 16–17, 20–22
sexuality of, 62, 78–79, 93
statues of, 1–3
telegraph development and, 285, 287, 382–388
Transvaal coup attempt (1895–1896) and, 329–330, 339, 344–345, 347, 358, 360–361
unification of South Africa colonies supported by, 93–94, 225, 228–229, 329, 342–343, 347, 367–368
voting laws in Cape Colony and, 164–168, 228, 232, 389–390
Warren Expedition in Bechuanaland (1884–1885) and, 103
white settler colonialism promoted by, 111, 160–161, 163–164, 171–172, 174–176, 182–184, 290, 302, 322, 324, 350, 414
wills of, 162, 272, 407–408
Rhodes, Edith, 12, 358–359
Rhodes, Elizabeth, 11–12
Rhodes, Elmhirst, 12, 358–359, 398–399, 401–402
Rhodes, Ernest, 12, 326

Rhodes, Francis William ("Frank," brother of Cecil Rhodes)
  birth of, 12
  diamond mining boom in Cape Colony and, 32–33
  education of, 12–13, 32
  funeral and grave site of Rhodes and, 357, 358f, 404, 406
  Sudan and, 382
  Transvaal coup (1895–1896) and, 330, 343–344, 347
Rhodes, Francis William (father of Cecil Rhodes)
  as Anglican priest, 11–12
  death of, 72–74, 162
  education of, 11
  education of children of, 12–13
  marriages of, 11
  Oriel College and, 39–40
  real estate holdings of, 162
Rhodes, Frederick, 12
Rhodes, Herbert
  birth of, 12
  cotton farming in Natal by, 14–17, 20, 22
  cricket and, 21
  death of, 74
  diamond mining industry in Cape Colony and, 16–20, 27–29, 32–34, 40
  education of, 12–13
Rhodes, Louisa Peacock, 11–12, 39–40
Rhodes, Samuel, 10–11
Rhodes, William, 10–11
"Rhodes Colossus" (Sambourne), 279, 280*of*
Rhodes House (Oxford University), 411–414
Rhodesia. *See also* Mashonaland; Matabeleland
  anticolonial rebellion (1960s) in, 406
  gold mining companies operating in, 350
  gold surveys in, 301, 375
  origins of names of, 269
  telegraph lines in, 283–284, 288
Rhodes Memorial (Cape Town, South Africa), 2
Rhodes Scholarships, 6–7, 61, 409–412
Rhodes Trust, 407–410
Ricarde-Seaver, Francisco, 179, 207–208
Ripon, Marquess of (George Robinson)
  Bechuanaland Protectorate and, 334–337
  Irish home rule and, 286
  Matabele War and, 293–294, 298–299
  secretary of colonies appointment of, 282–283
  Transvaal and, 329–331
Road to the North. *See also* Cape-to-Cairo connections
  Basutoland War (1880–1881) and, 91
  Bechuanaland and, 101–102, 108
  Boers' threats to Rhodes's plan for, 96–97
  Colonial Office of Great Britain and, 97–98
  railroad development and, 217, 220, 339
  Rhodes's promotion of, 90, 96–98, 101–103, 107–109, 121, 144–145, 162–164, 180
  telegraph development along, 104
  Warren Expedition and, 104
  Western Cape and, 90
  white settler colonialism and, 108–109, 111
Robinson, George. *See* Ripon, Marquess of
Robinson, Hercules
  appointment as governor of Cape Colony of, 333, 337
  appointment as high commissioner of Cape Colony, 98
  Bechuanaland and, 81, 100, 105
  British South Africa Company and, 213*t*, 216
  De Beers Consolidated Mining and, 307

gold mining concessions in
Matabeleland and, 209–210
Groote Schuur and, 244
photo of, 99f
Road to the North and, 98, 101–102, 324
Transvaal coup attempt and, 344–345, 347
United Concession Company and, 216
Warren Expedition (1884–1885) and, 103
Robinson, Joseph B.
biographical background of, 84
De Beers Mining Company buyout attempt (1886) and, 117–118
Diamond Trade Act of 1882, 94
Exploring Company and, 182–183
gold mining concessions in Matabeleland and, 185, 190, 192–193, 196–197, 207
gold mining industry and, 131–133, 136, 162–163
House of Assembly and, 87
sanitation facilities in Kimberley and, 76
Standard Company founded by, 84, 141–142
Transvaal electoral politics and, 328
Robinson Deep Mine, 326
Rockefeller, John D., 6–7, 410–411
Rolong people, 16–17, 19–20, 25–26, 97, 102
Roosevelt, Theodore, 393
Rosebery, Lord (Archibald Primrose)
appointment as prime minister of Great Britain of, 331
biographical background of, 331–332
Delagoa Bay purchase attempt and, 225–226
Imperial Federation League and, 331
resignation as prime minister of, 337
Rhodes Trust and, 408
sexuality of, 331–332

telegraph development in Africa and, 285, 287
Transvaal coup attempt and, 333
Rotberg, Robert, 32–33, 78–79, 271–272
Rothschild, Arthur de, 294
Rothschild, Nathaniel "Natty" (1st Lord Rothschild)
British imperialism supported by, 135–136, 162
British South Africa Company and, 206, 213t, 278, 281
Chamberlain and, 135–136
Churchill and, 281–282
De Beers Consolidated Mining and, 135, 143–146, 304, 306–307, 317, 324
Delagoa Bay purchase attempt and, 225–226
gold mining concessions in Matabeleland and, 192–193
Jewish identity of, 135–136
as member of British House of Commons, 135–136
Mozambique Company and, 262
philanthropy by, 135–136
railroad development and, 377, 388
Rhodes's business dealings with, 143–144
Rhodes's wills and, 272, 407
wealth of, 135–136
Rothschild family
De Beers Mining Company and, 135–136
gold mining investments by, 130–131
Panic of 1873 and, 35
Suez Canal and, 35
Roulina, Charles, 117–118
Royal Geographical Society, 276
Royal Niger Company, 181
Rudd, Charles
British South Africa Company and, 213t
diamond mining industry in Cape Colony and, 33–36, 42–47, 71, 80–81

Rudd, Charles (*Continued*)
  education of, 33
  gold mining industry and, 131–133, 136
  as House of Assembly member, 116–117, 150
  innovations in diamond mining promoted by, 44–47, 58, 113–116
  mining concession negotiations and, 185–190, 195
Rudd, Thomas, 33, 44, 136, 216
Rudd Concession
  British Parliament's discussion of, 195–196
  Central Search Association and, 202–203
  concerns about legitimacy of, 189–190
  Concession Company and, 295–296
  Gold Fields of South Africa and, 199–200, 207
  humanitarian concerns regarding, 196–197
  land ownership systems under, 269–275
  Lobengula's repudiation of, 209–210, 269–270, 287–288
  Mozambique border and, 212
  Shona people and, 247, 287–288
  weapons to Ndebele people as part of, 188, 190–192, 195–199, 253
Ruskin, John, 64–66, 90, 101, 163
Rutherfoord Harris, Frederick
  Bechuanaland Protectorate and, 338, 340
  British South Africa Company and, 213*t*
  gold mining concessions in Matabeleland and, 190–191, 198
  smallpox outbreaks in Kimberley and, 77
  Transvaal coup attempt and, 339

Salisbury, Lord (Robert Cecil)
  appointment as prime minister of, 337
  British alliance with Portugal and, 257–258, 263
  British imperialism supported by, 175
  British South Africa Company and, 204–206
  German East Africa and, 257
  Katanga and, 267
  Manicaland and, 263
  Mozambique and, 259, 262
  Nyasaland and, 172–173, 205
  railroad development and, 376–377
  Swaziland and, 249–250
  Transvaal coup attempt and, 360–361
Salt, Titus, 313
Sambourne, Linley, 279, 280*f*
Sampson, Victor, 232
San people, 17
Sauer, Johannes "Hans"
  gold mining industry and, 131–136
  Inyanga estate and, 372
  railroad development and, 290
  as Rhodes cabinet member, 229
  Rhodes's friendship with, 77
  smallpox outbreaks in Kimberley and, 77
Sauer, J. W., 166–167, 224, 229
Sauerdale, 372–373, 408–409
Scanlen, Sarah Ann, 224–225
Scanlen, Thomas, 91–93, 98, 101–102, 224–225
Schama, Simon, 3–4
Schreiner, Olive, 227, 227*f*, 363–364
Schreiner, Will, 166–167, 229, 390–391
Schulz, Aurel, 260, 262
Scully, William Charles, 30
Sebele, 339–341
Sechele, 96, 104–105
Second Boer War (1899–1902), 395–398
Sekgoma, 336–337
Sekhukhune, 88–89, 230
Selborne, Earl of (William Palmer), 338, 349–350
Selous, Frederick Courteney
  British South Africa Company and, 263
  gold mining concessions in Matabeleland and, 194

Great Zimbabwe ruins and, 275–276
Manicaland and, 261
Mashonaland and, 248–250
Ndebele attacks on white settlers
 and, 353
photo of, 248*f*
Pioneer Column and, 255–256
Road to the North and, 249
Shangani Patrol, 298, 406
Sharpe, Alfred, 267
Sharrer, Eugene, 380–381
Shaw, Flora, 202
Shaw, John, 36
sheep scab disease, 241–243
Shepstone, Theophilus, 15–16, 88–89
Shepstone, William E., 21
Shinn, Percy, 378–379
Shippard, Sidney
 attorney general of Cape Colony
  appointment of, 53
 British imperialist expansion in southern
  Africa supported by, 176–177
 British South Africa Company and,
  210
 gold mining negotiations and, 186–187,
  190, 192, 196–198
 Lobengula and, 178
 Ndebele people and, 187, 292
 Oriel College and, 39–40
 railroad development and, 180–181
 resident commissioner of
  Bechuanaland appointment of, 107
 Rhodes's friendship and business
  dealings with, 30, 53, 69–70
 Road to the North and, 324
Shire Valley, 204
Shona people
 Bechuanaland Protectorate and, 173–174
 British South Africa Company and,
  300, 355–356
 cattle and, 351–352
 Great Zimbabwe ruins and, 275–276

hut taxes and, 351
Matabele War and, 291–292
Maund Report (1885) and, 173
as migrant laborers, 6
Ndebele people and, 107, 189, 247, 282,
 287–288
Pioneer Column and, 255
Rudd Concession and, 247, 287–288
telegraph lines and, 283–284, 288
Shore, Miles, 271–272
Sidojiwa, 300
Silberbauer, Conrad Christian, 402
Simmer and Jack Mine, 326
Sivewright, James
 biographical background and, 171
 Delagoa Bay purchase attempt and,
  225–226
 Johannesburg water supply and, 327–328
 knighthood awarded to, 228–229
 Logan corruption case and, 229
 as member of Cape Parliament, 171
 as member of Rhodes's cabinet, 223–224
 racist views of, 223–224
 railroads and, 172, 217, 342–343
 Rhodes's business dealings with, 171–172
 Swaziland and, 249–250
 telegraph development and, 171, 223–224
 Transvaal and, 228–229
 white settler colonialism promoted by,
  171–172
Smartt, Thomas, 395, 401
Smith, Hamilton, 130–131, 134–135, 326
Smith, Harry, 36–37
Smyth, Henry, 197
Sobrero, Ascanio, 82–83
Social Darwinism, 51, 67, 70
Socrates, 61–62
Soga, Allan Kirkland, 389–390
Solomon, Richard, 307
Solomon, Saul, 90
Somabhulana, 356
Soshangane, 258

Sotho people, 90–92
"The Soul of the Man under Socialism" (Wilde), 410–411
South Africa Committee, 194–195, 202–204
South African Native National Congress, 389–390
South African Republic. *See* Transvaal
Southey, Richard
   Carnarvon's dismissal of, 51–52
   coup attempt (1875) against governorship of, 50
   Diamond Fields Commission and, 49–50
   diamond mining industry and, 46–49, 80–81
   European settlement promoted by, 48–49
   Griqua rebellion (1878) and, 74–75
   as House of Assembly member, 74–75
   land claim questions arbitrated by, 48–49, 75
   restrictions placed on gambling and prostitution in Kimberley by, 76
   segregation facilitated by, 48–49
Spencer, Herbert, 407
Spencer-Churchill, George (eight Duke of Marlborough), *see* Churchill, George Spencer,
Spencer-Churchill, Randolph, *see* Churchill, Randolph Spencer
Sprigg, John Gordon
   Afrikaner Bond, 226, 388–389
   Basutoland War (1880–1881) and, 91–92
   election of 1898 and, 390–391
   gold mining concessions in Matabeleland and, 190, 197
   Peace Preservation Act of 1878 and, 91, 163–164, 166
   racist views of Black Africans held by, 91
   railroads and, 169–170, 218, 220–221, 223
   resignation as prime minister of Cape Colony (1881) by, 91–92
   Rhodes's political dealings with, 90–91, 238, 322
   sheep farming and, 242
   voting laws in Cape Colony and, 166–167
   wine taxes and, 90
Standard Company, 84, 141–143
Stanley, Henry Morton, 69, 268, 285
Star of South Africa diamond, 18–19
Stead, William T., 194–195, 202, 272, 391–392, 408
Stellaland, 97–98, 100–102, 104–105
Stent, Sydney, 7, 313, 324
Stent, Vere, 356–357
Stevenson, Edmond Sinclair, 77, 401
Stockdale, Henrietta, 77
Stoic philosophers, 61
Stow, Frederic Philipson (Fred), 77, 80–82, 116–117, 120–121, 145–146, 306–307
Strangways, Henry, 69
Strop Bill of 1890, 226–227, 236–237
Sub Nigel Mine, 326
Sudan, 93, 284–285, 382
Suez Canal, 35, 284–285, 382
Sutherland, Peter, 20–22
Syfret, Edward Ridge, 224–225
Syfret, Stephen, 401

Tainton, William, 192
Tanzania, 96–97
Tarbutt, Percy, 318–319, 375
Taylor, James B., 162–163
Thembu people, 231–232
Thompson, Frank "Matabele"
   Bechuanaland and, 102
   British South Africa Company and, 213*t*
   compound housing for diamond miners and, 125–126
   gold mining concessions in Matabeleland and, 185–186, 188–192

Lobengula and Ndebele people's
  interaction with, 210
 United Concession Company and, 216
Thompson, John C., 32
Thompson, Wardlaw, 194–195
Thomson, Joseph, 266–268
Tlhaping people
 British offer of protectorate in
  Bechuanaland and, 102
 diamond mining industry in Cape
  Colony and, 17, 19–20, 44–45
 land claims in Cape Colony by, 24–26,
  48–49
 Warren's attack (1878) on, 75–76
Townsend, Helen, 376
Toynbee, Arnold, 63
Transkei region
 Black Africans voting rights and,
  165–166
 Cape Colony's incorporation (1885)
  of, 165–166, 230–231
 landholding practices in, 231
 Rhodes's travels in, 237–239
 white settlement in, 236
Transvaal
 Afrikaner Bond and, 216–217, 347
 Bechuanaland and, 101–102
 Boer nationalism in, 108–109, 322
 Boer republics in Stellaland and
  Goshen supported by, 98
 British suzerainty in, 17, 25–26, 88–89,
  101–102
 Cape Colony's annexation (1877) of, 72
 coal mining in, 85, 170
 coup attempt (1895–1896) in, 1, 6–7,
  329–331
 customs union in southern Africa
  refused by, 109, 169–170, 225, 329
 diamond mining industry in Cape
  Colony and, 17, 25–26
 election (1892) in, 328
 establishment of Boer republic in, 17
 First Anglo-Boer War and, 88–89
 gold mining in, 3–4, 129–135, 162, 172,
  220, 319
 Lobengula and, 177–179
 Mozambique and, 109
 racial discrimination and
  discriminatory laws in, 50–51,
  98–99, 217
 railroads in, 96–97, 109, 168–170, 172,
  216–217, 220, 223, 228–229,
  328–329, 342–343
 Road to the North and, 96–98, 101–102
 Stellaland and, 100–102
 Swaziland and, 249–250
 tariffs on Cape Colony and, 97, 101–102
 uitlanders (foreign-born population)
  in, 326–330, 342–343
 voting laws in, 167–168
Transvaal National Union, 328
Tregonning, William, 153–154
Trollope, Anthony, 87
Tsonga people, 258
Tswana people. See also *specific chiefdoms*
 Bechuanaland Protectorate and, 335,
  339–340
 Boer settlement movement in the
  lands of, 97–98, 100, 104–107
 British Bechuanaland Colony and,
  105–107
 Cape Colony control of Bechuanaland
  and, 337
 cattle ranching by, 101
 Christianity and missionaries among,
  96, 98–99
 diamond mining industry in Cape
  Colony and, 18–19
 European visitors to southern Africa
  and, 96
 Great Zimbabwe ruins and, 276
 ivory trade and, 264–265
 Matabeleland War and, 293–294
 Pioneer Column and, 249

Tswana people (*Continued*)
  railroad labor by, 275
  Road to the North and, 96–97, 337
  separate chiefdoms involved in governing, 96
  weapons obtained by, 197–198
Turner, Frederick Jackson, 184
Turner, Scott, 371, 387
Twain, Mark, 3

Uganda, 7–8, 257, 285, 287, 382, 387
Umtali
  British South Africa Company and, 263
  railroads and, 258, 264, 378
  telegraph lines and, 369–370, 387
Union-Castle Shipping Line, 142, 363–364
United Company, 119
United Concessions, 201, 203, 216, 283, 294–295
United States
  Civil War in, 14–16, 35, 325
  Rhodes's views regarding, 6–7, 67–68, 235
University of Cape Town, 1–3, 322–323, 408–409
University of Oxford. *See* Oxford University
Upington, Thomas, 165–167, 224

Vanderbilt, Cornelius, 6–7, 410–411
van Laun, Henry, 263–264, 278
van Niekerk, Gerrit, 102
van Niekerk, Schalk, 18
van Onselen, Charles, 325
Verschoyle, John, 202
Victoria (queen of England)
  African leaders' audience (1889) with, 194
  gold mining concessions in Matabeleland and, 196–197, 209–210, 212, 217
  letter to Lobengula (1890) addressed from, 218–219
  Rhodes's meetings with, 262, 332–333
  Salisbury premiership and, 337
Victoria Company, 83, 111–112, 119–121, 141
Vingoe, John, 155
Vintcent, Judge, 299–300
The Volksraad (legislature), 221–222, 327
Vooruitzigt mine, 19–20, 23–24, 47–48
Vorstman, Lambertus, 319
Voters' Registration Bill of 1887, 166–167
Vryburg
  British suzerainty over, 102
  railroads and, 108–109, 179–180, 217, 220, 275–276, 331, 334, 377
  Rhodes's funeral train and, 404
  Stellaland republic and, 97
  telegraph lines and, 104, 384

W.A. Hall and Company, 142
Wallop, John, 199–200, 216
Ward, William (Earl of Dudley), 18
Ware, Henry, 265–266
Warren, Charles
  Boer landholders in Stellaland and, 104–105
  expedition to Bechuanaland (1884–1885) led by, 103–104
  Freemasonry and, 103
  Griqua rebellion (1878) and, 74–76
  humanitarian imperialism promoted by, 173
  Kruger's meeting (1885) with, 104
  Rhodes's interactions with, 103–105
  Road to the North and telegraph developed by, 104
  Tlhaping forces attacked (1878) by, 75–76
  Tswana chiefdoms' negotiations with, 104–105
Waterboer, Andries, 24–26, 48–49
Webb, Henry Barlow, 58
Webster, Richard, 360–361
Wernher, Julius, 80
Wernher & Beit, 263–264, 306

Wesselton mine, 305–306
Westbeech, George, 264–265
Western Cape
   as Afrikaners' imagined homeland, 89, 231
   agriculture in, 7–8, 108–109, 163, 168–169, 242, 363–365
   Black African migrant workers in, 89
   "coloured" (mixed-race) population in, 231
   immigration politics in, 164
   railroads in, 41, 108–109
   Road to the North proposal and, 90
   vineyards in, 89–90, 164, 168, 243, 368
   voting laws and, 368
White, Robert, 346–347
"The White Man's Burden" (Kipling), 393–394
Wilde, Oscar, 64–66, 331–332, 410–411
Wilhelm II (kaiser of Germany), 286, 385, 409–410
Williams, Alpheus, 130–131, 134–135, 143
Williams, Basil, 27, 79
Williams, Gardner
   amalgamation of De Beers Mining Company and, 143
   Black African mining workers described by, 159–161
   compound housing system for African diamond miners and, 139, 314
   De Beers general manager appointment of, 135–136, 138, 144–145, 160, 324
   De Beers mine fire (1888) and, 147–148, 152–155, 159–161, 184
   dynamite supply for De Beers and, 366–367
   environmental impact of gold mining and, 321
   falsification of diamond mining data by, 306–307
   innovations in diamond mining introduced by, 42–43, 138, 140–141, 146–147, 303, 308–309, 324

   Kenilworth workers' village and, 313–314
   photo of, 135*f*
   profitability of De Beers Consolidated Mining and, 303
   Rhodes's business ventures with, 6–7, 130–131
   Second Boer War and, 395–396
   Transvaal coup attempt and, 343–344
   Transvaal gold mining operations and, 130–131, 134–135
   workplace safety at De Beers mines and, 303
Williams, Ralph, 107, 177
Williams, Robert, 375, 388
Willoughby, John
   British South Africa Company and, 213*t*, 252
   gold surveys in Rhodesia and, 375
   imprisonment in Great Britain of, 350
   incursion to Mozambique by, 262
   Matabele War and, 292–293, 298
   Rhodesia gold survey and, 301–302
   Transvaal coup attempt and, 344–347, 349–350
Willoughby, William, 333–334, 339–341
Wilson, Allan, 298, 406
Witwatersrand
   gold discovery (1886) at, 109, 130–131
   gold mining operations at, 6–7, 131–136, 162–163, 176–177, 258, 318
   innovations in mining at, 318–319, 324–325
   labor relations at, 320
   railroads and, 328
   Rhodes's farm at, 39
   telegraph lines and, 171
Wodehouse, John (Earl of Kimberley), 25, 32–33
Wodehouse, Philip, 18
Wolseley, Garnet, 179–180
Woolf, Samuel, 58

Wright, Henry Charles Seppings, 30
Wyndham, George, 360–361

Xhosa people, 74–75, 166–167, 230, 236, 316

Yerburgh, Robert, 66

Zambesi Company, 258–260
Zambia, 7–8, 264
Zimbabwe, 7–8, 203. *See also* Mashonaland; Matabeleland
Zulu people, 14–15, 74–76, 88–89
Zuma, Jacob, 1–2